A PEOPLE AND A NATION

A History of the United States

Brief Edition ◆ Volume A: To 1877 ◆ Third Edition

MARY BETH NORTON
Cornell University

DAVID M. KATZMAN
University of Kansas

PAUL D. ESCOTT
Wake Forest University

HOWARD P. CHUDACOFF
Brown University

THOMAS G. PATERSON
University of Connecticut

WILLIAM M. TUTTLE, JR.
University of Kansas

and

WILLIAM J. BROPHY
Stephen F. Austin State University

HOUGHTON MIFFLIN COMPANY   BOSTON

Dallas   Geneva, Illinois   Palo Alto   Princeton, New Jersey

Cover: Unknown artist, *He That Tilleth His Land Shall Be Satisfied.* Philadelphia Museum of Art, The Edgar William and Bernice Chrysler Garbisch Collection.

Cover photograph researched by Rose Corbett Gordon.

Text photographs researched by Pembroke Herbert/Picture Research Consultants.

Insert credits appear on page I-21.

Printed in the U.S.A.

Library of Congress Catalog Card Number: 90-83012

ISBN: 0-395-56298-8

CDEFGHIJ-RRD-95432

Contents

Contents

INDEX   I-1

Maps and Charts

Preface to the Brief Third Edition

This text is a condensation of the very successful Third Edition of *A People and a Nation*. We have preserved all the strengths of the full-length edition—its readability, its comprehensiveness, and, most important, its dynamic blend of social, political, diplomatic, and economic history—in a form approximately half as long. This condensation of the whole story of American history is ideally suited for short courses or courses in which additional readings are assigned.

The brief edition is available in both one-volume and two-volume formats. The two-volume format divides as follows: Volume A contains Chapters 1–15, beginning with a discussion of three cultures—Native American, African, and European—that intersected during the exploration and colonization of the New World and ending with a discussion of the Reconstruction era; Volume B contains Chapters 15–33, beginning its coverage at Reconstruction and extending to the present. The chapter on Reconstruction appears in both volumes to provide greater flexibility in matching a volume to the historical span covered by a specific course.

This brief edition is not a simple revision of the previous brief version: we have ensured that it reflects changes in content and organization incorporated into the full-length Third Edition (see the preface to the full-length edition, which follows). William J. Brophy, who prepared the condensation, collaborated closely with the six authors of the full-length edition to make all deletions with great care. Rather than simply cut entire sections, we took a line-by-line approach to the removal of material, paring down detail. Where two examples were given in the full-length edition, we deleted one; where many statistics were presented, we used a few. Although we abridged or deleted some excerpts from diaries and letters, we have retained many quotations and many individual accounts of everyday life. In the interest of concision, we also combined two chapters from the full-length edi-

Creation of the Brief Edition

tion—the chapter on the city from 1877 to 1920 and the chapter on everyday life during the same period.

Three aspects of this brief edition should be noted. First, we have used the occasion of a new edition to update the end-of-chapter bibliographies as well as the chapter that covers the Reagan and Bush years. Second, many pieces in the illustration and map program are new to the brief edition, including four maps, two figures, and numerous photographs. Finally, this edition includes four new full-color inserts that examine leisure in America during the years surrounding 1800, 1850, 1900, and 1950. The one-volume format contains all four inserts; each volume in the two-volume format includes two.

A full set of ancillaries is available with the brief edition. These include a *Study Guide* (in two volumes) by George C. Warren and Cynthia L. Ricketson; *Microstudy Plus,* an interactive computer study guide that gives students feedback on correct and incorrect answers; an *Instructor's Manual with Test Items* by George C. Warren; *Microtest,* a computerized test item file; map transparencies; and *Places in Time: Computer Exercises in Historical Geography,* a new computerized map study program.

Ancillaries

Each volume of the *Study Guide* includes an introductory chapter on study techniques as well as learning objectives, a thematic guide, and various kinds of study questions for each chapter in the text. The *Instructor's Manual with Test Items* includes learning objectives, chapter outlines, lecture suggestions and topics, lists of audio-visual resources, and a variety of test questions for each chapter in the text. *Places in Time,* the new map study program designed for the Macintosh computer, uses maps to explore various issues—territory acquisition, population patterns, economic development, and so on—during four time periods—1763, 1860, 1920, and 1980. Each map is paired with a three-part exercise that focuses on map analysis, identification, and discussion. (A for-sale student workbook is also available.)

Though each of us feels answerable for the whole of *A People and a Nation,* we take primary responsibility for particular chapters: Mary Beth Norton, Chapters 1–7; David M. Katzman, Chapters 8–9, 11–12; Paul D. Escott, Chapters 10, 13–15; Howard P. Chudacoff, Chapters 16–20, 23; Thomas G. Paterson, Chapters 21–22, 25, 28, 30, and the material on foreign relations in 32 and 33; and William M. Tuttle, Jr., Chapters 24, 26–27, 29, and 31–33.

Finally, we want to thank the many people who have contributed their thoughts and labors to this work, including the staff at Houghton Mifflin Company.

W.J.B.

Preface to the Full-Length Third Edition

In preparing for the third edition, the authors of *A People and a Nation* met in Boston with Houghton Mifflin editors and art researchers. In several sessions we re-evaluated and discussed every aspect of the book—themes, organization, emphases, coverage, interpretation, scholarship, writing style, and illustrations. In these planning meetings, we analyzed many instructors' reports and profited from their advice. Our goals for this edition were to improve the organization of the book, delineate themes even more sharply, clarify specific passages, and incorporate the best of recent scholarship. Our basic approach to American history as the story of all the people remains the same, and in the third edition we have preserved and strengthened those characteristics of the second edition that students and faculty have found so attractive.

As teachers and students we are always recreating our past, restructuring our memory, rediscovering the personalities and events that have shaped us, inspired us, and bedeviled us. This book is our rediscovery of America's past—its people and the nation they founded and have sustained. This history is sometimes comforting, sometimes disturbing. As with our own personal experiences, it is both triumphant and tragic, filled with injury as well as healing. As a mirror on our lives, it is necessarily revealing—blemishes and all. As memory, it is the way we identify ourselves.

We draw on recent research, authoritative works, and our own teaching experience to offer a comprehensive book that tells the whole story of American history. Politics, government, **Characteristics of the Book** diplomacy, wars, and economic patterns have been at the core of writing on American history for generations. Into this traditional fabric we weave social history in order to discuss both the public and private spheres of Americans. We investigate the everyday life of the American people, that of the majority of Americans— women—and that of minorities. We explore the many ways Americans have identified and still identify themselves: gender, race, class, ethnicity, religion, work, sexual preference, geographic region, politics.

From the ordinary to the exceptional—the factory worker, the slave, the office secretary, the local merchant, the small farmer, the plantation owner, the ward politician, the president's wife, the film celebrity, the scientist, the army general—Americans have personal stories that have intersected with the public policies of their governments. Whether victors or victims, all have been actors in their own right, with feelings, ideas, and aspirations that have fortified them in good times and bad. All are part of the American story; all speak in *A People and a Nation* through excerpts from letters, diaries, oral histories, and other historical materials that we have integrated into this narrative history.

Several questions guided us in this third edition. On the official, or public, side of American history, we emphasize Americans' expectations of their governments and the practices of **Major Themes** those local, state, and federal institutions. We look not only at politics but also at the culture of politics. We identify the mood and mentality of an era, searching for what Americans thought about themselves and their public officials. In our discussion of foreign relations, we ask why negotiations failed to prevent wars, why the United States became an expansionist, interventionist, global power, and how the domestic setting influenced diplomacy and vice versa.

In the social and economic areas, we emphasize patterns of change in the population, geographic and social mobility, and people's adaptation to new environments. We study the often friction-ridden interactions of people of different color, social class, national origin, religious affiliation, sectional identity, and gender, and the efforts made, often in reform movements, to reduce tensions. As well, we focus on the effects of technological development on the economy, the worker and the workplace, and lifestyles.

In the private, everyday life of the family and the home, we pay particular attention to gender roles, childbearing and childrearing, and diet and dress. We ask how Americans have entertained themselves, as participants or spectators, through sports, music, the graphic arts, reading, theater, film, radio, and television. Throughout American history, of course, this private sphere of American life and public policy have interacted and influenced one another.

Students and instructors have commended the book for its discussion of these many topics in clear, concrete language, and they have commented on how enjoyable the book is to read. We have appreciated hearing, too, that we challenged them to think about the meaning of American history, not just to memorize it; to confront one's own interpretations and at the same time to respect the views of others; and to show how the historian's mind works to ask questions and to tease conclusions out of vast amounts of information. We especially welcome these responses because they tell us that we have met our goal: to convey the excitement and fascination we feel as teacher-scholars in recreating and understanding the past.

For this third edition, literally hundreds of changes—major and minor—have been made throughout the book. Among the major changes,

Changes in the Third Edition the third edition is one chapter shorter than the second edition as a result of the merger of two chapters that covered the Hoover and Roosevelt periods. Now the Great Depression and the New Deal are presented in one chapter, 1929–1941. In addition, half of the stories that open chapters are new, and throughout we have provided new examples to illustrate themes.

A number of other revisions deserve special mention. Mary Beth Norton, who had primary responsibility for Chapters 1–7, has introduced new material on the Spanish and French colonies and on the soldiers who fought in colonial wars and the American Revolution. She has also revised the discussion of African migration and slavery and of early political parties. David M. Katzman, who had primary responsibility for Chapters 8–9 and 11–12, has expanded the coverage of the War of 1812, agriculture's adjustment to a market-oriented econ-

omy, city and country life, public disorder, Indian removal, abolitionism, and Jacksonian politics. He has reworked the discussion of reform to link it more closely to social and economic changes, religion, and politics. He has also introduced new material on how people experienced the market economy, public space, the growing gender divisions in work, asylums, single women, and Hispanics in Texas and California. Paul D. Escott, who had primary responsibility for Chapters 10 and 13–15, has expanded the treatment of the spread of market relations among southern yeomen and the influence of slavery on national life and, in the chapter on Reconstruction, of black activism in the South, splits among Republicans in Congress, and Supreme Court cases.

Howard P. Chudacoff, who had primary responsibility for Chapters 16–21 and 24, has added new material on Indians and the cultural conflict between their subsistence societies and the market-oriented economy; post–Civil War land policy; child labor; eating habits; and women's history. He has expanded the discussion of immigration and family life, urban reform, the new consumer society, and the origins of feminism. Chapter 20 especially has been reworked to develop the theme of inclusion versus exclusion in politics. Thomas G. Paterson, who had primary responsibility for Chapters 22–23, 26, 29, and 31, and the foreign relations parts of 33 and 34, has sharpened the discussion of expansionism and imperialism and expanded the treatment of the origins of the First World War in Europe and the clash of "systems" before the Second World War. He has added new material on the everyday lives of soldiers, Eisenhower's domestic policies and views on race relations, and the grass-roots nature of the civil rights movement. He has also reworked treatment of the world economy, termination policy toward Indians, and the Vietnam War—protest, lessons, and veterans. Paterson served as the coordinating author for *A People and a Nation* and also prepared the Appendix.

William M. Tuttle, Jr., who had primary responsibility for Chapters 25, 27–28, 30, and 32–34, has combined coverage of the Great Depression and the New Deal into one chapter. He has expanded discussion of the Second World War experience of soldiers, McCarthyism, women in higher education, the baby boom, and the 1970s economy. He also reworked treatment of the War on Poverty, the 1968 election, and the fragmentation of the Democratic party. New material on Asian-Americans appears in Chapter 33, and the foreign policy of Jimmy Carter has been relocated there. Finally, Chapter 34 on the Reagan years and the beginnings of the Bush administration has been thoroughly revised; besides carrying the story to the end of the 1980s, the last chapter includes new discussion of Reagan's popularity, AIDS, the Iran-contra scandal, feminization of poverty, and drugs.

We have also revised the "Important Events" lists and in this edition moved them toward the front of each chapter. The end-of-chapter bibliographies have been revised to reflect recent scholarship. The Appendix now includes the Articles of Confederation as well as updated information. New illustrations—many of them in color—have been introduced, and new maps have been added and other maps revised.

To make the book as useful as possible for students and instructors, several learning and teaching aids are available, including a *Study Guide* and *MicroGuide* (a computerized study **Study and** guide), an *Instructor's Manual*, a **Teaching** *Test Items* file, *Diploma III* (test **Aids** generator and class management software), and *Map Transparencies*. The *Study Guide,* which was prepared by George Warren and Cynthia Ricketson of Central Piedmont Community College, includes an introductory chapter on study techniques for history students, learning objectives and a thematic guide for each chapter in the text, exercises on evaluating and using information and on finding the main idea in passages from the text, map exercises where appropriate, new sections on organizing information for some chapters, and test questions (multiple choice and essay) on the content of each chapter. An answer key tells students not only which response is correct but also why each of the other choices is wrong. The *Study Guide* is available as *MicroGuide,* a computerized, tutorial version that also gives students feedback on incorrect as well as correct answers.

The *Instructor's Manual* contains chapter outlines, suggestions for lectures and discussion, and lists of audio-visual resources. The *Test Items* file, also by Professor Warren, offers more than 1,500 new multiple-choice and essay questions and more than 700 identification terms. The test items are available to adopters for IBM and Macintosh computers. In addition, there is a set of 93 full-color *Map Transparencies* available on adoption.

Acknowledgments Many instructors have read and criticized the several drafts of our manuscript. Their suggestions have made this a better book. We heartily thank:

John K. Alexander, *University of Cincinnati*
Sara Alpern, *Texas A & M University*
Dee Andrews, *California State University, Hayward*
Robert Asher, *University of Connecticut*
Edward L. Ayers, *University of Virginia*
Len Bailes, *El Paso Community College*
Delmar L. Beene, *Glendale Community College*
Michael Bellesiles, *Emory University*
Sidney R. Bland, *James Madison University*
Frederick J. Blue, *Youngstown State University*
Bill Cecil-Fronsman, *Washburn University*
William F. Cheek, *San Diego State University*
Michael S. Coray, *University of Nevada, Reno*
Donald T. Critchlow, *University of Notre Dame*
Bruce Dierenfield, *Canisius College*
Charles E. Dickson, *Clark State Community College*
Richard W. Etulain, *University of New Mexico*
Owen E. Farley, Jr., *Pensacola Junior College*
Lacy K. Ford, Jr., *University of South Carolina*
Donald E. Green, *Central State University*
L. Ray Gunn, *University of Utah*
Joseph M. Hawes, *Memphis State University*
Gary R. Hess, *Bowling Green State University*
Joseph P. Hobbs, *North Carolina State University*
Alan M. Kraut, *American University*
Monroe H. Little, Jr., *Indiana University, Purdue University at Indianapolis*
Cathy Matson, *University of Tennessee, Knoxville*
Michael N. McConnell, *University of Alabama, Birmingham*
Melissa L. Meyer, *University of Minnesota*
J. Bruce Nelson, *Dartmouth College*
Allan B. Spetter, *Wright State University*

Kathleen Xidis, *Johnson County Community College*

Charles A. Zappia, *San Diego Mesa College*

We also thank the following for their contributions to this third edition: Daniel H. Usner, Jr., Sharyn Brooks Katzman, Theodore A. Wilson, Eric Foner, Phillip Paludan, Nancy Fisher Chudacoff, Elizabeth Mahan, Ellen C. Garber, Kathryn N. Kretschmer, Samuel Watkins Tuttle, David Thelen, and Ronald Schlundt. We owe our special thanks to the many people at Houghton Mifflin who always set high standards, gave this book excellent guidance and care, and have become our friends.

T.G.P.

"It spread over the people as great destruction," the old man told the priest. "Some it quite covered [with pustules] on all parts—their faces, their heads, their breasts. . . . Great was its destruction. Covered, mantled with pustules, very many people died of them. And very many starved; there was death from hunger."

Four months earlier, Spanish troops led by Hernando Cortés had abandoned their siege of the Aztec capital of Tenochtitlán after failing in their first attempt to gain control of the city. The temples, desecrated during the siege, were cleaned and the images of the gods once again clothed with "godly ornaments"—turquoise mosaic masks and parrot and eagle feathers. But the European smallpox germs that would ensure the Spaniards' eventual triumph were already threatening the Aztecs. By the time the invaders returned, the epidemic described above had fatally weakened Tenochtitlán's inhabitants. Even so, the city held out for months. But in the Aztec year Three House, on the day One Serpent (August 1521), Tenochtitlán finally surrendered. The Spaniards had conquered Mexico, and on the site of the Aztec capital they built what is now Mexico City.

1

THE MEETING OF OLD WORLD AND NEW, 1492–1640

By the time Spanish troops occupied Tenochtitlán, the age of European expansion and colonization was already well under way. Over the next 350 years, Europeans would spread their civilization across the globe. Although they began by primarily seeking trade goods, they would eventually come to dominate native peoples in Asia and Africa, as well as in the New World of the Western Hemisphere. The history of the tiny colonies in North America that became the United States must be seen in this broader context of European exploration and exploitation.

After 1400, European nations sought to improve their positions relative to neighboring countries not only by fighting wars on their own continent, but also by acquiring valuable colonies and trading posts elsewhere in the world. At the same time, the warring tribes and nations of Asia, Africa, and the Americas attempted to use the alien intruders to their own advantage or, failing that, to adapt successfully to the Europeans' presence in their midst. All the participants in the resulting interaction of divergent cultures were indelibly affected. In the Americas and Africa, Europeans emerged politically dominant at the end of this long process of interaction. By no means, however, did they control every aspect of it.

Nowhere is that lack of European control shown more clearly than in the early history of the English settlements in North America. England's attempts to establish colonies on the mainland in the sixteenth century failed completely. In the early seventeenth century, the English succeeded only because neighboring Indians assisted the newcomers. The English colonists prospered by learning to grow such unfamiliar American crops as corn and tobacco and by developing extensive trading relationships with Native Americans. Eventually, they discovered a third source of prosperity—importing enslaved African laborers to work in their fields.

To achieve their first goal—feeding themselves—they had to adopt agricultural techniques suited both to the new crops and to an alien environment. Their second goal—maintaining lucrative trade networks—required them to deal regularly on a more or less equal basis with people who seemed very different from them and who were far more familiar with America than they were. The early history of the United States, in short, can best be understood as a series of complex interactions among different peoples and environments rather than as the simple story of a triumph by only one of those groups—the English colonists.

Societies of the Americas and Africa

In the Christian world, it was the year 1400; by the Muslim calendar, 802; and to the Mayas, who had the most accurate calendar of all, the era started with the date 1 Ahau 18 Ceh. Regardless of the name or reckoning system, the two-hundred-year period that followed changed the course of world history. For thousands of years, human societies had developed largely in isolation from each other. The era that began in the Christian fifteenth century brought the long-standing isolation to an end.

Although the civilizations had developed sepa-

rately, they shared several basic characteristics. All had political structures governing their secular affairs, kinship customs regulating their social life, economic systems defining their modes of subsistence, and one or more sets of indigenous religious beliefs. In addition, they all organized their work assignments on the basis of the sexual division of labor. However, these various societies exhibited basic economic differences. Some were nomadic, surviving by moving continually in search of wild animals and edible plants; others combined regular seasonal movements with a limited reliance on agriculture. In many areas, the cultivation of food crops provided most of the essential food supply. Such agricultural civilizations did not have to devote all their energies to subsistence. Instead, they were able to accumulate wealth, produce ornamental objects, and create elaborate rituals and ceremonies.

The differences in cultural traditions became the focal point for the interactions that occurred in the fifteenth century and thereafter among the various societies. Basic similarities were obscured by the shock of discovering that not all people were the same color as oneself, that other folk worshiped other gods, or that some people defined the separate roles of men and women differently from the way one's own society did. Because three major human groups—Native Americans, Africans, and Europeans—met and mingled on the soil of the Western Hemisphere, their relationships can be examined in that context.

Because the earliest known humanlike remains, about 3 million years old, have been found in what is now Ethiopia, it is likely that human beings originated on the continent of Africa. During many millennia, people slowly dispersed to the other continents. Some crossed a now-submerged stretch of land that joined Asia and North America at the site of the Bering Strait. These forerunners of the Native American population, known as Paleo-Indians, arrived in the Americas more than thirty thousand years ago. The Paleo-Indians were nomadic hunters of game and gatherers of wild plants. Over many centuries, they spread through North and South America, probably moving as extended families, or bands. Tribes were

Paleo-Indians

IMPORTANT EVENTS

1492	Christopher Columbus reaches Bahama islands	**1619**	First blacks arrive in Virginia
1518–30	Smallpox epidemic decimates Indian population of Central and South America	**1620**	Plymouth colony founded First group of English women arrives in Virginia
1521	Tenochtitlán surrenders to Cortés; Aztec empire falls to Spaniards	**1622**	Powhatan Confederacy attacks Virginia colony
1533	Henry VIII divorces Catherine of Aragon; English Reformation begins	**1625**	Charles I becomes king
		1630	Massachusetts Bay colony founded
1558	Elizabeth I becomes queen	**1634**	Maryland founded
1565	Establishment of St. Augustine	**1635**	Roger Williams expelled from Massachusetts Bay; founds Providence, Rhode Island
1587–90	Sir Walter Raleigh's Roanoke colony fails	**1636**	Connecticut founded
1603	James I becomes king	**1637**	Pequot war Anne Hutchinson expelled from Massachusetts Bay colony
1607	Jamestown founded		
1611	First Virginia tobacco crop		

composed of allied bands. Linguistic and cultural similarities linked tribes into even larger units, described by the name of the language they shared. East of the Mississippi River, the most important linguistic groups were the Algonkians and the Iroquoians, found primarily in the north, and the Muskogeans of the south.

Approximately 5,500 years ago, Indians living in central Mexico were already cultivating food crops. As knowledge of agricultural techniques spread, most Indian groups started to live a more sedentary existence. Some established permanent settlements; others moved several times a year among fixed sites. All the Native American cultures emphasized subsistence. Over the centuries, the North American Indians adapted their once-similar ways of life to specific and very different geographical settings. Thus they created the diversity of cultures that the Europeans encountered when they first arrived (see map, page 4).

The Indian bands that lived in environments not well suited to agriculture—for example, the Great Basin (now Nevada and Utah)—continued the nomadic lifestyle of their ancestors. Bands of such hunter-gatherers were small because it was difficult to find sufficient food for more than a few people. These bands usually consisted of one or more related families, with men hunting small animals and women gathering seeds and berries. Where large game was more plentiful and food supplies therefore more certain, bands of hunters could be somewhat larger.

In more favorable environments, still larger groups of Indians combined agriculture in varying degrees with gathering, hunting, and fishing. Tribes living near the seacoasts, such as the Chinooks of

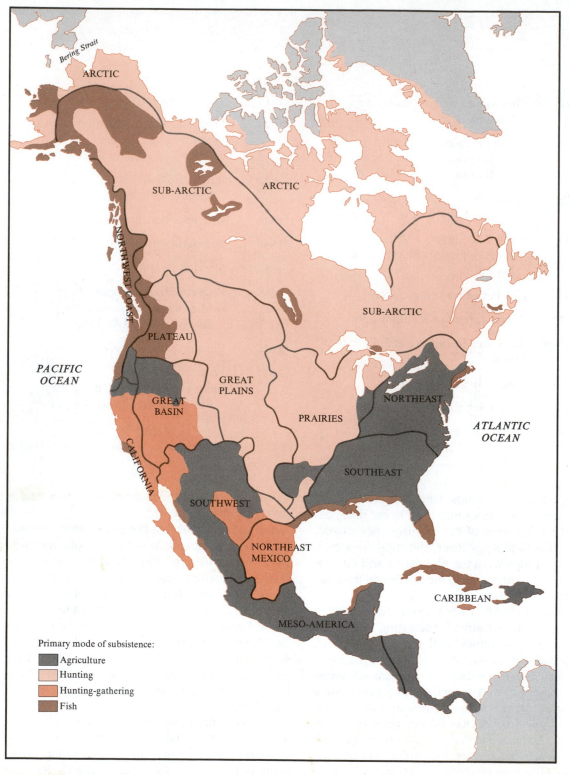

Indian Cultures of North America

John White, an artist who accompanied the exploratory mission Raleigh sent to America in 1585, sketched Pomeioc, a typical Algonkian village composed of houses made from woven mats stretched over poles, and surrounded by a defensive wooden palisade. *Library of Congress.*

the region that is now Washington and Oregon, consumed large quantities of fish and shellfish, in addition to growing crops and gathering seeds and berries. Tribes of the interior (for example, the Arikaras of the Missouri River valley) hunted large game animals while also cultivating fields of corn, squash, and beans. The Algonkian tribes, which inhabited much of what is now eastern Canada and the northeastern United States, also combined hunting and agriculture.

Societies that relied primarily on hunting large animals, such as deer and buffalo, for their food supply assigned that task to men, allotting food-processing and clothing-production chores to women. Before these nomadic bands acquired horses from the Spaniards, women—occasionally helped by dogs—also carried the family's belongings whenever the band relocated. Such a sexual division of labor was universal among hunting tribes,

Sexual Division of Labor in America

regardless of the linguistic group to which they belonged or their specific location.

By contrast, agricultural Indians differed in how they assigned cultivation of crops to the sexes. In what is now the southwestern United States, the Pueblo peoples defined agricultural labor as men's work. In the East, though, Algonkian, Iroquoian, and Muskogean peoples allocated agricultural chores to women. Among these eastern tribes, men's major assignments were hunting and clearing the land. In all the cultures, women gathered wild foods, prepared the food for consumption or storage, and cared for the children.

The southwestern and eastern agricultural Indians had similar social organizations. They lived in villages—sometimes sizable ones, with a thousand or more inhabitants. Pueblo villages were large, multistory buildings, constructed on terraces along the sides of cliffs or other easily defended sites. Most of the eastern villages were laid out defensively, often being surrounded by wood palisades and ditches. In these cultures, each dwelling housed an extended family defined matrilineally (through a female line of descent). Mothers, their married daughters, and their daughters' husbands and children all lived together. Matrilineal descent did not imply matriarchy, or the wielding of power by women; it was simply a means of reckoning kinship. The families in such dwellings were linked together into clans, again defined by matrilineal ties. On the other hand, nomadic bands of the Great Plains were most often related patrilineally—that is, through the male line.

In the southwestern and eastern cultures, the village supplied the most important political structures, but for the Plains dwellers, bands fulfilled that function. Among Pueblo and Muskogean peoples, the village council was the highest political authority; there was no government at the tribal level. That was also true of the nomadic hunters. The Iroquois, by contrast, had an elaborate political hierarchy, linking villages into tribes and tribes into a widespread confederation. In all the cultures, political power was divided between civil and war leaders, who had authority only so long as they retained the confidence of the people. Consensus rather than autocratic rule characterized the Indians' political systems.

Indian Politics and Religion

The political position of women varied from tribe to tribe. Women were more likely to assume leadership roles among the agricultural peoples than among nomadic hunters. For example, women could become the leaders of certain Algonkian bands, but they never held that position in the hunting tribes of the Great Plains. Iroquois women did not become chiefs, yet tribal matrons exercised political power. Probably the most powerful female chiefs were found in what is now the southeastern United States. In the mid-sixteenth century a female ruler, known as the Lady of Cofitachique, governed a large group of villages in the area that is now western South Carolina. Early English settlers on the Atlantic coast also noted the presence of female chiefs in nearby villages, most of them the wives, sisters, or widows of male leaders.

The Indian tribes varied in their religious beliefs even more than they did in their political systems. Yet they were all polytheistic, worshipping a multitude of gods. One common thread was their integration with nature. Thus the most important rituals related closely to each tribe's chief means of subsistence. The major deities of agricultural Indians and their chief festivals were linked to planting and harvest. On the other hand, the most important gods of hunting tribes were associated with animals, and their major festivals were related to hunting. The tribe's mode of subsistence and women's role in it helped to determine women's potential as religious leaders. Women held the most prominent positions in the agricultural societies (like the Iroquois) in which they were also the chief food producers.

The most highly centralized Indian civilizations on the North American continent inhabited what is now Mexico and Guatemala (Mesoamerica). The major Indian societies that the Spanish explorers encountered in the sixteenth century were the Aztecs and Mayas. The Aztecs, who entered central Mexico in the fourteenth century, were a warlike people who had consolidated their control over the entire region by the time of Cortés's arrival. The Mayas, who lived in what is now Guatemala and Mexico's Yucatan peninsula, were the intellectual leaders of Mesoamerica. They invented systems of writing and mathematics.

Aztecs and Mayas

Thus many different Indian cultures, comprising perhaps 4 to 6 million people, inhabited North America when Europeans arrived. Political systems varied among these cultures, as did means of sustenance. All told, these diverse groups spoke well over one thousand different languages. For obvious reasons, they did not consider themselves as one people.

Fifteenth-century Africa was also home to a variety of cultures adapted to different geographical settings (see map). In the north, along the Mediterranean Sea, lived the Berbers, a Muslim people of Middle Eastern origin. (Muslims are adherents of the Islamic religion, founded by the prophet Mohammed.) On the east coast of Africa, city-states dominated by Muslim merchants engaged in extensive trade with India, the Moluccas (part of modern Indonesia), and China. Through these ports passed a considerable share of the trade between the eastern Mediterranean and Far East;

Africa: Its Peoples

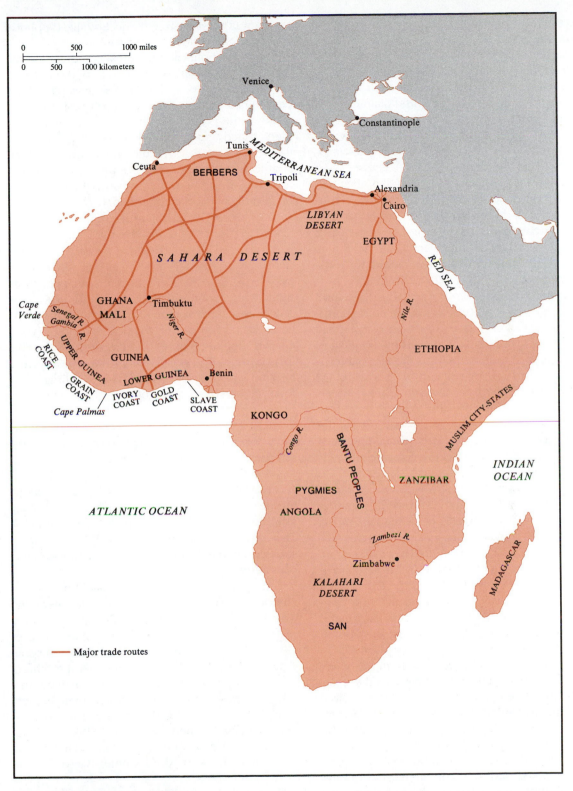

Africa and Its Peoples, ca. 1400

the rest followed the long land route across Central Asia known as the Silk Road.

In the African interior, south of the Mediterranean coast, lie the Sahara and Libyan deserts. Below the deserts, much of the continent is divided between tropical rain forests and grassy plains. People following quite different modes of subsistence lived in a wide belt south of the deserts. Below the Gulf of Guinea (see map), the fertile, forested landscape came to be dominated by Bantu-speaking peoples. About two thousand years ago, they had left their homeland in the region that now constitutes Nigeria and slowly migrated south and east across the continent, assimilating and conquering other ethnic groups as they went.

Most of the unwilling black migrants to North America came from West Africa, which the Europeans called Guinea, a land of tropical forests and small-scale agriculture. The northern region, or Upper Guinea, was heavily influenced by Islamic culture. As early as the eleventh century, many of its inhabitants had become Muslims; more important, the trans-Saharan trade between Upper Guinea and the Muslim Mediterranean was black Africa's major connection to Europe and the Middle East. In return for salt, dates, and such manufactured goods as silk and cotton cloth, Africans exchanged ivory, gold, and slaves with the northern merchants. (Slaves, who were mostly criminals and wartime captives, were in great demand as household servants in the homes of the Muslim Mediterranean elite.) This commerce was controlled first by the great kingdom of Ghana (ca. 900–1100), and then by its successor, the empire of Mali. Black Africa and Islam intersected at Timbuktu, the city that was the intellectual and commercial hub of the trade. A cosmopolitan center, Timbuktu attracted merchants and scholars from all parts of North Africa and the Mediterranean.

West Africa (Guinea)

Along the coast of West Africa and in the south, or Lower Guinea, most Africans continued to practice their indigenous religions, which revolved around rituals designed to ensure good harvests. The vast interior kingdoms of Mali and Ghana had no counterparts on the coast. Throughout Lower Guinea, individual villages composed of groups of kin were linked into small, hierarchical kingdoms. At the time of initial contact with Europeans, the region was characterized by decentralized political and social authority.

Just as the political structures varied, so too did the means of subsistence pursued by the different peoples of Guinea. In the northernmost part of Upper Guinea was the so-called Rice Coast, lying just south of the Gambia River. The people who lived there fished and cultivated rice. The Grain Coast, the next region to the south, was thinly populated and not readily accessible from the sea because it had only one good harbor. Its people concentrated on farming and animal husbandry. The Ivory Coast and the Gold Coast, in Lower Guinea, were each named by Europeans for the major trade goods they obtained there. The Gold Coast, comprising thirty little kingdoms known as the Akan States, later formed the basis of the great Asante kingdom. Initially many of the slaves destined for sale in the Americas came from the Akan States. By the eighteenth century, however, the next section of Lower Guinea supplied most of the slaves sold in the English colonies. The Adja kings of the region, which became known as the Slave Coast, encouraged the founding of slave-trading posts and served as middlemen in the trade.

Located east of the Slave Coast and west of the Niger River, the ancient kingdom of Benin was the strongest and most centralized coastal state in Guinea. Like Mali, it was a center of trade for West and North Africa. Those who lived in Benin along the delta of the Niger made much of their living from the water—like the peoples of the Rice Coast. They fished, made salt, and used skillfully constructed dugout canoes to carry on a wide-ranging commerce.

The societies of West Africa, like those of the Americas, assigned different tasks to men and women. In general, the sexes shared agricultural duties, but in some cultures women bore the primary responsibility for growing crops, whereas in others men assumed that chore. In addition, men hunted, managed livestock, and did most of the fishing. Women were responsible for childcare, food preparation, and cloth manufacture. Everywhere in West Africa women were the primary local traders.

Sexual Division of Labor in West Africa

Despite their different modes of subsistence and

Chapter 1: The Meeting of Old World and New, 1492–1640

A. *Guard-house for the Cattle.*
B. *Cotton.*
C. *Indian Corn.*
D. *A Native carrying a log of Timber.*

A West African village as drawn by a European observer. A wooden defensive palisade surrounds the circular houses made of woven plant materials. In this the African village resembles Pomeioc, the Indian village pictured on page 5. But note a major difference—a herd of livestock enclosed in a larger fence. Note also that the Africans are growing Indian corn, thus illustrating the exchange of plants between America and Africa (see page 14). *Library of Congress.*

deep political divisions, the peoples of West Africa had similar social systems. In the societies of West Africa, each sex handled its own affairs: just as male political and religious leaders governed the men, so females ruled the women. In the Dahomean kingdom, every male official had his female counterpart; in the Akan States, chiefs inherited their status through the female line, and each chief had a female assistant who supervised women's affairs. Religious beliefs likewise stressed the complementary nature of male and female roles. Both women and men served as heads of the cults and secret societies that directed the spiritual life of the villages.

The West Africans brought to the Americas, then, were agricultural peoples, skilled at tending livestock, hunting, fishing, and manufacturing cloth from plant fibers and animal skins. Both men and

women were accustomed to working communally, alongside other members of their own sex. They were also accustomed to a relatively egalitarian relationship between the sexes. In the New World, they entered societies that used their labor but had little respect for their cultural traditions. Of the three peoples whose experience intersected in the Americas, their lives were the most disrupted.

Europe and Its Explorations

After 1400, Europe began to recover from centuries of decline. Northern Europe had long been an intellectual and economic backwater, far outstripped in importance by the states of the Mediterranean, especially the great Italian city-states like Venice and Florence. The cultural flowering known as the Renaissance began in those city-states in the fourteenth century and spread northward. At the same time, the pace of economic activity quickened. Near-constant warfare promoted feelings of nationalism within the combatant countries. All these developments helped to set the stage for extraordinary political and technological change after the middle of the fifteenth century.

Yet in the midst of that change the life of Europe's rural people remained basically untouched for at least another century. European societies were hierarchical, with a few wealthy aristocratic families wielding arbitrary power over the majority of the people. Accordingly, Europe's kingdoms resembled those of Africa or Mesoamerica but differed greatly from the more egalitarian, consensus-based societies found in America north of Mexico. Most Europeans, like most Africans or Native Americans, lived in small agricultural villages. European farmers, or peasants, had separate landholdings, but worked their fields communally. Because fields had to lie fallow every second or third year to regain their fertility, all the villagers shared the work and the crop annually. Otherwise, individual families could not be sure of a regular supply of food.

In European cultures, men did most of the field work, with women helping out chiefly at planting and harvest. At other times, women's duties consisted primarily of childcare and household tasks, including preserving food for the winter, milking cows, and caring for poultry. If a woman's husband was an artisan or storekeeper, she might assist him in business. Since Europeans usually kept domesticated animals to use for meat, hunting had little economic importance in their cultures.

Sexual Division of Labor in Europe

In African or Native American societies, women often played major roles in politics and religion. In Europe, however, men were dominant in all areas of life. A few women from noble families—for example, Queen Elizabeth I of England—achieved status or power, but the vast majority of European women were excluded from positions of political authority. In the Catholic church, men served as bishops and priests; women served as nuns. At the familial level, husbands and fathers expected to control the lives of their wives, children, and servants (a patriarchal system of family governance).

The traditional hierarchical social structure of Europe changed little in the fifteenth century. But the same era witnessed rapid and dynamic political change. In England, Henry VII founded the Tudor dynasty in 1485 and began uniting a previously divided land. In France, the successors of Charles VII unified the kingdom. Most successful of all, at least in the short run, were Ferdinand of Aragon and Isabella of Castile. In 1469, they married and combined their kingdoms, thus creating the foundation of a strongly Catholic Spain. In 1492, they defeated the Muslims, who had lived on the Iberian peninsula for centuries, and expelled all Jews from their domain.

Political and Technological Change

The fifteenth century also brought significant technological change to Europe. Movable type and the printing press, invented in the 1450s, made information more widely and more readily accessible than ever before. Adapting designs from Arab sailors, Europeans created more maneuverable ships, which could sail against the wind. Of key importance was the perfecting of navigational instruments, so that sailors could estimate their position on the high seas. These developments stimulated Europeans' curiosity about fabled lands and spurred them to think about reaching exotic places by ship. The widespread dissemination of Marco Polo's *Travels,* published in 1477, convinced many educated Europeans that they could trade directly with China via oceangoing vessels, instead of relying on the Silk Road or the Muslim merchants of East Africa.

Thus the European explorations of the fifteenth and sixteenth centuries were made possible by technological advances and by the financial might of newly powerful national rulers. The primary motivation for the exploratory voyages was a desire for direct access to the wealth of the East. Another motive was to spread Christianity around the world. The linking of materialist and spiritual goals might seem con-

Motives for Exploration

tradictory today, but fifteenth-century Europeans saw no conflict between the two.

The seafaring Portuguese, whose land was located on the southwestern corner of the continent of Europe, began the age of European expansion in 1415, when they seized control of Ceuta, a Muslim city in North Africa (see map, page 7). Prince Henry the Navigator, son of King John I, realized that vast wealth awaited the first European nation to tap the riches of Africa and Asia directly. Each year he dispatched ships southward along the western coast of Africa, attempting to discover a passage to the East. Not until after Prince Henry's death did Bartholomew Dias round the southern tip of Africa (1488) and Vasco da Gama finally reach India (1498).

Although West African states successfully resisted European penetration of the interior, they allowed the Portuguese to establish trading posts along their coasts. Charging the traders rent and levying duties on the goods they imported, the African chiefdoms benefited considerably from their new access to European manufactures. The Portuguese, who no longer had to rely on the long trans-Saharan trade route, earned immense profits by transporting African goods swiftly to Europe. Among their most valuable cargoes were slaves. When they carried African Muslim prisoners of war back to the Iberian peninsula, the Portuguese introduced the custom of black slavery into Europe.

Spain, with its reinvigorated monarchy, was the next country to sponsor exploratory voyages. Envious of Portuguese successes, Queen Isabella hoped to gain a foothold in Asia for her nation, and so she agreed to finance a voyage by Christopher Columbus, a Genoese sea captain.

Christopher Columbus

Like other experienced sailors, Columbus believed the world to be round. But Columbus was regarded as a crackpot because of his estimate of the world's size. He believed that Japan lay only three thousand miles from the southern European coast and therefore concluded that it would be easier to reach the East by sailing west than by making the difficult voyage around the southern tip of Africa.

On August 3, 1492, with three ships under his command—the *Pinta*, the *Niña*, and the *Santa Maria*—Columbus sailed west from the port of Palos in Spain. On October 12, he landed on an island in the Bahamas, which he named San Salvador and claimed for the king and queen of Spain. Because he thought he had reached the Indies, he called the inhabitants of the region Indians.

Columbus made three more voyages to the west, during which he explored most of the major Caribbean islands and sailed along the coasts of Central and South America. Until the day he died in 1506, Columbus continued to believe that he had reached Asia. Even before his death, others knew better. Because the Florentine Amerigo Vespucci, who explored the South American coast in 1499, was the first to publish the idea that a new continent had been discovered, a mapmaker in 1507 labeled the land America. By then, in 1494, Spain, Portugal, and Pope Alexander VI had signed the Treaty of Tordesillas, which confirmed Portugal's dominance in Africa and Brazil, in exchange for Spanish pre-eminence in the rest of the New World.

More than five hundred years earlier, Norse explorers had briefly colonized the area that is now Newfoundland, but the voyages of Columbus and his successors finally brought the Old and New Worlds together. England dispatched John Cabot (1497) to the new lands. Giovanni da Verrazzano (1524), and Jacques Cartier (1534) explored the North American coast for the French. Henry Hudson (1609 and 1610) did likewise for a Dutch company. (See map, page 12.) Although they were primarily searching for the legendary, nonexistent "Northwest Passage" through the Americas, their discoveries prompted European nations to explore the New World further for its own sake.

Only Spain moved immediately to take advantage of the discoveries. On his first voyage, Columbus had established a base on the island of Hispaniola.

Conquistadores

From there, Spanish explorers fanned out around the Caribbean basin. In the 1520s, Spain's dreams of wealth were realized when Cortés conquered the Aztec empire, killing its ruler, Moctezuma, and seizing a fabulous treasure of gold and silver. And Francisco Pizarro, who explored the western coast of South America, acquired the richest silver mines in the world by conquering and enslaving the Incas in 1535. Other conquistadores, such as Juan Rodriguez Cabrillo

European Explorations in America

(who sailed along the California coast), Hernando de Soto (who discovered the Mississippi River), and Francisco Vásquez de Coronado (who explored the southwestern portion of what is now the United States), found little of value. Still, by 1550, Spain controlled the richest, most extensive empire Europe had known since ancient Rome.

Spain established the model of colonization that other countries later attempted to imitate, a model with three major elements. First, the crown maintained tight control over the colonies, establishing a hierarchical government that allowed little autonomy to New World jurisdictions. Second, most of the colonists sent from Spain were male. They married Indian—and later black—women, thereby creating the racially mixed population that characterizes Latin America to the present day. Third, the colonies' wealth was based on the exploitation of both the native population and slaves imported from Africa. The *encomienda* system, which granted tribute from Indian villages to individual

conquistadores as a reward for their services to the crown, ensured that the conquerors themselves did not have to engage in field work. Laws adopted in 1542 reformed the system, by forbidding Spaniards to enslave Indians. In response, the conquerors began to import Africans in order to increase the labor force under their direct control.

American civilizations suffered under Spanish rule. The Spaniards leveled Indian cities, building cathedrals and monasteries on sites once occupied by Aztec, Incan, and Mayan temples. Some conquistadores sought to erase all vestiges of the great Indian cultures by burning all the written records they found. With traditional ways of life in disarray, devastated by disease, and compelled to labor for their conquerors, many residents of Mesoamerica accepted the Christian religion brought to New Spain by Franciscan and Dominican missionaries. The friars devoted their initial energies to persuading the Indians to move into new towns and build Roman Catholic churches. There the Indians were

Chapter 1: The Meeting of Old World and New, 1492–1640

exposed to European lifestyles, newly elaborated religious rituals, and attempts to assimilate Christianity and pagan beliefs. These conversion efforts met with remarkable success.

The Spanish missionaries who ventured into the territory that is now the United States were less able to win Indian converts, for native cultures there remained largely intact, despite the European invasion. After several failed attempts to colonize the Atlantic coast, the Spanish established St. Augustine, Florida, in 1565. Efforts to Christianize the Indians succeeded only after Franciscans forced them to move to mission towns; even then, many resisted the friars' message. Still, by the end of the sixteenth century, a chain of Spanish missions stretched across what is now northern Florida.

Unlike the Spanish, other European nations did not immediately start to colonize the coasts that their sailors had explored. They were interested in exploiting the natural wealth of the region, not in conquering territories. Their mariners, who came to fish in the rich waters off Newfoundland, learned that they could supplement their profits by exchanging cloth and metal goods like pots and knives for the Indians' beaver pelts. At first the Europeans conducted their trading from ships sailing along the coast, but later they established permanent outposts on the mainland, to centralize and control the traffic in furs. Among the most successful of these were the French trading posts at Quebec (1608) and Montreal (1642), on the St. Lawrence River; the Swedish settlement at Fort Christina (1638) on the Delaware River; and the Dutch forts of New Amsterdam and Fort Orange on the Hudson River, both founded in 1624, which together constituted the colony of New Netherland. All were inhabited primarily by male adventurers, whose chief aim was to send as many pelts as possible home to Europe.

Northern Traders

The northern Europeans' trading activities had a significant effect on native societies. The Europeans' insatiable demand for furs, especially beaver, was matched by the Indians' desire for European goods that could make their lives easier and establish their superiority over neighboring tribes. Some tribes concentrated so completely on trapping for the European market that they abandoned their traditional modes of subsistence. The

Abenakis of Maine, for example, became partially dependent on food supplied by their neighbors to the south, the Massachusett tribe, because they devoted most of their energies to catching beaver to sell to French traders. The Massachusetts, in turn, intensified their production of foodstuffs, which they traded to the Abenakis in exchange for European metal tools.

The French in particular devoted considerable attention to converting Native Americans to Christianity. Jesuit missionaries in New France, known to the Indians as Black Robes, tried to persuade Native Americans to live near French settlements and to adopt European lifestyles and Roman Catholicism. When that effort failed, the Jesuits concluded that they could convert their new charges without insisting that the Indians alter their customary modes of existence. So the priests learned Indian languages and traveled to remote regions.

Jesuit Missions in New France

In their pursuit of conversions, the Jesuits sought to undermine the authority of village shamans (religious leaders) and to gain the confidence of leaders who could influence others. The Black Robes cleverly used a variety of weapons to attain the desired end. Seemingly immune to smallpox, they explained epidemics among the Native American peoples as God's punishment for sin. Drawing on a knowledge of European science, they predicted solar and lunar eclipses. Perhaps most important of all, they amazed the Indians by being able to communicate with each other over long distances and periods of time by employing marks on pieces of paper. The Indians' desire to learn how to harness the extraordinary power of literacy was probably the most critical factor in making them receptive to the Jesuits' message. Although the process took many years, the Jesuits slowly gained thousands of converts.

The Europeans' greatest impact on the Americas was unintended. The diseases carried from the Old World to the New by the alien invaders killed millions of Native Americans, who had no immunity to germs that had infested Europe, Asia, and Africa for centuries. The greatest killer was smallpox, which was spread by direct human contact. Other devastating diseases in-

Killer Diseases

cluded influenza and measles. The statistics are staggering. When Columbus landed on Hispaniola in 1492, more than 3 million Indians resided there. Fifty years later, only 500 were still alive.

Even in the north, where smaller Indian populations encountered only a few Europeans, disease ravaged the countryside. A great epidemic, most likely chicken pox, swept through the Indian villages along the coast north of Cape Cod in 1616–1618. The mortality rate may have been as high as 90 percent. Because of this dramatic depopulation of the area, just a few years later English colonists were able to establish settlements virtually unopposed by native peoples.

The Native Americans, though, took a revenge of sorts. They gave the Europeans syphilis, a virulent venereal disease. The first recorded case of the new disease in Europe occurred in Barcelona, Spain, in 1493, shortly after Columbus's return from the Caribbean. Although less likely to cause immediate death than smallpox, syphilis was extremely dangerous and debilitating. It spread quickly, even reaching China by 1505.

Columbus's voyages also brought about a broad mutual transfer of plants and animals between the Old World and the New. Europeans introduced large domesticated mammals to the Americas, and they obtained from the New World a variety of vegetables—particularly corn, beans, squash, and potatoes—that were more nutritious than Old World's wheat and rye. Thus, the diets of both peoples were enriched.

Exchange of Plants and Animals

The exchange of two other commodities significantly influenced European and American civilizations. In America, Europeans encountered tobacco, and smoking and chewing the "Indian weed" became a fad in the Old World. Tobacco cultivation was later to form the basis for the prosperity of the first successful English colonies in North America. But more important than tobacco's influence on Europe was the impact of the horse on some Indian cultures. Horses brought to America by the Spaniards inevitably fell into the hands of Native Americans. They were traded northward through Mexico into the Great Plains, where they eventually changed the lifestyles of some tribes—for example, the Apaches, Blackfeet, Comanches,

and Sioux, who made the horse a focal point of their existence.

England Colonizes the New World

English merchants and political leaders watched enviously as Spain's New World possessions immeasurably enriched that country. In the mid-sixteenth century, English "sea dogs," such as John Hawkins and Sir Francis Drake, began to raid Spanish treasure fleets. Their actions caused friction between the two countries and helped to foment a war that culminated in the defeat of the Spanish armada off the English coast in 1588. With the loss of the armada, Spain's fortunes began to ebb. England started to think about planting its own colonies in the Western Hemisphere, thereby preventing Spain from completely dominating the New World and simultaneously gaining direct access to valuable American commodities.

The first English colonial planners hoped to reproduce Spanish successes by dispatching to America men who would exploit the native peoples for their own and their nation's benefit. In the 1580s, a group including Sir Humphrey Gilbert and Sir Walter Raleigh promoted a scheme to establish outposts that could trade with the Indians and provide bases for attacks on New Spain. Approving the idea, Queen Elizabeth I authorized Raleigh and Gilbert to colonize North America. Gilbert failed to plant a colony in Newfoundland, and Raleigh was only briefly more successful. In 1587, he sent 117 colonists to the territory he named Virginia (for Elizabeth, the "Virgin Queen"). They established a settlement on Roanoke Island, in what is now North Carolina, but in 1590 a resupply ship could not find them. The colonists had vanished, leaving only the name of a nearby island carved on a tree.

Raleigh's Roanoke Colony

Raleigh's failure ended English efforts at settlement in North America for nearly two decades.

When, in 1606, the English decided to try once more, they again planned colonies that imitated the Spanish model. However, success came only when they abandoned that model and sent large numbers of men and women to set up agriculturally based colonies in the New World. Before discussing the history of those colonies, it is important to examine the two major developments that prompted approximately 200,000 ordinary English men and women to move to North America in the seventeenth century—with encouragement from their government.

The first development was a significant change in English religious practice—a transformation that eventually led large numbers of English dissenters to leave their homeland. In 1533, **English Reformation** Henry VIII, wanting a male heir, sought to annul his marriage to his Spanish-born queen, Catherine of Aragon. When the pope refused to approve the annulment, Henry left the Roman Catholic church, founded the Church of England, and, with Parliament's concurrence, proclaimed himself its head. At first the reformed Church of England differed little from Catholicism in its practices. Under Henry's daughter Elizabeth I, however, new currents of religious belief, which had originated on the European continent early in the sixteenth century, dramatically affected the English church.

The leaders of the continental Protestant Reformation were Martin Luther, a German monk, and John Calvin, a French cleric and lawyer. Combating the Catholic doctrine that priests had to serve as intermediaries between lay people and God, they both insisted that each person could interpret the Bible individually. Both Luther and Calvin rejected Catholic rituals, denied the need for an elaborate church hierarchy, and asserted that salvation came through faith alone, rather than, as Catholics believed, through faith and good works. Calvin, though, went further than Luther in stressing God's absolute omnipotence and emphasizing the need for people to submit totally to His will.

Elizabeth I tolerated religious diversity among her subjects as long as they generally acknowledged her authority as head of the Church of England. Accordingly, during her long reign (1558–1603) Calvin's ideas gained influence within the English church. By the late sixteenth century, many English Calvinists believed that the Reformation had not gone far enough. Because these English Calvinists said that they wanted to purify the church, they became known as Puritans.

Elizabeth I's Stuart successors, her cousin James I (1603–1625) and his son Charles I (1625–1649), were less tolerant of Puritans than she. As Scots, **Puritans** they also had little respect for the traditions of representative government that had developed in England under the Tudors and their predecessors. The Stuarts insisted that a monarch's power came directly from God and that his subjects had no alternative but to obey him. A king's authority, they argued, was absolute. Both James I and Charles I believed that their authority included the power to enforce religious conformity among their subjects. Thus they authorized the persecution of Puritans, who were challenging many of the most important precepts of the English church. Consequently, in the 1620s and 1630s a number of English Puritans decided to move to America, where they hoped to put their religious beliefs into practice unmolested by the Stuarts or the church hierarchy.

The second major development that led English folk to move to North America was the onset of dramatic social and economic change caused by the doubling of the English population in the 150-year period after **Social Change in England** 1530. All those additional people needed food, clothing, and other goods. The competition for goods led to high inflation, coupled with a fall in real wages as the number of workers increased. In these new economic and demographic circumstances, those with sizable landholdings frequently prospered. Others, particularly landless laborers or those with very small amounts of land, fell into unremitting poverty.

Well-to-do English people reacted with alarm to what they saw as the disappearance of traditional ways of life. The streets and highways were filled with steady streams of the landless and the homeless. Officials became obsessed with the problem of maintaining order and came to believe that England was overcrowded. They concluded that colonies established in the New World could siphon off England's "surplus population," thus easing the social strains at home. For similar reasons, many English people decided that they could improve their circumstances by migrating from a small, land-scarce, apparently overpopulated island to a large, land-rich continent.

The initial impetus for establishing what was to become England's first permanent colony in the Western Hemisphere came from a group of merchants and wealthy gentry. In 1606, envisioning the possibility of earning great profits from a New World settlement by finding precious metals and opening new trade routes, they set up a joint-stock company, the Virginia Company, to plant colonies in America.

Joint-stock companies had been developed in England during the sixteenth century as a mechanism for pooling the resources of a large number of small investors. These forerunners of modern corporations were funded through the sale of stock. Until the founding of the Virginia Company, they had been used primarily to finance trading voyages. For that purpose they worked well. No one person risked too much money, and investors usually received quick returns. But joint-stock companies turned out to be a poor way to finance colonies, because the early settlements required enormous amounts of capital and, with rare exceptions, failed to return much immediate profit. Accordingly, the colonies founded by joint-stock companies suffered from a chronic lack of capital.

Joint-Stock Companies

The Virginia Company was no exception to this rule. Chartered by King James I in 1606, the company tried but failed to start a colony in Maine and barely succeeded in planting one in Virginia. In 1607 it dispatched 144 men and boys to North America. Ominously, only 104 of them survived the voyage. In May of that year, they established the settlement called Jamestown. Many of the first migrants were gentlemen unaccustomed to working with their hands and artisans with irrelevant skills like glassmaking. They resisted living "like savages" and retained English dress and casual work habits despite their desperate circum-

Founding of Virginia

stances. Such attitudes, combined with the effects of chronic malnutrition and epidemic disease, took a terrible toll. Only when Captain John Smith, one of the colony's founders, imposed military discipline on the colonists in 1608 was Jamestown saved from collapse. But after Smith's departure, the colony experienced a severe "starving time" (the winter of 1609–1610), during which some colonists resorted to cannibalism. Although later conditions improved somewhat, by 1624 only 1,300 of the approximately 8,000 English migrants to Virginia remained alive.

That the colony survived at all was a tribute not to the English, but rather to a group of six Algonkian tribes known as the Powhatan Confederacy (see map). Powhatan, a powerful figure, was consolidating his authority over some twenty-five other small tribes in the area when the Europeans arrived. Fortunately for the Englishmen, Powhatan viewed them as potential allies. He found the English colony to be a reliable source of such items as steel knives and guns, which gave him a technological advantage over his Indian neighbors. In return, Powhatan's tribes traded corn and other foodstuffs to the starving colonists. The initially cordial relationship soon deteriorated, however. The colonists kidnaped Powhatan's daughter, Pocahontas, held her hostage, and forcibly married her off to one of their number, John Rolfe.

Powhatan Confederacy

Thereafter the relationship between the Jamestown colony and the coastal tribes was an uneasy one. English and Algonkian peoples had much in common: deep religious beliefs, a lifestyle oriented around agriculture, clear political and social hierarchies, and sharply defined sex roles. Yet both the English and the Indians usually focused on their cultural differences, not their similarities. English men saw Indian men as lazy because they hunted (hunting was a sport in English eyes) and did not work in the fields. Indian men thought English men effeminate because they did "women's work" of cultivation. In the same vein, the whites believed that Indian women were oppressed since they did heavy field labor.

Other differences between the two cultures caused serious misunderstandings. Although both

European Settlements and Indian Tribes in America, 1650

societies were hierarchical, the nature of the hierarchies differed considerably. Among the coastal Algonkian tribes, people were not born to positions of leadership, nor were political power and social status necessarily inherited through the male line. The English gentry inherited their position from their fathers, and English leaders tended to rule autocratically. By contrast, the authority of Indian leaders rested on the consent of their fellow tribesmen. Accustomed to the European concept of powerful kings, the English sought such figures within the tribes. Often (for example, when negotiating treaties) they willfully overestimated the ability of chiefs to make independent decisions for their people.

Algonkian and English Cultural Differences

Furthermore, the Indians and the English had very different notions of property ownership. In most eastern tribes, land was held communally by the entire group. It could not be bought or sold absolutely. The English, on the other hand, were accustomed to individual farms and to buying and selling land. In addition, the English refused to accept the validity of Indian claims to traditional hunting territories, insisting that only land intensively cultivated could be regarded as owned or occupied by a tribe.

Above all, the English settlers believed unwaveringly in the superiority of their civilization. They expected the Indians to adopt English customs and to convert to Christianity. They showed little respect for traditional Indian ways of life, especially when they believed their own interests were at stake. That attitude was clearly revealed in the Virginia colony's treatment of the Powhatan Confederacy in subsequent years.

What upset the balance between the English and the Indians was the spread of tobacco cultivation. In tobacco, the settlers and the Virginia Company found the salable commodity for which they had been searching. John Rolfe planted the first crop in 1611. In 1620, Virginians exported 40,000 pounds of cured leaves, and by the end of that decade shipments had jumped dramatically, to 1.5 million pounds. The great tobacco boom had begun, fueled

Tobacco: The Basis of Virginia's Success

by high prices and substantial profits for planters. Although the price of tobacco fluctuated wildly from year to year, it became the foundation of Virginia's prosperity. With an economic base, the colony developed from an all-male outpost into an agricultural settlement inhabited by both men and women (the first group of English women arrived in 1620).

Successful tobacco cultivation required abundant land, since the crop quickly drained soil of nutrients. Planters soon learned that a field could produce only about three crops before it had to lie fallow for several years to regain its fertility. Thus the once-small English settlements began to expand rapidly: eager planters applied to the Virginia Company for large land grants on both sides of the James River and its tributary streams.

Opechancanough, Powhatan's brother and successor, watched the English colonists steadily encroaching on Indian lands and attempting to convert members of the tribes to Christianity. He recognized the danger his brother had overlooked. On March 22, 1622, the confederacy launched coordinated attacks all along the river. By the end of the day, 347 colonists (about one-quarter of the total) lay dead, and only a timely warning from two Christianized Indians saved Jamestown itself from destruction. The colony survived both this war and one waged by Opechancanough in 1644. His defeat in the latter war ended the Powhatan Confederacy's efforts to resist the spread of white settlement.

Life in the Chesapeake: Virginia and Maryland

In 1624, James I revoked the charter and made Virginia a royal colony, ruled by the king through appointed officials. At the same time, though, he allowed the company's "headright" system and a representative assembly to survive. Under the headright system, every new arrival was promised a land grant of fifty acres; those who financed the passage of others received headrights for each. The assembly, called the House of Burgesses, had been created in 1619. It gave the settlers a representative

Advocates of colonization hoped to establish a silk industry in the Chesapeake and published tracts illustrating the production of silk. This one shows a man and a woman working together, but at different tasks. All the attempts to create such industries failed, despite the promoters' efforts. *John Carter Brown Library, Brown University.*

system of government, with considerable local autonomy. The continuance of the House of Burgesses ensured that the political structure of England's American possessions would differ from that of New Spain, which was ruled autocratically by the Spanish monarchs.

By the 1630s, tobacco was firmly established in Virginia as the staple crop and chief source of revenue. It quickly became just as important in the second English colony planted on Chesapeake Bay: Maryland, chartered by the king in 1632 and given to the Calvert family as a personal possession (proprietorship). The Calverts intended the colony to serve as a haven for their fellow Roman Catholics, who were being persecuted in England. Cecilius Calvert, second Lord Bal-

Founding of Maryland

timore, became the first colonizer to offer freedom of religion to all Christian settlers. In that respect Maryland differed from Virginia, where the Church of England was the only officially recognized church. The two Chesapeake colonies, however, resembled each other in most ways. In Maryland, as in Virginia, tobacco planters spread along the riverbanks, establishing isolated farms instead of towns.

The planting, cultivation, and harvesting of tobacco were essentially unskilled tasks that had to be done by hand. When the headright system was adopted in Maryland in 1640, a prospective tobacco planter anywhere in the Chesapeake could simultaneously obtain both land and the labor to work it. Through good management a planter could use his profits to pay for the passage of more workers and thus gain title to more land.

There were two possible sources of laborers for the tobacco farms of the Chesapeake: Africa and England. Nearby tribes could not supply the needed workers, since the region was not densely populated. Beginning in 1619, a few Africans were carried to the Chesapeake. Their numbers were small and their status uncertain; some appear to have been slaves, but others were not. As late as 1670, blacks constituted only about 5 percent of Virginia's population. Chesapeake tobacco planters looked instead to England to supply their labor needs. Workers migrated from England as indentured servants: that is, in return for their passage they contracted to work for planters for periods ranging from four to seven years.

Indentured servants accounted for 75 to 85 percent of the approximately 130,000 English migrants to Virginia and Maryland during the seventeenth century. Roughly three-quarters of them were men between the ages of fifteen and twenty-four. Most had been farmers and laborers. They were what their contemporaries called the "common" or "middling" sort. Judging by their youth, though, most had probably not yet established themselves in England.

Migrants to the Chesapeake

Many of the servants came from areas of England that were experiencing severe social disruption. Some had already moved several times within England before deciding to migrate to America. For such people the Chesapeake appeared to offer good prospects. Once they had fulfilled the terms of their indentures, servants were promised "freedom dues" consisting of clothes, tools, livestock, casks of corn and tobacco, and sometimes even land.

The migrants' lives were difficult. They typically worked six days a week, ten to fourteen hours a day, in a climate much warmer than they were accustomed to. Their masters could discipline or sell them, and they faced severe penalties for running away. Even so, the laws did offer them some protection. For example, their masters were supposed to supply them with sufficient food, clothing, and shelter, and they were not to be beaten excessively. Servants who were especially cruelly treated could turn to the courts for assistance.

Conditions of Servitude

Servants and planters alike had to contend with epidemic disease. After surviving a process called "seasoning"—a bout with disease (probably malaria)—immigrants were confronted with dysentery, influenza, typhoid, and recurrences of malaria. As a result, approximately 40 percent of the male servants did not survive long enough to become freedmen.

For those who survived the term of their indentures, however, the opportunities for advancement were real. Until the last decades of the century, former servants were usually able to become independent planters (freeholders) and to live a modest but comfortable existence. Some even assumed such positions of political prominence as justice of the peace or militia officer. But after 1670, tobacco prices fell, good land became expensive, and Maryland dropped its legal requirement that servants receive land as part of their freedom dues. By 1700, the Chesapeake was no longer the land of opportunity it had once been.

Life in the seventeenth-century Chesapeake was hard for everyone. Before being cultivated, fields had to be cleared of trees. Most settlers lived in houses that were little more than shacks, had few material possessions, and consumed a diet based on pork and corn. Indeed, the lack of a nutritious diet magnified the health problems caused by epidemic disease.

The predominance of males, the incidence of servitude, and the high mortality rates combined to produce unusual patterns of family life. Female servants normally were not allowed to marry during their terms of indenture, since masters did not want pregnancies to deprive them of workers. Many male ex-servants could not marry at all because there were so few women. On the other hand, nearly every adult free woman in the Chesapeake married, and the many widows commonly remarried within a few months of a husband's death. Yet because their marriages were delayed by servitude or broken by death, Chesapeake women bore only one to three children, in contrast to English women, who normally had at least five.

Family Life in the Chesapeake

As a result of the demographic patterns that led to a low rate of natural increase, migrants made up a majority of the Chesapeake population through-

Chesapeake Politics out the seventeenth century. That fact had important implications for politics in Maryland and Virginia. Since migrants dominated the population, they also composed the vast majority of the membership of Virginia's House of Burgesses and Maryland's House of Delegates (established in 1635). In each colony, they also dominated the governor's council, which was simultaneously part of the legislature, the colony's highest court, and executive adviser to the governor.

English-born colonists naturally tended to look to England for solutions to their problems, and migrants frequently relied on English allies to advance their cause. The seventeenth-century leaders of the Chesapeake colonies engaged in bitter and prolonged struggles for power and personal economic advantage. These struggles often thwarted the Virginia and Maryland governments' ability to function effectively. Consequently, the existence of representative institutions failed to lead to political stability. Thus the people of the Chesapeake paid a high price for the area's unusual population patterns.

The Founding of New England

The economic motives that prompted English people to move to the Chesapeake colonies also drew men and women to New England. But Puritans had organized the New England colonies. Moreover, the northern landscape and climate were more conducive to diversified small farms than to large production units yielding staple crops. For both these reasons, the northern settlements turned out very differently from those in the South.

Religion was a constant presence in the lives of pious Puritans. As followers of John Calvin, they believed that an omnipotent God predestined souls to heaven or hell before birth and **Puritan Beliefs** that Christians could do nothing to change their ultimate fate. One of their primary duties as Christians, though, was to assess the state of their own souls. Thus they devoted themselves to self-examination and Bible study. Yet even the most pious could never be absolutely certain that they were numbered among the saved. Consequently, devout Puritans were filled with anxiety about their spiritual state.

Some Puritans (called Congregationalists) wanted to reform the Church of England rather than abandon it. Another group, known as Separatists, believed the Church of England to be so corrupt that it could not be salvaged. The only way to purify it, they believed, was to start anew, establishing their own religious bodies, with membership restricted to the saved, as nearly as they could be identified.

In 1620, some Separatists, many of whom had earlier migrated to Holland in quest of the right to practice their religion freely, obtained permission to settle in part of the territory **Founding of Plymouth** controlled by the Virginia Company. In September 1620, more than one hundred people, only thirty of them Separatists, set sail from Plymouth, England, on the *Mayflower*. Two months later they landed in America, but farther north than they had intended. Because of the lateness of the season, they decided to stay where they were. They established their colony on a fine harbor and named it after the city from which they had sailed.

Even before they landed, the Pilgrims had to surmount their first challenge from the "strangers," or non-Puritans, who had sailed with them. Because they landed outside the jurisdiction of the Virginia Company, some of the strangers questioned the authority of the colony's leaders. In response, the Mayflower Compact, signed while everyone was still on board the ship, established a "Civil Body Politic" and a rudimentary legal authority for the colony. Later, after more towns had been founded and the population had increased, Plymouth created an assembly to which the landowning male settlers elected representatives.

A second challenge facing the Pilgrims in 1620 and 1621 was, quite simply, survival. Like the Jamestown settlers before them, they were poorly prepared to survive in the new environment. Their difficulties were compounded by the season of their arrival, for they barely had time to build shelters before winter descended on them. Only half of the *Mayflower*'s passengers were still alive by spring. But, again like the Virginians, the Pilgrims benefited from the political circumstances of their Indian neighbors.

The Pokanokets (also called Wampanoags), who controlled the area in which the Pilgrims had settled, had suffered terrible losses from an epidemic in 1616. To protect themselves from the powerful Narragansett Indians of the southern New England coast, the Pokanokets decided to ally themselves with the newcomers. In the spring of 1621, their leader, Massasoit, signed a treaty with the Pilgrims, and, during the colony's first difficult years, the Pokanokets supplied the English with essential foodstuffs. The settlers were also assisted by Squanto, an Indian whose village had been wiped out by the epidemic. Because he had been captured by traders and held prisoner in England for several years, Squanto spoke English. He served as the Pilgrims' interpreter, as well as their major source of information about the unfamiliar environment.

Before the 1620s had ended, a group of Congregationalists launched the colonial enterprise that would come to dominate New England. The

Founding of Massachusetts Bay

event that stimulated their interest in the New World was the accession of Charles I to the throne in 1625. Charles was more hostile to Puritan beliefs than his father had been. Consequently, some non-Separatists began to think of settling in America. A group of Congregationalist merchants sent out a body of settlers to Cape Ann, north of Cape Cod, in 1628. The following year, the merchants obtained a royal charter, constituting themselves as the Massachusetts Bay Company.

The new company quickly attracted the attention of Puritans of the "middling sort" who were becoming increasingly convinced that they could no longer practice their religion freely in England. Although still committed to the goal of reforming the Church of England, they came to believe that they should pursue it in America rather than at home. In a dramatic move, the Congregationalist merchants boldly decided to transfer the headquarters of the Massachusetts Bay Company to New England. The settlers would then be answerable to no one in the mother country and would be able to handle their affairs as they pleased.

The most important recruit to the new venture was John Winthrop, a pious but practical landed gentleman from Suffolk. In October 1629, the

Governor John Winthrop

members of the Massachusetts Bay Company elected the forty-one-year-old Winthrop as their governor. With the exception of a few isolated years, he served in that post until his death in 1649. It thus fell to Winthrop to organize the initial segment of the great Puritan migration to America. In 1630, more than one thousand English men and women settled in Massachusetts—most of them in Boston, which soon became the largest town in British North America. By 1643, nearly twenty thousand compatriots had followed them.

Winthrop's was a transcendent vision. The society he foresaw in Puritan America was a true commonwealth, a community in which each person put the good of the whole ahead of his or her private concerns. In America, he asserted, "we shall build a city upon a hill, the eyes of all people are upon us." People in this "city upon a hill" were to live according to the precepts of Christian charity, loving and aiding friends and enemies alike. Of course, such an ideal was beyond human reach.

The Puritans' communal ideal was expressed chiefly in the doctrine of the covenant. They believed God had made a covenant—that is an agree-

Ideal of the Covenant

ment or contract—with them when they were chosen for the special mission to America. In turn, they covenanted with each other, promising to work together toward their goals. The founders of churches and towns in the new land often drafted formal documents setting forth the principles on which such institutions would be based. The same was true of the colonial governments of New England.

The leaders of Massachusetts Bay likewise transformed their original joint-stock company charter into the foundation for a covenanted community based on mutual consent. Under pressure from the settlers, they gradually changed the General Court, officially merely the company's governing body, into a colonial legislature. They also opened the status of freeman, or voting member of the company, to all property-owning adult male church members residing in Massachusetts. Less than two decades after the first large group of Puritans had arrived in Massachusetts Bay, the colony had a functioning system of self-government composed of a governor and a two-house legislature. The General Court also established a judicial system modeled on England's.

The colony's method of distributing land helped to further the communal ideal. Groups of families, which often came from the same region of England,

New England Towns

applied together to the General Court for grants of land to establish towns. The men who received the original town grant had the sole authority to determine how the land would be distributed. Understandably, they copied the villages from which they had come. First they laid out town lots for houses and a church. Then they gave each family parcels of land scattered around the town center: pasture here, a woodlot there, an arable field elsewhere. They also reserved the best and largest plots for the most distinguished among them (usually including the minister); people who had been low on the social scale in England were given much smaller and less desirable allotments. Even when migrants began to move beyond the territorial limits of the Bay Colony into Connecticut (1636), New Haven (1638), and New Hampshire (1638), the same pattern of town land grants was maintained.

Thus New England settlements initially tended to be more compact than those of the Chesapeake. Town centers grew up quickly, developing in three distinctly different ways. Some, chiefly isolated agricultural settlements in the interior, tried to sustain Winthrop's vision of harmonious community life based on diversified family farms. A second group, the coastal towns like Boston and Salem, became bustling seaports. The third category, in the Connecticut River valley, developed as commercialized agricultural towns.

The migration to the Connecticut valley ended the Puritans' relative freedom from clashes with neighboring Indians. The first English settlers in the valley moved there from Newtown (Cambridge), under the direction of their minister, Thomas Hooker. Connecticut was fertile, though remote from the other English towns, and the wide river promised ready access to the ocean. The site had just one problem: it fell within the territory controlled by the Pequot Indians.

The Pequots' dominance was based on their role as primary middlemen in the trade between New England Indians and the Dutch in New Netherland.

Pequot War

The arrival of English settlers signaled the end of Pequot power over the regional trading networks, for their tributary bands could now trade directly with Europeans. Clashes between the Pequots and the English began even before the Connecticut valley settlements were established, but their founding tipped the balance toward war. After trying without success to galvanize other tribes to resist English expansion into the interior, the Pequots (after an English raid on their villages) attacked the new town of Wethersfield in April 1637, killing nine and capturing two of the colonists. In retaliation, a Massachusetts Bay expedition the following month attacked and burned the main Pequot town on the Mystic River. The Englishmen and their Narragansett Indian allies slaughtered at least four hundred people, mostly women and children. The few surviving Pequots were captured and enslaved.

Just five years later, the Narragansett leader Miantonomi realized that the Pequots had been correct in assessing the danger posed by the Puritan settlements. Miantonomi tried but failed to forge a pan-Indian alliance. He was killed in 1643 by other Indians, acting at the English colonists' behest.

For the next thirty years, the New England Indians tried to accommodate themselves to the spread of white settlement. They traded with the whites and sometimes worked for them, but for the most part they resisted acculturation or incorporation into English society. The Indians clung to their traditional farming methods, which did not employ plows, fertilizer, or fences; and women rather than men continued as the chief cultivators. The one European practice they did adopt was keeping livestock, for in the absence of game, domesticated animals provided excellent alternative sources of meat.

Although the official seal of Massachusetts Bay showed an Indian crying, "Come over and help us," most whites showed little interest in converting the Indians to Christianity. Only a few Puritan clerics, most notably John Eliot, seriously undertook missionary activities. Eliot insisted that converts reside in towns, farm the land in English fashion, assume

English names, wear European-style clothing and shoes, cut their hair, and stop observing a wide range of native customs. Since Eliot was demanding a total cultural transformation from his adherents, he understandably met with little success. At the peak of his efforts, only 1,100 Indians lived in the fourteen "Praying Towns" he established.

Puritan and Jesuit Missions Compared

The Jesuits' successful missions in New France contrasted sharply with the Puritans' failure to convert many Indians. Three factors account for the difference. First, the small French outposts along the St. Lawrence did not substantially encroach on Indian lands and therefore did not alienate potential converts. Second, Catholicism, unlike Puritanism, employed attractive rituals, instructed converts that through good works they could help earn their own salvation, and supplied Indian women with inspiring role models—the Virgin Mary and the communities of nuns who resided in Montreal and Quebec. Third, and perhaps most important, the Jesuits understood that Christian beliefs were to some extent compatible with native culture. Quite simply, Catholics were willing to accept converts without requiring them to wholly embrace European lifestyles; Puritans were not.

But what attracted Indians to these alien religious ideas? One primary motive must have been a desire to use the Europeans' religion as a means of coping with the dramatic changes the intruders had wrought on Indian society. The combination of disease, alcohol, new trading patterns, and the loss of territory disrupted customary ways of life to an unprecedented extent. Many Indians must have concluded that the Europeans' own ideas could provide the key to survival in the new circumstances.

Life in New England

White settlers in New England adopted lifestyles that differed considerably from the lifestyles of both their Indian neighbors and their counterparts in the Chesapeake. Unlike the mobile Algonkians, English people lived year-round in the same location. Unlike the residents of the Chesapeake, New Englanders constructed sturdy, permanent dwellings intended to last for many years. They used the same fields again and again, believing it was less arduous to employ fertilizer than to clear new fields every few years. Furthermore, they had to fence their croplands to prevent them from being overrun by the cattle, sheep, and hogs that were their chief sources of meat. When New Englanders began to spread out over the countryside, it was often to find additional pasturage for their livestock.

New England and the Chesapeake Compared

In contrast to the Chesapeake migrants, Puritans commonly moved to America in family groups. The age range of New Englanders was wide and the sexes were more balanced numerically, so the population could immediately begin to reproduce itself. Moreover, New England's climate was much healthier than the Chesapeake's. Indeed, New England proved to be even healthier than the mother country. Though adult male migrants to the Chesapeake lost about ten years from their English life expectancy, their Massachusetts counterparts gained about ten years.

Consequently, while Chesapeake population patterns gave rise to families that were few in number, small in size, and transitory, the demographic characteristics of New England made families there numerous, large, and long-lived. In New England, most men were able to marry; migrant women married young (at the age of twenty, on the average); and marriages lasted longer and produced more children, who were more likely to live to maturity. If seventeenth-century Chesapeake women could expect to rear one to three healthy children, New England women could anticipate raising five to seven.

Family Life in New England

The nature of the population had other major implications for family life. New England in effect created grandparents, since in England people rarely lived long enough to know their children's children. And whereas early southern parents normally died before their children married, northern parents exercised a good deal of control over their adult children. Young men could not marry without acreage to cultivate, and because of the communal land-grant system, they were dependent on their fathers to supply them with that land. Daughters, too, needed the dowry of household goods that their parents would give them when they married. Yet parents needed their children's labor and were often reluctant to see them marry and start their own households. These needs at times led to conflict between the generations. On the whole, though, children seem to have obeyed their parents' wishes, for they had few alternatives.

Another important difference lay in the influence of religion on New Englanders' lives. The governments of Massachusetts Bay, Plymouth, Connecticut, and the other early northern colonies were all controlled by Puritans. Congregationalism was the only officially recognized religion; members of other sects had no freedom of worship except in Rhode Island. Some non-Puritans appear to have voted in town meetings, but with the exception of Connecticut, church membership was a prerequisite for voting in colony elections. All households were taxed to build meetinghouses and pay ministers' salaries. Massachusetts's Body of Laws and Liberties (1641) incorporated regulations drawn from the Old Testament into the legal code of the colony.

In the New England colonies, then, church and state were intertwined. Puritans objected to secular interference in religious affairs but at the same time expected the church to influence the conduct of politics. They also believed that the state had an obligation to support and protect the one true church—theirs. As a result, though they came to America seeking freedom of worship, they saw no contradiction in refusing to grant that right to others. Indeed, the two most significant divisions in early Massachusetts were caused by Massachusetts Bay's unwillingness to tolerate religious dissent.

Roger Williams, a Separatist, migrated to Massachusetts Bay in 1631. Williams soon began to express the eccentric ideas that the king of England had no right to give away land belonging to the Indians, that church and state should be kept entirely separate, and that Puritans should not impose their religious beliefs on others. Ban-

Roger Williams

ished from Massachusetts in 1635, Williams founded the town of Providence on Narragansett Bay. Because of his beliefs, Providence and other towns in what became the colony of Rhode Island adopted a policy of tolerating all religions, including Judaism.

The other dissenter, and an even greater challenge to Massachusetts Bay orthodoxy, was Anne Marbury Hutchinson. She was a follower of John Cotton, a minister who stressed the covenant of grace, or God's free gift of salvation to unworthy humans. In 1636, Hutchinson began holding women's meetings in her home to discuss Cotton's sermons. Soon men also started to attend. Hutchinson emphasized the covenant of grace more than did Cotton himself, and she even adopted the belief that the elect could communicate directly with God and be assured of salvation. Because her ideas offered Puritans the certainty of salvation instead of a state of constant tension, they had an immense appeal.

Anne Hutchinson

Hutchinson's ideas were a dangerous threat to Puritan orthodoxy, so in November 1637 she was brought before the General Court of Massachusetts, charged with defaming the colony's ministers. For two days she defended herself cleverly against her accusers. Finally, in an unguarded moment, Hutchinson declared that God had spoken to her "by an immediate revelation." That assertion assured her banishment to Rhode Island. Equally significant was her challenge to traditional gender roles. Her judges were almost as outraged by her "masculine" behavior as by her heretical beliefs. As one judge told her bluntly, "You have stept out of your place, you have rather bine a Husband than a Wife and a preacher than a Hearer; and a Magistrate than a Subject."

The New England authorities' reaction to Anne Hutchinson reveals the depth of their adherence to European gender-role concepts. To them, an orderly society required the submission of wives to husbands, as well as the obedience of subjects to rulers. English people intended to change many aspects of their lives by colonizing North America, but not the sexual division of labor or the assumption of male superiority.

In 1630, John Winthrop wrote to his wife, Margaret, who was still in England, "my deare wife, we are heer in a paradise." He was, of course, exaggerating. Yet America was a place where English men and women could free themselves from Stuart persecution or attempt to better their economic circumstances. Many died, but those who lived laid the foundation for subsequent colonial prosperity. That they did so by dispossessing the Indians bothered few besides Roger Williams. By the middle of the seventeenth century, Europeans had unquestionably come to North America to stay, a fact that signaled major changes for the peoples of both the Old and the New World.

European political rivalries, once confined to Europe, now spread around the globe, as the competing nations of England, Spain, Portugal, France, and the Netherlands vied for control of the peoples and resources of Asia, Africa, and the Americas. France and the Netherlands earned their profits from Indian trade rather than imitating the Spanish example and engaging in wars of conquest. Although they, too, at first relied on trade, the English colonies soon took another form altogether when so many English people of the "common sort" decided to migrate to North America. In the years to come, the European rivalries would grow even fiercer, and residents of the Americas—whites, Indians, and blacks alike—would inevitably be drawn into them. Those rivalries would continue to affect Americans of all races until after France and England fought—in the mid-eighteenth century—the greatest war yet known and the thirteen Anglo-American colonies won their independence.

Suggestions for Further Reading

General

Charles M. Andrews, *The Colonial Period of American History: The Settlements,* 3 vols. (1934–1937); Leslie Bethel, ed., *The Cambridge History of Latin America,* vol. 2: *Colonial Latin America* (1984); D. W. Meinig, *Atlantic America, 1492–1800* (1986); Gary B. Nash, *Red, White, and Black: The Peoples of Early America,* 2nd ed. (1982); Eric Wolf, *Europe and the People Without History* (1982).

Indians

Harold E. Driver, *Indians of North America,* 2nd ed. (1969); Brian Fagan, *The Great Journey: The Peopling of Ancient America* (1987); Alvin Josephy, Jr., *The Indian Heritage of America* (1968); Alice B. Kehoe, *North American Indians* (1981); Smithsonian Institution, *Handbook of North American Indians,* 8: California (1978), 9, 10: *The Southwest* (1979, 1983), 15: *The Northeast* (1978).

Africa

Philip Curtin et al., *African History* (1978); J. D. Fage, *A History of Africa* (1978); Robert July, *Precolonial Africa* (1975); Richard Olaniyan, *African History and Culture* (1982); Roland Oliver, ed., *The Cambridge History of Africa,* vol. 3: c. 1050–c. 1600 (1977).

England

Kenneth Andrews, *Trade, Plunder and Settlement: Maritime Enterprise and the Genesis of the British Empire, 1480–1630* (1984); Peter Laslett, *The World We Have Lost,* 3rd ed. (1984); Wallace Notestein, *The English People on the Eve of Colonization, 1603–1630* (1954); Michael Walzer, *The Revolution of the Saints* (1965); Keith Wrightson, *English Society, 1580–1680* (1982).

Exploration and Discovery

Alfred W. Crosby, Jr., *The Columbian Exchange: Biological and Cultural Consequences of 1492* (1972); Samuel Eliot Morison, *The European Discovery of America: The Southern Voyages,* A.D. *1492–1616* (1974); *The Northern Voyages,* A.D. *1500–1600* (1971); J. H. Parry, *The Age of Reconnaissance* (1963); David B. Quinn, *North America from Earliest Discovery to First Settlements* (1977); John Super, *Food, Conquest, and Colonization in Sixteenth Century Spanish America* (1988).

Early Contact Between Whites and Indians

James Axtell, *The Invasion Within: The Contest of Cultures in Colonial North America* (1985); James Bradley, *Evolution of the Onondaga Iroquois* (1987); William Cronon, *Changes in the Land: Indians, Colonists, and the Ecology of New England* (1983); Francis Jennings, *The Invasion of America: Indians, Colonialism, and the Cant of Conquest* (1975); Karen O. Kupperman, *Roanoke, The Abandoned Colony* (1984); Neal Salisbury, *Manitou and Providence: Indians, Europeans, and the Making of New England, 1500–1643* (1982); Tzvetan Todorov, *The Conquest of America* (1984); Alden T. Vaughan, *The New England Frontier: Puritans and Indians 1621–1675 ,* rev. ed. (1979).

Chesapeake

Lois Green Carr and Lorena Walsh, "The Planter's Wife: The Experience of White Women in Seventeenth-Century Maryland," *William and Mary Quarterly,* 3rd ser., 34 (1977), 542–571; Wesley Frank Craven, *The Southern Colonies in the Seventeenth Century, 1607–1689* (1949); David Galenson, *White Servitude in Colonial America: An Economic Analysis* (1981); Ivor Noel Hume, *Martin's Hundred: The Discovery of a Lost Colonial Virginia Settlement* (1979); Gloria L. Main, *Tobacco Colony: Life in Early Maryland, 1650–1720* (1983); Edmund S. Morgan, *American Slavery, American Freedom: The Ordeal of Colonial Virginia* (1975); Darrett Rutman and Anita Rutman, *A Place in Time: Middlesex County, Virginia, 1650–1750* (1984); Thad W. Tate and David L. Ammerman, eds., *The Chesapeake in the Seventeenth Century* (1979); Alden T. Vaughan, *American Genesis: Captain John Smith and the Founding of Virginia* (1975).

New England

Ben Barker-Benfield, "Anne Hutchinson and the Puritan Attitude Toward Women," *Feminist Studies,* 1 (1972), 65–96; Charles Cohen, *God's Caress: The Psychology of Puritan Religious Experience* (1986); David Cressy, *Coming Over: Migration and Communication Between England and New England in the Seventeenth Century* (1987); John Demos, *A Little Commonwealth: Family Life in Plymouth Colony* (1970); Philip J. Greven, Jr., *Four Generations: Population, Land, and Family in Colonial Andover, Massachusetts* (1970); Philip Gura, *A Glimpse of Sion's Glory: Puritan Radicalism in New England, 1620–1660* (1984); Stephen Innes, *Labor in a New Land: Economy and Society in Seventeenth-Century Springfield* (1983); Lyle Koehler, *A Search for Power: The "Weaker Sex" in Seventeenth-Century New England* (1980); Kenneth A. Lockridge, *A New England Town: The First Hundred Years* (Dedham, Massachusetts, 1636–1736) (1970); Edmund S. Morgan, *The Puritan Family,* rev. ed. (1966); Roger Thompson, *Sex in Middlesex: Popular Mores in a Massachusetts County, 1649–1699* (1986).

Olaudah Equiano was eleven years old in 1756 when black raiders seeking slaves for white traders kidnapped him from his village in what is now Nigeria. As a captive, he was passed from master to master, finally arriving at the coast, where an English slave ship lay at anchor. Terrified by the light complexions, long hair, and strange language of the sailors, he was afraid that "I had gotten into a world of bad spirits and that they were going to kill me." Equiano was placed below decks, where "with the loathsomeness of the stench and crying together, I became so sick and low that I was not able to eat, nor had I the least desire to taste anything."

After a long voyage, during which many of the Africans died of disease, the ship arrived in the West Indies. Equiano was not purchased in the West Indies because planters there preferred older, stronger slaves. Instead, he was carried to Virginia, where his new owner separated him from the other Africans and put him to work weeding and clearing rocks from the fields. "I was now exceedingly miserable and thought myself worse off than any of the rest of my companions," Equiano remembered, "for they could talk to each other, but I had no person to speak to that I could understand. In this state I was constantly grieving and pining and wishing for death rather than anything else."

2

AMERICAN SOCIETY TAKES SHAPE, 1640–1720

But Equiano did not remain in Virginia for long. Bought by a sea captain, Olaudah Equiano eventually became an experienced sailor. He learned to read and write English, purchased his freedom at the age of twenty-one, and later actively supported the English antislavery movement. Until he was purchased by the sailor, Equiano's experiences differed very little from those of other Africans who were forced into slavery in the English colonies of the New World. Like him, many were sold by black slavers and taken first to the West Indies, then to North America.

Equiano's life story, which he published in 1789, illustrates one of the major developments in colonial life during the years after 1640: the importation of more than 200,000 unwilling, captive Africans into North America. The introduction of the institution of slavery and the arrival of large numbers of West Africans reshaped colonial society. Indeed, the geographic patterns of that migration still influence the United States.

The other important trends in colonial life between 1640 and 1720 involved the English colonists' relationships with their mother country and with their American neighbors. Dramatic events in England during this period affected its New World colonies. The Puritan victory in the civil war, which began in 1642, the restoration of the Stuart monarchy in 1660, and finally the Glorious Revolution of 1688–1689 indelibly affected the residents of England's American possessions. By the end of the seventeenth century, the New World colonies were no longer isolated outposts but an integral part of a far-flung mercantile empire. Further, as the Anglo-American settlements expanded, they came into violent conflict not only with powerful Indian tribes, but also with the Dutch, French, and Spanish. By 1720, war was an all-too-frequent feature of American life.

The English Civil War, the Stuart Restoration, and the American Colonies

In 1640, Charles I, who had ruled England arbitrarily for the previous eleven years, called Parliament into session because he needed money and wanted to propose new taxes. But Parliament passed laws limiting his authority, and tensions heightened. In 1642, civil war broke out between royalists and the supporters of Parliament. Four years later, Parliament triumphed, and Charles I was executed in 1649. Oliver Cromwell, the leader of the parliamentary army, then assumed control of the government, taking the title of Lord Protector in 1653. After Cromwell's death in 1658, Parliament decided to restore the monarchy if Charles I's son and heir would agree to certain restrictions on his authority. In 1660, Charles II ascended the throne, having promised to seek Parliament's consent for any new taxes and to support the Church of England. Thus ended the tumultuous chapter in English history known as the Interregnum (Latin for "between reigns"), or the Commonwealth, period.

The civil war, the Interregnum, and the reign of Charles II (1660–1685) had major significance for the English colonies in the Americas. During the Civil War and the Commonwealth period, Puritans dominated the English government. Therefore the migration to New England largely ceased. During the subsequent reign of Charles II, six of the thirteen colonies that eventually would form the American nation were either founded or came under English rule: New York, New Jersey, Pennsylvania (including Delaware), and North and South Carolina (see map, page 30). All were proprietorships granted in their entirety to one man or a group of men who held title to the soil and controlled the government. Charles II gave these vast American holdings as rewards to men who had supported him during his years of exile.

One of the first to benefit was Charles's younger brother James, the duke of York. In March 1664, acting as though the Dutch colony of New Netherland did not exist, Charles II gave James the region between the Connecticut and Delaware rivers, including the Hudson valley and Long Island. James immediately organized an invasion fleet. In late August the vessels anchored off Manhattan Island (New Amsterdam) and demanded New Netherland's surrender. The colony's director-general, Peter Stuyvesant, complied without offering resistance.

Thus England acquired a tiny but heterogeneous possession. Though founded in 1624, New Netherland had remained small in comparison with its English neighbors. Holland, the world's dominant commercial power in the first half of the seventeenth century, was primarily interested in trade rather than colonization. As a trading post of the Dutch West India Company, whose chief economic interests lay elsewhere, New Netherland was considered relatively unimportant. Furthermore, the Dutch did not experience the economic, demographic, and religious pressures that caused English people to move to the New World, and so migration was sparse. Even a company policy of 1629 that offered a large land grant, or patroonship, to anyone who would bring fifty settlers to the province failed to attract takers. In the mid-1660s,

New Netherland Becomes New York

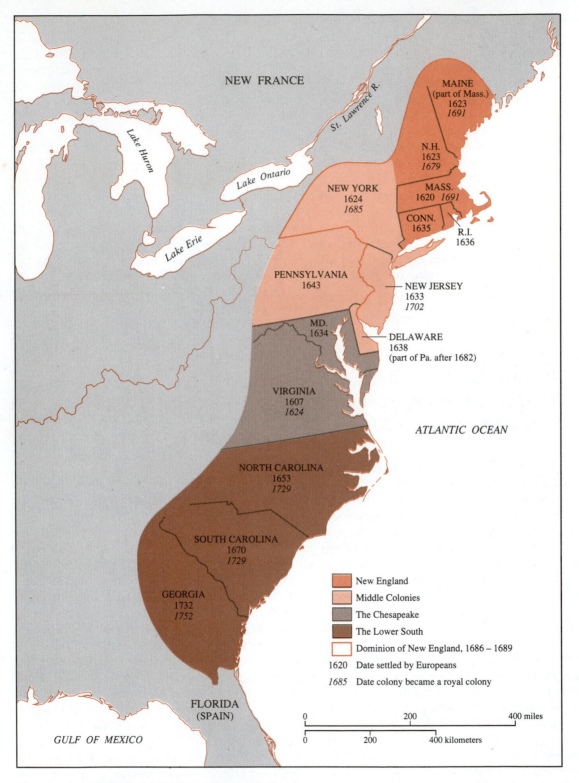

The American Colonies in the Early Eighteenth Century

IMPORTANT EVENTS

1642–46	English civil war
1649	Charles I executed
1651	First Navigation Act passed
1660	Stuarts restored to throne; Charles II becomes king
1662	Halfway Covenant drafted
1663	Carolina chartered
1664	English conquer New Netherland; New York founded New Jersey established
1675–76	King Philip's (Metacomet's) War (New England)
1676	Bacon's Rebellion (Virginia)
1680–92	Pueblo revolt (New Mexico)
1681	Pennsylvania chartered 1685 James II becomes king
1686–89	Dominion of New England
1688–89	James II deposed in Glorious Revolution; William and Mary ascend throne
1689–97	King William's War
1692	Witchcraft panic in Salem Village
1696	Board of Trade and Plantations established
1701	Iroquois adopt neutrality policy
1702–13	Queen Anne's War
1711–13	Tuscarora War (North Carolina)
1715	Yamasee War (South Carolina)
1732	Georgia chartered

when New Netherland became New York, it had only about five thousand inhabitants. The Dutch made up the largest segment of this population. The rest consisted of Puritans who had left New England, migrants from several areas of Europe, Indians, and Africans. Because the Dutch West India Company had imported slaves into the colony, almost one-fifth of Manhattan's approximately fifteen hundred inhabitants were black at the time of the English conquest. Thus at that point, New York's urban population had a higher proportion of slaves than the population of the Chesapeake.

Recognizing the diversity of the population, the duke of York's representatives moved cautiously in their efforts to establish English authority. The Duke's Laws, a legal code proclaimed in March 1665, at first applied only to the Puritan settlements on Long Island; they were later extended to the rest of the colony. Dutch forms of local government were maintained and Dutch land titles confirmed. Religious toleration was guaranteed through a sort of multiple establishment: each town was permitted to decide which church to support with its tax revenues. Furthermore, the Dutch were allowed to maintain their customary legal practices. Much to the chagrin of English residents of the colony, the Duke's Laws made no provision for a representative assembly. James was suspicious of legislative bodies. He did not agree to the colonists' requests for an elected legislature until 1683.

The English takeover thus had little immediate effect on the colony. Its population grew slowly, barely reaching eighteen thousand by the time of the first English census in 1698.

Founding of New Jersey One of the chief reasons the English conquest brought so little change to New York was that the duke of York quickly regranted the land between the Hudson and Delaware rivers—East and West

Jersey—to his friends Sir George Carteret and John Lord Berkeley. That left his own colony confined between Connecticut to the east and the Jerseys to the west and south, depriving it of much fertile land and hindering its economic growth. He also failed to promote migration. Meanwhile, the Jersey proprietors promised settlers generous land grants, limited freedom of religion, and—without authorization from the Crown—a representative assembly.

Within twenty years, Berkeley and Carteret sold their interests in the Jerseys to separate groups of investors. The purchasers of all of Carteret's share (West Jersey) and portions of Berkeley's (East Jersey) were Quakers seeking a refuge from persecution in England. The Quakers, formally known as the Society of Friends, denied the need for an intermediary between the individual and God. Anyone, they believed, could receive the "inner light" and be saved, and all were equal in God's sight. They had no formally trained clergy; any Quaker, male or female, who felt the call could become a "public Friend" and travel from meeting to meeting to discuss God's word. Moreover, any member of the society could speak in meetings if he or she desired. Thus the Quakers were true religious radicals, in the mold of Anne Hutchinson.

The Quakers obtained their own colony in 1681, when Charles II granted the region between Maryland and New York to William Penn, one of the sect's most prominent members. Penn's father, Admiral William Penn, had originally served Oliver Cromwell but later joined forces with Charles II and lent the monarch a substantial sum of money. The younger Penn became a Quaker in the mid-1660s, much to his father's dismay. But despite Penn's radical political and religious beliefs, he and Charles II were close personal friends. Had it not been for their friendship (and the desire of Charles's advisers to rid England of religious dissenters), the despised Quakers would never have won a charter for an American settlement.

Penn-sylvania: A Quaker Haven

William Penn held the colony as a personal proprietorship, and the vast property holdings earned profits for his descendants until the American Revolution. However, Penn viewed the province not merely as a source of revenue, but also as a haven for his persecuted coreligionists. Penn offered land to all comers on liberal terms, promised toleration to all religions (though only Christians were given the right to vote), guaranteed such English liberties as the right to bail and trial by jury, and pledged to establish a representative assembly.

Penn's activities and the natural attraction of his lands for Quakers gave rise to a migration whose magnitude was equaled only by the Puritan exodus to New England in the 1630s. By mid-1683, more than three thousand people—among them Welsh, Irish, Dutch, and Germans—had already moved to Pennsylvania, and within five years the population reached twelve thousand. Philadelphia, carefully planned to be the major city in the province, drew merchants and artisans from throughout the English-speaking world. From mainland and West Indian colonies alike came Quakers seeking religious freedom. Pennsylvania's lands were both plentiful and fertile, and the colony soon began exporting flour and other foodstuffs to the West Indies. Practically overnight, Philadelphia acquired more than two thousand citizens and began to challenge Boston's commercial dominance.

A pacifist with egalitarian principles, Penn was determined to treat the Indians of Pennsylvania fairly. He carefully purchased tracts of land from the Delawares (or Leni-Lenapes), the dominant tribe in the region, before selling them to settlers. Penn also established strict regulations for the Indian trade and forbade the sale of alcohol to tribesmen. His Indian policy provides a sterling example of the complexity of the interaction among whites and Indians, because it prompted several tribes to move to Pennsylvania. Most important were the Tuscaroras, whose experiences are described later in this chapter. Likewise, Shawnees and Miamis chose to move eastward from the Ohio valley. By a supreme irony, however, the same toleration that attracted Indians to Penn's domains also brought non-Quaker Europeans, who showed little respect for Indian claims to the soil. In effect, Penn's policy was so successful that it caused its own downfall. The Scotch-Irish, Palatine Germans, and Swiss who settled in Pennsylvania in the first half of the eighteenth century clashed repeatedly over land with tribes that had also recently migrated to the colony.

The other proprietary colony, granted by Charles

II in 1663, encompassed a huge tract of land, stretching from the southern boundary of Virginia to Spanish Florida. The area had

Founding of Carolina great strategic importance; a successful English settlement there would prevent the Spanish from pushing farther north. The proprietors named their new province Carolina in Charles's honor (in Latin his name was Carolus). The "Fundamental Constitutions of Carolina," which they asked the political philosopher John Locke to draft for them, set forth an elaborate plan for a colony governed by a hierarchy of landholding aristocrats and characterized by a carefully structured distribution of political and economic power. But Carolina failed to follow the course the proprietors laid out. Instead, it quickly developed two distinct population centers, which in 1729 split into two separate colonies.

The Albemarle region that became North Carolina was settled by Virginians. They established a society much like their own, with an economy based on tobacco cultivation and the export of such forest products as pitch, tar, and timber. Because North Carolina lacked a satisfactory harbor, its planters continued to rely on Virginia's ports and merchants to conduct their trade, and the two colonies remained tightly linked. Although North Carolina planters held some slaves, they never became as dependent on slave labor as did the other population center in Carolina.

In 1670, Charleston, South Carolina, was founded by a group of settlers from Barbados, which was already overcrowded less than fifty years after English people had first moved there. The white Barbadians brought with them the slaves who had worked on their sugar plantations and the legal codes that had governed those laborers. Thus they irrevocably shaped the future of South Carolina and the subsequent history of the United States.

The Forced Migration of Africans

Since England had no tradition of slavery, why did English settlers in the New World begin to enslave Africans around the middle of the seventeenth century? The answer to that question lies in the combined effect of economics and racial attitudes.

The English were an ethnocentric people who believed firmly in the superiority of their values and civilization. Furthermore, they believed that fair-skinned peoples like themselves were superior to the darker-skinned races. Those beliefs alone did not cause them to enslave Indians and Africans, but the idea that other races were inferior to whites helped them to justify slavery and the slave trade.

Although the English had not previously practiced slavery, the Spanish and Portuguese had long enslaved African Muslims and other "heathen" peoples. Further, Christian doctrine could be interpreted as allowing enslavement as a means of converting such people to the "true faith." European colonizers needed a large labor force to exploit the riches of the New World, and few free people were willing to work as wage laborers in the difficult and dangerous conditions of South American mines or Caribbean sugar plantations.

The most obvious source of workers would have been the Indians native to the Americas. But their familiarity with the American environment made them difficult to enslave, and when captured, they often managed to escape. Africans, however, were a different story. Transported to alien surroundings far from home, frequently they could not communicate with their fellow workers. They were also the darkest (and thus, to European eyes, the most inferior) of all peoples. Black Africans, therefore, seemed to be ideal candidates for perpetual servitude.

The first English colonists in the Americas to utilize slave laborers extensively were those who settled in the Caribbean. In the 1640s, the English

Slavery Established migrants to such islands as Barbados (colonized in 1627), Nevis (1628), and Antigua (1632) discovered that their soil and climate were ideally suited for the cultivation of cane sugar, previously a rare and expensive luxury food item. Caribbean planters made enormous profits by importing hundreds of thousands of African slaves to work in the cane fields. Until well into the eighteenth century, England's Caribbean colonies were far more valuable than those on the mainland.

The English colonies to the north did not immediately move to the slave system because white indentured servants filled their labor needs. Lack of evidence makes it difficult to determine the legal status of blacks during the first few decades of English settlement, but apparently many of them were also indentured, which meant that they eventually became free. After 1640, some blacks were being permanently enslaved in each of the English colonies. Massachusetts, in 1641, was the first to mention slavery in its legal code. By the end of the century, the slaves' status was fixed. Barbados adopted a comprehensive slave code in 1661, and the mainland provinces soon did the same.

Between 1492 and 1770 more Africans than Europeans came to the New World. But just 4.5 percent of them (about 275,000 persons during the eighteenth century) were imported into the region that became the United States. By contrast, 42 percent of the approximately 9.5 million enslaved blacks were carried to the Caribbean, and 49 percent went to South America. The magnitude of this trade in slaves raises three important and related questions. First, what was its impact on West Africa and Europe? Second, how was the trade organized and conducted? Third, what was its effect on the blacks it carried?

The West African coast was one of the most densely inhabited regions of the continent. Despite the extent of forced migration to the Western Hemisphere, the area was not seriously depopulated by the trade in human beings. Even so, because American planters preferred to purchase male slaves, the sex ratio of the remaining population was significantly affected by the trade. The relative lack of men increased the work demands on women and encouraged polygyny (the practice of one man having several wives). In Guinea, the primary consequences of the trade were political. The coastal kings who served as middlemen in the trade used it as a vehicle to consolidate their power and extend their rule over larger territories. They controlled both the European traders' access to slaves and the inland peoples' access to European trade goods. The centralizing tendencies of the trade thus helped in the formation of such powerful eighteenth-century kingdoms as Dahomey and Asante.

West Africa and the Slave Trade

These West African kings played a crucial role in the functioning of the slave trade. Europeans set up permanent slave-trading posts in Lower Guinea under the protection of local rulers, who then supplied the resident Europeans with slaves to fill the ships that stopped regularly at the coastal forts. In Upper Guinea, there was a somewhat different trading pattern: Europeans would sail along the coast, stopping to pick up cargoes when signaled from the shore. Most persons sold into American slavery were wartime captives, criminals sentenced to enslavement, or persons seized for nonpayment of debts. A smaller proportion had been kidnapped.

Europeans were the chief beneficiaries of this traffic in slaves. The expanding network of trade between Europe and its colonies in the seventeenth and eighteenth centuries was fueled by the sale and transportation of slaves, the exchange of commodities produced by slave labor, and the need to feed and clothe so many bound laborers. Planters in the New World eagerly purchased slaves from Africa, dispatched shiploads of valuable staple crops to Europe, and bought large quantities of cheap food and clothing, much of it from elsewhere in the Americas. The European economy, previously oriented toward the Mediterranean and the Far East, shifted its emphasis to the Atlantic Ocean. By the late seventeenth century, commerce in slaves and the products of slave labor constituted the basis of the European economic system.

Given the economic importance of the slave trade, it is hardly surprising that European nations fought bitterly over control of it. The Portuguese, who initially dominated the trade, were supplanted by the Dutch. The Dutch in turn lost out to the English, who eventually controlled the trade through the Royal African Company, a joint-stock company chartered in 1672. Holding a monopoly on all English trade with black Africa, the company transported more than 120,000 slaves to England's American colonies. Yet even before the company's monopoly expired in 1712, many individual English traders had illegally entered the market for slaves. By the early eighteenth century, independent traders were carrying most of the Africans imported into the colonies and earning immense profits.

The experience of the Middle Passage (so named because it was the middle section of the so-called

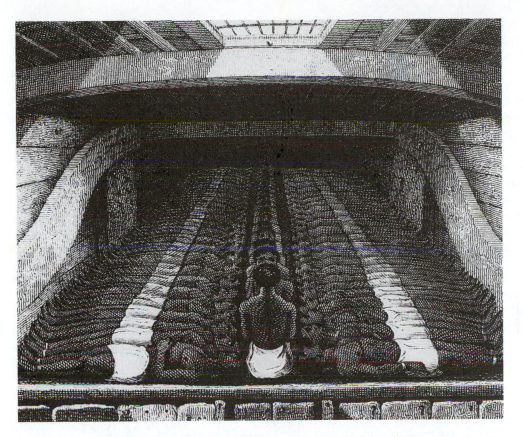

A contemporary print illustrating how slave-ship captains tightly packed their human cargo so as to achieve the greatest possible profits from each voyage. *American Antiquarian Society*.

triangular trade among England, Africa, and the Americas) was often fatal for the Africans who made up a ship's cargo. An average of 10 to 20 percent of the slaves died en route, but on voyages that were unusually long or had outbreaks of epidemic diseases, the mortality rates rose much higher. In addition, some slaves usually died either before the ships left Africa or shortly after their arrival in the New World. Their white captors died at the same, if not higher, rates, chiefly through exposure to alien African germs.

The Middle Passage

On shipboard, men were usually kept shackled in pairs; women and children were released from any bonds once the ship was well out at sea. The slaves were fed a vegetable diet of beans, rice, yams, and corn cooked together in various combinations to create a warm mush. In good weather, they were allowed on deck for fresh air, because only healthy slaves commanded high prices. Many ships also carried a doctor, whose primary role was to treat the slaves' illnesses. The average size of a cargo was about 250 slaves, but since the size of ships varied, so too did the number of slaves carried.

Records of slave traders reveal numerous instances of Africans' resistance to captivity. Some committed suicide; others participated in shipboard revolts. Yet most of the Africans who embarked on the slave vessels arrived in the Americas alive and still in captivity; the whites saw to that, for only then could they make a profit.

At first, most of the slaves imported into the English colonies went to various Caribbean islands. But after about 1675, Chesapeake planters could no longer obtain an adequate supply of English workers. A falling birthrate and improved economic conditions in England decreased the number of possible migrants to the colonies. At the same time, new English set-

Slavery in the Chesapeake

tlements in North America started to compete with the Chesapeake for settlers. When the shortage of servants became acute in the mid-1670s, imports of Africans increased dramatically. As early as 1690, the Chesapeake colonies contained more black slaves than white indentured servants, and by 1710 one-fifth of the region's population was black.

Yet not all white planters could afford to devote so much money to purchasing workers. Those whites with enough money could acquire slaves and accumulate greater wealth, while less-affluent whites could not. Consequently, as time passed, white Chesapeake society became more and more stratified—that is, the gap between the rich and the poor steadily widened.

Besides causing demographic and economic change, the introduction of large numbers of Africans into the Chesapeake affected cultural values as well. Without realizing it, Chesapeake whites adopted African modes of thought about the use of time and the nature of work. Africans were more accustomed than European migrants to life in a hot climate, and whites soon learned the benefits of following African patterns of time usage—working early and late, taking a long rest in the heat of midday. And unlike the colonists in New England, where the Puritan condemnation of leisure-time activities prevailed, Chesapeake whites learned, again from blacks, the importance of recreation.

In South Carolina, the first slaves arrived with the initial white settlers. Indeed, one-quarter to one-third of South Carolina's early population was black. The Barbados whites **Blacks in South Carolina** quickly discovered that Africans had a variety of skills well suited to South Carolina's semitropical climate. African-style dugout canoes became the chief means of transportation in the colony, which was crisscrossed by rivers. Fishing nets copied from African models proved to be more efficient than those of English origin. The settlers also adopted African techniques of cattle herding. Since meat and hides were the colony's chief exports in its earliest years, blacks contributed significantly to South Carolina's prosperity.

The similarity of South Carolina's environment to West Africa's, coupled with the large number of blacks in the population, ensured that more aspects of West African culture survived in that colony than elsewhere on the mainland of North America. Only in South Carolina did black parents continue to give their children African names; only there did a dialect develop that combined English words with African terms (known as Gullah, it has survived to the present day in isolated areas). African skills remained useful, and so techniques that in other regions were lost when the migrant generation died were here passed down from parents to children. In South Carolina, as in West Africa, black women were the primary traders, dominating the markets of Charleston as they did those of Gambia or Benin.

Significantly, the importation of large numbers of Africans near the end of the seventeenth century coincided with the successful introduction of rice as a staple crop in South Carolina. English people knew little about the techniques of growing and processing rice, but slaves from Africa's Rice Coast had spent their lives working with the crop. Although the evidence is circumstantial, it seems likely that the Africans' expertise enabled their English masters to cultivate the crop profitably. After rice had become South Carolina's major export, 43 percent of the Africans imported into the colony came from rice-producing regions, and blacks' central position in the colony's economy was firmly established.

South Carolina later developed a second staple crop, and it too made use of blacks' special skills. The crop was indigo, much prized in Europe as a blue dye for clothing. In the early 1740s, Eliza Lucas, a young white West Indian woman who was managing her father's South Carolina plantations, began to experiment with indigo cultivation. Drawing on the knowledge of white and black West Indians, she developed the planting and processing techniques later adopted throughout the colony. Indigo was grown on high ground, and rice was planted in low-lying swampy areas; rice and indigo also had opposite growing seasons. Thus the two crops complemented each other perfectly.

After 1700, white southerners were committed to black slavery as their chief source of labor; white northerners were not. Small-scale northern agriculture did not demand many bound **Slavery in the North** laborers. In northern urban areas, however, white domestic servants were hard to find and slaves were often used. In some northern colonial cities (notably Newport, Rhode Island, and New York City), black slaves accounted for more than 10 percent of the population.

The introduction of large-scale slavery in the South, coupled with its near-absence in the North, accentuated regional differences that had already begun to develop in England's American colonies. To the distinction between diversified agriculture and staple-crop production was now added a difference in the race and status of most laborers. That difference was one of degree, but it was crucial.

Relations Between Europeans and Indians

Everywhere in North America, European colonizers depended heavily on the labor of native peoples. But their reliance on Indians took varying forms in different parts of the continent. In the Northeast, France, England, and the Netherlands competed for the pelts supplied by Indian trappers. In the Southeast, England, Spain, and later France each tried to control a thriving trade with the tribes in deerskins and Indian slaves. Finally, in the Southwest, Spain attempted to exploit the agricultural and artisan skills of the Pueblo peoples.

In 1598, drawn northward by accounts that rich cities lay in the region, Juan de Oñate, a Mexican-born adventurer, led a group of about five hundred to colonize New Mexico. The emissaries from New Spain had three goals: to acquire personal wealth; to claim new territories for their monarch; and to convert the Indians to Catholicism. When it became apparent that New Mexico held little wealth and offered only a hard life, many of the first settlers returned to Mexico. In 1609, Spanish authorities decided to maintain only a small military outpost and a few Christian missions in the area, with the capital at Santa Fé (founded in 1610).

Franciscan friars set to work to convert the residents of the pueblos, with mixed success. The Pueblo peoples proved willing to add Christianity to their own religious beliefs but not to give up their indigenous rituals. Friars and secular colonists who held *encomiendas* also placed heavy labor demands on the In-

Popé and the Pueblo Revolt

dians. As the decades passed, conditions grew worse, for the Franciscans adopted brutal and violent tactics as they tried to wipe out all vestiges of the native religion. Finally, in 1680, the Pueblos revolted under the leadership of Popé, a respected shaman, and successfully drove the Spaniards out of New Mexico (see map, page 38). Although Spanish authority was restored in 1692, Spain had learned its lesson. From that time on, Spanish governors stressed cooperation with the Pueblos, and no longer attempted to reduce them to bondage or to violate their cultural integrity. The Pueblo revolt was the most successful and longest sustained Indian resistance movement in colonial North America.

When the Spanish expanded their territorial claims to the east (Texas) and the north (California), they followed the strategy they had used in New Mexico, establishing their presence through widely scattered military outposts and Franciscan missions. The army's role was to maintain order among the subject Indians and to guard the boundaries of the Spanish empire from possible incursions, especially by the French. The friars, of course, continued to concentrate on conversion efforts. By the late eighteenth century, Spain claimed a vast territory that stretched from California (initially colonized in 1769) through Texas (settled after 1700) to the Gulf Coast.

Along the eastern seaboard, Europeans valued the Indians as hunters and traders. The major Dutch settlements in North America were trading posts; the French settlements were trading posts allied to missions. In the earliest phase of settlement in each of the English mainland colonies, the primary exports were furs and skins obtained from neighboring Indians.

South Carolina provides a case in point. The Barbadians who colonized the region moved quickly to establish a vigorous trade in deerskins with nearby tribes. Between 1700 and 1710, South Carolina exported to Europe an average of 54,000 skins annually, a number that later climbed to a peak of 160,000. The trade gave rise to other exchanges that reveal the complexity of the economic relationships among Indians and Europeans. For example, white Carolinians carried those deerskins on horses, which they obtained from the Creek Indians, who had in turn acquired them from the Spaniards through trade and capture.

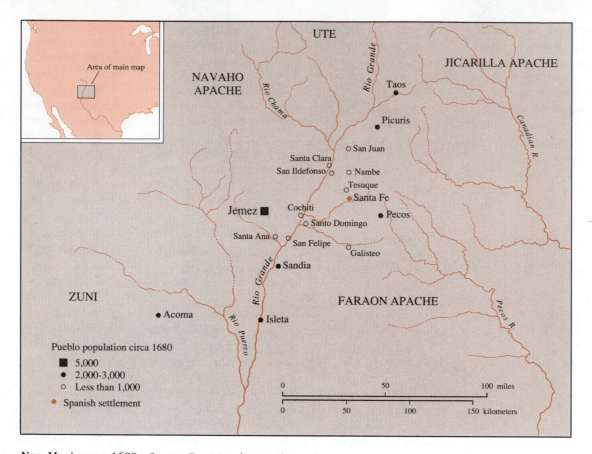

New Mexico, ca. 1680 *Source: From* Apache, Navaho, and Spaniard, *by Jack D. Forbes. Copyright © 1960, 1988 by the University of Oklahoma Press. Used by permission.*

Another important component of the Carolina trade was traffic in Indian slaves. The warring tribes of South Carolina (especially the Creeks) profited

Indian Slave Trade

from selling their captive enemies to the whites, who then either kept them in the colony as slaves or exported them to other mainland settlements or to the West Indies. There are no reliable statistics on the extent of the trade in Indian slaves, but in 1708 they made up 14 percent of the population of South Carolina.

A major conflict between white Carolinians and neighboring tribes added to the supply of Indian slaves. In 1711, the Tuscaroras, an Iroquoian people, attacked a settlement at New Bern, North Carolina, which had expropriated their lands without payment. The Tuscaroras had been avid slavers

and had sold to the whites many captives from the weaker Algonkian tribes. Those tribes seized the opportunity to settle old scores, joining with the English colonists to defeat their enemy in a bloody two-year war. In the end, more than a thousand Tuscaroras were themselves sold into slavery, and the remnants of the tribe drifted northward, where they joined the Five Nations Iroquois in New York.

The abuses of the slave trade led to the most destructive Indian war in the Carolinas. White traders regularly engaged in corrupt, brutal, and fraudulent practices. They were notorious for cheating the Indians, physically abusing them, and selling friendly tribesmen into slavery. In the spring of 1715, the Yamasees, aided by Creeks and a number of other tribes, retaliated by attacking the English colonists. At times, the Creek-Yamasee offensive came close to driving the intruders from the mainland altogether. But then colonial reinforcements arrived from the north, and the Cherokees joined the whites against their ancient enemies, the Creeks. The war pointed up both the difficulty of achieving unity among the tribes and the Indians' now-critical dependence on European weapons. When the tribal allies ran out of ammunition and could not repair their broken guns, their cause was lost. The Yamasees moved south to seek Spanish protection, and the Creeks retreated to villages in the west.

That the Yamasees could escape by migrating southward exposed the one remaining gap in the line of English coastal settlements, the area between the southern border of South Carolina and Spanish Florida. The gap was plugged in 1732 with the chartering of Georgia, the last of the colonies that would become part of the United States. Intended as a haven for debtors by its founder James Oglethorpe, Georgia was specifically designed as a garrison province. Since all its landholders were expected to serve as militiamen to defend English settlements, the charter prohibited women from inheriting or purchasing land in the colony. The charter also prohibited the use of alcoholic beverages and forbade the introduction of slavery. Such provisions reveal the founders' intention that Georgia should be peopled by sturdy, sober yeoman farmers who could take up their weapons against the Indians or Spaniards at a moment's notice. None of the conditions could be enforced, however, and all were abandoned by 1752, when Georgia became a royal colony.

Founding of Georgia

In the Northeast, the Iroquois hoped to become the major supplier of pelts to the Europeans. They achieved that goal in the 1640s by practically exterminating the Hurons, their chief trading rivals. The scope of the Iroquois victory was made possible by the use of guns obtained from the Dutch. By defeating the Hurons, the Iroquois established themselves as a force that the Europeans could not ignore.

The Iroquois nation was not one tribe, but five: Mohawks, Oneidas, Onondagas, Cayugas, and Senecas. (In 1722, the Tuscaroras became the sixth.) Under the terms of a defensive alliance forged early in the sixteenth century, key decisions of war and peace for the entire Iroquois Confederacy were made by a council composed of tribal representatives. Each tribe retained some autonomy, and no tribe could be forced to comply with a council directive against its will. The Iroquois were unique among Indians not only because of the strength and persistence of their alliance, but also because of the role played by their tribal matrons. The older women of each village chose its chief and could either start wars (by calling for the capture of prisoners to replace dead relatives) or stop them (by refusing to supply warriors with necessary foodstuffs).

Iroquois Confederacy

The war with the Hurons was just the first of a series of conflicts with other tribes—conflicts known collectively as the Beaver Wars—in which the Iroquois fought to maintain a dominant position in the fur trade. In the mid-1670s, just when it appeared that they would be successful, the French stepped in to prevent an Iroquois triumph, which would have destroyed France's plans to trade directly with the Indians of the Great Lakes and Mississippi valley regions. During the next twenty years, the French launched repeated attacks on Iroquois villages. The English offered little assistance other than weapons to their Iroquois trading partners. Their people and resources depleted by constant warfare, the Iroquois in 1701 negotiated neutrality treaties with France, England, and their tribal neighbors. For the next half-century they maintained their power through trade and skillful, often successful diplomacy.

Military action against the Iroquois Confederacy was part of French Canada's plan to penetrate the heartland of North America. The plan also included the explorations of Father Jacques Marquette, Louis Jolliet, and Robert Cavelier de La Salle in the Great Lakes and Mississippi valley regions. Officials in France approved the expeditions because they wanted to find a route to Mexico. La Salle, by contrast, hoped to make great personal profits by monopolizing the fur trade through establishing trading posts along the Mississippi River.

French Expansion

A French settler in Canada made this drawing of an Iroquois about 1700. The artist's fascination with his subject's mode of dress and patterned tattoos is evident. Such pictorial representations of "otherness" help to suggest the cultural gulf that divided the European and Indian residents of North America. *Library of Congress.*

Unlike the Spanish, these French adventurers did not attempt to subjugate the Indian peoples they encountered or even at first to claim the territory formally for France. Still, when France decided to strengthen its presence near the Gulf of Mexico by founding New Orleans in the early eighteenth century—to counter both the westward thrust of the English colonies and the eastward moves of the Spanish—the Mississippi posts became the glue of empire.

At each post lived a small military garrison and a priest, surrounded by powerful Indian nations (see map). The tribes permitted the French to remain among them because the traders gave them ready access to precious European goods. The French, for their part, sought political as well as economic ends, attempting to prevent the English from encroaching too far into the interior. Their goals, however, were limited; they did not engage in systematic efforts to convert the Indians of the region to Christianity.

The French learned to live in the midst of powerful tribes with relatively little friction because of the mutual needs of all parties to the arrangement. Matters were very different in the English colonies, where white colonists were interested in acquiring land. In Virginia, the conflict was especially acute because of the colonists' insatiable hunger for land on which to grow still more tobacco.

By the early 1670s, some Virginians were eagerly eyeing the rich lands north of the York River that had been reserved for Indians under earlier treaties. Using as a pretext the July 1675 killing of a white servant by some Doeg Indians, they attacked not only the Doegs, but also the powerful Susquehannocks. In retaliation, Susquehannock bands began to raid frontier plantations in the winter of 1676. The land-hungry whites rallied behind the leadership of Nathaniel Bacon, a planter who wanted, in his words, "to ruine and extirpate all Indians in general." Governor William Berkeley, however, hoped to avoid setting off a major war.

Bacon's Rebellion

Berkeley and Bacon soon clashed. After Bacon forced the House of Burgesses to authorize him to attack the Indians, Berkeley declared Bacon and his men to be in rebellion. As the summer of 1676 wore on, Bacon alternately pursued Indians and battled with the governor's supporters. In September, he marched on Jamestown itself and burned the capital to the ground. But after Bacon died of dysentery the following month, the rebellion collapsed. A new Indian treaty signed in 1677 opened much of the disputed territory to whites.

Not coincidentally, New England, which had also been settled more than fifty years earlier, was wracked by conflict with Indians at precisely the same time. In both areas, the whites' original accommodation with the tribes no longer satisfied both parties. But in New England the Indians, rather than the whites, felt aggrieved.

In the mid-1670s, Metacomet (known to the whites as King Philip) set out to expel the whites from New England. Metacomet, whose father, Mas-

King Philip's War sasoit, had signed the treaty with the Pilgrims in 1621 was troubled because the whites had com-

pletely surrounded the ancestral lands of the Pokanokets (Wampanoags) on Narragansett Bay. He was also concerned about the impact of European culture and Christianity on his people. In late June 1675, Metacomet led his warriors in attacks on nearby white communities.

Soon two other local tribes, the Nipmucks and the Narragansetts, joined Metacomet's forces. In the fall, the three tribes attacked settlements in the northern Connecticut River valley; in the winter and spring of 1676, they devastated well-established villages. Altogether, the alliance destroyed twelve of the ninety Puritan towns and attacked forty others. But the tide turned in the summer of 1676. The Indian alliance ran short of food and ammunition, and after Metacomet was killed in an ambush in August, the coalition crumbled. Many surviving Pokanokets, Nipmucks, and Narragansetts were captured and sold into slavery in the West Indies. The power of New England's coastal tribes was broken. From then on, they lived in small clusters, often working as servants or sailors.

New England and the Web of Imperial Trade

By the later years of the seventeenth century, the New England settlements had changed in three major ways since the early years of colonization. The population had grown dramatically; the nature of the residents' religious commitment had altered; and the economy had developed in unanticipated ways.

By 1700, New England's population had quadrupled to reach approximately 100,000. Such an increase placed great pressure on the available land,

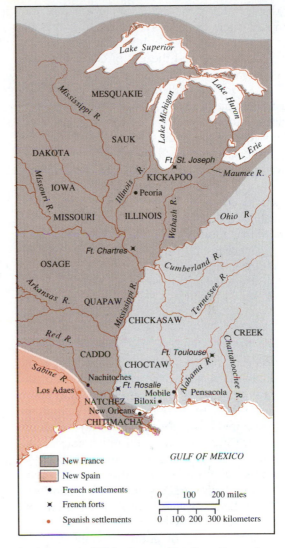

Louisiana, ca. 1720 *Source: Map from* France in America *by William J. Eccles. Copyright © 1972 by William J. Eccles. Reprinted by permission of Harper & Row, Publishers, Inc.*

Population Pressures and many members of the third and fourth generations of New Englanders had to migrate— north to New Hampshire or Maine, south to New York, or west beyond the Connecticut River— to find sufficient farmland for themselves and their children. Others abandoned agriculture and learned such skills as blacksmithing or carpentry.

Furthermore, second-generation Puritans did

not display the same religious fervor that had prompted their ancestors to cross the Atlantic.

Halfway Covenant
Many of them had not experienced the gift of God's grace, or "saving faith," which was required for full membership in the Congregational church. Yet they had been baptized as children, attended church services regularly, and wanted their own infants to be baptized, even though the sacrament of baptism was supposed to be available only to the children of church members. A synod of Massachusetts ministers, convened in 1662 to consider the problem, responded by establishing the Halfway Covenant. The clergymen declared that adults who had been baptized as children but were not full church members could have their children baptized. In return, such parents had to acknowledge the authority of the church and live according to moral precepts. "Halfway" members could neither vote in church affairs nor take communion.

By the 1660s, another change in church membership was evident: the proportion of women in the typical congregation was increasing. Indeed, by the end of the century, women constituted a majority in many churches. In response, Cotton Mather, the most prominent member of a family of distinguished ministers, began to deliver sermons outlining women's proper role in church and society—the first formal examination of that theme in American history. Mather urged women to be submissive to their husbands, watchful of their children, and attentive to religious duty.

The different rate of church membership for men and women in late-seventeenth-century New England suggests a growing division between pious women and their more worldly husbands. That split reflected significant economic changes—the third major way in which the Puritan colonies were being transformed.

New England's first commercial system had been based on two pillars: the fur trade and the constant flow of migrants. Through both these means, New Englanders could acquire the manufactured goods they needed. The fur trade gave them valuable pelts to sell in England, and the migrants were always willing to exchange clothing and other items for the earlier settlers' surplus seed, grains, and livestock. But New England's supply of furs was limited because the region lacked rivers giving ready access to the interior of the continent, and the migrants stopped coming after the English civil war began. Consequently, in 1640, that first economic system collapsed.

The Puritans then began a search for new salable crops and markets. They found such crops in the waters off the coast—fish—and on their own land—grain and wood products.

New England's Trading System
By 1643, they had also found the necessary markets: first the Wine Islands (Azores and Canaries) in the Atlantic and then the English colonies in the Caribbean. These islands lacked precisely the goods New England could produce in abundance: cheap food (corn and salted fish) to feed to slaves and wood to make barrels that would hold wine and molasses (the form in which sugar was shipped).

Thus developed the series of transactions that has become known, inaccurately, as the triangular trade. Since New England's products duplicated England's, the northern colonists sold their goods in the West Indies and elsewhere to earn the money with which to purchase English products. There soon grew up in New England's ports a cadre of merchants who acquired cargoes of timber and foodstuffs, which they then dispatched to the West Indies for sale. In the Caribbean the ships sailed from island to island, exchanging fish, barrel staves, and grains for molasses, fruit, spices, and slaves. Then the ships returned to Boston, Newport, or New Haven to dispose of their cargoes. The trading pattern was thus not a triangle but a shifting set of shuttle voyages (see map). Its sole constant was uncertainty, due to the weather, rapid changes of supply and demand in the small island markets, and the delicate system of credit on which the entire structure depended.

The Puritan New Englanders who ventured into commerce were soon differentiated from their rural counterparts by their ties to a wider transatlantic world and by their preoccu-

Puritans and Anglicans
pation with material endeavors. The gulf between commercial and farming interests widened after 1660, when Anglican merchants began to migrate to New England. Such men had little stake in the survival of Massachusetts Bay and

Atlantic Trade Routes

Connecticut in their original form, and some were openly antagonistic to Puritan traditions. As non-Congregationalists, they were denied the vote, and they resented their exclusion from the governing elite. Congregationalist clergymen returned their hostility in full measure and preached sermons called jeremiads, lamenting New England's new commercial orientation. But the ministers spoke for the past, not the future, because by the 1670s New England and the other American colonies were deeply enmeshed in an intricate international trading network.

The valuable American commerce also attracted the attention of English officials seeking a new source of revenue after the disruptions of the civil war. They realized that the colonies could make important contributions to England's economic well-being. Additional tax revenues could put the nation back on a sound financial footing, and English merchants wanted to ensure that they—not their Dutch rivals—reaped the benefits of trading with the English colonies. Accordingly, Parliament and the restored Stuart monarchs began to design a system of laws that would, they hoped, confine the profits of colonial trade primarily to the mother country.

They based their commercial policy on a series of assumptions about the operations of the world's economic system. Collectively, these assumptions are usually called *mercantilism*. The economic world was seen as a collection of national states, each government actively competing for shares of a finite amount of wealth. Each nation's goal was to become as economically self-sufficient as possible while maintaining a favorable balance of trade with other countries (that is, exporting more than it imported). Colonies had an important role to play in such a scheme. They could supply the mother country with valuable raw materials, and they could serve as a market for the mother country's manufactured goods.

Parliament applied mercantilist thinking to the American colonies in a series of laws known as the Navigation Acts. The major acts—passed in 1651, 1660, 1663, and 1673—established three main principles. First, only English or colonial merchants and ships could engage in trade in the colonies. Second, certain valuable American products (called enumerated goods) could be sold only in the mother country. Third, all foreign goods destined for sale in the colonies had to be shipped via England and were subject to English import duties. Some years later, a new series of laws declared a fourth principle: the colonies could not make or export items (such as wool clothing, hats, and iron) that competed with English products.

Navigation Acts

The intention of the Navigation Acts was clear: American trade was to center on England. The mother country was to benefit from colonial imports and exports. England had first claim on the most valuable colonial exports, and all foreign imports into the colonies had to pass through England first, enriching its customs revenues in the process. Moreover, English and colonial shippers were given a monopoly of the American trade. Even so, the American provinces produced many nonenumerated goods—such as fish, flour, and barrel staves—that could be traded directly to foreign purchasers as long as they were carried in English or American ships.

The English authorities soon learned that writing mercantilist legislation was easier than enforcing it. The many harbors of the American coast provided havens for smugglers, and colonial officials often looked the other way when illegally imported goods were offered for sale. In ports such as Curaçao in the Dutch West Indies, American merchants could easily dispose of enumerated goods and purchase foreign items on which duty had not been paid. Consequently, Parliament in 1696 enacted another Navigation Act designed to strengthen enforcement of the first four. This law established in America a number of vice-admiralty courts, which operated without juries. Since American juries had already demonstrated a tendency to favor local smugglers over customs officers, Parliament decided to remove Navigation Act cases from the regular colonial courts.

England took another major step in colonial administration in 1696 by creating the Board of Trade and Plantations, which from then on served as the chief organ of government concerned with the American colonies. (Previously, no one body had that responsibility.) It reviewed Crown appointments in America, scrutinized legislation passed by colonial assemblies, supervised trade policies, and advised successive ministries on colonial issues. Still, the Board of Trade did not have any direct powers of enforcement. It also shared jurisdiction over American affairs not only with the customs service and the navy, but also with the secretary of state for the southern department, the member of the ministry responsible for the colonies. In short, although the Stuart monarchs' reforms considerably improved the quality of colonial administration, supervision of the American provinces remained decentralized and haphazard.

Board of Trade

Even inefficient enforcement of the Navigation Acts was too much for many colonists, and they resisted the laws both by attempting to circumvent them and by formally protesting to the government in London. But protests had little effect, chiefly because policymakers in England were more concerned about preserving the revenues obtained from colonial trade than about any adverse impact the acts might have on the colonies.

Colonial Political Development and Imperial Reorganization

English officials who dealt with colonial administration in the 1670s and 1680s were confronted not only by resistance to the Navigation Acts, but also by a bewildering array of colonial governments. Massachusetts Bay still functioned under its original corporate charter, and its New England neighbors Connecticut and Rhode Island had been granted similar corporate status by Charles II in 1662 and 1663, respectively. Virginia was a royal colony, and New York became one when its proprietor ascended the throne in 1685 as James II. All the other mainland settlements were proprietorships.

Still, in political structure, the colonies shared certain characteristics. Most were ruled by a governor and a two-house legislature. In New England,

Colonial Political Structures

the governors were elected by property-holding men or by the legislature; in the Chesapeake, they were appointed by the king or the proprietor. A council, elected in some colonies and appointed in others, advised the governor on matters of policy and sometimes served as the province's highest court. The council also had a legislative function: initially, its members met jointly with representatives elected by their districts to debate and vote on laws affecting the colony. But as time passed, the fundamental differences between the two legislative groups' purposes and constituencies led them to separate into two distinct houses. Thus developed the two-house legislature still used in almost all the states.

While provincial governments were taking shape, so too were local political institutions. In New England, elected selectmen governed the towns at first, but by the end of the century the town meeting, held at least annually and attended by most adult white townsmen, handled most matters of local concern. In the Chesapeake, the same function was performed by the judges of the county court and by the parish vestry, a group of laymen charged with overseeing church affairs, whose power also encompassed secular concerns.

By late in the seventeenth century, therefore, the American colonists were accustomed to exercising a considerable degree of local political autonomy. The tradition of consent was especially firmly established in New England. Everywhere in the English colonies, white males owning more property than a stated minimum (which varied from province to

province) expected to have an influential voice in how they were governed, and especially in how they were taxed.

After James II became king, these expectations clashed with those of the monarch. The new king and his successors sought to bring order to the apparently chaotic state of colonial administration by tightening the reins of government and reducing the colonies' political autonomy. They began to chip away at the privileges granted in colonial charters and to reclaim proprietorships for the Crown. New Hampshire (1679), its parent colony Massachusetts (1691), New Jersey (1702), and the Carolinas (1729) all became royal colonies. The charters of Rhode Island, Connecticut, Maryland, and Pennsylvania were temporarily suspended as well but were ultimately restored to their original status.

The most drastic reordering of colonial administration was attempted in 1686 through 1689, and its chief target was Puritan New England. Reports from

Dominion of New England

America had convinced English officials that New England was a hotbed of smuggling. Moreover, the Puritans refused to allow freedom of religion and insisted on maintaining laws that often ran counter to English practice. New England thus seemed an appropriate place to exert English authority with greater vigor. The charters of all the colonies from New Jersey to Maine (then part of Massachusetts) were revoked and a Dominion of New England was established in 1686. Sir Edmund Andros, the governor, was given immense power: all the assemblies were dissolved, and he needed only the consent of an appointed council to make laws and levy taxes.

New Englanders endured Andros's autocratic rule for more than two years. Then came the dramatic news that James II had been overthrown in a bloodless rebellion (known as the Glorious Revolution) and had been replaced on the throne by his daughter Mary and her husband, the Dutch prince William of Orange. Seizing the opportunity to rid themselves of the hated Dominion, New Englanders jailed Andros and his associates, proclaimed their loyalty to William and Mary, and wrote to England for instructions about the form of government they should adopt.

In other American colonies, too, the Glorious Revolution proved to be a signal for revolt. In Maryland, the Protestant Association overturned the government of the Catholic proprietor, and in New York, Jacob Leisler, a militia officer of German origin, assumed control of the government. Like the New Englanders, the Maryland and New York rebels allied themselves with the supporters of William and Mary. They saw themselves as carrying out the colonial phase of the English revolt against Stuart absolutism. The problem was that the new monarchs and their colonial administrators did not view American events in the same light.

Glorious Revolution in America

The Glorious Revolution occurred in the mother country because members of Parliament feared that once again a Stuart king was attempting to seize absolute power. James II, like his father, had levied taxes without parliamentary approval. He had also announced his conversion to Roman Catholicism. The Glorious Revolution affirmed the supremacy of Parliament and of Protestantism when Parliament offered the throne to the Protestants William and Mary. But it did not directly affect English policies toward America. William and Mary, like James II, believed that the colonies were too independent and that England should exercise tighter control over its unruly American possessions.

Consequently, the only American rebellion that received royal sanction was that in Maryland, which was approved primarily because of its anti-Catholic thrust. In New York, Jacob Leisler was hanged for treason, and Massachusetts (including the formerly independent jurisdiction of Plymouth) became a royal colony, complete with an appointed governor. The province was allowed to retain its town meeting system of local government and to elect its council, but the new charter issued in 1691 removed the traditional Puritan religious test for voting. An Anglican parish was even established in the heart of Boston.

Compounding New England's difficulties in a time of political uncertainty and economic change was a war with the French and their Indian allies. King Louis XIV of France allied himself with the deposed James II, and England declared war on France in the summer of 1689. In Europe, the conflict, which lasted until 1697, was known as the War of the League of Augsburg, but the colonists called it King William's War. The American phase of the war was fought chiefly on the northern frontiers of New England and New York.

In this period of extreme stress, there occurred an outbreak of witchcraft accusations in Salem Village (now Danvers), Massachusetts, a rural community adjoining the bustling port of Salem Town. Like their contemporaries elsewhere, seventeenth-century New Englanders believed in the existence of witches. If people could not find rational explanations for their troubles, they tended to suspect they were bewitched. Before 1689, 103 New Englanders, most of them middle-aged women, had been accused of practicing witchcraft, chiefly by neighbors who had suffered misfortunes they attributed to the suspected witch, with whom they usually had an ongoing dispute. Although most such accusations occurred singly, on occasion a witchcraft panic could result when one charge set off a chain reaction of similar charges. But nothing else in New England's history ever came close to matching the Salem Village cataclysm.

Witchcraft in Salem Village

The crisis began in early 1692, when a group of adolescent girls accused some older women of having bewitched them. Before the hysteria spent itself ten months later, nineteen people (including several men, most of them related to accused female witches) had been hanged, one person pressed to death by heavy stones, and more than one hundred people jailed. Historians have proposed various explanations for this puzzling episode, but to be understood, the panic must be put in the proper context—the context of political and legal disorder, of Indian war, and of religious and economic change. It must have seemed to Puritan New Englanders as though their entire world was collapsing. At the very least, they could have had no sense of security about their future.

Nowhere was that more true than in Salem Village, a farming town torn between old and new styles of life because of its position on the edge of a commercial center. And no residents of the village could have had a sharper feeling of insecurity than the girls who issued the initial accusations. Many of

No seventeenth-century New Englander ever drew a picture of a witchcraft trial or execution, but an artist did record a hanging of several witches in England, ca. 1650. The multiple executions of Salem witches in the summer of 1692 probably resembled this gallows scene. *By permission of the Folger Shakespeare Library.*

them had been orphaned in the recent Indian attacks on Maine; they were living in Salem Village as domestic servants. Their involvement with witchcraft began when they experimented with fortunetelling as a means of foreseeing their futures, in particular the identity of their eventual husbands. As the most powerless people in a town that was apparently powerless to affect its fate, they offered their fellow New Englanders a compelling explanation for the seemingly endless chain of troubles afflicting them: their province was under direct attack from the Devil and his legion of witches. Accordingly, it is not perhaps the number of witchcraft prosecutions that seems surprising but rather their abrupt cessation in the fall of 1692.

There were two reasons for the rapid end to the crisis. First, the accusers had grown too bold. When they started to charge some of the colony's most respected residents with being in league with the Devil, members of the ruling elite began to doubt their veracity. Second, the new royal charter was fully implemented in late 1692, ending the worst period of political uncertainty and removing a major source of psychological stress. The war continued, and the Puritans were not entirely pleased with the charter, but at least order had formally been restored.

During the next three decades, Massachusetts and the rest of the English colonies in America accommodated themselves to the new imperial order. Most colonists did not like the class of alien officials who arrived in America determined to implement the policies of king and Parliament, but they adjusted to their demands and to the trade restrictions imposed by the Navigation Acts. They fought another imperial war—the War of the Spanish Succession, or Queen Anne's War—from 1702 to 1713, without enduring the psychological stress of the first, despite the heavy economic burdens the conflict imposed. Colonists who allied themselves with the royal government received patronage in the form of offices and land grants and composed "court parties" that supported English officials. Others, who were perhaps less fortunate in their friends or more principled in defense of colonial autonomy (opinions differ), made up the opposition, or "country," interest. By 1725 or so, most men in both groups were native-born Americans, members of elite families whose wealth derived from staple-crop production in the South and commerce in the North.

During the eighty years from 1640 to 1720, then, the European colonies in America changed dramatically. From a small outpost in Santa Fé, New Mexico, the Spanish had expanded their influence throughout the region as far east as Texas and—around the mid-century—as far north as California. The French had moved from a few settlements along the St. Lawrence to dominate the length of the Mississippi River and the entire Great Lakes region.

In 1640 there were just two isolated centers of English population, New England and the Chesapeake. In 1720, nearly the entire east coast of mainland North America was in English hands, and Indian power east of the Appalachian Mountains had been broken. What had been a migrant population was now mostly American-born; economies originally based on the fur trade had become far more complex and more closely linked with the mother country; and a wide variety of political structures had been reshaped into a more uniform pattern. Yet at the same time, the introduction of large-scale slavery into the Chesapeake and the Carolinas had irrevocably differentiated their societies from those of the colonies to the north.

By 1720, the essential elements of the imperial structure that would govern the English colonies until 1775 were in place. The regional economic systems originating in the late seventeenth and early eighteenth centuries continued to dominate North American life for another century—until after independence had been won. The period from 1640 to 1720, in other words, established the basic economic and political patterns that were to structure all subsequent changes in colonial American society.

Suggestions for Further Reading

General

Charles M. Andrews, *The Colonial Period of American History,* vol. 4 (1938); Carl Bridenbaugh, *Cities in the Wilderness: The First Century of Urban Life in America, 1625–1742* (1938); Nicholas Canny and Anthony Pagden, eds., *Colonial Identity in the Atlantic World, 1500–1800* (1987); Wesley Frank Craven, *The Colonies in Transition, 1660–1713* (1968); W. J. Eccles, *The Canadian Frontier, 1534–1760,* rev. ed. (1983); Jack P. Greene and J. R. Pole, eds., *Colonial British America: Essays in the New History of the Early Modern Era* (1984); John J. McCusker and Russell R. Menard, *The Economy of British America, 1607–1789* (1985); Gary Walton and James Shepherd, *The Economic Rise of Early America* (1979).

New Netherland and the Restoration Colonies

Edwin Bronner, *William Penn's "Holy Experiment": The Founding of Pennsylvania, 1681–1701* (1962); Thomas J. Condon, *New York Beginnings: The Commercial Origins of New Netherland* (1968); Wesley Frank Craven, *New Jersey and the English Colonization of North America* (1964); Michael Kammen, *Colonial New York: A History* (1975); Oliver Rink, *Holland on the Hudson: An Economic and Social History of Dutch New York* (1986); Robert C. Ritchie, *The Duke's Province: A Study of Politics and Society in Colonial New York, 1660–1691* (1977); Robert M. Weir, *Colonial South Carolina: A History* (1983).

Africa and the Slave Trade

Philip D. Curtin, *The Atlantic Slave Trade: A Census* (1969); David Brion Davis, *The Problem of Slavery in Western Culture* (1966); David W. Galenson, *Traders, Planters, and Slaves: Market Behavior in Early English America* (1986); Herbert Klein, *The Middle Passage* (1978); Paul Lovejoy, ed., *Africans in Bondage: Studies in Slavery and the Slave Trade* (1986); James Rawley, *The Transatlantic Slave Trade: A History* (1981).

Blacks in Anglo-America

T. H. Breen and Stephen Innes, *"Myne Owne Ground": Race and Freedom on Virginia's Eastern Shore, 1640–1676* (1980); Allan Kulikoff, *Tobacco and Slaves: The Development of Southern Cultures in the Chesapeake, 1680–1800* (1986); Edgar J. McManus, *Black Bondage in the North* (1973); Edmund S. Morgan, *American Slavery, American Freedom: The Ordeal of Colonial Virginia* (1975); Peter H. Wood, *Black Majority: Negroes in Colonial South Carolina from 1670 Through the Stono Rebellion* (1974).

European-Indian Relations

Henry Bowden, *American Indians and Christian Missions: Studies in Cultural Conflict* (1981); Judith K. Brown, "Economic Organization and the Position of Women Among the Iroquois," *Ethnohistory,* 17 (1970), 151–167; Verner W. Crane, *The Southern Frontier, 1760–1732* (1929); Francis Jennings, *The Ambiguous Iroquois Empire* (1984); Elizabeth A. H. John, *Storms Brewed in Other Men's Worlds: The Confrontation of Indians, Spanish, and French in the Southwest, 1540–1795* (1975); Douglas Leach, *Flintlock and Tomahawk: New England in King Philip's War* (1958); Daniel Richter and James Merrell, eds., *Beyond the Covenant Chain: The Iroquois and Their Neighbors in Indian America, 1600–1800* (1987); J. Leitch Wright, Jr., *The Only Land They Knew: The Tragic Story of the American Indians in the Old South* (1981).

New England

Bernard Bailyn, *The New England Merchants in the Seventeenth Century* (1955); Paul Boyer and Stephen Nissenbaum, *Salem Possessed: The Social Origins of Witchcraft* (1974); Richard Bushman, *From Puritan to Yankee: Character and the Social Order in Connecticut, 1690–1765* (1967); John Demos, *Entertaining Satan: Witchcraft and the Culture of Early New England* (1982); Carol Karlsen, *The Devil in the Shape of a Woman: Witchcraft in Early New England* (1987); Perry Miller, *The New England Mind: From Colony to Province* (1953); Robert Pope, *The Half-Way Covenant: Church Membership in Puritan New England* (1969); Laurel Thatcher Ulrich, *Good Wives: Image and Reality in the Lives of Women in Northern New England, 1650–1750* (1982).

Colonial Politics

Lois Green Carr and David W. Jordan, *Maryland's Revolution of Government, 1689–1692* (1974); Richard P. Johnson, *Adjustment to Empire: The New England Colonies, 1675–1715* (1981); David S. Lovejoy, *The Glorious Revolution in America* (1972); Jack M. Sosin, *English America and Imperial Inconstancy: The Rise of Provincial Autonomy, 1696–1715* (1985); Jack M. Sosin, *English America and the Revolution of 1688: Royal Administration and the Structure of Provincial Government* (1982); Jack M. Sosin, *English America and the Restoration Monarchy of Charles II: Transatlantic Politics, Commerce, and Kingship* (1980).

Imperial Trade and Administration

Ronald Hutton, *Charles II* (1990); Michael Kammen, *Empire and Interest: The American Colonies and the Politics of Mercantilism* (1970); Robert C. Ritchie, *Captain Kidd and the War Against the Pirates* (1986); I. K. Steele, *Politics of Colonial Policy: The Board of Trade in Colonial Administration* (1968); Stephen Saunders Webb, *1676: The End of American Independence* (1984); Stephen Saunders Webb, *The Governors-General: The English Army and the Definition of the Empire, 1569–1681* (1979).

In June 1744, Dr. Alexander Hamilton, a Scottish-born physician living in Annapolis, Maryland, paid his first visit to Philadelphia. There he encountered two quite different worlds. One consisted of men of his own status, the merchants and professionals he called "the better sort." The other comprised ordinary folk from different ethnic backgrounds and religious beliefs. Hamilton thought of these people as "rabble." To Hamilton, the "better sort" engaged in informed conversation; the "rabble," he thought, spoke "ignorantly," regardless of the subject.

And what of the women in Philadelphia? Hamilton met few of them, aside from his landlady and one of her friends. "The ladies," he explained, "seldom appear in the streets, never in publick assemblies except at the churches or meetings." Hamilton was referring to women of "the better sort." He could hardly have walked the streets of the city without seeing many female domestic servants, market women, and wives of ordinary laborers going about their daily chores.

Despite his biases, Dr. Hamilton was an astute observer. The Philadelphians' chief employment, he wrote, "is traffick and mercantile business"; and the richest merchants of all were the Quakers. Members of that sect also controlled the colony's government. But, Hamilton noted, "the standing or falling of the Quakers in the House of Assembly depends upon their making sure the interest of the Palatines [Germans] in this province, who of late have turned so numerous that they can sway the votes which way they please." Hamilton deplored the impact on the city of the Great Awakening, a religious revival then sweeping the colonies. "I never was in a place so populous where the gout [taste] for publick gay diversions prevailed so little," he remarked.

Hamilton's observations applied to other places as well. Non-English migrants were settling in many regions of the mainland colonies. Their arrival enlarged the population, altered political balances worked out before 1720, and affected the religious climate by increasing the number of sects. Moreover, others shared Philadelphians' assessment of the importance of commerce. Indeed, by the 1750s, Americans of all descriptions were tied to an international commercial system.

Like other well-educated men of his time, Dr. Hamilton was heavily

3

GROWTH AND DIVERSITY, 1720–1770

The portrait of an eighteenth-century family shows the typical colonial childbearing pattern in the large number of "stairstep" children, born at approximately two-year intervals. *National Gallery of Art, Washington, D.C., Gift of Edgar William and Bernice Chrysler Garbisch.*

influenced by the Enlightenment, the major European intellectual movement of the day. The Enlightenment stressed reason and empirical knowledge. Enlightened thinkers believed above all in rationality. From this perspective came Hamilton's distaste for the Great Awakening, the hallmark of which was emotion. To a believer in the primacy of reason, the passions of the newly converted were more than foolish—they were idiotic.

The Enlightenment had affected Dr. Hamilton in yet another way: it had helped create the elite world of which he was a part. Wealthy, well-read Americans participated in a transatlantic intellectual community, lived in comfortable houses, and entertained at lavish parties. The world of the ordinary folk was different. Working daily from dawn to dark, they struggled just to make ends meet. And most of the "lesser sort" could neither read nor write. The colonies had always been composed of people of different ranks, but by the last half of the eighteenth century the social and economic distance between those ranks had widened noticeably.

Above all, after 1720 the colonies presented a picture of growth and diversity. Population increased dramatically, and the area settled by whites and blacks expanded until it filled almost all of the region between the Appalachian Mountains and the Atlantic Ocean. At the same time, the colonies became more diverse; the two original economies, the Chesapeake and New England, became four through the addition of the middle colonies and the Lower South. Before 1720, the colonies were still inhabited mainly by English, African, and Indian peoples; by 1770, a large proportion of the white population was of non-English origin. The urban population, though tiny by today's standards, grew considerably larger after 1720; and in the cities were found the greatest extremes of wealth and poverty. Such changes transformed the character of England's North American possessions. The colonies that revolted in unison against British rule after 1765 were very different from the colonies that revolted separately against Stuart absolutism in 1689.

Population Growth and Ethnic Diversity

One of the most striking characteristics of the mainland colonies in the eighteenth century was their rapid population growth. Only about 250,000 European and African-Americans resided in the colonies in 1700; thirty years later, that number had more than doubled, and by 1775 it had become 2.5 million. Although migration accounted for a considerable share of the growth, most of it resulted from natural increase. Once the difficult early decades of settlement in each colony had passed, the American population doubled approximately every twenty-five years. Such a rate of growth was then unparalleled in human history. It had a variety of causes, the chief one being the youthful marriage age of women (early twenties for whites, late teens for blacks). Since married women became pregnant every two or three years, women normally bore five to ten children. Because the colonies, especially those north of Virginia, were healthful places to live, a large proportion of the children born reached maturity and began families of their own. As a result, in 1775, about half the American population, white and black, was under sixteen years old.

Such a dramatic phenomenon did not escape the attention of contemporaries. As early as the 1720s, Americans began to point with pride to their fertility, citing population growth as evidence of the advantageous conditions in the colonies. In 1755, Benjamin Franklin published his *Observations Concerning the Increase of Mankind,* which predicted that in another century "the greatest Number of Englishmen will be on this Side the Water." Franklin's purpose in writing his *Observations* was to argue that Britain should prevent Germans from migrating to Pennsylvania. Since the English population in America was increasing so rapidly, he asked, "Why should Pennsylvania, founded by the English, become a Colony of *Aliens,* who will shortly be so numerous as to Germanize us instead of our Anglifying them?"

Whether a majority of Franklin's American-born contemporaries shared his fears is not known. But the eighteenth-century migration to the English colonies was massive; it comprised approximately 375,000 whites and 275,000 blacks. Because some of the whites (for example, convicts sentenced to exile by English courts) and all the blacks did not choose freely to come to the colonies, nearly half the migrants moved to America against their will.

Newcomers from Europe and Africa

Africans made up the largest single racial or ethnic group that came to the colonies during the eighteenth century. More important than the number of black migrants, however, is the fact that in the first half of the century the black population of the Chesapeake began to grow faster through natural increase than through importation. In the slaveholding societies of South America and the Caribbean, a surplus of males over females and appallingly high mortality rates produced very different slave population patterns. There, only large, continuing importations from Africa could maintain the enslaved work force at adequate levels. South Carolina, where rice cultivation was difficult and unhealthy and where planters preferred to purchase males, bore some resemblance to such colonies in that it too required a constant influx of Africans. But in the Chesapeake, the black population grew primarily through natural increase after 1740.

The largest group of white non-English immigrants to America was the Scotch-Irish, chiefly descended from Presbyterian Scots who had settled in northern regions of Ireland during the seventeenth century. Perhaps as many as 250,000 Scotch-Irish people moved to the colonies. Fleeing economic distress and religious discrimination, they were lured as well by hopes of obtaining land. The Scotch-Irish

Scotch-Irish, Germans, and Scots

1720–21 Smallpox inoculation controversy (Boston)

1720–40 Black population of Chesapeake begins to grow by natural increase

1739 Stono Rebellion
George Whitefield arrives in America; Great Awakening broadens

1739–48 King George's War

1741 Slave revolt scare (New York City)

1765–66 Hudson River land riots

1767–69 Regulator movement (South Carolina)

1771 North Carolina Regulators defeated at Battle of Alamance

often arrived in Philadelphia. They moved west and south from that city, settling chiefly in the western portions of Pennsylvania, Maryland, Virginia, and the Carolinas. Frequently unable to afford to buy any acreage, they squatted on land belonging to Indian tribes, land speculators, or colonial governments.

The German migrants numbered about 100,000. Most of them emigrated from the Rhineland between 1730 and 1755, usually arriving in Philadelphia. Not all, however, remained in Pennsylvania. Some moved west and then south along the eastern slope of the Appalachian Mountains, eventually finding homes in western Maryland and Virginia. Others sailed first to Charleston or Savannah and settled in the interior of South Carolina or Georgia. The German immigrants belonged to a wide variety of Protestant sects—primarily Lutheran, German Reformed, and Moravian—and therefore added to the religious diversity of the middle colonies.

The 50,000 or more Scots who came directly to America from Scotland should not be confused with the Scotch-Irish. Many early Scottish immigrants were supporters of Stuart claimants to the throne of England, or Jacobites. After the death of William and Mary's successor, Queen Anne, in 1714, the British throne passed to the German house of Hanover, in the person of King George I. In 1715 and again in 1745, Jacobite rebels attempted unsuccessfully to capture the Crown for

the Stuart pretender, and many were exiled to America as punishment. Most of the Jacobites settled in North Carolina. Ironically, they tended to become loyalists during the Revolutionary War because of their strong commitment to monarchy.

The most concentrated period of immigration to the colonies fell between 1760 and 1775. Tough times in the home country led many to decide to seek a better life in America. In those fifteen years alone, more than 220,000 persons arrived—10 percent of the entire population of British North America. At least 125,000 of the migrants came from the British Isles: 55,000 Scotch-Irish, 40,000 Scots, and more than 30,000 English people. To them were added at least 12,000 Germans and 85,000 Africans. Late-arriving free immigrants had little choice but to remain in the cities or move to the far frontiers of settlement, for land elsewhere was fully occupied.

Because of the migration patterns of the different ethnic groups and the concentration of slaveholding in the South, half the colonial population south of New England was of non-English origin by 1775. Whether the migrants assimilated readily into Anglo-American culture depended on the patterns of settlement, the size of the group, and the strength of the migrants' ties to their common culture. For example, the Huguenots were French Protestants who settled in tiny enclaves in American cities but were unable to sustain either their language or their distinctive religious practices. Within two generations, they were almost wholly absorbed into Anglo-American culture. By contrast, the equally small group of colonial Jews maintained a separate identity. They established synagogues and strove to preserve their culture. Members of the larger groups of migrants (the Germans, Scotch-Irish, and Scots) found it easier to sustain Old World ways if they wished. Countless local areas of the colonies were settled almost exclusively by one or another of these groups.

Recognizing that it was to their benefit to keep other racial and ethnic groups divided, the dominant white elites on occasion deliberately fostered antagonisms among them. When the targets of their policies were European migrants, the goal was the maintenance of political and economic power. When the targets were Indians and blacks, as was the case in South Carolina, the stakes were considerably higher. South Carolina whites, a minority of the population, wanted to prevent Indians and blacks from making common cause against them. So that slaves would not run away to join the Indians, whites hired Indians as slave catchers. So that Indians would not trust blacks, whites used blacks as soldiers in Indian wars.

Although the dominant elites probably would have preferred to ignore the colonies' growing racial and ethnic diversity, they could not do so for long and still maintain their power. When these men decided to lead a revolution in the 1770s, they recognized that they needed the support of non-English Americans. Not by chance, then, did they begin to speak of "the rights of man," rather than "English liberties," when they sought recruits for their cause.

Economic Growth and Development

The eighteenth-century American economy was characterized more by sharp fluctuations than by a consistent long-term trend. Those fluctuations had two primary causes: the impact of European wars and variations in the overseas demand for American products. The only source of stability in the shifting economic climate was the dramatic increase in colonial population.

Each year the rising population generated greater demands for goods and services, which led to the development of small-scale colonial manufacturing and to the creation of a complex network of internal trade. As the area of settlement expanded, roads, mills, and stores were built to serve the new communities. A lively coastal trade developed; by the late 1760s, 54 percent of the vessels leaving Boston harbor were sailing to other mainland colonies. Such ships not only collected goods for export and distributed imports but also sold items made in America. The colonies thus began to move away from their earlier pattern of near-total dependence on Europe for manufactured goods. For the first time, the American population sustained sufficient demand to encourage manufacturing enterprises. The largest indigenous industry was iron making; by 1775, 82 American furnaces and 175 forges were producing more iron than was England itself. Almost all that iron was for domestic consumption.

The major energizing—yet destabilizing—influence on the colonial economy was foreign trade. Colonial prosperity still depended heavily on overseas demand for American products such as tobacco, rice, indigo, fish, and barrel staves, for it was through the sale of these items that the colonists earned the credit they needed to purchase English and European imports. If the demand for American exports slowed, the colonists' income dropped and so did their demand for imported goods.

Despite fluctuations, the economy grew during the eighteenth century. That growth produced higher standards of living for property-owning Americans. Early in the century, households began to acquire such amenities as crude earthenware dishes, chairs, and knives and forks. (Seventeenth-century colonists had used only spoons.) Diet also improved; inventories reveal larger quantities and wider varieties of stored foods. After 1750, luxury items, such as silver plate, appeared in the homes of the

Rising Standard of Living

wealthy, and the "middling sort" started to purchase imported English ceramics and teapots. Even the poorest property owners showed some improvement in the number and type of their household possessions.

Yet the benefits of economic growth were not evenly distributed: wealthy Americans improved their position relative to other colonists. The native-born elite families who dominated American society by 1750 were those who had begun the century with sufficient capital to take advantage of the changes caused by population growth. The rise of a group of monied families comprising urban merchants, large landowners, slave traders, and the owners of rum distilleries helped to make the social and economic structure of mid-eighteenth-century America more rigid than before. The new immigrants did not have the opportunities for advancement that had greeted their predecessors. Even so, there was little poverty among whites in the rural areas, where 90 percent of the colonists lived.

In the cities, however, the story was different. Families of urban laborers lived on the edge of destitution. In Philadelphia, for instance, a male laborer's average annual earnings

Urban Poverty fell short of the amount needed to supply his family with the bare necessities. Even in a good year, other family members had to do wage work; in a bad year, the family could be reduced to beggary. By the 1760s, urban poor-relief systems were overwhelmed with applicants for assistance, and some cities began to build workhouses or almshouses to shelter the growing number of poor people. How could that have happened while the lot of the average American family was improving?

Three answers to that question suggest themselves. First, some poor, unskilled colonists were not able to accumulate sufficient resources to acquire property. Such people clustered in the cities, where they could more easily find work. Second, poverty seems to have been a stage that people passed through at certain times in their lives rather than a constant condition. Third, women, mostly widows, predominated among the urban poor. Since women in the eighteenth century, like women today, were paid about half the wages

earned by men, it may be that urban poverty was primarily a sex-typed phenomenon, with poor white males being the exception rather than the rule.

Within this overall picture, it is important to distinguish among the various regions. In New England, three elements combined to exert a major influence on economic development: the quality of the land, the region's leadership in colonial shipping, and the impact of the imperial wars. New England's soil was rocky and thin, and farmers did not normally produce large surpluses to sell abroad. Farms were worked primarily by family members. New England had the lowest average wealth per freeholder in the colonies. But it also had its share of wealthy men: they were the merchants and professionals whose income was drawn from overseas trade.

Boston's central position in the New England economy and its role as a shipbuilding center ensured that it would be directly affected by any resumption of warfare. In 1739,

New England and King George's War English vessels began clashing with Spanish ships in the Caribbean, setting off a conflict that would merge with the European War of the Austrian Succession and become known in America as King George's War. Nominally, the war was fought to determine who would sit on the Austrian throne, but one of its causes was European commercial rivalries in the Americas. The war's first impact on Boston's economy was positive. Ships and sailors were in demand, and wealthy merchants profited from contracts to supply military expeditions.

But Boston suffered heavy losses of manpower. After France became Spain's ally, a Massachusetts force captured the French fortress of Louisbourg, which guarded the sea lanes leading to New France, but the colony had to levy heavy taxes on its residents to pay for the expensive effort. For decades, Boston's economy felt the continuing effects of King George's War. The city was left with unprecedented numbers of widows and children on its relief rolls, the boom in shipbuilding ended when the war did, and taxes remained high. As a final blow to the colonies, Britain gave Louisbourg back to France in the Treaty of Aix-la-Chapelle (1748).

Because of one key difference between the northern and middle colonies, the latter were more positively affected by King George's War and its aftermath. That difference was the

Prosperity of the Middle Colonies

greater fertility of the soil in New York and Pennsylvania, where commercial farming was the norm. With the outbreak of war, farmers in the middle colonies were able to profit from the increased demand for foodstuffs, especially in the West Indies. After the war, a series of poor grain harvests in Europe caused flour prices to rise even more rapidly. Philadelphia and New York, which could draw on large, fertile grain- and livestock-producing areas, took the lead in the foodstuffs trade, while Boston found its economy stagnating.

The increased European demand for grain also had a significant impact on the Chesapeake. After 1745, some Chesapeake planters began to convert tobacco fields to wheat and corn because the price of grain was rising faster than that of tobacco. By diversifying their crops, they could avoid dependence on just one product for their income. But tobacco still ruled the region and remained the largest single export from the mainland colonies.

The continuing concentration on tobacco in the Chesapeake had two major results by the mid-eighteenth century. The first stemmed from the substitution of enslaved for in-

Natural Increase of Black Population

dentured labor. The offspring of slaves were also slaves, whereas the children of servants were free. As the black population of the Chesapeake began to grow through natural increase between 1720 and 1740, the advantages for the slaveowners became evident. A planter who started with only a few slave families could watch the size of his labor force increase steadily without making additional major investments in workers. Not coincidentally, the first truly large Chesapeake plantations began appearing in the 1740s.

The second effect of tobacco cultivation on the Chesapeake was linked to patterns of trade. In the first half of the eighteenth century, wealthy planters served as middlemen in the tobacco trade. They collected and shipped tobacco grown by their less prosperous neighbors, extended credit to them, and ordered the English imports they wanted. This system changed in the 1740s, when Scottish merchants entered the tobacco trade. The Scots organized their efforts differently from their London-based competitors. They stationed representatives (called factors) in the Chesapeake to purchase tobacco, arrange for shipments, and sell imports. The arrival of the Scottish factors created genuine competition for the first time and thus pushed up tobacco prices. When the Chesapeake finally began to develop port towns later in the century, they grew up in centers of Scottish mercantile activity or in regions that had largely converted to grain production.

The Lower South, like the Chesapeake, depended on staple crops and slave labor, but its pattern of economic growth was distinctive. In contrast

Lower South Trade Patterns

to tobacco prices, which rose slowly through the middle decades of the century, rice prices climbed steeply. The sharp increase was caused primarily by a heavy demand for rice in southern Europe. Because Parliament removed rice from the list of enumerated products in 1730, South Carolinians were able to do what colonial tobacco planters never could: trade directly with continental Europe. But dependence on European sales had its drawbacks, as rice growers discovered at the outbreak of King George's War in 1739. Trade with the continent was disrupted, rice prices plummeted, and South Carolina entered a depression. Still, by the 1760s, prosperity had returned; indeed, in that period, the Lower South experienced more rapid economic growth than the other regions of the colonies. Partly as a result, it had the highest average wealth per freeholder in Anglo-America by the time of the Revolution.

Each region of the colonies, then, had its own economic rhythm derived from the nature of its export trade. King George's War initially helped New England and hurt the Lower South, but in the long run those effects were reversed. In the Chesapeake and the middle colonies, the war initiated a long period of prosperity. The variety of these economic experiences points up a crucial fact about the mainland colonies: they did not compose a unified whole. They were linked economically into regions, but they had few political or social ties beyond or even within those regions. Despite the growing coastal trade, the individual colonies' economic fortunes depended not on their neighbors in America, but rather on the shifting markets of Europe and the West Indies.

Daily Life

The basic unit of colonial society was the household. Headed by a white male (or perhaps his widow), the household was the chief mechanism of production and consumption. Its members—bound by ties of blood or servitude—worked together to produce goods for consumption or sale. The white male head of the household represented it to the outside world, serving in the militia or political posts, casting the household's sole vote in elections. He managed the finances and held legal authority over the rest of the family—his wife, his children, and his servants or slaves. (Eighteenth-century Americans used the word *family* for people who lived together in one house, whether or not they were blood kin.) Such households were considerably larger than American families today; in 1790, the average per home was 5.7 whites. Most of those large families were nuclear—that is, they did not include extended kin like aunts, uncles, or grandparents.

More than 90 percent of all colonial families lived in rural areas. Therefore, nearly all adult white men were farmers, and all adult white women farm wives. In colonial **Sexual Division of Labor Among White Americans** America, household tasks were allocated by sex. The master, his sons, and his male servants or slaves performed one set of chores; the mistress, her daughters, and her female servants or slaves, an entirely different set. So rigid were the gender classifications that when households for some reason lacked a master or mistress, the appropriate jobs were not done. Only in emergencies and for brief periods of time would women do "men's work" or men do women's.

The mistress of the rural household was responsible for what were termed indoor affairs. She and her female helpers prepared the food, cleaned the house, did the laundry, and often made the clothing. The phrase "indoor affair" is somewhat deceptive. For instance, the preparation of food, an "indoor" function, involved planting and cultivating a garden, harvesting and preserving vegetables, salting and smoking meat, drying apples and pressing cider, milking cows and making butter and cheese, not to mention cooking and baking.

The head of the household and his male helpers, responsible for outdoor affairs, also had a heavy workload. They had to plant and cultivate fields, build fences, chop firewood, harvest and market crops, and butcher livestock. Only in the plantation South and in northern cities could even a few adult white males lead lives free from arduous physical labor.

Farm households were governed by the seasons and by the hours of daylight. Men and boys had the most leisure in the winter, when there were no crops that needed care. Women **Rhythms of Rural Life** and girls were freest in the summer, before embarking on autumn food preservation and winter spinning and weaving. Other activities, including education, had to be subordinated to seasonal work. The seasons also affected travel plans. Because the roads were muddy in the spring and fall, most visiting took place in the summer and, in the North, in the winter, when sleighs could be used.

Because most farm families were relatively isolated from their neighbors and had these heavy seasonal work obligations, rural folk took advantage of every possible opportunity for socializing. Men taking grain to be milled would stop at a crossroads tavern for a drink and conversation. Women gathering to assist at childbirth would drink tea and exchange news. Work itself also provided opportunities for visiting. Corn-husking bees, barn raisings, quilting parties, and other communal activities brought together neighbors from miles around, often for several days of work, followed by feasting, dancing, and singing in the evenings.

The few eighteenth-century colonial cities were just large towns by today's standards. The largest, Boston, had only seventeen thousand inhabitants in

Rhythms of Urban Life

1750. Still, city life differed considerably from rural life. City dwellers were not as tied to the seasons. Year-round they could purchase foodstuffs and wood at city markets and cloth at dry-goods stores. They could see friends whenever they wished. Wealthy urbanites had plenty of leisure to read, take walks around town, play cards, or attend dances, plays, and concerts.

City people also had much more contact with the world beyond their own homes than did their rural compatriots. By the 1750s, every major city had at least one weekly newspaper. Newspapers printed the latest "advices from London" (usually two to three months old) and news of events in other English colonies, as well as reports on matters of local interest. However, contact with the outside world also had drawbacks. Sailors sometimes brought contagious diseases into port with them, causing epidemics, which the countryside largely escaped.

Cities attracted many migrants from rural areas. Young men seeking to become apprentices, laborers in need of work, and widows looking for a means to support their families often moved into the cities. Widows could sell their services as nurses, teachers, seamstresses, servants, or prostitutes, or (if they had some capital) open shops, inns, or boarding houses. In rural areas, where the economy was based on agriculture and families produced many of their own necessities, there was little demand for the services that landless women and men could perform. In the cities, though, someone always needed another servant, blacksmith, or laundress.

Only widows and the very few never-married women could legally run independent businesses. An unmarried colonial woman had the same legal

Status of Women

rights as a man (with the exception of voting), but an Anglo-American wife was subordinate to her husband in law as well as custom. Under the common-law doctrine of coverture, a married woman became one person with her husband. She could not sue or be sued, make con-

tracts, buy or sell property, or draft a will. Any property she owned prior to marriage became her husband's after the wedding; any wages she earned were legally his; and all children of the marriage fell under his control.

Anglo-American men expected their wives to defer to their judgment. Most wives seem to have accepted secondary status without murmuring. When girls married, they were commonly advised to devote themselves to their husbands' interests. A Virginia woman remarked, for example, that it was wives' responsibility "to give up to their husbands" whenever differences of opinion arose between them.

The man's legal and customary authority extended to his children as well. Indeed, child rearing was the one task regularly undertaken by both sexes in colonial America. The father set the general standards by which children were raised and usually had the final word on such matters as education or vocational training. White parents normally insisted on unquestioning obedience from their offspring, and many freely used physical punishment to break a child's will. In the homes of America's elite families, most burdensome chores were performed by white or black servants, freeing parents to spend more time with their offspring and reducing the need for strict disciplinary measures.

A white man's authority could include black families, as well as his own kin. More than 95 percent of colonial blacks were held in perpetual bondage. In South Carolina, a majority of the population was black; in Georgia, about half; and in the Chesapeake, 40 percent. The trend toward consolidation of landholding and slave ownership after 1740 had a profound effect on the lives of African-Americans. In areas with high proportions of blacks in the population, most slaves resided on plantations with at least nine other bondspeople. Although many southern blacks lived on farms with only one or two other slaves, the majority had the experience of living and working in a largely black setting.

The concentration of the slave population also had a profound effect on whites. Plantation housing styles, for example, were more African than English in origin, with clusters of small buildings—serving

Chapter 3: Growth and Diversity, 1720–1770

An Overseer Doing His Duty, by Benjamin H. Latrobe. Most slave women were field hands like these, sketched in 1798 near Fredericksburg, Virginia. White women were believed to be unsuited for heavy outdoor labor. *Maryland Historical Society, Baltimore.*

as kitchens, spinning rooms, and so forth—taking the place of one large structure. Just as blacks mimicked the whites' dances in their evening frolics, so too it became customary for whites to perform "Negro jigs" at the end of their cotillions. And words of African origin like *tote* and *okay* were readily incorporated into American English.

The size of such plantations allowed the specialization of labor. Encouraged by planters, whose goal was self-sufficiency, African-American men and women became highly skilled at tasks that whites believed appropriate to their sex. Each large plantation had its own male blacksmiths, carpenters, valets, shoemakers, and gardeners, and female dairymaids, seamstresses, cooks, and at least one midwife, who attended pregnant white and black women alike. These skilled slaves—between 10 and 20 percent of the black population—were essential to the smooth functioning of

Sexual Division of Labor Among Black Americans

the plantation. Most slaves, male or female, were assigned to work in the fields.

The typical Chesapeake tobacco plantation was divided into small "quarters" located at some distance from one another. White overseers supervised work on the distant quarters, while the planter personally took charge of the "home" quarter (which included the planter's house). Planters commonly assigned "outlandish" (African-born) slaves to do field labor in order to accustom them to plantation work routines and to enable them to learn some English. Artisans, on the other hand, were usually drawn from among the plantation's American-born blacks. In such families, skills like carpentry and midwifery were passed down from father to son and mother to daughter; such knowledge often constituted a slave family's most valuable possession.

All the English colonies legally permitted slavery, so discontented blacks had few places to go to escape bondage. Sometimes, recently arrived

Africans ran off in groups to the frontier, where they joined the Indians or attempted to establish traditional villages. Occasionally, slaves from South Carolina tried to reach Spanish Florida. But most slave runaways merely wanted to visit friends or relatives or to avoid their normal work routines for a few days or months. From the blacks' perspective, violent resistance had even less to recommend it than running away. Whites may have been in the minority in some areas, but they controlled the guns and ammunition.

African-Americans did try to improve the conditions of their bondage. Their chief vehicle for gaining some measure of control over their lives was the family. Planters' records reveal how members of extended-kin groups provided support, assistance, and comfort to each other.

Black Families

They asked to live on the same quarters, protested excessive punishment administered to relatives, and often requested special treatment for children. The extended-kin ties that developed among African-American families who had lived on the same plantation for several generations served as insurance against the uncertainties of existence under slavery. If a nuclear family was broken up by sale, there were always relatives around to help with child rearing and other tasks. Among colonial blacks, the extended family served a more important function than it did among whites.

By a variety of means, most black families managed to carve out a small measure of autonomy. On many plantations, slaves were allowed or required to plant their own gardens, hunt, or fish in order to supplement the standard diet of corn and salt pork. Some Chesapeake mistresses permitted their female slaves to raise chickens, which they could then sell or exchange for such items as extra clothing or blankets. In South Carolina, slaves were often able to accumulate personal property because most rice and indigo plantations operated on a task system. Once slaves had completed their assigned tasks for the day, they were free to work for themselves. In Maryland and Virginia, where by the end of the century whites had begun to hire out their slaves to others, blacks were sometimes allowed to keep a small part of the wages they earned. Such advances were slight, but against the bleak backdrop of slavery they deserve to be highlighted.

Yet blacks were always subject to white intrusions into their lives, since they had to serve white families rather than their own. In some households, masters and mistresses enforced their will chiefly through physical coercion. On other plantations, masters were more lenient and respectful of slaves' property and their desire to live with other members of their families. But even in households where whites and blacks displayed genuine affection for one another, there were inescapable tensions. Such tensions were caused not only by whites' uneasiness about the slave system, but also by the dynamics of day-to-day relationships in which a small number of whites wielded arbitrary power over the lives of many blacks.

Black-White Relations

Thomas Jefferson was deeply concerned about that issue. In 1780, he observed, "The whole commerce between master and slave is . . . the most unremitting despotism on the one part, and degrading submission on the other. Our children see this, and learn to imitate it." What troubled Jefferson most was the impact of the system on whites. Before the Revolution, only a tiny number of Quakers took a different approach, criticizing slavery out of sympathy for blacks. The other white colonists who questioned slavery took Jefferson's approach, stressing the institution's adverse effect on whites.

By the third quarter of the eighteenth century, the daily work routines of most Americans had changed little from those of their Old World ancestors. Ordinary white folk lived in farm households, their lives governed by the sexual division of labor. Most African-Americans were held in perpetual bondage, but their work was performed as it had been in West Africa, communally in the fields. Even in colonial cities, life differed little from European cities in previous centuries. Yet if the routines of daily life seemed fixed and unchanging, the wider context in which those routines occurred did not. In both Europe and America, the eighteenth century was a time of great cultural and intellectual ferment. The movement known as the Enlightenment at first primarily influenced the educated elites. Ordinary people seemed little touched by it. But since enlightened thinking played a major part in the ideology of the American Revolution, it eventually had an important impact on the lives of all Americans.

Colonial Culture

The traditional form of colonial culture was oral, communal, and—for at least the first half of the eighteenth century—intensely local. The newer culture of the elite was print-oriented, individualized, and self-consciously cosmopolitan. Although the two are discussed separately here, they mingled in a variety of ways, for people of both descriptions lived side by side in small communities.

A majority of the residents of British America could neither read nor write. That had important consequences for the transmission and development of American culture. In the **Oral Culture** absence of literacy, the primary means of communication was conversation. Information tended to travel slowly and within relatively confined regions. Different locales developed divergent cultural traditions, and those differences were heightened by racial or ethnic variations.

When Europeans or Africans migrated to the colonies, they brought with them assumptions about how society should work and how their own lives fitted into the broader social context. In North America, those assumptions influenced the way they organized their lives. Yet Old World customs usually could not be recreated intact in the New World, because people from different origins now resided in the same communities. Accordingly, the colonists had to forge new cultural identities for themselves, and they did so through public rituals.

Attendance at church was perhaps the most important such ritual in the colonies. In Congregational (Puritan) churches, seating was assigned by church leaders to reflect standing **Religious Rituals** in the community. In early New England, men and women sat on opposite sides of a central aisle, arranged in ranks according to age, wealth, and

church membership. By the middle of the eighteenth century, wealthy men and their wives sat in privately owned pews. In eighteenth-century Virginia, seating in Anglican parishes also revealed the local status hierarchy. Planter families purchased their own pews. Where one sat in colonial churches, in other words, symbolized one's place in society and the values of the local community.

Other aspects of the service also reflected communal values. In most colonial churches, trained clergymen delivered formal sermons, but in Quaker services members of the meeting spoke informally to each other. Communal singing in Congregational churches added an egalitarian element to an otherwise status-conscious experience. The first book printed in the colonies was the *Bay Psalm Book* (1640), consisting of Old Testament psalms recast in short, rhyming, metrical lines so they could be easily learned and sung even by people who could not read. Such singing helped to reduce the ritual significance of hierarchical seating arrangements, bringing a kind of crude democracy into the church.

Communal culture also centered on the civic sphere. In New England in particular, colonial governments proclaimed official days of thanksgiving **Civic Rituals** or days of fasting and prayer. Everyone in the community was expected to participate in the public rituals held on such occasions. Militia musters (known as training days), normally scheduled once a month, were similar moments that brought the community together, since all able-bodied men between the ages of sixteen and sixty were members of the militia.

In the Chesapeake, some of the most important cultural rituals occurred on court and election days. When the county court was in session, men would come from miles around to file suits, appear as witnesses, serve as jurors, or simply observe the goings-on. Attendance at court functioned as a method of civic education; from watching the proceedings men learned what behavior their neighbors expected of them. Elections served the same purpose, for freeholders voted in public. An election official, often flanked by the candidates for the office in question, would call each man forward to declare his preference. The voter would then be thanked politely by the gentleman for whom he had cast his oral ballot.

In such settings as church and courthouse, then, the elite and the ordinary folk alike participated in the oral culture that served as the cement holding their communities together. But the genteel residents of the colonies also took part in a newer kind of culture, one organized through the world of print and the message conveyed by reading, as well as by observing one's neighbors.

Literacy was certainly less essential in eighteenth-century America than it is today. People—especially women—could live their entire lives without ever being called upon to read a book or write a letter. Thus education beyond the bare rudiments of reading, writing, and "figuring" was usually regarded as a frill for either sex. Teaching slaves to read or write was forbidden as too subversive of the social order. Education was thus a sign of status. Only parents who wanted their children to be distinguished from less fortunate peers were willing to forgo their children's valuable labor to allow them to attend school. When parents did so, the education they gave their sons differed from that given their daughters. Girls received little intellectual training beyond the rudiments, though they might learn music, dancing, or fancy needlework. Boys studied with tutors or attended grammar schools that prepared them to enter college at the age of fourteen or fifteen.

Attitudes Toward Education

The colonial system of higher education for males was therefore more fully developed than the basic instruction for either sex. The first American colleges were designed to train young men for the ministry. But during the eighteenth century, the curriculum and character of colleges changed considerably. Their students, the sons of the colonial elite, were now interested in careers in medicine, law, and business instead of the ministry. And the learned men who headed the colleges, though ministers themselves, were deeply affected by the Enlightenment.

In the seventeenth century, some European thinkers began to analyze nature in an effort to determine the laws that govern the universe. They employed experimentation and abstract reasoning

The Enlightenment

to discover general principles behind such everyday phenomena as the motions of the planets and stars, the behavior of falling objects, and the characteristics of light and sound. Above all, Enlightenment philosophers emphasized acquiring knowledge through reason.

The Enlightenment had an enormous impact on well-to-do, educated people in Europe and America. It supplied them with a common vocabulary and a unified view of the world—a view stressing that the enlightened eighteenth century was better than all previous ages. It joined them in a common endeavor, the effort to make sense of God's orderly creation. Thus American naturalists supplied European scientists with information about New World plants and animals, so that they could be fitted into newly formulated universal classification systems.

Enlightenment rationalism affected politics as well as science. John Locke's *Two Treatises of Civil Government* (1691) challenged previous concepts of an unchanging and unchangeable political order. Government, declared Locke, was created by men and so could be altered by them. If a ruler broke his agreement with the people and refused to protect their rights, he could legitimately be ousted from power. Enlightenment theorists proclaimed that the aim of government was the good of the people, that a proper political order could prevent the rise of tyrants, and that even the power of monarchs was subject to God's natural laws.

These intellectual currents had a dramatic effect on the curriculum of the colonial colleges. Whereas in the seventeenth century Harvard courses had focused on the study of the ancient languages and theology, in the 1730s colleges began to introduce courses in mathematics, the natural sciences, law, and medicine. The young men educated in such colleges—and their sisters at home, with whom they occasionally shared their books and ideas—developed a rational outlook on life that differentiated them from their fellow colonists. This was the world of Dr. Alexander Hamilton and his associates. When he left Annapolis in 1744, he carried letters of introduction to "the better sort" in all the places he intended to visit. Such people had learned the value of reading, of regular correspondence with like-minded friends, and of conversation, which focused on recent books imported from Europe.

Well-to-do graduates of American colleges, along with others educated in Great Britain, formed the core of genteel culture in the colonies. Men and women from these families

Elite Culture

wanted to set themselves apart from ordinary folk. Beginning in the 1720s, they constructed grandiose residences and filled them with imported furnishings, entertained their friends at elaborate dinner parties and balls at which all present dressed in the height of fashion, cultivated polite manners, and saw themselves as part of a transatlantic and intercolonial network.

In what ways did this genteel, enlightened culture affect the lives of most colonists? Certainly no resident of the colonies could have avoided some contact with members of the elite. Ordinary folk were expected to doff their hats and behave in a deferential fashion when conversing with their "betters." Some were economically dependent on genteel folk; for example, the elite's demand for consumer goods of all kinds led to the growth of artisan industries like furniture making and silversmithing. But the Enlightenment's most immediate impact on all Americans was in the realm of medicine.

The key figure in the drama was the Puritan clergyman, Cotton Mather, who was a member of England's Royal Society, an organization of the intellectual elite. In a Royal Soci-

Smallpox Inoculations

ety publication, Mather read about the benefits of inoculation (deliberately infecting a person with a mild case of a disease) as a protection against the dreaded smallpox. In 1720 and 1721, when Boston suffered a major smallpox epidemic, Mather and a doctor ally urged people to be inoculated despite fervent opposition from Boston's leading physician. When the epidemic ended, the statistics bore out Mather's opinion: of those inoculated, fewer than 3 percent died; of those who became ill without inoculation, nearly 15 percent perished.

If the lives of genteel and ordinary folk in the eighteenth-century colonies seemed to follow different patterns, there was one man who in his per-

Benjamin Franklin, the Symbolic American

son appeared to combine their traits. That man was Benjamin Franklin. Born in Boston in 1706, he was the perfect example of a self-made, self-educated man. Apprenticed at an early age to his older brother James, a Boston printer, Franklin ran away to Philadelphia in 1723. There he eventually started his own publishing business, printing books, a newspaper, and *Poor Richard's Almanack*. The business was so successful that Franklin was able to retire from active control in 1748. He then devoted himself to intellectual endeavors and public service. Franklin's *Experiments and Observations on Electricity* (1751) was the most important scientific work by a colonial American; it established the terminology and the basic theory of electricity that is still in use today.

Franklin proposed the establishment of a new educational institution in Pennsylvania. The purpose of Franklin's "English School" was not to produce clerics or scholars, but to prepare young men "for learning any business, calling or profession." The College of Philadelphia (now the University of Pennsylvania), which he founded in 1755, was intended to graduate youths who would resemble Franklin himself—talented, practical men of affairs competent in a number of different fields.

Franklin and the student he envisioned thus fused the conflicting tendencies of colonial culture. Free of the Old World's traditions, the ideal American would achieve distinction through hard work and the application of common-sense principles. Like Franklin, he would rise from an ordinary family into the ranks of the genteel, thereby transcending the cultural boundaries that divided the colonists. The American would be a true child of the Enlightenment, knowledgeable about European culture yet not bound by its fetters, advancing through reason and talent alone. To him all things would be possible, all doors open.

The contrast with the original communal ideals of early New England could not have been sharper. Franklin's American was an individual, free to make choices about his future. John Winthrop's American had been a component of a greater whole that required his unquestioning submission. But the two visions had one point in common: both

In 1713, the colony of Massachusetts constructed its impressive State House in Boston. Here met the Assembly and the Council. The solidity and imposing nature of the building must have symbolized for its users the increasing consolidation of power in the hands of the Massachusetts legislature. *Library of Congress.*

described only white males. Not until many years later would America formally recognize what had been true all along: that females and nonwhites had participated in creating the nation's cultural tradition.

Politics and Religion: Stability and Crisis at Midcentury

In the first decades of the eighteenth century, colonial political life developed a new stability. Despite the large migration from overseas, most mainland colonists were now native-born. Men from genteel families dominated the political structures in each province, for voters (white males who met property-holding requirements) tended to defer to their well-educated "betters" on election days.

Colonial political leaders sought to increase the powers of the elected assemblies relative to those of the governors and other appointed officials. As-

Rise of the Assemblies semblies began to claim privileges associated with the British House of Commons, such as the right to initiate all tax legislation and to control the militia. The assemblies also developed effective ways of influencing British appointees, especially by threatening to withhold their salaries. In some colonies (for example, Virginia and South Carolina), the elite members of the assemblies usually presented a united front to royal officials, but in others (for example, New York), they fought with each other long and bitterly.

Yet eighteenth-century assemblies bore little resemblance to twentieth-century state legislatures. Much of their business was what today would be termed administrative; only on rare occasions did they formulate new policies or pass important laws. Unlike modern legislators, who act positively to improve the lives of their constituents, eighteenth-century assemblymen acted negatively, to prevent encroachments on the people's rights. In their minds, their primary function was to stop the governors or councils from enacting such measures as oppressive taxes, rather than to pass laws that would actively benefit their constituents.

By the middle of the century, politically aware colonists commonly drew analogies between their governments and the balance among king, lords, and commons found in Great Britain—a combination that was thought to produce a stable polity. Although the analogy was not exact, political leaders equated their governors with the monarch, their councils with the aristocracy, and their assemblies with the House of Commons. All three were thought essential to good government, but Americans did not regard them with the same degrees of approval. They saw the governors and appointed councils as representatives of England who posed a potential threat to colonial freedoms and customary ways of life. By contrast, they viewed assemblies as the people's protectors. The assemblies, for their part, regarded themselves as representatives of the people.

Again, such beliefs should not be equated with modern practice. Firmly controlled by dominant families, whose members were reelected year after year, the assemblies rarely responded to the concerns of their poorer constituents. Although settlement continually spread westward, assemblies failed to reapportion themselves to provide adequate representation for newer communities. Thus it is important to distinguish between the colonial ideal, which placed the assembly at the forefront in the protection of people's liberties, and the reality, in which the people protected tended chiefly to be the wealthy and the assembly members themselves.

At midcentury, the political structures that had stabilized in a period of relative calm confronted a series of crises. None affected all the mainland provinces, but no colony escaped wholly untouched by at least one. The crises foreshadowed the greater disorder of the revolutionary era. Most important, they demonstrated that the political accommodations arrived at in the aftermath of the Glorious Revolution were no longer adequate to govern Britain's American empire.

One of the first—and greatest—of the crises occurred in South Carolina. Early one morning in September 1739, about twenty slaves gathered near the Stono River, south of Charleston. After seizing guns and ammunition from a store, they killed the storekeepers and some nearby planter families. Then, joined by other slaves from the area, they headed south toward Florida, hoping to find refuge in that Spanish colony. Later the same day, the militia caught up with the fugitives (who numbered about one hundred) and attacked them, killing some and dispersing the rest. More than a week later, the whites finally captured most of the remaining conspirators. Those not killed on the spot were later executed.

Stono Rebellion

The Stono Rebellion shocked white South Carolinians and residents of other colonies as well. Laws governing the behavior of blacks were stiffened throughout British America. But the most immediate response came in New York, which itself had suffered a slave revolt in 1712. There the news from the South, coupled with fears of Spain generated by the outbreak of King George's War, set off a reign of terror in the summer of 1741. Hysterical whites transformed a biracial gang of thieves and arsonists into conspirators who wanted to foment a slave uprising under the guidance of a supposed priest in the pay of Spain. By the end of the summer, thirty-one blacks and four whites had been executed for participating in the "plot." The Stono Rebellion and the New York "conspiracy" revealed both the deepest fears about the dangers of slaveholding and the inability of assemblies to prevent serious internal disorder. Events of the next two decades confirmed that inability.

By midcentury, much of the fertile land east of the Appalachians had been purchased or occupied. As a result, conflicts over land titles and conditions of landholding grew in number and frequency as

Land Riots colonists competed for control of land good for farming. In 1746, for example, New Jersey farmers holding land under grants from the governor of New York (dating from the brief period when both provinces were owned by the duke of York) clashed violently with agents of the East Jersey proprietors. The proprietors claimed the land as theirs and demanded annual payments, called quitrents, for the use of the property. Similar violence occurred in the 1760s in the region that later became Vermont.

The most serious land riots of the period took place along the Hudson River in 1765 and 1766. Late in the seventeenth century, Governor Benjamin Fletcher of New York had granted several huge tracts in the lower Hudson valley to prominent colonial families. The proprietors in turn divided these estates into small farms, which they rented chiefly to poor Dutch and German migrants. After 1740, though, increasing migration from New England brought conflict to the great New York estates. The New Englanders squatted on vacant portions of the manors and resisted all attempts to evict them. In the mid-1760s, the Philipse family brought suit against the New Englanders, some of whom had lived on Philipse land for twenty or thirty years. New York courts upheld the Philipse claim and ordered the squatters to make way for tenants with valid leases. Instead of complying, the farmers organized a rebellion against the proprietors. For nearly a year, the insurgent farmers terrorized proprietors and loyal tenants, freed their friends from jail, and on one occasion battled a county sheriff and his posse. The rebellion was put down only after British troops dispatched from New York City captured its most important leaders.

Violent conflicts of a different sort erupted just a few years later in the Carolinas. The Regulator movements of the late 1760s (South Carolina) and early 1770s (North Carolina)

The Regulators pitted backcountry farmers against the wealthy eastern planters who controlled their provinces' governments. The frontier dwellers, most of whom were Scotch-Irish, protested their lack of an adequate voice in colonial political affairs. The South Carolinians for months policed the countryside in vigilante bands, contending that law enforcement in the region was too lax. The North Carolinians, many of whose grievances had their origin in heavy taxation, fought and lost a battle with eastern militiamen at Alamance in 1771.

The most widespread crisis occurred not in politics but in religion. From the late 1730s through the 1760s, waves of religious revivalism—known collectively as the Great Awaken-

First Great Awakening ing—swept over various parts of the colonies, primarily New England (1735–1745) and Virginia (1750s and 1760s). America was ripe for religious renewal at midcentury. Orthodox Calvinists were eager to combat Enlightenment rationalism, which denied innate human depravity. In addition, many recent immigrants and residents of the backcountry had no prior religious affiliation, thus presenting evangelists with a likely source of converts.

The first signs of what was to become the Great Awakening appeared in western Massachusetts, in Northampton Congregational Church, led by the Reverend Jonathan Edwards, a noted preacher and theologian. During 1734 and 1735, Edwards noticed a remarkable response among the young members of his flock to a message based squarely on Calvinist principles. Individuals, Edwards argued, could attain salvation only through recognition of their own depraved natures and the need to surrender completely to God's will. Such surrender brought an intensely emotional release from sin and came to be seen as a single identifiable moment of conversion.

The effects of such conversions remained isolated until 1739, when an English Methodist named George Whitefield arrived in America. For

George Whitefield fifteen months, Whitefield toured the colonies, preaching to large audiences from Georgia to New England, and he became the chief generating force behind the Great Awakening. At first, regular clerics welcomed Whitefield, as well as native evangelist preachers. Soon, however, many clergymen began to realize that "revived" religion ran counter to their own approach to matters of faith.

Opposition to the Awakening heightened rapidly, and large numbers of churches splintered in its wake. "Old Lights"—traditional clerics and their followers—engaged in bitter disputes with the "New Light" evangelicals. American religion, already characterized by numerous sects, became further divided as the major denominations split into Old Light and New Light factions and as new evangelical sects—Methodists and Baptists—quickly gained adherents. Paradoxically, the angry fights and the rapid rise in the number of distinct denominations eventually led to an American willingness to tolerate religious diversity.

The most important effect of the Awakening was its impact on American modes of thought. The revivalists' message directly challenged the colonial

Impact of the Awakening

tradition of deference. Itinerant preachers, many of whom were not ordained clergymen, claimed they understood the will of God better than orthodox clerics. The Awakening's emphasis on emotion rather than learning undermined the validity of received wisdom, and New Lights questioned not only religious, but also social and political, orthodoxy. For example, New Lights began to defend the right of groups and individuals to dissent from a community consensus and so challenged one of the most fundamental tenets of colonial political life up to that time.

Thus, at midcentury, the Great Awakening injected an egalitarian strain into American life and further disrupted traditional structures of existence. Although primarily a religious movement, the Awakening also had important social and political consequences. It called into question habitual modes of behavior in the secular, as well as the religious, realm. The Great Awakening, in short, helped to break Americans' ties to their limited seventeenth-century origins. So, too, did the newcomers from Germany, Scotland, Ireland, and Africa, who brought their languages, customs, and religions to North America. Also important were the changes in the economy that linked the colonies tightly to international markets, drawing them irrevocably into European wars and creating the wealthy class of merchants and landowners who dominated colonial life.

A century and a half after English people had first settled in North America, the colonies were only nominally English. In reality, they mixed diverse European, American, and African traditions into a novel cultural blend. That culture owed much to the Old World, but just as much, if not more, to the New. In the 1760s, Americans began to recognize that their interests were not necessarily identical with those of Great Britain or its monarch.

Suggestions for Further Reading

General

Wayne Craven, *Colonial American Portraiture* (1986); Jack P. Greene, *Pursuits of Happiness: The Social Development of the Early Modern British Colonies and the Formation of American Culture* (1988); Richard Hofstadter, *America at 1750: A Social Portrait* (1971).

Rural Society

T. H. Breen, *Tobacco Culture* (1985); Lois Green Carr et al., eds., *Colonial Chesapeake Society* (1988); Rhys Isaac, *The Transformation of Virginia, 1740–1790* (1982); Sung Bok Kim, *Landlord and Tenant in Colonial New York: Manorial Society, 1664–1775* (1978); James T. Lemon, *The Best Poor Man's Country: A Geographical Study of Early Southeastern Pennsylvania* (1972); Jackson Turner Main, *Society and Economy in Colonial Connecticut* (1985); Michael Zuckerman, *Peaceable Kingdoms: New England Towns in the Eighteenth Century* (1970).

Urban Society

Carl Bridenbaugh, *Cities in Revolt: Urban Life in America, 1743–1776* (1955); Christine L. Heyrman, *Commerce and Culture: The Maritime Communities of Colonial Massachusetts, 1690–1750* (1984); Gary B. Nash, *The Urban Crucible: Social Change, Political Consciousness, and the Origins of the American Revolution* (1979); Frederick B. Tolles, *Meeting House and Counting House: The Quaker Merchants of Colonial Philadelphia, 1682–1763* (1948).

Economic Development

Paul Clemens, *The Atlantic Economy and Colonial Maryland's Eastern Shore: From Tobacco to Grain* (1980); Alice Hanson Jones, *Wealth of a Nation to Be: The American Colonies on the Eve of the Revolution* (1980); John J. McCusker and Russell R. Menard, *The Economy of British America,*

1607–1789 (1985); Edwin J. Perkins, *The Economy of Colonial America* (1980); Gary M. Walton and James F. Shepherd, *The Economic Rise of Early America* (1979).

Politics

Bernard Bailyn, *The Origins of American Politics* (1968); Patricia U. Bonomi, *A Factious People: Politics and Society Colonial New York* (1971); Richard Bushman, *King and People in Provincial Massachusetts* (1985); Edward M. Cook, Jr., *The Fathers of the Towns: Leadership and Community Structure in Eighteenth-Century New England* (1976); Jack P. Greene, *The Quest for Power: The Lower Houses of Assembly in the Southern Royal Colonies, 1689–1776 (1963).*

Immigration

Bernard Bailyn, *The Peopling of British North America* (1986); Bernard Bailyn, *Voyagers to the West* (1986); Jon Butler, *The Huguenots in America* (1983); R. J. Dickson, *Ulster Immigration to Colonial America, 1718–1775* (1966); Ned Landsman, *Scotland and Its First American Colony* (1985); Sharon Salinger, *To Serve Well and Faithfully: Labor and Indentured Servants in Pennsylvania, 1682–1800* (1988).

Blacks

Ira Berlin, "Time, Space, and the Evolution of Afro-American Society in British Mainland America," *American Historical Review,* 85 (1980), 44–78; Thomas J. Davis, *A Rumor of Revolt: The "Great Negro Plot" in Colonial New York* (1985); Herbert Gutman, *The Black Family in Slavery and Freedom, 1750–1925* (1976); Gerald W. Mullin, *Flight and Rebellion: Slave Resistance in Eighteenth-Century Virginia* (1972); William Pierson, *Black Yankees: The Development of an Afro-American Subculture in Eighteenth-Century New England* (1988); Mechal Sobel, *The World They Made Together: Black and White Values in Eighteenth-Century Virginia* (1987).

Women and Family

J. William Frost, *The Quaker Family in Colonial America* (1972); Philip J. Greven, *The Protestant Temperament: Patterns of Child-rearing, Religious Experience, and the Self in Early America* (1977); Barry J. Levy, *Quakers and the American Family* (1988); Mary Beth Norton, *Liberty's Daughters: The Revolutionary Experience of American Women, 1750–1800* (1980); Marylynn Salmon, *Women and the Law of Property in Early America* (1986).

Colonial Culture and the Enlightenment

Daniel J. Boorstin, *The Americans: The Colonial Experience* (1958); Richard Beale Davis, *Intellectual Life in the Colonial South, 1585–1763 ,* 2 vols. (1978); Henry F. May, *The Enlightenment in America* (1976); Louis B. Wright, *The Cultural Life of the American Colonies, 1607–1763* (1957).

Education

James Axtell, *The School upon a Hill: Education and Society in Colonial New England* (1974); Bernard Bailyn, *Education in the Forming of American Society* (1960); Patricia Cline Cohen, *A Calculating People: The Spread of Numeracy in Early America* (1982); Lawrence A. Cremin, *American Education: The Colonial Experience, 1607–1783* (1970); Kenneth A. Lockridge, *Literacy in Colonial New England* (1974).

Science and Medicine

Jane Donegan, *Women and Men Midwives: Medicine, Morality, and Misogyny in Early America* (1978); John Duffy, *Epidemics in Colonial America* (1953); Raymond P. Stearns, *Science in the British Colonies of America* (1970).

Religion and the Great Awakening

Patricia U. Bonomi, *Under the Cope of Heaven: Religion, Society, and Politics in Colonial America* (1986); Carl Bridenbaugh, *Mitre and Sceptre: Transatlantic Faiths, Ideas, Personalities, and Politics, 1689–1775* (1962); J. M. Bumstead and John E. Van de Wetering, *What Must I Do to Be Saved? The Great Awakening in Colonial America* (1976); David S. Lovejoy, *Religious Enthusiasm in the New World* (1985); Harry S. Stout, *The New England Soul: Preaching and Religious Culture in Colonial New England* (1986); Patricia Tracy, *Jonathan Edwards, Pastor* (1980).

In late October 1769, the young Boston shopkeeper Betsy Cuming was visiting a sick friend when outside the house she heard "a voilint Skreeming Kill him Kill him." Betsy ran to the window and saw John Mein, a bookseller and newspaper publisher, being chased by "a larg Croud of those who Call themselves Gentleman." That same night, Mein fled to a vessel anchored in the harbor. He later sailed to England and never returned to the city.

Mein had aroused the wrath of the crowd by printing in his newspaper, the *Boston Chronicle,* lists of names of local merchants who had recently cleared imports through the Boston customs house. But why was the information Mein revealed so explosive? In the fall of 1769, many American merchants had signed an agreement not to import goods from Great Britain; Mein's lists indicated that some of the most vocal supporters of nonimportation (including the patriot leader John Hancock) had been violating the agreement. That was why the "gentlemen" of Boston had to silence the outspoken publisher.

John Mein was not the first, and he would be far from the last, resident of the colonies who found his life wholly disrupted by the growing political antagonism

SEVERING THE BONDS OF EMPIRE, 1754–1774

between England and her American possessions. Long afterward, John Adams identified the years between 1760 and 1775 as the period in which the true American Revolution had occurred. The Revolution, Adams declared, was completed before the fighting started, for it was "in the Minds of the people," involving not the actual winning of independence but rather a shift of allegiance from England to America. Today, not all historians would agree with Adams's assertion that that shift constituted the Revolution. But none would deny the importance of the events of those crucial years.

The story of the 1760s and early 1770s is one of an ever-widening split between England and America. In the long history of British settlement in the Western Hemisphere, there had been at times considerable tension in the relationship between individual provinces and the mother country. Still, that tension had rarely been sustained for long, nor had it been widespread, except in 1688 and 1689. In the 1750s, however, a series of

A LIST of the Names of *those*
who AUDACIOUSLY continue to counteract the UNIT-
ED SENTIMENTS of the BODY of Merchants thro'out
NORTH-AMERICA ; by importing British Goods
contrary to the Agreement.

John Bernard,
(In King-Street, almost opposite Vernon's Head.

James McMasters,
(On Treat's Wharf.

Patrick McMasters,
(Opposite the Sign of the Lamb.

John Mein,
(Opposite the White-Horse, and in King-Street.

Nathaniel Rogers,
(Opposite Mr. Henderson Inches Store lower End
King-Street.

William Jackson,
At the BrazenHead, Cornhill, near the Town-House.

Theophilus Lillie,
(Near Mr. Pemberton's Meeting-House, North-End.

John Taylor,
(Nearly opposite the Heart and Crown in Cornhill.

Ame & Elizabeth Cummings,
(Opposite the Old Brick Meeting House, all of Boston.

Israel Williams, Esq; & *Son*,
(Traders in the Town of Hatfield.

And, *Henry Barnes*,
(Trader in the Town of Marlboro'.

The following Names should have been inserted in
the List of Justices.

County of Middlesex.	County of Lincoln.
Samuel Hendley	
John Borland	John Kingsbury
Henry Barnes	
Richard Cary	County of Berkshire.
County of Bristol.	Mark Hopkins
George Brightman	Elijah Dwight
County of Worcester.	Israel Stoddard
Daniel Bliss	

A blacklist printed in the *North American Almanac* for
1770 identified those Boston merchants who had ignored
the nonimportation agreement. Among their number were
both John Mein, the object of the mob's wrath the previous October, and Betsy (Elizabeth) Cuming, the narrator
of the story, who—with her sister Anne—ran a small dry-
goods store. *Library of Congress.*

events began to change the situation. It all started
with the Seven Years' War (1754–1763).

Britain's overwhelming victory in that war
forever altered the balance of power in North
America. France was ousted from the continent, an
event with major consequences for both the Indian
tribes of the interior and the colonists. Northern
Indians could no longer play European powers off
against one another, and so they lost one of their

major diplomatic tools. Anglo-Americans, for their
part, no longer had to fear a French threat on
their borders. The British colonies would never
have dared to break with their mother country,
some historians have argued, if an enemy nation
and its Indian allies had controlled the interior of
the continent.

The British victory in 1763, then, constituted a
major turning point in American history because of
its direct effect on white and Indian residents of
North America. It also had a significant impact on
Great Britain, one that soon affected the colonies as
well. To win the war, Britain had gone heavily into
debt. To reduce the debt, Parliament for the first
time laid revenue-raising taxes on the colonies. That
decision exposed differences in the political thinking of Americans and Britons.

During the 1760s, a broad coalition of white
Americans, men and women alike, resisted new tax
levies and attempts by British officials to tighten
controls over the provincial governments. America's elected leaders became ever more suspicious
of Britain's motives as the years passed. They laid
aside intercolonial antagonisms to coordinate their
response to the new measures, and they slowly began to reorient their political thinking. As late as
the summer of 1774, though, most were still seeking a solution within the framework of the empire;
few harbored thoughts of independence. When independence did become the issue, as opposed to
loyal resistance, the coalition of the 1760s broke
down. That, however, did not happen until after the
battles of Lexington and Concord in April 1775.
Before then, only a few Americans closely connected to colonial administration or the Church of
England opposed the trend of resistance.

Renewed Warfare Among Europeans and Indians

The English colonies along the Atlantic seaboard
were surrounded by hostile, or potentially hostile,
neighbors: Indians everywhere, the Spanish in
Florida and along the coast of the Gulf of Mexico,
and the French along the great inland system of

1754	Albany Congress Seven Years' War begins		1767	Townshend Acts

1756	War officially declared		1770	Lord North becomes prime
				  minister
				Repeal of the Townshend duties,
				  except the tea tax
				Boston Massacre

1760	American phase of war ends George III becomes king			
1763	Treaty of Paris Pontiac's uprising Proclamation of 1763		1772	Boston Committee of Correspondence formed
1764	Sugar Act		1773	Tea Act Boston Tea Party
1765	Stamp Act Sons of Liberty formed		1774	Coercive Acts
1766	Repeal of the Stamp Act Declaratory Act			

rivers and lakes that stretched from the St. Lawrence to the Mississippi. The Spanish outposts posed little threat to the English, for Spain's days as a major power had passed, but the French were another matter. Their forts and settlements dominated the North American interior, facilitating trading partnerships and alliances with the tribes of the region. In none of the three wars fought between 1689 and 1748 was England able to shake France's hold on the American frontier. Under the Peace of Utrecht, which ended Queen Anne's War in 1713, the English won control of such peripheral northern areas as Newfoundland, Hudson's Bay, and Nova Scotia (Acadia). But Britain made no additional territorial gains in King George's War (see map, page 72).

During both Queen Anne's War and King George's War, the Iroquois Confederacy did not take sides. Instead, it skillfully played the Europeans off against one another. When the Iroquois went to war in those years, it was against a traditional southern enemy, the Catawbas. Since France repeatedly urged them to attack the Catawbas, who were allied with England, the Iroquois achieved three desirable goals. They kept the French happy and simultaneously consolidated their control over the entire interior region north of Virginia. In addition, these southern wars (by identifying a common enemy) enabled the confederacy to cement its alliance with its weaker tributaries, the Shawnees and Delawares. But even the careful Iroquois diplomats could not prevent the region inhabited by the Shawnees and Delawares (now western Pennsylvania and eastern Ohio) from providing the spark that set off a major war. That conflict spread from America to Europe and proved decisive in the contest for North America. Trouble began in 1752, when English fur traders ventured into the area known as the Ohio country. The French could not permit their English rivals to dominate the region. A permanent English presence in the Ohio country could challenge France's control of the western fur trade and even threaten its prominence in the Mississippi valley. Accordingly, in 1753 the French built fortified outposts at strategic points along the rivers of the Ohio country.

Iroquois Neutrality

Lake Superior

Lake Michigan

Lake Huron

Lake Ontario

Lake Erie

NEW FRANCE

CHIPPEWA

CHIPPEWA

OTTAWA

POTAWATOMI
MIAMI

WYANDOT

ILLINOIS CONFEDERATION

WEA

OHIO COUNTRY

SHAWNEE

Quebec

Montreal

St. Lawrence R.

Ft. Niagara

Ft. Detroit

Allegheny R.

Monongahela R.

SENECA

CAYUGA
ONONDAGA
TUSCARORA
ONEIDA

MOHAWK

Ft. Stanwix
Albany

NEW YORK

PENNSYLVANIA

DELAWARE
Ft. Duquesne
(Pitt)

*Ft.
Necessity*

Ohio R.

Mississippi R.

1720–1760

Tuscarora Migration

Proclamation Line of 1763

Philadelphia

New York

N.J.

New Castle

Baltimore

MD.

DEL.

Ft. Western
(Augusta)

MAINE
(Part of Mass.)
Falmouth
(Portland)

N.H. Portsmouth

Boston
MASS.

Hartford
CONN.

Providence
R.I.

Richmond

VIRGINIA

Williamsburg

ATLANTIC OCEAN

CHEROKEE

Salem

Hillsboro

NORTH CAROLINA

New Bern

CATAWBA

Camden

SOUTH CAROLINA

Wilmington

CHICKASAW

Ft. Augusta
(Augusta)

GEORGIA

Charleston

CREEK

Savannah

CHOCTAW

NEW SPAIN

St. Augustine

Total population of
English colonies: c.1.5 million

Extent of settlement

| 0 | | 100 | | 200 miles |

| 0 | 100 | 200 | | 300 kilometers |

European Settlements and Indian Tribes, 1750

In response to the threat posed by the French, delegates from seven northern and middle colonies gathered in Albany, New York, in June 1754.

Albany Congress With the backing of administrators in London, they sought to coordinate the defenses of the colonies and to persuade the Iroquois to abandon their traditional neutrality. They did not succeed in either aim. The Iroquois saw no reason to change a policy that had served them well for half a century. And although the Albany Congress delegates adopted a Plan of Union (which provided for an elected intercolonial legislature with the power to tax), the plan was uniformly rejected by their provincial governments—primarily because those governments feared a loss of autonomy.

As they deliberated, the delegates to the Albany Congress did not know that the war they sought to prepare for was already beginning. The governor of Virginia, which claimed ownership of the Ohio country, had sent a small militia force westward to counter the French moves. But the militiamen arrived too late. The French had already taken possession of the strategic point—now Pittsburgh—where the Allegheny and Monongahela rivers meet to form the Ohio, and they were busily constructing Fort Duquesne. The inexperienced young colonel who commanded the Virginians attacked a French detachment, then allowed himself to be trapped by the French in his crudely built Fort Necessity at Great Meadows, Pennsylvania. After the twenty-two-year-old George Washington surrendered and signed a document of capitulation, he and his men were allowed to return to Virginia.

Washington had blundered grievously. He had started a war that would eventually encompass nearly the entire world. He had also ensured that most tribes in the Ohio valley would support France in the coming conflict. The Indians took Washington's mistakes as an indication of Britain's inability to win the war, and nothing that occurred in the next four years made them change their minds. In July 1755, a combined force of French and Indians ambushed General Edward Braddock, two regiments of British regulars, and some colonial troops a few miles south of Fort Duquesne. Braddock was killed and his men demoralized by their complete defeat. After news of

Seven Years' War

the debacle reached London, Britain declared war on France in 1756, thus formally beginning the conflict that is known as the Seven Years' War.

Although the early years of the war were disastrous for the British, the tide began to turn in 1757. In that year, William Pitt was named secretary of state. Under his leadership, the British mounted the effort that won them the war in North America. By agreeing to reimburse the colonies for their military expenditures and placing troop recruitment wholly in local hands, Pitt gained wholehearted American support for the war effort. (Pitt's approach contrasted sharply with earlier British actions, when the British had commandeered supplies from American farmers and merchants and quartered royal troops in private homes.) In 1758, the British recaptured the fortress at Louisbourg. Then, in a surprise night attack in September 1759, General James Wolfe's soldiers defeated the French on the Plains of Abraham and broke down the defenses of Quebec. A year later, the British took Montreal, the last French stronghold on the continent, ending the American phase of the war.

When the Treaty of Paris was signed in 1763, France ceded its major North American holdings to Britain. Spain, an ally of France toward the end of the war, gave Florida to the victorious English. Since Britain feared the presence of France on its western borders, it also forced the French to cede the region west of the Mississippi (Louisiana) to Spain. The English seacoast colonies no longer had to worry about the threat to their existence posed by France's extensive North American territories, and the British gained control of the fur trade of the entire continent.

Because most of the fighting had been in the Northeast, the war had especially pronounced effects on New Englanders. Perhaps one-third of all

American Soldiers Massachusetts men between the ages of sixteen and twenty-nine served in the provincial army. Wartime service left a lasting impression on these soldiers. For the first time, ordinary Americans came into extended contact with Britons—and they did not like what they saw. The provincials thought the redcoats haughty, profane Sabbath-breakers who arbitrarily imposed overly harsh punishments on anyone who broke the rules.

The New England soldiers also learned that British regulars did not share their adherence to principles of contract and consensus. Colonial regiments mutinied or rebelled en masse if they believed they were being treated unfairly, as happened, for example, when they were not allowed to leave at the end of their formal enlistments. One private grumbled in his journal in 1759, "Although we be Englishmen born, we are debarred Englishmen's liberty. . . . [The British soldiers] are but little better than slaves to their officers. And when I get out of their [power] I shall take care how I get in again." Later, when they were deciding to support the Revolution, such men would draw on their personal experience of British "tyranny."

The overwhelming British triumph stimulated some Americans to think expansively about the colonies' future. Persons like Benjamin Franklin, who had long touted the colonies' wealth and potential, predicted a new, glorious future for British North America. Such men were to form the core of the leadership of resistance to British measures in the years after 1763. They uniformly opposed any laws that would retard America's growth and persistently supported steps to increase Americans' control over their own destiny.

1763: A Turning Point

The great victory over France had an irreversible impact on North America. Its effect was felt first by the interior tribes. With France excluded from the continent altogether and the Spanish confined to the area west of the Mississippi, the diplomatic strategy that had served the tribes so well could no longer be employed. The consequences were immediate and devastating.

Even before the Treaty of Paris, southern Indians had to adjust to the new circumstances. After the British gained the upper hand in the American war in 1758, the Creeks and Cherokees lost their ability to force concessions from them by threatening to turn instead to the French or the Spanish. In desperation and in retaliation for British atrocities, the Cherokees attacked the Carolina and Virginia frontiers in 1760. Although initially victorious, the tribesmen were defeated the following year. Late in 1761, the two sides concluded a treaty under which the Cherokees allowed the construction of English forts in tribal territories and also opened a large tract of land to white settlement.

In the Ohio country, the Ottawas, Chippewas, and Potawatomis became angry when Great Britain, no longer facing French competition, raised the price of trade goods and ended the practice of paying rent for forts. In addition, the British allowed settlers to move into the Monongahela and Susquehanna valleys.

Pontiac, the war chief of an Ottawa village near Detroit, understood the implications of such British actions. Only unity among the western tribes, he realized, could possibly prevent total dependence on and subordination to the victorious British.

Pontiac's Uprising

Using his considerable powers of persuasion, in the spring of 1763 he forged an unprecedented alliance among Hurons, Chippewas, Potawatomis, Delawares, and Shawnees, even gaining the participation of some Mingoes (Pennsylvania Iroquois). Pontiac laid siege to the fort at Detroit while his war parties attacked and took possession of most of the other British outposts in the Great Lakes region.

That was the high point of the uprising. The tribes raided the Virginia and Pennsylvania frontiers at will throughout the summer, killing at least two thousand whites. But they could not take the strongholds of Niagara, Fort Pitt (old Fort Duquesne), or Detroit. In early August, a combined force of Delawares, Shawnees, Hurons, and Mingoes was soundly defeated at Bushy Run, Pennsylvania, by troops sent from the coast. Conflict ceased when Pontiac broke off the siege of Detroit in late October, after most of his warriors had returned to their villages. A treaty ending the war was finally negotiated in 1766.

In the aftermath of the bloody summer of 1763, Scotch-Irish frontiersmen from Paxton Township, Pennsylvania, sought revenge on the only Indians within reach, a peaceful band of Christian converts living at Conestoga. In December, the whites raided the Indian village twice, killing twenty people. Two months later, hundreds of frontier dwellers known

Benjamin West, the first well-known American artist, engraved this picture of a prisoner exchange at the end of Pontiac's uprising, with Colonel Henry Bouquet supervising the return of whites captured during the war. In the foreground, a white child resists leaving the Indian parents he had grown to love. Many whites were fascinated by the phenomenon West depicted—the reluctance of captives to abandon their adoptive Indian families. *Rare Books and Manuscripts Division, New York Public Library, Astor, Lenox, and Tilden Foundations.*

to history as the Paxton Boys marched on Philadelphia to demand military protection against future Indian attacks. City officials feared violence and mustered the militia to repel the westerners, but the protesters presented their request in an orderly fashion and returned home.

Pontiac's uprising and the march of the Paxton Boys showed that Great Britain would not find it easy to govern the huge territory it had just acquired from France. In October, in a futile attempt to assert control over the interior, the ministry issued the Proclamation of 1763, **Proclamation of 1763** which declared the headwaters of rivers flowing into the Atlantic from the Appalachian Mountains to be the temporary western boundary for colonial settlement. The proclamation was intended to prevent clashes between Indians and colonists by forbidding whites to move onto Indian lands until the tribes had given up their land by treaty. But many whites had already established farms or purchased property west of the proclamation line. Thus the policy was doomed to failure from the outset.

Other decisions made in London in 1763 and thereafter had a wider impact in British North America. The victory in the Seven Years' War both created difficulties for the British government and offered it opportunities. The most pressing problem was Britain's immense war debt. The men who had to solve this problem were King George III and his new prime minister, George Grenville.

In 1760, George III, then twenty-two years old, assumed the English throne. A man of mediocre intellect and even more mediocre education, the young king was also an erratic judge of character. During the crucial period from 1763 to 1770, when the rift between England and the colonies kept widening, he replaced ministries with bewildering rapidity. Often acting stubbornly, the king viewed adherence to the status quo as the hallmark of patriotism.

George III

The man he chose as prime minister in 1763, George Grenville, confronted a financial crisis: England's burden of indebtedness had nearly doubled since 1754, from £73 million to £137 million. Obviously, Grenville's ministry had to find new sources of funds, and the English people themselves were already heavily taxed. Since the colonists had been major beneficiaries of the wartime expenditures, Grenville concluded that the Americans should be asked to pay a greater share of the cost of running the empire.

Grenville did not question Great Britain's right to levy taxes on the colonies. Like all his countrymen, he believed that the government's legitimacy derived ultimately from the consent of the people, but he defined consent far more loosely than did the colonists. Americans had come to believe that they could be represented only by men for whom they or their property-holding neighbors had actually voted. To Grenville and his English contemporaries, Parliament—king, lords, and commons acting together—by definition represented all English subjects, wherever they resided (even overseas) and whether or not they could vote. According to this theory of government, called *virtual representation,* the colonists were said to be virtually, if not actually, represented in Parliament. Thus their consent to acts of Parliament could be presumed.

Theories of Representation

Proceeding from the same theoretical starting point, the Americans and the English arrived at different conclusions in practice. In England, members of Parliament saw themselves as collectively representing the entire nation, composed of nobility and common folk. Only members of the House of Commons were elected, and the particular constituency that chose a member had no special claim on his vote. In the colonies, by contrast, members of the lower houses of the assemblies were viewed as individually representing the voters who had elected them.

The events following 1763 threw into sharp relief Americans' attitudes toward political power. The colonists had become accustomed to a government that wielded only limited authority over them and affected their daily lives very little. Consequently, they believed that a good government was one that largely left them alone, a view in keeping with the theories of a group of British writers known as the Real Whigs. These writers stressed the dangers inherent in a powerful government, particularly one headed by a monarch. They warned that political power was always to be feared, that rulers would try to corrupt and oppress the people, and that only the perpetual vigilance of the people and their elected representatives could preserve their fragile yet precious liberty.

Britain's attempts to tighten the reins of government and raise revenues from the colonies in the 1760s and early 1770s convinced many Americans that the Real Whigs' reasoning applied to their circumstances. Excessive and unjust taxation, they believed, could destroy their freedoms. They began to interpret British measures in the light of the Real Whigs' warnings and to see evil designs behind the actions of Grenville and his successors. In the mid-1760s, however, colonial leaders did not immediately accuse Grenville of an intent to oppress them. At first, they simply questioned the wisdom of the laws Grenville proposed.

The first such measures, the Sugar and Currency acts, were passed by Parliament in 1764. The Sugar Act revised the existing system of customs regulations; laid new duties on certain foreign imports into the colonies; established a vice-admiralty court at Halifax, Nova Scotia; and included special provisions aimed at stopping the widespread smuggling of molasses,

Sugar and Currency Acts

one of the chief commodities in American trade. Although the Sugar Act appeared to resemble the Navigation Acts, which the colonies had long accepted as legitimate, it broke with tradition because it was explicitly designed to raise revenue, not to channel American trade through Britain. The Currency Act, in effect, outlawed colonial issues of paper money. Americans could accumulate little hard cash, since they imported more than they exported; thus the act seemed to the colonists to deprive them of a useful medium of exchange.

Since the American economy was in the midst of a postwar depression, it is not surprising that both individual colonists and colonial governments decided to protest the new policies. But lacking any precedent for a united campaign against acts of Parliament, Americans in 1764 took only hesitant and uncoordinated steps. Eight colonial legislatures sent separate petitions to Parliament requesting repeal of the Sugar Act. They argued that the act placed severe restrictions on their commerce and that they had not consented to its passage. The protests had no effect. The law remained in force, and Grenville proceeded with another revenue plan.

The Stamp Act Crisis

The Stamp Act, Grenville's most important proposal, was modeled on a law that had been in effect in England for almost a century. It touched nearly every colonist by requiring tax stamps on most printed materials, but it placed the heaviest burden on colonial elites, who used printed matter more frequently than ordinary folk. Anyone who purchased a newspaper or pamphlet, made a will, transferred land, bought dice or playing cards, needed a liquor license, accepted a government appointment, or borrowed money would have to pay the tax. Never before had a revenue measure of such scope been proposed for the colonies. The act also required that tax stamps be paid for with hard money and that violators be tried in vice-admiralty courts, without juries. Finally, such a law broke decisively with the colonial tradition of self-imposed taxation.

The most important colonial pamphlet protesting the Sugar Act and the proposed Stamp Act was *The Rights of the British Colonies Asserted and Proved,* by James Otis, Jr., a brilliant young Massachusetts attorney. Otis starkly exposed the ideological dilemma that was to confound the colonists for the next decade. How could they justify their opposition to certain acts of Parliament without questioning Parliament's authority over them? On the one hand, Otis asserted that Americans were "entitled to all the natural, essential, inherent, and inseparable rights" of Britons, including the right not to be taxed without their consent. On the other hand, he was forced to admit that, under the British system, "the power of parliament is uncontrollable but by themselves, and we must obey."

Otis's Rights of the British Colonies

Otis's first contention, drawing on colonial notions of representation, implied that Parliament could not constitutionally tax the colonies because Americans were not represented in its ranks. Yet his second point both acknowledged political reality and accepted the prevailing theory of British government—that Parliament was the sole, supreme authority in the empire. Even unconstitutional laws enacted by Parliament had to be obeyed until Parliament decided to repeal them. Otis tried to find a middle ground by proposing colonial representation in Parliament, but his idea was never taken seriously on either side of the Atlantic. The British believed that the colonists were already virtually represented in Parliament, and the Americans realized that a handful of colonial delegates to London would simply be outvoted.

Otis wrote his pamphlet before the Stamp Act was passed. When Americans learned of its adoption in the spring of 1765, they did not at first know how to react. Few colonists publicly favored the law. But colonial petitions had already failed to prevent its adoption, and further lobbying appeared futile. Perhaps Otis was right, and the only course open to Americans was to pay the stamp tax, reluctantly but loyally.

Not all the colonists were resigned to paying the new tax. Among the dissenters was a twenty-nine-year-old lawyer serving his first term in the Virginia House of Burgesses. Patrick Henry

Patrick Henry and the Virginia Stamp Act Resolves later recalled that he was appalled by his fellow legislators' unwillingness to oppose the Stamp Act. Henry decided to act. "Alone, unadvised, and unassisted, on a blank leaf of an old law book," he wrote the Virginia Stamp Act Resolves.

Patrick Henry introduced his seven proposals in late May, near the end of the legislative session, when many members of the House of Burgesses had already departed for home. Henry's fiery speech in support of his resolutions led the Speaker of the House to accuse him of treason. (Henry quickly denied the charge, contrary to the myth that had him exclaiming in reply, "If this be treason, make the most of it!") The small number of burgesses remaining in Williamsburg adopted five of Henry's resolutions by a bare majority. Although they repealed the most radical resolution the next day, their action had far-reaching effects.

The four propositions adopted by the burgesses repeated the arguments that James Otis had already advanced. The colonists had never forfeited the rights of British subjects, they declared, and consent to taxation was one of the most important such rights. The other three resolutions went much further. The one that was repealed claimed for the burgesses "the only exclusive right" to tax Virginians. The final two asserted that residents of the colony did not have to obey tax laws passed by other legislative bodies (namely Parliament) and termed any opponent of that opinion "an Enemy to this his Majesty's Colony."

The burgesses' decision to accept only the first four of Henry's resolutions anticipated the position most Americans would adopt throughout the following decade. Though willing to contend for their rights, the colonists did not seek independence. They merely wanted some measure of self-government. Accordingly, they backed away from the assertions that they owed Parliament no obedience and that only their own assemblies could tax them.

During the next ten years, America's political leaders searched for a formula that would enable them to control their internal affairs, especially tax-

ation, but remain within the British Empire. The chief difficulty lay in British officials' inability to compromise on the issue of parliamentary power. The notion that Parliament could exercise absolute authority over all colonial possessions was basic to the British theory of government. In effect, the Americans wanted British leaders to revise their understanding of the workings of their government. That was simply too much to expect.

The ultimate effectiveness of Americans' opposition to the Stamp Act rested on more than ideological arguments over parliamentary power. What gave the resistance its primary force were the decisive and inventive actions of some colonists during the late summer and fall of 1765.

In August, the Loyal Nine, a Boston social club of printers, distillers, and other artisans, organized a demonstration against the Stamp Act. Hoping to

Loyal Nine show that people of all ranks opposed the act, they approached the leaders of the city's rival laborers' associations, based in the North End and the South End. The Loyal Nine convinced them to participate in the demonstration. After all, the stamp taxes would have to be paid by all colonists, not just affluent ones.

Early in the morning of August 14, the demonstrators hung an effigy of Andrew Oliver, the province's stamp distributor, from a tree on Boston Common. That night a crowd tore down a small building they thought was intended as the stamp office and built a bonfire near Oliver's house with the wood from the destroyed building. They then beheaded the effigy and added it to the flames. Members of the crowd broke most of Oliver's windows and threw stones at officials who tried to disperse them. The Loyal Nine's demonstration achieved its objective when Oliver publicly promised not to fulfill the duties of his office. Twelve nights later, another mob, reportedly led by the South End leader, Ebenezer MacIntosh, attacked the homes of several customs officers. This time the violence was almost universally condemned, for the mob completely destroyed Lieutenant Governor Thomas Hutchinson's townhouse.

The differences between the two Boston mobs of August 1765 exposed divisions that would continue to characterize colonial protests in the years that followed. The skilled craftsmen who composed the Loyal Nine and members of the educated elite like merchants and lawyers preferred orderly demonstrations confined to political issues. For the city's laborers, by contrast, economic grievances may have been paramount.

Colonists, like Britons, had a long tradition of crowd action in which disfranchised people took to the streets to redress deeply felt local grievances. But the Stamp Act controversy drew ordinary urban folk into the vortex of imperial politics for the first time. Matters that had previously been of concern only to genteel folk or to members of colonial legislatures were now discussed on every street corner. Sally Franklin observed as much when she wrote to her father, Benjamin, who was then serving as a colonial agent in London, that "nothing else is talked of, the Dutch [Germans] talk of the stompt act the Negroes of the tamp, in short every body has something to say."

The entry of lower-class whites, blacks, and women into the realm of imperial politics both threatened and afforded an opportunity to the elite white men who wanted to mount effective opposition to British measures. On the one hand, crowd action could have a stunning impact. Demonstrations against the Stamp Act occurred in cities and towns stretching from Halifax, Nova Scotia, to the Caribbean island of Antigua. They were so successful that by November 1, when the law was scheduled to take effect, not a single stamp distributor was willing to carry out the duties of his office. Thus the act could not be enforced. On the other hand, wealthy men recognized that mobs composed of the formerly powerless could endanger their own dominance of the society.

To channel resistance into acceptable forms, they created an intercolonial association, the Sons of Liberty. The first such group was established in New York in early November, and branches spread rapidly through the coastal cities. Composed of merchants, lawyers, prosperous tradesmen, and the like, the Sons of Liberty linked protest leaders from Charleston, South Carolina, to Portsmouth, New Hampshire, by early 1766.

Sons of Liberty

In Philadelphia, resistance leaders were dismayed when an angry mob threatened to attack Benjamin Franklin's house. The city's laborers believed Franklin to be partly responsible for the Stamp Act, since he had obtained the post of stamp distributor for a close friend. But Philadelphia's artisans—the backbone of the opposition movement there and elsewhere—were fiercely loyal to Franklin. They gathered to protect his home and family from the crowd. The house was saved, but the resulting split between the better-off tradesmen and the common laborers prevented the establishment of a successful workingmen's alliance like that of Boston.

During the fall and winter of 1765 and 1766, opposition to the Stamp Act proceeded on three separate fronts. Colonial legislatures petitioned Parliament to repeal the hated law and sent delegates to an intercolonial congress, the first since 1754. In October, the Stamp Act Congress met in New York to draft a unified but conservative statement of protest. At the same time, the Sons of Liberty held mass meetings in an effort to win public support for the resistance movement. Finally, American merchants organized nonimportation associations to put economic pressure on British exporters. By the 1760s, one-quarter of all British exports were being sent to the colonies, and American merchants reasoned that London merchants whose sales suffered severely would lobby for repeal. (Nonimportation also enabled colonial merchants to reduce bloated inventories.)

In March 1766, Parliament repealed the Stamp Act. The nonimportation agreements had the anticipated effect on London merchants. But boycotts, formal protests, and crowd actions were less important in winning repeal than was Grenville's replacement as prime minister in the summer of 1765. Lord Rockingham, the new head of the ministry, had opposed the Stamp Act, not because he believed that Parliament lacked power to tax the colonies, but because he thought the law unwise and divisive. Rockingham, however, linked repeal to passage of the Declaratory Act, which asserted Parliament's ability to tax and legislate for Britain's American possessions "in all cases whatsoever." As they celebrated the Stamp Act's repeal, few colonists saw the ominous implications of the Declaratory Act.

Repeal of the Stamp Act

BRITISH MINISTRIES AND THEIR AMERICAN POLICIES

Head of Ministry	Major Acts
George Grenville	Sugar Act (1764) Currency Act (1764) Stamp Act (1765)
Lord Rockingham	Stamp Act repealed (1766) Declaratory Act (1766)
William Pitt/Charles Townshend	Townshend Acts (1767)
Lord North	Townshend duties repealed, except the tea tax (1770) Coercive Acts (1774) Quebec Act (1774)

Resistance to the Townshend Acts

The colonists had accomplished their immediate aim, but the long-term prospects were unclear. Another change in the ministry, in the summer of 1766, revealed how fragile their victory had been. Charles Townshend, a Grenvillite, was named chancellor of the exchequer in a new administration headed by the ailing William Pitt. Townshend became the dominant force in the ministry and decided to renew the attempt to obtain additional funds from the colonies.

The taxes proposed by Townshend in 1767 were to be levied on trade goods such as paper, glass, and tea and thus seemed to be extensions of the existing Navigation Acts. But the Townshend duties differed from previous customs taxes in two ways. First, they were levied on items imported into the colonies from Britain, not from foreign countries. Thus they were at odds with mercantilist theory. Second, they were designed to raise money to pay the salaries of royal officials in the colonies. That posed a direct challenge to the colonial assemblies, which derived considerable power from threatening to withhold officials' salaries. In addition, Townshend's scheme provided for the establishment of an American Board of Customs Commissioners and for the creation of vice-admiralty courts at Boston, Philadelphia, and Charleston. Townshend also proposed the appointment of a secretary of state for American affairs and the suspension of the New York legislature for refusal to comply with the Quartering Act of 1765, which required colonial governments to supply certain items to British troops who were stationed permanently in America.

The Townshend Acts drew a quick response. One series of essays in particular, *Letters from a Farmer in Pennsylvania* by the prominent lawyer John Dickinson, expressed a broad consensus. Dickinson contended that Parliament could regulate colonial trade but could not exercise that power for the purpose of raising revenue. By drawing a distinction between the acceptable regulation of trade and unacceptable commercial taxation, Dickinson avoided the complicated question of colonial consent to parliamentary legislation. But his argument implied that the colonies would have to assess Parliament's motives in passing any law pertaining to imperial trade before deciding whether to obey it. That was clearly an unworkable position.

The Massachusetts assembly responded to the Townshend Acts by drafting a circular letter to the other colonial legislatures, calling for unity and suggesting a joint petition of protest. Not the letter itself but the ministry's reaction to it united the colonies. When Lord Hillsborough, the first secretary of

Massachusetts Assembly Dissolved

state for America, learned of the circular letter, he ordered Governor Francis Bernard of Massachusetts to insist that the assembly recall it. He also directed other governors to prevent their assemblies from discussing the letter. Hillsborough's order gave the colonial assemblies the incentive they needed to forget their differences and join forces to meet the new threat to their prerogatives. In late 1768, the Massachusetts legislature met, debated, and resoundingly rejected recall by a vote of 92 to 17. Bernard immediately dissolved the assembly, and other governors followed suit when their legislatures debated the circular letter.

During the two-year campaign against the Townshend duties, the Sons of Liberty and other American leaders made a deliberate effort to involve ordinary folk in the formal resistance movement, not just in occasional crowd actions. In a June 1769 Maryland nonimportation agreement, for instance, the signers (who were identified as "Merchants, Tradesmen, Freeholders, Mechanics [artisans], and other Inhabitants") agreed not to import or consume items of British origin. Such tactics helped to increase the number of colonists who were publicly aligned with the protest movement.

Just as the pamphlets by Otis, Dickinson, and others acquainted literate colonists with the issues raised by British action, public rituals taught illiterate Americans about the reasons for resistance and familiarized them with the terms of the argument. When Boston's Sons of Liberty invited hundreds of the city's residents to dine with them each August 14 to commemorate the first Stamp Act uprising and the Charleston Sons of Liberty held their meetings in public, crowds gathered to watch and listen. The participants in such events were expressing their commitment to the cause of resistance and urging others to join them.

Women, who had previously regarded politics as outside their proper sphere, now took a part in resisting British policy. In towns throughout America, young women calling themselves **Daughters of Liberty** met to spin in public in an effort to spur other women to make homespun and end the colonies' dependence on English cloth. These symbolic displays of patriotism served an important purpose. When young ladies from well-to-do families sat publicly at spinning wheels all day, eating only American food and drinking local herbal tea, and afterward listening to patriotic sermons, they were serving as political instructors.

Women also took the lead in promoting nonconsumption of tea. In Boston, more than three hundred matrons publicly promised not to drink tea, "Sickness excepted." The women of Wilmington, North Carolina, burned their tea after walking through town in a solemn procession. Housewives throughout the colonies exchanged recipes for tea substitutes or drank coffee instead. The best known of the protests (because it was satirized by a British cartoonist), the so-called Edenton Ladies Tea Party, actually had little to do with tea; it was a meeting of prominent North Carolina women who pledged formally to work for the public good and to support resistance to British measures.

But the colonists were by no means united in support of nonimportation. If the Stamp Act protests had occasionally revealed a division between artisans and merchants, on the one hand, and common laborers, on the other, resistance to the Townshend Acts exposed new splits in the American ranks. The most important divided the former allies of 1765 and 1766, the urban artisans and merchants, and it arose from a change in economic circumstances. The Stamp Act boycotts had helped to revive a depressed economy. In 1768 and 1769, by contrast, merchants were enjoying boom times and had no financial incentive to support a boycott. As a result, merchants signed the agreements only reluctantly. However, artisans, who recognized that the absence of British goods would create a ready market for their own manufactures, supported nonimportation enthusiastically. They also used coercion to enforce nonimportation.

Such tactics were effective: colonial imports from England dropped dramatically in 1769, especially in New York, New England, and Pennsylvania. But they also aroused significant opposition, creating a second major division among the colonists. Some Americans who supported resistance to British measures began to question the use of violence to force others to join the boycott. In addition, wealthier and more conservative colonists were frightened by the threat to private property inherent in the campaign. Moreover, political activism by ordinary colonists challenged the ruling elite's domination.

Americans were relieved when the news arrived in April 1770 that a new prime minister, Lord North, had persuaded Parliament to repeal the Townshend duties, except the tea tax, on the grounds that duties on trade within the empire were bad policy. Although some political leaders argued that nonimportation should be continued until the tea tax was repealed, merchants quickly resumed importing. The rest of the Townshend Acts remained in force, but repeal of the taxes made the other laws appear less objectionable.

Repeal of the Townshend Duties

Growing Rifts

At first, the new ministry did nothing to antagonize the colonists. Yet on the very day that Lord North proposed repeal of the Townshend duties, a clash between civilians and soldiers in Boston led to the deaths of five Americans. The origins of the event, which patriots called the Boston Massacre, lay in repeated clashes between customs officers and the people of Massachusetts. The Townshend Acts' creation of an American Board of Customs Commissioners had been error enough, but a decision to base the board in Boston severely compounded the mistake.

From the day of their arrival in November 1767, the customs commissioners were frequent targets of mob action. In June 1768, their seizure of the patriot leader John Hancock's sloop *Liberty* on suspicion of smuggling caused a riot. The riot in turn led the ministry in London to station two regiments in Boston. This act confirmed Bostonians' worst fears; the redcoats were a constant reminder of the oppressive potential of British power.

Bostonians, accustomed to leading their lives with a minimum of interference from government, now found themselves hemmed in at every turn. Guards on Boston Neck, the entrance to the city, checked all travelers and their goods. Redcoat patrols roamed the city day and night, questioning and sometimes harassing passers-by. But the greatest potential for violence lay in the uneasy relationship between the soldiers and Boston laborers. Many redcoats sought employment in their off-duty hours, competing for unskilled jobs with the city's ordinary workingmen, and members of the two groups brawled repeatedly.

On March 2, 1770, workers at a ropewalk (a ship-rigging factory) attacked some redcoats seeking jobs; a pitched battle resulted when both groups acquired reinforcements. Three days later, the tension exploded. Early on the evening of March 5, a crowd began throwing hard-packed snowballs at sentries guarding the Customs House. Goaded beyond endurance, the sentries fired on the crowd against express orders to the contrary, killing four and wounding eight, one of whom died a few days later. Resistance leaders idealized the dead rioters as martyrs for the cause of liberty. The best-known engraving of the massacre, by Paul Revere, was part of the propaganda campaign. It depicts a peaceful crowd, an officer ordering the soldiers to fire, and shots coming from the window of the Customs House.

Boston Massacre

The leading patriots wanted to make certain that the soldiers did not become martyrs as well. Despite the political benefits the patriots derived from the massacre, it is unlikely that they approved of the crowd action that provoked it. Thus, when the soldiers were tried for the killings in November, they were defended by John Adams and Josiah Quincy, Jr., both unwavering patriots. All but two of the accused men were acquitted, and those convicted were released after having been branded on the thumb. Undoubtedly, the favorable outcome of the trials prevented London officials from taking further steps against the city.

For more than two years after the Boston Massacre and the repeal of the Townshend duties, a superficial calm descended on the colonies. Local incidents, like the burning of the customs vessel *Gaspée* in 1772 by Rhode Islanders, marred the relationship of individual colonies and the mother country, but nothing caused Americans to join in a unified protest. Even so, the resistance movement continued to gather momentum. The most outspo-

The BLOODY MASSACRE perpetrated in King—†—Street BOSTON on March 5th 1770 by a party of the 29th REGT.

Paul Revere's engraving of the Boston Massacre, a masterful piece of propaganda. At right, the British officer seems to be ordering the soldiers to fire on a peaceful, unresisting crowd. The Customs House has been labeled Butcher's Hall. *Library of Congress.*

ken colonial newspapers, such as the *Boston Gazette,* the *Pennsylvania Journal,* and the *South Carolina Gazette,* published essays drawing on Real Whig ideology and accusing Great Britain of a deliberate plan to oppress America. Patriot writers played repeatedly on the word *enslavement.* Most white colonists had direct knowledge of slavery (either being slaveholders themselves or having slaveowning neighbors), and the threat of enslavement by Britain must have hit them with peculiar force.

Still, no one yet advocated complete independence from the mother country. Though the patriots were becoming increasingly convinced that they should seek freedom from parliamentary authority, they continued to acknowledge their British identity and to pledge their allegiance to George III. They began, therefore, to try to envision a system that would enable them to be ruled by their own elected legislatures while remaining loyal to the king. But any such scheme was totally alien to Britons' conception of the nature of their government, which was that Parliament held sole undivided sovereignty over the empire. Furthermore, in the British mind, Parliament encompassed the king, as well as lords and commons, and so separating the monarch from the legislature was impossible.

In the fall of 1772, the North ministry began to

implement the portion of the Townshend Acts that provided for governors and judges to be paid from customs revenues. In early November, voters at a Boston town meeting established a Committee of Correspondence to publicize the decision by exchanging letters with other Massachusetts towns. Samuel Adams, the man who had proposed its formation, became the committee's head. Adams was fifty-one years old in 1772, thirteen years the senior of his distant cousin John and a decade older than most other leaders of American resistance. An experienced political organizer, Adams continually stressed the necessity of prudent collective action. Thus his Committee of Correspondence undertook the task of creating an informed consensus among all the citizens of Massachusetts.

Committees of Correspondence

Such committees, which were soon established throughout the colonies, represented the next logical step in the organization of American resistance. Until 1772, the protest movement was largely confined to the seacoast and primarily to major cities and towns. Adams realized that the time had come to widen the movement's geographic scope and try to involve the residents of the interior in the struggle. Accordingly, the Boston town meeting directed the Committee of Correspondence "to state the Rights of the Colonists and of this Province in particular," to list "the Infringements and Violations thereof that have been, or from time to time may be made," and to send copies to the other towns in the province.

Samuel Adams, James Otis, Jr., and Josiah Quincy, Jr., prepared the statement of the colonists' rights. Declaring that Americans had absolute rights to life, liberty, and property, the committee asserted that the idea that "a British house of commons, should have a right, at pleasure, to give and grant the property of the colonists" was "irreconcileable" with "the first principles of natural law and Justice . . . and of the British Constitution in particular." The list of grievances, drafted by another group of prominent patriots, complained of taxation without representation, the presence of unnecessary troops and customs officers on American soil, the use of imperial revenues to pay colonial officials, the expanded jurisdiction of vice-admiralty courts, and even the nature of the instructions given to American governors by their superiors in London. No mention was made of obedience to Parliament. Patriots—at least in Boston—had placed American rights first, and loyalty to Great Britain a distant second.

The response of the Massachusetts towns to the committee's pamphlet must have caused Samuel Adams to rejoice. Some towns disagreed with Boston's assessment of the state of affairs, but most aligned themselves with the city. From Braintree came the assertion that "all civil officers are or ought to be Servants to the people and dependent upon them for their official Support, and every instance to the Contrary from the Governor downwards tends to crush and destroy civil liberty." The town of Holden declared that "the People of New England have never given the People of Britain any Right of Jurisdiction over us." The citizens of Petersham commented that resistance to tyranny was "the first and highest social Duty of this people." Such beliefs made the next crisis in Anglo-American affairs the final one.

The Boston Tea Party

The only one of the Townshend duties still in effect by 1773 was the tax on tea. Although a continuing tea boycott was less than fully effective, tea retained its explosive symbolic character. In May 1773, Parliament passed an act designed to save the East India Company from bankruptcy. The company was of critical importance to the British economy and to the financial well-being of many prominent British politicians. Resistance leaders were immediately suspicious. Under the Tea Act, certain duties paid on tea were to be returned to the company. Tea was to be sold only by designated agents, which would enable the East India Company to avoid colonial middlemen and undersell any competitors, even smugglers. The net result would be cheaper tea for American consumers. But many colonists interpreted the new measure as a pernicious device to make them admit Parliament's right to tax them, since the less expensive tea would still be taxed under the Townshend law. Others saw the Tea Act

Tea Act

as the first step in the establishment of an East India Company monopoly of all colonial trade.

New York City, Boston, Charleston, and Philadelphia were singled out to receive the first shipments of tea. Only Boston was the site of a dramatic confrontation. There both sides—the town meeting, joined by participants from nearby towns, and Governor Thomas Hutchinson—rejected compromise.

The first of three tea ships, the *Dartmouth,* entered Boston harbor on November 28. Under the customs laws, a cargo had to be landed and the appropriate duty paid within twenty days of a ship's arrival. If that was not done, the cargo would be seized by customs officers. After a series of mass meetings, Bostonians voted to prevent the tea from being unloaded and to post guards on the wharf. Hutchinson, for his part, refused to permit the vessels to leave the harbor.

On December 16, 1773, one day before the cargo would have to be confiscated, more than five thousand people (about a third of the city's population) crowded into Old South Church. The meeting, chaired by Samuel Adams, made a final attempt to persuade Hutchinson to send the tea back to England. But Hutchinson remained adamant. At about 6 P.M. Adams reportedly announced "that he could think of nothing further to be done—that they had now done all they could for the Salvation of their Country." As if his statement were a signal, cries rang out from the back of the crowd: "Boston harbor a teapot tonight! The Mohawks are come!" Small groups pushed their way out of the meeting. Within a few minutes, about sixty men crudely disguised as Indians assembled at the wharf, boarded the three ships, and dumped the cargo into the harbor. By 9 P.M. their work was done: 342 chests of tea worth approximately £10,000 floated in splinters on the ebbing tide.

At the news of the Tea Party, the North ministry proposed—in March 1774—the first of the four laws that became known as the Coercive, or Intoler-

Coercive and Quebec Acts

able, Acts. It called for closing the port of Boston until the tea was paid for and prohibiting all but coastal trade in food and firewood. Later in the spring, Parliament passed three other punitive measures. The Massachusetts Government Act altered the province's charter, substituting an appointed council for the elected one,

increasing the powers of the governor, and forbidding special town meetings. The Justice Act provided that a person accused of committing murder in the course of suppressing a riot or enforcing the laws could be tried outside the colony where the incident had occurred. Finally, a new Quartering Act gave broad authority to military commanders seeking to house their troops in private dwellings.

After passing the last of the Coercive Acts in early June, Parliament turned its attention to needed reforms in the government of Quebec. The Quebec Act, though unrelated to the Coercive Acts, thus became linked with them in the minds of the patriots. The law granted greater religious freedom to Catholics—alarming the Protestant colonists, who regarded Roman Catholicism as a mainstay of religious and political despotism. It also reinstated French civil law and established an appointed council as the governing body of the colony. To protect Indians from white settlement, the act annexed to Quebec the area east of the Mississippi River and north of the Ohio River. Thus that region, parts of which were claimed by individual seacoast colonies, was removed from their jurisdiction.

Members of Parliament who voted for the punitive legislation believed that the acts would be obeyed. But the patriots showed little inclination to bow to the wishes of Parliament. In their eyes, the Coercive Acts and the Quebec Act proved what they had feared since 1768: that Great Britain had embarked on a deliberate plan to oppress them. If the port of Boston could be closed, why not those of Philadelphia or New York? If the royal charter of Massachusetts could be changed, why not that of South Carolina? If troops could be forcibly quartered in private houses, did not that pave the way for the occupation of all of America? If the Roman Catholic church could receive favored status in Quebec, why not everywhere? It seemed as though the full dimensions of the plot against American rights and liberties had at last been revealed.

The Boston Committee of Correspondence urged all the colonies to join in an immediate boycott of British goods. But the other provinces were not yet ready to take such a drastic step. Instead, they suggested that another intercolonial congress be convened to consider an appropriate response to the Coercive Acts. Few people wanted to take hasty action; even the most ardent patriots still hoped for reconciliation with Great Britain. And so the colonies agreed to send delegates to Philadelphia in September.

During the preceding decade, momentous changes had occurred in the ways that politically aware colonists thought about themselves and their allegiance. Once linked unquestioningly to Great Britain, they had begun to develop a sense of their own identity as Americans. They had started to realize that their concept of the political process differed from that held by people in the mother country. They also had come to understand that their economic interests did not necessarily coincide with those of Great Britain. Colonial political leaders reached such conclusions only after a long train of events, some of them violent, had altered their understanding of the nature of their relationship with the mother country.

In the late summer of 1774, the Americans were committed to resistance but not to independence. Even so, they had started to sever the bonds of empire. During the next decade, they would forge the bonds of a new American nationality to replace those rejected Anglo-American ties.

Suggestions for Further Reading

General

Ian R. Christie and Benjamin W. Labaree, *Empire or Independence, 1760–1776: A British-American Dialogue on the Coming of the American Revolution* (1976); Marc Egnal, *A Mighty Empire: The Origins of the American Revolution* (1988); Merrill Jensen, *The Founding of a Nation: A History of the American Revolution, 1763–1776* (1968); Edmund S. Morgan, *The Birth of the Republic, 1763–1789* (1956).

Colonial Warfare and the British Empire

Fred Anderson, *A People's Army: Massachusetts Soldiers and Society in the Seven Years' War* (1984); Douglas Leach, *Roots of Conflict: British Armed Forces and Colonial Americans, 1677–1763* (1986); Howard H. Peckham, *The Colonial Wars, 1689–1762* (1963); Alan Rogers, *Empire and Liberty: American Resistance to British Authority, 1755–1763* (1974).

British Politics and Policy

John Brooke, *King George III* (1972); John L. Bullion, *A Great and Necessary Measure: George Grenville and the Genesis of the Stamp Act, 1763–1765* (1981); Bernard Donoughue, *British Politics and the American Revolution: The Path to War, 1773–1775* (1965); Lewis B. Namier, *England in the Age of the American Revolution,* 2nd ed. (1961); P. D. G. Thomas, *The Townshend Duties Crisis* (1987).

Indians and the West

Thomas P. Abernethy, *Western Lands and the American Revolution* (1959); Richard Aquila, *The Iroquois Restoration: Iroquois Diplomacy on the Colonial Frontier, 1701–1754* (1983); David H. Corkran, *The Cherokee Frontier: Conflict and Survival, 1740–1762* (1962); Francis Jennings, *Empire of Fortune: Crowns, Colonies and Tribes in the Seven Years' War in America* (1988); Howard H. Peckham, *Pontiac and the Indian Uprising* (1947); Jack M. Sosin, *Whitehall and the Wilderness: The Middle West in British Colonial Policy, 1760–1775* (1961).

Political and Economic Thought

Bernard Bailyn, *The Ideological Origins of the American Revolution* (1967); Jay Fliegelman, *Prodigals and Pilgrims: The American Revolution Against Patriarchal Authority, 1750–1800* (1982); Caroline Robbins, *The Eighteenth-Century Commonwealthman: Studies in the Transmission, Development, and Circumstance of English Liberal Thought from the Restoration of Charles II Until the War with the Thirteen Colonies* (1959); Clinton Rossiter, *Seedtime of the Republic: The Origin of the American Tradition of Political Liberty* (1953).

American Resistance

David Ammerman, *In the Common Cause: American Response to the Coercive Acts of 1774* (1974); Richard Beeman, *Patrick Henry: A Biography* (1974); Richard D. Brown, *Revolutionary Politics in Massachusetts: The Boston Committee of Correspondence and the Towns, 1772–1774* (1970); Dirk Hoerder, *Crowd Action in Revolutionary Massachusetts, 1765–1780* (1977); Rhys Isaac, *The Transformation of Virginia, 1740–1790* (1982); Benjamin W. Labaree, *The Boston Tea Party* (1964); Pauline R. Maier, *The Old Revolutionaries: Political Lives in the Age of Samuel Adams* (1980); Pauline R. Maier, *From Resistance to Revolution: Colonial Radicals and the Development of American Opposition to Britain, 1765–1776* (1972); Edmund S. Morgan and Helen M. Morgan, *The Stamp Act Crisis: Prologue to Revolution* (1953); Gary B. Nash, *The Urban Crucible: Social Change, Political Consciousness, and the Origins of the American Revolution* (1979); Peter Shaw, *American Patriots and the Rituals of Revolution* (1981); John W. Tyler, *Smugglers and Patriots: Boston Merchants and the Advent of the American Revolution* (1986); Hiller B. Zobel, *The Boston Massacre* (1970).

On November 20, 1837, Sarah Benjamin, then eighty-one years old, applied for a pension as the widow of a Revolutionary War soldier. She declared that she had married Aaron Osborn, a blacksmith, in Albany in 1780. After he enlisted, he insisted that she accompany him to the army. The narrative she dictated in 1837 is the only known autobiographical account left by one of the thousands of women who traveled with the revolutionary army as "camp followers."

For the first eighteen months of their service, Sarah and Aaron Osborn were stationed at West Point, on the Hudson River, where she did washing and sewing for the soldiers. Three other women were also attached to the company—an unmarried black woman and the wives of a sergeant and a lieutenant. This orderly existence changed abruptly in the fall of 1781, when their unit joined others marching hurriedly to Yorktown under the command of General George Washington.

There, she reported, she "busied herself washing, mending, and cooking for the soldiers, in which she was assisted by the other females." At intervals she carried beef, bread, and coffee to the front lines. Once she met Washington himself, who asked whether she was afraid of the cannonballs. Osborn staunchly replied, "It

5

A REVOLUTION, INDEED, 1775–1783

would not do for the men to fight and starve too." One day she heard the British drums "beat excessively" and inquired what had happened. "The British have surrendered," she was told. She then watched the redcoats' ceremonial capitulation: the army "marched out beating and playing a melancholy tune, their drums covered with black handkerchiefs and their fifes with black ribbands tied around them."

The Osborns returned north with the army and stayed until the troops were disbanded in early 1784. Soon afterward, Aaron Osborn deserted his wife, leaving her with two young children. After he contracted a bigamous second marriage, she decided she too was free to remarry. Her second husband, John Benjamin, was also an army veteran, and in response to her 1837 petition the government awarded her a double pension in honor of her two husbands. Her own service earned her nothing.

The Revolution was more than just a series of clashes between British and patriot armies. It uprooted thousands of families like the Osborns, disrupted the economy, reshaped society by forcing many colonists into permanent exile, led Americans to develop new conceptions of politics, and created a nation from thirteen separate colonies. Thus it marked a significant turning point in Americans' collective history.

The struggle for independence required revolutionary leaders to accomplish three separate but closely related tasks. The first was political and ideological: they had to transform the 1760s consensus favoring loyal resistance into a coalition supporting independence. The second task was diplomatic. To win their independence, the patriot leaders knew they needed international recognition and aid, particularly assistance from France. Thus they dispatched to Paris Benjamin Franklin, the most experienced American diplomat. Franklin skillfully negotiated the Franco-American alliance of 1778, which was to prove crucial to the winning of independence.

Only the third task directly involved the British. George Washington, commander-in-chief of the American army, quickly realized that his primary goal should be not to win battles but rather to avoid losing them decisively. He understood that, as long as his army survived to fight another day, the outcome of any individual battle was more or less irrelevant. Accordingly, the story of the Revolutionary War reveals British action and American reaction, British attacks and American defenses. The American war effort was aided by the failure of British military planners to analyze accurately the problem confronting them. Until it was too late, they treated the war against the colonists as they did wars against other Europeans—that is, they concentrated on winning battles and did not consider the difficulties inherent in achieving their main goal, retaining the colonies' allegiance. In the end, the Americans' triumph owed more to their own endurance and to Britain's mistakes than to their military prowess.

Government by Congress and Committee

When the fifty-five delegates to the First Continental Congress convened in Philadelphia in September 1774, they knew that any measures they adopted were likely to enjoy support among many of their fellow countrymen and countrywomen. During the summer of 1774, open meetings held throughout the colonies had endorsed the idea of another nonimportation pact. The committees of correspondence that had been established in many communities publicized these meetings so effectively that Americans everywhere knew about them. Most of the congressional delegates were selected by extralegal provincial conventions, whose members were chosen at such local gatherings, since the royal governors had forbidden the regular assemblies to conduct formal elections. Thus the very act of designating delegates to attend the Continental Congress involved Americans in open defiance of British authority.

The colonies' leading political figures—most of them lawyers, merchants, or planters—were sent to the Philadelphia Congress. The Massachusetts delegation included both Samuel Adams and his younger cousin John, an ambitious lawyer. Among others, New York sent John Jay, a talented young attorney. From Pennsylvania came the conservative Joseph Galloway and his long-time rival John Dickinson. Virginia elected Richard Henry Lee and Patrick Henry, both noted for their patriotic zeal, as well as George Washington.

First Continental Congress

The congressmen faced three tasks when they convened on September 5, 1774. The first two were explicit: defining American grievances and developing a plan for resistance. The third—outlining a theory of their constitutional relationship with England—proved troublesome. The most radical congressmen, like Lee of Virginia, argued that the colonists owed allegiance only to George III and that Parliament was nothing more than a local legislature for Great Britain, with no authority over the colonies. By contrast, the conservatives—Joseph Galloway and his allies—proposed a formal plan of union that would have required the joint consent of Parliament and a new general American legislature to all laws pertaining to the colonies. After a heated debate, the delegates rejected Galloway's proposal, but they were not prepared to accept the radicals' position either.

Finally, they accepted a compromise position

1774	First Continental Congress	**1778**	French alliance with the United States
1775	Battles of Lexington and Concord		British evacuate Philadelphia
	Second Continental Congress	**1779**	Sullivan expedition against Iroquois villages
	Lord Dunmore's Proclamation		
1776	Thomas Paine, *Common Sense*	**1780**	British take Charleston
	British evacuate Boston	**1781**	Cornwallis surrenders at Yorktown
	Declaration of Independence	**1782**	Peace negotiations begin
	New York campaign		
1777	British take Philadelphia	**1783**	Treaty of Paris
	Burgoyne surrenders at Saratoga		

worked out by John Adams. The crucial clause that Adams drafted in the congressional Declaration of

Declaration of Rights and Grievances

Rights and Grievances read in part: "From the necessity of the case, and a regard to the mutual interest of both countries, we cheerfully consent to the operation of such acts of the British parliament, as are bona fide, restrained to the regulation of our external commerce." Note the key phrases. "From the necessity of the case" declared that Americans had decided to obey Parliament only because they had decided that doing so was in the best interest of both countries. "Bona fide, restrained to the regulation of our external commerce" made it clear to Lord North that they would continue to resist taxes in disguise, like the Townshend duties. Most striking of all was the fact that such language, which only a few years before would have been regarded as irredeemably radical, could be presented and accepted as a compromise in the fall of 1774.

With the constitutional issue resolved, the delegates readily agreed on a list of the laws they wanted repealed (notably the Coercive Acts) and decided to implement an economic boycott while petitioning the king for relief. They adopted the Continental Association, which called for nonimportation of British goods (effective December 1, 1774), nonconsumption of British products (effec-

tive March 1, 1775), and nonexportation of American goods to Britain and the British West Indies (effective September 10, 1775, so that southern planters would have a chance to market their 1774 tobacco crop).

To enforce the Continental Association, Congress recommended the election of committees of observation and inspection in every county, city,

Committees of Observation

and town in America. Since Congress specified that committee members be chosen by all persons qualified to vote for members of the lower house of the colonial legislatures, the committees were guaranteed a broad popular base. The seven to eight thousand members selected in all the colonies became the local leaders of American resistance.

Officially, these committees were charged only with overseeing the implementation of the boycott, but over the next six months they became de facto governments. They examined merchants' records and published the names of those who continued to import British goods. They also promoted home manufactures and encouraged Americans to adopt simple modes of dress and behavior. Since expensive leisure-time activities were symbols of vice and corruption, Congress urged Americans to forgo dancing, gambling, horse racing, cock fighting, and other forms of "extravagance and dissipation." In enforcing these injunctions, the committees gradually extended their authority over many aspects of American life.

The committees also attempted to identify opponents of American resistance, developed elaborate spy networks, and investigated reports of dissident remarks and activities. Suspected dissenters were first urged to convert to the colonial cause; if they failed to do so, the committees had them watched, restricted their movements, or tried to force them to leave the area. People engaging in casual political exchanges with friends one day could find themselves charged with "treasonable conversation" the next.

While the committees of observation were expanding their power during the winter and early spring of 1775, the established governments of the colonies were collapsing. Only in **Provincial** Connecticut, Rhode Island, Dela-**Conventions** ware, and Pennsylvania did regular assemblies continue to meet without encountering patriot challenges to their authority. In every other colony, popularly elected provincial conventions took over the task of running the government, sometimes entirely replacing the legislatures and at other times holding concurrent sessions. In late 1774 and early 1775, these conventions approved the Continental Association, elected delegates to the Second Continental Congress (scheduled for May), organized militia units, and gathered arms and ammunition. The British-appointed governors and councils, unable to stem the tide of resistance, watched helplessly as their authority crumbled. Courts were prevented from holding sessions; taxes were paid to agents of the conventions rather than to provincial tax collectors; sheriffs' powers were questioned; and militiamen refused to muster except by order of the local committees. In short, during the six months preceding the battles at Lexington and Concord, independence was being won at the local level, but without formal acknowledgment and, for the most part, without shooting or bloodshed. Not many Americans fully realized what was happening. The vast majority still proclaimed their loyalty to Great Britain and denied that they sought to leave the empire. Among the few who did recognize the trend toward independence were those who opposed it.

Choosing Sides: Loyalists, Blacks, and Indians

The first protests against British measures, in the mid-1760s, had won the support of most colonists. Only in the late 1760s and early 1770s did a significant number of Americans begin to question both the aims and the tactics of the resistance movement. In 1774 and 1775, such people found themselves in a difficult position. Like their more radical counterparts, most of them objected to parliamentary policies and wanted some kind of constitutional reform. But their desire to uphold the legally constituted colonial governments and their fear of anarchy made them especially sensitive to the dangers of resistance. If forced to a choice, these colonists sympathized with Great Britain rather than with an independent America.

In 1774 and 1775, some conservatives began to publish essays and pamphlets critical of Congress and its allied committees. In New York City, a group of Anglican clergymen jointly wrote pamphlets and essays arguing the importance of maintaining a cordial connection between England and America. In Massachusetts, the young attorney Daniel Leonard, using the pseudonym Massachusettensis, engaged in a prolonged newspaper debate with Novanglus (John Adams). Leonard and the others realized that what had begun as a dispute over the extent of American subordination within the empire had now raised the question of whether the colonies would remain linked to Great Britain at all.

Some colonists heeded the conservative pamphleteers' warnings. About one-fifth of the white American population remained loyal to Great **Loyalists,** Britain, actively opposing in-**Patriots, and** dependence. With notable ex-**Neutrals** ceptions, most people of the following types remained loyal to the Crown: British-appointed government officials; merchants whose trade depended on imperial connections; Anglican clergy everywhere and lay Anglicans in the North; former officers and enlisted men from the British army; non-English ethnic minorities, especially Scots; tenant farmers, particularly those whose landlords sided with the patriots; members of persecuted religious sects; and many of the backcountry southerners who had rebelled against eastern rule in the 1760s and early 1770s. All these people had one thing in common: the patriot leaders were their long-standing enemies. Local and provincial disputes thus helped to determine which side a person chose in the imperial conflict.

The active patriots, who accounted for about two-fifths of the white population, came chiefly from the groups that had dominated colonial society, either numerically or politically. Among them were yeoman farmers, members of dominant Protestant sects, Chesapeake gentry, merchants dealing mainly in American commodities, city artisans, elected officeholders, and people of English descent. Wives usually, but not always, adopted their husbands' political beliefs.

The remaining two-fifths of the white population tried to avoid taking sides. This segment included sincere pacifist Quakers and those who simply wanted to be left alone. In the southern backcountry, many Scotch-Irish took a neutral position, for they had little love for either the patriot gentry or the English authorities.

To American patriots, that sort of apathy or neutrality was a crime as heinous as loyalism. Those who were not for them were against them; in their minds, there could be no conscientious objectors. By the winter of 1775–1776, the Second Continental Congress was recommending to the states that all "disaffected" persons be disarmed and arrested. The state legislatures quickly passed laws prescribing severe penalties for suspected loyalists. Many began to require all voters (or, in some cases, all free adult males) to take oaths of allegiance; the punishment for refusal was usually banishment or extra taxes. After 1777, many states confiscated the property of banished loyalists and used the proceeds for the war effort. Perhaps as many as 100,000 white loyalists were forced into exile, but they were not the only Americans to concern the patriots.

Slaves faced a dilemma at the beginning of the Revolution: how could they best achieve their goal of escaping perpetual servitude? Should they fight with or against their white masters? The correct choice was not immediately apparent, and so

The Blacks' Dilemma

blacks made different decisions. Some indeed joined the revolutionaries, but to most an alliance with the British appeared more promising. Thus news of slave conspiracies surfaced in different parts of the colonies in late 1774 and early 1775. All shared a common element: a plan to assist the British in return for freedom. A group of blacks petitioned General Thomas Gage, the commander-in-chief of the British army in Boston, promising to fight for the redcoats if he would liberate them. The governor of Maryland authorized the issuance of extra guns to militiamen in four counties where slave uprisings were expected. The most serious incident occurred during the summer of 1775, in Charleston, where Thomas Jeremiah, a free black harbor pilot, was brutally executed after being convicted of attempting to foment a slave revolt.

Concern over the slave population affected the level of revolutionary sentiment in the colonies. In the North, where whites greatly outnumbered blacks, revolutionary fervor was at its height. But in South Carolina, which was more than 60 percent black, and Georgia, where the racial balance was nearly even, whites were noticeably less enthusiastic about resistance. Georgia, in fact, sent no delegates to the First Continental Congress and reminded its representatives at the Second Continental Congress to consider its circumstances, "with our blacks and tories within us," when voting on the question of independence.

Racial Composition and Patriotic Fervor

The whites' worst fears were realized in November 1775, when Lord Dunmore, the governor of Virginia, offered to free any slaves and indentured servants who would leave their patriot masters to join the British forces. Dunmore hoped to use blacks in his fight against the revolutionaries and to disrupt the economy by depriving white Americans of their labor force. But fewer blacks than expected rallied to the British standard in 1775 and 1776 (there were at most two thousand), and many of them perished in a smallpox epidemic. Even so, Dunmore's proclamation led Congress in January 1776 to modify an earlier policy that had prohibited the enlistment of blacks in the Continental Army.

Although black Americans did not pose a serious threat to the revolutionary cause in its early

RUN away from *Hampton*, on *Sunday* laſt, a luſty Mulatto Fellow named ARGYLE, well known about the Country, has a Scar on one of his Wriſts, and has loſt one or more of his fore Teeth; he is a very handy Fellow by Water, or about the Houſe, &c. loves Drink, and is very bold in his Cups, but daſtardly when ſober. Whether he will go for a Man of War's Man, or not, I cannot ſay; but I will give 40 s. to have him brought to me. He can read and write.
NOVEMBER 2, 1775. JACOB WRAY.

An advertisement for a runaway slave suspected of joining Lord Dunmore—a common sight in Virginia and Maryland newspapers during the fall and winter of 1775 and 1776. *Virginia State Library and Archives.*

years, the patriots managed to turn rumors of slave uprisings to their own advantage. In South Carolina, they won adherents by promoting white unity under the revolutionary banner. The Continental Association was needed, they argued, to protect whites from blacks at a time when the royal government was unable to muster adequate defense forces. Undoubtedly, many wavering Carolinians were drawn into the revolutionary camp by fear that an overt division among the colony's whites would encourage a slave revolt.

A similar factor—the threat of Indian attacks—helped to persuade some reluctant westerners to support the struggle against Great Britain. In the years since the Proclamation of 1763, British officials had won the trust of the interior tribes by attempting to protect them from land-hungry whites. In 1768, the British-appointed superintendents of Indian affairs, John Stuart in the South and Sir William Johnson in the North, negotiated two treaties—signed at Hard Labor Creek, South Carolina, and at Fort Stanwix, New York—with the tribes. The treaties supposedly established permanent western borders for the colonies. But just a few years later, the British pushed the southern boundary even farther west to accommodate the demands of whites in western Georgia and Kentucky.

By the time of the Revolution, the Indians were impatient with white Americans' aggressive pressure on their lands. The relationship of the tribes

The Indians' Grievances and frontier whites was filled with bitterness, misunderstanding, and occasional bloody encounters. In combination with the tribes' confidence in Stuart and Johnson, such grievances predisposed most Indians toward an alliance with the British. Even so, the latter hesitated to make full and immediate use of their potential Indian allies. The superintendents were aware that tribal war aims and the Indians' style of fighting were not necessarily compatible with those of the British. Accordingly, they sought nothing more from the tribes than a promise of neutrality.

The patriots, recognizing that their standing with the tribes was poor, also sought the Indians' neutrality. In 1775, the Second Continental Congress sent a general message to the tribes describing the war as "a family quarrel between us and Old England" and requesting that they "not join on either side," since "you Indians are not concerned in it." A branch of the Cherokee tribe, led by Chief Dragging Canoe, nevertheless decided that the whites' "family quarrel" would allow them to settle some old scores. They attacked white settlements along the western borders of the Carolinas and Virginia in the summer of 1776. But a coordinated campaign by Carolina and Virginia militia destroyed many Cherokee towns, along with crops and large quantities of supplies. Dragging Canoe and his diehard followers fled west to the Tennessee River, where they established new outposts; the rest of the Cherokees agreed to a treaty that ceded more of their land to the whites.

The fate of the Cherokees—forced to fight alone without other Indian allies—foreshadowed the history of Indian involvement in the American Rev-

Lack of Unity Among Indians

olution. During the eighteenth century, the Iroquois had forcefully established their dominance over neighboring tribes. But the basis of their power started to disintegrate with the British victory over France in 1763, and their subsequent friendship with Sir William Johnson could not prevent the erosion of their position during the years before 1775. Tribes long resentful of Iroquois power (and of the similar status of the Cherokees in the South) saw little reason to ally themselves with those from whose dominance they had just escaped, even to prevent white encroachment on their lands. Consequently, most tribes pursued a course that aligned them with neither side and kept them out of active involvement in the war.

Thus, although the patriots could never completely ignore the threats posed by loyalists, blacks, neutrals, and Indians, only rarely did fear of these groups seriously hamper the revolutionary movement. Occasionally, militia on the frontier refused to turn out for duty on the seaboard because they feared Indians would attack in their absence. Indeed, the practical impossibility of a large-scale slave revolt, coupled with tribal feuds and the patriots' successful campaign to disarm and neutralize loyalists, ensured that the revolutionaries would remain firmly in control as they fought for independence.

War Begins

On January 27, 1775, Lord Dartmouth, secretary of state for America, addressed a fateful letter to General Thomas Gage in Boston. Expressing his belief that American resistance was nothing more than the response of a "rude rabble without plan," Dartmouth ordered Gage to arrest "the principal actors and abettors in the provincial congress." If such a step were taken swiftly and silently, Dartmouth observed, no bloodshed need occur."

By the time Dartmouth's letter reached Gage, on April 14, the major patriot leaders had already left Boston. Spurred to action by the letter, Gage

Battles of Lexington and Concord

decided to send an expedition to confiscate provincial military supplies stockpiled at Concord. Bostonians dispatched two messengers, William Dawes and Paul Revere (later joined by a third, Dr. Samuel Prescott), to rouse the countryside. Thus when the British vanguard approached Lexington at dawn on April 19, they found a straggling group of seventy militiamen—approximately half the adult male population of the town—drawn up before them on the town common. The Americans' commander, Captain John Parker, ordered his men to withdraw, realizing they could not halt the redcoat advance. But as they began to disperse, a shot rang out; the British soldiers then fired several volleys. When they stopped, eight Americans lay dead and another ten had been wounded. The British moved on to Concord, five miles away.

At Concord, British troops suffered their first casualties of the war when they were attacked by patriot militia at the North Bridge. Before the day ended, thousands of colonial militiamen harassed the British on their march back to Boston. The redcoats suffered 272 casualties (70 dead) and inflicted only 93 casualties on the patriots.

By the evening of April 20, perhaps as many as twenty thousand American militiamen had gathered around Boston, summoned by local committees that spread the alarm across the New England countryside. Many did not stay long, since they were needed at home for spring planting, but those who remained dug in along siege lines encircling the city. For nearly a year the two armies sat and stared at each other across those lines. The only battle occurred on June 17, when the British drove the Americans from trenches atop Breed's Hill in Charlestown. In that misnamed Battle of Bunker Hill, the British incurred their greatest losses of the entire war: more than 800 wounded and 228 killed. The Americans lost less than half that number. Elsewhere in the first eleven months of the war, the patriots captured Fort Ticonderoga, a British fort on Lake Champlain, acquiring much-needed cannon. In the hope of bringing Canada into the war on the American side, they also mounted a northern campaign that ended in disaster at Quebec in early 1776. Most significantly, the lull of the first year of the war gave both sides a chance to regroup, organize, and plan their strategies.

Lord North and his new American secretary, Lord George Germain, made three major assumptions about the war they faced. First, they concluded that patriot forces could **British** not withstand the assaults of **Strategy** trained British regulars. Accordingly, they dispatched to America the largest single force Great Britain had ever assembled anywhere: 370 transport ships carrying 32,000 troops and tons of supplies, accompanied by 73 naval vessels and 13,000 sailors. Such an extraordinary effort would, they thought, ensure a quick victory. Second, British officials and army officers persisted in comparing this war to wars they had fought successfully in Europe. Thus they adopted a conventional strategy of capturing major American cities. Third, they assumed that a clear-cut military victory would automatically bring about their goal of retaining the colonies' allegiance.

All these assumptions proved false. North and Germain, like Lord Dartmouth before them, vastly underestimated the Americans' commitment to armed resistance. Defeats on the battlefield did not lead the patriots to abandon their political aims and sue for peace. At one time or another during the war, the British controlled all major American ports, but with fifteen hundred miles of coastline, their actions did not halt essential commerce. Since less than 5 percent of the population lived in those cities, their loss did little damage to the American cause.

Most of all, the British did not grasp at first that a military victory would not necessarily bring a political victory. Securing the colonies permanently would require hundreds of thousands of Americans to return to their original allegiance. The conquest of America was thus a far more complicated task than the defeat of France twelve years earlier. The British needed not only to overpower the patriots, but also to convert them. They never fully realized that they were fighting an entirely new kind of conflict: the first modern war of national liberation.

The British at least had a bureaucracy ready to supervise the war effort. The Americans had only the Second Continental Congress, originally intended merely as a brief gathering **Second** of colonial representatives to con- **Continental** sider the British response to the **Congress** Continental Association. Instead, the delegates who convened in Philadelphia on May 10, 1775, found that they had to assume the mantle of intercolonial government. Yet as the summer passed, Congress slowly organized the colonies for war. It authorized the printing of money with which to purchase necessary goods, established a committee to supervise relations with foreign countries, and took steps to strengthen the militia. Most important of all, it created the Continental Army and appointed its generals.

Until Congress met, the Massachusetts provincial congress had taken responsibility for organizing the massive army of militia encamped at Boston. Because the cost of maintaining that army was too great, Massachusetts asked the Continental Congress to assume control of the army. Until then, the war had been a wholly northern affair. To ensure unity, Congress selected a non–New Englander to be the commander-in-chief. The only obvious and unanimous choice was a fellow delegate, George Washington of Virginia.

Washington was no fiery radical, nor was he a reflective political thinker. He had not played a prominent role in the prerevolutionary agitation, but his devotion to the Ameri- **George** can cause was unquestioned. **Washington:** He was dignified, conservative, **A Portrait of** and respectable—a man of un- **Leadership** impeachable integrity. Though unmistakably an aristocrat, Washington was unswervingly committed to representative government. Moreover, he both looked and acted like a leader. Six feet tall in an era when most men were five inches shorter, he had a stately and commanding presence. Other patriots praised his judgment, steadiness, and discretion, and even a loyalist admitted that Washington could "atone for many demerits by the extraordinary coolness and caution which distinguish his character."

Washington needed all the coolness and caution he could muster when he took command of the army outside Boston in July 1775. It took him months to impose hierarchy and discipline on the unruly troops and to bring order to the supply system. But by March 1776, the army was prepared to act. As it happened, an assault on Boston proved unnecessary. Sir William Howe, who had replaced Gage, had been considering an evacuation for some time; he wanted to transfer his troops to New York City. The patriots' bombardment of Boston early in the month decided the matter. On March 17, the British and more than a thousand of their loyalist allies abandoned Boston forever.

That spring of 1776, as the British fleet left Boston for the temporary haven of Halifax, Nova Scotia, the colonies were moving inexorably toward the unthinkable—a declaration of independence. But already in January 1776, a pamphlet had appeared, written by a man who both thought the unthinkable and advocated it.

Thomas Paine's *Common Sense* exploded on the American scene like a bombshell. Within three months of publication, it sold 120,000 copies. The

Thomas Paine's Common Sense

author, a radical English printer who had lived in America only since 1774, called stridently and stirringly for independence. More than that: Paine rejected the notion that a balance of monarchy, aristocracy, and democracy was necessary to preserve freedom and advocated instead the establishment of a republic. Instead of acknowledging the benefits of a connection with the mother country, Paine insisted that Britain had exploited the colonies unmercifully. In place of the frequently heard assertion that an independent America would be weak and divided, he substituted an unlimited confidence in America's strength when freed from European control.

There is no way of knowing how many people were converted to the cause of independence by reading *Common Sense*. But by late spring, independence had clearly become inevitable. On May 10, 1776, the Second Continental Congress formally recommended that individual colonies "adopt such governments as shall, in the opinion of the representatives of the people, best conduce to the happiness and safety of their constituents in particular,

and America in general." From that source grew the first state constitutions.

Then, on June 7, came confirmation of the movement toward independence. Richard Henry Lee of Virginia, seconded by John Adams of Massachusetts, introduced the crucial resolution: "that these United Colonies are, and of right ought to be, free and independent States, that they are absolved of all allegiance to the British Crown, and that all political connection between them and the State of Great Britain is, and ought to be, totally dissolved." Congress debated the resolution and directed a committee composed of Thomas Jefferson, John Adams, Benjamin Franklin, Robert R. Livingston of New York, and Roger Sherman of Connecticut to draft a declaration of independence. The committee in turn assigned primary responsibility for writing the declaration to Jefferson, a Virginia lawyer widely read in history and political theory and well known for his apt and eloquent style.

The draft of the declaration was laid before Congress on June 28. The delegates officially voted for independence four days later, then debated the

Declaration of Independence

wording of the declaration for two more days, adopting it with some changes on July 4. Since Americans had long since ceased to see themselves as legitimate subjects of Parliament, the Declaration of Independence concentrated on George III (see the Appendix). That focus also provided a single identifiable villain on whom to center the charges of misconduct.

The declaration's long-term importance, however, did not lie in its catalogue of grievances against George III but rather in its ringing statements of principle. These statements have served ever since as the ideal to which Americans aspire: "We hold these truths to be self-evident: That all men are created equal; that they are endowed by their Creator with certain unalienable rights; that among these are life, liberty and the pursuit of happiness; that, to secure these rights, governments are instituted among men, deriving their just powers from the consent of the governed; that whenever any form of government becomes destructive of these ends, it is the right of the people to alter or to abolish it, and to institute new government." The phrases have echoed down through American history like no others.

After listening to the first formal reading of the Declaration of Independence in New York City on July 9, 1776, a crowd of American soldiers and civilians pulled down a statue of George III that stood on the Bowling Green in the heart of the city. Most of the statue was later melted down into bullets, but a British officer rescued the head, which was later taken to London. *Library of Congress.*

The delegates in Philadelphia who voted to accept the Declaration of Independence did not have the advantage of our two hundred years of hindsight. When they adopted the declaration, they risked their necks: they were committing treason. Thus when they concluded the declaration with the assertion that they "mutually pledge[d] to each other our lives, our fortunes, and our sacred honor," they spoke no less than the truth. The real struggle still lay before them.

The Long Struggle in the North

On July 2, 1776, the day Congress voted for independence, the first of Sir William Howe's troops from Halifax landed on Staten Island. But Howe delayed his attack on New York City until mid-August, when additional troops arrived from England. The delay gave Washington sufficient time to march his army south to meet the threat. To defend New York, Washington had ten thousand Continentals, who had promised to serve until the end of the year, and seven thousand militiamen, who had enlisted for shorter terms. Neither he nor most of his men had ever fought a major battle against the British, and their lack of experience led to disastrous mistakes. The difficulty of defending New York City only compounded the errors.

Washington's problem was as simple as the geography of the region was complex (see map). To protect the city adequately, he would have to divide his forces among Long Island, Manhattan Island, and the mainland. But the British fleet under Admiral Lord Richard Howe, Sir William's brother, controlled the harbors and rivers that divided the American

Battle for New York City

The War in the North, 1775–1777

forces. The patriots thus constantly courted catastrophe, for swift action by the British navy could cut off the possibility of retreat and perhaps even communication. But despite these dangers, Washington could not afford to surrender New York to the Howes without a fight. Not only did the city occupy a strategic location, but the region that surrounded it was known to contain many loyalist sympathizers. A show of force was essential if the revolutionaries were to retain any hope of persuading waverers to join them.

On August 27, Sir William Howe's forces attacked the American positions on Brooklyn Heights, pushing the untried rebel troops back into their defensive entrenchments. But Howe failed to press his advantage, even neglecting to send his brother's ships into the East River to cut off a retreat. Consequently, the Americans were able to escape. Washington then moved north on the island, retreating onto the mainland. But the nearly three thousand men he left behind in the supposedly impregnable Fort Washington on the west shore of Manhattan had to surrender to Howe in early November.

George Washington had defended New York, but badly. He had repeatedly broken a basic rule of military strategy: never divide your force in the face of a superior enemy. In the end, though, the Howe brothers' failure to move quickly prevented a decisive defeat of the Americans. Although Washington's army had been seriously reduced by casualties, the surrender of Fort Washington, and the loss of most of the militiamen (who had returned home for the harvest), its core remained. Through November and December, Washington led his men in a retreat across New Jersey. Howe followed at a leisurely pace, setting up a string of outposts manned mostly by Hessian mercenaries. After Washington crossed the Delaware River into Pennsylvania, the British commander turned back and settled into comfortable winter quarters in New York City.

The British controlled most of New Jersey, and hundreds of Americans accepted the pardons offered by the Howes. Occupying troops met little opposition, and the revolutionary cause appeared to be in disarray. "These are the times that try men's souls," wrote Thomas Paine in his pamphlet *The Crisis*.

In the aftermath of battle, as at its height, the British commanders let their advantage slip away. The redcoats stationed in New Jersey went on a rampage of rape and plunder. Because loyalists and patriots were indistinguishable to the British and Hessian troops, families on both sides suffered nearly equally. Houses were looted and burned, churches and public buildings desecrated. But nothing was better calculated to rally doubtful Americans to the cause than the wanton murder of innocent civilians and the rape of women.

The soldiers' marauding alienated potentially loyal New Jerseyites and Pennsylvanians, whose allegiance the British could ill afford to lose. It also spurred Washington's determination to strike back. With the enlistments of most of the Continental troops scheduled to expire on December 31, Washington decided to strike quickly. He first struck the Hessian encampment at Trenton early on the morning of December 26. The patriots captured more than nine hundred Hessians and killed another thirty; only three Americans were wounded. A few days later, Washington attacked Princeton. Having buoyed American spirits with the two victories, Washington set up winter quarters at Morristown, New Jersey.

Battle of Trenton

The campaign of 1776 established patterns that were to persist throughout much of the war. British forces, although usually numerically superior to the Americans, engaged in ponderous maneuvering, lacked familiarity with the terrain, and antagonized the populace. Furthermore, although Washington always seemed to lack regular troops—the Continental Army never numbered more than 18,500 men—he could usually count on the militia to join him at crucial times. American militiamen did not like to sign up for long terms of service or to fight far from home, but when their homes were threatened they would rally to the cause.

As the war dragged on, the Continental Army and the militia took on decidedly different characters. State governments, responsible for filling military quotas, discovered that most men willing to enlist for long periods in the regular army were young, single, and footloose. Farmers with families tended to prefer short-term militia duty. As the supply of whites willing to sign up with the Continentals diminished, recruiters in the northern states turned increasingly to blacks, both slave and free. Perhaps as many as five thousand blacks eventually served in the revolutionary army, and most of them won their freedom as a result. Camp followers, like Sarah Osborn, also rendered service to the army. These women, usually the wives and widows of poor soldiers, worked as cooks, nurses, and launderers for rations and low pay. The American army was unwieldy and difficult to manage, yet this shapelessness provided an almost unlimited reservoir of man and woman power.

The American Army

The officers of the Continental Army developed an intense sense of pride and commitment to the revolutionary cause. The hardships they endured, the battles they fought, the difficulties they overcame all helped to forge an esprit de corps that was to outlast the war. The realities of warfare were often dirty, messy, and corrupt, but the officers drew strength from a developing image of themselves as professionals who sacrificed personal gain for the good of the entire nation.

In 1777, the chief British effort was planned by the flashy "Gentleman Johnny" Burgoyne, a playboy general who had gained the ear of Lord George Germain. Burgoyne convinced Germain that he

Deborah Sampson (1760–1827), who disguised herself as a man and enlisted in the Continental Army as Robert Shurtleff. She served from May 1782 to October 1783, when her sex was discovered and she was discharged. In later years she gave public lectures describing her wartime experiences. After her death her husband became the only man to receive a pension as the "widow" of a revolutionary soldier. *Courtesy of The Rhode Island Historical Society.*

could lead an invading force of redcoats and Indians down the Hudson River from Canada, cutting off New England from the rest of the states. He proposed to rendezvous near Albany with a similar force that would move east from Niagara along the Mohawk River valley. The combined forces would then presumably link up with Sir William Howe's troops in New York City.

That Burgoyne's scheme would give "Gentleman Johnny" all the glory and relegate Howe to a supporting role did not escape Sir William's notice. While Burgoyne was plotting in London, Howe was

Campaign of 1777

the 1777 campaign was virtually over, and far to the north, Burgoyne was going down to defeat.

Burgoyne and his men set out from Montreal in mid-June 1777, floating down Lake Champlain into New York in canoes and flat-bottom boats. They

Burgoyne's Campaign in New York

easily took Fort Ticonderoga from its outnumbered and outgunned defenders. Trouble began, however, as Burgoyne started his overland march. Because of his clumsy artillery carriages and baggage wagons, Burgoyne's troops took twenty-four days to travel the twenty-three miles. Moreover, the eight hundred German mercenaries he sent to forage the countryside were nearly wiped out near Bennington. Yet Burgoyne failed to recognize the seriousness of his predicament and continued to dawdle. By the time he finally crossed the Hudson in mid-September, bound for Albany, his fate was sealed. After several bloody clashes with the American force commanded by Horatio Gates, Burgoyne was surrounded near Saratoga, New York. On October 17, 1777, he surrendered his entire force of more than six thousand men.

Two months before, the fourteen hundred redcoats and Indians marching along the Mohawk River from Niagara toward Albany had also been turned back. The troops, under the command of Colonel Barry St. Leger, ambushed the patriots at Oriskany on August 6. The British claimed victory in the ensuing battle, one of the bloodiest of the war, but they and their Indian allies lost their taste for further fighting.

The Battle of Oriskany marked a split of the Iroquois Confederacy. In 1776, the Six Nations had formally pledged to remain neutral in the Anglo-

Split of the Iroquois Confederacy

American struggle. But two influential Mohawk leaders, Joseph Brant and Mary Brant, worked tirelessly to persuade their fellow Iroquois to join the British. Mary Brant, a powerful tribal matron, was also the widow of the Indian superintendent Sir William Johnson. Her younger brother Joseph, a renowned warrior, was convinced that the Six Nations should ally themselves with the British in order to prevent American encroachment on their lands. The Brants won over to the British the Senecas, Cayugas, and Mohawks. But the Oneidas preferred the American

laying his own plans to take Philadelphia. Just as Burgoyne left Howe out of his plans, so Howe left Burgoyne out of his. Thus the two major British armies in America would operate independently in 1777, and the result would be a disaster (see map).

Howe accomplished his objective in an inexplicable fashion. Instead of marching his forces from New York, he waited for months and then transported them by sea. The six-week

Howe Takes Philadelphia

voyage brought him only forty miles closer to Philadelphia, debilitated his men, depleted his supplies, and gave Washington time to prepare a defense of the city. Washington engaged the enemy at Brandywine Creek and again at Germantown. Although the British won both engagements, the Americans handled themselves well. By the time the redcoats took Philadelphia in late September, side, bringing the Tuscaroras with them. At Oriskany, the three-hundred-year league of friendship was torn apart, as confederation warriors fought on both sides.

The collapse of Iroquois unity and the confederacy's abandonment of neutrality had important consequences for both whites and Indians in subsequent years. In 1778, Iroquois warriors allied with the British raided the frontier villages of Wyoming, Pennsylvania, and Cherry Valley, New York. Retaliating in the summer of 1779, the whites dispatched an expedition under General John Sullivan to burn Iroquois crops, orchards, and settlements. The destruction was so thorough that many bands had to leave their ancestral homeland to seek food and shelter with the British north of the Great Lakes. A large number of Iroquois people never returned to New York but settled permanently in British Canada.

For the Indians, Oriskany was the most significant battle of the northern campaign; for the whites, it was Saratoga. The news of Burgoyne's surrender brought joy to patriots, discouragement to loyalists, and prompted Lord North to authorize a peace commission to offer the Americans everything they had requested in 1774—in effect, a return to the imperial system of 1763. It was, of course, far too late for that. The patriots rejected the overture, and the peace commission sailed back to England empty-handed in mid-1778.

Most important of all, the American victory at Saratoga drew France formally into the conflict. Ever since 1763, the French had sought to avenge their defeat in the Seven Years' War, and the American Revolution gave them that opportunity. Even before Benjamin Franklin arrived in Paris in late 1776, France was covertly supplying the revolutionaries with military necessities.

Franklin worked tirelessly to strengthen ties between the two nations. By presenting himself as a representative of American simplicity, Franklin played upon the French image of Americans as virtuous yeomen. His effort culminated in February 1778, when the countries signed two treaties. In the Treaty of Amity and Commerce, France recognized American independence and established **Franco-American Alliance of 1778** trade ties with the new nation; the second treaty provided for a formal alliance between the two nations. In this Treaty of Alliance, France and the United States promised—assuming that France would go to war with Britain, which it soon did—that neither country would negotiate peace with the enemy without consulting the other. France also abandoned all its claims to North American territory east of the Mississippi River and to Canada.

The French alliance had two major benefits for the patriot cause. First, France began to aid the Americans openly, sending troops and naval vessels, in addition to arms, ammunition, clothing, and blankets. Second, the British could no longer focus their attention on the American mainland alone, for they had to fight the French in the West Indies and elsewhere. Spain's entry into the war in 1779 as an ally of France (but not the United States) further magnified Britain's problems.

The Long Struggle in the South

In the aftermath of the Saratoga disaster, Lord George Germain and the military officials in London reassessed their strategy. Maneuvering in the North had done them little good; perhaps shifting the field of battle southward would bring success. The new British commander-in-chief, Sir Henry Clinton, became convinced that a southern strategy would work. In late 1779, he sailed down the coast from New York with 8,500 troops to attack Charleston, the most important American city in the South (see map).

Although the Americans worked hard to bolster Charleston's defenses, the city fell to the British on May 12, 1780. General Benjamin Lincoln surrendered the entire southern army of 5,500 men to the invaders. The **Fall of Charleston** redcoats then spread throughout South Carolina. As hundreds of South Carolinians proclaimed their loyalty to the Crown, Clinton organized loyalist regiments. Yet the British triumph was less complete than it ap-

The War in the South

dom. Indeed, slaves ran away from their patriot masters in such numbers that they seriously disrupted planting and harvesting in 1780 and 1781. Many of the thousands who ran away served the British well as scouts, guides, and laborers.

After the defeat at Camden, Washington gave command of the southern campaign to General Nathanael Greene of Rhode Island. Greene

Greene Rallies South Carolina

adopted a conciliatory policy toward loyalists and neutrals. He ordered his troops not to loot loyalist property and to treat captives fairly. Greene recognized that the patriots could win only by convincing the people that they could bring stability to the region. He thus helped the shattered provincial congresses of Georgia and South Carolina to begin re-establishing civilian authority in the interior.

Greene also took a conciliatory approach to the southern Indians. With his desperate need for soldiers, he could not afford to have frontier militia companies occupied in defending their homes against Indian attacks. Since he had so few regulars (only sixteen hundred men when he took command), Greene had to rely on western volunteers. Therefore, he negotiated with the Indians. By the end of the war, only the Creeks remained British allies.

Even before Greene took command of the southern army in December 1780, the tide had begun to turn. In October, at King's Mountain, near the North Carolina–South Carolina border, a force of "overmountain men" from the settlements west of the Appalachians defeated a large party of redcoats and loyalists. Then, in January 1781, Greene's trusted aide Brigadier General Daniel Morgan brilliantly defeated the crack British regiment Tarleton's Legion at Cowpens, also near the border of the Carolinas. In March, Greene engaged the main body of British troops at Guilford Court House, North Carolina. Although the Americans lost, most of Cornwallis's army had been destroyed. He had to retreat to the coast in order to receive supplies and fresh troops from New York.

Cornwallis had already ignored explicit orders not to leave South Carolina unless the state was safely in British hands. He headed north into

peared. The success of the southern campaign depended on British control of the seas, for only by sea could the widely dispersed British armies remain in communication with one another. For the moment, the Royal Navy safely dominated the American coastline, but French naval power posed a threat to the entire southern enterprise. Moreover, the redcoats never managed to establish full control of the areas they seized. As a result, patriot bands operated freely throughout the state. Last but not least, the fall of Charleston did not dishearten the patriots; instead, it spurred them to greater exertions.

Nevertheless, the war in South Carolina went badly for the patriots. In August 1780, a reorganized southern army under the command of Horatio Gates was defeated at Camden by the forces of Lord Cornwallis, who had been placed in charge of the southern campaign. The British army was joined wherever it went by blacks seeking free-

Surrender at Yorktown Virginia, where he joined forces with a detachment of redcoats commanded by the American traitor Benedict Arnold. Instead of acting decisively with his new army of 7,200 men, Cornwallis withdrew to the edge of the peninsula between the York and James rivers; there he fortified Yorktown and, in effect, waited for the end. Seizing the opportunity, Washington quickly moved more than 7,000 troops south from New York City. When a French fleet under the Comte de Grasse arrived from the West Indies in time to defeat the Royal Navy vessels sent to rescue Cornwallis, the British general was trapped (see map, page 101). On October 19, 1781, Cornwallis surrendered to the combined American and French forces.

When news of the surrender reached England, Lord North's ministry fell. Parliament voted to cease offensive operations in America and authorized peace negotiations. But guerrilla warfare between patriots and loyalists continued to ravage the Carolinas and Georgia for more than a year, and in the North vicious retaliatory raids by Indians and whites kept the frontier aflame. The persistence of conflict between whites and Indians after the Battle of Yorktown, all too often overlooked in accounts of the Revolution, serves to underline the degree to which the Indians were the real losers in the war initiated by whites.

The fighting finally ended when Americans and Britons learned of the signing of a preliminary peace treaty at Paris in November 1782. The American negotiators—Benjamin Franklin, John Jay, and John Adams—ignored their instructions from Congress to be guided by France and instead struck a separate agreement with Great Britain. Their instincts were sound: the French government was more an enemy to Britain than a friend to the United States. In fact, French ministers worked secretly behind the scenes to try to prevent the establishment of a strong, unified, independent government in America. The new British ministry, headed by Lord Shelburne, was weary of war and made numerous concessions.

Treaty of Paris

Under the treaty, signed formally on September 3, 1783, the Americans were granted unconditional independence and unlimited fishing rights off Newfoundland. The boundaries of the new nation were generous: to the north, approximately the present-day boundary with Canada; to the south, the 31st parallel; to the west, the Mississippi River. Florida, which the British had acquired in 1763, was returned to Spain. In ceding so much land unconditionally to the Americans, the British entirely ignored the territorial rights of their Indian allies. Once again, the tribes' interests were sacrificed to the demands of European power politics. Loyalists and British merchants were also poorly served by the British negotiators. The treaty's ambiguously worded clauses pertaining to the payment of prewar debts and the postwar treatment of loyalists caused trouble for years to come and proved impossible to enforce.

The long war finally over, the victorious Americans could look back on their achievement with satisfaction and awe. In 1775, with an inexperienced, ragtag army, they had taken on the greatest military power in the world—and eight years later they had won. They had accomplished their goal more through persistence and commitment than through brilliance on the battlefield. Actual victories had been few, but their army had always survived defeats and standoffs to fight again. Ultimately, the Americans had simply worn their enemy down.

Achieving independence in military terms, however, was only half the battle. The Americans still faced perhaps even greater challenges: establishing stable republican governments at the state and national levels, and ensuring their governments' continued existence in a world filled with bitter rivalries among the major powers—England, France, and Spain. Those European rivalries had worked to the Americans' advantage during the war, but in the decades to come they would pose significant threats to the survival of the new nation.

Suggestions for Further Reading

General

Edward Countryman, *The American Revolution* (1985); Stephen G. Kurtz and James H. Hutson, eds., *Essays on the*

American Revolution (1973); Edmund S. Morgan, *The Challenge of the American Revolution* (1976); Alfred F. Young, ed., *The American Revolution: Explorations in the History of American Radicalism* (1976).

Military

John Richard Alden, *The American Revolution, 1775–1783* (1964); John C. Dann, ed., *The Revolution Remembered: Eyewitness Accounts of the War for Independence* (1980); Don Higginbotham, *The War of American Independence: Military Attitudes, Policies, and Practice, 1763–1789* (1971); Piers Mackesy, *The War for America, 1775–1783* (1964); James K. Martin and Mark Lender, *"A Respectable Army": The Military Origins of the Republic, 1763–1789* (1982); Charles Royster, *A Revolutionary People at War: The Continental Army and American Character, 1775–1783* (1980).

Local and Regional

Edward Countryman, *A People in Revolution: The American Revolution and Political Society in New York, 1760–1790* (1981); Elaine F. Crane, *A Dependent People: Newport, R.I., in the Revolutionary Era* (1985); Jeffrey Crow and Larry Tise, eds., *The Southern Experience in the American Revolution* (1978); Thomas Doerflinger, *A Vigorous Spirit of Enterprise: Merchants and Economic Development in Revolutionary Philadelphia* (1986); Robert A. Gross, *The Minutemen and Their World* (1976); Ronald Hoffman, *A Spirit of Dissension: Economics, Politics, and the Revolution in Maryland* (1973); Ronald Hoffman, Thad W. Tate, and Peter Albert, eds., *An Uncivil War: The Southern Backcountry During the American Revolution* (1985); Stephen Rosswurm, *Arms, Country, and Class: The Philadelphia Militia and the "Lower Sort" During the American Revolution* (1988); John Selby, *The Revolution in Virginia, 1775–1783* (1988).

Indians and Blacks

Barbara Graymont, *The Iroquois in the American Revolution* (1972); Isabel T. Kelsey, *Joseph Brant, 1743–1807: Man of Two Worlds* (1984); Duncan J. MacLeod, *Slavery, Race, and the American Revolution* (1974); James H. O'Donnell III, *Southern Indians in the American Revolution* (1973); Benjamin Quarles, *The Negro in the American Revolution* (1961).

Loyalists

Bernard Bailyn, *The Ordeal of Thomas Hutchinson* (1974); Robert McCluer Calhoon, *The Loyalists in Revolutionary America, 1760–1781* (1973); William H. Nelson, *The American Tory* (1961); Mary Beth Norton, *The British-Americans: The Loyalist Exiles in England, 1774–1789* (1972); Janice Potter, *The Liberty We Seek: Loyalist Ideology in Colonial New York and Massachusetts* (1983).

Women

Richard Buel and Joy Buel, *The Way of Duty: A Woman and Her Family in Revolutionary America* (1984); Linda Grant DePauw and Conover Hunt, *"Remember the Ladies": Women in America, 1750–1815* (1976); Linda K. Kerber, *Women of the Republic: Intellect and Ideology in Revolutionary America* (1980); Mary Beth Norton, *Liberty's Daughters: The Revolutionary Experience of American Women, 1750–1800* (1980).

Foreign Policy

Jonathan Dull, *A Diplomatic History of the American Revolution* (1985); Felix Gilbert, *To the Farewell Address* (1961); Ronald Hoffman and Peter Albert, eds., *Peace and the Peacemakers: The Treaty of 1783* (1986); Ronald Hoffman and Peter Albert, eds., *Diplomacy and Revolution: The Franco-American Alliance of 1778* (1981); Lawrence Kaplan, ed., *The American Revolution and a "Candid World"* (1977); Richard B. Morris, *The Peacemakers: The Great Powers and American Independence* (1965); Richard W. Van Alstyne, *Empire and Independence: The International History of the American Revolution* (1965).

Patriot Leaders

Fawn M. Brodie, *Thomas Jefferson: An Intimate History* (1974); Verner W. Crane, *Benjamin Franklin and a Rising People* (1954); Marcus Cunliffe, *George Washington: Man and Monument* (1958); Noble Cunningham, *In Pursuit of Reason: The Life of Thomas Jefferson* (1987); James T. Flexner, *George Washington*, 4 vols. (1965–1972); Eric Foner, *Tom Paine and Revolutionary America* (1976); Claude A. Lopez and Eugenia Herbert, *The Private Franklin: The Man and His Family* (1975); Dumas Malone, *Jefferson and His Time*, 6 vols. (1948–1981); Peter Shaw, *The Character of John Adams* (1976).

On January 25, 1787, an army of fifteen hundred farmers in western Massachusetts advanced on the federal armory at Springfield. Inside the arsenal, General William Shepard prepared his group of one thousand militiamen to resist the assault. First, though, he warned the farmers that they would soon "inevitably" draw the fire of men who had been their officers during the Revolutionary War. "That is all we want, by God!" replied one of the rebels. The farmers moved toward the armory, urged on by the commands of Daniel Shays, one of their leaders. Shepard fired two cannon over the heads of the farmers. When that did not frighten them, he directed his men to shoot directly at the straggling ranks. Four men died; twenty were wounded; and the rebels withdrew from the field.

6

FORGING A NATIONAL REPUBLIC, 1776–1789

What had caused this violent clash between former comrades in arms? The Massachusetts farmers were angered by high taxes and the scarcity of money. Since the preceding summer, they had used committees and crowd actions—adopting the tactics used so successfully in the 1760s and early 1770s—to halt court proceedings in which the state was trying to seize property for nonpayment of taxes. Many of the insurgents were respected war veterans. Daniel Shays, their nominal leader, had been a captain in the Continental Army. Clearly, the episode could not be dismissed as the work of an unruly rabble. What did the uprising mean for the future of the republic? Was it a sign of impending anarchy?

The protesters explained their position to the governor and council of Massachusetts. They proclaimed their loyalty to the nation but objected to the state's fiscal policies, which, they said, prevented them from providing adequately for their families. One rebel sympathizer explained, "Whenever any encroachments are made either upon the liberties or properties of the people, if redress cannot be had without, it is virtue in them to disturb government." The Massachusetts government, Shays asserted, was "tyrannical" and, like that of Great Britain, deserved to be overthrown.

To the state's elected leaders, the most frightening aspect of the uprising was the rebels' attempt to forge direct links with the earlier struggle for independence. The state legislature issued an address to the people, asserting that "in a republican government the majority must govern. If the minor part governs it becomes aristocracy; if every one opposed at his pleasure, it is . . . anarchy and confusion." Thus Massachusetts officials insisted that crowd actions, which had once been a justifiable response to British tyranny, were no longer legitimate. In a republic, reform had to come about through the ballot box rather than by force.

For many Americans, the confrontation at the Springfield armory symbolized the trials facing the new nation. That the rebels were dispersed easily, that their leaders (including Shays) were forced to flee to neighboring states for asylum, and that a newly elected Massachusetts legislature adopted conciliatory measures—all those facts were almost irrelevant to American political leaders' interpretation of the events in western Massachusetts. In Shays's Rebellion, they thought they discerned the first signs of disintegration of the republic they had worked so hard to establish.

Republicanism—the idea that governments should be based wholly on the consent of the people—had first been discussed by political theorists in ancient Greece and Rome. Republics, such writers declared, were desirable yet fragile forms of government. Unless their citizens were especially virtuous and largely in agreement on key issues, republics were doomed to failure. When they left the British Empire, Americans committed themselves to republicanism. Now they had to deal with the potentially unwelcome consequences of that decision. How could they best ensure political stability? How could they create a virtuous republic?

America's leaders worked hard to inculcate virtue in their fellow countrymen and countrywomen. After 1776, American literature, theater, art, architecture, and education all had explicitly moral goals. The education of women was particularly important, for as the mothers of the republic's children, they were primarily responsible for ensuring their nation's future. On such matters Americans could agree, but they disagreed on many other critical issues. Although almost all white men concurred that women, Indians, and blacks should be excluded from formal participation in politics, they found it difficult to reach a consensus on how many of their own number should be included. And

when should consent be sought: semiannually? annually? at intervals of two or more years? Further, how should governments be structured so as to reflect the people's consent most accurately? Americans replied to these questions in different ways.

Republican citizens had to answer many other questions as well. Should a republic conduct its dealings with Indian tribes and foreign countries any differently from other types of governments? Did republics, in other words, have an obligation to negotiate fairly and honestly at all times? And how could white republicans reconcile the conflict between slavery and Jefferson's words in the Declaration of Independence, "all men are created equal"? Some resolved the dilemma by freeing their slaves; others denied that blacks were "men" in the same sense as whites.

The most important task facing Americans in these years was the construction of a national government. Before 1765, the English mainland colonies had rarely cooperated on common endeavors. Many things separated them: their diverse economies, varying religious traditions and ethnic compositions, competing land claims, and differences in their political systems. But fighting the Revolutionary War brought them together and created a new nationalistic spirit. Wartime experiences broke down at least some of the boundaries that had previously divided Americans, replacing loyalties to state and region with loyalties to the nation.

Still, forging a national republic was neither easy nor simple. America's first framework for such a government, the Articles of Confederation, proved to be inadequate. But some of the nation's political leaders learned from their experiences and tried another approach when they drafted the Constitution in 1787. Some historians have argued that the Articles of Confederation and the Constitution reflected opposing political philosophies, the Constitution representing an "aristocratic" counterrevolution against the "democratic" Articles. The two documents are more accurately viewed as separate and successive attempts to solve the same problems. Both in part applied theories of republicanism to practical problems of governance; neither was entirely successful in resolving those difficulties.

Creating a Virtuous Republic

Many years after the Revolution, John Dickinson recalled that in 1776, when the colonies declared their independence from Great Britain, "there was no question concerning forms of Government, no enquiry whether a Republic or a limited Monarchy was best. . . . We knew that the people of this country must unite themselves under some form of Government and that this could be no other than the republican form." But how could that goal be implemented?

Three different definitions of *republicanism* emerged in the new United States. The first, held chiefly by members of the educated elite, was

Varieties of Republicanism

based directly on ancient history and political theory. The histories of popular governments in Greece and Rome seemed to prove that republics could succeed only if they were small in size and homogeneous in population. Furthermore, unless the citizens of a republic were willing to sacrifice their own private interests for the good of the whole, the government would inevitably collapse. In return for sacrifices, though, a republic offered its citizens equality of opportunity. Under such a government, society would be ruled by a "natural aristocracy" of men whose rank would be based upon merit rather than inherited wealth or status.

A second definition, advanced both by members of the elite and by some skilled craftsmen, drew more on economic than political thought. Instead of perceiving the nation as an organic whole composed of people sacrificing to the common good, this version of republicanism followed the English theorist Adam Smith in emphasizing individuals' pursuit of rational self-interest. When republican men sought to improve their own economic and social circumstances, the entire nation would benefit. Republican virtue would be achieved through the advancement of private interests, rather than through their subordination to some communal ideal.

The third notion of republicanism was less influential because it was popular primarily with people who were illiterate or barely literate and who thus wrote little to promote their beliefs. But it involved a more egalitarian approach to governance than did either of the other two, both of which contained considerable potential for inequality. Some Americans (like Thomas Paine) emphasized the importance of widespread participation in political activities, wanted government to be responsive to their needs, and openly questioned the gentry's ability to speak for them. They can, in fact, be termed democrats in more or less the modern sense.

It is important to recognize that the three strands of republicanism were part of a unified whole and shared many of the same assumptions. For example, all three contrasted a virtuous, industrious America to the corrupt luxury of England and Europe. In the first version, that virtue manifested itself in frugality and self-sacrifice; in the second, it would prevent self-interest from becoming vice; in the third, it was the justification for including even propertyless white men in the ranks of voters.

As the citizens of the United States set out to construct their republic, they believed they were embarking on an unprecedented enterprise. With

Virtue and the Arts

great pride in their new nation, they expected to exchange the vices of monarchical Europe for the virtues of republican America. They wanted to embody republican principles not only in their governments, but also in their society and their culture. They looked to painting, literature, drama, and architecture to convey messages of nationalism and virtue to the public.

But Americans faced a crucial contradiction at the very outset of their efforts. To some republicans, the fine arts themselves were manifestations of vice. What need did a frugal yeoman have for a painting—or, worse yet, a novel? Why should anyone spend hard-earned wages to see a play in a lavishly decorated theater? The first American artists, playwrights, and authors were thus trapped in a dilemma from which escape was nearly impossible. They wanted to produce works embodying virtue, but those very works, regardless of their content, were viewed by many as corrupting.

Still, they tried. William Hill Brown's *The Power of Sympathy* (1789), the first novel written in the

1776	Second Continental Congress directs states to draft constitutions	1787	Northwest Ordinance Constitutional Convention
1777	Articles of Confederation sent to states for ratification	1788	Hamilton, Jay, and Madison, *The Federalist* Constitution ratified
1781	Articles of Confederation ratified	1794	Battle of Fallen Timbers
1786	Annapolis Convention	1795	Treaty of Greenville
1786–87	Shays's Rebellion	1800	Weems, *Life of Washington*

United States, was a lurid tale of seduction intended as a warning to young women, who made up a large proportion of America's fiction readers. In Royall Tyler's *The Contrast* (1787), the first successful American play, the virtuous conduct of Colonel Manly was contrasted (hence the title) with the reprehensible behavior of the fop Billy Dimple. The most popular book of the era, Mason Locke Weems's *Life of Washington,* published in 1800, shortly after George Washington's death, was, the author declared, designed to "hold up his great Virtues . . . to the imitation of Our Youth."

Painting, too, was expected to embody high moral standards. Gilbert Stuart, one of the era's major artists, painted portraits of upstanding republican citizens. And John Trumbull's vast canvases depicted such milestones of American history as the Battle of Bunker Hill, Burgoyne's surrender at Saratoga, and Cornwallis's capitulation at Yorktown. Both men attempted to instill patriotic virtues in their viewers.

Architects likewise hoped to convey in their buildings a sense of the young republic's ideals, and most of them consciously rejected British models. When the Virginia government asked Thomas Jefferson, then ambassador to France, for advice on the design of a state capitol in Richmond, Jefferson unhesitatingly recommended copying a Roman building. "It is very simple," he explained, "but it is noble beyond expression." Jefferson set forth ideals that would guide American architecture for a generation to come: simplicity of line, harmonious proportions, a feeling of grandeur. Nowhere were these rational goals of republican art manifested more clearly than in Benjamin H. Latrobe's plans for the majestic, domed United States Capitol in Washington, built in the early 1800s.

Despite the artists' efforts, or perhaps, some would have said, because of them, some Americans were beginning to detect signs of luxury and corruption by the mid-1780s. The end of the war and resumption of European trade brought a return to fashionable clothing styles and the abandonment of the homespun garments patriots had once worn with pride. Well-dressed elite families attended balls and concerts. Parties no longer seemed complete without gambling and card playing. Especially alarming to fervent republicans was the establishment in 1783 of the Society of the Cincinnati, a hereditary organization of Revolutionary War officers and their descendants. Many feared that the group would become the nucleus of a native-born aristocracy. All these developments directly challenged the image of the United States as a virtuous republic.

The deep-seated concern for the future of the infant republic focused Americans' attention on their children, the "rising generation." Education

Im: *Do you want to kill the Colonel ?*
I feel chock full of fight.

A scene from Royall Tyler's *The Contrast,* as performed in New York City in 1787. The play both satirized English aristocrats and celebrated the virtuous simplicity of its American hero and heroine. *Harvard Theatre Collection.*

Educational Reform acquired new significance in the context of the republic. Since the early days of the colonies, education had been seen chiefly as a private means to personal advancement. Now, though, it would serve a public purpose. If young people were to resist the temptation of vice, they would have to learn the lessons of virtue at home and at school. In fact, the very survival of the nation depended on it. The early republican period was thus a time of major educational reform.

The 1780s and 1790s brought two significant changes in American educational practice. First, some northern states began to use tax money to support public elementary schools. Nearly all education in the colonies had been privately financed. In the republic, though, schools could lay claim to tax dollars.

Second, schooling for girls was improved. Americans' recognition of the importance of the rising generation led to the realization that mothers would have to be properly educated if they were to instruct their children adequately. Therefore Massachusetts, the first state to require towns to supply their citizens with free public elementary education, insisted that the schools be open to girls as well as boys. Throughout the United States, private academies were founded to give teenage girls from well-to-do families an opportunity for advanced schooling. No one yet proposed opening colleges to women, but a few fortunate girls could study history, geography, rhetoric, and mathematics.

The chief theorist of women's education in the early republic was Judith Sargent Murray of Gloucester, Massachusetts. In a series of essays published in the 1780s and 1790s, **Judith Sargent Murray on Education** Murray argued that women and men had equal intellectual capacities. Therefore, concluded Murray, boys and girls should be offered equivalent scholastic training. She further contended that girls should be taught to support themselves by their own efforts. Because she rejected the prevailing notion that a young woman's chief goal in life should be finding a husband, Judith Sargent Murray deserves the title of the first American feminist. (That distinction is usually accorded to better-known nineteenth-century women, such as Margaret Fuller or Sarah Grimké.)

Murray's direct challenge to the traditional colonial belief that (as one man put it) girls "knew quite enough if they could make a shirt and a pudding" was part of a general rethinking of women's position stemming from the Revolution. Male patriots who enlisted in the army or served in Congress were away from home for long periods of time. In their absence, their wives, who had previously handled only the "indoor affairs" of the household, had to shoulder the responsibility for "outdoor affairs" as well.

In many households, the necessary shift of responsibilities during the war caused men and women to rethink their notions of proper gender roles. Both John and Abigail Adams took great pride in Abigail's developing skills as a "farmeress." Abigail Adams, like her female contemporaries, stopped calling the farm "yours" in letters to her husband and began referring to it as "ours"—a revealing change of pronoun. Both men and women realized that female patriots had made a vital contribution to winning the war. Thus, in the years after the Revolution, Americans began to develop new ideas about the role women should play in a republican society.

The best-known example of those new ideas came in a letter Abigail Adams addressed to her husband in March 1776. "In the new Code of Laws

Abigail Adams: "Remember the Ladies"

which I suppose it will be necessary for you to make I desire you would Remember the Ladies," she wrote. "If perticuliar care and attention is not paid to the Laidies we are determined to foment a Rebelion, and will not hold ourselves bound by any Laws in which we have no voice, or Representation."

With these words, Abigail Adams took a step that was soon to be duplicated by other disfranchised Americans. She employed the ideology that had been developed to combat Great Britain's claims to political supremacy, but she applied it to purposes white male leaders had never intended. Abigail Adams did not ask that women be allowed to vote. But other women wanted to claim that right, as events in New Jersey proved. The men who drafted the state constitution in 1776 defined voters loosely as "all free inhabitants" who met certain property qualifications. They thereby unintentionally gave the vote to property-holding white spinsters and widows, as well as to free blacks. In the 1780s and 1790s qualified women regularly voted in New Jersey's local and congressional elections. They continued to exercise that right until 1807, when women and blacks were disfranchised by the state legislature on the grounds that their votes could be easily manipulated. Yet the fact that they had voted at all made plain their altered perception of their place in political life.

Such dramatic episodes were unusual. On the whole, the re-evaluation of women's position had its greatest impact on private life. The traditional

Woman's Role in the Republic

colonial view of marriage had stressed the subordination of wife to husband. But in 1790, a female "Matrimonial Republican" asserted that "marriage ought never to be considered as a contract between a superior and an inferior, but a reciprocal union of interest. . . . The obedience between man and wife is, or ought to be mutual." This new understanding of the marital relationship seems to have contributed to a rising divorce rate after the war. Dissatisfied wives proved less willing to remain in unhappy marriages than they had been previously. At the same time, state judges became more sympathetic to women's desires to be freed from abusive or unfaithful husbands. Even so, divorces were still rare; most marriages were for life, and married women continued to suffer serious legal handicaps.

After the war, then, most white Americans still assumed that women's place was in the home and that their primary function was to be good wives and mothers. They accepted the notion of equality, broadly defined, but within the context of men's and women's separate roles in life. Seeing such differences between the male and female characters eventually enabled Americans to resolve the conflict between the two most influential strands of republican thought. Because married women could not own property or participate directly in economic life, women in general came to be seen as the embodiment of self-sacrificing, disinterested republicanism. Through female-run charitable and other social welfare groups, they assumed responsibility for the welfare of the community as a whole. Thus men were freed from any naggings of conscience as they pursued their economic self-interest (that other republican virtue), secure in the knowledge that their wives and daughters were fulfilling the family's obligation to the common good. The ideal republican man, therefore, was an individualist, seeking advancement for himself and his family; the ideal republican woman, by contrast, always put the well-being of others ahead of her own.

Together white men and women established the context for the creation of a virtuous republic. But nearly 20 percent of the American population was black. How did approximately 700,000 African-Americans fit into the developing national plan?

Emancipation and the Growth of Racism

Revolutionary ideology exposed one of the primary contradictions in American society. Both blacks and whites saw the irony in slaveholding Americans' claims that one of their aims in taking up arms was to prevent Britain from "enslaving" them.

As early as 1764, James Otis, Jr., had identified the basic problem in his pamphlet *The Rights of the British Colonies Asserted and Proved.* If, according to natural law, all people were born free and equal, that meant *all* humankind, black and white. "Does it follow that 'tis right to enslave a man because he is black?" Otis asked. The same theme was later voiced by other revolutionary leaders. In 1773, the Philadelphia doctor Benjamin Rush warned that "the plant of liberty is of so tender a nature that it cannot thrive long in the neighborhood of slavery." Common folk, too, noticed the contradiction. When a Connecticut soldier saw Washington's plantation, he observed in his journal: "Alas! That persons who pretend to stand for the rights of mankind . . . can delight in oppression, & that even of the worst kind!"

African-Americans themselves were quick to recognize the implications of revolutionary ideology. In 1779, a group of slaves from Portsmouth, New Hampshire, asked the state legislature "from what authority [our masters] assume to dispose of our lives, freedom and property" and pleaded "that the name of slave may not more be heard in a land gloriously contending for the sweets of freedom." That same year, several black residents of Fairfield, Connecticut, petitioned the legislature for their freedom, characterizing slavery as a "dreadful Evil" and "flagrant Injustice."

Both legislatures responded negatively. But the postwar years did witness the gradual abolition of slavery in the North. Vermont abolished slavery in its 1777 constitution. Massachu-

Gradual Emancipation

setts courts decided in the 1780s that the clause in the state constitution declaring that "all men are born free and equal, and have certain natural, essential, and unalienable rights" prohibited slavery in the state. Pennsylvania passed an abolition law in 1780; four years later, Rhode Island and Connecticut provided for gradual emancipation, followed by New York (1799) and New Jersey (1804).

No southern state adopted similar general emancipation laws, but the legislatures of Virginia (1782), Delaware (1787), and Maryland (1790 and 1796) did decide to change laws that had restricted masters' ability to free their slaves. South Carolina and Georgia never considered adopting such acts, and North Carolina insisted that all manumissions (emancipations of individual slaves) be approved by county courts.

Thus revolutionary ideology had limited impact on the well-entrenched economic interests of large slaveholders. Only in the North, where there were few slaves, could state legislatures vote to abolish slavery with relative ease. Even there, legislators' concern for property rights led them to favor gradual emancipation over immediate abolition. Most states provided only for the freeing of children born after passage of the law. And even those children were to remain slaves until ages ranging from eighteen to twenty-eight. Still, by 1840 in only one northern state—New Jersey—were black persons legally held in bondage.

Despite the slow progress of abolition, the free black population of the United States grew dramatically in the first years after the Revolution. Before

Growth of the Free Black Population

the war there had been few free blacks in America. Most prewar free blacks were mulattos, born of unions between white masters and enslaved black women. But wartime disruptions radically changed the size and composition of the free black population. Slaves who had escaped from plantations during the war, others who had served in the American army, and still others who had been emancipated by their owners or by state laws were now free. By 1790, there were nearly 60,000 free people of color in the United States; ten years later, they numbered more than 108,000, nearly 11 percent of the total black population.

In the 1780s and later, freed people often made their way to the port cities of the North. Boston and Philadelphia, where slavery was abolished sooner than it was in New York City, were particularly popular destinations. Women outnumbered men among the migrants by a margin of three to two. Like female whites, black women found more opportunities for employment, particularly as domestic servants, in the cities than in the countryside. Some black men also worked in domestic service, but larger numbers were employed as unskilled laborers or seamen. A few of the women and a sizable proportion of the men (nearly one-third of those in Philadelphia in 1795) were skilled workers or retailers. As soon as possible, these freed people established independent two-parent nuclear families instead of continuing to live in white households. They also began to cluster their residences in certain neighborhoods, probably as a result of both discrimination by whites and a desire for black solidarity.

Emancipation did not bring equality. Even whites who recognized African-Americans' right to freedom were unwilling to accept them as equals.

Discrimination Against Blacks Laws discriminated against emancipated blacks—South Carolina, for example, did not permit free blacks to testify against whites in court. Public schools often refused to educate free black children. Freedmen found it difficult to purchase property and find good jobs. And whites rarely allowed them an equal voice in church affairs.

Gradually, free blacks developed their own separate institutions, often based in the neighborhoods in which they lived. In Charleston, mulattos formed the Brown Fellowship Society, which provided insurance coverage for its members, financed a school for free children, and helped to support black orphans. In 1794, blacks in Philadelphia and Baltimore founded societies that eventually became the African Methodist Episcopal (AME) denomination. AME churches later sponsored schools in a number of cities and, along with African Baptist, African Episcopal, and African Presbyterian churches, became cultural centers of the free black community.

Their endeavors were all the more important because the postrevolutionary years ironically witnessed the development of a coherent racist theory in the United States. Whites had

Development of Racist Theory long regarded blacks as inferior, but the most influential writers on race had attributed that inferiority to environmental rather than hereditary factors. After the Revolution, white southerners needed to defend their holding other human beings in bondage against the notion that "all men are created equal." Consequently, they began to argue that blacks were less than fully human and that the principles of republican equality applied only to whites.

Their racism had several intertwined elements. First was the insistence that, as Thomas Jefferson suggested in 1781, blacks were "inferior to the whites in the endowments both of body and mind." Second came the belief that blacks were congenitally lazy, dishonest, and uncivilized (or uncivilizable). Third, and of crucial importance, was the notion that all blacks were sexually promiscuous and that black men lusted after white women. The specter of interracial sexual intercourse involving black men and white women haunted early American racist thought. The reverse situation, which occurred with far greater frequency (as white masters sexually exploited their female slaves), aroused little comment.

African-Americans did not allow these developing racist notions to pass unnoticed. Benjamin Banneker, a free black surveyor, astronomer, and mathematical genius, directly challenged Thomas Jefferson's belief in blacks' intellectual inferiority. In 1791, Banneker sent Jefferson a copy of his latest almanac (which included his astronomical calculations) as an example of blacks' mental powers. Jefferson's response admitted Banneker's capability but implied that he regarded Banneker as an exception.

At its birth, then, the republic was defined by

A woodcut portrait of Benjamin Banneker adorned the cover of his almanac for 1795. *Maryland Historical Society, Baltimore.*

whites as an exclusively white enterprise. Indeed, some historians have argued that the subjection of

A Republic for Whites Only blacks was a necessary precondition for equality among whites. They have pointed out that identifying a common racial antagonist helped to create white solidarity and to lessen the threat to gentry power posed by the enfranchisement of poorer whites. It was less dangerous to allow whites with little property to participate formally in politics than to open the pos-

sibility that they might combine with freed blacks to question the rule of the "better sort." That was one reason why, in the postrevolutionary years, the division of American society between slave and free was transformed into a division between blacks—some of whom were free—and whites. The white male wielders of power ensured their continued dominance in part by making certain that race replaced enslavement as the primary determinant of African-Americans' status.

Designing Republican Governments

On May 10, 1776, the Second Continental Congress directed the states to devise new republican governments to replace the provincial congresses and committees that had met since 1774. Thus Americans initially concentrated on drafting state constitutions and devoted little attention to their national government. At the state level, they immediately faced the problem of defining just what a constitution was. The British constitution could not serve as a model because it was an unwritten mixture of law and custom; Americans wanted tangible documents specifying the fundamental structures of government. Several years passed before the states agreed that their constitutions, unlike ordinary laws, could not be drafted by regular legislative bodies. Following the lead established by Massachusetts in 1780, they called conventions for the sole purpose of drafting constitutions. Thus the states sought direct authorization from the people—the theoretical sovereigns in a republic—before establishing new governments.

Those who wrote the state constitutions concerned themselves primarily with outlining the distribution and limitations of government power. As

Drafting of State Constitutions colonists, Americans had learned to fear the power of the governor—in most cases the appointed agent of the king or the proprietor—and to trust the legislature. Accordingly, the first state constitutions typically provided for the governor to be elected annually (usually by the legislature), limited the number of terms any one governor could serve, and gave him little independent authority. At the same time, the constitutions expanded the powers of the legislature. All the states except Pennsylvania retained the two-house organization common in the colonial years and provided that members of the upper house would have longer terms and be required to meet higher standards of property holding. But they also redrew the lines of electoral districts to reflect population patterns more accurately and increased the numbers of members in both the upper and the lower houses. Finally, most states lowered property qualifications for voting. Thus the revolutionary era witnessed the first deliberate attempt to broaden the base of American government.

The authors of the state constitutions knew that governments designed to be responsive to the people would not necessarily provide sufficient protection if tyrants were elected to office. Consequently, they included limitations on government authority in the documents they composed. Seven of the constitutions contained formal bills of rights, and the others had similar clauses. Most of them guaranteed citizens freedom of the press and of religion, the right to a fair trial, the right of consent to taxation, and protection against general search warrants. An independent judiciary was charged with upholding such rights.

In sum, the constitution makers put far greater emphasis on preventing state governments from becoming tyrannical than on making them effective wielders of political authority. Their approach to the process of shaping governments was understandable, given the American experience with Great Britain. But establishing such weak political units, especially in wartime, practically ensured that the constitutions would soon need revision. Invariably, the revised versions increased the powers of the governor and reduced the scope of the legislature's authority. Only in the 1780s did Americans start to develop a formal theory of checks and balances as the primary means of controlling government power. Once they realized that legislative supremacy did not in itself guarantee good government, Americans attempted to achieve that goal by balancing the powers of the legislative, executive, and judicial branches against one another.

The constitutional theories that Americans applied at the state level did not at first influence their conception of the nature of a national government. The powers and structure of the Continental Congress evolved by default early in the war, since Americans had little time to devote to legitimizing their de facto government while organizing the military struggle against Britain. Not until late 1777, after Burgoyne's defeat at Saratoga, did Congress send the Articles of Confederation to the states for ratification.

The chief organ of national government was a unicameral (one-house) legislature in which each state had one vote. Its powers included the conduct of foreign relations, the settlement of disputes between states, control over maritime affairs, the regulation of Indian trade, and the valuation of state and national coinage. The Articles did not give the national government the ability to tax effectively or to enforce a uniform commercial policy. The United States of America was described as "a firm league of friendship" in which each state "retains its sovereignty . . . and every Power . . . which is not by this confederation expressly delegated to the United States, in Congress assembled."

Articles of Confederation

The Articles required the unanimous consent of the state legislatures for ratification or amendment, and a clause concerning western lands turned out to be troublesome. The draft accepted by Congress allowed the states to retain all land claims derived from their original colonial charters. Because Maryland did not want to be overpowered by states with land claims deriving from their colonial charters, the state refused to accept the Articles until 1781. Only when Virginia promised to surrender its western holdings to national jurisdiction did Maryland accept the Articles (see map, page 114). Other states followed Virginia, establishing the principle that western lands would be held by the nation as a whole.

The fact that a single state could delay ratification for three years was a portent of the fate of American government under the Articles of Confederation. The authors of the Articles had not given

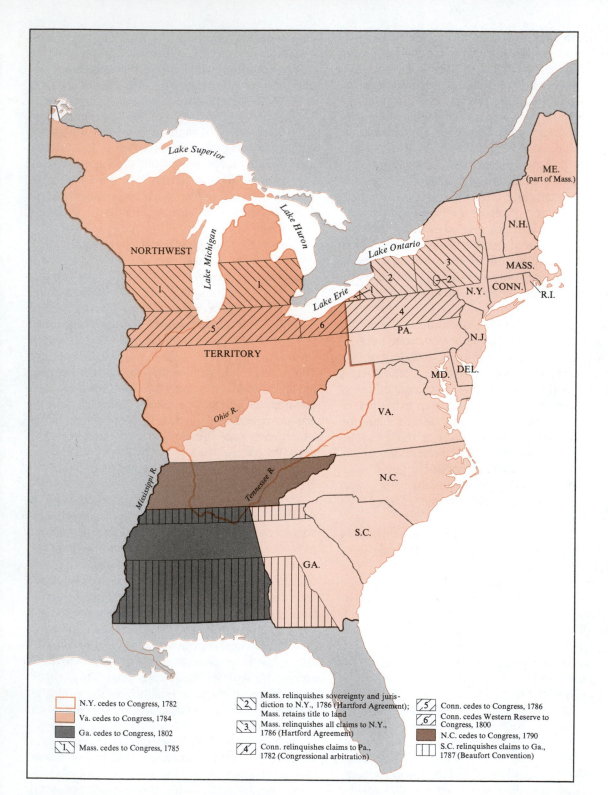

Western Land Claims and Cessions, 1782–1802

adequate thought to the distribution of power within the national government or to the relationship between the Confederation and the states. The Congress they created was simultaneously a legislative body and a collective executive, but it had no independent income and no authority to compel the states to accept its rulings. What is surprising, in other words, is not how poorly the Confederation functioned in the following years, but rather how much the government was able to accomplish.

Trials of the Confederation

During and after the war, the most persistent problem faced by the American governments, state and national, was finance. Because of a reluctance to

Financial Problems levy taxes, both Congress and the states tried to finance the war by printing currency. Even though

the money was backed by nothing but good faith, it circulated freely and without excessive depreciation during 1775 and most of 1776. But in late 1776, as the American army suffered major battlefield reverses, prices began to rise and inflation set in. The value of the currency rested on Americans' faith in their government, a faith that was sorely tested in the years that followed. Both Congress and the states attempted to control inflation, but in 1780 it took forty paper dollars to purchase one silver dollar. A year later, Continental currency was worthless.

Although many suffered from inflation, especially those on fixed incomes, some benefited from such economic conditions. Military contractors, large-scale farmers, and investors could make sizable profits. More risky, but potentially even more profitable, was privateering against enemy shipping. Privateering attracted venturesome sailors and wealthy merchants alike.

Accumulation of private wealth in the country, however, did not help Congress with its financial problems. In 1781, faced with the total collapse of the monetary system, the delegates undertook major reforms. After establishing a department of finance under the wealthy Philadelphia merchant

Robert Morris, they asked the states to amend the Articles of Confederation so that Congress could levy a duty on imported goods. Morris put national finances on a solid footing, but the customs duty was never adopted.

Congress also faced major diplomatic problems at the close of the war. Chief among them were issues involving the peace treaty itself. Article 4,

Weakness in Foreign Affairs and Commerce which promised the repayment of prewar debts (most of them owed by Americans to British merchants), and Article 5, which recommended that states allow loyalists to recover their confis-

cated property, aroused considerable opposition. States passed laws denying British subjects the right to sue for recovery of debts or property in American courts, and since most of the purchasers of the confiscated loyalist property were prominent patriots, state governments had no desire to enforce Article 5.

The failure of state and local governments to comply with Articles 4 and 5 gave Britain an excuse to maintain military posts on the Great Lakes long after it was supposed to withdraw its troops. Furthermore, the inability of Congress to convince the states to implement the treaty pointed up its lack of power. Concerned nationalists argued publicly that enforcement of the treaty, however unpopular, was a crucial test for the republic. "Will foreign nations be willing to undertake anything with us or for us," asked Alexander Hamilton, "when they find that the nature of our governments will allow no dependence to be placed on our engagements?"

The weakness of Congress was especially evident in the realm of trade because the Articles of Confederation specifically denied it the power to establish a national commercial policy. Immediately after the war, Britain, France, and Spain restricted American trade with their colonies. When Britain closed the West Indies to American goods and flooded the United States with British products, Congress watched helplessly. Although Americans reopened trade with northern European countries and started a profitable trade with China in 1784, neither substituted for access to closer and larger markets.

Congress also had difficulty in dealing with the

threat posed by Spain's presence on the southern and western borders of the United States. Determined to prevent the new nation's expansion, Spain in 1784 closed the Mississippi River to American navigation. It thus deprived the growing settlements west of the Appalachians of their major access route to the rest of the nation and the world. If Spain's policy were not reversed, westerners might have to accept Spanish sovereignty as the necessary price for survival. Congress opened negotiations with Spain in 1785 but could not win the necessary concessions on navigation.

Diplomatic problems of another sort confronted congressmen when they considered the status of the land on the western borders of the United States. In the Treaty of Paris (1783), Britain ceded all land east of the Mississippi (except for that held by Spain) to the United States. The Indian tribes, however, had made no such cession. To eliminate that problem, representatives signed treaties of questionable legality with Iroquois at Fort Stanwix, New York, in 1784 and with the Choctaws, Chickasaws, and Cherokees at Hopewell, South Carolina, in 1785 and 1786. When whites poured over the southern Appalachians, the Creek tribe—which had not agreed to the Hopewell treaties—declared war. Only in 1790, when the Creek chief Alexander McGillivray traveled to New York to negotiate a treaty, did the tribe finally come to terms with the United States.

Encroachment on Indian Lands

In 1786, the Iroquois Confederacy formally repudiated the Fort Stanwix treaty and threatened new attacks on frontier settlements, but both whites and Indians knew that the threat was an empty one. The flawed treaty was permitted to stand by default. At intervals during the remainder of the decade, the state of New York purchased large amounts of land from individual Iroquois tribes. By 1790, the once-proud Iroquois Confederacy was confined to a few scattered reservations. In the West, tribes like the Shawnees, Chippewas, Ottawas, and Potawatomis formed their own confederacy and demanded direct negotiations with the United States. Their aim was to present a united front, so as to avoid the piecemeal surrender of land by individual tribes.

Congress, though, ignored the western Indian confederacy and organized the Northwest Territory, bounded by the Mississippi River, the Great Lakes, and the Ohio River. Ordinances passed in 1784, 1785, and 1787 outlined the process through which the land could be sold to settlers and formal governments organized. To ensure orderly development, Congress in 1785 directed that the land be surveyed into townships 6 miles square, each divided into thirty-six sections of 640 acres (1 square mile). Revenue from the sale of the sixteenth section of each township was to be reserved for the support of public schools—the first instance of federal aid to education in American history. The minimum price per acre was set at $1, and the minimum sale was to be 640 acres. Congress was not especially concerned about helping the small farmer: the minimum outlay of $640 was beyond the reach of most Americans. The proceeds from the land sales were the first independent revenues available to the national government.

The most important ordinance was the third, passed in 1787. The Northwest Ordinance contained a bill of rights guaranteeing settlers in the territory freedom of religion and the right to a jury trial, prohibiting cruel and unusual punishments, and abolishing slavery. It also specified the process by which residents of the territory could eventually organize state governments and seek admission to the Union "on an equal footing with the original States." Early in the nation's history, therefore, Congress laid down a policy of admitting new states on the same basis as the old and assuring residents of the territories the same rights as citizens of the original states.

The Northwest Ordinance

In a sense, though, the ordinance was purely theoretical at the time it was passed. The Miamis, Shawnees, and Delawares refused to acknowledge American sovereignty and insisted on their right to the land. They opposed white settlement violently, attacking pioneers who ventured too far north of the Ohio River. In 1788, the Ohio Company, to which Congress had sold a large tract of land at reduced rates, established the town of Marietta at the juncture of the Ohio and Muskingum rivers. But the Indians prevented the company from extending settlement very far into the interior. After General Arthur St. Clair, the first governor of the Northwest Territory, failed to negotiate a meaningful treaty with the tribes in early 1789, it was apparent that the United States and the Miami-led western confederacy would clash.

Little Turtle, the war chief of the Miami Confederacy, defeated General Josiah Harmar (1790) and then St. Clair himself (1791) in major battles near the present border between Indiana and Ohio. More than six hundred of St. Clair's men were killed and scores more wounded; it was the whites' worst defeat in the entire history of the American frontier. In 1793, the Miami Confederacy declared that peace could be achieved only if the United States recognized the Ohio River as the boundary between white and Indian lands. But the government refused to relinquish its claim to the Northwest Territory. A new army under the command of General Anthony Wayne defeated the tribesmen in 1794 at the Battle of Fallen Timbers (near Toledo, Ohio). This victory made serious negotiations possible.

War in the Northwest

The Treaty of Greenville (1795) gave each side a portion of what it wanted. The United States gained the right to settle much of what was to become the state of Ohio, the tribes retaining only the northwest corner of the region. The Indians received the acknowledgment they had long sought: American recognition of their rights to the soil. At Greenville, the United States formally accepted the principle of Indian sovereignty, by virtue of residence, over all lands the tribes had not yet ceded. Never again would the United States government claim that it had acquired Indian territory solely through negotiation with a European or American country.

The problems the United States encountered in ensuring safe settlement of the Northwest Territory pointed up, once again, the basic weakness of the Confederation government. Not until a new constitution was adopted could the United States muster sufficient force to implement all the provisions of the Northwest Ordinance. Thus, although the ordinance is often viewed as one of the few major accomplishments of the Confederation Congress, it must be seen within a context of political impotence.

From Crisis to a Constitution

The most obvious deficiencies of the Articles of Confederation involved overseas trade and foreign affairs. Congress could not impose its will on the states to establish a uniform commercial policy or to ensure the enforcement of treaties. The problems involving trade were particularly serious. Less than a year after the war ended, the American economy slid into a depression. Exporters of staple crops and importers of manufactured goods were adversely affected by the postwar restrictions that European powers imposed on American commerce. Although recovery had begun by 1786, the war's effects proved impossible to erase entirely.

The war had wrought permanent change in the American economy. The near-total cessation of commerce in nonmilitary items during the war years proved a great stimulus to domestic manufacturing. Consequently, despite the influx of European goods after 1783, the postwar period witnessed the stirrings of American industrial development—for example, the first American textile mill began production in Pawtucket, Rhode Island, in 1793. Moreover, foreign trade patterns shifted from Europe and toward the West Indies. Foodstuffs shipped to the French and Dutch Caribbean islands became America's largest single export.

Economic Change

Recognizing the inability of the Confederation Congress to deal with commercial matters, Virginia invited the other states to a convention at Annapolis, Maryland, to discuss trade policy. Although eight states named representatives to the meeting in September 1786, only five delegations attended. Those present realized that they were too few in number to have any real impact on the political system. They issued a call for another convention, to be held in Philadelphia in nine months, "to devise such further provisions as shall . . . appear necessary to render the constitution of the federal government adequate to the exigencies of the Union." The other states did not respond immediately to the summons to another general meeting, but then Shays's Rebellion occurred.

The reaction to Shays's Rebellion hastened the movement toward comprehensive revision of the Articles of Confederation. In February 1787, after most of the states had already appointed delegates, the Confederation Congress belatedly endorsed the convention. In May, fifty-five men, representing all the states except Rhode Island, assembled in Philadelphia to begin their deliberations.

The vast majority of the delegates to the Constitutional Convention were men of property and substance. Among their number were merchants, planters, physicians, generals, governors, and especially lawyers. Most had been born in America, and many came from families that had arrived in the seventeenth century. In an era when only a tiny proportion of the population had any advanced education, more than half had attended college. A few had been educated in Britain, but most were graduates of American institutions. The youngest delegate was twenty-six, the oldest—Benjamin Franklin—eighty-one. Like George Washington, whom they elected chairman, most were in their middle years. Of the dozen men who did the bulk of the convention's work, James Madison of Virginia was the most important. He truly deserves the title Father of the Constitution.

Constitutional Convention

Madison was unique among the delegates in his systematic preparation for the Philadelphia meeting. Through Jefferson in Paris he bought more than two hundred books on history and government and carefully analyzed their accounts of past confederacies and republics. In April 1787, a month before the Constitutional Convention began, he summed up the results of his research in a lengthy paper, entitled "Vices of the Political System of the United States." After listing the eleven major flaws he perceived in the current structure of the government, Madison set forth the principle of checks and balances.

James Madison

The government, he believed, had to be constructed in such a way that it could not become tyrannical or fall wholly under the influence of a particular interest group. He regarded the large size of a potential national republic as an advantage in that respect. Rejecting the common assertion that republics had to be small to survive, Madison argued that a large, diverse republic was in fact to be preferred. Because the nation would include many different interest groups, no single interest group would be able to control the government. Political stability would result from compromises among the contending parties.

Madison's conception of national government was embodied in the so-called Virginia Plan, introduced on May 29 by his colleague Edmund Randolph. The plan provided for a two-house legislature—one house elected directly by the people and the other selected by the first, with proportional representation in both houses, an executive elected by Congress, a national judiciary, and congressional veto over state laws. The Virginia Plan gave Congress the broad power to legislate "in all cases to which the separate states are incompetent." Had it been adopted intact, it would have created a government in which national authority reigned unchallenged and state power was greatly diminished.

Virginia and New Jersey Plans

But the convention included many delegates who, while recognizing the need for change, believed that the Virginians had gone too far in the direction of national consolidation. The disaffected delegates united under the leadership of William Paterson. On June 15, Paterson presented an alternative scheme, the New Jersey Plan, calling for modifications in the Articles of Confederation rather than a complete overhaul of the government. Paterson proposed retaining the unicameral Confederation Congress but giving it new powers of taxation and trade regulation. Although the delegates rejected Paterson's narrow interpretation of their task, he and his allies won a number of major victories.

The delegates began their work by discussing the structure and functions of Congress. They readily agreed that the new national government should have a two-house (bicameral) legislature. But then they discovered that they differed widely in their answers to three key questions: Should representation in both houses of Congress be proportional to population? How was representation in either or both houses to be apportioned among the states?

And, finally, how were the members of the two houses to be elected?

The last issue was the easiest to resolve. In the words of John Dickinson, the delegates thought it "essential" that members of one branch of Congress be elected directly by the people and "expedient" that members of the other be chosen by the state legislatures. Since the legislatures had selected delegates to the Confederation Congress, they would expect a similar privilege in the new government.

Considerably more difficult was the matter of proportional representation. The delegates accepted without much debate the principle of proportional representation in the lower house. The nature of representation to the Senate, however, was another matter. Delegates from the smaller states argued for equal representation; those from the large states favored proportional representation. For weeks, the convention was deadlocked on the issue, neither side being able to obtain a majority. A committee appointed to work out a compromise recommended equal representation in the Senate, coupled with a proviso that all appropriation bills had to originate in the lower house. The dispute was finally resolved when the convention agreed that the two senators from each state could vote as individuals rather than as a unit.

Another critical question remained: how was representation in the lower house to be apportioned among the states? Delegates from states with large numbers of slaves wanted all people, black and white, to be counted equally; delegates from states with few slaves wanted only free people to be counted. The issue was resolved by using a formula developed by the Confederation Congress in 1783 to allocate financial assessments among the states: three-fifths of the slaves would be included in the population totals. (The formula reflected the delegates' judgment that slaves were less efficient producers of wealth than free people, not that they were 60 percent human and 40 percent property.) The three-fifths compromise was unanimously accepted by the convention.

Slavery and the Constitution

Although the words *slave* and *slavery* do not appear in the Constitution (the framers used euphemisms like "other persons"), direct and indirect protections for slavery were deeply embedded in the document. The three-fifths clause, for example, ensured not only that white southern voters would be represented in Congress out of all proportion to their numbers, but also that they would have a disproportionate influence in the selection of the president, since the number of each state's electoral votes was determined by the size of its congressional delegation. Congress was prevented from outlawing the slave trade for at least twenty years. Furthermore, by guaranteeing that the national government would help any states threatened with "domestic violence," the Constitution promised aid in putting down slave revolts.

Once agreement was reached on the problems of slavery and representation, the delegates resolved the other issues more easily. They agreed to enumerate the powers of Congress but to allow it to pass all laws "necessary and proper" to carry out its functions. Foreign policy was placed in the hands of the executive, who was also made the commander-in-chief of the armed forces. The idea of a legislative veto over state action was rejected, but an implied veto was included. Moreover, the Constitution, national laws, and treaties were made the supreme law of the land. Finally, the delegates established the electoral college and a four-year term for the chief executive, who could seek re-election.

Separation of Powers

The key to the Constitution was the distribution of political authority—separation of powers among the executive, legislative, and judicial branches of the national government, and division of powers between the states and the nation. The system of checks and balances would make it difficult for the government to become tyrannical. At the same time, though, the elaborate system would sometimes prevent the government from acting quickly and decisively. Furthermore, the line between state and federal powers was so ambiguously drawn that it would take a civil war to fully resolve the issue.

The convention held its last meeting on September 17, 1787. Of the forty-two delegates, only three

In July 1788, New York City's leaders celebrated their state's ratification of the Constitution at an elaborate banquet served in a pavilion erected for the occasion. Their hopes for an orderly government were symbolized by the orderly arrangement of the tables, separate but linked into a semicircle by the central structure displaying flags and banners. *The New-York Historical Society.*

refused to sign the Constitution. (Two of the three declined because of the lack of a bill of rights.) Though the delegates had accepted the Constitution, the question remained as to whether the states would ratify it.

Opposition and Ratification

The ratification clause of the Constitution provided for the new system to take effect once it was approved by special conventions in at least nine states. The delegates to each state convention were to be elected by the qualified voters. Thus the national Constitution, unlike the Articles of Confederation, would rest directly on popular authority.

As the states began to elect delegates to the special conventions, discussions of the proposed government grew more heated. Federalists, who supported the Constitution, and Antifederalists, who opposed it, wrote newspaper essays and pamphlets vigorously defending or attacking the convention's decisions. The extent of the debate was unprecedented.

The Antifederalist camp included those who emphasized the threat to the states embodied in the new national government and those who stressed the dangers to individuals posed by the lack of a bill of rights. All **Anti-** **federalists** Antifederalists saw the states as the chief protectors of individual rights and their weakening as the onset of arbitrary power. Fearing a too powerful central government, they rejected the Federalists' emphasis on the need for national leadership by a disinterested elite. Their arguments against the Constitution often consisted of lists of potential abuses of the national government's authority. The Antifederalists were the heirs of the Real Whig ideology of the late 1760s and early 1770s, which stressed the need for the people's constant vigilance to avert oppression.

Indeed, some of the Antifederalists were the very men who had originally promulgated those ideas; for example, Samuel Adams and Richard Henry Lee were both leaders of the opposition to the Constitution. Antifederalist ranks were also peopled by small farmers, who hoped to guard their property against excessive taxation, and by ambitious, upwardly mobile men, who knew that they would reap financial benefits from a less tightly controlled economic and political system that the Constitution promised to establish.

With each passing month, the Antifederalist attack focused more sharply on the Constitution's lack of a bill of rights. Even if the states were weakened by the new system, the Antifederalists believed, the people could still be protected from tyranny if their rights were specifically guaranteed. *Letters of a Federal Farmer,* perhaps the most widely read Antifederalist pamphlet, listed the rights that should be protected: freedom of the press and of religion, the right to trial by jury, and guarantees against unreasonable search warrants.

As the state conventions met to consider ratification, the lack of a bill of rights loomed larger and larger as a flaw in the new form of government. Four of the first five states to ratify did so unanimously, but serious disagreement then began to surface. Massachusetts ratified by a majority of only 19 votes out of 355 cast. In New Hampshire, the Federalists won by a majority of 57 to 47. When New Hampshire ratified, in June 1788, the requirement of nine states had been satisfied. But New York and Virginia had not yet voted, and everyone realized that the new Constitution could not succeed unless those key states accepted it.

Ratification of the Constitution

In Virginia, despite a valiant effort by the Antifederalist Patrick Henry, the pro-Constitution forces won 89 to 79. In New York, James Madison, John Jay, and Alexander Hamilton campaigned for ratification by publishing *The Federalist,* a political tract that explained the theory behind the Constitution and masterfully answered its critics. Their reasoned arguments, coupled with the promise that a bill of rights would be added to the Constitution, helped win the battle. On July 26, 1788, New York ratified the Constitution by the slim margin of 3 votes. The new government was a reality, even though the last state (Rhode Island, which had not participated in the convention) did not formally join the Union until 1790.

The experience of fighting a war and of struggling for survival as an independent nation in the 1780s had altered the political context of American life. Whereas at the outset of the war most politically aware Americans believed that "that government which governs best governs least," by the late 1780s many had changed their minds. These were the drafters and supporters of the Constitution, who won their point when the Constitution was adopted, however narrowly.

Leading Federalists and Antifederalists did share one key common characteristic: they were all white males. The era of the formation of the Union was also the age of the systematic formulation of American racist thought, and the two processes were intimately linked. One way to preserve the freedom of all whites was to ensure the continued subjection of all blacks, slave or free. Likewise, one way to preserve the unchallenged economic independence of white men was to ensure the economic and political dependence of white women. Independence had been fought for and won by many Americans—white, black, and red, male and female—but in the new republic only white males would hold political power.

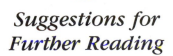

Suggestions for Further Reading

General

Richard Beeman et al., eds., *Beyond Confederation: Origins of the Constitution and American National Identity* (1987); Staughton Lynd, *Class Conflict, Slavery, and the United States Constitution: Ten Essays* (1967); Forrest McDonald, *Novus Ordo Seculorum: The Intellectual Origins of the Constitution* (1985); Forrest McDonald, *E Pluribus Unum: The Formation of the American Republic, 1776–1790* (1965); Edmund S. Morgan, *Inventing the People: The Rise of Popular Sover-*

eignty in England and America (1988); William and Mary Quarterly, 3rd ser., 44, No. 3 (July 1987), The Constitution of the United States; Gordon S. Wood, The Creation of the American Republic, 1776–1787 (1969).

Continental Congress and Articles of Confederation

H. James Henderson, Party Politics in the Continental Congress (1974); Merrill Jensen, The Articles of Confederation, 2nd ed. (1959); Merrill Jensen, The New Nation: A History of the United States During the Confederation, 1781–1789 (1950); Jerrilyn G. Marston, King and Congress: The Transfer of Political Legitimacy, 1774–1776 (1987); Jack N. Rakove, The Beginnings of National Politics: An Interpretive History of the Continental Congress (1979).

State Politics

Willi Paul Adams, The First American Constitutions: Republican Ideology and the Making of the State Constitutions in the Revolutionary Era (1980); Ronald Hoffman and Peter Albert, eds., Sovereign States in an Age of Uncertainty (1981); Jackson Turner Main, Political Parties Before the Constitution (1973); Jackson Turner Main, The Sovereign States, 1775–1783 (1973); J. R. Pole, Political Representation in England and the Origins of the American Republic (1966); David P. Szatmary, Shays' Rebellion: The Making of an Agrarian Insurrection (1980).

The Constitution

Charles A. Beard, An Economic Interpretation of the Constitution of the United States (1913); Forrest McDonald, We the People: The Economic Origins of the Constitution (1958); Jackson Turner Main, The Anti-Federalists: Critics of the Constitution, 1781–1788 (1961); Frederick W. Marks III, Independence on Trial: Foreign Affairs and the Making of the Constitution (1973); Clinton Rossiter, 1787: The Grand Convention (1973); Robert A. Rutland, The Ordeal of the Constitution: The Antifederalists and the Ratification Struggle of 1787–88 (1966).

Education and Culture

Lawrence A. Cremin, American Education: The National Experience, 1783–1876 (1981); Joseph M. Ellis, After the Revolution: Profiles of Early American Culture (1979); Russell B. Nye, The Cultural Life of the New Nation: 1776–1803 (1960); Kenneth Silverman, A Cultural History of the American Revolution (1976).

Women

Charles Akers, Abigail Adams: An American Woman (1980); Linda K. Kerber, Women of the Republic: Intellect and Ideology in Revolutionary America (1980); Mary Beth Norton, Liberty's Daughters: The Revolutionary Experience of American Women, 1750–1800 (1980); Lynn Withey, Dearest Friend: A Life of Abigail Adams (1980).

Blacks and Slavery

Ira Berlin and Ronald Hoffman, eds., Slavery and Freedom in the Age of the American Revolution (1983); David Brion Davis, The Problem of Slavery in the Age of Revolution, 1770–1823 (1975); Carol V. R. George, Segregated Sabbaths: Richard Allen and the Emergence of Independent Black Churches, 1760–1840 (1973); Winthrop Jordan, White over Black: American Attitudes Toward the Negro, 1550–1812 (1968); Gary Nash, Forging Freedom: The Formation of Philadelphia's Black Community, 1720–1840 (1988); Donald L. Robinson, Slavery in the Structure of American Politics, 1765–1820 (1971); Arthur Zilversmit, The First Emancipation: The Abolition of Slavery in the North (1967).

Indians

Harvey L. Carter, The Life and Times of Little Turtle (1987); Dorothy Jones, License for Empire: Colonialism by Treaty in Early America (1982); Bernard Sheehan, Seeds of Extinction: Jeffersonian Philanthropy and the American Indian (1973); Anthony F. C. Wallace, The Death and Rebirth of the Seneca (1969).

Abigail Adams was furious. "I am at a loss to know how the people who were formerly so much alive to the usurpation of one Nation can crouch so tamely to a much more dangerous and dareing one," she wrote to her sister in January 1798. France, she asserted, "aims not only at our independance and libe[r]ty, but a total annihilation of the Christian Religion." Yet every state except Connecticut had elected French sympathizers to Congress.

Abigail Adams's anger stemmed from the way in which American opinion had divided over the French Revolution, which had begun in 1789. She and her husband, along with many others, viewed the violent tactics of the French revolutionaries with deep alarm and saw the former ally of the United States as the major threat to freedom in the world, even though other Americans continued to sympathize with the French. "There is no end to their audaciousness," she informed her sister in the spring of 1798; "French emissaries are in every corner of the union sowing and spreading their Sedition."

Opinionated and fiercely loyal to her husband, John, elected president of the United States in 1796, Abigail Adams found herself in the middle of the first truly heated partisan battle in the new republic. She knew her husband had devoted his life to the nation's welfare. What then could be the source of the bitter invective directed at him by his opponents, the political faction now called Republicans? For her and her husband, there was only one answer: the criticism must have been instigated by France, whose revolutionary government saw the Adams administration as its enemy.

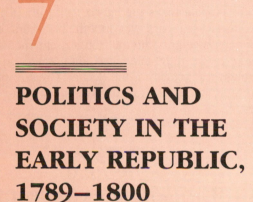

7

POLITICS AND SOCIETY IN THE EARLY REPUBLIC, 1789–1800

The failure of Americans' quest for unity and unqualified independence during the 1790s was nowhere more evident than in the political battles that absorbed Abigail Adams's attention. The fight over the Constitution was the precursor of an even wider division over the major political, economic, and diplomatic questions confronting the young republic. To make matters worse, Americans had not anticipated the political disagreements that would mark the decade. Believing that the Constitution would resolve the problems that had arisen during the Confederation period, they expected the new government to rule by consensus. They could not understand or fully accept the division of America's political leaders into two factions—not yet political parties—known as Federalists and Republicans.

Attaining prosperity and expanding were not easy tasks either. The United States economy depended on the export trade. When warfare between England and France resumed in 1793, Americans found their commerce disrupted once again. Moreover, the strength of the Miami Confederacy blocked the westward expansion of white settlement north of the Ohio River until after the Treaty of Greenville in 1795. South of the Ohio, settlements were established west of the mountains as early as the 1770s, but the geographical barrier of the Appalachians tended to isolate them from the eastern seaboard. Not until the first years of the nineteenth century did the frontier settlements become more fully integrated into American life through the vehicle of the Second Great Awakening, a religious revival that swept both east and west.

Building a Workable Government

In 1788, Americans celebrated the ratification of the Constitution with a series of parades, held in many cities on the Fourth of July. The processions were carefully planned to symbolize the unity of the new nation and to recall its history to the minds of the watching throngs. Like prerevolutionary protest meetings, the parades served as political educators for literate and illiterate Americans alike. Men and women who could not read learned about the significance of the new Constitution in the life of the nation. They were also instructed about political leaders' hopes for industry and frugality on the part of a virtuous American public.

The nationalistic spirit expressed in the ratification processions carried over into the first session of Congress. In the congressional elections held late in 1788, only a few Antifederalists ran for office, and even fewer were elected. Thus the First Congress consisted chiefly of men

First Congress

who supported a strong national government. Since the Constitution had deliberately left many key issues undecided, the nationalists' domination of Congress meant that their views on those points quickly prevailed.

Congress faced four immediate tasks when it convened in April 1789: raising revenue to support the new government, responding to the state ratification conventions' call for the addition of a bill of rights to the Constitution, setting up executive departments, and organizing the federal judiciary. The last task was especially important. The Constitution established a Supreme Court but left it to Congress to decide whether to have other federal courts as well.

James Madison, who had been elected to the House of Representatives, soon became as influential in Congress as he had been at the Constitutional Convention. Only a few months into the first session, he persuaded Congress to impose a 5-percent tariff on certain imported goods. Thus, the First Congress quickly achieved what the Confederation Congress never had: an effective national tax law. The new government would have problems, but lack of revenue in its first years was not one of them.

Madison also took the lead on the issue of constitutional amendments, introducing nineteen proposed amendments, of which Congress accepted twelve and the states ten. The two not ratified by the states dealt with the number of congressmen and their salaries. The other ten amendments officially became part of the Constitution on December 15, 1791. Not for many years, though, did they become known collectively as the Bill of Rights.

Bill of Rights

The First Amendment specifically prohibited Congress from passing any law restricting the people's right to freedom of religion, speech, press, peaceable assembly, or petition. The next two arose directly from the former colonists' fear of standing armies as a threat to freedom. The Second Amendment guaranteed the people's right "to keep and bear arms" because of the need for a "well regulated Militia." The Third Amendment defined the circumstances in which troops could be quartered in private homes. The next five pertained to judicial procedures. The Fourth Amendment prohibited

1789	George Washington inaugurated Judiciary Act of 1789 French Revolution begins	**1795**	Jay Treaty
1790	Alexander Hamilton's *Report on Public Credit*	**1796**	First contested presidential election: John Adams elected president, Thomas Jefferson vice president
1791	First ten amendments (Bill of Rights) ratified	**1798**	XYZ affair Alien and Sedition Acts Virginia and Kentucky resolutions
1793	France declares war on Britain, Spain, and Holland Neutrality Proclamation Democratic-Republican societies founded	**1798–99**	Quasi-War with France
		1800	Franco-American Convention Jefferson elected president Second Great Awakening begins Gabriel's Rebellion
1794	Whiskey Rebellion		

"unreasonable searches and seizures"; the Fifth and Sixth established the rights of accused persons; the Seventh specified the conditions for jury trials in civil, as opposed to criminal, cases; and the Eighth forbade "cruel and unusual punishments." Finally, the Ninth and Tenth Amendments reserved to the people and the states other unspecified rights and powers. In short, the authors of the amendments made clear that in listing some rights explicitly they did not mean to preclude the exercise of others.

While debating the proposed amendments, Congress also concerned itself with the organization of the executive branch. It readily agreed to continue the three administrative departments established under the Articles of Confederation: War, Foreign Affairs (renamed State), and Treasury. Congress also instituted two lesser posts: the attorney general—the nation's official lawyer—and the postmaster general. The only serious controversy arose over whether the president alone could dismiss officials whom he had originally appointed with the consent of the Senate. After some debate, the House and Senate agreed that he had such authority. Thus was established the important principle that the heads of the executive departments are responsible to the president.

Aside from the constitutional amendments, the most far-reaching piece of legislation enacted by the First Congress was the Judiciary Act of 1789. That act provided for the Supreme Court to have six members: a chief justice and five associate justices.

Judiciary Act of 1789

It also defined the jurisdiction of the federal judiciary and established thirteen district courts and three circuit courts of appeal. The act's most important provision may have been Section 25, which allowed appeals from state courts to the federal court system when certain types of constitutional issues were raised. This section was intended to implement Article VI of the Constitution, which stated that federal laws and treaties were to be considered "the supreme Law of the Land." If Article VI was to be enforced uniformly, the national judiciary clearly had to be able to overturn state court decisions involving the Constitution, federal laws, or treaties.

During the first decade of its existence, the Supreme Court handled few cases of any importance.

But in a significant 1796 decision, *Ware* v. *Hylton,* the Court—acting on the basis of Section 25 of the Judiciary Act of 1789—for the first time declared a state law unconstitutional. That same year, it also reviewed the constitutionality of an act of Congress, upholding its validity in the case of *Hylton* v. *U.S.* The most important case of the decade, *Chisholm* v. *Georgia* (1793), established that states could be freely sued in federal courts by citizens of other states. This decision, unpopular with the state governments, was overruled five years later by the Eleventh Amendment to the Constitution.

Domestic Policy Under Washington and Hamilton

George Washington did not seek the presidency. When in 1783 he returned to Mount Vernon, his plantation on the Potomac River, he was eager for

Election of the First President
the peaceful life of a Virginia planter. Yet his fellow countrymen never regarded Washington as just another private citizen. Americans agreed that only George Washington had sufficient prestige to serve as the republic's first president. The unanimous vote of the electoral college was just a formality.

During his first months in office, Washington acted cautiously, knowing that whatever he did would set precedents for the future. For example, he concluded that he should exercise his veto power over congressional legislation very sparingly—only, indeed, if he was convinced that a bill was unconstitutional. His first major task as president was to choose the men who would head the executive departments. For the War Department, he selected an old comrade-in-arms, Henry Knox. His choice for the State Department was his fellow Virginian Thomas Jefferson, who had just returned to the United States from his post as minister to France. For the crucial position of secretary of the treasury, the president chose the brilliant, intensely ambitious Alexander Hamilton.

Two traits distinguished Hamilton from most of

John Trumbull painted "Washington at Verplanck's Point" in the spring of 1790, when George Washington was completing his first year as president. Washington's stepgrandson later wrote that this portrait was "the most perfect extant" of its subject, whom Trumbull depicted wearing a Continental Army uniform. *The Henry Francis du Pont Winterthur Museum.*

his contemporaries. First, he displayed an undivided, unquestioning loyalty to the nation as a

Alexander Hamilton
whole. As a West Indian who had lived on the mainland only briefly before the war, Hamilton had no ties to an individual state. He showed little sympathy for, or understanding of, demands for local autonomy. Thus the aim of his fiscal policies was always the consolidation of power at the national level. Further, he never feared the exercise of centralized executive authority, as did his older counterparts who had clashed repeatedly with colonial governors.

Second, he regarded his fellow human beings

Chapter 7: Politics and Society in the Early Republic, 1789–1800 with cynicism. Perhaps because of his own poverty in his early years and his overriding ambition, Hamilton believed people to be motivated primarily, if not entirely, by self-interest—particularly economic self-interest. He placed absolutely no reliance on people's capacity for virtuous and self-sacrificing behavior. That outlook set him apart from those republicans who foresaw a rosy future, in which public-spirited citizens would pursue the common good rather than their own private advantage.

In 1789, Congress ordered the new secretary of the treasury to study the state of the public debt and to submit recommendations for supporting the government's credit. Hamilton **National Debt** discovered that the country's remaining war debts fell into three categories: those owed by the national government to foreign governments and investors, mostly to France (about $11 million); those owed by the national government to merchants, former soldiers, holders of revolutionary bonds, and the like (about $27 million); and, finally, similar debts owed by state governments (roughly estimated at $25 million). With respect to the national debt, there was little disagreement: politically aware Americans recognized that if their new government was to succeed it would have to repay at full face value the financial obligations the nation had incurred while winning independence.

The state debts were quite another matter. Some states—notably Virginia, Maryland, North Carolina, and Georgia—had already paid off most of their war debts. They would oppose the national government's assumption of responsibility for other states' debts, since their citizens would be taxed to pay such obligations. Massachusetts, Connecticut, and South Carolina, on the other hand, still had sizable unpaid debts and would welcome a system of national assumption. The possible assumption of state debts also had political implications. Consolidation of the debt in the hands of the national government would help to concentrate economic and political power at the national level.

Hamilton's first *Report on Public Credit*, sent to Congress in January 1790, reflected both his national loyalty and his cynicism. He proposed that

Hamilton's First *Report on Public Credit* Congress assume outstanding state debts, combine them with national obligations, and issue new securities covering both principal and accumulated unpaid interest. Current holders of state or national debt certificates would have the option of taking a portion of their payment in western lands. Hamilton's aims were clear: he wanted to expand the financial reach of the United States government and reduce the economic power of the states. He also wanted to ensure that the holders of public securities—many of them wealthy merchants and speculators—would have a significant financial stake in the survival of the national government.

Hamilton's plan stimulated lively debate in Congress. The opposition coalesced around his former ally James Madison. Well aware that speculators had purchased large quantities of debt certificates at a small fraction of their face value, Madison proposed that the original holders of the debt also be compensated by the government. Madison's plan, though fairer than Hamilton's—because it would have directly repaid those people who had actually supplied the revolutionary governments with goods or services—would have been difficult, perhaps impossible, to administer. The House of Representatives rejected it.

At first, the House also rejected the assumption of state debts. Since the Senate, by contrast, had adopted Hamilton's plan largely intact, a series of compromises followed. Hamilton agreed to some changes in the assumption plan that would benefit Virginia in particular. The assumption bill also became linked in a complex way to another controversial issue: the location of the permanent national capital. Both northerners and southerners wanted the capital in their region. The traditional story that Hamilton and Madison agreed over Jefferson's dinner table to exchange assumption of state debts for a southern site is not supported by the surviving evidence, but a political deal was undoubtedly struck. The Potomac River was designated as the site for the capital. Simultaneously, the four congressmen from Maryland and Virginia whose districts contained the most likely locations for the new city switched from opposition to support for assumption. The first part of Hamilton's financial program became law in August 1790.

Four months later, Hamilton submitted to Congress a second report on public credit, recommending the chartering of a national bank. **Hamilton modeled his bank on the Bank of England.** The Bank of the United States was to be capitalized at $10 million, of which only $2 million would come from public funds. Private investors would supply the rest. The bank's charter was to run for twenty years, and one-fifth of its directors were to be named by the government. Its bank notes would circulate as the nation's currency; it would also act as the collecting and disbursing agent for the Treasury and lend money to the government. Most political leaders recognized that such an institution would benefit the country. But there was another issue: did the Constitution give Congress the power to establish such a bank?

First Bank of the United States

James Madison, for one, answered that question with a resounding no. He pointed out that the delegates at the Constitutional Convention had specifically rejected a clause authorizing Congress to issue corporate charters. Consequently, he argued, that power could not be inferred from other parts of the Constitution.

Disturbed by Madison's contention, Washington decided to request other opinions before signing the bill. Edmund Randolph, the attorney general, and Thomas Jefferson, the secretary of state, agreed with Madison that the bank was unconstitutional. Jefferson referred to Article I, Section 8, of the Constitution, which gave Congress the power "to make all Laws which shall be necessary and proper for carrying into Execution the foregoing Powers." The key word, Jefferson argued, was "necessary": Congress could do what was needed, but not what was merely desirable, without specific constitutional authorization. Thus Jefferson formulated the strict-constructionist interpretation of the Constitution.

Washington asked Hamilton to reply to these negative assessments of his proposal. Hamilton's *Defense of the Constitutionality of the Bank,* presented to Washington in February 1791, was a brilliant exposition of what has become known as the broad-constructionist view of the Constitution. Hamilton argued forcefully that Congress could choose any means not specifically prohibited by the Constitution to achieve a constitutional end. In short, if the end was constitutional and the means was not unconstitutional, then the means was also constitutional. Washington was convinced and signed the bill.

In December 1791, Hamilton presented to Congress his *Report on Manufactures,* the third and last of his prescriptions for the American economy. In it, he outlined an ambitious plan for encouraging and protecting the country's infant industries, such as shoemaking and textile manufacturing. Hamilton urged Congress to promote the immigration of technicians and laborers, enact protective tariffs, and support industrial development. Most congressmen, being convinced that America's future was agrarian, rejected Hamilton's report.

That same year, Congress did accept another part of Hamilton's financial program, **an excise tax on whiskey.** Congressmen both recognized the need for additional government revenues and hoped to reduce the national consumption of distilled spirits. The new tax most directly affected western farmers, who sold their grain crops in the form of distilled spirits as a means of avoiding the high costs of transporting wagonloads of bulky corn over the mountains.

Whiskey Rebellion

News of the excise law set off protests in frontier areas of Pennsylvania. But matters did not come to a head until July 1794, when western Pennsylvania farmers resisted a federal marshal and a tax collector who were trying to enforce the law. About seven thousand rebels convened on August 1 to plot the destruction of Pittsburgh but decided not to face the heavy guns of the fort guarding the town. Unrest nevertheless continued for months on the frontiers of Pennsylvania, Maryland, and Virginia. Crowds of men drafted petitions protesting the excise, raised liberty poles (in deliberate imitation of the 1760s), and occasionally harassed tax collectors. But the Whiskey Rebellion remained largely leaderless and unorganized. Washington, determined to prevent another Shays's Rebellion, ordered the insurgents to disperse by September 1

Leisure in America, **1800**

SIMPLE PLEASURES

In almost all early American societies, the tasks of daily life demanded great investments of energy and time. Struggles for food, shelter, personal security, or political stability necessarily took precedence over frivolous pursuits. Nevertheless, the need to balance work with play is a human trait, and leisure had its place in even the most rigorous societies.

In Indian communities, ritual provided opportunities for recreation. In 1736, a German artist, Philip Georg Friedrich von Reck, painted several watercolors of the Yuchi, a tribe that occupied the coastal regions of South Carolina and Georgia, including this festival scene. Indians in the southeastern colonies were typically agriculturalists; their largest ceremonies usually coincided with the late-summer harvest and incorporated singing, dancing, the lighting of sacred fires, the creation of new clothes and household items, and the destruction of last year's goods. Although these thanksgiving rituals certainly served a religious purpose, they also afforded participants a well-earned physical and emotional release.

Previous page: Philip Georg Friedrich von Reck, *Indian Festival,* 1736. Right: Cutwork valentine (watercolor and ink on paper), 1753. Below: Corncob doll, probably eighteenth century.

Colonial children, like their more modern counterparts, enjoyed playing with dolls, though eighteenth-century toys tended to be made simply, from available materials. Indians probably taught the colonists how to make little corncob figures, using wrapped or woven cornhusks for head, limbs, clothes, and doll-sized accessories.

Not surprisingly, romance, a perennial leisure-time activity, flourished in the colonies. The valentine above is thought to have been one of the first made in America, given to Elizabeth Sandwith, a Philadelphia Quaker, in 1753. Not only did Elizabeth's industrious suitor skillfully wield scissors to snip this intricate design from painted paper, he filled the valentine's interior scallops and arcs with lines of verse dedicated to her. (Elizabeth must have been pleased but not entirely persuaded; she married someone else eight years later.)

Families with money enjoyed portraying themselves surrounded by the pleasures of a European-style culture. For instance, the portraits of self-possessed young ladies often included handsome harps or pianofortes. The pianoforte was a relatively new invention, and some mechanical difficulties—for instance, the ease with which the strings and hammers might break—had yet to be resolved; nevertheless, pianofortes were fairly common items in well-to-do American homes by the end of the century.

Elaborate needlework pictures, in themselves a leisure-time pursuit, also hint at the degree of elegance and luxury some wealthy colonists aspired to. The lush example below was stitched by a thirty-year-old Salem, Massachusetts, woman. Though wonderfully detailed, its idyllic depiction may be more a reflection of the popular pictorial motifs of the period than a faithful representation of a garden party's ambience.

Above: Philippe Abraham Peticolas, *Musical Ladies* **(watercolor-on-ivory miniature), 1798. Below: Needlework picture, stitched by Love Rawlins, ca. 1740**

A social scene of a more modest character appears on the painted pie plate from Pennsylvania, shown left. The charm of the plate's craftsmanship reminds us, too, of the pleasures that baking and small domestic decorations must have afforded some eighteenth-century women.

Finally, contemporary depictions of slaves help prove that men and women create diversion in the midst of severe repression, that fun and relaxation are essential to human survival. From necessity, African-Americans invented simple entertainments. Juba dances could be performed without the use of any musical instruments; singing, foot tapping, hand clapping, and body slapping sometimes provided the only rhythmic accompaniment. Slave dances contrasted markedly with the slow steps practiced at plantation cotillions, and white observers often admired the dancers' remarkable ability and vitality.

Above: Pie plate, 1786. Below: Artist unknown, *The Old Plantation*, ca. 1790–1800.

and summoned nearly thirteen thousand militiamen. By the time the troops arrived, the disturbances were over.

The chief importance of the Whiskey Rebellion was the message it forcefully conveyed to the American public. The national government, Washington had demonstrated, would not allow violent organized resistance to its laws. In the new republic, change would be effected peacefully, by legal means.

By 1794, a group of Americans were already beginning to seek change systematically within the confines of electoral politics, even though traditional political theory regarded organized opposition—especially in a republic—as illegitimate. The leaders of the opposition, Jefferson and Madison, saw themselves as the true heirs of the Revolution. To emphasize their point, they and their followers in Congress began calling themselves Republicans. Hamilton and his supporters claimed to be the rightful interpreters of the Constitution and took the name Federalists. Each group contended that the other was a faction bent upon subversion. (By traditional definition, a faction was opposed to the public good.)

Partisan Politics and Foreign Policy

The first years under the Constitution were blessed by international peace. Eventually, however, the French Revolution, which began in 1789, brought about the resumption of hostilities between France, America's wartime ally, and Great Britain, America's most important trading partner.

At first, Americans welcomed the news that France was turning toward republicanism. But by the early 1790s, the reports from France were disquieting. Outbreaks of violence continued; ministries succeeded each other with bewildering rapidity; and executions were commonplace. The king himself was beheaded in early 1793. Although many Americans, including Jefferson and Madison, retained their sympathy for the French revolutionaries, others began to view France as a prime example of the perversion of republicanism. As might be expected, Hamilton fell into the latter group.

At that juncture, France declared war on Britain, Spain, and Holland. The Americans thus faced a dilemma. The 1778 Treaty of Alliance with France bound them to that nation "forever," and a mutual commitment to republicanism created ideological bonds. Yet the United States was connected to Great Britain as well. Aside from sharing a common history and language, America and England were economic partners. Indeed, since the nation's financial system depended heavily on import tariffs as a source of revenue and America's imports came primarily from Britain, the economic health of the United States required uninterrupted trade with the former mother country.

The political and diplomatic climate was further complicated in April 1793, when Citizen Edmond Genêt, a representative of the French government,

Citizen Genêt

landed in Charleston. As Genêt made his leisurely way northward to New York City, he was wildly cheered and lavishly entertained at every stop. En route, he recruited Americans for expeditions against British and Spanish possessions in the Western Hemisphere and distributed privateering commissions with a generous hand. Genêt's arrival raised a series of key questions for President Washington. Should he receive Genêt, thus officially recognizing the French revolutionary government? Should he acknowledge an obligation to aid France under the terms of the 1778 Treaty of Alliance? Or should he proclaim American neutrality in the conflict?

For once, Hamilton and Jefferson saw eye to eye. Both told Washington that the United States could not afford to ally itself firmly with either side. Washington agreed. He received Genêt officially but also issued a proclamation informing the world that the United States would adopt "a conduct friendly and impartial toward the belligerent powers." However, the domestic divisions Genêt helped to widen were perpetuated by clubs called Democratic-Republican societies.

Americans sympathetic to France formed more than forty of these Democratic-Republican societies between 1793 and 1800. Their members saw themselves as heirs of the Sons of Liberty, seeking the same goal as their predecessors: protection of the people's liberties against encroachments by corrupt and evil rulers. To that end, they publicly protested government policies and warned the people of impending tyranny. Like the Sons of Liberty, the Democratic-Republican societies were composed chiefly of artisans and craftsmen of various kinds, although professionals, farmers, and merchants also joined.

Democratic-Republican Societies

The rapid growth of such groups, outspoken in their criticism of the Washington administration, deeply disturbed Hamilton and eventually Washington himself. Newspapers sympathetic to the Federalists charged that the societies were subversive agents of a foreign power. The climax of the attack came in the fall of 1794, when Washington accused the societies of having fomented the Whiskey Rebellion.

In retrospect, Washington's and Hamilton's reaction to the Democratic-Republican societies seems hysterical and overwrought. But it must be kept in mind that the Democratic-Republican societies were the first formally organized political dissenters in the United States. As such, they aroused the fear and suspicion of elected officials, who had not yet accepted the idea that one component of a free government was an organized loyal opposition.

That same year, George Washington decided to send Chief Justice John Jay to England to try to reach agreement on four major unresolved questions affecting Anglo-American affairs. The first point at issue was recent British seizures of American merchant ships trading in the French West Indies. The United States wanted to establish the principle of freedom of the seas and to assert its right, as a neutral nation, to trade freely with both sides. Second, Great Britain had not yet carried out its promise, made in the Treaty of Paris (1783), to evacuate its posts in the American Northwest. Third and fourth, the Americans hoped for a commercial treaty and sought compensation for the slaves who had left with the British army at the end of the war.

Jay Treaty

The negotiations in London proved difficult, since Jay had little to offer Britain in exchange for the concessions he wanted. In the end, Britain did agree to evacuate the western forts and ease the restrictions on American trade to England and the West Indies. No compensation for lost slaves was agreed to, but Jay accepted a provision establishing an arbitration commission to deal with the matter of prewar debts owed to British creditors. A similar commission was to handle the question of compensation for the seizures of American merchant ships. Under the circumstances, Jay did remarkably well: the treaty averted war with England. Nevertheless, most Americans, including the president, were dissatisfied with at least some parts of the treaty.

At first, potential opposition was blunted because the Senate debated and ratified the treaty in secret. Not until after it was formally approved on June 24, 1795, was the public informed of its provisions. The Democratic-Republican societies led protests against the treaty. Once President Washington signed the treaty, though, there seemed to be little the Republicans could do to prevent it from taking effect. Just one opportunity remained: Congress had to appropriate funds to carry out the treaty provisions.

When the House took up the money issue in March 1796, opponents of the treaty tried to prevent approval of the appropriations. They called on Washington to submit to the House all documents pertinent to the negotiations. In successfully resisting the House request, Washington established the doctrine of executive privilege—that is, the power of the president to withhold information from Congress if he believes circumstances warrant doing so. At first, the treaty's opponents appeared to be in the majority. But the desire of frontier residents to have British posts evacuated and of merchants to trade with the British Empire weakened the opposition. Finally, Federalist senators threatened to reject the treaty that Thomas Pinckney of South Carolina had negotiated with Spain unless the funds for the Jay Treaty were approved. Since Pinckney's Treaty had secured American navigation rights on the Mississippi, it was popular with southerners and westerners, for it would be an economic boost to their regions. For all these reasons the House approved the necessary funds by a vote of 51 to 48.

Analysis of the vote reveals both the regional nature of the division and the growing cohesion of the Republican and Federalist factions in Congress.

Republicans and Federalists Forty-four Federalists and seven Republicans voted in favor of the appropriations and forty-five Republicans and three Federalists voted against them. Southerners cast most of the votes against the bill. Except for two South Carolina Federalists, the bill's supporters came from New England and the middle states.

The small number of defectors revealed a new force at work in American politics: partisanship. Voting statistics from the first four Congresses show the ever-increasing tendency of members of the House of Representatives to vote as coherent groups, rather than as individuals. If factional loyalty is defined as voting together at least two-thirds of the time on national issues, the percentage of nonaligned congressmen dropped from 42 percent in 1790 to just 7 percent in 1796.

The growing division cannot be accurately explained in the terms used by Jefferson and Madison (aristocrats versus the people) or by Hamilton and Washington (true patriots versus subversive rabble). Nor do simple economic differences between agrarian and commercial interests provide the answer, since more than 90 percent of Americans in the 1790s lived in rural areas.

Yet certain distinctions can be made. Republicans, who were especially prominent in the southern and middle states, tended to be self-assured, confident, and optimistic about both politics and the economy. They did not fear instability and sought to widen the people's participation in government. Included in the Republican ranks were southern planters and small farmers, urban artisans, and non-English ethnic groups, especially Irish, Scots, and Germans.

By contrast, Federalists, who were concentrated in New England, were insecure, uncertain of the future. They stressed the need for order, authority, and regularity in the political world. Unlike Republicans, they had no grassroots political organization and put little emphasis on involving ordinary people in government. The nation was, in Federalist eyes, perpetually threatened by potential enemies, both internal and external, and best protected by a continuing alliance with Great Britain. The Federalists drew support from northern merchants and commercially oriented farmers, subsistence farmers in New England, and people of English stock.

The presence of the two organized groups—though not yet parties in the modern sense—made the presidential election of 1796 the first that was seriously contested. George Wash-

Washington's Farewell Address ington, tired of the criticism to which he had been subjected, decided to retire from office. (Presidents had not yet been limited to two terms by constitutional amendment.) In September, Washington published his famous Farewell Address, most of which was written by Hamilton. Washington outlined two principles that guided American foreign policy at least until the late 1940s: maintain commercial but not political ties with other nations and enter no permanent alliances. He also attacked the legitimacy of the Republican opposition.

To succeed Washington, the Federalists in Congress put forward Vice President John Adams, with the diplomat Thomas Pinckney of South Carolina as his vice-presidential running

Election of 1796 mate. Congressional Republicans caucused and chose Thomas Jefferson as their presidential candidate; the lawyer, Revolutionary War veteran, and active Republican politician Aaron Burr of New York agreed to run for vice president.

That the election was contested did not mean that its outcome was decided by the people. Under the Constitution, electors—not the people—voted. Though in most cases the people chose their electors, in 1796 more than 40 percent of the members of the electoral college were chosen by state legislatures. As the Constitution required members of the electoral college to vote for two persons without specifying the office, the system tended to work against the new parties. There was no way an elector could explicitly support one person for president and another for vice president. The man with the highest total became president; the second highest, vice president. Thus Adams, the Federalist with 71 votes, became the new president and Jefferson, the Republican with 68 votes, became vice president.

John Adams and Political Dissent

John Adams took over the presidency peculiarly blind to the partisan developments of the previous four years. As president, he never abandoned an outdated notion discarded by George Washington as early as 1794: that the president should be above politics, an independent and dignified figure who did not seek petty factional advantage. Thus Adams kept Washington's cabinet intact, despite its key members' allegiance to his chief rival, Alexander Hamilton. Adams often adopted a passive posture, letting others (usually Hamilton) take the lead, when he should have acted decisively. When Adams's term ended, the Federalists were severely divided and the Republicans had won the presidency. But Adams's detachment from Hamilton's maneuverings enabled him to weather the greatest international crisis the republic had yet faced: the so-called Quasi-War with France.

The Jay Treaty improved America's relationship with England, but it provoked retaliation from France. When French vessels began seizing American ships carrying British goods, Adams appointed three special commissioners to try to reach a settlement with France: Elbridge Gerry of Massachusetts, John Marshall of Virginia, and Charles Cotesworth Pinckney of South Carolina. At the same time, Congress increased military spending. The negotiations never materialized, however, because French agents demanded a bribe of $250,000 before talks could begin. The Americans retorted, "No, no; not a sixpence." When Adams received word of the incident in March 1798, he informed Congress of the impasse and recommended increased appropriations for defense.

Convinced that Adams had deliberately sabotaged the negotiations, congressional Republicans insisted that the dispatches be turned over to Congress. Aware that releasing **XYZ Affair** the reports would work to his advantage, Adams complied. He withheld only the names of the French agents, referring to them as X, Y, and Z. The revelation that the Americans had been treated with utter contempt stimulated a wave of anti-French sentiment in the United States. Cries for war filled the air. Congress formally abrogated the Treaty of Alliance and authorized American ships to seize French vessels.

Thus began the undeclared war with France. This Quasi-War was fought in the West Indies, between French privateers seeking to capture American merchant vessels and warships of the United States Navy. Although initial American losses of merchant shipping were heavy, by early 1799 the navy had established its superiority in Caribbean waters. Its ships captured a total of eight French privateers and naval vessels, easing the threat to America's vital West Indian trade.

The Republicans, who opposed war and continued to sympathize with France, could do little to stem the tide of anti-French feelings. The Federalists saw this climate of opinion as an opportunity to deal a death **Alien and Sedition Acts** blow to their Republican opponents. Now that the country seemed to see the truth of what they had been saying ever since the Whiskey Rebellion in 1794— that the Republicans were subversive foreign agents—the Federalists sought to codify that belief into law. In the spring and summer of 1798, the Federalist-controlled Congress adopted a set of four laws known as the Alien and Sedition Acts, intended to suppress dissent and prevent further growth of the Republican party.

Three of the acts were aimed at immigrants, whom the Federalists quite correctly suspected of being Republican in their sympathies. The Naturalization Act lengthened the residency period required for citizenship from five to fourteen years and ordered all resident aliens to register with the federal government. The Alien Enemies Act provided for the detention of enemy aliens in time of war. The Alien Friends Act, to be in effect for two years, gave the president almost unlimited authority to deport any alien he deemed dangerous to the nation's security. (Adams never used that authority. The Alien Enemies Act was not implemented either, since war was never formally declared.)

The fourth law, the Sedition Act, sought to control both citizens and aliens. It outlawed conspiracies to prevent the enforcement of federal

Matthew Lyon, the congressman convicted of violating the Sedition Act, had a fiery temper. In January 1798, before his arrest and trial, he engaged in this brawl with a congressman from Connecticut in the chamber of the House of Representatives. *Library of Congress.*

laws and set the maximum punishment for such offenses at five years in prison and a $5,000 fine. The act also tried to control speech. Writing, printing, or uttering "false, scandalous and malicious" statements "against the government of the United States, or the President of the United States, with intent to defame" became a crime punishable by as much as two years' imprisonment and a fine of $2,000.

In all, there were fifteen indictments and ten convictions under the Sedition Act. Most of the accused were outspoken Republican newspaper editors who failed to mute their criticism of the administration in response to the law. But the first victim—whose story may serve as an example of the rest—was a Republican congressman from Vermont, Matthew Lyon. The Irish-born Lyon was fined $1,000 and given a four-month prison sentence for declaring in print that John Adams had displayed "a

continual grasp for power" and "an unbounded thirst for ridiculous pomp, foolish adulation, and selfish avarice."

Faced with the prosecutions of their major supporters, Jefferson and Madison sought an effective means of combating the Alien and Sedition Acts.

Virginia and Kentucky Resolutions
They turned to constitutional theory and the state legislatures. Carefully concealing their own role (it would hardly have been desirable for the vice president to be indicted for sedition), Jefferson and Madison each drafted a set of resolutions. Introduced into the Kentucky and Virginia legislatures respectively in the fall of 1798, the resolutions differed somewhat, but their import was the same. Since the Constitution was created by a compact among the states, they contended, the people speaking through their states had a legitimate right to judge

the constitutionality of actions taken by the federal government. Both sets of resolutions pronounced the Alien and Sedition Acts null and void and asked other states to join in the protest.

Although no other state replied positively to the Virginia and Kentucky resolutions, they nevertheless had major significance. In the first place, they were superb political propaganda, rallying Republican opinion throughout the country. They placed the opposition party squarely in the revolutionary tradition of resistance to tyrannical authority. Second, the theory of union they proposed was expanded on by southern states' rights advocates in the 1830s and later.

Meanwhile, Adams's decision not to seek a declaration of war against France had split the Federalists, for Hamilton wanted a declared war. When the French government privately indicated that it regretted the treatment of the three American commissioners, Adams dispatched an envoy to Paris. The United States asked two things of France: nearly $20 million in compensation for ships the French had seized since 1793 and abrogation of the treaty of 1778. The Convention of 1800, which ended the Quasi-War, included the latter but not the former. The results of the negotiations, however, were not known until after the election of 1800. By then, the split in Federalist ranks had already cost Adams his re-election.

In sharp contrast, the Republicans entered the 1800 presidential race firmly united behind Jefferson and Burr. Although they won the election, their lack of foresight almost cost them dearly. The problem was caused by the system of voting in the electoral college. All Republican electors voted for both Jefferson and Burr, giving each of them 73 votes (Adams had 65). Because neither Republican had a plurality, the Constitution required that the contest be decided in the House of Representatives, with each state's congressmen voting as a unit. Federalist congressmen decided the election by selecting Jefferson on the thirty-fifth ballot. As a result of the tangle, the Twelfth Amendment to the Constitution (1804) changed the method of voting in the electoral college to allow for a party ticket.

Election of 1800

Westward Expansion, Social Change, and Religious Ferment

In the postrevolutionary years, the United States experienced a dramatic increase in internal migration. As much as 5 to 10 percent of the population moved each year, half of the movers relocating to another state. Young white men were the most mobile segment of the populace. The major population shifts were from east to west (see map): from New England to upstate New York and Ohio, from New Jersey to western Pennsylvania, from the Chesapeake to the new states of Kentucky and Tennessee, which entered the union in 1792 and 1796, respectively. Very few people moved north or south.

The first permanent white settlements beyond the mountains were established in western North Carolina in 1771. But not until after the defeat of the Shawnees in 1774 and the Cherokees in 1776 did significant numbers of settlers move west of the mountains and south of the Ohio River. By 1790, more than a hundred thousand residents lived in the future states of Kentucky and Tennessee. North of the Ohio River, white settlements grew more slowly because of the strength of the Miami Confederacy. But once the Treaty of Greenville was signed in 1795, the Ohio country, too, grew rapidly.

White Settlement in the West

The transplanted New Englanders did their best to recreate the societies they had left behind, laying out farms and towns in neat checkerboard patterns, founding libraries and Congregational churches. Early arrivals recruited others to join them through enthusiastic letters about Ohio's rich soil and potential for growth, setting off a phenomenon known in New England as Ohio Fever. The New Englanders, proud of their literate, orderly culture, viewed their neighbors with disdain. Ohioans, said one, were "intelligent, industrious, and thriving," whereas the Virginians who had settled across the river in Kentucky were "ignorant, lazy, and poor."

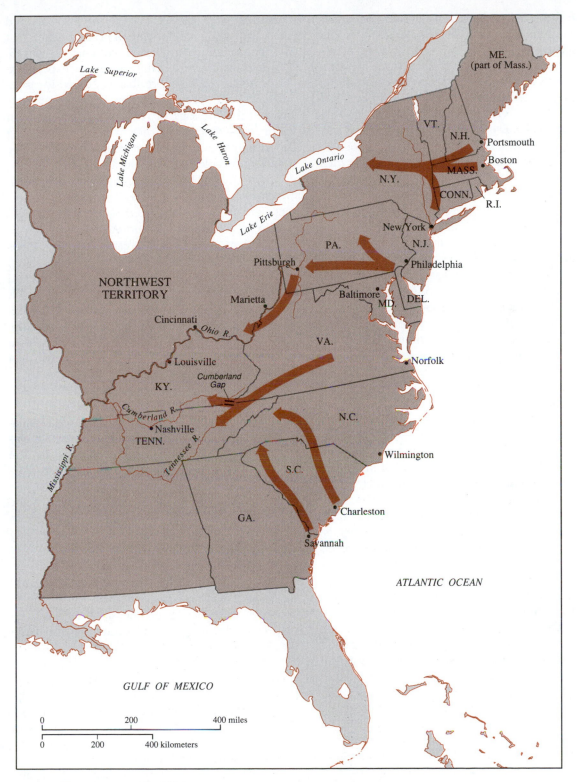

Western Expansion, 1785–1805

The westward migration of slaveholding whites, first to Kentucky and Tennessee, then to the rich lands of western Georgia, and eventually to the Gulf Coast, tore apart the web of family connections African-Americans had built up over several generations of residence in the Chesapeake. Even those few large planters who moved their entire slave force west could not have owned all the members of every family on their plantations. Far more commonly, the white migrants were younger sons of eastern slaveholders, whose inheritance included only a portion of the family's slaves, or small farmers who owned just one or two blacks. In the early years of American settlement in the West, the population was widely dispersed; accordingly, Chesapeake blacks, who had been raised in the midst of large numbers of kin, had to adapt to lonely lives on isolated farms. The approximately one hundred thousand African-Americans forcibly moved west by 1810 had to begin building new families there to replace those unwillingly left behind in the East.

Blacks in the West

The mobility of both blacks and whites created a volatile population mix in southern frontier areas. Since most of the migrants were young single men just starting to lead independent lives, western society was at first unstable. Like the seventeenth-century Chesapeake, the American West in the late eighteenth century was a society in which single women married quickly. The other side of the same coin was that the few women among the migrants lamented their lack of congenial female friends. Isolated, far from familiar surroundings, women and men both strove to create new communities to replace those they had left behind.

Perhaps the most meaningful of the new communities was that supplied by evangelical religion. Among the migrants to Kentucky and Tennessee were clergymen and committed lay members of the evangelical sects that arose in America after the First Great Awakening: Baptists, Presbyterians, and Methodists. At camp meetings, sometimes attended by thousands of people and usually lasting from three days to a week, clergymen exhorted their audiences to repent their sins and become genuine

Second Great Awakening

Christians. They stressed that salvation was open to all, downplaying the doctrine of predestination that had characterized orthodox colonial Calvinism. The emotional nature of the conversion experience was emphasized far more than the need for careful study and preparation. Such preachers thus brought the message of religion to the people in more ways than one. They were democratizing American religion, making it available to all, rather than to a preselected and educated elite.

The sources of the Second Great Awakening, which began around 1800 and revitalized Protestant Christianity in the United States, were embedded in late-eighteenth-century American society in the East, as well as the West. From the 1760s through the 1780s, religious concerns had been subordinated to secular affairs. Indeed, clerics had created a "civil religion" for the nation, in which the fervor of the veneration for the public sometimes surpassed the fervor of religious worship. Most churches, influenced by Enlightenment thought, had for decades stressed reason more than revelation. Circumstances were thus ripe for a movement of spiritual renewal that would appeal to the emotional side of people's natures.

Besides, America's largest Protestant denominations had to find new sources of financial and membership support after the Revolution. In the colonial period, most of the provinces had had established, or state-supported, churches. Many states dissolved their ties to churches during or immediately after the war, and others vastly reduced state support for established denominations.

Disestablishment of Religion

These changes meant that congregations could no longer rely on tax revenues and that all churches were placed on the same footing with respect to the government. Church membership became entirely voluntary, as did monetary contributions from members. If congregations were to survive, they had to generate new sources of support and increase the size of their membership. Revivals proved a convenient means of doing so. The revivals represented genuine outpourings of religious sentiment, but their more mundane function must not be overlooked.

An analysis of secular society can help explain

Chapter 7: Politics and Society in the Early Republic, 1789–1800 the conversion patterns of the Second Awakening. Unlike the First Great Awakening, when converts were evenly divided by sex, more

Women and the Second Awakening

women than men—particularly young women—answered the call of Christianity during the Second Awakening. The increase in female converts seems to have been directly related to major changes in women's circumstances at the end of the eighteenth century. In some areas of the country, especially New England, women outnumbered men after 1790. Thus eastern girls could no longer count on finding marital partners. The uncertainty of their social and familial position seems to have led them to seek spiritual certainty through religion. In the churches, they formed hundreds of female associations to aid widows and orphans, collect money for foreign missions, or improve the quality of maternal care. Thus American women collectively assumed the role of keepers of the nation's conscience, taking the lead in charitable enterprises and freeing their husbands from concern for such moral issues.

The religious ferment among blacks and whites in frontier regions of the Upper South contributed to racial ferment as well. People of both races attended camp meetings to hear

Blacks and the Second Awakening

black and white preachers. When revivals spread eastward into more heavily slaveholding areas, white planters became fearful of the egalitarianism implied in the evangelical message of universal salvation and harmony. At the same time, revivals created a group of respected black leaders—the preachers—and provided them with a ready audience.

Events in the West Indies gave whites ample reason for apprehension. In 1793, mulattos and blacks in the French colony of Saint Domingue (Haiti) overthrew European rule under the leadership of a mulatto, Toussaint L'Ouverture. In an attempt to prevent the spread of such unrest to their own slaves, southern state legislators passed laws forbidding white Haitian refugees from bringing their slaves with them. But North American blacks learned about the revolt anyway. And the preconditions for racial upheaval already existed in the South.

In Virginia, a revolt was planned by Gabriel Prosser, a blacksmith who argued that blacks should fight to obtain the same rights as whites and who

Gabriel's Rebellion

explicitly placed himself in the tradition of the French and Haitian revolutions. At revival meetings led by his brother Martin, a preacher, Gabriel recruited other blacks like himself—artisans who moved easily in both black and white circles and who lived in semifreedom under minimal white supervision. The artisan leaders then enlisted rural blacks in the cause. The conspirators planned to attack Richmond on the night of August 30, 1800, setting fire to the city, seizing the state capitol, and capturing the governor. Their plan showed considerable political sophistication, but heavy rain made it impossible to execute the plot as scheduled. Several whites then learned of the plan from their slaves and spread the alarm. Gabriel avoided capture for some weeks, but most of the other leaders of the rebellion were quickly arrested and interrogated. The major conspirators, including Prosser himself, were hanged, but in the months that followed other insurrectionary scares continued to frighten Virginia slaveowners.

Significantly, the Iroquois were affected by a religious revival at the same time as American whites and blacks were experiencing the Second Great Awakening. Led by their prophet,

Handsome Lake

Handsome Lake, the remaining American Iroquois, who were scattered on small reservations, embraced the traditional values of their culture and renounced such destructive white customs as drinking alcohol and playing cards. At the same time, though, they began abandoning their ancient way of life. With Handsome Lake's approval, Quaker missionaries taught the Iroquois Anglo-American styles of agricultural subsistence; men were now to be cultivators rather than hunters and women housekeepers rather than cultivators. Since the tribes had lost their hunting territories to white farmers, Iroquois men accepted the changes readily. But many women, especially the powerful tribal matrons, resisted the shift in the gender division of labor. They realized that when they surrendered control over food production they would jeopardize their status in the tribe. But Handsome Lake

Around 1790, an unknown artist painted Benjamin Hawkins, an Indian trader, and a group of Creeks at his trading post in northern Florida. Such commerce with the Indians, long a part of American life, continued to play an important role in the national economy during the early years of the republic. *Courtesy of the Greenville County Museum of Art, S.C.*

branded as "witches" any women who opposed the changes too vigorously, and eventually he triumphed.

As the new century began, white, red, and black inhabitants of the United States were moving toward an accommodation to their new circumstances. Indians east of the Mississippi learned that they would have to give up some parts of their traditional culture to preserve others. Blacks and whites tried to create new lives in the West and adjust to changed economic circumstances in the East. Building on successful negotiations with both Britain (the Jay Treaty) and France (the Convention of 1800), the United States charted its own diplomatic course, striving to avoid dependence on the European powers. The 1790s spawned vigorous de-

bates over foreign and domestic policy and saw the beginnings of a system of political parties. Religious revivals again swept portions of the countryside, and again those revivals contributed to social unrest.

At the end of the decade, after years of struggle, the Jeffersonian interpretation of republicanism finally prevailed over Hamilton's approach. As a result, in the years to come the country would be characterized by a decentralized economy, minimal government (especially at the national level), and maximum freedom of action and mobility for individual white men. Jeffersonian Republicans, like white male Americans before them, failed to extend to white women, Indians, and blacks the freedom and individuality they recognized as essential for themselves.

Suggestions for Further Reading

National Government and Administration

Ralph Adams Brown, *The Presidency of John Adams* (1975); Forrest McDonald, *Alexander Hamilton* (1979); Forrest McDonald, *The Presidency of George Washington* (1974); John C. Miller, *The Federalist Era, 1789–1801* (1960); John R. Nelson, Jr., *Liberty and Property: Political Economy and Policymaking in the New Nation, 1789–1812* (1987); Merrill D. Peterson, *Thomas Jefferson and the New Nation* (1970); Garry Wills, *Cincinnatus: George Washington and the Enlightenment* (1984).

Partisan Politics

Lance Banning, *The Jeffersonian Persuasion: Evolution of a Party Ideology* (1978); Richard Buel, Jr., *Securing the Revolution: Ideology in American Politics, 1789–1815* (1972); William Nisbet Chambers, *Political Parties in a New Nation: The American Experience, 1776–1809* (1963); Joseph Charles, *The Origins of the American Party System* (1956); Richard Hofstadter, *The Idea of a Party System: The Rise of Legitimate Opposition in the United States, 1780–1840* (1970); Adrienne Koch, *Jefferson and Madison: The Great Collaboration* (1950); Norman K. Risjord, *Chesapeake Politics, 1781–1800* (1978); John Zvesper, *Political Philosophy and Rhetoric: A Study of the Origins of American Party Politics* (1977).

Foreign Policy

Jerald A. Combs, *The Jay Treaty* (1970); Alexander DeConde, *The Quasi-War: Politics and Diplomacy of the Undeclared War with France, 1797–1801* (1966); Alexander DeConde, *Entangling Alliance: Politics and Diplomacy Under George Washington* (1958); Felix Gilbert, *To the Farewell Address: Ideas of Early American Foreign Policy* (1961); Reginald Horsman, *The Diplomacy of the New Republic, 1776–1815* (1985); Lawrence Kaplan, *"Entangling Alliances with None": American Foreign Policy in the Age of Jefferson* (1987); William Stinchcombe, *The XYZ Affair* (1981); Paul A. Varg, *Foreign Policies of the Founding Fathers* (1963).

Civil Liberties

Leonard W. Levy, *Emergence of a Free Press* (1985); Leonard W. Levy, *Origins of the Fifth Amendment* (1968); Robert A. Rutland, *The Birth of the Bill of Rights, 1776–1791,* rev. ed. (1983); James Morton Smith, *Freedom's Fetters: The Alien and Sedition Laws and American Civil Liberties* (1956).

Women, Blacks, and the Family

Ira Berlin and Ronald Hoffman, eds., *Slavery and Freedom in the Age of the American Revolution* (1983); Nancy F. Cott, *The Bonds of Womanhood: "Woman's Sphere" in New England, 1780–1835* (1977); Toby Ditz, *Property and Kinship: Inheritance in Early Connecticut, 1750–1820* (1986); Gerald W. Mullin, *Flight and Rebellion: Slave Resistance in Eighteenth-Century Virginia* (1972).

Social Change and Westward Expansion

Andrew Cayton, *The Frontier Republic: Ideology and Politics in the Ohio Country, 1789–1812* (1986); Howard Rock, *Artisans of the New Republic: The Tradesmen of New York City in the Age of Thomas Jefferson* (1979); Malcolm Rohrbough, *The Trans-Appalachian Frontier: Peoples, Societies, and Institutions, 1775–1850* (1979); W. J. Rorabaugh, *The Alcoholic Republic: An American Tradition* (1979); Thomas Slaughter, *The Whiskey Rebellion* (1986); Charles G. Steffen, *The Mechanics of Baltimore: Workers and Politics in the Age of Revolution, 1763–1812* (1984); Sean Wilentz, *Chants Democratic: New York City and the Rise of the American Working Class, 1788–1850* (1984).

Religion

Catharine Albanese, *Sons of the Fathers: The Civil Religion of the American Revolution* (1976); Ruth Bloch, *Visionary Republic: Millennial Themes in American Thought* (1985); Fred J. Hood, *Reformed America, 1783–1837* (1980); William McLoughlin, *Revivals, Awakenings, and Reform* (1978).

"I have this morning witnessed one of the most interesting scenes a free people can ever witness," Margaret B. Smith, a Philadelphian, wrote on March 4, 1801, to her sister-in-law. "The changes of administration, which in every government and in every age have most generally been epochs of confusion, villainy and bloodshed, in this our happy country take place without any species of distraction, or disorder." On that day, Thomas Jefferson strolled from his New Jersey Avenue boarding house in the new federal capital of Washington, D.C., to take the oath as president at the Capitol. The precedent of an orderly and peaceful change of government had been established.

Jefferson's inauguration marked a change of style in government. Almost overnight, the formality of the Federalist presidencies of Washington and Adams disappeared as Jefferson set the tone for the Republican government. Jefferson abandoned the aristocratic wigs and breeches (knee-length trousers) of his predecessors and rejected the wealthy pretensions he associated with the Federalists. Republican virtue would be restored.

Carved out of Maryland and Virginia, the new district had been chosen because of its central location. Washington was thus beholden neither to the colonial past nor to any single state. The small government, which essentially collected tariffs, delivered mail, and defended the nation's borders, suited the republic. Even for the Federalists, the adoption of the Constitution had been more a result of dissatisfaction with the Articles of Confederation than a sign of confidence in central government. Though Jefferson, after his inauguration in 1801, cut the federal budget and operations, he and his Republican successors invigorated the federal government over the next two decades.

The transfer of power to the Republicans from the Federalists intensified political conflict and voter interest. Republican presidents sought to restrain government. Federalists prized a stronger national government with more centralized order and authority. With both factions competing for adherents and popular support, the basis was laid for the evolution of democratic politics. But factionalism, personal disputes, and suspicion of partisanship within each group prevented the development of modern political parties.

8

THE EMPIRE OF LIBERTY, 1801–1824

Events abroad and on the frontier encouraged and threatened the expansionism of the young nation. Seizing one opportunity, the United States purchased the Louisiana Territory, pushing the frontier farther west. But then from the high seas came war. Caught between the British and the French, the United States found itself a victim of European conflict, with its shipping rights as a neutral, independent nation ignored and violated. When the humiliation became too great, Americans took up arms in the War of 1812, both to defend their rights as a nation and to expand farther to the west and north.

The War of 1812 unleashed a wave of nationalism and self-confidence. War stimulated the development of domestic manufacturing and internal transportation. After the war, the federal government championed business and promoted road and canal building. The new spirit encouraged economic growth, western expansion at home, and assertiveness throughout the Western Hemisphere. By the 1820s, the United States was no longer an experiment; a new nation had emerged.

Rembrandt Peale's 1805 portrait of President Thomas Jefferson. Charles Willson Peale and his five sons helped establish the reputation of American art in the new nation. Rembrandt Peale was most famous for his presidential portraits; here he captures Jefferson in a noble pose without the usual symbols of office or power, befitting the Republican age. *The New-York Historical Society.*

Jefferson in Power

Jefferson delivered his inaugural address in the Senate chamber, the only part of the Capitol that had been completed. "We are all Republicans, we

Jefferson's Inaugural Address

are all Federalists," he told the assembly in an appeal for unity. Confidently addressing those with little faith in the people's ability to govern themselves, he called America's republican government "the world's best hope."

The new president went on to outline his goals:

A wise and frugal government, which shall restrain men from injuring one another, which shall leave them otherwise free to regulate their own pursuits. . . . Equal and exact justice to all men, of whatever state or persuasion, religious or political. . . . The support of the state governments in all their rights, as the most competent administrators for

our domestic concerns and the surest bulwarks against antirepublican tendencies.

At the same time, he assured Federalists that he shared some of their concerns:

The preservation of the general government in its whole constitutional vigor. . . . The honest payment of our debts and sacred preservation of the public faith.

. . . Encouragement of agriculture and of commerce as its handmaid.

Still, the Federalists and Republicans distrusted each other. Republicans considered the Federalists antidemocratic and antirepublican at heart. One of Jefferson's first acts was to extend the Republicans' grasp over the federal government. Virtually all officials appointed under Washington and Adams were loyal Federalists. To counteract Federalist power, Jefferson refused to recognize Adams's last-minute "midnight appointments" to local offices in the District of Columbia. He also dismissed Federalist customs collectors from New England ports, and awarded vacant treasury and judicial offices to Republicans. By July 1803, Federalists held only 130 of the 316 presidentially controlled offices. In restoring political balance in government, Jefferson used patronage to reward his friends, build a party organization, and compete with the Federalists.

The Republican Congress, too, proceeded to affirm its republicanism. Guided by Secretary of the Treasury Albert Gallatin and Representative John Randolph of Virginia, it put the federal government on a diet. Congress repealed all internal taxes, including the whiskey tax. Gallatin cut the army budget in half, to just under $2 million, and reduced the 1802 navy budget from $3.5 to $1 million. Moreover, Gallatin planned to reduce the national debt—Alexander Hamilton's engine of economic growth—from $83 million to $57 million, as part of a plan to retire it altogether by 1817.

More than frugality, however, separated Republicans from Federalists. Opposition to the Alien and Sedition laws of 1798 had helped unite Republicans. Now Congress let the acts expire in 1801 and 1802 and repealed the Naturalization Act of 1798. The 1802 act that replaced it required only five years of residency, acceptance of the Constitution, and the renouncing of foreign allegiance and titles.

The Republicans turned next to the judiciary, the last stronghold of unchecked Federalist power. During the 1790s, not a single Republican had been appointed to the federal bench. Moreover, the Judiciary Act of 1801, passed in the last days of the Adams administration, had created fifteen new judgeships (which Adams filled in his midnight appointments, signing appointments until his term was just hours away from expiring) and would reduce by attrition the number of justices on the Supreme Court from six to five. Since that reduction would have denied Jefferson any Supreme Court appointments until two vacancies had occurred, the new Republican-

Attacks on the Judiciary

dominated Congress, in one of its first moves, repealed the 1801 act.

Republicans also targeted opposition judges for removal. Federalist judges had refused to review the Sedition Act and prosecuted critics of the administration under the act. At Jefferson's suggestion, the House impeached (indicted) Federal District Judge John Pickering of New Hampshire; in 1804, the Senate removed him from office. Pickering had not committed any crime, although he was an alcoholic and was emotionally disturbed.

The day Pickering was convicted, the House impeached Supreme Court Justice Samuel Chase for judicial misconduct. Chase had repeatedly denounced Jefferson's administration from the bench. The Republicans, however, failed to muster the necessary two-thirds majority of senators to convict him. Their failure to remove Chase preserved the Court's independence by establishing the precedent that criminal actions, not political disagreements, were the proper grounds for impeachment. Although Jefferson did appoint three new Supreme Court justices, under Chief Justice John Marshall the Court remained a Federalist stronghold.

Marshall, a Virginia Federalist, was an astute lawyer with keen political sense. Under his domination, the Supreme Court retained a Federalist viewpoint even after Republican justices achieved a majority in 1811. Throughout his tenure (from 1801 until 1835), the Court upheld federal supremacy over the states and protected the interests of commerce and capital. More important, Marshall made the Court an equal branch of government in practice as well as theory. First, he made service on the Court a coveted honor. Second, he unified the Court, influencing the justices to issue single majority opinions rather than individual concurring judgments. Marshall himself became the voice of the majority. From 1801 through 1810, he wrote 85 percent of the 171 opinions, including every important decision.

John Marshall

Marshall also increased the Court's power. *Marbury* v. *Madison* (1803) was the landmark case that enabled Marshall to strengthen the Court. William Marbury had been designated a justice of the peace in the District of Columbia as part of Adams's midnight appointments. Marbury sued the new secre-

Chapter 8: The Empire of Liberty, 1801–1824

IMPORTANT EVENTS

1801	John Marshall becomes chief justice Jefferson inaugurated	**1813**	Death of Tecumseh
1801–05	Tripoli War	**1814**	Treaty of Ghent
1803	*Marbury* v. *Madison* Louisiana Purchase	**1814–15**	Hartford Convention
1804	Jefferson re-elected	**1815**	Battle of New Orleans
1804–06	Lewis and Clark expedition	**1816**	Monroe elected president Second Bank of the United States chartered
1805	Prophet emerges as Shawnee leader	**1817**	Rush-Bagot Treaty
1807	*Chesapeake* affair Embargo Act	**1819**	*McCulloch* v. *Maryland* Adams-Onís Treaty
1808	Madison elected president	**1819–23**	Financial panic; depression
1808–13	Prophet and Tecumseh: Indian resistance	**1820**	Missouri Compromise Monroe re-elected
1812–15	War of 1812	**1823**	Monroe Doctrine

Marbury v. Madison tary of state, James Madison, for failing to certify his appointment so that Jefferson could appoint a Republican. In his suit, Marbury requested a writ of mandamus (a court order forcing Madison to appoint him).

At first glance, the case presented a political dilemma. If the Supreme Court issued a writ of mandamus, the president might not comply. After all, why should the president, sworn to uphold the Constitution, allow the Court to decide for him what was constitutional? However, if the Court refused to issue the writ, it would be handing the Republicans a victory. Marshall avoided both alternatives. Speaking for the Court, he ruled that Marbury had a right to his commission but that the Court could not compel Madison to honor it, because the Constitution did not grant the Court power to issue a writ of mandamus. Thus Marshall declared unconstitutional Section 13 of the Judiciary Act of 1789, which authorized the Court to issue such writs. Marbury lost his job and the justices denied themselves the power to issue writs of mandamus, but the Supreme Court established its great power to judge the constitutionality of laws passed by Congress.

In succeeding years, Marshall fashioned the theory of judicial review. Since the Constitution was the supreme law, he reasoned, any act (federal or state) contrary to the Constitution must be null and void. And since the Supreme Court was responsible for upholding the law, the Court had a duty to decide whether a conflict existed between a legislative act and the Constitution. If such a conflict existed the Court would declare the act unconstitutional.

Marshall's decision rebuffed Republican criticism of the Court as a partisan instrument. He avoided a confrontation with the Republican-dominated Congress by not ruling on its repeal of the 1801 Judiciary Act. And he enhanced the Court's independence by claiming the power of judicial review.

While President Jefferson fought with the Federalist judiciary and struggled to reduce federal spending, Americans in search of land had trekked into the rich Mississippi and Ohio valleys. Western settlers—there were hundreds of thousands of them by 1800—depended on the Mississippi and Ohio rivers to get their products to New Orleans for export. Thus, whoever controlled the port of New Orleans had a hand on the throat of the American economy.

Louisiana Purchase

As long as Spain owned Louisiana, Americans had no fear. But in 1802, Napoleon acquired the vast territory in an ambitious bid to rebuild France's empire in the New World. The acquisition, Jefferson lamented, "works most sorely" on the United States. On the eve of ceding control to the French, Spain violated Pinckney's Treaty by denying Americans the privilege of storing their products at New Orleans before transshipment to foreign markets. Western farmers and eastern merchants thought a devious Napoleon had closed the port; they grumbled and talked war.

To relieve the pressure for war and to prevent westerners from joining Federalists in opposition to his administration, Jefferson simultaneously prepared for war and accelerated talks with the French. In January 1803, he sent James Monroe to France to join Robert Livingston in negotiating to buy New Orleans. Meanwhile, Congress authorized the call-up of eighty thousand militia if it proved necessary. Arriving in Paris in April, Monroe was astonished to learn that France had already offered to sell all 827,000 square miles of Louisiana to the United States for $15 million. On April 30, Monroe and Livingston signed a treaty to purchase the vast territory, whose borders were undefined and whose land was uncharted (see map).

The Louisiana Purchase doubled the size of the nation and opened the way for westward expansion across the continent. The acquisition was the single most popular achievement of Jefferson's presidency. But its legality was questionable. The Constitution gave him no clear authority to acquire new territory and incorporate it into the nation. Jefferson considered requesting a constitutional amendment to allow the purchase, but finally he justified it on the grounds that he was exercising the president's implied powers to protect the nation. The people, he knew, would accept or reject the purchase on election day in 1804.

The president had a long-standing interest in Louisiana and the West. As secretary of state, he had commissioned a French emigré, André Michaux, to explore the Missouri River. Allegations of Michaux's complicity in the Genêt Affair aborted this mission. In 1803, Jefferson sent Meriwether Lewis and William Clark to the Pacific Ocean via the Missouri and Columbia rivers. Lewis and Clark, from 1804 to 1806, headed the nearly fifty-strong "Corps of Discovery," which was aided by trappers and American Indians along the way.

Lewis and Clark

The Lewis and Clark expedition, planned in secrecy before the Louisiana Purchase, reflected Jefferson's scientific curiosity and his interest in western commercial development, especially the fur and China trades. Other explorers soon followed Lewis and Clark, led in 1805 and 1806 by Lieutenant Zebulon Pike in search of the source of the Mississippi. Pike attempted to find a navigable water route to the Far West and sought the headwaters of the Arkansas River. He and his men reached the Rocky Mountains in present-day Colorado and wandered into Spanish territory to the south, where the Spanish arrested them and held them captive for several months in Santa Fe. After his release, Pike wrote an account of his experiences that set commercial minds spinning. He described a potential commercial market in southwestern Spanish cities, as well as the bounty of furs and precious minerals to be had. The vision of the road to the Southwest became a reality with the opening of the Santa Fe Trail in the 1820s.

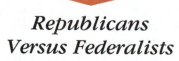

Republicans Versus Federalists

Campaigning for re-election in 1804, Jefferson claimed credit for western expansion and the resto-

Louisiana Purchase

ration of republican values. He had removed the
Federalist threat to liberty by end-

Election of 1804 ing the Alien and Sedition Acts
and the Judiciary Act. He had re-
duced the size and cost of govern-
ment by cutting spending. Despite his opponents'
charges, he had proved that Republicans supported
commerce by having Congress repeal Federalist excise and property taxes.

The Federalist candidate was Charles Cotesworth
Pinckney, a wealthy South Carolina lawyer and former Revolutionary War aide to General George
Washington. Pinckney had been Adams's vice-
presidential candidate in 1800, thereby inheriting
the Federalist leadership. Jefferson and his running
mate, George Clinton of New York, defeated Pinckney and Rufus King in the electoral college with 162
votes to 14.

Jefferson's re-election was both a personal and
an organizational triumph. The political dissenters
of the 1790s had used their Democratic-Republican
societies to win elections. More than anything else,
opposition to the Federalists had molded and
unified them. Indeed, it was in the parts of the

country where the Federalists were strongest—in
commercial New York and Pennsylvania in the
1790s and in New England in the 1800s—that the
Republicans had organized most effectively.

Until the Republican successes in 1800 and 1804,
most Federalists had disdained popular campaigning. They believed in government by the "best"
people—those whose education, wealth, and experience marked them as leaders. For candidates to
debate their qualifications before their inferiors—
the voters—was unnecessary and undignified. The
direct appeals of the Republicans struck the
Federalists as a subversion of the natural political
order.

After the resounding Federalist defeat in 1800, a
younger generation of Federalists began to imitate
the Republicans. They organized statewide and, led
by men like Josiah Quincy, a

Younger Federalists young congressman from Massachusetts, campaigned for popular
support. Quincy cleverly identi-
fied the Federalists as the people's party, attacking Republicans as autocratic planters. In attacking frugal government, the self-styled Younger

John Lewis Krimmel, *Election Day in Philadelphia* (1815). Citizens crowded outside the State House in Philadelphia on election day in 1815 to whip up support for their candidates and to await the results. The painting suggests the overwhelmingly white, male composition of the electorate. *The Henry Francis du Pont Winterthur Museum.*

Federalists played on fears of a weakened army and navy. Merchants depended on a strong navy to protect ocean trade while westerners, encroaching on Indian tribes, looked for federal support.

In the states where both factions organized and ran candidates, participation in elections increased markedly. In some states, more than 90 percent of the eligible voters cast ballots between 1804 and 1816. People became more interested in politics generally, especially at the local level; and as participation in elections increased, the states expanded suffrage. Nevertheless, the popular base remained restricted. Property qualifications for voting and holding office persisted, and in six states the legislatures still selected presidential electors in 1804.

Yet political competition, spurred on by a vigorous press that saw its primary role as partisan advocacy, prompted grassroots campaigning. The political barbecue symbolized the new style as the factions responded to increasing voter involvement in politics. During the barbecue, candidates and party leaders spoke from the stump. Oratory was a popular form of entertainment, and speeches were lengthy and uninhibited. Although both factions used the political barbecue, the Federalist party never fully mastered the art of wooing voters.

Older Federalists still opposed such blatant campaigning. And though they were strong in a few states like Connecticut and Delaware, the Federalists never offered the Republicans sustained competition. Divisions between Older and Younger

Federalists often hindered them, and the extremism of some Older Federalists tended to discredit the organization. A case in point was Timothy Pickering, a Massachusetts congressman who urged the secession of New England in 1803 and 1804. Pickering won some support among the few Federalists in Congress, but others opposed his plan for a northern confederacy. When Vice President Aaron Burr lost his bid to become governor of New York in 1804, the plan collapsed. Burr, more an opportunist than a loyal Republican, was to have led New York into secession, with the other states to follow.

Both political groups suffered from divisions and individuals' personal ambitions. For a long time, for instance, Aaron Burr and Alexander Hamilton had crossed swords in political con-

Hamilton-Burr Duel flict. It seemed to Burr that Hamilton always blocked his path. Hamilton had thwarted Burr's attempt to steal the election of 1800 from Jefferson, and in the 1804 New York gubernatorial race the Federalist Hamilton backed a rival Republican faction against Burr. Again a loser, Burr turned his resentment on Hamilton and challenged him to a duel. Hamilton accepted Burr's challenge and was killed. Indicted for murder, Burr became involved in a conspiracy to build an empire in the Southwest. After being tried and acquitted on the charge of treason, he fled to Europe.

The controversies surrounding Burr highlight some of the limitations of the emerging political system. Personal animosities were as strong a force as ideology and political differences, and new, temporary factions flourished. Moreover, although politicians appealed for voter support, the electoral base remained narrow. As the election of 1804 revealed, the Federalists could offer only weak competition at the national level. And where Federalists posed no threat, Republicans fought among themselves.

Thus, although this period is commonly called the era of the first party system, parties as such were not fully developed. Competition encouraged party organization, but personal ambition, personality clashes, and local, state, and regional loyalties worked against it. Increasingly, external events intruded and occupied most of Jefferson's time in his second administration.

Preserving American Neutrality in a World at War

"Peace, commerce, and honest friendship with all nations, entangling alliance with none," President Jefferson had proclaimed in his first inaugural address. Jefferson's efforts to stand clear of European conflict were successful until 1805. Indeed, for two years after the renewal of the Napoleonic wars in May 1803, American commerce benefited from the conflict. As the world's largest neutral carrier, the United States became the chief supplier of food to Europe. American merchants also gained control of most of the West Indian trade, which was often transshipped though American ports to Europe.

Meanwhile, the United States victory over Tripolitan pirates on the north coast of Africa (the Barbary states) provided Jefferson with his one clear success in protecting American trading rights. In 1801, Jefferson had refused the demands of the sultan of Tripoli for payment to exempt American ships and sailors from being taken hostage. Instead, he sent a naval squadron to the Mediterranean to protect American merchant ships. The United States signed a peace treaty with Tripoli in 1805 but continued to pay tribute to other Barbary states until 1815, when the navy, under Captain Stephen Decatur, forced Algiers and Tunis to renounce attacks against Americans.

American merchants were more concerned about Anglo-French interference with trade. In October 1805, Britain tightened its control of the high seas with its victory over the French and Spanish fleets at the Battle of Trafalgar. Two months later Napoleon defeated the Russian and Austrian armies at Austerlitz. Stalemated, France and Britain waged commercial war, blockading and counterblockading each other's trade. As a trading partner of both countries, the United States paid a high price.

The British navy stepped up impressments of American sailors. Britain, whose navy was the

Impressment of American Sailors world's largest, was suffering a severe shortage of sailors. Few men enlisted, and those already in service frequently deserted, discouraged by poor food and living conditions and brutal discipline. The Royal Navy resorted to stopping American ships and forcibly removing British deserters, British-born naturalized American seamen, and other unlucky sailors suspected of being British. It is estimated that six to eight thousand Americans were drafted in this manner between 1803 and 1812.

In February 1806, the Senate denounced British impressment as aggression and a violation of neutral rights. To protest the insult, Congress passed the Non-Importation Act, prohibiting importation from Great Britain of a long list of cloth and metal articles. In November, Jefferson suspended the act temporarily while William Pinckney, a Baltimore lawyer, joined James Monroe in London in an attempt to negotiate a settlement. The treaty Monroe and Pinckney carried home violated their instructions—it did not mention impressment—and Jefferson never submitted it to the Senate for ratification.

Less than a year later, the *Chesapeake* affair exposed American military weakness. In June 1807, the forty-gun frigate U.S.S. *Chesapeake* left Norfolk,

Chesapeake Affair Virginia. About ten miles out, still inside American territorial waters, it met the fifty-gun British frigate *Leopard*. When the *Chesapeake* refused to be searched for deserters, the *Leopard* repeatedly emptied its guns broadside into the American ship. Three Americans were killed and eighteen wounded, including the ship's captain. The British impressed four sailors—three of them American citizens, all of them deserters from the Royal Navy. Damaged and humiliated, the *Chesapeake* crept back into port.

Had the United States been better prepared militarily, the howl of public indignation that resulted might have brought about a declaration of war. But the United States was ill equipped to fight a war. Jefferson responded instead by strengthening the military and putting economic pressure on Great Britain. In July, he closed American waters to British warships to prevent similar incidents, and soon afterward he increased military and naval expenditures. On December 14, 1807, Jefferson again invoked the Non-Importation Act, and it was followed eight days later by a new law, the Embargo Act.

Intended as a short-term measure, the Embargo Act forbade virtually all exports from the United States to any country. Imports came to a halt as well,

Embargo Act since foreign ships delivering goods had to leave American ports with empty holds. Smuggling blossomed overnight.

Few American policies were as well intentioned but as unpopular and unsuccessful as Jefferson's embargo. The lucrative American merchant trade collapsed; between 1807 and 1808, exports fell by 80 percent. Federalist New England felt the brunt of a depression, and in the winter of 1808–1809, talk of secession spread through the region's port cities. Great Britain, in contrast, was only mildly affected by the embargo. Finally, the policy gave France an excuse to set privateers against the American ships that had managed to escape the embargo by avoiding American ports. The French argued that such ships must be British ships in disguise, since the embargo barred American ships from the seas.

In the election of 1808, the Republicans faced the Federalists, the embargo, and internal factional dissent. Jefferson followed Washington's example in renouncing a third term and supported James Madison, his secretary of state, as the Republican standard-bearer. Madison won the endorsement of the congressional caucus. Madison and his running mate, George Clinton, defeated the Federalist ticket of Charles C. Pinckney and Rufus King.

As for the embargo, it eventually collapsed under the pressure of domestic opposition. Jefferson withdrew the embargo in his last days in office, replacing it with the Non-

Non-Intercourse Act Intercourse Act of 1809. The act reopened trade with all nations except Britain and France and authorized the president to resume trade with either country if it ceased to violate neutral rights. But the new act solved only the problems that had been created by the embargo; it did not convince Britain and France to change their policies.

When the Non-Intercourse Act expired in the spring of 1810, Congress created a variant, labeled Macon's Bill Number 2. The bill reopened trade with both Great Britain and France, but it provided that if either nation ceased to violate American rights, the president could shut down American commerce with the other. Madison, eager to use the bill rather than go to war, was tricked at his own game. When Napoleon declared that French edicts against United States shipping would be lifted, Madison declared nonintercourse against Great Britain in March 1811. But Napoleon did not keep his word. The French continued to seize American ships, and nonintercourse failed a second time.

Britain, not France, was the main target of American hostility because the Royal Navy controlled the Atlantic. New York harbor was virtually blockaded by the British, so reopening trade with any nation had little practical effect. Angry American leaders tended to blame even Indian resistance in the West on British agitation, ignoring the Indians' legitimate protests against white encroachment and treaty violations. Frustrated and having exhausted all efforts to alter British policy, the United States in 1811 and 1812 drifted into war with Great Britain.

Meanwhile, unknown to the president and Congress, Great Britain was changing its policy. The Anglo-French conflict had ended much of British commerce with the European continent, and exports to the United States had fallen by 80 percent. Depression had hit the British Isles. On June 16, 1812, Britain opened the seas to American shipping. But two days later, before word had crossed the Atlantic, Congress declared war.

The War of 1812 was the logical outcome of United States policy after the renewal of war in Europe in 1803. The grievances enumerated in President Madison's message to Congress on June 1, 1812, were old ones: impressment, interference with neutral commerce, and British alliances with western Indians. Unmentioned was the resolve to defend American independence and honor—and the thirst of expansionists for British Canada.

Yet Congress and the country were divided. Much of the sentiment for war came from the War Hawks, land-hungry southerners and westerners led by Henry Clay of Kentucky and John C. Calhoun of South Carolina. Most representatives from the coastal states opposed war, since armed conflict with the great naval power threatened to close down all American shipping. The vote for war—79 to 49 in the House, 19 to 13 in the Senate— reflected these sharp regional differences. The split

would also be reflected in the way Americans fought the war.

The War of 1812

War was a foolish adventure for the United States in 1812; despite six months of preparation, American forces remained ill equipped. Because the army had neither an able staff nor an adequate force of enlisted men, the burden of fighting fell on the state militias, and not all the states cooperated. The navy did have a corps of well-trained, experienced officers but next to the Royal Navy, the ruler of the seas, the United States Navy was minuscule.

For the first time, the United States waged a general land war. It had an ill-equipped regular army, with only a few professionally trained soldiers; West Point had produced only eighty-nine regular officers by 1812. The army expanded by appointing political leaders to organize volunteer companies and by depending on the state militias. The government offered enlistees a $16 sign-up bonus, $5 monthly pay, a full set of clothes, and a promise of three months' pay and 160 acres of land upon discharge.

Recruiting an Army

Conditions in the army could be dismal. The Kentucky volunteers who constituted the majority of General William Henry Harrison's command at the Battle of the Thames were a ragtag group. Recruited as volunteers in the Kentucky militia, they were drafted into the regular army and sent to fight against Lower Canada. They marched twenty to thirty miles a day from Kentucky to join Harrison's forces in Ohio. They received no training, carried only swords and knives on the march, and were undisciplined.

In the South, Andrew Jackson's Tennessee volunteers were no better organized in their first fifteen months of service. Jackson had raised his militia in December 1812 with the promise that they would serve one year. By the late fall of 1813, his anti-Creek campaign was stalled, and his men were talking of disbanding and going home. Jackson refused to discharge the men. In March 1814, Jackson executed John Woods, a militiaman, for disobedience and mutiny. This broke the opposition in the ranks, and his men defeated the Creek nation at the Battle of Horseshoe Bend.

In Federalist New England, where the conflict was viewed as a Republican war, raising an army proved even more difficult. Those officials who agreed to raise volunteer companies, promised the men that they would serve only in a defensive role. Indeed, the inability of the United States to mount a successful invasion of Canada was due, in part, to the army's failure to assemble an effective force. State militias in New England and New York often declined to fight outside the borders of their own state.

Canada was important because it offered the United States the only readily available battlefront on which to challenge Great Britain. The mighty Royal Navy was useless on the waters separating the United States and Canada, since no river afforded it access from the sea. Canada, thousands of miles from British supply sources, was vulnerable.

Invasion of Canada

Begun with high hopes, the invasion of Canada ended as a disaster. The American strategy was to concentrate on the West, splitting Canadian forces and isolating the Shawnees, Potawatomis, and other tribes that supported the British. General William Hull marched his troops into Lower Canada, near Detroit. But the British anticipated the invasion, mobilized their Indian allies, moved troops into the area, and demanded Hull's surrender. When a pro-British, mostly Potawatomi, contingent captured Fort Dearborn, near present-day Chicago, Hull capitulated (see map). Farther to the west, other American forts surrendered. By the winter of 1812–1813, the British controlled about half of the Old Northwest.

The United States had no greater success on the Niagara front, where New York borders Canada. At the Battle of Queenstown, north of Niagara, the United States regular army met defeat because the New York state militia refused to leave the state. This scene was repeated near Lake Champlain, where American plans to attack Montreal were foiled when the militia declined to cross the border.

The navy provided the only bright note in the first year of the war: the U.S.S. *Constitution,* the U.S.S. *Wasp,* and the U.S.S. *United States* all bested British warships on the Atlantic. But their victories gave the United States only a brief advantage. In defeat, the British lost just 1 percent of their strength; in victory, the Americans lost 20 percent. The British admiralty simply shifted its fleet away from the American ships, and by 1813 the Royal Navy again commanded the seas.

In 1813, the two sides also vied for control of the Great Lakes, the key to the war in the Northwest. The contest was largely a shipbuilding race. Under Master Commandant Oliver Hazard Perry and shipbuilder Noah Brown, the United States outbuilt the British on Lake Erie and defeated them at the bloody Battle of Put-in-Bay on September 10. With this costly victory, the Americans gained control of Lake Erie.

Great Lakes Campaign

General William Henry Harrison then began the march that proved to be the most successful moment in the war for the United States. Harrison's force of forty-five hundred men, mostly Kentucky volunteers, crossed Lake Erie and pursued the British, Shawnee, and Chippewa forces into Canada, defeating them on October 5 at the Battle of the Thames. This victory gave the United States control of the Old Northwest.

An important by-product of the war at this stage was the defeat of effective Indian resistance to American expansion. In the decade before the War of 1812, the Shawnee leaders Prophet and Tecumseh had attempted to build a pan-Indian federation, but in the end they failed. With their failure died the most significant resistance to the federal government's treaty-making tactics.

Prophet's early experiences mirror the fate that befell many frontier tribes. Born in 1775, a few months after his father had died in battle, Prophet was raised by his sister and called Lalawethika (Noisemaker) as a young man. He was among the Shawnees defeated at the Battle of Fallen Timbers and expelled to Ohio under the 1795 Treaty of Greenville. Within the shrunken territory granted to the Shawnees under the treaty, game became scarce. Encroachment by whites and the periodic

Prophet

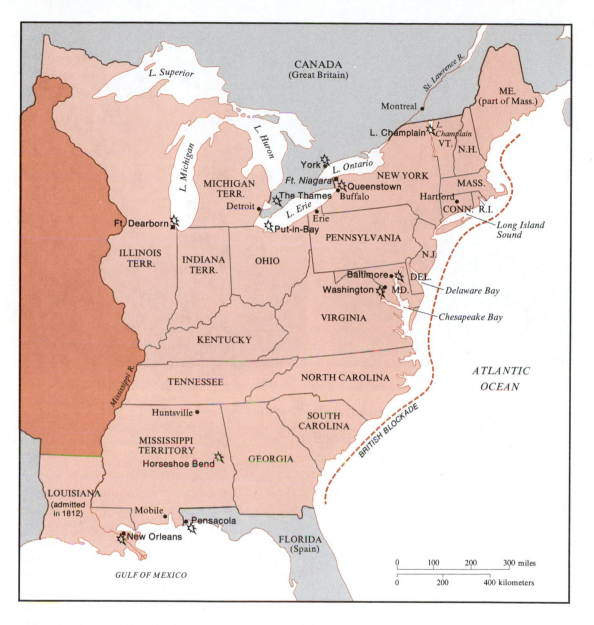

Major Campaigns of the War of 1812

ravages of disease brought further misery to Indian villages and tribes.

In 1804, Lalawethika became a tribal medicine man. But his medicine could not stop the white man's viral illness from ravaging his village. Lalawethika emerged from his own battle with ill-

ness in 1805 as a new man, called Prophet. Claiming to have died and been resurrected, he told a visionary tale of this experience and warned of damnation for those who drank whiskey. In the following years, Prophet traveled widely in the Northwest as a religious leader, attacking the de-

The Shawnee Chiefs Prophet (left) and Tecumseh (right). The two brothers led a revival of traditional Shawnee culture and preached Indian federation against white encroachment. In the War of 1812, they allied themselves with the British, but Tecumseh's death at the Battle of Thames (1813) and British indifference thereafter caused Indian resistance and unity to collapse. *Prophet: National Museum of American Art, Smithsonian Institution, Gift of Mrs. Joseph Harrison, Jr.; Tecumseh: Field Museum of Natural History, FMNH Neg. #A93851.*

cline of moral values among Indians, condemning intertribal battles, and stressing harmony and respect for elders. In essence he preached the revitalization of traditional Shawnee culture. Return to the old ways, he told the Indians of the Old Northwest, abandon white customs.

Prophet's message was a reassuring one to the tribes of the Old Northwest who felt unsettled and threatened by whites. Prophet won converts by performing miracles—he seemed to darken the sun by coinciding his activities with a solar eclipse—and used opposition to federal Indian policy to draw others into his camp.

The government and white settlers were alarmed by the religious revival led by Prophet. With his brother, Tecumseh, who was seven years older, he refused to leave lands claimed by the government. In 1808, Prophet

Tecumseh

and his brother began to turn from a message of spiritual renewal to one of resistance to American aggression. When he repudiated land cessions to the government made under the Treaty of Fort Wayne (1809), Tecumseh told Indiana's Governor William Henry Harrison in 1810 that "the only way to check and stop this evil is, for all the red men to unite in claiming a common and equal right in the land. . . . No part has a right to sell, even to each other, much less to strangers." Tecumseh then warned Harrison that the Indians would resist white occupation of the 2.5 million acres on the Wabash that they had ceded in the Treaty of Fort Wayne.

A year later, using a Potawatomi raid on an Illinois settlement as an excuse, Harrison attacked and demolished Tecumseh's headquarters on Tippecanoe Creek in Indiana Territory. Losses on both sides were heavy. When the War of 1812 started, Tecumseh joined the British in return for a promise of an Indian country in the Great Lakes region. Tecumseh, however, was killed in the Battle of the Thames in October 1813, and with his death Indian unity collapsed.

Outside the Old Northwest, the British set Americans back. In December 1812, the Royal Navy blockaded the Chesapeake and Delaware bays. By **British Naval Blockade** May 1814, the blockade extended southward from New England down the Atlantic coast and then westward along the Gulf of Mexico. It was so effective that between 1811 and 1814 American trade had declined nearly 90 percent.

After their defeat of Napoleon in April 1814, the British stepped up the land campaign against the United States, concentrating their efforts in the Chesapeake Bay region. To retaliate for the burning of York (now Toronto) and divert American troops from Lake Champlain, where the British planned a new offensive, royal troops occupied Washington in August and set it ablaze. The attack on the capital, however, was only a raid. The major battle occurred at Baltimore, in September, where the Americans held firm. Francis Scott Key, witnessing the British fleet's bombardment of Fort McHenry in Baltimore harbor, was inspired to write the verses of "The Star-Spangled Banner." (In 1931, it became the national anthem.) Although the British inflicted heavy damage both materially and psychologically, they achieved no more than a stalemate. The British offensive at Lake Champlain proved equally unsuccessful. An American fleet forced a British flotilla to turn back at Plattsburgh on Lake Champlain, and the offensive was discontinued.

The last campaign of the war was waged in the South, along the Gulf of Mexico. It began when Andrew Jackson, a Tennessee militia general, defeated the Creek Indians at the Battle of Horseshoe Bend in March 1814. The battle ended the year-long Creek War. As a result, the Creeks had to cede two-thirds of their land and withdraw to southern and western Alabama. Jackson became a major general in the regular army and continued south toward the Gulf. To forestall a British invasion at Pensacola

Bay, which guarded an overland route to New Orleans, Jackson seized Pensacola—in Spanish Florida—on November 7, 1814. After securing Mobile, he marched on to New Orleans and prepared for a British attempt to capture the city.

The Battle of New Orleans was the final military engagement. Early in December, the British fleet landed fifteen hundred men east of New Orleans, **Battle of New Orleans** hoping to gain control of the Mississippi River. They faced an American force of regular army troops, plus a larger contingent of Tennessee and Kentucky frontiersmen and two companies of free black volunteers from New Orleans. For three weeks, the British and the Americans played cat and mouse, each trying to gain a major strategic position. Finally, on January 8, 1815, the two forces met head-on. Jackson and his mostly untrained army held their ground against two suicidal frontal assaults and a reinforced British contingent of six thousand. At day's end, more than two thousand British soldiers lay dead or wounded. The Americans suffered only twenty-one casualties. Andrew Jackson emerged a national hero. Ironically, the Battle of New Orleans was fought two weeks after the end of the war; unknown to Jackson, a treaty had been signed in Ghent, Belgium, on December 24, 1814.

The Treaty of Ghent did not mention the issues that had led to war. The United States received no satisfaction on impressment, blockades, or other **Treaty of Ghent** maritime rights for neutrals. Likewise, British demands for an Indian buffer state in the Northwest and territorial cessions from Maine to Minnesota were not satisfied. Essentially, the treaty restored the prewar status quo. It provided for an end to hostilities with the British and with Indian tribes, as well as for the release of prisoners, the restoration of conquered territory, and arbitration of boundary disputes. Other questions—notably compensation for losses and fishing rights—would be negotiated by joint commissions.

Why did the negotiators settle for so little? Events in Europe had made peace and the status quo acceptable at the end of 1814, as they had not been in 1812. Napoleon's fall from power allowed the

United States to abandon its demands, since peace in Europe made impressment and interference with American commerce moot questions. Similarly, war-weary Britain, its treasury nearly depleted, ceased striving for a military victory.

The War of 1812 reaffirmed the independence of the young American republic. Although conflict with Great Britain continued, it never again led to war. The experience strengthened America's resolve to steer clear of European politics, for it was the British-French conflict that had drawn the United States into war.

Results of War of 1812

For the rest of the century, the United States shunned involvement in European political issues and wars. The war also convinced the American government to maintain a standing army of ten thousand men—three times its size under Jefferson.

The war had disastrous results for most Indian tribes. Although Indians were not a party to the Treaty of Ghent, the ninth article pledged the United States to end hostilities and to restore "all the possessions, rights, and privileges" that the tribes had enjoyed before the war. Treaties were signed in 1815 with midwestern tribal leaders, but they had little meaning. With the death of Tecumseh, the Indians lost their most powerful political and military leader; with the withdrawal of the British, they lost their strongest ally. The midwestern tribes thus lost the resources with which they could have resisted American expansion.

Possibly most important of all, the war stimulated economic change. The embargo, the Non-Importation and Non-Intercourse acts, and the war itself spurred the production of manufactured goods to replace banned imports. In the absence of commercial opportunities abroad, New England capitalists began to invest in manufactures. These changes had far-reaching effects (see Chapter 9).

The war also sealed the fate of the Federalist party. Its presidential nominee in 1812, De Witt Clinton, lost to James Madison despite a hard campaign by the Younger Federalists.

Hartford Convention

The extremism of the Older Federalists—not the 1812 defeat—was the party's undoing. During the war, Older Federalists had revived talk of secession, and from December 15, 1814, to January 5, 1815, Federalist delegates from New England met in Hartford, Connecticut. With the war in a stalemate and trade in ruins, they plotted to revise the national compact or pull out of the republic. Moderates prevented a resolution of secession, but convention members endorsed radical changes in the Constitution. They wanted to restrict the presidency to one term and to require a two-thirds congressional vote to admit new states. These proposals were designed to weaken the Republicans.

The timing of the Hartford Convention proved fatal. The victory at New Orleans and news of the peace treaty made the convention, with its talk of secession and proposed constitutional amendments, look ridiculous, if not treasonous. Rather than harassing a beleaguered wartime administration, the Federalists retreated before a rising tide of nationalism. Though Federalism remained strong in a handful of states until the 1820s, the Federalists began to dissolve.

Postwar Nationalism and Diplomacy

With peace came a new sense of American nationalism. Self-confidently, the nation asserted itself at home and abroad as Republicans aped Federalists in encouraging economic development and commerce. In his message to Congress in December 1815, President Madison embraced Federalist doctrine by recommending military expansion and a program to stimulate economic growth. Wartime experiences, he said, had demonstrated the need for a national bank (the charter of the first Bank of the United States had expired) and for better transportation. To raise government revenues and perpetuate the wartime growth in manufacturing, Madison called for a protective tariff—a tax on imported goods. Though straying from Jeffersonian Republicanism, Madison did so within limits. Only a constitutional amendment, he argued, could give the federal government authority to build roads and canals that were less than national in scope.

The congressional leadership pushed Madison's nationalist program energetically. Representative John C. Calhoun and Speaker of the House Henry Clay, who named the program the American System, believed it would unify the country. They looked to the tariff on imported goods to stimulate industry. New mills would purchase raw materials; new millworkers would buy food from the agricultural South and West. New roads would make possible the flow of produce and goods, and tariff revenues would provide the money to build them. A national bank would facilitate all these transactions.

American System

In 1816, Congress enacted much of the nationalistic program. The Second Bank of the United States was chartered. Like its predecessor, the bank had a twenty-year charter, was a blend of public and private ownership, and had one-fifth of its directors appointed by the government. The nation's first protective tariff was also passed. Duties were placed on imported cottons and woolens and on iron, leather, hats, paper, and sugar. Some New England representatives viewed the tariff as interference in free trade, and southern representatives (except Calhoun and a few others) opposed it because it raised the cost of imported goods to southern families. But the western and Middle Atlantic states backed it.

Congress did not share Madison's reservations about the constitutionality of using federal funds to build local roads. "Let us, then, bind the republic together," Calhoun declared, "with a perfect system of roads and canals." But Madison vetoed Calhoun's internal improvements bill, which provided for the construction of roads of mostly local benefit, insisting that it was unconstitutional. Internal improvements were the province of the states and of private enterprise. (Madison did, however, approve funds for the continuation of the National Road, which began in Maryland, to Ohio, on the grounds that it was a military necessity.)

James Monroe, Madison's successor as president, retained Madison's domestic program, supporting the national bank and tariffs and vetoing internal improvements on constitutional grounds. After he

easily defeated Rufus King, the last Federalist candidate, Monroe declared that "discord does not belong to our system." The American people were, he said, "one great family with a common interest." A Boston newspaper dubbed the one-party period the "Era of Good Feelings." For Monroe's first term, that label seemed appropriate.

Under Chief Justice John Marshall, the Supreme Court during this period became the bulwark of a nationalist point of view. In *McCulloch* v. *Maryland* (1819), the Court struck down a Maryland law taxing a branch of the federally chartered Second Bank of the United States. Maryland had adopted the tax in an effort to destroy the bank's Baltimore branch. The issue was thus one of state versus federal power. Speaking for a unanimous Court, Marshall asserted the supremacy of the federal government over the states.

McCulloch v. Maryland

Having established federal supremacy, the Court in *McCulloch* v. *Maryland* went on to consider whether Congress could issue a bank charter. No such power was specified in the Constitution. But Marshall noted that Congress had the authority to pass "all laws which shall be necessary and proper for carrying into execution" the enumerated powers of the government. Therefore, Congress could legally exercise "those great powers on which the welfare of the nation essentially depends." If the ends were legitimate and the means were not prohibited, Marshall ruled, a law was constitutional. The bank charter was declared legal.

In *McCulloch* v. *Maryland,* Marshall combined Federalist nationalism with Federalist economic views. By asserting federal supremacy, he was protecting the commercial and industrial interests that favored a national bank. This was federalism in the tradition of Alexander Hamilton. The decision was only one in a series. In *Fletcher* v. *Peck* (1810), the Court voided a Georgia law that violated individuals' right of contract. Similarly, in *Dartmouth College* v. *Woodward* (1819), the Court nullified a New Hampshire act altering the charter of Dartmouth College, which, Marshall ruled, constituted a contract. In protecting such contracts, Marshall thwarted state interference in commerce and business.

John Quincy Adams, Monroe's secretary of state,

matched the self-confident Marshall Court in nationalism and assertiveness. From 1817 to 1825, he managed the nation's foreign

John Quincy Adams as Secretary of State

policy brilliantly. Adams stubbornly pushed for expansion, fishing rights for Americans in Atlantic waters, political distance from the Old World, and peace. An ardent expansionist, he nonetheless placed limits on expansion, believing that it must come through negotiations, not war, and that newly acquired territories must not permit slavery. In appearance a small, austere man, Adams was a superb diplomat.

Despite being an Anglophobe, Adams worked to strengthen the peace with Great Britain. In April 1817, the two nations agreed in the Rush-Bagot Treaty to limit their Great Lakes naval forces to one ship each on Lakes Ontario and Champlain and two vessels each on the other lakes. The first disarmament treaty of modern times led to the demilitarization of the United States–Canadian border. Adams then pushed for the Convention of 1818, which fixed the United States–Canadian border from the Lake of the Woods in Minnesota west to the Rockies along the 49th parallel. When agreement could not be reached on the territory west of the mountains, the two nations settled on joint occupation of Oregon for ten years.

Adams's next move was to settle long-term disputes with Spain. During the War of 1812, the United States seized Mobile and the remainder of

Adams-Onís Treaty

West Florida. Afterward, it took advantage of Spain's preoccupation with domestic and colonial troubles to negotiate for the purchase of East Florida. Talks took place in 1818, while General Andrew Jackson's troops occupied much of present-day Florida on the pretext of suppressing Seminole raids against American settlements across the border. Adams was furious with Jackson but defended his brazen act. The following year, Don Luís de Onís, Spanish minister to the United States, agreed on behalf of Spain to cede Florida to the United States without payment. In this Transcontinental, or Adams-Onís, Treaty, the United States also defined the southwestern boundary of the Louisiana Purchase. In return, the United States government assumed $5 million's worth of claims by American citizens against Spain and gave up its dubious claim to Texas. Expansion was thus achieved at little cost and without war, and American territorial claims stretched from the Atlantic to the Pacific.

While these treaties with Great Britain and Spain temporarily resolved conflict between the United States and European nations, events to the south still threatened American interests. John Quincy Adams's desire to insulate the United States and the Western Hemisphere from European conflict led to his greatest achievement: the Monroe Doctrine.

The thorny issue of the recognition of new governments in Latin America had to be confronted. Between 1808 and 1822, the United Provinces of the Río de la Plata (present-day northern Argentina, Paraguay, and Uruguay), Chile, Peru, Colombia, and Mexico had all broken free from Spain. Although many Americans wanted to recognize the independence of these former colonies, Monroe and Adams moved cautiously. They sought to avoid conflict with Spain and its allies and to assure themselves of the stability of the revolutionary regimes. But in 1822, shortly after the Adams-Onís Treaty with Spain was safely signed and ratified, the United States became the first nation outside Latin America to recognize the new states.

Soon events in Europe again threatened the stability of the New World. Spain suffered a domestic revolt, and France occupied Spain in an attempt to bolster the weak Spanish monarchy against the rebels. The United States feared that France would seek to restore the new Latin American states to Spanish rule. Similarly distrustful of France, Great Britain proposed a joint United States–British declaration against European intervention in the hemisphere. Adams rejected the British overture; he insisted that the United States act independently in accordance with the principle of avoiding foreign entanglements.

The result was the Monroe Doctrine, a unilateral declaration against European interference in the

Monroe Doctrine

New World. The president enunciated the famous doctrine in his last message to Congress on December 2, 1823. First, Monroe called for *non-colonization* of the Western

Hemisphere by European nations, a principle that expressed American anxiety not only about Latin America but also about Russian expansion on the West Coast. Second, he demanded *nonintervention* by Europe in the affairs of independent New World nations. Finally, Monroe pledged *noninterference* by the United States in European affairs, including those of Europe's existing New World colonies.

Monroe words, however, carried no force. Indeed, the policy could not have succeeded without the support of the British, who were already committed to keeping other European nations out of the New World. Europeans ignored the doctrine. It was the Royal Navy they respected, not American policy.

The Panic of 1819 and Renewed Sectionalism

Monroe's domestic achievements could not match the diplomatic successes that John Quincy Adams brought to his administration. In 1819, a financial panic interrupted the postwar nationalism and confidence and stimulated sectional loyalties. Neither the panic nor the resurgence of sectionalism hurt Monroe politically; without a rival political party to rally opposition, he won a second term in 1820 unopposed.

But hard times spread. The postwar expansion was built on loose money and widespread speculation. State banks extended credit and printed notes too freely, fueling a speculative **Hard Times** western land boom. When expansion slowed, the manufacturing depression that had begun in 1818 deepened. The Second Bank of the United States, in order to protect its assets, reduced loans, thus accelerating the contraction in the economy. Distressed urban workers lobbied for relief and began to take a more active role in politics. Farmers clamored for lower tariffs on manufactured goods. Hurt by a sharp decline in the price of cotton, southern planters railed at the protective Tariff of 1816, which had raised prices while their incomes were falling sharply.

Western farmers suffered too. Those who had purchased public land on credit could not repay their loans. To avoid mass bankruptcy, Congress delayed payment of the money, and western state legislatures passed "stay laws" restricting mortgage foreclosures. Many westerners blamed the panic on the Second Bank of the United States and its tightening of the money supply.

Even more divisive was the question of slavery. Ever since the drafting of the Constitution, most political leaders had avoided the issue. The one exception was the 1807 act closing **Slavery Question** the foreign slave trade after January 1, 1808, which passed without much opposition. In February 1819, however, slavery finally crept onto the political agenda when Missouri residents petitioned Congress for admission to the Union as a slave state. For the next two and a half years the issue dominated all congressional action.

The debate transcended slavery in Missouri. At stake was the undoing of the compromises that had kept the issue quarantined since the Constitutional Convention. Five new states had joined the Union since 1812—Louisiana (1812), Indiana (1816), Mississippi (1817), Illinois (1818), and Alabama (1819). Missouri was on the same latitude as free Illinois, Indiana, and Ohio (a state since 1803), and its admission as a slave state would thus thrust slavery farther northward. It would also tilt the political balance in the Senate toward the states committed to slavery. In 1819, the Union consisted of an uneasy balance of eleven slave and eleven free states. If Missouri entered as a slave state, the slave states would have a two-vote edge in the Senate.

What made the issue so deeply felt was not the politics of admission to statehood but white people's emotional attitudes toward slavery. Many northerners had come to the conclusion that it was evil. Thus, when Representative James Tallmadge, Jr., of New York introduced an amendment providing for gradual emancipation in Missouri, it led to passionate and sometimes violent debate over moral and political concerns. The House, which had a northern majority, passed the Tallmadge amendment, but the Senate rejected it. The two sides were deadlocked.

A compromise emerged in 1820 under pressure

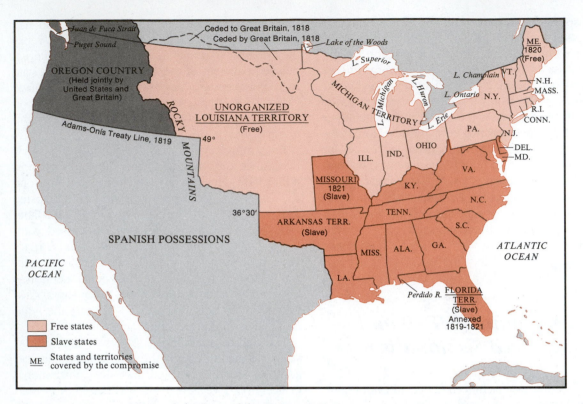

The Missouri Compromise and the State of the Union, 1820

from House Speaker Henry Clay: the admission of free Maine, carved out of Massachusetts, was linked with that of slave Missouri. In the

Missouri Compromise rest of the Louisiana Territory north of 36°30' (Missouri's southern boundary), slavery was prohibited forever (see map). Though the compromise carried, the issue ultimately undermined Republican unity and ended the Virginia dynasty that had begun with Jefferson's election in 1800.

Sectionalism and the question of slavery would ultimately threaten the Union itself. Still, the first decades of the nineteenth century were a time of nationalism and growth for the young republic. Political parties increased white, male involvement in government and channeled and limited partisan divisions. Moreover, a tradition of peaceful transition of power through presidential elections was established. A second war with Britain—the War of 1812—had to be fought to reaffirm American independence and to thwart Indian opposition to

United States expansion; thereafter, the nation was able to settle many disputes at the bargaining table.

The foreign policy problems confronting the infant republic from the turn of the century through the mid-1820s strikingly resemble those faced today by the newly established nations of the Third World. Mother countries often treat their former colonies as if they had not won their independence. Like Third World nations today, the young United States steered clear of alliances with the great powers, preferring neutrality and unilateralism.

After the war, all branches of the government, responding to the popular mood, pursued a vigorous national policy. The Supreme Court further advanced national unity by extending federal power over the states and encouraging commerce and economic growth. Moreover, disruption of trade during the war had promoted the manufacturing of goods in the United States. Developments in transportation further stimulated the economy, and old cities expanded in the market-oriented North as new ones sprouted up in the West on trade and transportation routes.

Along with nationalism and geographic expansion came the problem of sectionalism. While the manufacturers and commercial interests in the North were becoming increasingly connected with the agricultural producers in the West through transportation and trade, the South was developing its own economy and culture based on cotton crops, export markets, a plantation system, and slavery. Politicians kept the question of slavery off the national agenda as long as possible and worked out the Missouri Compromise as a stopgap measure. However, new land acquisitions and further westward expansion in the 1840s and 1850s, combined with a rising tide of reform, made the question of slavery unavoidable (see Chapters 12 and 13).

Suggestions for Further Reading

General

George Dangerfield, *The Awakening of American Nationalism, 1815–1828* (1965); John Mayfield, *The New Nation, 1800–1845* (1981); Marshall Smelser, *The Democratic Republic, 1801–1815* (1968).

Party Politics

Joyce Appleby, *Capitalism and a New Social Order: The Republican Vision of the 1790s* (1984); Noble E. Cunningham, Jr., *The Jeffersonian Republicans in Power: Party Operations, 1801–1809* (1963); David Hackett Fischer, *The Revolution of American Conservatism: The Federalist Party in the Era of Jeffersonian Democracy* (1965); Linda K. Kerber, *Federalists in Dissent* (1970); Richard P. McCormick, *The Presidential Game: The Origins of American Presidential Politics* (1982); James Sterling Young, *The Washington Community, 1800–1828* (1966).

The Virginia Presidents

Harry Ammon, *James Monroe: The Quest for National Identity* (1971); Noble E. Cunningham, Jr., *In Pursuit of Reason: The Life of Thomas Jefferson* (1987); Noble E. Cunningham, Jr., *The Process of Government Under Jefferson* (1978); Ralph Ketcham, *Presidents Above Party: The First American Presidency, 1789–1829* (1984); Forrest McDonald, *The Presidency of Thomas Jefferson* (1976); Merrill D. Peterson, *Thomas Jefferson and the New Nation* (1970); Merrill D. Peterson, *The Jefferson Image in the American Mind* (1960); Robert Allen Rutland, *James Madison: The Founding Father* (1987).

The Supreme Court and the Law

Richard E. Ellis, *The Jeffersonian Crisis: Courts and Politics in the Young Republic* (1971); Charles G. Haines, *The Role of the Supreme Court in American Government and Politics, 1789–1835* (1944); Morton J. Horowitz, *The Transformation of American Law, 1780–1860* (1977); R. Kent Newmyer, *The Supreme Court Under Marshall and Taney* (1968); Francis N. Stites, *John Marshall: Defender of the Constitution* (1981).

Expansion and the War of 1812

Roger H. Brown, *The Republic in Peril: 1812* (1964); Alexander De Conde, *This Affair of Louisiana* (1976); R. David Edmunds, *Tecumseh and the Quest for Indian Leadership* (1984); Clifford L. Egan, *Neither Peace nor War: Franco-American Relations, 1803–1812* (1983); Reginald Horsman, *The War of 1812* (1969); James P. Ronda, *Lewis and Clark Among the Indians* (1984); J. C. A. Stagg, *Mr. Madison's War: Politics, Diplomacy, and Warfare in the Early Republic, 1783–1830* (1983).

The Monroe Doctrine

Samuel F. Bemis, *John Quincy Adams and the Foundations of American Foreign Policy* (1949); Walter LaFeber, ed., *John Quincy Adams and American Continental Empire* (1965); Ernest R. May, *The Making of the Monroe Doctrine* (1976); Dexter Perkins, *Hands Off: A History of the Monroe Doctrine* (1941).

John Jervis's life bridged the old and the new. His roots lay in the farm country of upstate New York. Born at Huntington, Long Island, in 1795, he was taken to western New York in 1798 by his father. John learned to read and write during occasional attendance at common school. His father taught him to farm and handle an axe. But in 1817, he left behind much of that tradition and became involved in undertakings that would lead to a new and different nation. Hired to clear a cedar swamp for the Erie Canal, Jervis had to acquire skills not used on the farm. As he learned new skills, he advanced from axeman to surveyor to engineer and then to superintendent of a division. He was the most famous engineer to receive his training from the Erie Canal "School of Engineering."

When the 363-mile Erie Canal was completed in 1825, Jervis signed on as second-in-command of the Delaware and Hudson Canal project. Later, as a supervisor of an early railroad experiment, Jervis redesigned the locomotive's wheel assembly, and his design became standard throughout America. Jervis spent the next two decades building the 98-mile Chenango Canal and the freshwater system for New York City—consisting of the Croton Reservoir, a 33-mile aqueduct, and pumps. Later, he helped build other railroads, including the Michigan Southern, the Rock Island, and the Nickel Plate. In 1864, at the age of sixty-nine, Jervis returned home to Rome, New York, and organized an iron mill. He had spent his life constructing the mechanisms—canals and railroads—that would change America and connect its far-flung regions.

9

RAILS, MARKETS, AND MILLS: THE NORTH AND WEST, 1800–1860

The canals and railroads that John Jervis and others built were the most visible signs of economic development and the best-known links in the growing national economy from 1800 through 1860. The canal boat, the steamboat, the locomotive, and the telegraph were all agents of change and economic growth. They helped to open up the frontier and expand farm production for markets at home and abroad. They made it possible for New England mill girls to turn slave-produced southern cotton into factory-made cloth that was purchased by women from New York to San Francisco. Although transportation was the most visible change, less tangible but equally significant was the increased specialization in agriculture, manufacturing, and finance, which fostered a national, capitalist, market-oriented economy.

The dramatic transformation of the United States in the nineteenth century began in the first decades of the century and spread nearly everywhere. In 1800, most of the 5.3 million Americans earned a living working the land or serving those who did. Except in Kentucky and Tennessee, settlement had not stretched far to the west. By 1860, 31.4 million Americans had spread across the continent. A continental nation had been forged. Though still primarily agricultural, the economy was being transformed by commercial and industrial expansion.

Promotion of economic growth became the hallmark of government, especially in the nationalist mood after the War of 1812. Government sought to encourage individual freedom and choice by promoting an environment in which farming and industry could flourish. New financial institutions amassed the capital for large-scale enterprises like factories and railroads. Mechanization took root; factories and precision-made machinery successfully competed with home workshops and handmade goods, while reapers and sowers revolutionized farming.

Transportation and Regionalization

From 1800 through 1860, the North, South, and West followed distinctly different economic paths. Everywhere agriculture remained the foundation of the American economy. Nevertheless, industry, commerce, and finance came to characterize the North, plantations and subsistence farms the South, and commercialized family farms, agricultural processing, and implement manufacturing the West. This tendency toward regional specialization made the sections both different and more dependent on each other.

The revolution in transportation and communications was probably the single most important cause of these changes. The North's heavy investment in canals and railroads made the region the center of American commerce. With most of its capital invested in slave labor, the South built fewer canals, railroads, and factories and remained mostly rural and undeveloped.

Before the canal and railroad fevers, it was by no means certain that New England and the Middle Atlantic states would dominate American economic life. Indeed, the southward-flowing Ohio and Mississippi rivers oriented the frontier of 1800—Tennessee, Kentucky, and Ohio—to the South. At first, westerners floated their products on flatboats down the rivers to New Orleans. In 1815, the steamboat *Enterprise* first carried cargo upstream on the Mississippi and the Ohio, further strengthening southern and western ties. This happened just eight years after Robert Fulton successfully introduced the steamboat by paddling up the Hudson River in the *Clermont*.

Change in Trade Routes

But the pattern changed in the 1820s. New arteries opened up east-west travel. The National Road, a stone-based, gravel-topped highway beginning in Cumberland, Maryland, reached Wheeling (then in Virginia) in 1818 and Columbus, Ohio, in 1833. More important, the Erie Canal, completed in 1825, forged an east-west axis from the Hudson River to Lake Erie, linking the Great Lakes with New York City and the Atlantic Ocean. Railroads and later the telegraph would solidify these east-west links. By contrast, only at one place—Bowling Green, Kentucky—did a northern railroad connect with a southern one. By 1850, the bulk of western trade flowed eastward. Thus, on the eve of the Civil War, the northern and Middle Atlantic states were closely tied to the former frontier of the Old Northwest.

Construction of the 363-mile-long Erie Canal was a visionary enterprise. Vigorously promoted by Governor De Witt Clinton, the Erie cost $7 million, much of it raised by loans from British investors. The canal shortened the journey between Buffalo and New York City from twenty to six days and reduced freight charges from $100 to $5 a ton. By 1835, traffic was so heavy that the canal had to be widened from 40 to 70 feet and deepened from 4 to 7 feet.

Canals

The Erie Canal triggered an explosion of canal building. Other states and cities, sensing the advantage New York had gained, rushed to follow suit. By 1840, canals crisscrossed the Northeast and Midwest, and canal mileage in the United States reached 3,300—an increase of more than 2,000 miles in a single decade. Unfortunately for investors, none of these canals enjoyed the financial success achieved by the Erie. As a result, investment in canals began to slump in the 1830s. By 1850, more miles were being abandoned than built, and the canal era had ended.

Meanwhile, railroad construction boomed, and visionaries like John Jervis left canals for railroads. The railroad era in the United States began in 1830, when Peter Cooper's locomotive

Railroads *Tom Thumb* first steamed along 13 miles of track constructed by the Baltimore and Ohio Railroad. In 1833, a second railroad ran 136 miles from Charleston to Hamburg, South Carolina. By 1850, the United States had nearly 9,000 miles of railroad; by 1860, roughly 31,000.

The earliest railroads connected two cities or one city and its surrounding area. But in the 1850s, technological improvements, competition, economic recovery, and a desire for national unity prompted the development of regional and, eventually, national rail networks. By 1853, rail lines linked New York to Chicago, and a year later track had reached the Mississippi River. In 1860, the rails stretched as far west as St. Joseph, Missouri—the edge of the frontier. In 1853, seven short lines combined to form the New York Central system, and the Pennsylvania Railroad was unified from Philadelphia to Pittsburgh. Most lines, however, were still independently run, separated by gauge, scheduling, differences in car design, and a commitment to serve their home towns first and foremost.

Railroads did not completely replace water transportation. By the midcentury, steamships still carried bulk cargo more cheaply than railroads, except during freezing weather. The sealike Great Lakes permitted the construction of giant ships with propellers in place of paddle wheels; these leviathans carried heavy bulk cargoes like lumber, grain, and ore.

Gradually, steamships replaced sailing vessels on the high seas. In 1818, steam-powered packets made four round trips a year between New York and Liverpool, sailing on schedule

Steamboats rather than waiting for a full cargo as ships had done before then. The breakthrough came in 1848, though, when Samuel Cunard introduced regularly scheduled steamships to the Atlantic run between Liverpool and New York, reducing travel time from twenty-five days eastbound and forty-nine days westbound to between ten and fourteen days each way. Sailing ships quickly lost first-class passengers and light cargo to these swift steamships.

By far the fastest-spreading technological advance of the era was the magnetic telegraph. Samuel F. B. Morse's invention freed long-distance messages from the restraint of

Telegraph traveling no faster than the messenger. By 1853, only nine years after the construction of the first experimental line, 23,000 miles of telegraph wire spread across the United States; by 1860, 50,000. In 1861, the telegraph bridged the continent, connecting the east and west coasts. The new invention revolutionized news gathering, provided advance information for railroads and steamships, and altered patterns of business and finance. Rarely has an innovation had so great an impact so quickly.

The changes in transportation and communications between 1800 and 1860 were revolutionary. Railroads reduced the time of travel, were cheap to build over difficult terrain, and remained in use all year, unlike water transport, which was frozen out in winter. But time was the key factor. In 1800, it took four days to travel by coach from New York City to Baltimore and nearly four weeks to reach Detroit. By 1830, Baltimore was only a day and a half away, and Detroit, via the Erie Canal, was only a two-week journey. By 1857, Detroit was just an overnight train ride from New York City. The reduction in travel time saved money and facilitated commerce. During the first two decades of the century, wagon transportation cost 30 to 70 cents per ton per mile. By 1860, wheat moved from Chicago to New York for 1.2 cents per ton-mile. In sum, the transportation revolution had transformed the economy.

1807	Fulton's steamboat, *Clermont*	**1837**	*Charles River Bridge* v. *Warren Bridge*
1812–15	War of 1812	**1839–43**	Hard times
1813	Boston Manufacturing Company founded	**1848**	Regularly scheduled steamship passage between Liverpool and New York
1818	National Road reaches Wheeling, Virginia	**1849**	California gold rush
1819–23	Depression	**1853**	British study American system of manufacturing
1824	*Gibbons* v. *Ogden*	**1854**	Railroad reaches the Mississippi
1825	Erie Canal completed	**1857**	Hard times
1830	Baltimore and Ohio Railroad begins operation		
1834	Mill workers strike at Lowell		

The Market Economy

Prior to the transportation revolution, most farmers in the early nineteenth century had geared production to family needs. They lived in interdependent communities and kept detailed account books of labor and goods exchanged with neighbors. Farm families tended to produce much of what they needed, but they traded agricultural surpluses for or purchased items that they could not produce. On such farms, men selling cordwood and women selling eggs, butter, cheese, and poultry produced the family's only cash. By the start of the Civil War, however, the United States had an industrializing economy, in which an increasing number of men and women worked for wages and in which most people outside the South—farmers and townspeople alike—increasingly purchased store-bought goods produced in workshops and factories.

In the market economy, crops were grown and goods produced for sale in the marketplace, at home or abroad. The money received in market transactions, whether from the sale of goods or of a person's labor, purchased items produced by other people. Such a system encouraged specialization. Formerly self-sufficient farmers began to grow just one or two crops or to concentrate on raising only cows, pigs, or sheep for market. Farm women gave up spinning and weaving at home and purchased fabric produced by wage-earning farm girls in Massachusetts textile mills.

Definition of a Market Economy

The United States experienced enormous economic growth. Improvements in transportation and technology, the division of labor, and new methods of financing all fueled expansion of the economy—that is, the multiplication of goods and services. In turn, this growth prompted new improvements. The effect was cumulative; by the 1840s, the economy was growing more rapidly than in the previous four decades. Per capita income doubled between 1800 and 1860, while the price of manufactured goods and food fell between 1809 and 1860. An expanding economy provided greater opportunities for wage labor.

Despite the great economic change and growth, the pace was uneven. Prosperity reigned during two long periods, from 1823 to 1835 and from 1843 to 1857. But there were also long stretches of economic contraction. During the time from Jefferson's 1807 embargo through the War of 1812, the growth rate was negative—that is, fewer goods and services were produced. Contraction and deflation occurred again during the hard times of 1819 through 1823, 1839 through 1843, and 1857. These periods were characterized by the collapse of banks, business bankruptcies, and a decline in wages and prices. For workers, the down side meant lower wages and higher unemployment rates.

Boom-and-Bust Cycles

Tens of thousands suffered during the hard times. In 1857, the Mercantile Agency—the forerunner of Dun and Bradstreet—recorded 5,123 bankruptcies, or nearly double the number in the previous year. Contemporary reports estimated 20,000 to 30,000 unemployed in Philadelphia and 30,000 to 40,000 in New York City. Female benevolent societies expanded their soup kitchens and distributed free firewood to the needy. In Chicago, charities reorganized to meet the needs of the poor; in New York, the city hired the unemployed to fix streets and develop Central Park. And in Fall River, Massachusetts, a citizens' committee disbursed public funds on a weekly basis to nine hundred families. The soup kitchen, the bread line, and public aid had become fixtures in urban America.

What caused the cycles of boom and bust that brought about such suffering? In general, they were a direct result of the new market economy. Prosperity stimulated greater demand for staples and finished goods. Increased demand led in turn to higher prices and still higher production, to speculation in land, and to the flow of foreign currency into the country. Eventually, production surpassed demand, leading to lower prices and wages; and speculation inflated land and stock values. The inflow of foreign money led first to easy credit and then to collapse when unhappy investors withdrew their funds.

Cause of Boom-and-Bust Cycles

Some early economists considered this process beneficial—a self-adjusting cycle in which unprofitable economic ventures were eliminated. In theory, people concentrated on the activities they did best, and the economy as a whole became more efficient. Advocates of the system argued also that it furthered individual freedom, since ideally each seller, whether of goods or labor, was free to determine the conditions of the sale. But in fact the system put workers on a perpetual roller coaster. They became dependent on wages—and the availability of jobs—for their very existence.

Government Promotes Economic Growth

The eighteenth-century political ideas that had captured the imagination of the Revolutionary War generation and found expression in the ideal of republican virtue were paralleled in economic thought by the writings of Adam Smith, a Scottish political economist. Smith's *The Wealth of Nations* first appeared in 1776, the year of the Declaration of Independence. Both works emphasized individual liberty, one economic, the other political. Both were reactions against forceful government: Jefferson attacked monarchy and distant government; Smith attacked mercantilism (government regulation of the economy to benefit the state). They believed that virtue was lodged in individual freedom and that the entire community would benefit most from individuals pursuing their own self-interest. As president, Jefferson put these political and economic beliefs into action by reducing the role of government.

Jefferson, however, recognized that government was nonetheless a necessary instrument in promoting individual freedom. Freedom, he believed, thrived where individuals had room for independence, creativity, and choices; individuals fettered by government, monopoly, or economic dependence could not be free. Committed to the idea that a republican democracy would flourish best in a nation of independent farmers and artisans and in an atmosphere of widespread political participation, Jefferson worked to realize those ideals. Beginning with the purchase of Louisiana in 1803, Republican policy, no less than that of the Federalists, turned to using the federal government to promote economic growth. Belief in limited government was not an end in itself, but only a means to greater individual freedom. The result was faith in a market economy in which government also played an active role.

Once Louisiana had been acquired, the federal government facilitated economic growth and geographic expansion by encouraging westward exploration and settlement and by promoting agriculture. The Lewis and Clark expedition from 1804 to 1806 was the beginning of a continuing federal interest in geographic and geologic surveying and the first step in the opening of western lands to exploitation and settlement.

To encourage western agriculture, the federal government offered public lands for sale at reasonable prices and evicted Indian tribes from their traditional lands. Because transportation was crucial to the development of the frontier, the government first financed roads and then canals and later subsidized railroad construction through land grants; it also surveyed about fifty railroad routes between 1827 and 1840. Even the State Department aided agriculture: its consular offices overseas collected horticultural information, seeds, and cuttings and published technical reports in an effort to improve American farming.

The federal government played a key role in technological and industrial growth. Federal arsenals pioneered new manufacturing techniques and helped to develop the machine-tool industry. The United States Military Academy at West Point, founded in 1802, emphasized technical and scientific subjects in its curriculum. The U.S. Post Office stimulated interregional trade and played a brief but crucial role in the development of the telegraph: the first telegraph line was constructed in 1844 under a government grant, and during 1845 the Post Office ran it. Finally, to create an atmosphere conducive to economic growth and individual creativity, the government protected inventions and domestic industries. Patent laws gave inventors a seventeen-year monopoly on their inventions, and

tariffs protected American industry from foreign competition.

The federal judiciary validated government promotion of the economy and encouraged business enterprise. In *Gibbons* v. *Ogden* (1824), the Supreme Court overturned a New York state law that had given Robert Fulton and Robert Livingston a monopoly on the New York–New Jersey steamboat trade. Ogden, their successor, lost his monopoly when Chief Justice John Marshall ruled that existing congressional licensing took precedence over New York's grant of monopoly rights to Fulton and Livingston. Marshall declared that congressional power under the commerce clause of the Constitution extended to "every species of commercial intercourse," including the transportation systems. In defining interstate commerce broadly, the Marshall Court expanded federal powers over the economy while limiting the ability of states to control economic activity within their borders.

Legal Foundations of Commerce

Federal and state courts, in conjunction with state legislatures, also encouraged the proliferation of corporations—groups of investors that could hold property and transact business as one person, with limited liability for the owners. In 1800, the United States had about three hundred incorporated firms. By 1830, the New England states alone had issued nineteen hundred charters. At first, each firm needed a special legislative act to incorporate, but after the 1830s applications became so numerous that incorporation was authorized by general state laws.

A further encouragement to economic development, corporate development, and free enterprise was the Supreme Court's ruling in *Charles River Bridge* v. *Warren Bridge* (1837) that new enterprises could not be restrained by implied privileges under old charters. The case involved issues of great importance. Should a new interest be able to compete against existing, older privileges, and should the state protect existing privilege or encourage innovation and the growth of commerce through competition?

In 1785, the Massachusetts legislature chartered the Charles River Bridge Company and in 1791 extended its charter to a seventy-year term. In return for assuming the risk of building the bridge between Charlestown and Boston, the owners received the privilege of collecting tolls. In 1828, the legislature chartered another company to build the Warren Bridge across the Charles, with the right to collect tolls for six years, after which the bridge would be turned over to the state and be toll-free. With the terminus of the new span only ninety yards away from its own bridge, the Charles River Bridge Company sued, claiming that the new bridge breached the earlier charter. Roger Taney, Marshall's successor as chief justice, speaking for the Court majority, noted that the original charter did not confer the privilege of monopoly and therefore exclusivity could not be implied. Focusing on the question of corporate privilege rather than the right of contracts, Taney ruled that charter grants should be interpreted narrowly and that ambiguities would be decided in favor of the public interest. New enterprises should not be restricted under old charters.

State Promotion of the Economy State governments far surpassed the federal government in promoting the economy. From 1815 through 1860, for example, 73 percent of the $135 million invested in canals was government money, mostly from the states. In the 1830s, the states started to invest in rail construction. Even though the federal government played a larger role in constructing railroads than in building canals, state and local governments provided more than half of southern rail capital. State governments also invested in corporation and bank stocks, providing those institutions with much-needed capital. Finally, state governments at a minimum equaled and may have exceeded private enterprise in their investments.

From the end of the War of 1812 until 1860, the United States experienced uneven but sustained economic growth largely as a result of these government efforts. Although political controversy raged over questions of state versus federal activity—especially with regard to internal improvements and banking—all parties agreed on the general goal of economic expansion. Indeed, the major restraint on government action during these years was not philosophical but financial: both the government purse and the public purse were small.

The Rise of Manufacturing and Commerce

In 1851, hundreds of American products made their international debut at the London Crystal Palace Exhibition, the first modern world's fair. There the design and quality of American machines and wares astonished observers. American manufacturers returned home with dozens of medals. Most impressive to the Europeans were three simple machines: Alfred C. Hobb's unpickable padlocks, Samuel Colt's revolvers, and Robbins and Lawrence's six rifles with completely interchangeable parts. All were machine- rather than hand-tooled products of what the British called the American system of manufacturing. This American system so impressed the British—the leading industrial nation of the time—that in 1853 they sent a parliamentary commission to study it. Soon other nations were sending delegations across the Atlantic to bring back American machines.

American System of Manufacturing The American system of manufacturing used precision machinery to produce interchangeable parts that needed no filing or fitting. In 1798, Eli Whitney promoted the idea of interchangeable parts when he contracted with the federal government to make ten thousand rifles in twenty-eight months. By the 1820s, the U.S. Ordnance Department, through the national armories at Springfield, Massachusetts and Harpers Ferry, Virginia, introduced machine-made interchangeable parts for firearms. From the arsenals, the American system spread, giving birth to the machine-tool industry—the mass manufacture of specialized machines for other industries. One by-product was an explosion in the production of inexpensive consumer goods of uniformly high quality.

Interchangeable parts and the machine-tool industry were uniquely American contributions to the industrial revolution. Both paved the way for America's swift industrialization after the Civil War. The process of industrialization began, however, in a simple and traditional way. In 1800, manufacturing was relatively unimportant to the American

F. B. Locke adapted to the new market for ready-made clothing by becoming a manufacturer, wholesaler, and retailer of men's shirts. Though continuing to make shirts to order, the Shirt Depot's staple was mass-produced shirts, as this advertisement from the *Boston Directory, 1848–49* indicates. *Collection of Advertising History, Archives Center, National Museum of American History.*

economy. What manufacturing there was took place mostly in small workshops or homes. Journeymen and apprentices worked with and under master craftsmen; women working alone at home spun thread and wove cloth. Tailors, shoemakers, and blacksmiths made articles by hand for a specific customer.

The clothing trades illustrate well the nineteenth-century changes in manufacturing and distribution and the reliance on the market economy. The machine-tool industry produced **Clothing Trades** new machinery that transferred textile and clothing production from kitchens and home workshops to mills and factories. Production, which had been based on artisan shops and female family labor, now depended on workers who were paid by the piece or by the hour. The manufactured product, first cloth, then cloth and finished clothing, was sold throughout the United States.

In the eighteenth century, most men wore clothes made at home, or they occasionally bought used clothing. Wealthy men had clothing made by tailors who cut unique garments to fit them. A tailor was a master craftsman whose journeymen and apprentices worked with him to produce goods made to order. By the 1820s and 1830s, clothiers and clothing manufacturers replaced most, though not all, of the old system. Typically, a journeyman cut the fabric panels in the factory, and the sewing was put out at piece rates to unskilled or semiskilled labor, often women working in their own homes. In 1832, Boston manufacturers employed three hundred journeymen tailors at $2 per day and a hundred boys and thirteen hundred women at 50 cents a day. Most of the women sewed straight seams at home. Previously women often had sewn an entire garment, but by the late 1850s, as many as seventeen different pairs of hands were involved in making a single pair of pants. Apprentices, if used at all, were no longer learning a trade but were a permanent source of cheap labor.

Merchants adapted to the changes in production. In the 1820s, clothiers appeared with stocks of ready-made clothes. T. S. Whitmarsh of Boston advertised in 1827 that "he keeps constantly for Sale, from 5 to 10,000 Fashionable ready-made Garments." Upon entering Whitmarsh's, a customer found row after row of ready-made apparel without a sign of tailors or a workshop. The merchant often bought the goods wholesale, though many merchants manufactured garments in their own factories apart from the retail stores. Lewis and Hanford of New York City boasted of cutting more than 100,000 garments in the winter of 1848–1849. The firm sold most of its clothing in the South and owned its own retail outlet in New Orleans. A New Orleans competitor, Paul Tulane, owned a New York factory that made goods for his Louisiana store. In the West, Cincinnati became the center of the new men's clothing industry.

The rise of cotton textile mills made possible the changes in the clothing industry. The first American textile mill, built in Pawtucket, Rhode Island, in 1790, used water-powered spinning machines constructed from British models by the English immigrant Samuel Slater. Slater employed women and children as cheap labor and sold thread from Maine to Maryland. Soon other mills sprang up, stimulated by the embargo on British imports from 1807 through 1815.

Early mills also used the "putting-out" system. Traditionally, women had spun their own thread and woven it into cloth for their own families; now many women received thread from the mills and returned finished cloth. The change was subtle but significant: although the work itself was familiar, women operated their looms for piece-rate wages and produced cloth for the market, not for their own use.

Textile manufacturing was radically transformed in 1813 by the construction of the first American power loom and the chartering of **Waltham (Lowell) System** the Boston Manufacturing Company. The corporation was capitalized at $400,000—ten times the amount behind the Rhode Island mills—by Francis Cabot Lowell and other Boston merchants. Its goal was to eliminate problems of timing, shipping, coordination, and quality control inherent in the putting-out system. The owners erected their factories in Waltham, Massachusetts, combining all the manufacturing processes at a single location. They also employed a resident manager to run the mill, thus separating ownership from management. The company produced cloth so inexpensively that many women began to purchase rather than make their own cloth.

In the rural setting of Waltham not enough hands could be found to staff the mill, so the managers recruited New England farm daughters, accepting responsibility for their living conditions. To persuade young women to come, they offered cash wages, company-run boarding houses, and such cultural events as evening lectures—none of which was available on the farm. This paternalistic approach, called the Waltham (or Lowell) system, was adopted in other mills erected alongside New England rivers.

By the 1850s, though, another work force had entered the mills—Irish immigrants. With a surplus of cheap labor available, Lowell and the other mill towns abandoned their model systems. Within a few years, the typical mill had become a modern factory, and work relationships in American society had been radically altered.

Textile manufacturing changed New England. Lowell, the "city of spindles," symbolized early American industrialization as it grew from 2,500 people in 1826 to 33,000 in 1850. The textile industry became the most important in the nation before the Civil War, employing 115,000 workers in 1860, more than half of whom were women and immigrants. The key to its success was that the machines, not the women, spun the thread and wove the cloth. The workers watched the machines and intervened to maintain smooth operation. When a thread broke, the machine stopped automatically; the worker would find the break, piece the ends together, and restart the machine. The mills used increasingly specialized machines, relying heavily on advances in the machine-tool industry. Technology enabled American firms to compete successfully with British cotton mills. Here was the American system of manufacturing applied.

Textile mills were in the vanguard of industrialization, but manufacturing grew in many areas. The manufacture of woolen textiles, farm implements, machine tools, iron, glass, and finished consumer goods all became major industries. "White coal"—water power—was widely used to run the machines. Yet by 1860, the United States was still predominantly an agricultural nation; just over one-half of the work force was engaged in agriculture. Manufacturing accounted for only a third of total production, even though that fraction had doubled in twenty years.

Several factors stimulated industrial development. They included the need for home manufactures created by the War of 1812, population growth, government policy (protective tariffs, for example), the rise of commercial agriculture, and the transportation revolution. Commercial growth accompanied the rise of manufacturing and was in many ways essential to it.

Cotton, for instance, had once been traded by plantation agents who handled all the goods produced and bought by the owners, extending credit where needed. As cotton became a great staple export following the invention of the cotton gin in 1793, exports rose from half a million pounds in that year to 83 million pounds in 1815. Gradually, some agents came to specialize in finance alone: cotton brokers appeared, men who for a commission brought together buyers and sellers. Similarly, wheat and hog brokers sprang up in the West—in Cincinnati, Louisville, and St. Louis. The supply of finished goods also became more specialized. Wholesalers bought large quantities of a particular item from manufacturers, and jobbers broke down the wholesale lots for retail stores and country merchants.

Commercial specialization made some traders in the big cities, especially New York, virtual merchant princes. When the Erie Canal opened, the city be-

Specialization of Commerce

came a standard stop on every major trade route—from Europe, the ports of the South, and the West. New York traders were the middlemen in southern cotton and western grain trading; in fact, New York was the nation's major cotton-exporting city. Merchants in other cities played a similar role within their own regions.

Newly rich traders invested their profits in processing and then manufacturing, further stimulating the growth of northern cities. Some cities became leaders in specific industries: Rochester became a milling center and Cincinnati—"Porkopolis"—the first meat-packing center.

Banking and other financial institutions played a significant role in the expansion of commerce and manufacturing and were also an important indus-

Banking and Credit Systems

try. Financial institutions (banks, insurance companies, and corporations) linked savers with those who wished to borrow money for equipment. The expiration of the first Bank of the United States in 1811, after Congress refused to renew its charter, acted as a stimulus to state-chartered banks, and in the next five years the number of banks more than doubled. Nonetheless, state banks proved inadequate to spur national growth. Consequently, in 1816 Congress chartered the Second Bank of the United States. But many farmers, local bankers, and politicians denounced the bank as a monster and in 1836 finally succeeded in killing it.

The closing of the Second Bank in 1836 caused a nationwide credit shortage that, along with the Panic of 1837, stimulated major reforms in banking. Michigan and New York introduced charter laws promoting what was called *free banking*. Previously, every new bank had required a special legislative charter, and so each bank incorporation was in effect a political decision. Under the new laws, any proposed bank that met certain minimum conditions—capital invested, notes issued, and types of loans to be made—would automatically receive a state charter. Although banks in Michigan and New York were thus freer to incorporate, restrictions were placed on their practices, slightly reducing the risk of bank failure. Many other states soon followed suit.

Free banking proved a significant stimulus to the economy in the late 1840s and 1850s. New banks sprang up everywhere, providing merchants and manufacturers with the credit they needed. The free banking laws also served as a precedent for general incorporation statutes, which allowed manufacturing firms to receive state charters without special acts of the state legislature. Investors in

The young mill women who worked in this New England textile mill stopped work to pose for this early view, ca. 1850. New England farm daughters, and later Irish immigrants, comprised much of the nation's first factory workforce. *International Museum of Photography, George Eastman House.*

corporations, called shareholders, were granted *limited liability,* or freedom from responsibility for the company's debts. An attractive feature to potential investors, limited liability encouraged people to back new business ventures.

In the 1850s, with credit and capital both easily obtainable, the pace of industrialization increased. In the North, industry began to rival agriculture and commerce in dollar volume. Meanwhile, commercial farming, financed by the credit boom, integrated the early frontier into the northern economy. By 1860, six northern states—Massachusetts, New York, Pennsylvania, Connecticut, Rhode Island, and Ohio—were highly industrialized. The clothing, textile, and shoe industries employed more than 100,000 workers each, lumber 75,000, iron 65,000, and woolens and leather 50,000. Although agriculture still predominated even in these states, industrial employment would soon surpass it.

Mill Girls and Mechanics

Oh, sing me the song of the Factory Girl!
So merry and glad and free!
The bloom in her cheeks, of health how it
   speaks,
Oh! a happy creature is she!
She tends the loom, she watches the spindle,
And cheerfully toileth away,
Amid the din of wheels, how her bright eyes
   kindle,
And her bosom is ever gay.

This idyllic portrait of factory work appeared in the Chicopee, Massachusetts, *Telegraph* in 1850. It was a fitting song for the teenage, single women who first left the villages and farms of New England to work in the mills. The mill owners, believing that the degradation of English factory workers arose from their living conditions and not from the work itself, designed a model community, offering airy courtyards and river views, secure dormitories, prepared meals, and cultural activities.

Kinship ties, the promise of steady work, and good pay at first lured rural young women into the mills. Many pairs of sisters and cousins worked in the same mills and lived in the same boarding houses. They helped each other adjust, and letters home brought other kin to the mills. Girls then had few opportunities for work outside their own homes, and at the same time their families had less need for their labor. The commercial production of thread and cloth had reduced a good part of the work done in farm households by New England daughters, who averaged sixteen and one-half years of age when they entered the mills and usually stayed there only about five years. Few intended to stay longer. Most left the mills to marry and were replaced by other women interested in earning a wage.

By the 1840s, however, the paternalism of the Lowell system was beginning to be replaced by exploitation. In their race for profits, mill owners lengthened the workday, cut **Mill Girl** wages, and tightened discipline. **Protests** They also introduced the speedup and the stretch-out to expand production. The speed-up increased the speed of the machines, and the stretch-out increased the number of machines a worker had to operate. These and other actions led to worker protests. In 1834, in reaction to a 25-percent wage cut, the mill women unsuccessfully "turned out" (struck) against the Lowell mills. Two years later, when boarding-house rates were raised, they turned out again. And in the 1840s, Massachusetts mill women joined forces with other workers to press for legislation mandating a ten-hour day.

What happened in the New England mills occurred in a less dramatic fashion throughout the nation. Work tasks and workplaces changed, as did relations between workers and supervisors. In the traditional workshops and households, work relationships were intensely personal. People worked within family settings and shared a sense of unity and purpose; men and women had a feeling of control over the quality, value (wages), and conditions of their labor.

The new textile mills, insurance companies, wholesale stores, and railroads, however, were the antithesis of the old workshop and household production tradition. Large factories **Changes** lacked the reciprocity that had **in the** characterized earlier relation- **Workplace** ships. Factory workers lost their sense of autonomy, and impersonal market forces seemed to dominate. Stiff competition among mills in the growing textile industry led to layoffs and replacement of operatives with cheaper, less skilled workers or children. The formal rules of the factory contrasted sharply with the conditions in artisan or farm households. Supervisors separated the workers from the owners. The division of labor and the use of machines reduced the skills required of workers. And the coming and going of the large work forces was governed by the bell, the steam whistle, or the clock.

Changes in the workplace transformed workers. Initially, mill girls used kinship, village, and gender ties to build supportive networks in factories. In the 1840s and after, as Irish women came to predominate, more workers were strangers to each other before they entered the mills. Once employed, what they had in common—the bases for friendship and mutual support—were their work and job experiences. As a sense of distance from their employers increased, so did deep-seated differences among workers. Nationality, religion, education, and future prospects separated Irish and Yankee millworkers. For many Irish women, mill work was permanent employment, not a stage in their lives, as it was for their Yankee sisters.

Organized labor's greatest achievement during this period was gaining relief from the threat of conspiracy laws. When journeymen shoemakers organized in the first decade of the **Emergence** century, employers turned to the **of a Labor** courts, charging criminal conspiracy. **Movement** acy. The cordwainers' (shoemakers') cases, which involved six trials from 1806 through 1815, left labor organizations in a tenuous position. Although the journeymen's right to organize was recognized, the courts ruled as unlawful any coercive action that harmed other businesses or the public. In effect, strikes were illegal. Eventually, a Massachusetts case, *Commonwealth* v. *Hunt* (1842), reversed that decision, when Chief Justice Lemuel Shaw ruled that Boston journeymen bootmakers could combine and strike. Conspiracy laws no longer thwarted unionization.

Yet permanent organizations were difficult to maintain. Outside the crafts, most workers were unskilled or, at best, semiskilled. Moreover, religion, race, and ethnicity divided workers. The early labor unions tended to be local in nature. The strongest resembled medieval guilds. They were created by journeymen craftsmen who sought to protect themselves against the competition of inferior workmen by regulating apprenticeship and establishing minimum wages. In the 1820s and 1830s, craft unions forged larger umbrella organizations in the cities, including the National Trades Union (1834). But in the hard times of 1839–1843, the movement fell apart amid wage reductions and unemployment. In the 1850s, the deterioration of working conditions strengthened the labor movement again. Workers won a reduction in hours, and the ten-hour day became standard. Though the Panic of 1857 wiped out the umbrella organizations, some of the new national unions for specific trade groups survived.

The impact of economic and technological change, however, fell more heavily on individual workers than on their organizations. As a group, the workers saw their share of the national wealth decline after the 1830s. Individual producers—craftsmen, factory workers, and farmers—had less economic power than they had had a generation or two before. And workers were increasingly losing control over their own work.

Commercial Farming

Beyond the town and city limits, agriculture (the nation was still overwhelmingly rural) remained the backbone of the economy. Indeed, it was rural population growth that transformed so many farm villages into bustling small cities. Moreover, the market orientation of farm families and their ability to feed the growing town and village populations made possible the concentration of population and the development of commerce and industry.

In 1800, New England and Middle Atlantic farmers worked as their fathers and mothers had. Life centered around a household economy in which the needs of the family and the labor it supplied mostly determined what was produced and in what amounts. But then canals and railroads began transporting grains eastward from the fertile Old Northwest. At the same time, northeastern agriculture developed some serious problems. Northeastern farmers had already cultivated all the land they could; expansion was impossible. Moreover, small New England farms with their uneven terrain did not lend themselves to the new labor-saving farm implements introduced in the 1830s—mechanical sowers, reapers, threshers, and balers. Many northeastern farms also suffered from soil exhaustion.

Northeastern Agriculture

In response to these problems and to competition from the West, many northern farmers either went west or gave up farming for jobs in the merchant houses and factories. Between 1820 and 1860, the percentage of people in the North living on farms declined from 71 to 40 percent. Those farmers who remained proved to be quite adaptable. By the 1850s, New England and Middle Atlantic farm families were successfully adjusting to western competition. Many abandoned the commercial production of wheat and corn and stopped tilling poor land. Instead, they improved their livestock, especially cattle, and specialized in vegetable and fruit production and dairy farming. They financed these changes through land sales or borrowing. In fact, their greatest potential profit was from rising land values, not from farming itself.

Increasingly, farm families everywhere adjusted to market conditions. In 1820, about one-third of the food produced was intended for market; by 1860, about two-thirds. As agriculture grew commercialized, women's production and earnings became essential to the survival of the family farm. As noted earlier, in New England, women did put-out work for income. In the Middle Atlantic states, especially near towns and cities, and in Ohio, women's dairy production was crucial to family income.

Butter and cheese making for local and regional markets replaced spinning and weaving as a major activity.

Most farm families seemed to welcome the opportunities offered by the market economy. Although they took pride in self-sufficiency and rural serenity, they shifted toward specialization and market-oriented production. The rewards in this period for such flexibility were great: produce sold at market financed land and equipment purchases and made credit arrangements possible. Many farm families flourished.

Americans saw great promise in railroads and industry, but they still valued agrarian life. State governments energetically promoted commercial agriculture in order to spur economic growth and sustain the values of an agrarian-based republic. Massachusetts in 1817 and New York in 1819 subsidized agricultural prizes and county fairs. New York required contestants to submit written descriptions of how they grew their prize crops; the state then published the best essays to encourage the use of new methods and to promote specialization.

Even so, the Old Northwest gradually and inevitably replaced the northeastern states as the center of American family agriculture. Farms in the Old Northwest were much larger than northeastern ones and better suited to the new mechanized farming implements. The farmers of the region bought machines, such as the McCormick reaper, on credit and paid for them with the profits from their high yields. By 1847, Cyrus McCormick was selling 1,000 reapers a year. Using interchangeable parts, he expanded production to 5,000 a year. Similarly, John Deere's steel plow, invented in 1837, replaced the inadequate iron plow; steel blades kept the soil from sticking and were tough enough to break the roots of prairie grass. By 1856, Deere's 65 employees were making 13,500 plows a year.

Mechanization of Agriculture

Mechanized farming was the basis of expanded production. In the 1850s alone, wheat production surged 70 percent. By that time the area that had been the western wilderness in 1800 had become one of the world's leading agricultural regions. Midwestern farm families fed an entire nation and had food to export.

The Western Frontier

Integral to the development of the market economy was the steady expansion of the United States. In 1800, the edge of settlement had formed an arc from western New York through the new states of Kentucky and Tennessee, south to Georgia. By 1820, it had shifted to Ohio, Indiana, and Illinois in the North and Louisiana, Alabama, and Mississippi in the South. By 1860, settlement reached the Southwest and the West Coast. Unsettled land remained—mostly between the Mississippi River and the Sierra Nevada—but the old frontier and its native inhabitants, the Indians, had given way to white settlement. Still, the plains and mountain territories were only sporadically settled by whites.

The lore of the frontier and of pioneers forms a part of the mythology of America. James Fenimore Cooper used the frontier setting and ordinary people in his Leatherstocking tales, a series of novels, the first of which appeared in 1823. The protagonist, Hawkeye (Natty Bumppo), was the first popular fictional hero in America. At heart a romantic, Hawkeye preferred the freedom of the virgin forest to domesticated society. Popular legends, songs, and dime novels in the nineteenth century, like movies, television, and paperbacks in the twentieth, glorified fur trappers, explorers and scouts, and pioneers. Major themes included pioneers crossing the arid plains and snow-covered Rockies to bring civilization to the wilderness; Mormons finding Zion in the Great American Desert; and gold seekers sailing on clipper ships to California.

Legends of Pioneers

Americans have only recently come to recognize that there are other sides to these familiar stories. Women, Indians, and blacks, as well as white men, were pioneers. Explorers and pioneers did not discover North America by themselves, nor did the wagon trains fight their way across the plains—Indians guided them along traditional paths and led them to food and water. Rather than civilizing the frontier, settlers at first brought a rather primitive economy and society, which did not compare favorably with the well-ordered Indian civilizations.

All those who sought furs, gold, and lumber spoiled the natural landscape in the name of progress and development.

No figure has come to symbolize the frontier more aptly than the footloose, rugged fur trapper, who roamed the wilderness in search of pelts. The trapper, with his backpack, rifle, **Fur Trade** and kegs of whiskey, spearheaded America's manifest destiny (see page 232), extending the United States presence to the Pacific Slope. Indeed, the history of trapping was in essence the history of the opening of the frontier. Early fur traders exploited friendly Indian tribes. Then pioneers—mountain trappers—monopolized the trade through the systematic organization and backing of trading companies. Soon settlements and towns sprang up along the trappers' routes. By the 1840s, with demand at a low ebb and the beaver nearing extinction, fur trading decreased and some trappers settled down. In Oregon in 1843, former trappers helped organize the first provisional government and pressured for United States statehood. In the mountain states, the mining and cattle frontiers lasted another half-century, following the development of the fur-trading frontier.

But not all regions followed that pattern. Anglos settled newly acquired California almost overnight. In January 1848, James Marshall, a carpenter, spotted a few goldlike particles in **California** the millrace at Sutter's Mill (now **Gold Rush** Coloma, California). Word of the discovery spread, and other Californians rushed to garner instant fortunes. By 1849, the news had spread eastward; hundreds of thousands of fortune seekers flooded in. Success in the market economy required capital, hard labor, and time; by contrast, gold mining seemed to promise instant riches. Most forty-niners never found enough gold to pay their expenses. "The stories you hear frequently in the States," one gold seeker wrote home, "are the most extravagant lies imaginable—the mines are a humbug. . . . the almost universal feeling is to get home." But many stayed, unable to afford the passage back home or tempted by the growing labor shortage in California's cities and agricultural districts. San Francisco, the gateway from the West Coast to the interior, became an instant city, ballooning from one

The gold rush brought treasure seekers—black and white, men and women, native and foreign born—to California. Few found their fortune in gold, but most stayed to settle the West Coast. *California State Library*.

thousand people in 1848 to thirty-five thousand just two years later.

About one-seventh of the travelers on the overland trails were women, many of whom found their domestic skills in great demand. They received high fees for cooking, laundering, **Frontier** and sewing. Inevitably, boarding **Women** houses and hotels were run by women, as men shunned domestic work. Not all women were entrepreneurs, however. Some wives, at their spouses' commands, cooked for and served their husbands' friends. The women did the work while their husbands built reputations as hosts.

Abigail Scott Duniway, a leading western crusader for women's suffrage and a veteran of the Overland Trail to Oregon, wrote of one woman's experience. She lived in a "neighborhood composed chiefly of bachelors," Duniway wrote in 1859, "who found comfort in mobilizing at meal time at the homes of the few married men of the township, and seemed especially fond of congregating at the hospitable cabin home of my good husband, who was never quite so much in his glory as when entertaining men at this fireside, while I, if not washing, scrubbing, churning, or nursing the baby, was preparing their meals in our lean-to kitchen."

Gold altered the pattern of settlement along the entire Pacific coast. Before 1848, most overland traffic flowed north over the Oregon Trail; few pioneers turned south to California or used the Santa Fe Trail. By 1849, a pioneer observed that the Oregon Trail "bore no evidence of having been much traveled this year." Instead, traffic was flowing south, and California was becoming the new population center of the Pacific Slope. One measure of the shift was the overland mail routes. In the 1840s, the Oregon Trail had been the major communications link between the Pacific and the Midwest. But the Post Office officials who organized mail routes in the 1850s terminated them in California, not in Oregon; there was no route farther north than Sacramento.

By 1860, California, like the Great Plains and prairies to the east, had become a farmers' and merchants' frontier linked to the market economy.

Land Grants and Sales What made farm settlement possible was the availability of land and credit. Some public lands were granted as a reward for military service: veterans of the War of 1812 received 160 acres; veterans of the Mexican War could purchase land at reduced prices. Until 1820, civilians could buy government land at $2 an acre (a relatively high price) on a liberal four-year payment plan. More important, from 1800 to 1817, the government successively reduced the minimum purchase from 640 to 80 acres. However, when the availability of land prompted a flurry of land speculation that ended in the Panic of 1819, the government discontinued credit sales. Instead, it reduced the price further, to $1.25 an acre.

Some eager pioneers settled land before it had been surveyed and put up for sale. Such illegal settlers, or squatters, then had to buy the land they lived on at auction, and they faced the risk of being unable to purchase it. In 1841, to facilitate settlement, simplify land sales, and end property disputes, Congress passed the Pre-emption Act, which legalized settlement prior to surveying.

Since most settlers, squatters or not, needed to borrow money, private credit systems arose. Banks, private investors, country storekeepers, and speculators all extended credit to farmers. Railroads also sold land on credit—land they had received from the government as construction subsidies. Indeed, nearly all economic activity in the West involved credit, from land sales and the shipping of produce to railroad construction.

Frontier Cities Towns and cities were the life lines of the agricultural West. Steamboats connected eastern markets and ports with river cities like Louisville, Cincinnati, and St. Louis and lake cities such as Cleveland and Chicago. These western cities eventually developed into manufacturing centers when merchants shifted their investments from commerce to industry. Chicago became a center for the manufacture of farm implements, Louisville of textiles, and Cleveland of iron.

For the North and the West, the period from 1800 through 1860 was one of enormous growth. Population increased sixfold. Settlement extended beyond the Mississippi by 1860 and was spreading east from the Pacific Ocean as well. By then, Cincinnati, St. Louis, and Chicago had populations exceeding a hundred thousand, and Buffalo, Louisville, San Francisco, Pittsburgh, Detroit, Milwaukee, and Cleveland has surpassed forty thousand. Thus commerce, urbanization, and industrialization overtook the farmers' frontier, wedding western areas to the Northeast. By the midcentury, farming was also challenged by a booming manufacturing sector. And agriculture itself was becoming not only mechanized but also more market-oriented.

Economic development changed the American landscape and the way people lived. Canals, railroads, steamboats, and telegraph lines linked economic activities hundreds and thousands of miles apart. The market economy brought sustained growth and cycles of boom and bust. Hard times and unemployment became frequent occurrences.

At the same time, commercial and industrial growth altered production and consumption. The market economy changed farm work as farmers began to purchase goods formerly produced by wives and daughters and farm families geared production to faraway markets. Farm women increasingly contributed wages and income from market sales to the family farm. In New England many farm daughters left to become the first factory workers in the new textile industry. As the master-journeyman-apprentice system faded away, workplace relations became more impersonal and conditions harsher. Immigrants began to form a new industrial group, and some workers organized labor unions.

The American people, too, were changing. Immigration and western expansion made the population and society more diverse. Urbanization, commerce, and industry produced significant divisions among Americans, affecting the home as well as the workshop. The South was not totally insulated from these changes, but its dependence on slave rather than free labor set it apart. Above all else, slavery defined the South.

Suggestions for Further Reading

General

Stuart Bruchey, *The Roots of American Economic Growth, 1607–1861: An Essay in Social Causation* (1965); David Klingaman and Richard Vedder, eds., *Essays in Nineteenth-Century History* (1975); Otto Mayr and Robert C. Post, eds., *Yankee Enterprise: The Rise of the American System of Manufactures* (1981); Douglass C. North, *Economic Growth of the United States, 1790–1860* (1966).

Transportation

Robert G. Albion, *The Rise of New York Port, 1815–1860* (1939); Carter Goodrich, *Government Promotion of American Canals and Railroads, 1800–1890* (1960); Harry N. Scheiber, *Ohio Canal Era: A Case Study of Government and the Economy, 1820–1861* (1969); Ronald E. Shaw, *Erie Water West: Erie Canal 1797–1854* (1966); George R. Taylor, *The Transportation Revolution, 1815–1860* (1951); James A. Ward, *Railroads and the Character of America, 1820–1887* (1986).

Commerce and Manufacturing

Alfred D. Chandler, Jr., *The Visible Hand: Managerial Revolution in American Business* (1977); Thomas C. Cochran, *Frontiers of Change: Early Industrialization in America* (1981); Robert F. Dalzell, Jr., *Enterprising Elite: The Boston*

Associates and the World They Made (1987); Louis Hartz, *Economic Policy and Democratic Thought: Pennsylvania, 1776–1860* (1954); David J. Jeremy, *Transatlantic Industrial Revolution: The Diffusion of Textile Technologies Between Britain and America, 1790s–1830s* (1981); Stanley I. Kutler, *Privilege and Creative Destruction: The Charles River Bridge Case* (1971); Merritt Roe Smith, *Harpers Ferry Armory and the New Technology* (1977); Barbara M. Tucker, *Samuel Slater and the Origins of the American Textile Industry, 1790–1860* (1984).

Agriculture

Jeremy Atack and Fred Bateman, *To Their Own Soil: Agriculture in the Antebellum North* (1987); Allen G. Bogue, *From Prairie to Corn Belt: Farming on the Illinois and Iowa Prairies in the Nineteenth Century* (1963); Clarence Danhof, *Change in Agriculture: The Northern United States, 1820–1870* (1969); John Mack Faragher, *Sugar Creek: Life on the Illinois Prairie* (1986); Paul W. Gates, *The Farmer's Age: Agriculture, 1815–1860* (1962); Benjamin H. Hibbard, *A History of Public Land Policies* (1939); Joan M. Jensen, *Loosening the Bounds: Mid-Atlantic Farm Women, 1750–1850* (1986); Robert Leslie Jones, *History of Agriculture in Ohio to 1880* (1983).

The Western Frontier

Ray A. Billington and Martin Ridge, *Westward Expansion,* 5th ed. (1982); John Mack Faragher, *Women and Men on the Overland Trail* (1979); William H. Goetzmann, *Exploration and Empire: The Explorer and the Scientist in the Winning of the American West* (1966); Julie Roy Jeffrey, *Frontier Women: The Trans-Mississippi West, 1840–1880* (1979); Theodore J. Karamanski, *Fur Trade and Exploration: Opening the Far Northwest, 1821–1852* (1983); John D. Unruh, Jr., *The Overland Emigrants and the Trans-Mississippi West, 1840–1860* (1979); David J. Wishart, *The Fur Trade of the American West, 1807–1840* (1979).

Workers

Mary H. Blewett, *Men, Women, and Work: Class, Gender, and Protest in the New England Shoe Industry, 1780–1910* (1988); Alan Dawley, *Class and Community: The Industrial Revolution in Lynn* (1977); Thomas Dublin, *Women at Work: The Transformation of Work and Community in Lowell, Massachusetts, 1826–1860* (1979); Alice Kessler-Harris, *Out to Work; A History of Wage-earning Women in the United States* (1982); W. J. Rorabaugh, *The Craft Apprentice: From Franklin to the Machine Age in America* (1986); Steven J. Ross, *Workers on the Edge: Work, Leisure, and Politics in Industrializing Cincinnati, 1788–1890* (1985); Norman Ware, *The Industrial Worker, 1840–1860* (1924); Sean Wilentz, *Chants Democratic: New York City and the Rise of the American Working Class, 1788–1850* (1984).

He was weeping, sobbing. In a humble voice he had begged his master not to give him to Mr. King, who was going away to Alabama, but it had done no good. Now his voice rose and he uttered "an absolute cry of despair." Raving and "almost in a state of frenzy," he declared that he would never leave the Georgia plantation that was home to his father, mother, wife, and children. He would kill himself, he said, before he lost his family and all that made life worth living.

To Fanny Kemble, watching from the doorway, it was a horrifying and disorienting scene. One of the most famous British actresses ever to tour America, Fanny had grown up breathing England's antislavery tradition as naturally as the air. In New England, she had become friends with enlightened antislavery thinkers. Then the man she married took her away from New England to a Georgia rice plantation.

Pierce Butler, Fanny's husband, was everything that a Philadelphia gentleman should be. He had lived all his life in the North, though part of his family's fortune had always sprung from southern slavery. When Fanny chose him, he had seemed an attractive exemplar of American culture. Yet now he shattered his slave's hopes without hesitation. Butler advised the distraught black man not to "make a fuss about what there was no help for." Only with tears and vehement pleas was she able to convince Butler to keep the slave family together. He finally agreed as a favor to her, not on principle or because she had a right to be consulted.

10

SLAVERY AND THE GROWTH OF THE SOUTH, 1800–1860

This incident, which occurred in 1839, illustrates both the similarities between South and North and the differences that were beginning to emerge. Although racism existed in the North, its influence was far more visible in the South. And although some northerners, like Pierce Butler, were undisturbed by the idea of human bondage, a growing number considered it shocking and backward. After the Revolution, these northerners, possessing few slaves and influenced by the revolutionary ideal of natural rights, had adopted gradual emancipation laws.

While the North grew and changed between 1800 and 1860, economically the South merely grew. New lands were settled and new states peopled, but southern growth only reinforced existing economic patterns.

One force behind the South's growth was soaring world demand for cotton. John Stobart's painting shows a steam packet, heavily laden with bales of cotton, arriving in New Orleans. *Courtesy Maritime Heritage Prints.*

Steadily, the South emerged as the world's most extensive and vigorous slave economy. Its people were slaves, slaveholders, and nonslaveholders rather than farmers, merchants, mechanics, and manufacturers. Its well-being depended on agriculture alone, rather than on agriculture, plus commerce and manufacturing. Its population was almost wholly rural rather than rural and urban.

Migration, Growth, and the Cotton Boom

Between 1800 and 1860, the South grew dramatically. Small farmers and slaveowning planters migrated westward and brought new territory under cultivation. Farms and plantations spread across the

landscape as human labor, both voluntary and coerced, built a vastly larger, slaveholding society.

The attraction of rich, new lands drew thousands of southerners across the Appalachian Mountains. Both small farmers and ambitious slaveowners poured across the mountains, pushing the Indians off their lands in the Gulf region. The floodtide of migration reached Alabama and Mississippi in the 1830s, then spilled into Texas in the 1850s. The earliest settlers were often yeomen—small farmers who generally owned no slaves. Yeomen pioneered the southern wilderness, moving into undeveloped regions and building their log cabins. They came first as herders of livestock and then as farmers. After the War of 1812, they moved in successive waves down the southern Appalachians into new Gulf lands. The herdsmen, who fattened their cattle and pigs on the abundant natural vegetation in the woods, generally moved on as farmers filled up an area and broke ground for crops. These yeomen farmers forced many herdsmen farther west and eventually across the Mississippi.

Some yeomen acquired large tracts of level land and became wealthy planters. Others clung to the beautiful mountainous areas they loved. As they moved, they tended to stick to the climate and soils they knew best. Yeomen could not afford the richest bottomlands, which were swampy and required expensive draining, but they acquired land almost everywhere else.

For slaveholding southerners, another powerful motive impelled westward movement: the chance to profit from a spectacular cotton boom. Southern planters were not sentimentalists who held onto their slaves for noneconomic reasons. Like other Americans, they were profit-oriented. But the cotton boom caused nonmechanized, slave-based agriculture to remain highly profitable in the South, sustaining the plantation economy.

Rise of the Cotton South

This had not always seemed likely. At the time of the Revolution, slave-based agriculture was not very profitable in the Upper South. Persistent debt hung heavily over Virginia's tobacco growers. Farther south, slaves grew rice and some indigo, but cotton was a profitable crop only for sea-island planters, who grew the luxurious long-staple variety. The short-staple cotton that grew readily in the interior was unmarketable because its sticky seeds lay tangled in the fibers.

Then England's burgeoning textile industry changed the southern economy. English mills consumed more and more cotton. Sea-island cotton was so profitable between 1785 and 1795 that thousands of farmers in the interior tried growing the short-staple variety. Most of this cotton was grown in the hope that some innovation would make the crop salable to the English. Eli Whitney responded to the need in 1793 with a simple machine that removed the seeds from the fibers. By 1800, cotton was spreading rapidly westward from the seaboard states.

The voracious appetite of English mills caused a meteoric rise in cotton production (see maps, page 180). Despite occasional periods of low prices, the demand for cotton surged ahead every decade. This inspired southerners with capital to buy more land, buy more slaves, and plant ever more cotton. Cotton growers boosted production so successfully that by 1825 the South was the world's dominant supplier of cotton. By the 1850s, the South sent Britain more than 70 percent of all the cotton it imported.

Thus the antebellum South, or Old South before the Civil War, became primarily a cotton South. Tobacco continued to be grown in Virginia and North Carolina, and rice and sugar were very important in certain coastal areas. But cotton was the largest crop and the force behind the South's hunger for new territory.

Small slaveowners and planters (those who owned at least twenty bondsmen) sought out alluvial bottomland and other fertile soils, eager to grasp the opportunity for wealth that came with the cotton boom. As demand for cotton increased, slaveowners pushed feverishly to grow more. Their desire to plant more cotton and buy more slaves often caused men with new wealth to postpone the enjoyment of luxuries. Many first-generation planters lived for decades in their original log cabin, improved only by clapboards or a frame addition. Yet the planters' wealth put ease and refinement within their grasp, and for the lucky, riches and high social status could come quickly.

The rise of new aristocrats in the Gulf and the migration of aspiring slaveholders across the Appalachians meant another kind of migration—involuntary movement—for black southerners. Cotton planters in the Gulf region generated a steady demand for more slaves, but Congress had closed the international slave trade in 1808. Despite some smuggling, slave labor from abroad was essentially unavailable. Thus new slaves for the Lower South had to come from the older states of the Upper South.

As it happened, slaveowners there often had more slaves than they needed. Their slave population had grown, but tobacco prices had fallen and soil exhaustion had become a serious problem. Thus planters in Virginia and North Carolina were shifting toward wheat and corn, crops that were less labor-intensive. Slaveowners on worn-out tobacco lands were glad to sell excess slaves to the expanding black belt areas of the cotton South.

Consequently, the expansion of slaveholding

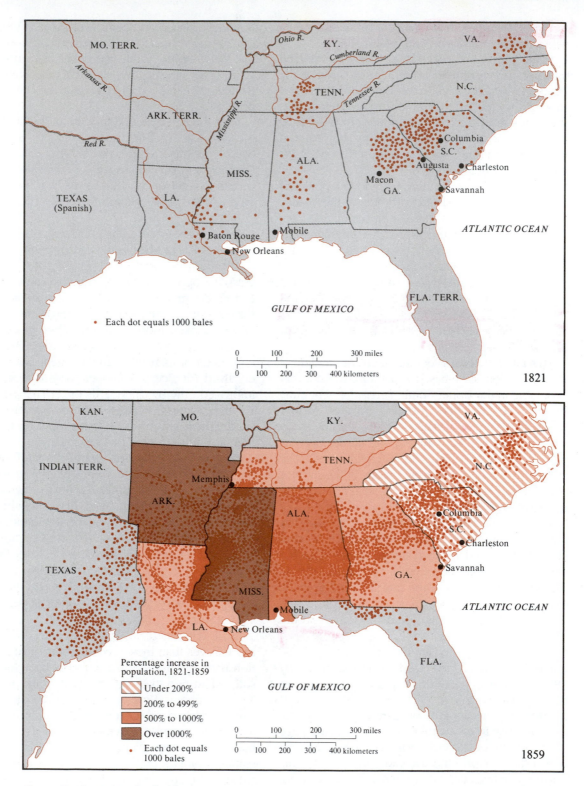

1821

MO. TERR.

Ohio R.

KY.

Cumberland R.

VA.

Arkansas R.

TENN.

Tennessee R.

N.C.

ARK. TERR.

Mississippi R.

Columbia

S.C.

Red R.

MISS.

ALA.

Augusta

Charleston

TEXAS (Spanish)

LA.

Macon

GA.

Savannah

Baton Rouge

Mobile

ATLANTIC OCEAN

New Orleans

FLA. TERR.

GULF OF MEXICO

• Each dot equals 1000 bales

0   100   200   300 miles

0   100   200   300   400 kilometers

1859

KAN.

MO.

KY.

VA.

INDIAN TERR.

TENN.

N.C.

Memphis

ARK.

ALA.

Columbia

S.C.

TEXAS

Charleston

MISS.

GA.

Savannah

Mobile

ATLANTIC OCEAN

LA.

New Orleans

FLA.

Percentage increase in population, 1821-1859

▨ Under 200%

▨ 200% to 499%

▨ 500% to 1000%

▨ Over 1000%

• Each dot equals 1000 bales

GULF OF MEXICO

0   100   200   300 miles

0   100   200   300   400 kilometers

Cotton Production in the South

across the Appalachians caused a large interregional movement of the black population. Between 1810 and 1820 alone, 137,000 slaves were forced to move from North Carolina and the Chesapeake states to Alabama, Mississippi, and other western regions. From 1820 to 1860, an estimated 2 million persons were sold in this interregional slave trade. Each year, thousands of African-American families were disrupted to serve the needs of the cotton economy.

Thus the South was growing and expanding, driven by excitement over new lands and energies related to the cotton boom. To white southerners, the period from 1800 to 1860 was a time of great change and progress, no less so than in the North. But the South was different. The distinguishing features of its social system were those of an agricultural and a slave society.

An Agrarian Society

The South did share some of the diversity of the bustling, urbanizing, commercial North. It had merchants, artisans, and craftsmen in the larger cities and men of commerce who promoted railways and transportation improvements. But the largest patterns of southern development reflected the dominance of agriculture and slavery and the prominence of rural slaves, slaveholders, and yeomen farmers in the population.

In the South, population distribution remained thin. Cotton growers spread out over as large an area as possible in order to maximize production and income. Because farms were **Population Distribution** far apart, rather than clustered around villages, southern society remained predominantly rural. Population density, low even in the older plantation states, was extremely low in the frontier areas being brought under cultivation. In 1860, there were only 2.3 people per square mile in Texas, 15.6 in Louisiana, and 18.0 in Georgia. By contrast, the Northeast averaged 65.4 persons per square mile,

and in some places the density was much higher. Massachusetts had 153.1 people per square mile.

Society in such rural areas was characterized by relatively weak institutions, for it takes people to create and support organized activity. Where the concentration of people was low, it was difficult to finance and operate schools, churches, libraries, or even hotels, restaurants, and other urban amenities. Southerners were strongly committed to their churches, and some believed in the importance of universities, but all such institutions were far less developed than in the North.

The southern cities were likewise smaller and less developed than those in the North. As exporters, southerners did not need large cities; a small **Weak Urban Sector** group of merchants working in conjunction with northern brokers sufficed to ship the cotton overseas and to import necessary supplies and luxuries. As planters, southerners invested most of their capital in slaves. They had little money left to build factories—another source of urban growth. A few southerners did invest in iron or textiles on a small scale. But the largest southern "industry" was lumbering, and the largest factories were cigar factories, where slaves finished tobacco products.

More important, the South did not develop a unified market economy or regional transportation network, as the North did. Far less money was spent on canals, turnpikes, or railroads. As a result, urban growth after 1820 was far less vigorous than in the North. In 1860, the population of Charleston was only 41,000, Richmond 38,000, and Mobile 29,000. New Orleans, by far the largest southern city, had only 169,000 residents; it was at an economic disadvantage because it was not part of the national railroad network.

Thus the South was only semideveloped in comparison with other sections of the country. Its white people were prospering, but neither as rapidly nor as independently as residents of the North. To prosper, southern planters increased their acreage and hoped for continued high demand from foreign customers—decisions that worked to the ultimate disadvantage of the region. Subsistence farmers merely worked harder and hoped to grow a bit more.

Farmers, Planters, and Free Blacks

A large majority of white southern families (three-quarters in 1860) owned no slaves. Some of them lived in towns and ran stores or businesses, but most were yeomen farmers who owned their own land and grew their own food. They were the typical whites, but typical in a society of extremes. The social distance between different groups of whites could be great; still greater was the distance between whites and blacks.

Southern yeomen farmers occupied a relatively autonomous position within the slavery-based, staple-crop economy that was expanding around them. Independent and motivated by a hearty share of frontier individualism, they provided for themselves in the traditional way of American farm families, prospering slowly from improvements on their acreage or the settlement of new and better land. And this meant steady progress for thousands of yeomen as the South expanded.

But the lives of most southern yeomen, as compared to northern farmers, had not been transformed by improvements in transportation. Because few railroads penetrated the southern interior, yeomen generally had little connection with the market or its type of progress. Families might raise a small surplus to trade for needed items or spending cash, but they were not particularly concerned about larger cash income. They valued instead their self-reliance and freedom from others' control. Absorbed in an isolated but demanding rural life, they formed an important, though sometimes silent, part of southern society.

The yeomen enjoyed a folk culture based on family, church, and community. They spoke with a drawl, and their inflections were reminiscent of **Folk Culture of the Yeoman** their Scottish and Irish backgrounds. Once a year they flocked to religious revivals, which they called protracted meetings or camp meetings, and in between they enjoyed events such as house-raisings, log-rollings, quilting bees, and corn shuckings. Such community events provided a fellowship that was especially welcome to isolated rural dwellers.

Beyond these basic facts, historians know little about the yeomen. Because their means were modest, they did not generate the voluminous legal papers—wills, contracts, and inventories of estates—that document the activities of the rich. Only a few letters have found their way into libraries and archives. It is reasonable to suppose, though, that yeomen held a variety of opinions and pursued individual goals. Many of them did aspire to wealth and were eager to join the race for slaves, land, and profits from cotton. Others were content with their independence, recreation, family life, and religion. But whether they strove to become rich or were satisfied with their status, they worked hard.

Toil was also the lot of two other groups of white southerners: landless whites and free blacks. From 25 to 40 percent of the white workers in the South **Landless Whites** were laborers who owned no land. Their property consisted of a few household items and some animals—most often pigs—that could feed themselves on the open range. In addition to unskilled laborers in the countryside and towns, the landless included some immigrants, especially the Irish, who did heavy and dangerous work such as building railroads and digging ditches.

The white farm laborers were people struggling to become yeomen. They faced low wages or, if they rented, were dependent on the unpredictable market price for their crops. Some fell into debt and were frequently sued; others managed to climb into the ranks of yeomen. When James and Nancy Bennitt of North Carolina succeeded in their ten-year struggle to buy land, they decided to avoid the unstable market in cotton as much as possible; instead, they raised extra corn and wheat as sources of cash.

Nearly a quarter of a million free blacks lived in the South in 1860. Their situation was generally worse than the yeoman's and often little better than the slave's. The free blacks of the **Free Blacks** Upper South were usually descendants of men and women emancipated by their owners in the 1780s and 1790s, a period of postrevolutionary idealism that coincided with a decline in tobacco prices. Usually, they did not own land and had to labor in someone else's field, frequently beside slaves. By law they could not own a gun or liquor, violate curfew, assemble except in church, testify in court, or (everywhere after 1835) vote. Despite these obstacles, a minority bought land, and others found jobs as artisans, draymen, boatmen, and fishermen. A few owned slaves, who were almost always their wives and children, purchased from bondage.

Farther south, in the cotton and Gulf regions, a large proportion of free blacks were mulattos, the privileged offspring of wealthy planters. Some received a good education and financial backing from their fathers, who recognized a moral obligation to them. In a few cities such as New Orleans and Mobile, extensive interracial sex had produced a mulatto population that was recognized as a distinct class. These mulattos formed a society of their own and sought a status above slaves and other freedmen, if not equal to planters. But outside New Orleans, Mobile, and Charleston, such groups were rare, and most mulattos encountered disadvantages more frequently than they enjoyed benefits from their light skin tone.

At the opposite end of the spectrum from free blacks were the slaveholders. As a group, slave-owners lived well, on incomes that enabled them to enjoy superior housing, food, clothing, and luxuries. But most did not live on the opulent scale that legend suggests. A few statistics tell the story: 88 percent of southern slaveholders had fewer than twenty slaves; 72 percent had fewer than ten; 50 percent had fewer than five. Thus the average slaveholder was not a man of great wealth but an aspiring farmer. Rather than a polished aristocrat, he was more often a person of humble origins, with little formal education and many rough edges to his manner.

The wealth of the greatest planters gave ambitious men something to aspire to. Most planters lived in spacious, comfortable farmhouses, but some did live in mansions. Most slaveowners sat down at mealtimes to an abundance of tempting country foods—pork and ham, beef and game, fresh vegetables and fruits, tasty breads and biscuits, cakes and jams—but the sophisticated elite consumed such delights as "gumbo, ducks and olives, *supreme de volaille,* chickens in jelly, oysters, lettuce salad, chocolate cream, jelly cake, claret cup, etc."

Slaveholding men held the dominant position in society and, especially among the wealthiest and oldest families, they justified their dominance through a paternalistic ideology.

Southern Paternalism Instead of stressing the acquisitive aspects of commercial agriculture, they focused on *noblesse oblige.* They viewed themselves as custodians of the welfare of society as a whole and of the black families who depended on them. The paternalistic planter viewed himself not as an oppressor but as the benevolent guardian of an inferior race. He developed affectionate feelings toward his slaves (as long as they kept in their place) and was genuinely shocked at outside criticism of his behavior.

The letters of Paul Carrington Cameron, North Carolina's largest slaveholder, illustrate this mentality. After a period of sickness among his one thousand North Carolina slaves, Cameron wrote, "I fear the Negroes have suffered much from the want of proper attention and kindness under this late distemper . . . no love of lucre shall ever induce me to be cruel, or even to make or permit to be made any great exposure of their persons at inclement seasons." On another occasion, he described to his sister the sense of responsibility he felt: "I cannot better follow the example of our venerated Mother than in doing my duty to her faithful old slaves and their descendants."

There is no doubt that the richest southern planters saw themselves in this way. It was comforting to do so, and slaves, accommodating themselves to the realities of power, encouraged their masters to think that their benevolence was appreciated. Paternalism also provided a welcome defense against abolitionist criticism. Still, for most planters, paternalism affected the manner and not the substance of their behavior. It was a matter of style. Its softness and warmth covered harsher assumptions: blacks were inferior; planters should make money.

Relations between men and women in the planter class were similarly paternalistic. Typically, an upper-class southern woman was raised and educated to be the subordinate companion of men. Her proper responsibility was home management. She was not to venture into politics and other worldly affairs. In a social system based on the coercion of an entire race, no women could be allowed to challenge

Elite Women's Role

society's rules, on sexual or racial relations. If she defied or questioned the status quo, she risked universal condemnation.

Within the domestic circle, the husband reigned supreme. For the fortunate women, like North Carolina diarist Catherine Devereux Edmondston, whose marriage joined two people of shared tastes and habits, the husband's authority weighed lightly or not at all. But other women were acutely conscious of that authority. "He is master of the house," wrote South Carolina's Mary Boykin Chesnut. "To hear is to obey . . . all the comfort of my life depends upon his being in a good humor." In a darker mood, Chesnut once observed that "there is no slave . . . like a wife." Unquestionably, there were some, possibly many, close and satisfying relationships between men and women in the planter class, but many women were dissatisfied.

The upper-class southern woman had to clear several barriers in the way of happiness. Making the right choice of a husband was especially important. Once married, she lost most of her legal rights to her husband, became part of his family, and was expected to get along with numerous in-laws during extended visits. On the plantation, she was expected to oversee the cooking and preserving of food, manage the house, care for the children, and attend sick slaves. As a woman, she was forbidden to travel and visit unless accompanied by a man. All the circumstances of her future life depended on the man she chose.

Childbearing brought grief and sickness, as well as joy, to southern women. In 1840, the birthrate for southern women in their fertile years was almost 20 percent higher than the national average. At the beginning of the nineteenth century, the average southern woman could expect to bear eight children; by 1860, the figure had decreased only to six, and one or more miscarriages were likely among so many pregnancies. The high birthrate took a toll on women's health, for complications of childbirth were a major cause of death. Moreover, a mother had to endure the loss of many of the infants she bore. In the South in 1860, almost five out of ten children died before the age of five, and in South Carolina more than six in ten failed to reach the age of twenty.

Slavery was another source of trouble, a source of problems that women had to endure but were not supposed to notice. "Violations of the moral law . . . made mulattoes as common as blackberries," protested a woman in Georgia, but wives had to play "the ostrich game." "A magnate who runs a hideous black harem," wrote Mrs. Chesnut, "under the same roof with his lovely white wife, and his beautiful accomplished daughters . . . poses as the model of all human virtues to these poor women whom God and the laws have given him. From the height of his awful majesty, he scolds and thunders at them, as if he never did wrong in his life."

In the early 1800s, some southern women, especially Quakers, had spoken out against slavery. Although most white women did not criticize the "peculiar institution," they often approached it differently from men, seeing it less as a system and more as a series of relationships with individuals. Perhaps southern men sensed this, for they wanted no discussion of the slavery issue by women. In the 1840s and 1850s, as national and international criticism of slavery increased, southern men published a barrage of articles stressing that women should restrict their concerns to the home.

But southern women were beginning to chafe at their customary exclusion from financial matters. A study of women in Petersburg, Virginia, has revealed behavior that amounted to an implicit criticism of the institution of marriage and the loss of autonomy it entailed. During several decades before 1860, the proportion of women who had not married, or not remarried after the death of a spouse, grew to exceed 33 percent. Likewise, the number of women who worked for wages, controlled their own property, or even ran businesses increased. In managing property, these women benefited from legal reforms, beginning with Mississippi's Married Women's Property Act of 1839, that were not designed to increase female independence. Rather, the law gave women some property rights in order to protect families from ruin caused by the husband's indebtedness. But some women saw the resulting opportunity and took it.

Restrictions on freedom and the use of education were not limited to upper-class women. For a large category of southern men and women, freedom was wholly denied and education in any form was not allowed. Male or female, slaves were expected to accept bondage and ignorance as their condition.

Slaves and the Conditions of Their Servitude

For African-Americans, slavery was a curse unrelieved by blessings, except the strengths they developed to survive it. Slaves knew a life of poverty, coercion, toil, heartbreak, and resentment. They had few hopes that were not denied; often they had to bear separation from their loved ones; and they were despised as an inferior race. That they endured and found loyalty and strength among themselves is a tribute to their courage, but it could not make up for a life without freedom or opportunity.

Southern slaves enjoyed few material comforts beyond the bare necessities. Their diet was plain and limited, although generally they had enough to eat. The basic ration was corn-

Slaves' Diet, Clothing, and Housing meal, fat pork, molasses, and occasionally coffee. Many masters allowed slaves to tend gardens, which provided the variety and extra nutrition of greens and sweet potatoes. Fishing and hunting benefited some slaves. Despite the occasional supplements of green vegetables and fish, their diet was nutritionally deficient; many slaves suffered from beriberi and pellagra. Clothing too was plain, coarse, and inexpensive. The few clothes issued to slaves were made either of light cotton or a coarse, heavy material called osnaburg. Because shoes were normally not issued until the weather became cool, slaves frequently contracted parasitic diseases such as hookworm.

Slaves typically lived in small one-room cabins with a door and possibly a window opening but no glass. Logs chinked with mud formed the walls; dirt was the only floor; and a wattle-and-daub or stone chimney vented the fireplace, which provided heat and light. Bedding consisted of heaps of straw, straw mattresses, or wooden bedframes lashed to the walls with rope. A few crude pieces of furniture and cooking utensils completed the furnishings of most cabins. The gravest drawback of slave cabins

was not their appearance and lack of comfort but their unhealthfulness. In each small cabin lived one or two whole families. Crowding and lack of sanitation fostered the spread of infection and contagious diseases.

Hard work was the central fact of the slaves' existence. In Gulf Coast cotton districts, long hours and large work gangs suggested factories in the

Slaves' Work Routines field rather than the small-scale, isolated work patterns of slaves in the eighteenth-century Chesapeake. Overseers rang the morning bell before dawn, making it possible for slaves to be in the fields at first light. Except in urban settings and on some rice plantations, where slaves were assigned daily tasks to complete at their own pace, working from "sun to sun" became universal in the South. These long hours and hard work were at the heart of the advantage of slave labor. As one planter put it, slaves were the best labor because "you could command them and *make* them do what was right." White workers, by contrast, were few and could not be *driven*; "they wouldn't stand it."

Planters aimed to keep all their laborers busy all the time. Profit took precedence over paternalism's "protection" of women: slave women did heavy field work, often as much as the men and even during pregnancy. Old people—of whom there were few—were kept busy caring for young children, doing light chores, or carding, ginning, or spinning cotton. Children had to gather kindling for the fire, carry water to the fields, or sweep the yard. But slaves had a variety of ways to keep themselves from being worked to death. It was impossible for the master to supervise every slave every minute, and slaves slacked off when they were not being watched.

Of course, slaves could not slow their labor too much, because the owner enjoyed a monopoly on force and violence. Whites throughout the South

Physical and Mental Abuse of Slaves believed that Negroes "can't be governed except with the whip." Evidence suggests that whippings were less frequent on small farms than on large plantations, but the reports of former slaves show that a large majority even of small farmers plied the

Coercion was the essence of slavery. To enforce their will, masters relied on whips and instruments like this pronged collar to inflict pain or restrict the slaves' movements. A slave girl in nineteenth-century New Orleans had to wear the collar shown as punishment for attempting to run away. The painting suggests that such sights were not unusual. *Painting: The Historic New Orleans Collection, Museum/Research Center; slave collar: Massachusetts Historical Society.*

lash. These beatings symbolized authority to the master and tyranny to the slaves, who made them a benchmark for evaluating a master. In the words of former slaves, a good owner was one who did not "whip too much," whereas a bad owner "whipped till he's bloodied you and blistered you."

As this testimony suggests, terrible abuses could and did occur. The master wielded virtually absolute authority on his plantation, and courts did not recognize the word of a chattel. Pregnant women were whipped, and there were burnings, mutilations, tortures, and murders. Yet the physical cruelty of slavery may have been less in the United States than elsewhere in the New World. In sugar-growing or mining regions of the Western Hemisphere in the 1800s, slaves were regarded as an expendable resource to be replaced after seven years. Treatment was so poor and families so uncommon that death rates were high and the heavily male slave population did not replace itself but in-stead rapidly shrank in size. In the United States, by contrast, the slave population showed a steady natural increase, as births exceeded deaths, and each generation grew larger.

The worst evil of American slavery was not its physical cruelty but the fact of slavery itself: coercion, loss of freedom, belonging to another person with virtually no hope for change. A woman named Delia Garlic cut to the core when she said, "It's bad to belong to folks that own you soul an' body. I could tell you 'bout it all day, but even then you couldn't guess the awfulness of it." American slaves hated their oppression, and contrary to some whites' perceptions, they were not grateful to their oppressors. Although they had to be subservient and speak honeyed words in the presence of their masters, they talked quite differently later on among themselves. The evidence of their resistant attitudes comes from their actions and from their own life stories.

Chapter 10: Slavery and the Growth of the South, 1800–1860

Former slaves reported some kind feelings between masters and slaves, but the overwhelming picture was one of antagonism and resistance.

Slaves' Attitudes Toward Whites Slaves mistrusted kindness from whites and suspected self-interest in their owners. A woman whose mistress "was good to us Niggers" said her owner was kind "'cause she was raisin' us to work for her." Christmas presents of clothing from the master did not mean anything, observed another, "'cause he was going to [buy] that anyhow."

Slaves were sensitive to the thousand daily signs of their degraded status. One man recalled the general rule that slaves ate cornbread and owners ate biscuits. If blacks did get biscuits, "the flour that we made the biscuits out of was the third-grade shorts." A woman reported that on her plantation "Old Master hunted a heap, but us never did get none of what he brought in." If the owner took slaves' garden produce to town and sold it for them, the slaves suspected him of pocketing part of the profits.

Suspicion and resentment often grew into hatred. According to a former slave from Virginia, "the white folks treated the nigger so mean that all the slaves prayed God to punish their cruel masters." When a yellow fever epidemic struck in 1852, many slaves saw it as God's retribution. As late as the 1930s, an elderly woman named Minnie Fulkes cherished the conviction that God was going to punish white people for their cruelty to blacks. She described the whippings that her mother had had to endure and then exclaimed, "Lord, Lord, I hate white people and the flood waters goin' to drown some more."

Slave Culture and Everyday Life

The force that helped slaves to maintain such defiance was their culture. They had their own view of the world, a body of beliefs and values born of both their past and their present, as well as the fellowship and support of their own community. With power overwhelmingly in the hands of whites, it was not possible for slaves to change their world. But drawing strength from their culture, they could resist their condition and struggle on against it.

Slave culture changed significantly after the turn of the century. Between 1790 and 1808, when Congress banned further importation of slaves, there was a rush to import Africans. After that the proportion of native-born blacks rose steadily, reaching 96 percent in 1840 and almost 100 percent in 1860. With time the old African culture faded farther into memory as an African-American culture matured.

In one sense, African influences remained primary, for African practices and beliefs reminded the slaves that they were and ought to be different from their oppressors and thus **Remnants of African Culture** encouraged them to resist. The most visible aspects of African culture were the slaves' dress and recreation. Some slave men plaited their hair into rows and fancy designs; slave women often wore their hair "in string"—tied in small bunches with a string or piece of cloth. A few men and many women wrapped their heads in kerchiefs of the styles and colors of West Africa. For entertainment slaves made musical instruments with carved motifs that resembled some African stringed instruments. Their drumming and dancing clearly followed African patterns.

Many slaves continued to see and believe in spirits. Whites also believed in ghosts, but the belief was more widespread among slaves. It closely resembled the African concept of the living dead— the idea that deceased relatives visited the earth for many years until the process of dying was complete. Slaves also practiced conjuration, voodoo, and quasi-magical root medicine. By 1860, the most notable conjurers and root doctors were reputed to live in South Carolina, Georgia, Louisiana, and other isolated coastal areas of heavy slave importation.

These cultural survivals provided slaves with a sense of their separate past. Black achievement in music and dance was so exceptional that whites felt entirely cut off from it; in this one area some whites became aware that they did not "know" their slaves.

Sunday was a precious time for slaves to worship, rest, play, and spend time with the members of their families. *The Historic New Orleans Collection, Museum/Research Center.*

Conjuration and folklore directly fed resistance; slaves could cast a spell or direct the power of a hand (a bag of articles belonging to the person to be conjured) against the master. Not all masters felt confident enough to dismiss such a threat.

In adopting Christianity, slaves fashioned it, too, into an instrument of support and resistance. Theirs was a religion of justice quite unlike that of the propaganda their masters pushed at them. Former slaves scorned the preaching arranged by their masters. "You ought to have heard that preachin'," said one man. "'Obey your master and mistress, don't steal chickens and eggs and meat,' but nary a word about havin' a soul to save." The slaves believed that Jesus cared about their souls and their present plight. They rejected the idea that in heaven whites would have "the colored folks . . . there to wait on 'em." Instead, when God's justice came, the slaveholders would be "broilin' in hell for their sin."

For slaves Christianity was a religion of personal and group salvation. Beyond seeking personal guidance, blacks prayed "for deliverance of the slaves." Some waited "until the overseer got behind a hill" and then laid down their hoes and called on God to free them. Others held fervent secret prayer meetings that lasted far into the night. From such activities many slaves gained the unshakable belief that God would end their bondage. This faith and the joy and emotional release that accompanied their worship sustained blacks.

Slaves also developed a sense of racial identity. The whole experience of southern blacks taught them that whites despised their race. Blacks naturally drew together, helping each other in danger, need, and resistance. "We never told on each other," one woman declared. Although some slaves did tell on others, former slaves were virtually unanimous in denouncing those who betrayed the group or sought personal advantage through allegiance to whites. And because most slaves lived on small units, there was no overriding class system within the black community.

Slaves' Religion

The main source of support for individuals was the family. Slave families faced severe dangers. At any moment, the master could sell a husband or wife, give a slave child away as a wedding present, or die in debt, forcing a division of his property. Many families were broken up in such ways. Others were uprooted in the trans-Appalachian expansion of the South. When the Union Army registered thousands of black marriages in Mississippi and Louisiana in 1864 and 1865, 25 percent of the men over forty reported that they had been forcibly separated from a previous wife. Probably a substantial minority of slave families suffered disruption of one kind or another.

Slaves' Family Life

But this did not mean that slave families could not exist. American slaves clung tenaciously to the personal relationships that gave meaning to life, for although American law did not protect slave families, masters permitted them. In fact, slaveowners expected slaves to form families and have children. As a result, there was a normal ratio of men to women, young to old.

Following African kinship taboos, African-Americans avoided marriage between cousins (a frequent occurrence among aristocratic slaveowners). Adapting other West African customs to the circumstances of their captivity, they did not condemn unwed mothers, although they did expect a young girl to form a stable marriage after one pregnancy, if not before. By naming their children after relatives of past generations, African-Americans emphasized their family histories. If they chose to bear the surname of a slaveowner, it was often not their current master's name but that of the owner under whom their family had begun in America.

Slaves abhorred interference in their family lives. Some of their strongest protests sought to prevent the breakup of a family. Rape was a horror for both men and women. Some husbands faced death rather than permit their wives to be sexually abused, and women sometimes fought back. In other cases slaves seethed with anger at the injustice but could do nothing except soothe each other with human sympathy and understanding. Significantly, blacks condemned the guilty party, not the victim.

Slave men did not dominate their wives in a manner similar to white husbands, but it is misleading to say that slave women enjoyed equality of power in sex roles and family life. The larger truth is that all black people, men and women, were denied the opportunity to provide for or protect their families. Slavery's cruelties put black men and women in the same dilemma. Under the pressures of bondage, they had to share the responsibilities of parenthood. Each might have to stand in for the other and assume extra duties. Similarly, uncles, aunts, and grandparents sometimes raised the children of those who had been sold away.

Sex Roles in Slavery

In two other respects, however, distinct gender roles remained very important in slave families and experience. First, after work in the fields was done, men's activities focused on traditional "outdoor" tasks while women did "indoor" work. Second, the life cycle and pattern of work routines frequently placed slave women in close associations with each other, which heightened their sense of sisterhood. Female slaves lived significant portions of their lives as part of a group of women, a fact that emphasized the gender-based element of their experience.

Slaves brought to their efforts at resistance the same common sense, determination, and practicality that characterized their family lives. American slavery produced some fearless and implacable revolutionaries. Gabriel Prosser's conspiracy apparently was known to more than a thousand slaves when it was discovered in 1800, just before it was put into motion. A similar conspiracy in Charleston in 1822, headed by a free black named Denmark Vesey, involved many of the most trusted slaves of leading families. The most famous rebel of all, Nat Turner, rose in violence in Southampton County, Virginia, in 1831.

Resistance to Slavery

The son of an African woman who passionately hated her enslavement, Nat was a precocious child who learned to read at a very young age. Encouraged by his first owner to study the Bible, he enjoyed some special privileges but also knew changes of masters and hard work. In time, young Nat became a preacher. He also developed a tendency toward mysticism and became increasingly withdrawn. After nurturing his plan for several years, Turner led a band of rebels from house to house in the predawn darkness of August 22, 1831. The group severed limbs and crushed skulls with axes or killed their victims with guns. Before they were stopped, Nat Turner and his followers had slaughtered sixty whites of both sexes and all ages. About two hundred blacks, including Turner, lost their lives as a result of the rebellion.

But most slave resistance was not violent because the odds against revolution were especially poor in North America. Consequently, slaves directed their energies toward creating means of survival and resistance. A desperate slave could run away for good, but probably in more instances slaves ran off temporarily to hide in the woods. Every day that a slave "lay out" in this way, the master lost a day's labor. Most owners chose not to mount an exhaustive search and sent word instead that the slave's grievances would be redressed. The runaway would then return to bargain with the master. Most owners would let the matter pass, for, like the owner of a valuable cook, they were "glad to get her back."

Other modes of resistance had the same object: to resist but survive under bondage. Appropriating food (stealing, in the master's eyes) was so common that even whites sang humorous songs about it. Blacks were also alert to the attitudes of individual whites and learned to ingratiate themselves or play off one white person against another. Field hands frequently tested a new overseer to intimidate him or win more favorable working conditions.

Harmony and Tension in a Slave Society

Not only for blacks but for whites, too, slave labor stood at the heart of the South's social system, and its importance grew as the century advanced. Slavery affected the organization of society, the values of individuals, and—increasingly—every aspect of politics in the region.

Ever since the seventeenth century, slavery had placed severe restrictions on black southerners, but these deepened as the 1800s advanced. In all things, from their workaday movements to Sunday worship, slaves fell under the supervision of whites. Courts held that a slave "has no civil right" and could not even hold property "except at the will and pleasure of his master." When slaves revolted, legislators tightened the legal straitjacket: after the Nat Turner insurrection of 1831, for example, they prohibited owners from teaching their slaves to read. As the sectional crisis developed, fears of slave revolt grew and restrictions on slaves increased accordingly.

Slavery imposed responsibilities on nonslaveholders, as well as on slaveowners. All white male citizens bore an obligation to ride in patrols to discourage slave movements at night. White ship captains and harbor masters were required to scrutinize the papers of blacks who might be attempting to escape bondage. Urban residents who did not supervise their domestic slaves as closely as planters did found themselves subject to criticism for endangering the community. And the South's few manufacturers often felt pressure to use slave rather than free labor.

Slavery had a deep effect on southern values because it was the main determinant of wealth in the South. Ownership of slaves guaranteed the labor to **Slavery as the Basis of Wealth and Social Standing** produce cotton and other crops on a large scale. Slaves were therefore vital to the acquisition of a fortune. In fact, for southern society as a whole, slaveholding indicated wealth in general with remarkable precision. Important economic enterprises not based on slavery were so rare that variations in wealth from county to county followed very closely variations in slaveholding.

It was therefore not surprising that slaveholding was the main determinant of a white man's social position. Wealth in slaves was also the foundation on which the ambitious built their reputations. Ownership of slaves brought political power: a solid majority of political officeholders were slaveholders, and the most powerful of them were generally large slaveholders. Lawyers and newspaper editors were sometimes influential, but they did not hold independent positions in the economy or society. Dependent on the planters for business and support, they served planters' interests and reflected their outlook.

Slavery's influence spread throughout the social system until even the values and mores of non-slaveholders bore its imprint. For one thing, the availability of slave labor tended to devalue free labor. Consequently, nonslaveholders preferred to work for themselves rather than to hire out. Whites who had to sell their labor tended to resent or reject tasks that seemed degrading. This kind of thinking engendered an aristocratic value system ill suited to a newly established democracy.

In modified form, the attitudes characteristic of the planter elite gained a considerable foothold among the masses. The ideal of the aristocrat emphasized lineage, privilege, power, pride, and refinement of person and manner. Some of those qualities were in short supply in the recently settled, expanding cotton kingdom, however; they mingled with and were modified by the tradition of the frontier. In particular, independence and defense of one's honor were highly valued by planter and frontier farmer alike. Thus, instead of gradually disappearing, as it did in the North, duelling hung on in the South and gained an acceptance that spread throughout the society.

Aristocratic Values and Frontier Individualism

Other aristocratic values that marked the planters as a class were less acceptable to the average citizen. Planters believed that they were better than other people. In their pride, they expected not only to wield power but to receive special treatment. By the 1850s, some planters openly rejected the democratic creed, vilifying Thomas Jefferson for his statement that all men are equal.

Belief in its own superiority shaped the outlook of the southern elite for generations, but this attitude was never acceptable to the individualistic members of the yeoman class. Independent and proud of their position, yeomen resisted any infringement of their rights. They believed that they were as good as anyone and knew that they lived in a nation in which democratic ideals were gaining strength. Thus there were occasional conflicts between aristocratic pretensions and democratic zeal.

Yeomen farmers and citizens resented their underrepresentation in state legislatures, corrup-

tion in government, and undemocratic control over local government. After vigorous debate, the reformers won most of their battles. Five southern states—Alabama, Mississippi, Tennessee, Arkansas, and Texas—adopted white manhood suffrage and other reforms, including popular election of governors, legislative apportionment based on the white population, and locally chosen county government. Only South Carolina and Virginia effectively defended property qualifications for office, legislative malapportionment, appointment of county officials, and selection of the governor by the lawmakers. The formal structure of government was more democratic than many planters would have wished.

Movements for Electoral Reform

Slaveowners knew that an open structure could permit troubling issues to arise. In Virginia, nonslaveholding westerners raised a basic challenge to the slave system in the year following the Nat Turner rebellion. Advocates of gradual abolition forced a two-week legislative debate on slavery, arguing that the institution was injurious to the state and inherently dangerous. When the House of Delegates finally voted, the motion favoring abolition lost by just 73 to 58. This was the last major debate on slavery in the antebellum South.

With such tension in evidence, it was perhaps remarkable that slaveholders and nonslaveholders did not experience frequent and serious conflict. Why were class confrontations among whites so infrequent? Historians who have considered this question have given many answers. One of the most important factors was race. The South's racial ideology stressed whites' superiority to blacks and declared that race, not class, was the social dividing line. Besides, in a rural society family bonds and kinship ties are valued, and some of the poor nonslaveholding whites were related to the rich new planters. The experience of frontier living must also have created a relatively informal, egalitarian atmosphere. Moreover, the South was an expanding, mobile society in which yeomen and planters rarely depended on each other. Yeomen farmed mainly for themselves; planters farmed for themselves and for the market.

But suppression of dissent also played a significant, and increasingly greater, role. White southern-

ATTENTION
SOUTHERN MEN !
DOWN WITH
THE ABOLITION PRESS
MEET AT
SCHNEIDER'S
At 8 o'clock This Night,
Augusta Ga.
DECEMBER 26, 1560.

Run off in haste and anger, with a misprinted date, this handbill illustrates the determination of southern slaveholders in Augusta, Georgia, to tolerate no criticism of their peculiar institution. *Library of Congress.*

ers who criticized the slave system out of moral conviction or class resentment were intimidated, attacked, or legally prosecuted. Southern cities impounded abolitionist literature and sought to bar any antislavery influences. Intellectuals developed elaborate justifications for slavery as newspapers railed at any antislavery threat. By the 1850s, the defense of slavery's interests dominated discussion, and all groups in society felt pressure to uphold the slave system.

Still, there were signs that the relative lack of conflict between slaveholders and nonslaveholders was coming to an end. As the region grew older, nonslaveholders saw their op-portunities beginning to narrow; meanwhile, wealthy planters enjoyed an expanding horizon. The risks of cotton production were becoming too great and the cost of slaves too high for many yeomen to rise in society. Thus from 1830 to 1860, the percentage of white southern families holding

Hardening of Class Lines

slaves declined steadily from 36 to 25 percent. At the same time, the monetary gap between the classes widened. In 1860, slaveowners' share of the South's agricultural wealth remained at between 90 and 95 percent. The average slaveholder was almost fourteen times as rich as the average nonslaveholder.

Urban artisans and mechanics felt the pinch acutely. Their numbers were few; their place in society was hardly recognized; and in bad times they were often the first to lose work. Moreover, they faced stiff competition from urban slaves, whose masters wanted them to hire their time and bring in money by practicing a trade. White workers demanded that economic competition from slaves be forbidden. This demand was always ignored—the powerful slaveowners would not tolerate interference with their property or the income they derived from it. But the angry protests of white workers resulted in harsh restrictions on *free* black workers and craftsmen.

Pre–Civil War politics reflected these tensions. Facing the prospect of a war to defend slavery, slaveowners expressed growing fear about the loyalty of nonslaveholders and discussed schemes to widen slave ownership. In North Carolina, a prolonged and increasingly bitter controversy over the combination of high taxes on land and low taxes on slaves erupted; a class-conscious nonslaveholder named Hinton R. Helper attacked the institution of slavery in his book *The Impending Crisis,* published in New York in 1857. Discerning planters knew that such fiery controversies lay close at hand in every southern state.

But for the moment, slaveowners stood secure. They held from 50 to 85 percent of the seats in state legislatures and a similarly high percentage of the South's congressional seats. In addition to their near-monopoly on political office, they had established their point of view in all the other major social institutions. Professors who criticized slavery had been dismissed from colleges; school books that contained "unsound" ideas had been replaced. And almost all the clergy had given up preaching against the institution. In fact, except for a few obscure persons of conscience, southern clergy had become slavery's most vocal defenders. Society as southerners knew it seemed to be stable.

In the nation generally, however, society was anything but stable. Change had become one of the major characteristics of the northern economy and society, as the rise of the market and industry produced a more diverse population. The American people were changing, and the currents of change would eventually affect the South.

Suggestions for Further Reading

Southern Society

W. J. Cash, *The Mind of the South* (1941); Clement Eaton, *The Growth of Southern Civilization, 1790–1860* (1961); Clement Eaton, *Freedom of Thought in the Old South* (1940); William W. Freehling, *Prelude to Civil War* (1965); Eugene D. Genovese, "Yeoman Farmers in a Slaveholders' Democ-

racy," *Agricultural History,* 49 (April 1975), 331–342; William Sumner Jenkins, *Pro-Slavery Thought in the Old South* (1935); Peter Kolchin, *Unfree Labor: American Slavery and Russian Serfdom* (1987); Robert McColley, *Slavery and Jeffersonian Virginia* (1964); Donald G. Mathews, *Religion in the Old South* (1977); James Hebron Moore, *The Emergence of the Cotton Kingdom in the Old Southwest: Mississippi, 1770–1860* (1987); Frederick Law Olmsted, *The Slave States,* ed. Harvey Wish (1959); Frederick F. Siegel, *The Roots of Southern Distinctiveness: Tobacco and Society in Danville, Virginia, 1780–1865* (1987); Charles S. Sydnor, *The Development of Southern Sectionalism, 1819–1848* (1948); Ralph A. Wooster, *Politicians, Planters, and Plain Folk* (1975); Ralph A. Wooster, *The People in Power* (1969); Gavin Wright, *The Political Economy of the Cotton South* (1978); Bertram Wyatt-Brown, *Southern Honor* (1982).

Slaveholders and Nonslaveholders

Bennet H. Barrow, *Plantation Life in the Florida Parishes of Louisiana, as Reflected in the Diary of Bennet H. Barrow,* ed. Edwin Adams Davis (1943); Malcolm Bell, Jr., *Major Butler's Legacy: Five Generations of a Slaveholding Family* (1987); Ira Berlin, *Slaves Without Masters* (1974); Randolph B. Campbell, "Intermittent Slave Ownership: Texas as a Text Case," *Journal of Southern History,* 30, No. 1 (February 1985), 15–30; William J. Cooper, *The South and the Politics of Slavery, 1828–1856* (1978); Everett Dick, *The Dixie Frontier* (1948); Clement Eaton, *The Mind of the Old South* (1967); Drew Faust, *A Sacred Circle: The Dilemma of the Intellectual in the Old South* (1977); John Hope Franklin, *The Free Negro in North Carolina, 1790–1860* (1943); Luther P. Jackson, *Free Negro Labor and Property Holding in Virginia, 1830–1860* (1942); Michael P. Johnson and James L. Roark, *Black Masters* (1984); Frances Anne Kemble, *Journal of a Residence on a Georgia Plantation in 1838–1839* (1863); Robert Manson Myers, ed., *The Children of Pride* (1972); James Oakes, *The Ruling Race* (1982); Frank L. Owsley, *Plain Folk of the Old South* (1949); J. Mills Thornton III, *Politics and Power in a Slave Society: Alabama, 1800–1860* (1978).

Southern Women

Carol Bleser, *The Hammonds of Redcliffe* (1981); Jane Turner Censer, *North Carolina Planters and Their Children, 1800–1860* (1984); Catherine Clinton, *The Plantation Mistress* (1982); Elizabeth Fox-Genovese, *Within the Plantation Household* (1988); Jean E. Friedman, *The Enclosed Garden* (1985); Jacqueline Jones, *Labor of Love, Labor of Sorrow* (1985); Suzanne Lebsock, *Free Women of Petersburg* (1984); Elisabeth Muhlenfeld, *Mary Boykin Chesnut* (1981); Mary D. Robertson, ed., *Lucy Breckinridge of Grove Hill* (1979); Ann Firor Scott, *The Southern Lady* (1970); Deborah G. White, *Arn't I a Woman?* (1985); C. Vann Woodward and Elisabeth Muhlenfeld, eds., *The Private Mary Chesnut* (1985).

Conditions of Slavery

Kenneth F. Kiple and Virginia H. Kiple, "Black Tongue and Black Men," *Journal of Southern History,* XLIII (August 1977), 411–428; Ronald L. Lewis, *Coal, Iron, and Slaves* (1979); Richard G. Lowe and Randolph B. Campbell, "The Slave Breeding Hypothesis," *Journal of Southern History,* XLII (August 1976), 400–412; Willie Lee Rose, ed., *A Documentary History of Slavery in North America* (1976); Todd L. Savitt, *Medicine and Slavery* (1978); Kenneth M. Stampp, *The Peculiar Institution* (1956); Robert S. Starobin, *Industrial Slavery in the Old South* (1970).

Slave Culture and Resistance

Herbert Aptheker, *American Negro Slave Revolts* (1943); John W. Blassingame, *The Slave Community* (1979); Judith Wragg Chase, *Afro-American Art and Craft* (1971); Paul D. Escott, *Slavery Remembered: A Record of Twentieth-Century Slave Narratives* (1979); Eric Foner, ed., *Nat Turner* (1971); Eugene D. Genovese, *From Rebellion to Revolution* (1979); Eugene D. Genovese, *Roll, Jordan, Roll* (1974); Herbert G. Gutman, *The Black Family in Slavery and Freedom, 1750–1925* (1976); Vincent Harding, *There Is a River* (1981); Charles Joyner, *Down by the Riverside* (1984); Lawrence W. Levine, *Black Culture and Black Consciousness* (1977); Stephen B. Oates, *The Fires of Jubilee* (1975); Albert J. Raboteau, *Slave Religion* (1978); Robert S. Starobin, *Denmark Vesey* (1970); Sterling Stuckey, *Slave Culture* (1987).

In 1844, English immigrant George Martin of Rochester, New York, a carpenter, fell ill at the age of thirty-three and suddenly had a sense of his own mortality. "A very few years hence and not one of us will be among the living," he wrote his brother in England. "You cannot imagine what the feeling is," he went on, "to think that you will die . . . in a foreign land far from your kindred and home, and no friendly hand to close your eyes." Eight years later, in 1852, George Martin's worst fears were realized. Save for his wife, Betsy, and their children, he died among strangers, away from kin and old friends.

George and Betsy Martin came to the United States in 1834 from an agricultural hamlet twenty-two miles from London. George thought New York harbor "the most beautiful that ever was seen." After two days of touring New York City, the Martins traveled by canal boat, railroad, and lake steamer to their new home on the north shore of Lake Ontario in Upper Canada. They moved permanently to Rochester in 1838, when George found work as a carpenter. Opportunities were good in Canada he wrote his father, but "there is more spirit of enterprise" in the United States.

When he died in 1852, George Martin left very little. His spare time and money

11

DIVERSITY AND CONFLICT: PEOPLE AND COMMUNITIES, 1800–1860

had gone into building his own house in Rochester, but it was unfinished. His relatives in England paid $500 to complete it, so that his widow and children would have a place to live. In the last four years of his life, Martin had become openly intolerant of ethnic diversity; his neighbors and fellow workmen, the butt of his anger, did nothing to help his family after his death.

The United States had changed so much and so rapidly in the decades before George Martin's death that most Americans, like him, were newcomers and strangers where they lived and where they worked. The largest cities grew to enormous size and numbered diverse ethnic, religious, and racial populations in the hundreds of thousands. Millions of immigrants settled in the expanding nation, and countless new and old Americans moved internally as the nation stretched from ocean to ocean.

As the market economy and economic opportunity attracted immigrants and energized the native-born, the American people drew apart. Increasingly, they lived in towns and cities, where diversity became the rule. And the nature of community was changing in the United States. Civic and public institutions had to offer services, such as education, once provided by private families. The face of the city changed too. Opulent mansions existed within sight of notorious slums, and both wealth and poverty reached extremes unknown before in agrarian America.

Private space—the family—also experienced change. With the growth of commerce and industry, the home began to lose its function as a workplace. Especially among the middle and upper classes, the home became woman's domain, a haven from man's world. Working-class women found no such refuge. At the same time, birth control was more widely practiced and families were smaller.

To a great degree, many Americans were uncomfortable with the new direction of American life. Antipathy toward immigrants was common among native-born Americans, who feared competition for jobs. Some blacks fought unceasingly for equality, and many Indians tried unsuccessfully to resist forced removal. In a society growing ever more diverse and complex, conflict became common.

Although the United States remained an agricultural country, the traditional economy and society were yielding to the spreading influence of the market economy, urban growth, and immigration. This process of change continued through the rest of the nineteenth century, accelerating and intensifying in the last three decades. But the path that led to the great industrial, urban, pluralist society had begun before the Civil War.

Country Life

Communities and life within them changed significantly in the first half of the nineteenth century. Within a generation, many frontier settlements became sources, rather than recipients, of migration. Villages in western New York state had lured the sons and daughters of New England in the first two decades of the century. But in the 1820s and 1830s, young people moved from New York villages to the new frontier in the Old Northwest. Later, Ohio and Michigan towns and farms would send their young people farther west. Similarly, migrants from the Upper South went to Illinois and Ohio as people on the move farther south settled the Gulf states.

Although they lived in isolation on individual farms, farm families found a sense of community in the neighborhood and village. The farm village was the center of rural life. But rural social life was not limited to trips to the village; families gathered on each other's farms to do as a community what they could not do individually. Barnraising was among the activities that regularly brought people together. In preparation for the event, the farmer and an itinerant carpenter built a platform and cut beams, posts, and joists. When the neighbors arrived by buggy and wagon, they put together the sides and raised them into position. After the roof was up, everyone celebrated with a communal meal and perhaps with singing, dancing, and folk games. Similar gatherings took place at harvest time and on special occasions.

Farm Communities

Women especially sought to counter rural isolation. Farm men had frequent opportunities to mix at general stores, markets, and taverns and in hunting and fishing. Some women, too, met at market, but more typically they came together at regular work and social gatherings: after-church dinners; sewing, quilting, and cornhusking bees; and preparations for marriages and baptisms. These were times to exchange experiences and thoughts, offer each other support, and swap letters, books, and news.

Traditional country bees had their town counterparts. Fredrika Bremer, a Swedish visitor to the United States, described a sewing bee in 1849 in Cambridge, Massachusetts, at which neighborhood women made clothes for "a family who had lost all their clothing by fire." Yet town bees were neither the all-day family affairs typical of the countryside nor held as often. Life was changing, and town dwellers purchased their goods at the store.

Increasingly, Americans were conscious of such changes. One response was an interest in utopian communities, which offered an antidote to the market economy and to the untamed growth of large

IMPORTANT EVENTS

1819	Indian "civilization act"
1823	Hartford Female Seminary established by Catharine and Mary Beecher
1824	President Monroe proposes removal of Indians
1827	*Freedom's Journal* first published
1830s –50s	Urban riots
1831	*Cherokee Nation* v. *Georgia*
1831–38	Trail of Tears
1835–42	Second Seminole War
1837	Boston employs paid policemen
1837–48	Horace Mann heads the Massachusetts board of education
1841–47	Brook Farm
1842	Knickerbocker baseball club formed
1845	Start of the Irish potato famine
1846–47	Mormon trek to the Great Salt Lake
1847–57	Peak period of immigration before the Civil War

urban communities and an opportunity to restore tradition and social cohesion. Whatever their particular philosophy, utopians sought order and regularity in their daily lives and a cooperative rather than a competitive environment.

The Shakers, who derived their name from the way they danced and swayed at worship services, were an early, lasting utopian experiment. Founder Ann Lee brought this offshoot of the English Quakers to America in 1774. Shakers believed that the end of the world was near and that sin entered the world through sexual intercourse. They regarded existing churches as too worldly and considered the Shaker family the instrument of salvation.

Shakers

In 1787, the Shakers "gathered in" at New Lebanon, New York, to live, worship, and work communally. Other colonies soon followed. At its peak, between 1820 and 1860, the sect had about six thousand members living in twenty settlements in eight states. It was the largest and most permanent of the utopian experiments. Though economically conservative, the Shakers were social radicals. They abolished individual families, practiced celibacy, and pioneered new roles for women. Each colony

was one large family. The Shaker ministry was headed by a woman, Lucy Wright, during its period of greatest growth. Celibacy, however, led to the withering away of the communities.

The most successful communitarians were the Mormons. Organized by Joseph Smith in 1830 as the Church of Jesus Christ of Latter-day Saints, the church spread from its birthplace in New York and established communities dedicated to Christian cooperation. Fleeing persecution in Ohio, Illinois, and Missouri because of their claims of continuous divine revelation and their newly adopted practice of polygyny, the Mormons trekked across the continent in 1846 and 1847 to found a New Zion in the Great Salt Lake Valley. There, under Brigham Young, head of the Twelve Apostles (their governing body), they established a cohesive community of Saints—a heaven on earth. The Mormons created agricultural settlements and distributed land according to family size. An extensive irrigation system, constructed by men who contributed their labor according to the quantity of land they received and the amount of water they expected to use, transformed the arid

Mormon Community of Saints

Shaker meetinghouse at Pleasant Hill, Kentucky, 1820, designed by Micajah Burnett. Marked by a simplicity and beauty of design, the meetinghouse exemplifies the Shaker sense of order. Their code of behavior required separate entrances for men and women. *Linda Butler.*

valley into a rich oasis. As the colony developed, the church elders came to control water, trade, industry, and even the territorial government of Utah.

Not all utopian communities were founded by religious groups. Robert Owen's New Harmony was a well-known, short-lived attempt to found a socialist utopia in Indiana. A wealthy Scottish industrialist, Owen established the cooperative community in 1825. According to his plan, its nine hundred members were to exchange their labor for goods at a communal store. Handicrafts (hat and boot making) flourished at New Harmony, but its textile mill, the economic base of the community, failed after Owen gave it to the community to run. By 1827, the experiment had ended.

More successful were the New Englanders who lived and worked at the Brook Farm cooperative in West Roxbury, Massachusetts. Inspired by the transcendental philosophy that the spiritual rises above

Brook Farm the worldly, its members rejected materialism and sought satisfaction in a rural communal life combining spirituality, work, and play. Though short-lived (1841–1847), Brook Farm played a significant part in the romantic movement in the United States. There Nathaniel Hawthorne, Ralph Waldo Emerson, and the editor of the *Dial* (the leading transcendentalist journal), Margaret Fuller, joined Henry David Thoreau, James Fenimore Cooper, and others in creating what is known today as the American Renaissance—the flowering of a national literature. In poetry and prose, these romanticists favored faith and emotion over reason. Rebelling against convention, both social and literary, they celebrated the American character and experience.

Utopian communities were a reaction against contemporary society; they attempted to recapture the cohesiveness of traditional agricultural and artisan life. Utopians resembled Puritan perfectionists: like the Separatists of seventeenth-century New England, they sought to start anew in their own colonies. Communal work and life offered alternatives to the market economy and urbanizing society.

City Life

Everywhere cities were growing, especially in the North. The transportation revolution and the expansion of commerce and manufacturing, fed by immigration and internal migration, caused the population of cities to rise geometrically. Between 1800 and 1860, the number of Americans increased from 5.3 million to 31.4 million. As the population expanded, the frontier receded, and small rural settlements became towns. In 1800, the nation had only 33 towns with 2,500 or more people and only 3 with more than 25,000. By 1860, 392 towns exceeded 2,500 in population, 35 had more than 25,000, and 9 exceeded 100,000 (see maps below and on page 200).

New York City became the nation's premier urban place. It grew from 60,500 in 1800 to 813,600 in 1860. That year, the combined population of New York City and Brooklyn exceeded 1 million. Many were just passing through; a majority would not stay ten years. Although contemporary bird's-eye views of New York depict an almost pastoral urban life, the city emitted energy and aromas that make twentieth-century cities seem sanitized in comparison. It was an immigrant port city, mostly Irish and German by the 1850s.

New York City

In the 1820s, New York City literally burst its boundaries. Up to that time, New Yorkers could still envision the city as a village, because in an hour's walk they could reach every corner. Mass transit,

Major American Cities, 1820

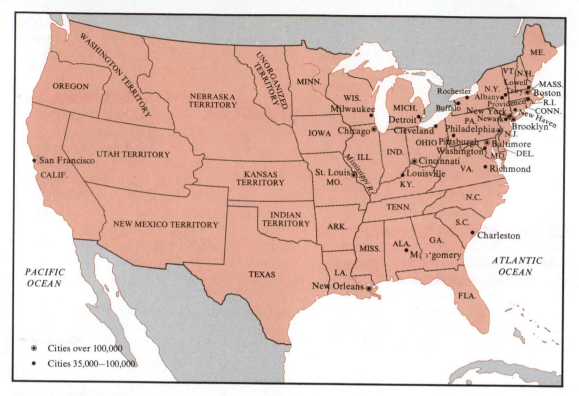

Major American Cities, 1860

however, made it possible for cities to expand. Horse-drawn buses appeared in New York in 1827, and the Harlem Railroad, completed in 1832, ran the length of Manhattan. By the 1850s, all big cities had horse-drawn streetcars.

By twentieth-century standards, early-nineteenth-century cities certainly were disorderly, unsafe, and unhealthy. Expansion occurred so rapidly that few cities could handle the problems it brought. For example, migrants from rural areas were used to relieving themselves and throwing refuse in any vacant area. In the city, such waste spread disease, created water pollution, and gave off obnoxious odors.

New York City solved part of the problem in the 1840s by abandoning wells in favor of reservoir water piped into buildings and outdoor fountains. In some districts, scavengers and refuse collectors carted away garbage and human waste, but in much of the city it just rotted on the ground. Only one-quarter of New York City's streets had sewers by 1857.

New York and other cities did not have the taxing power to raise the sums needed for providing adequate services to all. The best the city could do was to charge the cost of sewers, street paving, and water mains to adjoining property. Thus the spread of new services and basic sanitation depended on residents' ability or willingness to pay, and so those most in need of the services often got them last. Another solution was to depend on private companies. This worked well with gas service. Baltimore first chartered a private gas company in 1816; by the midcentury, all major cities were lit by private gas suppliers. The private sector, however, failed to supply the water that the cities needed. It did not have the capital to build adequate systems and laid pipe only in commercial and well-to-do residential areas, ignoring the poor. As cities grew, water service did not keep pace. Eventually, city governments had to take over.

Probably the most important and widespread service was the public school. In 1800, there were no public schools outside New England; by 1860,

Horace Mann and Public Schools

every state had some public education. Massachusetts took the lead, especially under Horace Mann, secretary of the state board of education from 1837 to 1848. Under Mann, Massachusetts established a minimum school year of six months, increased the number of high schools, formalized the training of teachers, and emphasized secular subjects and applied skills rather than religious training.

Horace Mann's preaching on behalf of free state education changed schooling throughout the nation. "If we do not prepare children to become good citizens," Mann prophesied, "then our republic must go down to destruction." The abolition of ignorance, Mann claimed, would end misery, crime, and suffering. "The only sphere . . . left open for our patriotism," he wrote, "is the improvement of our children—not the few, but the many; not a part of them but all."

In laying the basis of free public schools, Mann also broadened the scope of education. Previously, education had focused on literacy, religious training, and discipline. Under Mann's leadership, the school curriculum became more secular and appropriate for future clerks, farmers, and workers. Students studied geography, American history, arithmetic, and science. Moral education was retained, but direct religious indoctrination was dropped.

Mann and others responded to the changes wrought by a market economy, urbanization, and immigration. The typical city dweller was a newcomer, whether from abroad or from a country district. The new public schools would take the nation of strangers and inculcate them with common values, ones shared by many native Protestant political leaders. The basic texts—McGuffey's readers—used the Protestant scriptures to teach children to accept their position in society. A good child, McGuffey taught, does not envy the rich: "it is God who makes some poor and others rich." Catholics, immigrants, blacks, and working-class people sought community control of the schools, but they lost out to state control under Protestant educators.

Theater was a major institution in American life. After a church, a theater was often the second public building constructed in town. Large cities

Leisure Activities

boasted of two or more theaters that catered to different classes. In New York City, the Park Theater enjoyed the patronage of the carriage trade, the Bowery drew the middle class, and the Chatham attracted workers. The opera house generally became the playhouse of the upper class. Yet some theater cut across class lines. Shakespeare was performed so often and appreciated so widely that even illiterate theatergoers knew his blank verse well.

Sports, like theater, increasingly involved city dwellers as spectators. Horse racing, boxing, pedestrianism (walking races), and, in the 1850s, baseball began to attract large urban crowds. Entertainment became part of specialized commerce; one purchased a ticket—to the theater, the circus, P. T. Barnum's American Museum, the racetrack, or the ballpark.

Sports and recreation mirrored the growing divisions in American urban society. They had become less spontaneous; increasingly they involved organization and formal rules and attracted spectators who paid an admission fee. Most important, they frequently depended on exclusive associations and clubs, which advanced the interests of particular groups. In 1829, for instance, a group of Ohio merchants organized the Cincinnati Angling Club, with a formal constitution and bylaws, and limited the membership to twenty-five. A group of Wall Street office workers formed the Knickerbocker Club in 1842 and in 1845 set down formal rules for the game of baseball. Their written rules were widely adopted and are the basis for the game of baseball today.

Middle- and upper-class Americans formed clubs and associations to avoid being strangers to each other and to defend themselves against the culture of other groups—immigrants,

City Life

migrants, blacks, and artisans—that spilled onto the city streets. Many native-born New Yorkers felt alienated in the city of their birth. Some neighborhoods seemed dominated by foreigners, others by artisans. In the 1840s, even a youth culture developed in the Bowery. Older New Yorkers feared the "Bowery boy," whose ostentatious dress and behavior seemed threatening. The Bowery boy had close-cut hair in the back and long locks in front, greased into a roll. He wore a broad-brimmed black hat, an open shirt collar, a black frock coat that reached below the knee, and as much jewelry as he could afford. His swaggering step, especially when he had a girlfriend on his arm, frightened many in the middle class.

Voluntary associations and clubs offered the middle and upper classes an opportunity to recapture the city. Some, like the Masonic order, provided comfort and leisure activity to middle- and upper-class members. The Masons offered everything that the bustling city did not: an elaborate hierarchy, an orderly system of deference between ranks, and harmony and shared values. Masons marched in the parades that were a regular part of the city's public and political life. Most parades contained artisan and working-class organizations, and the Masons believed that they, too, had a stake in the street life of the city.

Most working people spent much of their lives outdoors—they worked, paraded, and carried out ordinary social and domestic affairs on the streets. Young people courted there, neighbors argued, and ethnic groups defended their turf. Urban streets served as a political arena. Extreme behavior found a home there as well; mob violence took place in the streets.

Inequality, urbanization, and immigration gave rise to urban conflict as rioting and incidents of violence became frequent. The colonial tradition of crowd action, in which disfranchised people took to the streets, had diminished in the first three decades of the nineteenth century. In the 1830s and 1840s riots again became commonplace. "Gentlemen of property and standing," unnerved by antislavery proponents, sacked abolitionist and antislavery organizations. In the 1840s, "respectable" citizens waged war against the Mormons, driving them from Illinois and Missouri. Workers raged against new migrants to the cities and other symbols of the new industrial order. In Philadelphia, for instance, native-born workers fought Irish weavers in 1828, and whites and blacks rioted on the docks in 1834 and 1835. Philadelphia's disturbances climaxed in the riots of 1844, in which mostly Protestant skilled workers fought Irish Catholics. Other cities, too, became battlegrounds as

Urban Riots

nativist riots peaked in the 1850s. By 1840, more than 125 people had died in urban riots, and by 1860 more than 1,000.

Public disorder spread in the city. To keep order and provide for public safety, Boston supplemented (1837) and New York replaced (1845) part-time watchmen and constables with uniformed policemen. Nonetheless, middle-class men and women did not venture out alone at night, and during the day they stayed clear of many city districts. And the influx of immigrants to the cities worsened social tensions by pitting people of different backgrounds against each other in the contest for jobs and housing. Ironically, in the midst of the dirt, the noise, the crime, and the conflict rose the opulent residences of the very rich.

Extremes of Wealth

Some observers, notably the young French visitor Alexis de Tocqueville, viewed the United States before the Civil War as a place of equality and opportunity. Tocqueville thought that American equality—the relative fluidity of the United States social order—derived from Americans' geographic mobility. Migration offered people opportunities to start anew regardless of where they came from or who they were. Prior wealth or family mattered little; a person could be known by deeds alone. Talent and hard work, many Americans believed, found their just reward in such an atmosphere.

But other observers recorded the rise of a new aristocracy based on wealth and power and the growth of class and ethnic divisions. Among those who disagreed with the egalitarian view of American life was *New York Sun* publisher Moses Yale Beach, author of twelve editions of *Wealth and Biography of the Wealthy Citizens of New York City.* In 1845, Beach listed 750 New Yorkers with assets of $100,000 or more. John Jacob Astor led the list of 19 millionaires with a fortune of $25 million. Ten years later, Beach reported that more than 1,000 New Yorkers were worth $100,000—28 of them were millionaires. Tocqueville himself, ever sensitive to the conflicting trends

Differences in Wealth

Chapter 11: Diversity and Conflict: People and Communities, 1800–1860

The infamous Five Points section of New York City's Sixth Ward, probably the worst slum in pre–Civil War America. Immodestly dressed prostitutes cruise the streets or gaze from windows, while a pig roots for garbage in their midst. *The New-York Historical Society.*

in American life, had described the growth of an American aristocracy based on industrial wealth. The rich and well educated "come forward to exploit industries," Tocqueville wrote, and become "more and more like the administrators of a huge empire. . . . What is this if not an aristocracy?"

Wealth throughout the United States was becoming concentrated in the hands of a relatively small number of people. In New York City between 1828 and 1845, the wealthiest 4 percent of the city's population increased their holdings from an estimated 63 percent to 80 percent of all individual wealth. By 1860, the top 5 percent of American families owned more than half the nation's wealth.

A cloud of uncertainty hung over working men and women. Many were afraid that during hard times they would become unemployed. They feared the competition of immigrant and slave labor. They feared the insecurities and indignities of poverty, chronic illness, disability,

Urban Poverty

old age, widowhood, and desertion. And they had good reason.

Poverty and squalor stalked the urban working class as cities grew. Cities were notorious for the dilapidated districts where newly arrived immigrants, indigent free blacks, the working poor, and thieves, beggars, and prostitutes lived. New York City's Five Points, a few blocks from City Hall, became the worst slum in pre–Civil War America. The neighborhood was predominantly Irish and black. Ill suited to human habitation and lacking such amenities as running water and sewers, Five Points exemplified the worst of urban life.

A world apart from Five Points and the people of the streets lived the upper-class elite society of Philip Hone, one-time mayor of New York. Hone's diary, meticulously kept from 1826 until 1851, records the activities of an American aristocrat. On February 28, 1840, for instance, Hone attended a masked ball at the Fifth Avenue

The Urban Elite

mansion of Henry Breevoort, Jr., and Laura Carson Breevoort. The ball began at the fashionable hour of 10 P.M., and the five hundred ladies and gentlemen who filled the mansion wore costumes adorned with ermine and gold. Few balls attained such grandeur, but at one time or another similar parties were held in Boston, Philadelphia, Baltimore, and Charleston.

Much of this new wealth was inherited. For every John Jacob Astor who made millions in the western fur trade, there were ten who built additional wealth on money they had inherited or married. Many of the wealthiest bore the names of the colonial commercial elite—Beekman, Breevoort, Roosevelt, Van Rensselaer, and Whitney. These rich New Yorkers were not an idle class; they devoted energy to increasing their fortunes and power. Hardly a major canal, railroad, bank, or mill venture lacked the names and investments of the fashionable elite. Wealth begot wealth, and family ties through inheritance and marriage were essential in that world.

More modest in wealth, though hard working, were those in the expanding middle class. The growth and specialization of trade had rapidly increased their numbers, and they **The Middle** were a distinct part of the urban **Class** scene. The men were businessmen or professionals, the women homemakers. Middle-class families enjoyed the fruits of the advances in consumption—wool carpeting, fine wallpaper, rooms full of furniture, and indoor toilets. If they dreamed of entering Philip Hone's world, they were mindful to keep their distance from the working class and the poor.

Women and the Family

Economic change and urbanization transformed women and families in the nineteenth century; work, class, gender roles, ethnicity, race, and religion created greater distinctions among families and among women. In the eighteenth century, the range of differences among females had been

much less; they had much more in common then.

Increasingly, women's and men's work grew apart. As manufacturing left the home, so did wage workers, except for those doing putting-out work. On farms, there was still an overlap between women's and men's work, but in the new stores and workshops tasks diverged. Specialization in business and production accompanied specialization in work tasks; men acquired new, narrow skills that they applied outside the home in set ways with purposefully designed tools and systems. Authority within the workplace, removed from the household, became formal and impersonal.

Some women shared these experiences for brief periods in their lives. New England farm daughters, who were the first textile mill workers, performed new, specialized tasks. **Working** The new urban department stores **Women** hired young women as clerks and cash runners. Many women worked for a few years as teachers. Paid employment represented a stage in their lives, a brief period before they left their paternal households and entered their marital households.

Working-class women—the poor, widows, free blacks—worked for wages to support themselves and their families. Leaving their parental homes as early as the age of twelve or thirteen, they earned wages most of their lives. Unlike men and New England farm daughters, however, most of these women did not work in the new shops and factories. Instead, they worked as domestic servants in other women's homes and as laundresses, seamstresses, cooks, and boarding-house keepers. Few of the available occupations allowed them to support themselves or a family at an acceptable level. Widowhood, especially, was synonymous with poverty.

Increasingly, work took on greater gender meaning and segregation. Most women's work centered, as it always had, on the home. As the urban family lost its significance in the production of goods, household upkeep and child rearing grew in importance and required women's full-time attention. Education, religion, morality, domestic arts, and culture began to overshadow the economic functions of the family. These areas came to be known as the woman's sphere. For a woman to achieve mastery in these areas was to live up to the middle-class ideal of the cult of domesticity of the nineteenth century.

Middle-class American women and men placed great importance on the family. The role of the mother was to ensure the nation's future by rearing her children and providing the home with a spiritual and virtuous environment. The family was to be a moral institution characterized by selflessness and cooperation. Thus women were idealized as the embodiment of self-sacrificing republicanism. This view was in sharp contrast to the world outside the home—a sphere identified with men and dominated by base self-interest. In the rapidly changing world, in which single men and women left their parental homes and villages, and factories and stores replaced traditional means of production and distribution, the family was supposed to be a rock of stability and traditional values.

The domestic ideal limited the paying jobs available to middle-class women outside the home. Most paid work was viewed with disapproval because it conflicted with the ideal of domesticity. One occupation came to be recognized as consistent with the genteel female nature: teaching. In 1823, Catharine and Mary Beecher established the Hartford Female Seminary and added philosophy, history, and science to the traditional women's curriculum of domestic arts and religion. A decade later, Catharine Beecher campaigned to establish training seminaries for female teachers. Viewing formal education as an extension of women's nurturing role, Beecher had great success in spreading her message. By the 1850s, teaching was a popular vocation for women, and women—usually unmarried—constituted the majority of teachers in most cities. Their pay, however, was often half that of male teachers.

While woman's work outside the home remained limited, family size was shrinking due to a number of factors. Increasingly, small families were viewed as desirable. Children would have greater opportunities in smaller families; parents could pay more attention to them and would be better able to educate them and help them financially. Besides, contemporary marriage manuals stressed the harmful ef-

Decline in the Birthrate

fects of too many births on a woman's health; too many children weakened women physically and overworked them as mothers.

All this evidence suggests that wives and husbands made deliberate decisions to limit the size of families. In areas where farmland was relatively expensive, families were smaller than in other agricultural districts. It appears that parents who foresaw difficulty in setting up their children as independent farmers chose to have fewer children. Similarly, in urban areas, children, as consumers and not producers, were more an economic burden than an asset.

How did men and women limit the size of their families in the early nineteenth century? Many married later, thus shortening the period of childbearing. Women had their last child at a younger age, suggesting that family planning was becoming more common. Many couples used traditional forms of birth control, such as coitus interruptus, or withdrawal of the male before completion of the sexual act. Medical devices, however, were beginning to compete with this ancient practice. Cheap rubber condoms were widely adopted when they became available in the 1850s. Some couples used the rhythm method—attempting to confine intercourse to a woman's infertile periods. Knowledge of the "safe period," however, was uncertain even among physicians. Another method was abstinence, or less frequent sexual intercourse. For those desiring to terminate a pregnancy, surgical abortions became common after 1830. By 1860, however, twenty states had outlawed abortions.

Birth Control

Significantly, the birth-control methods that women themselves controlled—douching, the rhythm method, abstinence, and abortion—were the ones that were increasing in popularity. The new emphasis on women's domesticity encouraged women's autonomy in the home and gave women greater control over their own bodies. According to the cult of domesticity, the refinement and purity of women ruled the household, including the bedroom.

Sarah Ripley of Massachusetts, a young girl in the eighteenth century and an adult in the nineteenth, revealed in her diaries the changes that American society was experiencing. Daughter of a Greenfield

Sarah Ripley Stearns shopkeeper, Ripley had a privileged childhood. After completing boarding school, she returned home to work as an assistant in her father's store. In 1812, after a five-year courtship, she married Charles Stearns. "I have now . . . left the protection of my parents and given up the name I have always borne," she recorded in her diary. "May the grace of God enable me to fulfill . . . the great and important duties which now dissolve [fall] on me." Yet she missed the bustle of the shop, as she confessed in her diary.

Sarah Ripley Stearns's life was not a settled one; change was everywhere. During the six years after her marriage, she bore three children, moved three times, became a widow, and found an anchor in religion. For Stearns, as well as for other middle-class women, social interaction within the church made it possible to extend the bounds of ideal domesticity. For example, she and her neighbors sponsored a school society and a juvenile home. Such benevolent society work not only aided poor children, but also provided its female participants with experience in organizing and chairing meetings, raising funds, and cultivating an extended women's network.

Women who made the decision to stay single rejected both the cult of domesticity and the traditional pattern in which women moved as **Single Women** dependents from their fathers' households to those of their husbands. Louisa May Alcott (1832–1888), the author of *Little Women* (1868), sought independence and financial security for herself. Alcott worked as a seamstress, governess, teacher, housemaid, and author; her writing brought her success. "Things go smoothly, and I think I shall come out right," she wrote her father in 1856. "I like the independent feeling; and though not an easy life, it is a free one, and I enjoy it."

Louisa May Alcott had forsworn marriage, risking the opprobrium of being a spinster. She and other women took a path of independence that made them less dependent on men. They chose to pursue vocational identities outside of home and marriage, to explore their own personal growth, and to follow their own abilities. Given the difficulty women had in finding work that would allow them to be self-supporting, they undertook their independence at great risk. Nonetheless, there was a significant increase in single women in the first three quarters of the nineteenth century.

Independent white women helped establish new roles for women. They were responding to changes and opportunities offered by the market economy and expanding cities. Immigration, too, had an enormous impact in remaking American life; ethnic and religious diversity became a hallmark of nineteenth-century America.

Immigrant Lives in America

No less than gender, ethnic and religious differences divided Americans. In numbers alone, immigrants drastically altered the United States. Five million strangers came to the states between 1820 and 1860. They came from all continents, though Europeans made up the vast majority. The peak period of pre–Civil War immigration was from 1847 through 1857; in those eleven years, 3.3 million immigrants entered the United States, 1.3 million from Ireland and 1.1 million from the German states. By 1860, 15 percent of the white population was foreign-born.

This massive migration had been set in motion decades earlier. In Europe, around the turn of the nineteenth century, the Napoleonic wars had begun one of the greatest population shifts in history; it was to last more than a hundred years. War, revolution, famine, industrialization, and religious persecution led many Europeans to leave home. The United States beckoned, offering them economic opportunity and religious freedom.

American institutions, both public and private, actively recruited European emigrants. Western states lured potential settlers in the interest of promoting their economies. In the **Promotion of Immigration** 1850s, for instance, Wisconsin appointed a commissioner of emigration, who advertised the state's advantages in American and European newspapers. Wisconsin also opened an office in New York and hired European agents to compete with other states and with firms for immigrants' attention.

Chapter 11: Diversity and Conflict: People and Communities, 1800–1860

Large construction projects and mines needed strong young laborers. Textile mills and cities attracted young women workers. Europeans' awareness of the United States heightened as employers, states, and shipping companies advertised the opportunities to be found across the Atlantic. With regularly scheduled sailing ships plying the ocean after 1848, the cost of transatlantic travel was within easy reach of millions of Europeans.

So they came, enduring the hardships of travel and of settling in a strange land. The journey was difficult. The average transatlantic crossing took six weeks; in bad weather it could take three months. Disease spread unchecked among people huddled together like cattle in steerage. More than seventeen thousand immigrants, mostly Irish, died from "ship fever" in 1847. On disembarking, immigrants became fair game for the con artists and swindlers who worked the docks. In 1855, in response to the immigrants' plight, New York State's commissioners of emigration established Castle Garden as an immigrant center. There immigrants were somewhat sheltered from fraud. Authorized transportation companies maintained offices in the large rotunda and assisted immigrants with their travel plans.

Most immigrants, like the George Martin family, gravitated toward cities, since only a minority had farming experience or the means to purchase land and equipment. Many stayed in New York itself. By 1855, 52 percent of the city's 623,000 inhabitants were immigrants. Boston, an important entry port for the Irish, took on a European tone. Throughout the 1850s, the city was about 35 percent foreign-born, and the Irish constituted more than two-thirds of this segment. In the South, too, major cities had large immigrant populations. In 1860, New Orleans was 44 percent foreign-born, Savannah 33 percent, and the border city of St. Louis, 61 percent. On the West Coast, San Francisco had a foreign-born majority.

Some immigrants, however, did settle in rural areas. In particular, German, Dutch, and Scandinavian farmers gravitated toward the Midwest. Greater percentages of Scandinavians and Netherlanders took up farming than did other nationalities; both groups came mostly as religious dissenters and migrated in family units. The Dutch, under such leaders as Albertus C. Van Raalte, fled persecution in their native land to establish new and more pious communities—Holland and Zeeland, Michigan, among them.

Not all immigrants found success in the United States; hundreds of thousands returned to their homelands with disappointment. Before the potato blight hit Ireland, recruiters lured many Irish to swing picks and shovels on American canals and railroads and to work in construction. Among them was Michael Gaugin, who had the misfortune to arrive in New York City during the financial panic of 1837. Gaugin, for thirteen years an assistant engineer in the construction of a Dublin canal, had been attracted to the United States by the promise that "he should soon become a wealthy man." Within two months of arriving in the United States, Gaugin became a pauper. In August 1837, he declared that he was "now without means for the support of himself and his family . . . and has already suffered great deprivation since he arrived in this country; and is now soliciting means to enable him to return with his family home to Ireland."

Immigrant Disenchantment

Such experiences did not deter Irish men and women from coming to the United States. Ireland was the most densely populated European country and among the most impoverished. From 1815 on, small harvests prompted a steady stream of Irish to emigrate to America. Then, in 1845 and 1846, potatoes—the basic Irish food—rotted in the fields. From 1845 to 1849, death from starvation, malnutrition, and typhus spread. In all, 1 million died and about 1.5 million fled.

Irish Immigrants

In the 1840s and 1850s, a total of 1.7 million Irish men and women entered the United States. At the peak of Irish immigration, from 1847 to 1854, 1.2 million came. Between 1820 and 1854, except for two years, the Irish constituted the largest single group of immigrants annually. By the end of the century, there were more Irish in the United States than in Ireland.

The new Irish immigrants differed greatly from those who had left Ireland to settle in the American colonies. In the eighteenth century, the Scotch-Irish had predominated, and their journey had involved moving from one part of the British Empire to another. The nineteenth-century Roman Catholic Irish travelers to America, however, moved from colonial Ireland to an independent republic, and the political and religious differences made their cultural adaptation that much more difficult. In comparison with the Scotch-Irish, the new immigrants from Ireland tended to be younger, increasingly female, and mostly from the rural provinces.

In the urban areas, where they clustered in poverty, most Irish immigrants met growing anti-immigrant, anti-Catholic sentiment. "No Irish Need Apply" signs were common. During the colonial period, white Protestant settlers had feared "popery" as a system of tyranny and had discriminated against the few Catholics in America. After the Revolution, anti-Catholicism receded; but in the 1830s, the trend reversed, and anti-Catholicism appeared wherever the Irish did. Attacks on the papacy and the church circulated widely in the form of libelous texts like *The Awful Disclosures of Maria Monk* (1836), which alleged sexual orgies among priests and nuns. Nowhere was anti-Catholicism more open and nasty than in Boston, though such sentiments were widespread.

Anti-Catholicism

The native-born who embraced anti-Catholicism were motivated largely by anxiety. They feared that a militant Roman church would subvert American society, that unskilled Irish workers would displace American craftsmen, and that the slums inhabited in part by the Irish were undermining the nation's values. Every American problem from immorality and alcoholism to poverty and economic upheaval was blamed on immigrant Irish Catholics. Friction increased as Irish-American men fought back by entering politics.

In 1854, Germans replaced the Irish as the single largest group of arriving immigrants. Potato blight also sent many from the German states to the United States in the 1840s, but other hardships contributed to the steady stream. Many came from areas where small landholdings made it hard to eke out a living and to pass on land to their sons. Others were craftsmen displaced by the industrial revolution. These refugees were joined by middle-class Germans who emigrated to the United States after the abortive revolution of 1848.

German Immigrants

Unlike the Irish, who tended to congregate in towns and cities, Germans settled everywhere. Many came on cotton boats, disembarked at New Orleans, and traveled up the Mississippi. In the South, they became peddlers and merchants; in the North and West, they worked as farmers, urban laborers, and businessmen. They, more than the Irish, tended to migrate in families and groups; that tendency helped maintain German culture.

Native-born Americans treated immigrants from the German states with greater respect than they did the Irish. Stereotypes of Germans often included such terms as "industrious," "hard-working," "self-reliant," and "intelligent." Many believed that Germans would "harmonize" better with American culture. This contrasted with the almost universal dislike of the Irish, as most Americans seemed to accept the negative British stereotypes of Irish people.

Nonetheless, Germans, too, met antiforeign attitudes. More than half the German immigrants were Catholic, and their Sabbath practices differed from those of Protestants. On Sundays, many urban German immigrant families gathered at beer gardens to eat and drink beer, to dance, sing, and listen to band music, and sometimes to play cards. Protestants were outraged by such violations of the Lord's Day.

These immigrants' persistence in using the German language and their different religious beliefs set them apart. Besides the Catholic majority, a significant number of German immigrants were Jewish. And even the German Protestants—mostly Lutherans—founded their own churches and often educated their children in German-language schools. Not all Germans, however, were religious. The failure of the revolution in 1848 had sent to the United States a whole generation of liberals and freethinkers, some of whom were socialists, communists, and anarchists.

Not all immigrants came to the United States voluntarily. After the annexation of Texas, the Mexican War, and the Gadsden Purchase (which in 1853 added southern Arizona and New Mexico), many Hispanics found themselves in the United States, some against their will, because of boundary changes. The development of Texas apart from Mexico after 1836, the discovery of gold in Califor-

Hispanics

Chapter 11: Diversity and Conflict: People and Communities, 1800–1860

nia, and the extension of railroads broke the linkage of the Southwest with Mexico and reoriented the Southwest toward the United States.

Hispanic culture continued in the region, but Anglos and European immigrants seized economic and political power. Anglos overwhelmed Hispanics in Texas and in California. Hispanics retained their language, Roman Catholic religion, and community through newspapers, mutual aid societies, and the church, but they lost power and status. In Nueces County, Texas, at the time of the Texas Revolution (1836), Mexicans held all the land; twenty years later, they had lost it all. Although many Hispanics had fought for Texas independence, the settlers coming in tended to treat Mexicans as inferior people. Within two generations, Hispanics became second-class citizens and strangers in their own land.

For immigrants, conflict centered on the desire to be part of American society, although in some cases, on their own terms. Once here, they claimed their right to a fair economic and political share. Indians, however, like Hispanics in the Southwest, defended what they conceived of as prior rights. Their land, their religion, their way of life came under constant attack because they were most often viewed as obstacles to expansion and economic growth.

Indian Resistance and Removal

The clash between Indians and the larger society was inherited from the colonial past. Population growth, westward expansion, the transportation revolution, and market orientation underlay the designs and demands on Indian land. Under the Constitution, the federal government had the responsibility for dealing with Indians. For better or worse, there had to be a federal Indian policy. As territorial expansion came at the Indians' expense, it was for the worse. The result was removal of the great Indian nations to lands west of the Mississippi.

While the population of other groups increased by leaps and bounds, the Indian population shrank.

War, forced removal, disease, and malnutrition reduced many tribes by half. In the 1830s alone, more than half of the Pawnees, Omahas, Ottoes, Missouris, and Kansas died.

As the colonial powers in North America had done, the United States treated Indian tribes as sovereign nations, until Congress ended the practice in 1871. In its relations with tribal leaders, the government followed the ritual of international protocol. Indian chiefs and delegations visiting Washington were received with the appropriate pomp and ceremony. Agreements between a tribe and the United States were signed, sealed, and ratified like any international pact.

In practice, however, Indian sovereignty was a fiction. Protocol seemed to acknowledge independence and mutual respect, but treaty negotiations exposed the sham. Essentially, treaty making was a process used by the American government to acquire Indian land. Differences in power made it less than the bargaining of two equal nations. Treaties were often made between victors and vanquished. In a context of coercion, many old treaties gave way to new ones, in which the Indians ceded their traditional holdings in return for different lands in the West.

The War of 1812 snuffed out whatever realistic hopes eastern Indian leaders might have had of resisting American expansion by warfare. Armed resistance persisted and was bloody on both sides. Resistance, however, only delayed the inevitable. The Shawnee chiefs Prophet and Tecumseh led the most significant movement against the United States, but after Tecumseh's death, Prophet failed to sustain the movement.

The experiences of Prophet and other Shawnees were typical of the wanderings of an uprooted people. When the Shawnees gave up 17 million acres in Ohio in the 1795 Treaty of Greenville, they scattered to Indiana and eastern Missouri. After the War of 1812, Prophet's Indiana group withdrew to Canada. In 1822, other Shawnees sought Mexican protection and moved from Missouri to present-day eastern Texas. With the United States government promoting western removal, Prophet returned from Canada and led a group to the new Shawnee lands established in eastern Kansas in 1825. When Missouri achieved statehood, the Shawnees there

Prophet

were forced to move to Kansas. In the 1830s, Shawnees in Ohio were removed to Kansas and were joined there by others expelled from Texas. By 1854, Kansas was open to white settlement, and the Shawnees had to cede back seven-eighths of their land.

Removal had a profound impact on all Shawnees. The men had to give up their traditional role as providers; their methods of hunting and knowledge of woodland animals were useless in prairie Kansas. Shawnee women played a greater role as providers as grains became the tribe's dietary staple. Yet, remarkably, the Shawnees preserved their language and culture in the face of these drastic changes.

In the 1820s, under pressure, Indians in Ohio, southern Indiana and Illinois, southwestern Michigan, most of Missouri, central Alabama, and southern Mississippi ceded their lands.

Indian Policy They gave up nearly 200 million acres for pennies an acre. But white settlers wanted more Indian land, and they wanted the Indians to assimilate. One instrument that served both purposes was the Indian agency system, which monopolized trade with Indians in a designated locality and paid out the rations, supplies, and annuities that Indians received in exchange for abandoning their land. With time, the tribes became dependent on these government payments.

Ever since the early days of European colonization, assimilation of Native Americans through education and Christianity had been an important goal. It found renewed interest as the United States expanded westward. In 1819, under missionary lobbying, Congress appropriated $10,000 annually for the "civilization of the tribes adjoining the frontier settlements." This "civilization act" was a means to teach Indians to live like white settlers. Protestant missionaries administered the "civilizing fund" and established mission schools.

To settlers eyeing Indian land, assimilation through education was too slow a process, and Indians themselves questioned the instruction. Some tribes found the missionary message repugnant. The Creek nation permitted the schools only after being assured that there would be no preaching. Zealous missionaries, however, violated the agreement, preaching to the Creeks and their black slaves. In response, a band of Creeks sacked the school.

It became apparent in the 1820s that neither economic dependency, nor education, nor even Christianity, could force Indians to cede much more land voluntarily to meet the demands of expansionists. Attention focused on Cherokees, Creeks, Choctaws, Chickasaws, and Seminoles in the South because much of their land remained intact after the War of 1812 and because they aggressively resisted white encroachment.

In his last annual message in December 1824, President James Monroe suggested to Congress that all Indians be moved beyond the Mississippi River.

Indian Removal Three days later, the president sent a special message to Congress proposing removal. The southern tribes unanimously rejected Monroe's offer.

Pressure from Georgia had prompted Monroe's policy. Most Cherokees and some Creeks lived in northwestern Georgia, and in the 1820s, the state accused the federal government of not fulfilling its 1802 promise to remove the Indians in return for the state's renunciation of its claim to western lands. Georgia sought complete expulsion and was satisfied neither by Monroe's removal messages nor by further Creek cessions. In 1826, the Creek nation, under federal pressure, ceded all but a small strip of its Georgia acreage. Governor George M. Troup, however, wanted all the Creek land. When President John Quincy Adams threatened to send the army to protect the Indians' claims, Troup countered with his own threats. Only the removal of the Georgia Creeks to the West in 1826 prevented a clash between the state and the federal government.

If "civilizing" Indians was the goal, none met that test better than the Cherokees. During the Cherokee renaissance from 1819 to 1829, the tribe became economically self-sufficient and politically self-governing. The twelve thousand to fifteen thousand adult Cherokees in the 1820s came to think of themselves as a nation. During that decade, they created a formal government with a bicameral legislature, elected representatives, a

Cherokees

French genre painter Alfred Boisseau recorded the passage of the Choctaw through Louisiana from Mississippi to Indian Territory. With dignity they made the forced march. *New Orleans Museum of Art, gift of Mr. William E. Groves.*

court system, a salaried bureaucracy, and a written constitution, modeled after that of the United States. Cherokee land laws, however, differed from United States law. The tribe owned all land, and complex provisions covered the sale of land (forbidden to outsiders). Nonetheless, the Cherokees assimilated American cultural patterns well. By 1833, they held fifteen hundred black slaves, whose legal status under the Cherokees was the same as that of slaves held by southern whites. Moreover, missionaries had been so successful that the Cherokees could be considered a Christian community.

Although the tribe developed a way of life similar to that of an American state, it failed to win acceptance from southerners. Georgia pressed the Cherokees to sell the 7,200 square miles of land they held in the state. Most Cherokees, however, preferred to stay where they were. Then, in 1828 and 1829, Georgia annulled the Cherokee constitution, extended the state's sovereignty over the tribe, and ordered the tribal lands seized.

In 1829, the Cherokees turned to the federal courts to defend their treaty with the United States and prevent Georgia's seizure of their land. In

Cherokee Nation v. Georgia

Cherokee Nation v. *Georgia* (1831), Chief Justice John Marshall ruled that under the federal Constitution an Indian tribe was neither a foreign nation nor a state and therefore had no standing in federal courts. Nonetheless, said Marshall, the Indians had an unquestioned right to their lands; they could lose title only by voluntarily giving it up. A year later, in *Worcester* v. *Georgia*, Marshall defined the Cherokee position more clearly. The Indian nation was, he declared, a distinct political community in which "the laws of Georgia can have no force" and into which Georgians could not enter without permission or treaty privilege.

President Andrew Jackson had little sympathy for the Indians and ignored the Supreme Court's ruling. Keen to open up new lands for settlement, he was determined to remove the Cherokees at all

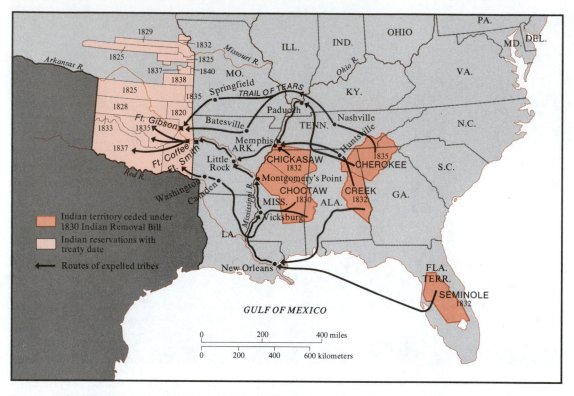

Removal of the Indians from the South, 1820–1840 *Source: Acknowledgment is due to Martin Gilbert and George Weidenfeld and Nicholson Limited for permission to reproduce the map above, taken from American History Atlas.*

costs. In the Removal Act of 1830, Congress provided Jackson with the funds he needed to negotiate new treaties and resettle the resistant tribes west of the Mississippi.

The infamous Trail of Tears (see map) had begun. The Choctaws in the winter of 1831 and 1832 were the first to go. Soon other tribes joined the

Trail of Tears trail: the Creeks in Alabama in 1836 and the Chickasaws in 1837. The Cherokees, having fought through the courts to stay, found themselves divided. Some recognized the hopelessness of further resistance and accepted removal as the only chance to preserve their civilization. The leaders of this minority signed a treaty in 1835, in which they agreed to exchange their southern home for western land. But when the time for evacuation came in 1838, most Cherokees refused to move. President Martin Van Buren then sent federal troops to round up the Indians. About twenty thousand Cherokees were evicted, held in detention camps, and

marched to present-day Oklahoma under military escort. Nearly one-quarter died of disease and exhaustion on the Trail of Tears. When the forced march to the West ended, the Indians had traded about 100 million acres of land east of the Mississippi for 32 million acres west of the river, plus $68 million. Only a few scattered remnants of the tribes, among them the Seminoles, remained in the East and South.

What was the impact of removal? Change had been thrust on these tribes so suddenly and drastically that they had to transform much of their culture. In the West, they occupied an alien environment; they had no generational ties with the new land. Many could not be at peace with the land or get used to the strange animals and plants they found there. Many Indians became dependent on government payments for survival. Finally, removal brought new internal conflicts that would ultimately shatter Cherokee tribal unity.

In the Southeast, a small band of Seminoles suc-

Chapter 11: Diversity and Conflict: People and Communities, 1800–1860

cessfully resisted removal and remained in Florida. In 1832, in the Treaty of Payne's Landing, some of the Seminole tribal leaders agreed to relocate to the West within three years. A minority under Osceola refused to vacate their homes, and in 1835 they initiated a fierce guerrilla war against the federal troops. The army in turn waged an unsuccessful effort to exterminate the Seminoles. In 1842, the United States finally abandoned the Seminole War; it had cost the lives of fifteen hundred soldiers and $20 million. Most of Osceola's followers agreed to move west to Indian Territory in 1858, but many Seminoles remained in the Florida Everglades, prideful that they had successfully resisted conquest.

Second Seminole War

A complex set of attitudes drove whites to force Indian removal. Most merely wanted Indian lands. Others were aware of the injustice but believed that Indians must inevitably give way to white settlement. Some, like John Quincy Adams, believed that the only way to preserve Indian civilization was to remove the tribes and establish a buffer zone between Indians and whites. Others hoped to "civilize" Indians and assimilate them slowly into American culture. Whatever the source of white behavior in the United States, the outcome was the devastation of Native American peoples and their cultures.

Another minority experienced insecurity and struggled for recognition and legal rights. Like most Indians, they, too, were involuntarily a part of American society. Unlike Indians, however, they wished to be fully a part of the American people.

Free People of Color

No black person was safe, wrote the abolitionist and former slave Frederick Douglass after the Philadelphia riot of 1849. "His life—his property—and all that he holds dear are in the hands of a mob." Between 1832 and 1849, five major antiblack riots occurred in Philadelphia. Mobs stormed black dwellings and churches, set them on fire, and killed the people inside. The mobs intimidating free blacks could be made up of slave hunters seeking runaways but were as likely to kidnap a free black as a slave. Or they could represent civil authority. In 1829 in Cincinnati, frightened by the growing black population, officials drove as many as two thousand blacks from the city by enforcing a law requiring cash bonds to ensure good behavior. Free blacks faced insecurity daily.

Under federal law, the blacks' position was uncertain. The Fifth Amendment specified that "no person shall . . . be deprived of life, liberty, or property, without due process of law." Yet the racist theory of the eighteenth century that defined a republic as being only for whites seemed to exclude blacks. This exclusion was reflected in early federal legislation. In 1790, naturalization was limited to white aliens, and in 1792, the militia was limited to white male citizens. Moreover, Congress approved the admission to the Union of states whose constitutions restricted the rights of blacks. After the admission of Missouri in 1821, every new state admitted until the Civil War banned blacks from voting. When the Oregon and New Mexico territories were organized, public land grants were limited to whites.

In the North, blacks faced legal restrictions nearly everywhere. Only in Massachusetts, New Hampshire, Vermont, and Maine could blacks vote on an equal basis with whites throughout the pre–Civil War period. Blacks gained the right to vote in Rhode Island in 1842, but they had lost it earlier in Pennsylvania and Connecticut. No state but Massachusetts permitted blacks to serve on juries; four midwestern states and California did not allow blacks to testify against whites. In Oregon, blacks could not own real estate, make contracts, or sue in court.

Legal status was important, but practice and custom were crucial. Although Ohio repealed its law barring black testimony against whites in 1849, the exclusion persisted as custom in southern Ohio counties. Throughout the North, free people of color were either excluded from or segregated in public places. Hotels and restaurants were closed to blacks, as were most theaters and churches. Probably no practice inflicted greater injury than the general discrimination in hiring. Counting houses, retail stores, and factories refused to hire black

Exclusion and Segregation of Blacks

men except as janitors and general handymen. New England textile mills hired only whites.

Free people of color faced especially severe legal and social barriers in the southern slave states, where their presence was often viewed as an incentive to insurrection. Indeed,

Southern Free Blacks southern states responded to fear of mass rebellion by tightening the restrictions on free blacks and forcing them to leave small towns and interior counties. After the Nat Turner rebellion in 1831, the position of free blacks weakened further. Within five years, nearly all the southern states prohibited the freeing of any slaves without legislative or court approval; by the 1850s, Texas, Mississippi, and Georgia had banned manumission altogether.

To restrict free blacks and encourage them to migrate north, southern states adopted elaborate "black codes." Blacks, who provided most of the South's skilled labor, encountered licensing requirements and bans restricting work opportunities. Virginia and Georgia banned black river captains and pilots. Some states forbade blacks to assemble without a license; some prohibited blacks from being taught to read and write. In the late 1830s, when these black codes were first enforced with vigor, free blacks increasingly moved northward, even though northern states discouraged the migration.

In spite of these obstacles, the free black population rose dramatically in the first part of the nineteenth century, from 108,000 in 1800 to almost 500,000 in 1860. Nearly half lived in the North, occasionally in rural settlements, but more often in cities like Philadelphia, New York, and Cincinnati. Baltimore had the largest free black community; sizable free black populations also existed in New Orleans, Charleston, and Mobile.

The ranks of free blacks were constantly increased by ex-slaves. Some, like Frederick Douglass and Harriet Tubman, were fugitives. Tubman, a slave on the eastern shore of Maryland, escaped to Philadelphia in 1849, when her master's death led to rumors that she would be sold out of the state. Within the next two years, she returned twice to free her two children, her sister, her mother, and her brother and his family. Other slaves were voluntarily freed by their owners. Some, like a Virginia planter named Sanders, who settled his slaves as freedmen in Michigan, sought to cleanse their souls by freeing their slaves in their wills. Some freed elderly slaves after a lifetime of service rather than support them in old age.

In response to their oppression, free blacks founded strong, independent self-help societies to meet their unique needs and fight against their less-than-equal status. In every

Founding of Black Institutions African-American community, people organized churches, fraternal and benevolent associations, literary societies, and schools. Many leaders believed that these mutual aid societies would encourage thrift, industry, and morality and thus equip the members to improve their lot. No amount of effort could counteract white prejudice, however.

The network of societies among urban free black men and women provided a base for black protest. From 1830 to 1835, and thereafter irregularly, free blacks held national conventions, with delegates drawn from city and state organizations. Under the leadership of the small black middle class, which included a Philadelphia sail manufacturer, James Forten, and an orator, the Reverend Henry Highland Garnet, the convention movement served as a forum to attack slavery and agitate for equal rights. The struggle was joined by new militant black newspapers, such as *Freedom's Journal* (1827) and the *Weekly Advocate* (1837).

Although ending slavery and attaining equal rights remained at the top of blacks' agenda, the mood of free blacks began to shift in the late 1840s

Black Nationalism and 1850s. Some were swept up in a tide of black nationalism that stressed racial solidarity and unity, self-help, and a growing interest in Africa. Before this time, efforts to send African-Americans "back to Africa" had originated with whites seeking to solve racial problems by ridding the United States of blacks. But in the 1850s, blacks held emigrationist conventions of their own under the leadership of Henry Bibb and Martin Delany. With the coming of the Civil War and emancipation, however, all but a few African-Americans lost interest in migrating to Africa.

The United States in 1860 was a far more diverse and turbulent society than it had been in 1800. The market economy, urbanization, and immigration had altered the ways people lived and worked. Economic growth created new jobs, but inequality increased everywhere. Cities housed both ostentatious wealth and abject poverty, and violence and disorder became commonplace.

In the midst of these changes, middle-class families sought to insulate their homes from the competition of the market economy. Many women found fulfillment in the domestic ideal, although others found it confining. More and more, middle-class urban women became associated with nurturing roles, first in homes and schools, then in churches and reform societies. Working-class women had more modest goals: escaping poverty and winning respect.

In Europe, famine and religious and political oppression sent millions of people across the Atlantic. They were drawn to the United States by the promise of jobs and political and religious toleration. Yet most found the going rough, even though conditions were often better than in their native lands. In the process, they changed the profile of the American people. Competition and diversity bred intolerance and prejudice. None were to feel that more painfully than Indians and free blacks, who were most often made to feel like aliens in their own land.

As the economy and society changed, conflict became commonplace and entered the public arena. The utopian communities, conflict over public space, the backlash against immigrants, black protest, and Indian resistance were manifestations of the divisions in America. But conflict took other forms as well, as in the widespread reform movements that came to characterize American life from the 1820s through the 1850s. Through reform and politics, many Americans sought to harness and control the forces of change.

Suggestions for Further Reading

Rural and Utopian Communities

Leonard J. Arrington and Davis Bitton, *The Mormon Experience: A History of the Latterday Saints* (1979); Priscilla J.

Brewer, *Shaker Communities, Shaker Lives* (1986); Don H. Doyle, *The Social Order of a Frontier Community: Jacksonville, Illinois, 1825–1870* (1978); Laurence Foster, *Religion and Sexuality: Three American Communal Experiments of the Nineteenth Century* (1981); Steven Hahn and Jonathan Prude, eds., *The Countryside in the Age of Capitalist Transformation* (1985); Joan M. Jensen, *Loosening the Bonds: Mid-Atlantic Farm Women, 1750–1850* (1986); Wallace Stegner, *The Gathering of Zion: The Story of the Mormon Trail* (1964); Anthony F. C. Wallace, *Rockdale: The Growth of an American Village in the Early Industrial Revolution* (1978).

Urban Communities and Inequality

Melvin A. Adelman, *A Sporting Time: New York City and the Rise of Modern Athletics, 1820–1870* (1986); Stuart M. Blumin, *The Urban Threshold: Growth and Change in a Nineteenth-Century American Community* (1976); Lawrence A. Cremin, *American Education: The National Experience, 1783–1876* (1980); Susan G. Davis, *Parades and Power: Street Theater in Nineteenth-Century Philadelphia* (1986); Karen Halttunen, *Confidence Men and Painted Women: A Study of Middle-Class Culture in America, 1830–1870* (1982); Carl Kaestle, *Pillars of the Republic: Common Schools and American Society, 1780–1860* (1982); Gary B. Nash, "The Social Evolution of Preindustrial American Cities, 1700–1820: Reflections and New Directions," *Journal of Urban History,* 13 (February 1987), 115–145; Edward Pessen, *Riches, Class and Power Before the Civil War* (1973); Christine Stansell, *City of Women: Sex and Class in New York, 1789–1860* (1986); Stephen Thernstrom, *Poverty and Progress: Social Mobility in a Nineteenth Century City* (1964); Alexis de Tocqueville, *Democracy in America,* 2 vols. (1835–1840); Richard C. Wade, *The Urban Frontier: 1790–1830* (1957).

Women and the Family

Lee Virginia Chambers-Schiller, *Liberty, A Better Husband: Single Women in America: The Generations of 1780–1840* (1984); Nancy F. Cott, *The Bonds of Womanhood: "Woman's Sphere" in New England, 1780–1835* (1977); Carl N. Degler, *At Odds: Women and the Family in America from the Revolution to the Present* (1980); Hasia R. Diner, *Erin's Daughters in America: Irish Immigrant Women in the Nineteenth Century* (1983); Linda Gordon, *Woman's Body, Woman's Rights: A Social History of Birth Control in America* (1976); Suzanne Lebsock, *The Free Women of Petersburg: Status and Culture in a Southern Town, 1784–1860* (1984); Mary P. Ryan, *Cradle of the Middle Class: The Family in Oneida County, New York, 1790–1865* (1981); Kathryn Kish Sklar, *Catharine Beecher: A Study in American Domesticity* (1973); Robert V. Wells, *Revolutions in Americans' Lives* (1982); Barbara Welter, "The Cult of True Womanhood, 1820–1860," *American Quarterly,* 18 (Summer 1966), 151–174.

Immigrants

Rowland Berthoff, *British Immigrants in Industrial America* (1953); Kathleen Neils Conzen, *Immigrant Milwaukee: 1836–1860* (1976); Arnoldo De León, *The Tejano Community, 1836–1900* (1982); Charlotte Erickson, *Invisible Immigrants* (1972); Robert Ernst, *Immigrant Life in New York City, 1825–1863* (1949); John Gjerde, *From Peasants to Farmers: The Migration from Balestrand, Norway, to the Upper Middle West* (1985); Oscar Handlin, *Boston's Immigrants: A Study in Acculturation,* rev. ed. (1959); Walter D. Kamphoefner, *The Westfalians: From Germany to Missouri* (1987); Dale T. Knobel, *Paddy and the Republic: Ethnicity and Nationality in Antebellum America* (1986); Philip Taylor, *The Distant Magnet: European Emigration to the United States of America* (1971); Mark Wyman, *Immigrants in the Valley: Irish, Germans, and Americans in the Upper Mississippi, 1830–1860* (1984).

Indians

Robert F. Berkhofer, Jr., *The White Man's Indian* (1978); Grant Foreman, *Indian Removal: The Emigration of the Five Civilized Tribes of Indians,* rev. ed. (1953); Michael D. Green, *The Politics of Indian Removal: Creek Government and Society in Crisis* (1982); Florette Henri, *The Southern Indians and Benjamin Hawkins, 1796–1816* (1986); Charles Hudson, *The Southeastern Indians* (1976); William G. McLoughlin, *Cherokee Renascence in the New Republic* (1986); Francis P. Prucha, *The Great Father: The United States Government and the American Indians,* 2 vols. (1984); Francis P. Prucha, *American Indian Policy in the Formative Years* (1967); Herman J. Viola, *Thomas L. McKenney: Architect of America's Early Indian Policy: 1816–1830* (1974); J. Leitch Wright, Jr., *Creeks and Seminoles: The Destruction and Regeneration of the Muscogulge People* (1986).

Free People of Color

Ira Berlin, *Slaves Without Masters: The Free Negro in the Antebellum South* (1974); Leonard P. Curry, *The Free Black in Urban America, 1800–1850* (1981); Luther Porter Jackson, *Free Negro Labor and Property Holding in Virginia, 1830–1860* (1942); David M. Katzman, *Before the Ghetto: Black Detroit in the Nineteenth Century* (1973); Rudolph M. Lapp, *Blacks in Gold Rush California* (1977); Leon Litwack, *North of Slavery: The Negro in the Free States, 1790–1860* (1961); Gary B. Nash, *Forging Freedom: The Formation of Philadelphia's Black Community, 1720–1840* (1988); Julie Winch, *Philadelphia's Black Elite: Activism, Accommodation, and the Struggle for Autonomy, 1787–1848* (1988); Arthur Zilversmit, *The First Emancipation: The Abolition of Slavery in the North* (1967).

The Tappan brothers, Arthur and Lewis, amassed a fortune from the War of 1812 through the 1840s. Born in Massachusetts in the 1780s, they were merchants and investors whose businesses included dry goods, textile mills, an importing house, the *New York Journal of Commerce,* and the Mercantile Agency (the first commercial-credit rating agency in the United States). Their wealth grew with the expansion of the market economy.

They shunned the balls and elaborate dinners of the urban elite. Instead, they lived by their mother's Calvinist tenet that this world was preparation for the next. Both believed that they would have to submit their accounts to God and that "luxurious living" would count against them. Nonetheless, they spent large sums, contributing generously to evangelical churches and missions, to temperance and antigambling societies, to Bible printing, to the Antimasons, and to antislavery.

The lives of the Tappan brothers and many other reformers were changed by one overriding issue: antislavery. Drawn to abolitionism by their religious concerns and the work of William Lloyd Garrison, Arthur and Lewis Tappan became the leaders of religious antislavery. They deservedly earned their reputations as being among the most committed reformers in the period from the 1820s through the 1850s, which became known as an age of reform.

12

REFORM, POLITICS, AND EXPANSION, 1824–1844

Reform was, in part, a response to the unsettling effect of the enormous transformation that the United States experienced after the War of 1812. Population growth, immigration, internal migration, urbanization, the market economy, growing inequality, loosening family and community ties, the advancing frontier, and territorial expansion all contributed to the remaking of the country. Many people felt that they were no longer masters of their own fate and that the changes in society were undermining traditional values.

Religious reformers such as the Tappans sought to find order or to impose it on a society in which economic change and discord had reached a crescendo. Prompted by the evangelical ardor of the Second Great Awakening and convinced of their moral rectitude, they crusaded for individual improvement. Everywhere benevolent and reform societies multiplied. Reform soon took on a much more active role than benevolent work and became an instrument for restoring discipline and order in a changing society. Women were prominent in the reform movement, and the role of women in public life became an issue in itself.

As reform organizations spread, they turned to the government as an effective instrument of social and economic change. Temperance, institutional reform, and most notably Antimasonry and abolition brought new voters into politics. The line between social reform and politics was not always distinguishable. Opponents were no less concerned with social problems. What set them apart from reformers was their skepticism about human perfectibility and their distrust of institutions and power. To them, coercion was the greater evil. They sought to reverse, not shape, change.

Two issues in particular provided the bridge between reform and politics: the brief Antimasonry frenzy and the crusade for immediate emancipation. Antimasons organized the first third-party movement, but abolition eventually overrode other concerns. No single issue evoked the depth of passion that slavery did. Territorial expansion in the 1840s and 1850s made it even more politically explosive.

Political leaders attempted to grapple with change. In the late 1820s, the opponents of religious reform found a champion in Andrew Jackson and a home in the Democratic party. Yet the Jacksonians saw themselves as reformers; they responded to change by attempting to foster individualism and to restore restraint in government. They fought special privileges and the Second Bank of the United States with the same vigor as the Tappan brothers opposed sin. President Jackson sought to restrain the national government, believing that a strong federal government restricted individual freedom by favoring one group over another. In response, reformers rallied around the new Whig party, which became the vehicle for humanitarian reform. Democrats and Whigs competed in the second party system, which was marked by strong organizations, intensely loyal followings, religious and ethnic differences, and popular bases among the electorate.

During the economically prosperous 1840s, both parties eagerly promoted westward expansion to further their goals. The idea of expansion from coast to coast seemed to Americans to be the inevitable manifest destiny of the United States. In the 1850s and 1860s, the politics of territorial expansion and the antislavery movement collided, with explosive results.

◀▬

From Revival to Reform

The prime motivating force behind organized benevolence and reform was probably religion. Starting in the late 1790s, a tremendous religious revival, the Second Great Awakening, galvanized Protestants, especially women. The Awakening began in small villages in the East, intensified after the War of 1812, then spread over western New York, and continued to grow through the late 1840s. Under its influence, Christians tried to right the wrongs of the world.

Revivals were the lifeblood of evangelical Christianity, and they drew converts to a religion of the heart, not the head. In 1821, Charles G. Finney, "the

Second Great Awakening

father of modern revivalism," experienced a soul-shaking conversion, which, he said, brought him "a retainer from the Lord Jesus Christ to plead his cause." In everyday language, he told his audiences that "God has made man a moral free agent." In other words, evil was avoidable; Christians were not doomed by original sin. Hence anyone could achieve salvation. The Second Great Awakening also raised people's hopes for the Second Coming of the Christian messiah and the establishment of the Kingdom of God on earth. Revivalists set out to speed the Second Coming by creating a heaven on earth. They joined the forces of good and light—reform—to combat those of evil and darkness.

Regardless of theology, all shared a belief in individual improvement and self-reliance as moving forces. In this way, the Second Great Awakening bred reform, and evangelical Protestants became missionaries for both religious and secular salvation. Wherever they preached, voluntary reform societies arose. Evangelists organized an association for each issue—temperance, education, Sabbath

IMPORTANT EVENTS

1790s–1840s	Second Great Awakening
1820s	Model penitentiaries
1825	House of Representatives elects John Quincy Adams president
1826	American Society for the Promotion of Temperance founded
1828	Tariff of Abominations Jackson elected president
1830	Webster-Hayne debate
1830s–40s	Second party system
1831	*Liberator* begins publication First national Antimason Convention
1832	Veto of Second Bank of the United States recharter Jackson re-elected
1832–33	Nullification crisis
1836	Republic of Texas established Specie Circular Van Buren elected president
1837	Financial panic
1838–39	U.S.–Canada border tensions
1839–43	Hard times
1840	Whigs under Harrison win presidency
1841	Tyler assumes the presidency Oregon fever
1844	Polk elected president
1845	Texas admitted to the Union
1848	Woman's Rights Convention, Seneca Falls, New York
1851	Maine adopts Prohibition

observance, and later antislavery; collectively, these groups formed a national web of benevolent and moral reform societies.

Women were the earliest converts, and they tended to sustain the Second Great Awakening. When Finney led daytime prayer meetings in Rochester, New York, for instance, **Role of Women** pious middle-class women visited families while the men were away at work. Slowly, they brought those families and husbands into the churches and under the influence of reform. Women more than men tended to feel personally responsible for the increasingly secular orientation of the expanding market economy. Many women felt guilty for neglecting their religious duties, and the emotionally charged conversion experience set them on the right path again.

Beyond conversion, the great impact of the Second Great Awakening was the spread of women's involvement in benevolent activities to ameliorate the growing social ills. In the cities, women responded both to inner voices and to the growing inequality, turbulence, and strains of change around them. By the turn of the nineteenth century, most of the expanding cities had women's benevolent societies to help needy women and orphans. Increasingly, the spread of poverty and vice that accompanied urbanization touched the hearts of women, especially those caught up in the fervor of revival.

An 1830 exposé of prostitution in New York City revealed the diverging concerns and responses of reform men and women, on the one hand, and political organizations, on the other hand, and demonstrated the convergence of urban problems, revival, and reform. In response to the report on how prostitution had taken hold in New York City, prominent male leaders united to defend the city's good name. Women, on the other hand, moved by the plight of "fallen women" and supported by the Tappans, responded by forming two new societies concerned with prostitutes and prostitution.

The Female Moral Reform Society led the crusade against prostitution. During the 1830s, the New York–based association expanded its activities and geographical scope as the American Female Moral Reform Society. By 1840, it had 555 affiliated societies across the nation. These women not only fought the evils of prostitution but also assisted poor women and orphans and entered the political sphere. In New York State in the 1840s, the movement fostered public morality by successfully crusading for criminal sanctions against seducers and prostitutes.

As the pace of social change increased in the 1830s and 1840s, so did efforts at reform. In western New York and Ohio, Finney's preaching was a catalyst to reform. Western New York experienced such continuous and heated waves of revivalism that it became known as the "burned-over" district. The opening of the Erie Canal and the migration of New Englanders carried the reform ferment farther westward. There, revivalist institutions—Ohio's Lane Seminary and Oberlin College were the most famous—sent committed graduates out into the world to spread the gospel of reform. Evangelists also organized grassroots political movements. In the late 1830s and 1840s, they rallied around the Whig party in an attempt to use government as an instrument of reform.

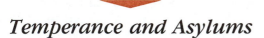

Temperance and Asylums

One of the most successful reform efforts was the campaign against the consumption of alcohol. As a group, American men liked to drink alcoholic spirits. They gathered in public houses, saloons, and rural inns to gossip, discuss politics, play cards, escape work and home pressures, and drink. And though respectable women did not drink in public, many regularly tippled alcohol-based patent medicines promoted as cure-alls.

This certificate of membership in a temperance society, for display, announced the virtues of the household to all visitors. In this illustration, the man signs with the support of wife and child; demon rum and its accompanying evils were banished from this home. *Library of Congress.*

Why then did temperance become such a vital issue? And why were women especially active in the movement? Like all reform, temperance had a strong religious base. To evangelicals, the selling of whiskey was a chronic symbol of Sabbath violation, for workers commonly labored six days a week, then spent Sunday at the public house drinking and socializing. Alcohol was seen as a destroyer of families. Temperance literature was laced with domestic images—abandoned wives, prodigal sons, drunken fathers. Outside the home, the habit of drinking could not be tolerated in the new world of the factory. Employers complained that drinkers took "St. Monday" as a holiday to recover from Sunday.

Demon rum thus became a major target of reformers. As the movement gained momentum, they shifted their emphasis from temperate use of spirits to voluntary abstinence and finally to legally enforced prohibition. The American Society for the Promotion of Temperance, organ-

Temperance Societies

ized in 1826 to urge drinkers to sign a pledge of abstinence, shortly afterward became a pressure group for state prohibition legislation. Within a few years, more than a million people had taken the pledge. By the 1840s, the annual per capita consumption of alcohol had fallen from more than five gallons to less than two gallons. Furthermore, many northern states, beginning with Maine in 1851, prohibited the manufacture and sale of alcohol except for medicinal purposes.

Another aspect of the temperance movement was the attack on gambling. People gathered at taverns to drink and gamble, and reformers believed that both drinking and gambling undermined independence and self-reliance. Of special concern in the nineteenth century was the spread of lotteries.

Lotteries had been brought by English colonists to the New World at the turn of the eighteenth century. In the New World, lotteries were a useful way of selling extremely valuable **Lotteries** property in an age when few single buyers could raise the large purchase price. Hundreds of small investors could participate in a lottery for the prize, enabling a merchant to dispose of inventory or a homeowner to sell a house. Local governments used lotteries to ease the tax burden by raising money for capital improvements. The Continental Congress had tried to use a grand lottery to raise $1.5 million to wage revolutionary war against England, but it failed to raise the anticipated revenue.

Lotteries became a target of reform, and between 1830 and 1860 every state in the Union banned them. To some, lotteries were among such vices as slavery and alcohol. Other opponents objected to the abuses inherent in the common pattern of states delegating their lottery powers to private sponsors. For instance, a Pennsylvania investigation (1831) revealed that a state-authorized lottery to raise $27,000 a year for internal improvement generated enormous profits for the lottery company. On $5-million annual sales, the state received its $27,000 and the sponsors $800,000.

Another important part of the reform impulse was the development of new social institutions. The age of reform prompted the establishment and construction of asylums and other institutions to house prisoners, the insane and ill, orphans, delinquent children, and the poor. Many believed that such institutions would provide the victims of instability and turbulence with an environment of order, stability, and discipline, thus giving them an opportunity to become self-reliant and responsible.

The penitentiary movement exemplified this approach. In the 1820s, New York and Pennsylvania offered similar models for reforming criminals. **Penitentiaries** Both systems sought to remove criminals from evil societal and individual influences and to place them in an ordered, disciplined regimen. It was commonly believed that criminals came from unstable families, in which lack of discipline and restraint led to vice and drink. Idleness was believed to be both a symptom and a cause of individual corruption and crime; thus the clock governed a prisoner's day, and idleness was banished.

Similar approaches were employed by societies promoting other asylums, from insane asylums and hospitals to orphanages and houses of refuge. Doctors linked mental illness to the stress and strain of contemporary urban life. The prescribed treatment was to remove individuals from families and society, to isolate them among strangers. The asylum would impose discipline and order on patients, but in a humane fashion. In response to organized reform societies, states began to erect asylums for the insane in the 1830s. They built them in tranquil, rural settings, away from the turbulent cities.

Antimasonry

Far more intense than the asylum movement, though of shorter duration, was the crusade against Masonry. The Antimasonry movement arose overnight in 1826, in the burned-over district of western New York, and it stirred political activity before virtually disappearing in the 1830s. Like other reforms, it sought political change. Indeed, it became more of a political than a reform movement. It created the first third-party movement and brought new white voters into politics at a time when male suffrage was being extended. Antimasons sought to liberate society from what they considered a secret, powerful, antirepublican fraternity. The political arena quickly absorbed Antimasonry, and its short life illustrates the close tie between politics and reform from the 1820s through the 1840s.

Antimasonry was a reaction to Freemasonry, which had come to the United States from England in the eighteenth century. Freemasonry was a secret middle- and upper-class fraternity that attracted the sons of the Enlightenment with its emphasis on individual belief in a deity (as opposed to organized religion) and on brotherhood (as opposed to one church). In the early nineteenth century, Freemasonry attracted many commercial and political leaders.

Opponents of Masonry charged that the order's secrecy was antidemocratic and antirepublican, as was its elite membership and its use of regalia and such terms as "knights" and "priests." As church leaders took up the moral crusade against Masonry, evangelicals labeled the order satanic. Antimasons argued that Masonry threatened the family because it encouraged men to spend time at the lodges, neglecting the family for alcohol and ribald entertainments.

The Morgan affair was the catalyst for Antimasonry as an organized movement. In 1826, William Morgan, a disillusioned Mason, wrote an exposé of Masonry, to which his **Morgan** printer David Miller added a **Affair** scathing attack on the order. On September 12, 1826, before the book appeared, a group of Masons abducted Morgan outside the jail in Canandaigua, New York. It was widely believed that some Masons murdered Morgan, whose body was never found.

What energized the Antimasonry crusade was that its worst fears about Masonry as a conspiracy seemed to be confirmed. Many of the officeholders in western New York, especially prosecutors, were Masons, and they appeared to obstruct the investigation of Morgan's abduction. Public outcry and opposing political factions pressed for justice, and a series of notorious trials from 1827 through 1831 led many to suspect a conspiracy. The cover-up became as much the issue as distrust of Masonry itself, and the movement spilled over to other states. In the Morgan affair, Antimason claims of a secret conspiracy seemed to be justified.

As a moral crusade, however, Antimasonry crossed over into politics almost immediately. The issue itself was a political one because the perceived obstruction of justice was a signal element. Antimasonry attracted the lower and middle classes, pitting them against higher-status Masons and exploiting the general public's distrust and envy of local political leaders.

Unwittingly, the Masons stoked the fires of Antimasonry. The silence of the order seemed to condone the murder of Morgan, and the construction of monumental lodges advertised their determination to remain a public force. When editors who were Masons ignored the crusade against Masonry, the Antimasons started their own newspapers. The struggle aroused further public interest in politics.

Antimasonry spread as a popular movement and introduced the convention system in place of caucuses for choosing political candidates. To defend public morality and the republic, **Convention** the Antimasons held conventions **System** in 1827. The following year the conventions supported the National Republican candidate and opposed Andrew Jackson because he was a Mason. In 1831, the Antimasons held the first national political convention in Baltimore and a year later nominated in convention William Wirt as their presidential candidate. Thus the Antimasons became one rallying point for those opposed to President Jackson.

By the mid-1830s, Antimasonry had lost force as a moral and political movement. A single-issue party, it declined along with Freemasonry. Yet the movement left its mark on the politics of the era. It inspired and welcomed wider participation in the political process. Moreover, the revivalist and reform impulses in movements such as Antimasonry further stimulated or awakened disagreements about values and ideology—disagreements that were reinforced by conflicts over wealth, religion, and status. These differences helped polarize politics and shape parties as organizations to express those differences. The Antimasons contributed specifically to party development by pioneering the convention system and by stimulating grassroots involvement.

Abolitionism and the Women's Movement

Sparked by territorial expansion, the issue of slavery eventually became so overpowering that it consumed all other reforms. Passions grew so heated that they threatened the nation itself. Above all else, those who advocated immediate emancipation saw slavery as a moral issue—evidence of the sinfulness of the American nation.

Before the 1830s few whites advocated the immediate abolition of slavery. Some, most notably the Quakers who had led the first antislavery movement in the eighteenth century, hoped that moral suasion would convince slaveholders to free their chattels. Others favored gradual abolition coupled with the resettling of blacks in Africa. The American Colonization Society had been founded in 1816 with this in mind.

Only free blacks pushed for an immediate end to slavery. By 1830, there were at least fifty black abolitionist societies in major African-American communities. These associations assisted fugitive slaves, attacked slavery at every turn, and reminded the nation that its mission as defined in the Declaration of Independence remained unfulfilled. A free black press helped to spread their word. Black abolitionists Frederick Douglass, Sojourner Truth, and Harriet Tubman then joined forces with white reformers in the American Anti-Slavery Society. These crusaders also stirred European support for their militant and unrelenting campaign.

Black Antislavery Movement

In the 1830s, a small minority of white reformers made immediate, complete, and uncompensated emancipation their primary commitment. William Lloyd Garrison, though clearly not the most representative, was the most prominent and uncompromising immediatist. Recruited to the abolitionist cause in 1828 by Benjamin Lundy, a gradualist, Garrison broke with the moderate abolitionists in 1831. That year, contributions from the Tappans and others helped him

William Lloyd Garrison

publish the first issue of the *Liberator,* which was to be his major weapon against slavery for thirty-five years. "I am in earnest—I will not equivocate—I will not excuse—I will not retreat a single inch—*and I will be heard,*" he wrote in the first issue. Garrison's refusal to work with anyone who even indirectly delayed emancipation left him isolated from most people opposed to slavery. Still, through sheer force of rhetoric, Garrison helped to make antislavery a national issue.

Most benevolent workers and reformers kept their distance from the immediatists. Many thought the intensity of the immediatist approach was unchristian. They shared the view that slavery was a sin, but they believed that it had to be eradicated slowly. If they moved too fast, if they attacked sinners too harshly or conflicted too much with community customs and beliefs, they would destroy the harmony and order that they sought to bring in benevolent and reform work.

Immediatists

Immediatists' greatest recruitment successes came from defending their own constitutional and natural rights, not those of slaves. Wherever they went, immediatists found their civil rights in danger, especially their right of free speech. For example, Southern mobs seized and destroyed much of the propaganda mailed by the American Anti-Slavery Society (organized by the immediatists in 1833), and the state of South Carolina (with the approval of the United States postmaster general) intercepted and burned abolitionist literature that entered the state. In 1837, Elijah P. Lovejoy, an abolitionist editor, was murdered in Alton, Illinois, by a mob that had come to sack his office.

The opposition saw many dangers in abolitionism. At a rally in Boston's Faneuil Hall in August 1835, former Federalist Harrison Gray Otis portrayed abolitionists as subversives. He attacked Garrison's American Anti-Slavery Society as a "dangerous association," a "revolutionary society" with branches in every community in the nation. Otis predicted that the abolitionists would soon turn to politics, causing unpredictable "trouble and calamity." "What will become of the union?" Otis asked. Others believed that the immediatist attack on colonization undermined the best solution. Keeping blacks in America, they believed, eventually would foment slave rebellions and lead to racial amalgamation.

Another civil rights confrontation developed in Congress. Exercising their constitutional right to petition Congress, abolitionists mounted a campaign to abolish slavery and the **Gag Rule** slave trade in the District of Columbia. But Congress responded in 1836 by adopting the so-called gag rule, which automatically tabled abolitionist petitions, effectively preventing debate on them. In a dramatic defense of the right of petition, former President John Quincy Adams, then a Massachusetts representative, took to the floor repeatedly to defy the detested gag rule and eventually succeeded in getting it repealed in 1844. Public outrage at the gag rule, censorship of the mails, and Lovejoy's murder broadened the base of antislavery support in the North.

Frustration with the federal government also fed northern support for antislavery. By and large, politicians and government officials sought to avoid the question of slavery. The Missouri Compromise of 1820 had been an effort to make debate on the slave or free status of new states unnecessary. Censorship of the mails and the gag rule were similar attempts to keep the issue out of the political arena. Yet the more national leaders, especially Democrats, sought to avoid the matter, the more they hardened the resolve of the antislavery forces.

The effect of the unlawful, violent, and obstructionist tactics used by proslavery advocates and anti-immediatists cannot be overestimated. This opposition, however, helped unify the abolition movement by forcing the factions to work together for mutual defense. At the outset, antislavery was not a unified movement. Its adherents were divided over Garrison's emphasis on "moral suasion" versus the more practical political approach of James G. Birney, the Liberty party's candidate for president in 1844 (see page 235). They disagreed about the place of free black people in American society and split on other reforms, especially the rights of women.

Women had less success when it came to their own position in society. At its inception, the American Anti-Slavery Society resembled most other benevolent societies; it was gender segregated, with

Women Abolitionists women in a subordinate role. Slowly over time, the pattern changed. By the late 1840s, women abolitionists were breaking free of the domestic sphere—many of them were single women—and becoming genuine colleagues to men in the movement. Men like Garrison came to accept their women colleagues' contributions in providing moral direction. Lydia Child, Maria Chapman, and Lucretia Mott all joined the American Anti-Slavery Society executive committee; Child edited its official organ, the *National Anti-Slavery Standard,* from 1841 to 1843, and Chapman co-edited it from 1844 until 1848.

Negative reaction to the growing involvement of women in reform movements led some women to re-examine their position in society. In 1837, two antislavery lecturers, Angelina and Sarah Grimké, became particular objects of controversy. Natives of South Carolina, they moved north in the 1820s to speak and write against slavery. They were received with hostility for speaking before mixed groups of men and women. This reaction turned the Grimkés' attention from slavery to women's condition. The two attacked the concept of "subordination to man," insisting that men and women had the "same rights and same duties." Sarah Grimké's *Letters on the Condition of Women and the Equality of the Sexes* (1838) and her sister's *Letters to Catharine E. Beecher* (1838) were the opening volleys in the war against the legal and social inequality of women.

Unlike other reform movements, which succeeded in building a broad base of individual and organizational support, the movement for women's **Women's Rights** rights was limited. Some men joined the ranks, notably Garrison and ex-slave Frederick Douglass, but most actively opposed the movement. The Woman's Rights Convention at Seneca Falls, New York, in 1848, led by Elizabeth Cady Stanton and Lucretia Mott, issued a much-published indictment of the injustices suffered by women. The Seneca Falls Declaration of 1848 paralleled the 1776 Declaration of Independence, asserting as a self-evident truth "that all men and women are created equal." The document listed the record of male tyranny against women and the inequalities

Chapter 12: Reform, Politics, and Expansion, 1824–1844

Leisure in America, **1850**

SHARED EXPERIENCE

Between 1800 and 1860, the American population increased from 5.3 to 31.4 million. Large cities grew even larger, villages became small towns, and the frontier and the countryside sprouted countless new settlements. People were able to interact more frequently with other people, and recreational activities often became social events, shared with participants beyond the family circle.

New York City, by 1810 the most populous city in the United States, provided the ultimate example of a burgeoning metropolis, growing from 60,500 people in 1800 to 813,600 in 1860. A view of Central Park painted by Winslow Homer during the winter of 1859–1860 provides a small glimpse of that crowded city. Recreational space had become limited, and skating time with the family had to be enjoyed in the midst of scores of like-minded neighbors.

Capitalizing on the growing concentrations of would-be patrons, entrepreneurs organized concerts in cities throughout the young nation. Jenny Lind (1820–1887) was perhaps the most famous singer of the nineteenth century, renowned for the purity of her voice and its remarkable range. Already extremely successful on European opera stages, Lind toured the United States between 1850 and 1852, visiting 137 cities in all. P. T. Barnum, the circus impressario who managed the initial leg of her tour, publicized his star so well that thousands of enthusiasts surrounded her New York hotel within minutes of her arrival in America. Currier and Ives produced a lithograph of her first appearance on an American stage, at Castle Garden in Manhattan's Battery Park.

Lind's fame was so complete that her name was affixed to various items of clothing and furniture, and china-head dolls mimicking her hair style and facial features were widely manufactured. She also inspired larger tokens of devotion; one San Francisco fan, disappointed when Lind failed to include his town on her itinerary, consoled himself by building a theater and naming it after her.

Out-of-the-way locations were not without their own concert performances. Itinerant musicians, particularly in the South, traveled from farm to farm, playing for small family groups. Eastman Johnson's 1866 painting *Fiddling His Way* evokes a sense of the quiet pleasure such visits provided. Fiddles and banjos provided much of the music in rural America. Banjos, in particular, produced a music that was uniquely American in sound and style, a hybrid of African and European influences.

First page: Winslow Homer, *Skating in Central Park, 1859–60*, 1860. Previous page, top: Currier and Ives lithograph, *First Appearance of Jenny Lind in America*, 1850. Previous page, bottom: Jenny Lind doll, ca. 1860. This page, right: Banjo, ca. 1840–1860. Below: Eastman Johnson, *Fiddling His Way*, 1866.

Despite the rapidly changing demographics, life in the country and on the frontier was frequently still an isolated one. To combat the loneliness of widely separated homesteads, families gathered for harvestings, barn-raisings, and communal bees. At a quilting bee, for instance, young and old came together to socialize, gossip, eat, court, and, incidentally, make quilts. Ordinarily, the top of the quilt had already been pieced together; the partygoers helped stitch the top to the cotton batting and backing underneath.

Although the quilt shown in the painting below looks like a simple affair, others displayed far more elaborate designs, often patterned after natural forms. See the detail of a design known as "peony and prairie flower," at right. The lovely meticulousness of this work suggests that the quiet domestic pleasures had not gone out of style in American homes.

Above: Detail of quilt, stitched by Parnel R. Grumley, 1847. Below: Artist unknown, *Quilting Party*, 1854.

and indignities that women suffered from the government and the law. If women had the vote, these early advocates of women's rights argued, they could protect themselves and realize their potential as moral and spiritual leaders.

Jacksonianism and the Beginnings of Modern Party Politics

The distinction between reform and politics eroded in the 1820s and after as reform pushed its way into politics. Politicians no less than reformers sought to control and direct change in an expanding, urbanizing, market-oriented nation. They, too, shared the unease caused by change and the corruption in private and public life. After a brief flirtation with single-party politics after the War of 1812, the United States entered a period of intense and heated political competition. By the 1830s, politics had become the great nineteenth-century American pastime.

The election of 1824, in which John Quincy Adams and Andrew Jackson faced each other for the first time, heralded the start of a new, more open political system. From 1800 through 1820, the presidential system in which a congressional caucus chose Jefferson, Madison, and Monroe as the Republican nominees had worked well. Such a system restricted voter involvement, but this was not a drawback at first, because in 1800 the people in only five of sixteen states voted for their presidential electors. (In most, state legislators designated the electors.) By 1824, however, eighteen out of twenty-four states chose electors by popular vote.

End of the Caucus System

In 1824, the caucus chose William H. Crawford, secretary of the treasury. But other Republicans, encouraged by the opportunity to appeal directly to the voters in most states, challenged Crawford as sectional candidates. Secretary of State John Quincy Adams drew support from New England, and westerners backed Speaker of the House Henry Clay of Kentucky. Secretary of War John C. Calhoun looked to the South for support and hoped to win Pennsylvania as well. Andrew Jackson, a popular military hero whose political views were unknown, was nominated by resolution of the Tennessee legislature and had the most widespread support. By boycotting the deliberations of the caucus and by attacking it as being undemocratic, these men and their supporters ended the role of the congressional caucus in nominating presidents.

Andrew Jackson led in both electoral and popular votes in the four-way presidential election of 1824, but no one received a majority in the electoral college (see map, page 226). Adams finished second, and Crawford and Clay trailed far behind. (Calhoun dropped out of the race before the election.) Under the Constitution, the selection of a president in such circumstances fell to the House of Representatives, on the basis of one vote to a state. Clay, who had received the fewest votes, was dropped; Crawford, a stroke victim, never received serious consideration. Clay, as Speaker of the House and leader of the Ohio Valley states, backed Adams, who received the votes of thirteen out of twenty-four state delegations. Clay became secretary of state in the Adams administration—the traditional steppingstone to the presidency. With angry Jacksonians denouncing the arrangement as a "corrupt bargain" in which the office had been stolen from the front runner, the Republican party divided. The Adams wing emerged as the National Republicans, and the Jacksonians became the Democratic-Republicans (shortened to Democrats).

The Jacksonians immediately laid plans for 1828, while John Quincy Adams took the oath as the sixth president. Adams proposed a strong nationalist policy emphasizing Henry Clay's American System of protective tariffs, a national bank, and internal improvements. Adams believed that the federal government should take an activist role not only in the economy, but also in education, science, and the arts; accordingly, he proposed a national university in Washington, D.C.

Brilliant as a diplomat and secretary of state, Adams was inept as president. He underestimated the lingering effects of the Panic of 1819 and the ensuing bitter opposition to a national bank and protective tariffs. Meanwhile, supporters of Andrew

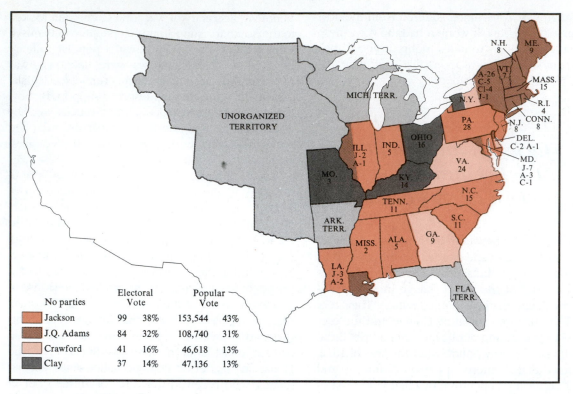

No parties	Electoral Vote		Popular Vote	
![Jackson] Jackson	99	38%	153,544	43%
![J.Q. Adams] J.Q. Adams	84	32%	108,740	31%
![Crawford] Crawford	41	16%	46,618	13%
![Clay] Clay	37	14%	47,136	13%

Presidential Election, 1824

Jackson sabotaged Adams's administration at every opportunity.

The 1828 campaign between Adams and Jackson was an intensely personal conflict. Whatever principles the two men stood for were obscured by the mudslinging on both sides. A month after the election, Rachel Jackson died, and the president-elect attributed his wife's death to the abuse heaped upon him in the campaign. He never forgave her "murderers."

Jackson polled 56 percent of the popular vote and won in the electoral college, 178 to 83. For him and his supporters, the will of the people had been served, as it had not been in 1824. Through a lavishly financed coalition of state parties, political leaders, and newspaper editors, a popular movement elected a president. An era ended, and the Democratic party became the first truly political party in the United States. Well-organized parties became the hallmark of nineteenth-century American politics.

Andrew Jackson was nicknamed "Old Hickory," after the toughest American hardwood. A rough-and-tumble, ambitious man, he rose from humble birth to become a wealthy planter and slaveholder. Jackson was the first American president from the West and the first not born into comfortable circumstances; he was a self-made man at ease among both frontiersmen and southern planters. Though he had a violent temper and was often vindictive, he could charm those opposed to him and allay their suspicions. He had an instinct for politics and picked issues and supporters shrewdly.

Andrew Jackson

Jackson and his Democratic supporters offered a distinct alternative to the strong national government Adams had advocated. The Democrats represented a wide range of beliefs but shared some common ideals. Fundamentally, they sought to foster the Jeffersonian concept of an agrarian society, har-

Democrats

Jacques Amans's 1840 oil portrait of former President Andrew Jackson. Jackson appears to look into the viewer's eyes, suggesting the directness that earned so deep a loyalty from his supporters. *The Historic New Orleans Collection Museum/Research Center.*

kening back to the belief that a strong central government was the enemy of individual liberty, a tyranny to be feared. Thus, like Jefferson, they favored limited central government.

Jacksonians feared the concentration of economic power as much as the concentration of political power and viewed government intervention in the economy as a boon to special-interest groups and the rich. Consequently, they sought to restore the independence of the individual—the artisan and the yeoman farmer—by ending federal support of banks and corporations and restricting the use of paper currency.

Finally, Jackson and his supporters were hostile to reform as a movement and an ideology. Reformers were increasingly calling for an activist and interventionist government as they organized to turn their programs into legislation. But Democrats tended to oppose programs such as educational reform and the establishment of public education. They believed, for instance, that public schools restricted individual liberty by interfering with parental responsibility and undermined freedom of religion by replacing church schools. Nor did Jackson share reformers' humanitarian concerns.

Jackson and the Jacksonians considered themselves reformers in a different way. In following Jefferson's notion of restraint in government and in emphasizing individualism, Jackson and his followers sought to bring back old republican virtues, prizing such individual traits as industriousness, prudence, and economy. No less than the reformers, Jackson sought to restore a harmony and unity that had been displaced by economic and social change.

Like Jefferson, Jackson strengthened the executive branch of government at the same time as he tended to weaken the federal role. Given his popularity and the strength of his personality, this concentration of power in the presidency was perhaps inevitable; but his deliberate policy of combining the roles of party leader and chief of state centralized even greater power in the White House. Invoking the principle that rotating officeholders would make government more responsive to the public will, Jackson used the spoils system to reward loyal Democrats with appointments to office. Though he removed fewer than one-quarter of federal officeholders in his two terms, his use of patronage nevertheless strengthened party organization and loyalty.

Jackson himself stressed his rejection of elitism and special favors, his use of rotation in office, and his belief in popular government. He declared repeatedly that sovereignty resided with the people and not with the states or with the courts. Summoning the electorate to support him, he confidently claimed to represent the people's will. In this context, Jackson was a reformer; he returned government to majority rule. Yet it is hard to distinguish between Jackson's belief in himself as the instrument of the people and simple egotism and demagogic arrogance. After all, his opponents, too, claimed to represent the people.

Jackson invigorated the philosophy of limited government. In 1830, he vetoed the Maysville Road bill, which would have provided a federal subsidy to construct a sixty-mile turnpike from Maysville to Lexington, Kentucky. Jackson insisted that a federally subsidized internal improvement confined to one state was unconstitutional and that such projects were properly a state responsibility. The veto undermined Henry Clay's American System and personally embarrassed Clay because the project was in his home district.

The Nullification and Bank Controversies

Jackson had to face more directly the question of the proper division of sovereignty between state and central government. The slave South, especially South Carolina, was fearful of federal power. To protect their interests, South Carolinian political leaders articulated the doctrine of *nullification,* according to which a state had the right to overrule federal legislation. The act that directly inspired this doctrine was the passage of the protectionist 1828 Tariff of Abominations. In his unsigned *Exposition and Protest,* John C. Calhoun argued that in any disagreement between the federal government and a state, a special state convention—like the conventions called to ratify the Constitution—would decide the conflict by either nullifying or accepting the federal law. Only the power of nullification could protect the minority against the tyranny of the majority, Calhoun asserted.

In public, Calhoun let others take the lead in advancing nullification. As Jackson's running mate in 1828, he avoided publicly identifying with nullification and thus embarrassing the ticket. As vice president, he hoped to win Jackson's support as the Democratic presidential heir apparent. Thus a silent Calhoun presided over the Senate and its packed galleries when Senators Daniel Webster of New Hampshire and Robert Y. Hayne of South Carolina debated nullification in January 1830. The debate explored North-South frictions and the nature of the Union. Though debating Hayne, Webster aimed

Webster-Hayne Debate

his remarks at Calhoun as he depicted the nation as a compact of people, not merely states. In this climax of his career as a debater, he invoked two images. One, which he hoped he would not see, was the outcome of nullification: "states dissevered, discordant, belligerent; on a land rent with civil feuds, or drenched . . . in fraternal blood!" The other was a patriotic vision of a great nation flourishing under the motto "Liberty and Union, now and forever, one and inseparable."

Though sympathetic to states' rights, Jackson rejected the idea of state sovereignty. Moreover, he was deeply committed to union. Thus he shared Webster's dread and distrust of nullification. Soon after the Webster-Hayne debate, the president made his position clear at a Jefferson Day dinner with the toast: "Our Federal Union, it *must* and *shall* be preserved." Calhoun, when his turn came, offered: "The Federal Union—next to our liberty the most dear."

South Carolina invoked its theory of nullification against the Tariff of 1832. Although this tariff had the effect of reducing some duties, it retained high

Nullification Crisis

taxes on imported iron, cottons, and woolens. A majority of southern representatives supported the new tariff, but South Carolinians refused to go along. In their view, their constitutional right to control their own destiny had been sacrificed to the demands of northern industrialists. They feared the consequences of accepting such an act; it could set a precedent for congressional legislation on slavery. In November 1832, a South Carolina state convention nullified the tariff, making it unlawful for officials to collect duties in the state after February 1, 1833.

"Old Hickory" responded with toughness. On December 10, 1832, Jackson issued his own proclamation, nullifying nullification. He moved troops to federal forts in South Carolina and prepared United States marshals to collect the required duties. At Jackson's request, Congress passed the Force Act, which supposedly renewed Jackson's authority to call up troops; it was actually a scheme to avoid the use of force by collecting duties before ships reached South Carolina. At the same time, Jackson extended the olive branch by recommending tariff reductions. Calhoun, disturbed by South Carolina's drift toward separatism, resigned as vice president and became a United States senator from South Carolina. In the Senate, he worked with Henry Clay to draw up the compromise Tariff of 1833. Quickly passed by Congress and signed by the president, the revision lengthened the list of duty-free items and reduced duties over the next nine years. Satisfied, South Carolina's convention repealed its nullification law and in a final salvo nullified Jackson's Force Act. Jackson ignored the gesture.

The nullification controversy represented a genuine debate on the true nature and principles of the republic. Each side believed it was upholding the Constitution. Neither side won a clear victory, though both claimed to have done so. Another issue, that of a central bank, would define the powers of the federal government more clearly.

At stake was the rechartering of the Second Bank of the United States, whose twenty-year charter expired in 1836. One of the bank's functions was to

Second Bank of the United States act as a clearing-house for state banks, keeping them honest by refusing to accept their notes if they had insufficient gold in reserve. Most state banks resented the central bank's police role; by presenting state bank notes for redemption all at once, the Second Bank could easily ruin a state bank. Moreover, state banks, with less money in reserve, found themselves unable to compete on an equal footing with the Second Bank.

Many state governments regarded the national bank, with its headquarters in Philadelphia, as unresponsive to local needs. Westerners and urban workers remembered with bitterness the bank's conservative credit policies during the Panic of 1819. Although the Second Bank served some of the functions of a central bank, it was still a private profit-making institution, and its policies reflected the self-interest of its owners. To many westerners, the bank's eastern, conservative president, Nicholas Biddle, symbolized all that was wrong with the bank.

Although the bank's charter would not expire until 1836, Biddle got Congress to approve an early rechartering. This strategy, encouraged by Henry Clay, the National Republican presidential candidate, was designed to create public pressure to force Jackson to sign the bill or to secure a veto override. The plan backfired when Jackson, in July 1832, vetoed the rechartering bill and the Senate failed to override. Jackson's veto message was an emotional attack on the undemocratic nature of the bank. The bank became the major symbol and issue in the presidential campaign of 1832, and Jackson used it to attack special privilege and economic power.

In 1833, after his sweeping victory and second inauguration, Jackson moved not only to dismantle the Second Bank of the United States but to ensure that it would not be resurrected.

Jackson's Second Term He deposited federal funds in favored state-chartered ("pet") banks; without federal money, the Second Bank shriveled. When its federal charter expired in 1836, it became just another Pennsylvania-chartered private bank. In 1841, it closed its doors.

In the aftermath of the fight against the bank, Congress in 1836 passed the Deposit Act. Under this act, the secretary of the treasury designated one bank in each state and territory to provide the services formerly performed by the Bank of the United States. The act provided that the federal surplus in excess of $5 million be distributed to the states as interest-free loans beginning in 1837.

The surplus had derived from wholesale speculation in public lands. Purchasers bought public land on credit, borrowed from banks against the land to purchase additional acreage, and repeated the cycle. Jackson feared that the speculative craze threatened the state banks while shutting out settlers, who could not compete with speculators in bidding for the best land.

Following his hard-money instinct and his opposition to paper currency, President Jackson ordered Treasury Secretary Levi Woodbury to issue the

Specie Circular Specie Circular. It provided that after August 15, 1836, only specie—gold or silver—or Virginia land scrip would be accepted as payment for federal lands. By ending credit sales, the circular significantly reduced public land purchases and the budget surplus. As a result, the government suspended the loan payments to the states soon after they were begun.

The policy was a disaster on many fronts. Although federal land sales dropped sharply, speculation continued as available land for sale became a scarce commodity. The ensuing increased demand for specie squeezed banks, and many suspended specie payment (the redemption of bank notes for specie). This led to further credit contraction as banks issued fewer notes and gave less credit. In the waning days of Jackson's administration, Congress voted to repeal the circular, but the president pocket-vetoed the bill. Finally, in May 1838, a joint resolution of Congress overturned the circular. Restrictions on land sales ended, but the speculative fervor was over. The federal government did not revive loans to states.

From George Washington to John Quincy Adams, presidents had vetoed nine bills; Jackson vetoed twelve. Previous presidents believed that vetoes were justified only on constitutional grounds, but Jackson stressed policy disagreement as well. He made the veto an important weapon in controlling Congress, since senators and representatives had to consider the possibility of a presidential veto on any bill. In effect, he made the executive a rival branch of government equal to Congress.

The Whig Challenge and the Second Party System

At one time, historians described the 1830s and 1840s as the Age of Jackson, and the personalities of the leading political figures dominated historical accounts. Increasingly, however, historians have viewed these years as an age of popularly based political parties and reformers, for only when the passionate concerns of reformers and abolitionists spilled into politics did party differences become paramount and party loyalties solidify. For the first time, grassroots political groups, organized from the bottom up, set the tone of political life.

In the 1830s, the Democrats' opponents found shelter under a common umbrella, the Whig party. Resentful of Jackson's domination of Congress, the

Whigs Whigs borrowed their name from the British party that had opposed the tyranny of Hanoverian monarchs in the eighteenth century. From the congressional elections of 1834 through the 1840s, they and the Democrats competed nearly equally. They fought at every level—city, county, and state—and achieved a stability previously unknown in American politics. The rise of political party competition in this period—commonly called the Second Party System—was a renewal of the organized political competition that had marked the First Party System of the Republicans and Federalists.

The two parties took different approaches to numerous fundamental issues during these years. Although both favored economic expansion, the Whigs sought it through an activist government and the Democrats through limited central government. Thus the Whigs supported corporate charters, a national bank, and paper currency, all of which the Democrats opposed. The Whigs also favored more humanitarian reforms than did the Democrats—public schools, abolition of capital punishment, temperance, and prison and asylum reform.

In general, Whigs were more optimistic than Democrats and more enterprising. They did not hesitate to help one group if doing so would promote the general welfare. The chartering of corporations, they argued, expanded economic opportunity for everyone, including laborers and farmers. Meanwhile, the Democrats, distrustful of the concentration of economic power and of moral and economic coercion, held fast to their Jeffersonian principle of limited government.

Ironically, the basic economic issues of the era were not the key determinants of party affiliation. Instead, religion and ethnicity determined party membership. In the North, the Whigs' concern for energetic government and humanitarian and moral reform won the favor of native-born and British-American evangelical Protestants, as well as the relatively small number of free black voters. Democrats, on the other hand, tended to be foreign-born Catholics and nonevangelical Protestants, both groups that preferred to keep religious and secular affairs separate.

The Whig party thus became the vehicle of revivalist Protestantism. Indeed, Whigs practiced a kind of political revivalism. Their rallies resembled camp meetings; their speeches echoed evangelical rhetoric; their programs embodied the perfectionist beliefs of reformers. In unifying evangelicals, the Whigs alienated members of other faiths. The evangelicals' ideal Christian state had no room for Catholics, Mormons, Unitarians, Universalists, or religious freethinkers. Sabbath laws and temperance legislation threatened the religious freedom and individual liberty of these groups, which generally opposed state interference in moral and religious questions. As a result, more than 95 percent of Irish Catholics, 90 percent of Reformed Dutch, and 80 percent of German Catholics voted Democratic.

Whigs and Reformers

Jackson hand-picked Vice President Martin Van Buren to head the Democratic ticket in the presidential election of 1836. The Whigs, who in 1836 had not yet coalesced into a national party, entered three sectional candidates: Daniel Webster of New England, Hugh White of the South, and William Henry Harrison of the West. By splintering the vote, they hoped to throw the election into the House, but Van Buren comfortably captured the electoral college, even though he held only a 25,000-vote edge out of a total of 1.5 million votes cast.

Van Buren took office just weeks before the American credit system collapsed. The economic boom of the 1830s was over. In May 1837, New York banks stopped redeeming paper currency with gold, responding to the impact of the Specie Circular. Soon all banks suspended payments in hard coin. Suspension of specie began a cycle that led to banks curtailing loans and reduced business confidence. The credit contraction only made things worse; after a brief recovery, hard times set in and persisted from 1839 to 1843.

Martin Van Buren and Hard Times

Unfortunately, Van Buren followed Jackson's hard-money policies. He curtailed federal spending, thus accelerating deflation, and opposed the Whigs' advocacy of a national bank, which would have expanded credit. Even worse, Van Buren proposed a new regional treasury system for holding government deposits, replacing banks; Van Buren wanted to prevent further government losses from failing banks. The treasury branches would accept and pay out only gold and silver coin; they would not accept paper currency or checks drawn on state banks. Van Buren's independent treasury bill was passed in 1840. By creating a constant demand for hard coin, it deprived banks of gold and added to the general deflation.

With the nation in hard times, the Whigs confidently prepared for the election of 1840. The Democrats renominated President Van Buren. The Whigs rallied behind the military hero General William Henry Harrison, conqueror of Prophet Town, or Tippecanoe Creek, in 1811, and his running mate, John Tyler of Virginia. In a huge turnout, in which 80 percent of eligible voters cast ballots, Harrison won the popular vote by a narrow margin but swept the electoral college 234 to 60.

Election of 1840

Unfortunately for the Whigs, the sixty-eight-year-old Harrison died within a month of his inauguration. His successor, John Tyler, a former Democrat who had left the party in opposition to Jackson's nullification proclamation, turned out to be more a Democrat than a Whig. He consistently opposed the Whig congressional program, vetoing bills that provided for protective tariffs, a revived Bank of the United States, and internal improvements. Two days after Tyler's second veto of a bank bill, the entire cabinet, except Secretary of State Daniel Webster, resigned. Webster, involved in negotiating a new treaty with Great Britain, left shortly thereafter. Tyler became a president without a party, and the Whigs lost the presidency without an election.

Hard times in the late 1830s and early 1840s deflected attention from the renewal of Anglo-American tensions. Northern commercial rivalry with Britain, the default of state governments and corporations on British-held debts during the Panic of 1837, rebellion in Canada, boundary disputes, southern alarm over West Indian emancipation, and American expansionism—all caused Anglo-American conflict.

Anglo-American Tensions

A major dispute with Great Britain emerged over the imprecisely defined border between Maine and

Using many of the techniques of twentieth-century politics, General William Henry Harrison ran a "log cabin and hard cider" campaign—a popular crusade—against Jackson heir, President Martin Van Buren. This campaign handkerchief shows Harrison welcoming two of his comrades to his log cabin, with a barrel of cider outside. *The New-York Historical Society.*

New Brunswick. In the winter of 1838 and 1839, Canadian lumbermen moved into the disputed area. Shortly afterward, Maine attempted to expel them. After the Canadians captured the Maine land agent, both sides mobilized their militia and Congress authorized a call-up of fifty thousand men. Fortunately, war was avoided. General Winfield Scott, who was dispatched to Aroostook, Maine, arranged a truce between the warring state and province, and the two sides compromised on their conflicting claims in the Webster-Ashburton Treaty (1842).

The border conflict with Great Britain prefigured an issue that became prominent in national politics in the second half of the 1840 decade: the westward expansion of the United States. Tyler's succession to power in 1841 and a Democratic victory in the presidential election of 1844 ended an activist fed-

eral government in the domestic sphere for the rest of the decade. Attention turned to the debate over territorial expansion.

Manifest Destiny

Americans had been hungry for new lands ever since the colonists first turned their eyes westward. There lay fertile soil, valuable minerals, and the chance for a better life or a new beginning. Agrarian Democrats saw the West as an antidote to urbanization and industrialization. Enterprising Whigs looked to the new commercial opportunities the West offered. Equally important was a fierce national pride and a desire to acquire western

Chapter 12: Reform, Politics, and Expansion, 1824–1844

lands to secure the nation from external enemies. Finally, Americans idealistically believed that westward expansion would extend American freedom and democracy "to less fortunate people." In the 1840s, *manifest destiny*—the belief that American expansion westward was inevitable, divinely ordained, and just—served the nation's expansionists (see map, page 234).

Manifest destiny was more than simply self-serving; it contained an undercurrent of racism. Indians were perceived as savages best confined to small areas in the West. Mexicans and Central and South Americans were also seen as inferior peoples, to be controlled or conquered. Thus the same racism that justified slavery in the South and discrimination in the North supported expansion in the West.

Among the long-standing objectives of expansionists was the Republic of Texas. Originally part of Mexico, Texas attracted thousands of Americans in the 1820s and 1830s. The Mexican government's extremely generous land policy enticed settlers into the area. In return for the right to settle in Texas, immigrants were expected to become Mexican citizens and adopt the Catholic religion.

Republic of Texas

By 1835, thirty-five thousand Americans, including many slaveholders, lived in Texas. These new settlers ignored local laws and oppressed native Mexicans, and when the Mexican government attempted to tighten its control over the region, Anglos and insurgent Hispanics rebelled. At the Alamo in San Antonio in 1836, fewer than two hundred Texans made a heroic stand against three thousand Mexicans under General Antonio López de Santa Anna. All the defenders of the mission died in the battle, and "Remember the Alamo" became the Texans' rallying cry. The desires of Texans to avenge the defeat at the Alamo and to secure their independence were fulfilled later in 1836, through Sam Houston's victory in the Battle of San Jacinto.

Americans were generally delighted with the revolution's success, but joy did not mean that the Texas request for annexation into the Union was welcomed. Texas was a slave republic and this made annexation a potentially explosive political issue. President Jackson delayed recognition of Texas until after the election of 1836, and President Van Buren ignored annexation altogether. Texans then talked about developing close ties with the British and extending their republic all the way to the Pacific Coast. President Tyler feared that a Texas alliance with the British might threaten American independence. He was also committed to expansion and hoped to build support in the South by enlarging the area of slavery. Therefore, he pushed for annexation. But in a sectional vote, the Senate in April 1844 rejected a treaty of annexation.

Just as southerners sought expansion to the Southwest, northerners looked to the Northwest. In 1841, "Oregon fever" struck thousands. Lured by the glowing reports of missionaries, migrants organized hundreds of wagon trains and embarked on the Oregon Trail. The 2,000-mile journey took six months or more, but within a few years five thousand settlers had arrived in the fertile Willamette Valley, south of the Columbia River.

Oregon Fever

Since the Anglo-American convention of 1818, Britain and the United States had jointly occupied the disputed Oregon Territory. Beginning with the administration of President John Quincy Adams, the United States had tried to fix the boundary at the 49th parallel, but Britain refused. Time only increased the American appetite. In 1843, a Cincinnati convention demanded that the United States obtain the entire Oregon Country, up to its northernmost border of 54°40′. Soon "Fifty-four Forty or Fight" had become the rallying cry of American expansionists.

The expansion into Oregon and the rejection of the annexation of Texas, both favored by antislavery forces, heightened southern pessimism. Southern leaders became anxious about their diminishing ability to control the debate over slavery. They persuaded the 1844 Democratic convention to adopt a rule that the presidential nominee had to receive two-thirds of the convention votes. In effect, the southern states acquired a veto, and they used it to block Van Buren as the nominee; most southerners objected to Van Buren's antislavery stance and opposition to Texas annexation. Instead, the party chose House Speaker James K. Polk, a hard-money Jacksonian and

Election of 1844

Western Expansion, 1800–1860

expansionist from Tennessee. The Whig leader Henry Clay, the Whig nominee, believed that the Democrats would provoke a war with Great Britain or Mexico. He favored expansion through negotiation, not force.

The Democrats captured the executive mansion with 170 electoral votes to 105 (they won the popular vote by just 38,000 out of 2.7 million). Polk carried New York's 36 electoral votes by just 6,000 votes; abolitionist James G. Birney, the Liberty party candidate, drew almost 16,000 votes away from Clay, handing New York and the election to Polk. Thus abolitionist forces unwittingly influenced the choice of a slaveholder as president.

Interpreting Polk's victory as a mandate for annexation, President Tyler proposed in his last days in office that Texas be admitted by joint resolution of Congress. Proslavery and antislavery congressmen debated the extension of slavery into the territory, and the resolution passed the House 120 to 98 and the Senate 27 to 25. Three days before leaving office, Tyler signed the measure. Mexico immediately broke relations with the United States; war loomed.

Politics, the reform spirit, and expansionism commingled in the 1830s and 1840s. Reform imbued with revivalism sought to bring order in a rapidly changing society. But reformers had no monopoly on claims of republican virtue; their opponents, too, claimed descent from the revolutionary values that held individual liberty dear. Once reform forced itself into politics, it sparked a broader-based interest. Political organization and conflict stimulated even greater interest in campaigns and political issues. Expansion and territorial questions further intensified conflict. Eventually, however, one issue absorbed nearly all attention and created a crisis in the Union: slavery.

Suggestions for Further Reading

Religion, Revivalism, and Reform

Michael Barkun, *Crucible of the Millennium: The Burned-over District of New York in the 1840s* (1986); Terry Bilhartz,

Urban Religion and the Second Great Awakening: Church and Society in Early National Baltimore (1986); Whitney R. Cross, *The Burned-Over District* (1950); Clifford S. Griffen, *Their Brother's Keepers: Moral Stewardship in the United States, 1800–1865* (1960); Keith J. Hardman, *Charles Grandison Finney, 1792–1875: Revivalist and Reformer* (1987); Paul E. Johnson, *A Shopkeeper's Millennium: Society and Revivals in Rochester, New York, 1815–1837* (1978); William G. McLoughlin, *Revivals, Awakenings, and Reform: An Essay on Religion and Social Change in America, 1607–1977* (1978); Randolph A. Roth, *The Democratic Dilemma: Religion, Reform, and the Social Order in the Connecticut Valley of Vermont, 1791–1850* (1987); Richard D. Shiels, "The Scope of the Second Great Awakening: Andover, Massachusetts, as a Case Study," *Journal of the Early Republic,* 5 (Summer 1985), 223–246; Timothy L. Smith, *Revivalism and Social Reform in Mid-Nineteenth Century America* (1957); Alice Felt Tyler, *Freedom's Ferment* (1944); Ronald G. Walters, *American Reformers, 1815–1860* (1978).

Temperance, Asylums, and Antimasonry

Paul Goodman, *Towards a Christian Republic: Antimasonry and the Great Transition in New England, 1826–1836* (1988); Gerald N. Grob, *Mental Institutions in America: Social Policy to 1875* (1973); Kathleen Smith Kutolowski, "Antimasonry Reexamined: Social Bases of the Grass-Roots Party," *Journal of American History,* 71 (September 1984), 269–293; W. J. Rorabaugh, *The Alcoholic Republic: An American Tradition* (1979); Charles E. Rosenberg, *The Care of Strangers: The Rise of America's Hospital System* (1987); David J. Rothman, *The Discovery of the Asylum: Social Order and Disorder in the New Republic* (1971); Ian R. Tyrrell, *Sobering Up: From Temperance to Prohibition in Antebellum America, 1800–1860* (1979); William Preston Vaughn, *The Antimasonic Party in the United States, 1826–1843* (1983).

Women and Reform

Barbara J. Berg, *The Remembered Gate: Origins of American Feminism: The Woman and the City, 1800–1860* (1977); Anne M. Boylan, "Women in Groups: An Analysis of Women's Benevolent Organizations in New York and Boston, 1797–1840," *Journal of American History,* 71 (December 1984), 497–523; Ellen C. Du Bois, *Feminism and Suffrage: The Emergence of an Independent Woman's Movement in America, 1848–1869* (1978); Barbara Leslie Epstein, *The Politics of Domesticity: Women, Evangelism, and Temperance in Nineteenth-Century America* (1981); Elisabeth Griffith, *In Her Own Right: The Life of Elizabeth Cady Stanton* (1984); Nancy A. Hewitt, *Women's Activism and Social Change: Rochester, New York, 1822–1872* (1984); Gerda Lerner, *The Grimké Sisters of South Carolina* (1967); Ian R. Tyrrell, "Women and Temperance in Antebellum America, 1830–1860," *Civil War History,* 28 (June 1982), 128–152.

Antislavery and Abolitionism

David Brion Davis, *Slavery and Human Progress* (1984); Frederick Douglass, *Life and Times of Frederick Douglass* (1881); Aileen S. Kraditor, *Means and Ends in American Abolitionism: Garrison and His Critics on Strategy and Tactics* (1967); Lewis Perry and Michael Fellman, eds., *Antislavery Reconsidered* (1979); Benjamin Quarles, *Black Abolitionists* (1969); Leonard L. Richards, *The Life and Times of Congressman John Quincy Adams* (1986); Leonard L. Richards, *"Gentlemen of Property and Standing": Anti-Abolition Mobs in Jacksonian America* (1970); Ronald G. Walters, *The Antislavery Appeal: American Abolitionism After 1830* (1976); Bertram Wyatt-Brown, *Lewis Tappan and the Evangelical War Against Slavery* (1969).

Andrew Jackson and the Jacksonians

Lee Benson, *The Concept of Jacksonian Democracy: New York as a Test Case* (1964); Donald B. Cole, *Martin Van Buren and the American Political System* (1984); Mary W. M. Hargreaves, *The Presidency of John Quincy Adams* (1985); Richard B. Latner, *The Presidency of Andrew Jackson* (1979); John Niven, *Martin Van Buren* (1983); Edward Pessen, *Jacksonian America: Society, Personality, and Politics,* rev. ed. (1979); Robert V. Remini, *The Legacy of Andrew Jackson: Essays on Democracy, Indian Removal, and Slavery* (1988); Robert V. Remini, *The Life of Andrew Jackson* (1988); Robert V. Remini, *Andrew Jackson and the Bank War* (1967); John William Ward, *Andrew Jackson: Symbol for an Age* (1955); Harry L. Watson, *Jacksonian Politics and Community Conflict: The Emergence of the Second American Party System in Cumberland County, North Carolina* (1981); Major L. Wilson, *The Presidency of Martin Van Buren* (1984).

Democrats and Whigs

Ronald P. Formisano, *The Transformation of Political Culture: Massachusetts Parties, 1790s–1840s* (1983); Daniel Walker Howe, *The Political Culture of the American Whigs* (1979); Merrill D. Peterson, *The Great Triumvirate: Webster, Clay, and Calhoun* (1987); James Roger Sharp, *The Jacksonians Versus the Banks: Politics in the States After the Panic of 1837* (1970).

Manifest Destiny and Foreign Policy

John M. Belohlavek, *"Let the Eagle Soar!" The Foreign Policy of Andrew Jackson* (1985); Norman B. Graebner, ed., *Manifest Destiny* (1968); Thomas R. Hietala, *Manifest Design: Anxious Aggrandizement in Late Jacksonian America* (1985); Reginald Horsman, *Race and Manifest Destiny* (1981); Frederick Merk, *Manifest Destiny and Mission in American History* (1963); David M. Pletcher, *The Diplomacy of Annexation: Texas, Oregon, and the Mexican War* (1973); Paul A. Varg, *United States Foreign Relations, 1820–1860* (1979).

He was free at last. Escaping from slavery in Virginia, Anthony Burns had stowed away on a ship and safely reached Boston. Breathing the free air in a city well known for its abolitionists, Burns seemed out of danger. He found a job in a clothing store, and his future for once looked bright.

Then Burns made a serious mistake. He wrote a letter and tried to route it to his brother, still enslaved in Virginia. Their master intercepted the letter and left for Boston, intending to seize his wayward human property.

In so doing, he counted on government enforcement of the Fugitive Slave Act. In May 1854, a deputy marshal arrested Burns. Predictably, Boston's abolitionists went into action, organizing public protests at Faneuil Hall. Then, in an attempt to free Burns by force, someone fired a shot and killed a deputy.

President Franklin Pierce decided on emphatic enforcement of federal law. "Incur any expense," Pierce telegraphed officials, "to insure the execution of the law." To demonstrate his determination, he sent marines, cavalry, and artillery to Boston and ordered a federal ship to stand ready to return Burns to Virginia. On June 2, a formidable contingent of troops marched Burns to the harbor through streets draped in black and hung with American flags at half mast. At a cost of $100,000, a single black man was sent back into slavery through the power of federal law.

The polarizing effects of this demonstration of federal support for slavery reached far and wide. In Boston, conservatives found that the spectacle of the national government enforcing bondage had radicalized them. A textile manufacturer, Amos A. Lawrence, observed that "we went to bed one night old fashioned, conservative, Compromise Union Whigs & waked up stark mad Abolitionists." New England states passed personal liberty laws designed to impede or block federal power. The southern states, in turn, reacted with outrage at every sign of northern "faithlessness" about the Fugitive Slave Act. The slavery issue was driving the sections apart. Northerners feared that the Slave Power was dominating American government, and white southerners demanded that their rights be upheld.

13

SLAVERY AND AMERICA'S FUTURE: THE ROAD TO WAR, 1845–1861

What brought these issues to center stage more than anything else was territorial expansion. Between 1845 and 1853, the United States added Texas, the West Coast, and the Southwest to its domain and launched the settlement of the Great Plains. But each time the nation expanded, it confronted a thorny issue—whether new territories and states should be slave or free. Disagreements on this question were too violent for compromise. A host of political leaders, including Henry Clay, Lewis Cass, Stephen A. Douglas, and Presidents Jackson and Van Buren, tried from the 1830s through the 1850s to postpone or compromise disagreements about slavery in the territories. But these disputes injected into national politics the bitterness surrounding slavery. Indeed, battles over slavery in the territories broke the second party system apart and then shaped a realigned system that emphasized sectional enmity. Sectional parties replaced nationwide organizations, which had tried to compromise differences.

As parties clamored for support, the feeling grew in both North and South that America's future was at stake. The new Republican party charged that southerners were taking over the federal government and trying to make slavery legal in every part of the Union. Republicans believed that America's future depended on the free labor of free men, whose rights were protected by a government devoted to liberty. By contrast, southern leaders charged the North with lawless behavior and failure to respect the Constitution. To these southerners, slavery was the foundation of white equality and republicanism, and a government that failed to protect slavery seemed un-American and unworthy of their loyalty.

Not all citizens were obsessed with these conflicts. In fact, the results of the 1860 presidential election indicated that most voters hoped for neither disunion nor civil war. Yet within six months they had both. What had begun as a dark cloud over the territories grew into a storm. Both sections felt threatened and anxious and believed that the future hung in the balance. At the last minute, neither the victorious Republican party nor defensive southern slaveholders could agree on any of the desperate compromises proposed and thus a vast civil war began.

Conflict Begins: The Mexican War

Territorial expansion surged forward under the leadership of President James K. Polk. The annexation of Texas just before his inauguration had not cooled Polk's interest in acquiring California and the Southwest, and he desired Oregon as well. But though Polk was an effective president, he was unaware of the price that expansion would exact in domestic harmony. The addition of a huge domain to the nation's boundaries had major side effects. It divided the Whig party, drove southern Whigs into a full embrace of slavery, and brought into the open an aggressive new southern theory about slavery's position in the territories. It also elicited northern protests and proposals that revealed profound disagreement between the sections.

Although his supporters had belligerently demanded all of the Oregon Territory, Polk found as president that diplomacy had its advantages. Congress's annexation of Texas had outraged Mexican leaders, who severed relations with the United States. Knowing that war with Mexico could break out at any time, Polk decided to try to avoid a conflict with Great Britain in the Northwest. Dropping the demand for a boundary at 54°40', he kept up pressure on the British to accept the 49th parallel. Eventually, in 1846, Great Britain agreed. In the Oregon Treaty, the United States gained all of present-day Oregon, Washington, and Idaho and parts of Wyoming and Montana.

Toward Mexico, Polk was much more aggressive. He ordered American troops to defend the border claimed by Texas—but contested by Mexico—and offered to buy a huge tract of land in the Southwest from the resentful Mexicans. After purchase failed, Polk resolved to ask Congress for a declaration of war and set to work compiling a list of grievances. This task became unnecessary when word arrived that Mexican forces had engaged a body of American troops in disputed territory. American blood had been shed. Eagerly, Polk declared that "war exists by the act of Mexico itself" and summoned the nation to arms.

Congress voted to recognize a state of war be-

IMPORTANT EVENTS

1846	War with Mexico Oregon Treaty Wilmot Proviso
1847	Lewis Cass proposes idea of popular sovereignty
1848	Taylor elected president Free-Soil party formed
1849	California applies for admission to Union as free state
1850	Compromise of 1850
1852	Publication of *Uncle Tom's Cabin* Pierce elected president
1854	Kansas-Nebraska Act Republican party formed Democrats lose ground in congressional elections
1856	Preston Brooks attacks Charles Sumner in Senate chamber "Bleeding Kansas" Buchanan elected president
1857	*Dred Scott* v. *Sanford* Lecompton Constitution
1858	Voters reject Lecompton Constitution Lincoln-Douglas debates Freeport Doctrine
1859	John Brown raids Harpers Ferry
1860	Democratic party splits in half Lincoln elected president Crittenden Compromise fails South Carolina secedes from Union
1861	Six more southern states secede Confederacy established Attack on Fort Sumter

tween Mexico and the United States in May 1846, but controversy grew. Public opinion about the war was sharply divided, with southwesterners enthusiastic and New Englanders strenuously opposed. In Congress, Whigs charged that Polk had "literally provoked" an unnecessary war and "usurped the power of Congress by making war upon Mexico." The aged John Quincy Adams passionately opposed the war and a tall young Whig from Illinois, named Abraham Lincoln, questioned its justification. Moreover, a small minority of antislavery Whigs agreed with abolitionists—the war was no less than a plot to extend slavery.

These charges fed fear of the Slave Power. Abolitionists long had warned that there was a Slave Power—a slaveholding oligarchy in control of the South and intent on control-

Idea of a Slave Power ling the nation. The Slave Power's assault on northern liberties, abo-

litionists argued, had begun in 1836, when Congress passed the gag rule. Many white northerners, even those who saw nothing wrong with slavery, had viewed John Quincy Adams's stand against the rule as a valiant defense of free speech and the right to petition. The battle over free speech first made the idea of a Slave Power credible.

Now the Mexican War increased fears of this sinister power. Antislavery northerners asked why claims to all of Oregon had been abandoned but a questionable war begun for slave territory. Steadily these arguments had an effect on northern opinion. But the impact of events on southern opinion and southern leaders was even more dramatic.

At first, many southern leaders criticized the war with Mexico. Southern Whigs attacked the Democratic president for causing the war, and southern congressmen did not immediately see defense of

Wilmot Proviso slavery as the paramount issue. But no southern Whig could oppose it once slavery became the central issue. That happened in August 1846, when a Democratic representative from Pennsylvania, David Wilmot, offered an amendment to a military appropriations bill. Wilmot attached a condition, or proviso, to the bill: that "neither slavery nor involuntary servitude shall ever exist" in any territory gained from Mexico. His proviso did not pass both houses of Congress, but it immediately transformed the debate.

John C. Calhoun drew up resolutions on the territories that staked out a radical, new southern position. According to these resolutions, the territories belonged to all the states, and the federal government could do nothing to limit the spread of slavery there. Southern slaveholders had a constitutional right, Calhoun claimed, to take their slaves anywhere in the territories. This position, which quickly became orthodox for every southern politician, was a radical reversal of history. The founding fathers, under the Articles of Confederation, had excluded slavery from the Northwest Territory. Moreover, the Constitution authorized Congress to make "all needful rules and regulations" for the territories, and the Missouri Compromise had barred slavery from most of the Louisiana Purchase. But southern leaders now demanded protection for slavery.

In the North, meanwhile, the Wilmot Proviso soon became a rallying cry for abolitionists and Free-Soilers. Eventually, the legislatures of fourteen northern states endorsed it—and not because all its supporters were abolitionists. Like Wilmot, most white northerners were racists, not abolitionists, but it was possible to be racist and an opponent of slavery. Fear of the Slave Power was building a potent antislavery movement that united abolitionists and antiblack voters. The latter's concern was to protect themselves, not southern blacks, from the Slave Power.

Despite profound disagreement at home, events on the battlefield went well for American troops, who, as in previous wars, were mainly volunteers furnished by the states. General Zachary Taylor's forces attacked and occupied Monterrey, securing northeastern Mexico (see map). Polk then ordered Colonel Stephen Kearny and a small detachment to invade the remote and relatively unpopulated provinces of New Mexico and California. Taking Santa Fe without opposition, Kearny pushed into California, where he joined forces with rebellious American settlers, led by Captain John C. Frémont, and a couple of United States naval units. A quick victory was followed by reverses, but American soldiers soon re-established their dominance in distant and thinly populated California.

Meanwhile, General Winfield Scott's daring invasion of Mexico City brought the war to an end. On February 2, 1848, representatives of both countries signed the Treaty of Guadalupe Hidalgo. The United States gained California and New Mexico (including present-day Nevada, Utah, and Arizona) and recognition of the Rio Grande as the southern boundary of Texas. In return, the American government agreed to settle the claims of its citizens against Mexico and to pay Mexico a mere $15 million.

Treaty of Guadalupe Hidalgo

The cost of the war included thirteen thousand American and fifty thousand Mexican dead, plus Mexican-American enmity lasting into the twentieth century. But the domestic cost was even higher. As sectional distrust and bitterness grew, party unity for both Democrats and Whigs began to loosen.

In the presidential election of 1848, slavery in the territories was the one overriding issue. Both parties tried to push this question into the background, but it dominated the conventions, the campaign, and the election. The Democrats tried to avoid sectional conflict by nominating General Lewis Cass of Michigan for president and General William Butler of Kentucky for vice president. Cass had devised the idea of *popular sovereignty* for the territories—letting residents in the territories decide the question of slavery for themselves. His party's platform declared that Congress did not have the power to interfere with slavery and criticized those who pressed the question. The Whigs nominated General Zachary Taylor, who was a southern slaveholder, as well as a military hero, with Congressman Millard Fillmore of New York as his running mate. Their convention similarly refused to assert that Congress had power over slavery in the

Election of 1848 and Popular Sovereignty

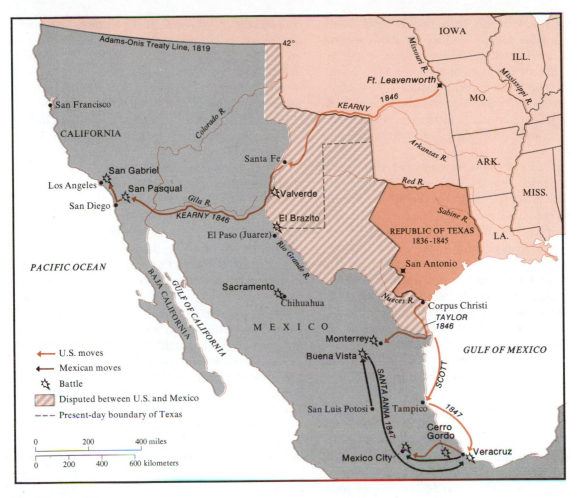

The Mexican War

territories. But the issue would not stay in the background.

In the North, concern about slavery led to the formation of a new party. First, New York Democrats devoted to the Wilmot Proviso rebelled and nominated former President Martin Van Buren. Antislavery Whigs and former supporters of the Liberty party then joined them to organize the Free-Soil party, with Van Buren as its candidate. This party, whose slogan was "Free soil, free speech, free labor, and free men," won almost 300,000 northern votes. Taylor polled enough votes to win the White House, but the results were ominous. Sectional concerns, especially slavery in the territories, posed a dangerous threat to the party system.

The election of 1848 and the conflict over slavery in the territories shaped politics in the 1850s. At the national level, all issues would be seen though the prism of sectional conflict over slavery in the territories. The nation's uncertain attempts to deal with economic and social change would give way to more pressing questions about the nature of the Union itself. And the second party system would succumb to crisis over slavery.

Territorial Problems Are Compromised but Re-emerge

The first sectional battle of the decade involved the territory of California. More than eighty thousand

Americans flooded into California in 1849. With Congress unable to agree on a formula to govern the territories, President Taylor urged these settlers to apply directly for admission to the Union. The proposed state constitution submitted by California, however, prohibited slavery, and southerners objected. At a minimum, southerners wanted the Missouri Compromise line extended through California.

Sensing that the Union was in peril, the venerable Whig leader Henry Clay marshaled his energies. To hushed Senate galleries, the Great Pacificator presented a series of compromise measures. In the weeks that followed, Clay and Senator Stephen A. Douglas of Illinois steered through the Congress compromises balancing the issues of California and the nearby territories, the Texas boundary claim, fugitive slaves, and the slave trade in the District of Columbia. The problems to be solved were thorny indeed and made more so by conflicting theories about settlers' rights in the territories. These theories proved most troublesome in the continuing debate over the territories.

Clay and Douglas hoped to avoid a specific formula and preserve the ambiguity that existed about settlers' rights in the territories. Lewis Cass's idea of popular sovereignty, for example, had both an attractive ring to it and a useful vagueness. Cass had observed that Congress could stay out of the territorial wrangle. Ultimately it would have to approve statehood for a territory, but Congress should "in the meantime," Cass said, allow the people living there "to regulate their own concerns in their own way." These seemingly clear words proved highly ambiguous. When could settlers bar slavery? Southerners claimed that neither Congress nor a territorial legislature could bar slavery. Only when settlers framed a state constitution could they take that step. Northerners, meanwhile, argued that Americans living in a territory could outlaw slavery at any time, if they allowed it at all. To avoid dissension within their party, northern and southern Democrats explained Cass's statement to their constituents in these two incompatible ways.

When Clay and Douglas finally brought their package to a vote, they met defeat. Even the support of Senator Daniel Webster, with all his power and prestige, was not enough to carry the day. Then, with Clay sick and absent from Washington, Doug-

las brought the compromise measures up again, one at a time. Congress lacked a majority to approve the package, but Douglas shrewdly realized that different majorities might be created for each of the measures. The strategy worked. The Compromise of 1850, as it was called, became law.

Under the terms of its various measures, California was admitted as a free state, and the Texas boundary was set at its present limits. The United

Compromise of 1850

States paid Texas $10 million in consideration of the boundary agreement. The territories of New Mexico and Utah were organized with power to legislate on "all rightful subjects . . . consistent with the Constitution." A stronger fugitive slave law and an act to suppress the slave trade in the District of Columbia completed the compromise.

Jubilation greeted passage of the Compromise of 1850. But in reality there was less cause for celebration than citizens thought. The compromise was at best an artful evasion of sectional disputes. It did not solve the problems but just postponed them. Furthermore, the compromise had two basic flaws. The first pertained to popular sovereignty. What were "rightful subjects of legislation, consistent with the Constitution"? During debate, southerners asserted that this meant that there would be no prohibition of slavery during the territorial stage; northerners declared that settlers could bar slavery whenever they wished.

The second flaw lay in the Fugitive Slave Act, which empowered slaveowners to go into court in their own states and present evidence that a slave who owed them service had es-

Fugitive Slave Act

caped. The transcript of such a proceeding, including a description of the fugitive, was to be taken as conclusive proof of a person's slave status, even in free states and territories. Legal authorities had to decide only whether the black person brought before them was the person described, not whether he or she was indeed a slave. Fees and penalties encouraged United States marshals to assist in apprehending fugitives and discouraged citizens from harboring them. (Authorities were paid ten dollars if the alleged fugitive was turned over to the slaveowner, five dollars if he or she was not.)

At this point, a relatively unknown writer dram-

The Webb family toured the North, presenting dramatic readings of *Uncle Tom's Cabin.* Performances by the Webbs and others deepened the already powerful impact of Harriet Beecher Stowe's novel. *Stowe-Day Foundation, Hartford, Conn.*

atized the plight of the slave in a way that captured the sympathies of millions of northerners.

Uncle Tom's Cabin
Harriet Beecher Stowe, daughter of a religious New England family, wrote *Uncle Tom's Cabin* out of deep moral conviction. Her book, published in 1852, showed how slavery brutalized the men and women who suffered under it. Stowe also portrayed slavery's evil effects on slaveholders. By mid-1853, more than a million copies had been sold. Stowe brought slavery home to many who had never before given it much thought.

Because southerners saw threats to their way of life in the territorial controversies and in the popularity of *Uncle Tom's Cabin,* they were alarmed. At the root of southern claims about territorial rights lay fear—fear that if nearby areas became free soil, they would be used as bases from which to spread abolitionism into the slave states. To defend slavery against political threats, the South's leaders relied on Calhoun's territorial theories and on the dogma of states' rights and strict construction.

To protect slavery in the arena of ideas, it was vital to counter indictments of the institution as a moral wrong. Accordingly, proslavery theorists elaborated numerous arguments based on pseudoscientific data. Southern writers or politicians readily discussed anthropological evidence for the separate origin of the races, physicians' views on the inferiority of the black body, and sociological arguments about the superiority of the slave-labor system. Proslavery spokesmen also expounded the new "science" of phrenology. Its data on the external dimensions of human skulls and the volume of the cranial cavity "proved" that blacks were a separate and inferior race. Yet in private and in their hearts, most southern leaders fell back on two rationales for slavery: the belief that blacks were inferior and biblical accounts of slaveholding. Some, such as Jefferson Davis, reverted to the eighteenth-century argument that southerners were doing the best they could with a situation they had inherited.

Proslavery Theories

Davis was troubled but far from despair in 1852. He and other southerners had reason to hope that slavery would be secure and allowed to expand under the administration of a new president. Franklin Pierce, a Democrat from New Hampshire, won a smashing victory that year over the Whig presidential nominee, General Winfield Scott. Pierce's victory derived less from his strengths than from his opponents' weaknesses. Though viable in Congress, the Whigs lacked commanding presidents in an era of strong leaders. The deaths of President Taylor (1850), Daniel Webster (1852), and Henry Clay (1852) and discord between the party's northern and southern wings dealt a lethal blow to the Whigs. The Whig party ran its last presidential candidate in 1852.

Election of 1852

Americans, northern and southern alike, hoped that the election of Pierce would end sectional divisions. Because Pierce had given firm support to the Compromise of 1850, his victory seemed to confirm the public's support for the compromise.

But Pierce did not seem able to avoid sectional conflict. His proposal for a transcontinental railroad ran into congressional dispute over where it should be built, in the North or in the South. His vigorous enforcement of the fugitive slave law appalled and

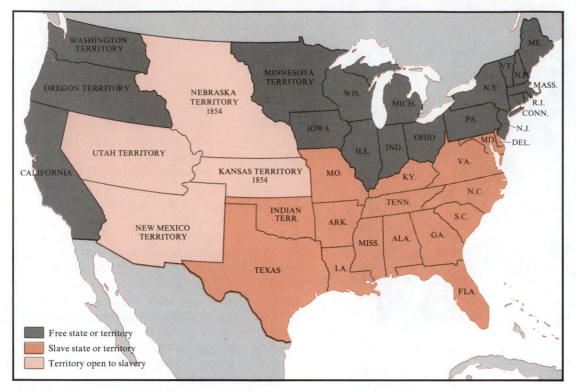

The Kansas-Nebraska Act, 1854

Free state or territory

Slave state or territory

Territory open to slavery

alarmed many northerners. His attempts to acquire foreign territory stirred up more trouble. An annexation treaty with Hawaii failed because southern senators would not vote for another free state, and Pierce's efforts to annex Cuba angered antislavery northerners. The shattering blow to sectional harmony, however, came from Congress rather than from the White House.

Territorial Problems Shatter the Party System

In 1854, Stephen A. Douglas, one of the architects of the Compromise of 1850 and a potential presidential nominee, introduced a bill to establish the Kansas and Nebraska territories. As a senator from Illinois, Douglas hoped for a midwestern transcontinental railroad to boost Chicago's economy and encourage settlement on the Great Plains. A neces-

sary precondition for such a railroad was the organization of the territory it would cross. Thus, it was probably in the interest of building such a railroad that Douglas introduced a bill that inflamed sectional passions, completed the destruction of the Whig party, damaged the northern Democrats, gave birth to the Republican party, and thwarted his own ambitions for national office.

The Kansas-Nebraska bill exposed the first flaw of the Compromise of 1850: the conflicting interpretations of popular sovereignty. Douglas's bill

Kansas-Nebraska Bill

left "all questions pertaining to slavery in the Territories . . . to the people residing therein," but northerners and southerners still disagreed violently over what territorial settlers could constitutionally do. Moreover, the Kansas-Nebraska bill opened a Pandora's box by repealing the Missouri Compromise of 1820. Douglas's bill, which became law in May 1854, threw land open to slavery where it had been prohibited (see map).

Northern reaction to the law was immediate and widespread. Abolitionists charged a sinister aggression by the Slave Power, and northern fears about slavery's influence deepened. Opposition to the fugitive slave law grew dramatically. Between 1855 and 1859, seven states—Connecticut, Rhode Island, Massachusetts, Michigan, Maine, Ohio, and Wisconsin—passed personal liberty laws. These laws interfered with the Fugitive Slave Act by providing counsel for alleged fugitives and requiring trial by jury. Southerners saw the personal liberty laws as signs of bad faith. Finally, the Kansas-Nebraska Act had a devastating impact on political parties.

The act divided the Whig party into northern and southern wings that could no longer cooperate as a national organization. One of the two great parties

The New Republican Party

in the second party system was now gone. The Democrats survived, but their support in the North fell drastically in the 1854 elections. Moreover, anger over the territorial issue created a new political party. During the summer and fall of 1854, antislavery Whigs and Democrats, Free-Soilers, and other reformers throughout the Old Northwest met to form a new Republican party, dedicated to keeping slavery out of the territories. The Republicans' influence rapidly spread to the East, and they won a stunning victory in the 1854 elections by capturing a majority of House seats in the North.

For the first time, too, a sectional party had gained significant power in the political system. When Whigs and Democrats had competed throughout the country, the national base of each had moderated sectional conflict. Party leaders compromised to achieve unity and subordinated sectional differences to partisan needs. But now the Whigs were gone, and politics in the 1850s would never be the same.

Nor were Republicans the only new party. An anti-immigrant organization, the American party, also seemed likely for a few years to replace the Whigs. This party, popularly

Know-Nothings

known as the Know-Nothings (because its members at first kept their purposes secret, answering all queries with the words "I know nothing"), exploited nativist fear of foreigners. By the mid-1850s, the American party was powerful and growing; in 1854 so many new congressmen won office with anti-immigrant, as well as antislavery, support

that Know-Nothings could claim that they outnumbered Republicans. But like the Whigs, the Know-Nothings could not keep their northern and southern wings together, and they melted away after 1856. That left the field to the Republicans.

Republicans, Know-Nothings, and Democrats were all scrambling to attract former Whig voters. The demise of that party ensured a major realignment of the political system, with

Realignment of Political System

nearly half the old electorate up for grabs. To woo these homeless Whigs, the remaining parties stressed a variety of issues, chosen to appeal to the Whigs for one reason or another. Immigration, temperance, homestead bills, the tariff, internal improvements—all played an important role in attracting voters during the 1850s.

The Republicans appealed strongly to groups interested in the economic development of the West. Commercial agriculture was booming in the Ohio–

Republican Appeals

Mississippi–Great Lakes area, but residents of that region needed more canals, roads, and river and harbor improvements to reap the full benefit of their labors. There was also widespread interest in a federal land-grant program that would provide free western land to homesteaders. Whigs had favored and Democrats had opposed all these things. Following long-standing party principles, Democratic presidents vetoed internal improvements bills and a homestead bill as late as 1859. Seizing their opportunity, the Republicans added internal improvements and land-grant planks to their platform. They also backed higher tariffs as an enticement to industrialists and businessmen.

Another major feature of the realigned political system was ideology. In the North, Republicans attracted many voters through effective use of ideology. They spoke to the image that northerners had of themselves, their society, and their future when they preached "Free Soil, Free Labor, Free Men." These phrases resonated with traditional ideals of equality, liberty, and opportunity under self-government—the heritage of republicanism.

"Free Soil, Free Labor, Free Men" seemed to fit in with a northern economy that was energetic, expanding, and prosperous. In the eyes of many, free labor was the key to northern progress. Any hard-working, virtuous person, it was thought, could improve his condition and gain economic independence by applying himself to opportunities that the country had to offer. Republicans pointed out that the South, which relied on slave labor and had little industry, appeared backward and retrograde in comparison. Praising both laborers and opportunity, the Republicans captured much of the spirit of the age in the North.

Thus, the Republican party attracted support from a variety of sources. Opposition to the extension of slavery had brought the party together, but party members carefully broadened their appeal by adopting the causes of other groups. They were wise to do so. As the newspaper editor Horace Greeley wrote in 1860, "an Anti-Slavery man *per se* cannot be elected." But, he added, "a Tariff, River-and-Harbor, Pacific Railroad, Free Homestead man, *may* succeed *although* he is Anti-Slavery." As these elements joined the Republican party, they also learned more about the dangers of slavery, and thus the process of party building deepened the sectional conflict.

A similar process was under way in the South. The disintegration of the Whig party had left many southerners at loose ends politically. Some of these people gravitated to the American **Southern** party, but not for long. By advocat-**Democrats** ing states' rights, Democratic leaders managed to convert most of the formerly Whig slaveholders. Democrats spoke to the class interests of slaveholders, and the slaveholders responded.

In the South, however, yeomen rather than slaveholders were the heart of the party. Thus, Democratic politicians, though often slaveowners themselves, had lauded the common man and argued that their policies advanced his interests. Yeomen were told that a well-ordered South was the true defender of constitutional principles, and that runaway change in the North was threatening to subvert the nation. And according to the southern version of republicanism, white citizens in a slave society enjoyed liberty and social equality because the black race was enslaved. As Jefferson Davis put it in 1851, slavery elevated every white person's status and allowed the nonslaveholder to "*stand upon the broad level of equality with the rich*

man." Slaveholders warned that the overriding issue was "shall negroes govern white men, or white men govern negroes?"

These arguments had their effect, and racial fears and traditional political loyalties helped keep the political alliance between yeoman farmers and planters intact through the 1850s. No viable party emerged in the South to replace the Whigs. The result was a one-party system there that emphasized sectional issues. In the South, as in the North, political realignment sharpened sectional divisions.

In both sections, political leaders argued that opportunity was threatened. The *Montgomery* (Alabama) *Mail* warned southern whites that the Republicans intended "to free the negroes and force amalgamation between them and the children of the poor men of the South." Republicans warned northern workers that if slavery entered the territories the great reservoir of opportunity for decent people without means would be poisoned. These charges aroused fears and anxieties in both sections. But events in Kansas did even more to deepen the conflict. Put into practice, the Kansas-Nebraska Act spawned hatred and violence. Abolitionists and religious groups sent armed Free-Soil settlers to make Kansas free; southerners sent their reinforcements to establish slavery and prevent "northern hordes" from stealing Kansas. Clashes between the two groups caused bloodshed, and soon the whole nation was talking about "Bleeding Kansas."

Politics in the territory resembled war more than democracy. When elections for a territorial legislature were held in 1855, thousands of proslavery Missourians invaded the polls and **Bleeding** ran up a large but unlawful major-**Kansas** ity for slavery candidates. The legislature that resulted promptly legalized slavery, and in response Free-Soilers called an unauthorized convention and created their own government and constitution. A proslavery posse sent to arrest the Free-Soil leaders sacked the town of Lawrence; in revenge, John Brown, a zealot who saw himself as God's instrument to destroy slavery, murdered five proslavery settlers. Soon armed bands of guerrillas roamed the territory.

The passion generated by this conflict erupted in

The earliest known photograph of John Brown, probably taken in 1846 in Massachusetts, shows him pledging his devotion to an unidentified flag, possibly an abolitionist banner. Already Brown was aiding runaway slaves and pondering ways to strike at slavery. *Ohio Historical Society.*

the chamber of the United States Senate in May 1856, when Charles Sumner of Massachusetts denounced "the Crime against Kansas." In doing so, Sumner bitterly assailed the president, the South, and Senator Andrew P. Butler of South Carolina. Soon afterward Butler's nephew, Representative Preston Brooks, approached Sumner at the latter's Senate desk, raised his arm, and began to beat Sumner over the head with a cane. Voters in the North and the South seethed; the country was becoming polarized.

The election of 1856 showed how far the polarization had gone. When Democrats met to select a nominee, they chose James Buchanan of Pennsylvania, whose chief virtue was that he had been serving as ambassador in Britain for four years. Thus he had not been embroiled in territorial controversies. This anonymity and superior party organization helped Buchanan win the election, but he owed his victory to southern support. Republican

candidate, John C. Frémont, won eleven of sixteen free states; Republicans had become the dominant party in the North. The Know-Nothing candidate, Millard Fillmore, received more than 20 percent of the vote, but this election was his party's last hurrah. The future battle was between a sectional Republican party and an increasingly divided Democratic party.

Slavery and the Nation's Future

For years, the issue of slavery in the territories had convulsed Congress, and for years the members of Congress had tried to settle the issue with vague formulas. In 1857, a different branch of government stepped onto the scene with a different approach. The Supreme Court addressed this emotion-charged subject and attempted to lay controversy to rest with a definitive verdict.

A Missouri slave named Dred Scott had sued his owner for his freedom. Scott based his suit on the fact that his former owner, an army surgeon, had taken him for several years into Illinois, a free state, and into the Wisconsin Territory, from which slavery had been barred by the Missouri Compromise. Scott first won and then lost his case as it moved on appeal through the state courts, into the federal system, and finally to the Supreme Court.

Dred Scott Case

Was a black person like Dred Scott a citizen and eligible to sue? Had residence in free territory made him free? Did Congress have the power to prohibit slavery in a territory or to delegate that power to a territorial legislature?

Each of these questions was answered by Chief Justice Roger B. Taney in *Dred Scott* v. *Sanford*. Taney wrote that Scott was not a citizen of either Missouri or the United States; that residence in a free territory did not make Scott free; and, most important, that Congress lacked the power to bar slavery from a territory, as it had done in the Missouri Compromise. The latter point suggested that the basic ideas of the Wilmot Proviso, and probably popular sovereignty, were invalid.

The Slave Power seemed to have gained vital constitutional ground. Black Americans were especially dismayed, for Taney's decision also declared that the founding fathers had never intended that black people be citizens. Though historically erroneous (black people had been citizens in several of the original states), the Dred Scott decision seemed to shut the door permanently on black people's hopes for justice and equal rights.

A storm of angry reaction broke in the North. The decision alarmed a wide variety of northerners—abolitionists, would-be settlers in the West, and those who hated black people but feared the influence of the South. Every charge against the aggressive Slave Power seemed now to be confirmed. "There is such a thing as THE SLAVE POWER," warned the *Cincinnati Daily Commercial*. And the *Cincinnati Freeman* asked, "What security have the Germans and the Irish that their children will not, within a hundred years, be reduced to slavery in this land of their adoption?" Echoed the *Atlantic Monthly*, "Where will it end?"

To Abraham Lincoln, the territorial question affected every citizen. "The whole nation," he declared as early as 1854, "is interested that the best use shall be made of these Territories. We want them for homes of free white people. This they cannot be, to any considerable extent, if slavery shall be planted within them." The territories must be reserved, he insisted, "as an outlet for *free white people everywhere.*" After the Dred Scott decision, Lincoln charged, it was clear that slavery's advocates were trying to "push it forward, till it shall become lawful in *all* the states . . . *North* as well as *South.*" He further asserted that the next step in the unfolding Slave Power conspiracy would be a Supreme Court decision "declaring that the Constitution does not permit a State to exclude slavery from its limits." This charge was not mere imagination, for cases soon were in the courts challenging state laws that gave freedom to slaves brought within their borders.

Lincoln's most eloquent statement against the Slave Power was his famous "House Divided"

Abraham Lincoln on the Slave Power

speech. In it, Lincoln declared: "I do not expect the Union to be dissolved—I do not expect the House to fall—but I do expect it to cease to be divided. It will become all one thing or all the other. Either the opponents of slavery will arrest the further spread of it, and place it where the public mind shall rest in the belief that it is in the course of ultimate extinction; or its advocates will push it forward, till it shall become alike lawful in all the States, old as well as new, North as well as South." Lincoln warned repeatedly that the latter possibility was well on the way to realization, and events convinced countless northerners that slaveholders were close to their goal of making slavery a national institution.

Politically, the force of Republican arguments offset the difficulties that the Dred Scott decision posed for party leaders. By endorsing southern constitutional theories, the Court had invalidated the central position of the Republican party: no extension of slavery. Republicans could only repudiate the decision, appealing to a "higher law," or hope to change the personnel of the Court. They did both and probably gained politically as public fear of the Slave Power increased.

Meanwhile, Stephen Douglas, a northern Democrat, faced an awful dilemma. He had to find a way to ease the fear of northerners without alienating southern Democrats. Douglas chose to stand by his principle of popular sovereignty, which encountered a second test in Kansas in 1857. There, after Free-Soil settlers boycotted an election, proslavery forces met at Lecompton and wrote a constitution that permitted slavery. New elections to the territorial legislature, however, returned an antislavery majority, and the legislature promptly called for a popular vote on the new constitution, which was defeated by more than 10,000 votes. Despite this overwhelming evidence that Kansans did not want slavery, President Buchanan tried to force the Lecompton Constitution through Congress. Douglas threw his weight against a document the people had rejected. He gauged their feelings correctly, for in 1858 Kansas voters rejected the constitution a third time. But his action infuriated southern Democrats.

In his well-publicized debates with Abraham Lincoln, his challenger for the Illinois Senate seat in

1858, Douglas further alienated the southern wing of his party. Speaking at Freeport, Illinois, he attempted to revive the notion of popular sovereignty with some tortured extensions of his old arguments. Asserting that the Supreme Court had not ruled on the powers of a *territorial* legislature, Douglas claimed that a territorial legislature could bar slavery either by passing a law against it or by doing nothing. Without the patrol laws and police regulations that support slavery, he reasoned, the institution could not exist. This argument, called the Freeport Doctrine, temporarily shored up Douglas's crumbling position in the North, but it alarmed southern Democrats. Some, like William L. Yancey of Alabama, studied the trend in northern opinion and concluded that southern rights would be safe only in a separate nation.

Stephen Douglas Proposes the Freeport Doctrine

The immediate consequence for politics, however, was the likelihood of division in the Democratic party. Northern Democrats could not support the territorial protection for slavery that southern Democrats insisted was their constitutional right. Thus the territories continued to generate wider conflict, even though the issue had little practical significance. In territories outside Kansas, the number of settlers was small, and everywhere the number of blacks was negligible—less than 1 percent of the population in Kansas and New Mexico. Nevertheless, the general public in both North and South moved from anxiety to alarm and anger. The situation had become explosive.

The Breakup of the Union

One year before the 1860 presidential election, violence inflamed passions further when John Brown led a small band of whites and blacks in an attack on Harpers Ferry, Virginia. Hoping to trigger a slave rebellion, Brown failed miserably and was quickly captured, tried, and executed. Yet his attempted insurrection struck fear into the South. Then it came to light that Brown had financial backing from several prominent abolitionists, and northern intellectuals praised him as a hero and a martyr. These disclosures and northern praise of Brown multiplied southerners' fears and anger many times over. The unity of the nation was now in peril.

Many observers feared that the election of 1860 would decide the fate of the Union. By that year, the Democratic party was the only remaining organization that was truly national in scope. "One after another," wrote a Mississippian, "the links which have bound the North and South together, have been severed . . . [but] the Democratic party looms gradually up, its nationality intact, and waves the olive branch over the troubled waters of politics." At its 1860 convention, however, the Democratic party broke in two.

Stephen A. Douglas wanted the party's presidential nomination, but he could not afford to alienate northern opinion by accepting the southern position on the territories. Southern Democrats like William L. Yancey, on the other hand, were determined to have their rights recognized, and they moved to block Douglas's nomination. When Douglas marshaled a majority for his version of the platform, delegates from eight slave states walked out of the convention hall in Charleston. Efforts at compromise failed, and so the Democrats presented two nominees: Douglas for the northern wing, Vice President John C. Breckinridge of Kentucky for the southern. The Republicans nominated Abraham Lincoln. A Constitutional Union party, formed to preserve the nation but strong only in the Upper South, nominated John Bell of Tennessee.

Splintering of the Democratic Party

The results of the balloting were sectional in character, with Lincoln the winner but with Douglas, Breckinridge, and Bell together receiving most of the votes. Douglas had broad-based support but won few states; Breckinridge carried nine southern states, with his strength concentrated in the Deep South; Bell won pluralities in Virginia, Kentucky, and Tennessee. Lincoln prevailed in the North, but in the states that ultimately remained loyal to the Union, he won only a plural-

Election of 1860

These soldiers, photographed in 1859, were helping the Federal government protect slavery. The Richmond Grays, a militia company in the 1st Regiment, Virginia Volunteers, helped suppress John Brown's raid. Eighteen months later many of these men were wearing gray for the Confederacy. *The Valentine Museum, Richmond, Virginia.*

ity, not a majority (see table). He gained his victory in the electoral college.

Given the heterogeneous nature of Republican voters, it is likely that many of them did not view the issue of slavery in the territories as paramount. But opposition to extending slavery was the core issue of the Republican party, and Lincoln's alarm over slavery's growing power in the nation was genuine. The slavery issue would not go away. While abolitionists and Free-Soilers in the North worked to keep the Republicans from compromising on their territorial stand, proslavery advocates and secessionists whipped up public opinion in the South and shrewdly manipulated state conventions.

Lincoln made the crucial decision not to soften his party's position on the territories. His refusal to compromise probably derived both from his convictions and from his concern for the unity of the Republican party. Although many conservative Republicans—eastern businessmen and former Whigs who did not feel strongly about slavery—hoped for a compromise, the original and strongest Republicans—antislavery voters and "conscience Whigs"—would not abandon free soil. Lincoln chose to preserve the unity of his party and to take a stand against slavery.

Southern leaders in the Senate were willing, conditionally, to accept a compromise formula drawn up by Senator John J. Crittenden of Kentucky. Crittenden had suggested that the two sections divide the territories between them at 36°30′. But the southerners would agree to this *only* if the Republicans did too. When Lincoln ruled out concessions on the territorial issue, Crittenden's peacemaking effort collapsed. Virginians called for a special convention in Washington, to which several states sent representatives. But this gathering, too, failed to find a suitable formula or to reach unanimity on disputed questions.

Furthermore, political leaders in the North and the South misjudged each other. Lincoln and other prominent Republicans believed that southerners were bluffing when they threatened secession; they expected a pro-Union majority in the South to assert itself. On their side, moderate southern leaders had become convinced, with more accuracy, that

PRESIDENTIAL VOTE IN 1860		
	Lincoln	Other Candidates
Entire United States	1,866,452	2,815,617
North plus border and southern states that rejected secession prior to war[1]	1,866,452	2,421,752
North plus border states that fought for union[2]	1,864,523	1,960,842

Note the large vote for other candidates in the righthand column.
[1] Kentucky, Missouri, Maryland, Delaware, Virginia, North Carolina, Tennessee, Arkansas
[2] Kentucky, Missouri, Maryland, Delaware

Source: From David Potter, Lincoln and His Party in the Secession Crisis. Copyright 1942, 1967 by Yale University Press. Reprinted by permission.

northern leaders were not taking them seriously and that a posture of strength was necessary to win respect for their position. Thus, southern leaders who hoped to preserve the Union did not offer compromise, for fear of inviting aggression. Northern leaders who loved the Union believed compromise would be unnecessary and unwise. With such attitudes controlling leaders' actions, the prospects for a solution were dim.

Meanwhile the Union was being destroyed. On December 20, 1860, South Carolina passed an ordinance of secession amid jubilation and cheering.

Secession of South Carolina This step marked the inauguration of a strategy known as separate-state secession. Foes of the Union, knowing the difficulty of persuading all the southern states to challenge the federal government simultaneously, had concentrated their hopes on the most extreme proslavery state. With South Carolina out of the Union, they hoped other states would follow and build momentum toward disunion.

Southern extremists soon got their way. Overwhelming their opposition, they quickly called conventions and passed secession ordinances in six other states: Mississippi, Florida, **Confederate States of America** Alabama, Georgia, Louisiana, and Texas. By February 1861, these states had joined with South Carolina to form a new government in Montgomery, Alabama: the Confederate States of America. Choosing Jefferson Davis as their president, they began to function independently of the United States.

Yet this apparent unanimity of action was deceiving. Confused and dissatisfied with the alternatives, many voters who had cast a ballot for president stayed home rather than vote for delegates who would consider secession. In some conventions, the vote to secede had been close, the balance tipped by the overrepresentation of plantation districts. Furthermore, the conventions were noticeably reluctant to seek ratification of their acts by the people. Four states in the Upper South—Virginia, North Carolina, Tennessee, and Arkansas—flatly rejected secession and did not join the Confederacy until after the fighting had started. In Kentucky and Missouri, popular sentiment was too divided for decisive action; these slave states remained under Union control, along with Maryland and Delaware (see map, page 252).

Misgivings about secession were not surprising, since it posed new and troubling issues for southerners, not the least of them being the possibility of war and the question of who would be sacrificed. A careful look at election returns indicates that slaveholders and nonslaveholders were beginning to part company politically. Heavily slaveholding counties gave strong support to secession, but many counties with few slaves took an antisecession position or were staunchly Unionist. In other words, nonslaveholding yeomen were beginning to

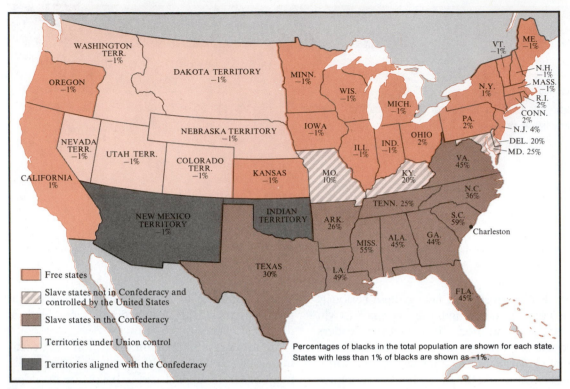

The Divided Nation—Slave and Free Areas, 1861

Legend:
- Free states
- Slave states not in Confederacy and controlled by the United States
- Slave states in the Confederacy
- Territories under Union control
- Territories aligned with the Confederacy

Percentages of blacks in the total population are shown for each state. States with less than 1% of blacks are shown as –1%.

act on their class interests. Finally, there was still considerable love for the Union in the South.

The dilemma facing President Lincoln on inauguration day in March 1861 was how to maintain the authority of the federal government without provoking war in the states that had left the Union. He decided to proceed cautiously; by holding onto federal fortifications, he reasoned, he could assert federal sovereignty while waiting for a restoration of relations. But Jefferson Davis, who could not claim to lead a sovereign nation if its ports and military facilities were under foreign control, would not cooperate. A collision was inevitable.

It came in the early morning hours of April 12, 1861, at Fort Sumter in Charleston harbor. A federal garrison there was running low on food. Lin-

Attack on Fort Sumter

coln notified the South Carolinians that he was sending a ship to resupply the fort. For the Montgomery government, the alternatives were to attack the fort or to acquiesce to Lincoln's authority. Accordingly, orders were sent to obtain surrender or attack the fort. Under heavy

bombardment for two days, the federal garrison finally surrendered. Confederates then permitted the soldiers, none of whom had been killed, to sail away on unarmed vessels while the residents of Charleston celebrated. The bloodiest war in America's history thus began in a deceptively gala spirit.

Throughout the 1840s and 1850s, many able leaders had worked diligently to avert armed conflict. Most people in both the North and the South had hoped to keep the nation together. As late as 1858, even Jefferson Davis had declared, "This great country will continue united." He had explained sincerely that the United States "is my country and to the innermost fibers of my heart I love it all, and every part." Why, then, had the war occurred?

Slavery was an issue that could not be compromised. The conflict over slavery was fundamental and beyond adjustment. Too many powerful emotions were engaged in attacking or defending it. Too many important interests and principles were involved in maintaining or destroying it. It was deeply entwined with almost every major policy question of the present and the future. Ultimately, each section regarded slavery as too important to ignore.

Even after extreme views were put aside, the North and the South had fundamentally different attitudes toward the institution. The logic of Republican ideology tended in the direction of abolishing slavery, though Republicans denied any such intention. Similarly, the logic of arguments by southern leaders led toward establishing slavery everywhere, though southern leaders denied that they sought any such thing. Lincoln put the problem succinctly. Soon after the 1860 election, he assured his old friend Alexander Stephens of Georgia that the Republican party would not attack slavery in the states where it existed. But Lincoln continued, "You think slavery is *right* and ought to be expanded; while we think it is *wrong* and ought to be restricted. That I suppose is the rub."

The issue of slavery in the territories made conflict impossible to avoid. Territorial expansion generated disputes so frequently that the nation never gained a breathing space. As the conflict recurred, it deepened its influence on policy and its effect on the government. Every southern victory increased fear of the Slave Power, and each increase in Free-Soil sentiment made alarmed slaveholders more insistent in their demands.

Concerns about slavery had driven all the other conflicts, but the fighting began with this central issue shrouded in confusion. How would the Civil War affect slavery, its place in the law, and black people's place in society?

Suggestions for Further Reading

Politics: General

Thomas B. Alexander, *Sectional Stress and Party Strength* (1967); Maurice G. Baxter, *One and Inseparable: Daniel Webster and the Union* (1984); Paul Bergeron, *The Presidency of James K. Polk* (1987); Ray Allen Billington, *The Protestant Crusade, 1800–1860* (1938 and 1964); Stanley W. Campbell, *The Slave Catchers* (1968); Avery O. Craven, *The Coming of the Civil War* (1942); Don E. Fehrenbacher, *The Dred Scott Case* (1978); Holman Hamilton, *Prologue to Con-*
flict: The Crisis and Compromise of 1850* (1964); Michael F. Holt, *The Political Crisis of the 1850s* (1978); James M. McPherson, *Battle Cry of Freedom* (1988); Stephen E. Maizlish and John J. Kushma, eds., *Essays on American Antebellum Politics, 1840–1860* (1982); Roy F. Nichols, *The Disruption of American Democracy* (1948); Russell B. Nye, *Fettered Freedom* (1949); Merrill D. Peterson, *The Great Triumvirate: Webster, Clay, and Calhoun* (1987); David M. Potter, *The Impending Crisis, 1848–1861* (1976); Joel H. Silbey, *The Transformation of American Politics, 1840–1960* (1967); Gerald W. Wolff, *The Kansas-Nebraska Bill* (1977).

The South and Slavery

William L. Barney, *The Secessionist Impulse* (1974); Daniel W. Crofts, *Reluctant Confederates: Upper South Unionists in the Secession Crisis* (1989); Drew G. Faust, *The Ideology of Slavery* (1981); Drew G. Faust, *A Sacred Circle: The Dilemma of the Intellectual in the Old South* (1978); Eugene D. Genovese, *The World the Slaveholders Made* (1969); Eugene D. Genovese, *The Political Economy of Slavery* (1967); William Sumner Jenkins, *Pro-Slavery Thought in the Old South* (1935); John Niven, *John C. Calhoun and the Price of Union* (1988); David M. Potter, *The South and the Sectional Conflict* (1968); Thomas E. Schott, *Alexander H. Stephens of Georgia* (1988); J. Mills Thornton III, *Politics and Power in a Slave Society* (1978).

The North and Antislavery

Eugene H. Berwanger, *The Frontier Against Slavery* (1967); Louis Filler, *The Crusade Against Slavery, 1830–1860* (1960); Eric Foner, *Free Soil, Free Labor, Free Men* (1970); William E. Gienapp, *The Origins of the Republican Party, 1852–1856* (1986); Henry V. Jaffa, *Crisis of the House Divided* (1959); Robert W. Johannsen, *The Frontier, the Union, and Stephen A. Douglas* (1989); Aileen S. Kraditor, *Means and Ends in American Abolitionism* (1969); Lewis Perry and Michael Fellman, eds., *Antislavery Reconsidered* (1979); Jeffrey Rossbach, *Ambivalent Conspirators* (1982); Alice Felt Tyler, *Freedom's Ferment* (1944); Ronald G. Walters, *American Reformers* (1978).

The Mexican War and Foreign Policy

K. Jack Bauer, *Zachary Taylor* (1985); Reginald Horsman, *Race and Manifest Destiny* (1981); Ernest M. Lander, Jr., *Reluctant Imperialists: Calhoun, the South Carolinians, and the Mexican War* (1980); Robert E. May, *The Southern Dream of a Caribbean Empire, 1854–1861* (1973); Frederick Merk, *The Oregon Question* (1967); David M. Pletcher, *The Diplomacy of Annexation: Texas, Oregon, and the Mexican War* (1973); John H. Schroeder, *Mr. Polk's War: American Opposition and Dissent* (1973); Otis A. Singletary, *The Mexican War* (1960).

Moncure Conway, a Virginian who had converted to abolitionism and settled in New England, saw the Civil War as an opportunity to bring justice to human affairs. He urged northerners to accept slavery's challenge and defeat it, so that "the rays of Freedom and Justice" could shine throughout America. Then the United States would stand as a beacon not only of commercial power, but also of moral righteousness.

Conway's idealism was far removed from the motives that drove most federal soldiers to march grimly to their death. Although slaves believed that they were witnessing God's "Holy War for the liberation," Union troops often took a different perspective. When a Yankee soldier ransacked a slave family's cabin, the mother exclaimed, "Why you nasty, stinkin' rascal. You say you come down here to fight for the niggers, and now you're stealin' from 'em." The soldier replied, "You're a G____ D____ liar, I'm fightin' for $14 a month and the Union."

Southerners, too, acted from limited and pragmatic motives, fighting in self-defense or out of regional loyalty. A Union officer interrogating Confederate prisoners noticed the poverty of one captive. Clearly, the man was no slaveholder, so the officer asked him why he was fighting. "Because y'all are down here," replied the Confederate.

14

TRANSFORMING FIRE: THE CIVIL WAR, 1861–1865

For each of these people and millions of others, the Civil War was a life-changing event. It obliterated the normal circumstances of life, sweeping millions of men into training camps and battle units. Armies numbering in the hundreds of thousands marched over the South, devastating once-peaceful countrysides. Families struggled to survive without their men; businesses tried to cope with the loss of workers. Women in both North and South faced added responsibilities in the home and moved into new jobs in the work force. Nothing seemed untouched.

Change was more drastic in the South, where the leaders of the secession movement had launched a revolution for the purpose of keeping things unchanged. Never were men so mistaken. The Civil War forced changes in every phase of southern society, and the leadership of Jefferson Davis, president of the Confederate States of America, resulted in policies more objectionable to the elite than any proposed by President Lincoln.

War altered the North as well, but not as deeply. Because most of the fighting took place on southern soil, most northern farms and factories remained physically unscathed. The drafting of workers and the changing needs for products slowed the pace of industrialization somewhat, but factories and businesses remained busy. Workers lost ground to inflation, but the economy hummed. A new probusiness atmosphere dominated the United States Congress. To the discomfort of many, the powers of the federal government and the president increased during the war.

Ultimately, the Civil War forced new social and racial arrangements on the nation. Its greatest effect was to compel leaders and citizens to deal with an issue that they had often tried to avoid: slavery. This issue had, in complex and indirect ways, given rise to the war; now the war forced Americans to grapple with it.

The South Goes to War

In the first bright days of the southern nation, few foresaw the changes that were in store. Lincoln's call for troops to put down the Confederate insurrection stimulated an outpouring of regional loyalty that unified the classes. In the South, half a million men volunteered to fight for the Confederate cause. There were so many would-be soldiers that the Confederate government could not arm them all.

The ground swell of popular support for the Confederacy generated a mood of optimism and gaiety. Confident recruits boasted of whipping the Yankees and returning home in **Battle of** time for dinner, and the first ma-
Bull Run jor battle of the war only increased such cockiness. On July 21, 1861, 30,000 federal troops attacked 22,000 southerners at a stream called Bull Run, near Manassas Junction, Virginia. Both armies were ill trained, and confusion reigned on the battlefield. But 9,000 Confederate reinforcements and a timely stand by General Thomas Jackson (thereafter known as "Stonewall" Jackson) won the day for the South. Union troops fled back to Washington in

disarray, and shocked northern congressmen and spectators, who had been following the battle from two miles away, suddenly feared that their capital would be taken.

In the wake of Bull Run, the North undertook a massive build-up of troops in northern Virginia. Lincoln gave command of the army to General George B. McClellan, who proved to be better at organization and training than at fighting. McClellan devoted the fall and winter of 1861 to readying a formidable force of a quarter of a million men. The North also moved to blockade southern ports in order to choke off the Confederacy's avenues of commerce and supply. At first, the Union blockade was woefully inadequate. But the Union Navy gradually increased the blockade's effectiveness, though it never completely bottled up southern commerce.

In the late summer and fall of 1861, Union naval power came ashore in the South. Federal squadrons captured Cape Hatteras and Hilton Head, part of the Sea Islands off Port Royal,
Union Naval South Carolina (see map, page
Campaign 256). A few months later, similar operations secured Albemarle and Pamlico sounds, Roanoke Island, and New Bern in North Carolina. The coastal victories, especially those off the coast of South Carolina, caused frightened planters to abandon their lands and flee. Their slaves thus became the first to escape slavery through military action. Ironically, the federal government, unwilling at first to wage a war against slavery, did not acknowledge the slaves' freedom.

With the approach of the spring of 1862, the military outlook for the Confederacy darkened again. In April 1862, ships commanded by Admiral David Farragut smashed through log
Grant's booms on the Mississippi River
Campaign in and fought their way upstream to
Tennessee capture New Orleans. In northern Tennessee, land forces won significant victories for the Union. There, General Ulysses S. Grant captured Fort Henry and Fort Donelson, securing two prime routes into the Confederacy's heartland. A path into Tennessee, Alabama, and Mississippi now lay open before the Union Army.

On April 6, Confederate General Albert Sidney

The Civil War, 1861–1863

1861	Battle of Bull Run
	General McClellan organizes Union Army
	Union blockade begins
	First confiscation act
1862	Capture of Fort Henry and Fort Donelson
	Capture of New Orleans
	Battle of Shiloh
	Confederacy enacts conscription
	McClellan attacks Virginia
	Second confiscation act
	Confederacy mounts offensive
	Battle of Antietam
1863	Emancipation Proclamation
	National Banking Act
	Union enacts conscription
	Black soldiers join Union Army
	Food riots in southern cities
	Battle of Chancellorsville
	Battle of Gettysburg and surrender of Vicksburg
	Draft riots in New York City
1864	Battle of Cold Harbor
	Lincoln requests party plank abolishing slavery
	General Sherman enters Atlanta
	Lincoln re-elected
	Jefferson Davis proposes Confederate emancipation
	Sherman marches through Georgia
1865	Congress approves Thirteenth Amendment
	Hampton Roads Conference
	Lee surrenders at Appomattox
	Lincoln assassinated

Johnston caught Grant's army at Pittsburg Landing in southern Tennessee. The Confederates inflicted heavy damage, but Johnston was killed. The next day, a reinforced Union Army forced the enemy to withdraw to Corinth, Mississippi. There was no clear victor in the Battle of Shiloh, but destruction reigned. Northern troops lost 13,000 of 63,000 men; southerners sacrificed 11,000 out of 40,000.

The losses at Shiloh foreshadowed the enormous costs of the war. Never before in Europe or America had such massive forces pummeled each other with weapons of such destructive power. Yet the armies in the Civil War seemed virtually indestructible. Even in the bloodiest engagements, the losing army was never destroyed, even though thousands of men died. The improved range of modern rifles multiplied casualties, and because medical knowledge was rudimentary, minor wounds often led to death through infection.

The scope and duration of the conflict began to have unexpected effects. Tens of thousands of Confederate soldiers had volunteered for just one year's service, planning to return home in the spring of 1862 to plant their crops. To keep southern armies in the field, the War Department of the Confederacy offered bounties and furloughs to all who would re-enlist. When "the spirit of volunteering . . . died out," the Confederate government enacted the first national conscription law in American history. Thus, the war forced an unprecedented change on the states that had seceded out of fear of change.

Confederacy Resorts to a Draft

With their ranks reinforced, southern armies moved into heavier fighting. The Confederacy had relocated its capital from Montgomery, Alabama, to Richmond, Virginia. General McClellan sailed his troops to the York peninsula and advanced on Richmond from the east. But General Stonewall Jackson and General Robert E. Lee managed to stave off McClellan's attacks. First, Jackson maneuvered into the Shenandoah Valley, behind Union forces, and

Antietam was the bloodiest day of the war. Nearly 6,000 men died—far more than in the War of 1812 and the Mexican War combined—and another 17,000 were wounded. The northern victory helped prevent European recognition of the Confederacy. *Tharpe Collection of American Military History.*

threatened Washington, drawing some of the federals away from Richmond to protect their own capital. Then, in a series of engagements culminating in the Seven Days' battles, Lee held McClellan off. On August 3, McClellan withdrew to the Potomac, and Richmond was safe for almost two more years.

Buoyed by these results, Jefferson Davis conceived an ambitious plan to turn the tide of the war and compel the United States to recognize the Confederacy. He ordered a general of-

Davis Orders an Offensive fensive, sending Lee north to Maryland and General Kirby Smith and General Braxton Bragg to Kentucky. The South would go on the offensive and take the war north. The plan was promising, but every part of the offensive failed. In the bloodiest single day of fighting, September 17, 1862, McClellan turned Lee back in the Battle of Antietam, near Sharpsburg, Maryland. Smith and Bragg had to withdraw from Kentucky. The entire effort collapsed.

But southern armies were not exhausted. General James E. B. ("Jeb") Stuart executed a daring cavalry raid into Pennsylvania on October 10 through 12, and Lee decimated General Ambrose Burnside's soldiers as they charged his fortified positions at Fredericksburg, Virginia, on December 13. Nevertheless, the Confederacy had marshaled all its strength for a breakthrough and had failed.

Profoundly disappointed, Davis admitted to a committee of Confederate representatives that southerners had entered "the darkest and most dangerous period we have yet had."

War Transforms the South

Even more than the fighting, changes in civilian life robbed southerners of their gaiety and nonchalance. The war fundamentally altered southern society. One of the first traditions to fall was the southern preference for local government.

The South had been an area of limited government. States' rights had been its motto, but by modern standards the state governments were weak and sketchy affairs. To withstand the massive power of the North, the South had to centralize. No one saw the necessity of centralization more clearly than Jefferson Davis. If the states insisted on fighting separately, said Davis, "we had better make terms as soon as we can."

From the outset, Davis pressed to bring all arms, supplies, and troops under his control. He advocated conscription when the states failed to enroll enough new soldiers. He took a strong

Chapter 14: Transforming Fire: The Civil War, 1861–1865

Centralization of Power in the South

leadership role toward the Confederate congress, which raised taxes and later passed a tax-in-kind—a tax paid not in money, but in wheat, corn, oats, cotton, and other farm products. Where opposition arose, the government suspended the writ of habeas corpus and imposed martial law. In the face of a political opposition that cherished states' rights, Davis proved unyielding.

Soon the Confederate administration in Richmond was taking virtually complete control of the southern economy. Because it controlled the supply of labor through conscription, the administration could regulate industry, compelling factories to work on government contracts to supply government needs. In addition, the Confederate congress passed laws giving the central government almost full control of the railroads; in 1864, shipping, too, came under extensive regulation. New statutes even limited corporate profits and dividends. A large bureaucracy sprang up to administer these operations; by the war's end, the southern bureaucracy was proportionally larger than its northern counterpart.

The mushrooming bureaucracy expanded the cities. Clerks and subordinate officials, many of them women, crowded the towns and cities where

Effects of War on Southern Cities and Industries

Confederate departments had their offices. These sudden population booms stretched the existing housing supply and stimulated new construction. The pressure was especially great in Richmond, whose population increased two and a half times.

Another prime cause of urban growth was industrialization. Because of the Union blockade, the traditionally agricultural South became interested in industry. Davis exulted that southerners were manufacturing their own goods, thus "becoming more and more independent of the rest of the world." Indeed, though the Confederacy started almost from scratch, it achieved tremendous feats of industrial development.

As a result of these changes, southerners adopted new ways. Women, sheltered in the patriarchal antebellum society, gained substantial new

Change in the Southern Woman's Role

responsibilities. The wives and mothers of soldiers became heads of households and undertook what had previously been considered men's work. In slaveowning families, women assumed management roles. In the cities, white women, who had been virtually excluded from the labor force, found a limited number of new, respectable, paying jobs. "Government girls" staffed the Confederate bureaucracy, and female schoolteachers became a familiar sight for the first time in the South. Such experiences undermined the image of the omnipotent male and gave thousands of women new confidence in their abilities.

The Confederate experience introduced and sustained many other new values. Legislative bodies yielded power to the executive branch of government, which could act more decisively in time of war. The traditional emphasis on aristocratic lineage gave way to respect for achievement and bravery under fire. Finally, sacrifice for the cause discouraged the pursuit of pleasure.

For the elite such sacrifice was symbolic, but for millions of ordinary southerners it was terrifyingly real. Mass poverty descended on the South, afflicting for the first time a large minority of the white population. Many yeoman families had lost their breadwinners to the army. As a South Carolina newspaper put it, "The duties of war have called away from home the sole supports of many, many families. . . . Help must be given, or the poor will suffer." The poor sought help from relatives, neighbors, friends, anyone. Sometimes they took their cases to the Confederate government.

Human Suffering in the South

Other factors aggravated the effect of the labor shortage. The South was in many places so sparsely populated that the conscription of one skilled craftsman could work a hardship on the people of an entire county. Often, they begged in unison for the exemption or discharge of the local miller, tanner, wheelwright, or potter. Most serious, however, was the loss of a blacksmith.

Inflation became a problem as prices increased by almost 7,000 percent. Indeed, rising prices imperiled those who could no longer provide for themselves. As early as 1861 and 1862, newspapers were reporting that "the poor of our . . . country will be unable to live at all" and that "want and starvation are staring thousands in the face." As their fortunes declined, people of once-modest means looked around them and found abundant evidence that all classes were not sacrificing equally. They saw that the wealthy gave up only their luxuries, while many poor families went without necessities. They saw that the government contributed to these inequities through policies that favored the upper class. Until the last year of the war, for example, prosperous southerners could avoid military service by hiring substitutes. Well over fifty thousand upper-class southerners purchased such substitutes.

Anger at such discrimination exploded in October 1862, when the Confederate congress exempted from military duty anyone who was

Inequities of the Confederate Draft

supervising at least twenty slaves. Immediately, protests arose from every corner of the Confederacy, and North Carolina's legislators formally condemned the law. Its defenders argued, however, that the exemption preserved order and aided food production, and the statute remained on the books.

Dissension spread as growing numbers of citizens concluded that the struggle was "a rich man's war and a poor man's fight." Alert politicians and newspaper editors warned that class resentment was building to a dangerous level; letters to Confederate officials during this period contained a bitterness that suggested the depth of the people's anger. "If I and my little children suffer [and] die while there Father is in service," threatened one woman, "I invoke God Almighty that our blood rest upon the South." War was magnifying social tensions in the Confederacy.

The Northern Economy Copes with War

With the onset of war, the tidal wave of change rolled over the North just as it did over the South. Factories and citizens' associations geared up to support the war, and the federal government and its executive branch gained power they had never had before. The energies of an industrializing, capitalist society were harnessed to serve the cause of the Union. Idealism and greed flourished together, but the northern economy proved its awesome productivity.

At first, the war was a shock to business. With the sudden closing of southern markets, firms could no longer predict the demand for their goods, and

Initial Slump in Northern Business

many companies had to redirect their activities in order to remain open. Southern debts became uncollectible, jeopardizing not only northern merchants, but many western banks as well. In farming regions, families struggled with an aggravated shortage of labor. For reasons such as these, the war initially caused an economic slump.

Overall, the war slowed industrialization in the North, but its economic impact was not all negative. Certain entrepreneurs, such as wool producers, benefited from shortages of competing products, and soaring demand for war-related goods swept some businesses to new heights of production. To feed the hungry war machine, the federal government pumped unprecedented amounts of money into the economy. As a result, firms producing weapons, munitions, uniforms, boots, camp equipment, saddles, ships, and other war necessities prospered.

War production also promoted the development of heavy industry in the North. The output of coal rose substantially. Iron makers improved the quality of their product while boosting

Effects of War on Northern Industry and Agriculture

the production of pig iron. Although new railroad construction slowed, the manufacture of rails increased. Of considerable significance for the future were the railroad industry's adoption of a standard gauge for track and foundries' development of new and less expensive ways to make steel.

Another strength of the northern economy was the complementary relationship between agriculture and industry. The mechanization of agriculture had begun before the war. Wartime recruitment and conscription, however, gave western farmers an added incentive to purchase labor-saving ma-

Despite initial problems, the task of supplying a vast war machine kept the northern economy humming. This photograph shows the west side of Hudson Street, New York City, in 1865. *The New-York Historical Society.*

chinery. The shift from human labor to machines created new markets for industry and expanded the food supply for the urban industrial work force. Finally, farm families whose breadwinners went to war did not suffer as they did in the South. "We have seen," one magazine observed, "a stout matron whose sons are in the army, cutting hay with her team . . . and she cut seven acres with ease in a day, riding leisurely upon her cutter."

Northern industrial and urban workers did not fare as well. Jobs were plentiful following the initial slump, but inflation took much of a worker's pay. Studies of the cost of living indicate that between 1860 and 1864 consumer prices rose by at least 76 percent; wages rose by only 42 percent. Consequently, workers' families suffered a substantial decline in their standard of living.

Concurrent with the decline in real income was a loss of job security. To increase production, some employers replaced workers with labor-saving machines. Other employers urged the government to liberalize immigration procedures so that they could import cheap labor. Workers responded by forming unions and sometimes by striking. Skilled workers organized to combat the loss of their jobs and status to machines; women and unskilled workers, excluded by the craftsmen, formed their own unions. In recognition of the increasingly national scope of business activity, thirteen groups—including coal miners and railway engineers—formed national unions during the Civil War.

New Militancy Among Northern Workers

Employers reacted negatively to this new spirit among workers. Manufacturers, for example, formed statewide or craft-based associations to pool information. These employers compiled blacklists of union members and required new workers to sign "yellow dog" contracts, or promises not to join a union. To put down strikes, they hired strikebreakers from the ranks of the poor—blacks, immigrants, and women—and sometimes received additional help from federal troops.

Troublesome as unions were, they did not prevent many employers from making a profit. The highest gains came from profiteering on government contracts. Unscrupulous businessmen took advantage of the sudden immense demand for goods for the army by selling clothing and blankets made of "shoddy"—wool fibers reclaimed from rags or worn cloth. Shoddy goods often came apart in the rain; most of the shoes purchased in the early months of the war were worthless, too. Contractors sold inferior guns for double the usual price and tainted meat for the price of good meat. Corruption was so widespread that it led to a year-long investigation by the House of Representatives.

Legitimate enterprises also made healthy profits. The output of woolen mills increased so dramatically that dividends in the industry nearly tripled.

Wartime Benefits to Northern Business Some cotton mills made record profits on what they sold, even though they reduced their output. Railroads carried immense quantities of freight and passengers, increasing their business to the point that railroad stocks doubled or even tripled in value.

In fact, railroads were a leading beneficiary of government largesse. In the 1850s, Congress had failed to resolve the question of a northern versus a southern route for the first transcontinental railroad. With the South out of Congress, the northern route quickly prevailed. In 1862 and 1864, Congress chartered two corporations, the Union Pacific Railroad and the Central Pacific Railroad, and assisted them financially in connecting Omaha, Nebraska, with Sacramento, California. For each mile of track laid, the railroads received a loan ranging from $16,000 to $48,000, plus twenty square miles of land along a free 400-foot-wide right of way. Overall, the two corporations gained approximately 20 million acres of land and nearly $60 million in loans.

Higher tariffs also pleased many businessmen. Northern businesses did not uniformly favor high import duties; some manufacturers desired cheap imported raw materials more than they feared foreign competition. But northeastern congressmen traditionally supported higher tariffs, and after southern lawmakers left Washington, they had their way: the Tariff Act of 1864 raised tariffs generously. As one might expect, some healthy industries made artificially high profits by raising their prices to a level just below that of the foreign competition. By the end of the war, tariff increases averaged 47 percent, and rates were more than double those of 1857.

Wartime Society in the North

The outbreak of war stimulated patriotism in the North, just as it initially had in the South. Northern society, which had felt the stresses associated with urban growth, industrialization, and immigration, found a unifying cause in the preservation of the nation. Throughout thousands of towns and communities, northern citizens had participated in local government and local office holding. They worked in their government and felt it worked for them. Secession threatened to destroy this American system of representative government, and northerners rallied to its defense.

But there were other aspects of the northern response to war. The frantic wartime activity, the booming economy, and the Republican alliance with business combined to create a new atmosphere in Washington. The balance of opinion shifted against wage earners and toward large corporations; the notion spread that government should aid businessmen but not interfere with them. Noting the favorable atmosphere, railroad builders and industrialists took advantage of government loans, grants, and tariffs.

As long as the war lasted, the powers of the federal government and the president continued to grow. At the beginning of the conflict, Lincoln **Wartime Powers of the U.S. Executive** launched a major shipbuilding program without waiting for Congress to assemble. The lawmakers later approved his decision, and Lincoln continued to act in advance of Congress when he deemed it necessary. In one striking exercise of executive power, Lincoln suspended the writ of habeas corpus for all people living between Washington and Philadelphia. There was scant legal justification for this act, but Lincoln's motive was practical: to ensure the loyalty of Maryland. Lincoln also used his wartime authority to bolster his political power. He and his generals proved adept at arranging furloughs for soldiers who could vote in close elections. Needless to say, the citizens in arms whom Lincoln helped to vote usually voted Republican.

Among the clearest examples of the wartime expansion of federal authority were the National Banking Acts of 1863, 1864, and 1865. Prior to the Civil War the nation did not have a uniform currency. Banks operating under state charters issued no fewer than seven thousand different kinds of notes. Under the new laws, Congress established a national banking system empowered to issue a maximum number of national bank notes. At the close of the war in 1865, Congress laid a prohibitive tax on state bank notes and forced most major state institutions to join the national system.

The increasing scale of things may have been best sensed by soldiers, whose first experiences with large organizations were often unfortunate. Blankets, clothing, and arms were often of poor quality. Vermin were commonplace. Hospitals were badly managed at first. Rules of hygiene in large camps were badly written or unenforced; latrines were poorly made or carelessly used. Indeed, conditions were such that 224,000 Union troops died from disease or accidents, far more than the 140,000 who died in battle.

Such conditions would hardly have predisposed the soldier to sympathize with changing social attitudes on the home front. Amid the excitement of

Self-Indulgence Versus Sacrifice in the North

moneymaking, a gaudy culture of vulgar display flourished in the largest cities. A writer for the New York *Herald* observed, "This war has entirely changed the American character. . . . The individual who makes the most money—no matter how—and spends the most—no matter for what—is considered the greatest man. . . . The world has seen its iron age, its silver age, its golden age, and its brazen age. This is the age of shoddy."

Yet strong elements of idealism coexisted with ostentation. After initial uncertainty about whether to let the South go, abolitionists campaigned to turn the war into a war against slavery. Free black communities and churches both black and white responded to the needs of slaves who flocked to the Union lines. They sent clothing, ministers, and teachers in generous measure to aid the runaways.

Northern women, like their southern counterparts, took on new roles. Those who stayed home organized more than ten thousand soldiers' aid societies, rolled innumerable bandages, and raised $3 million. Thousands served as nurses in front-line hospitals, where they pressed for better care of the wounded. The professionalization of medicine since the Revolution had created a medical system dominated by men; thus, able female nurses had to fight both military regulations and professional hostility to win the chance to make their contribution. In the hospitals, they quickly proved their worth, but only the wounded welcomed them. Even Clara Barton, the most famous female nurse, was ousted from her post during the winter of 1863.

Thus, northern society embraced strangely contradictory tendencies. Materialism and greed flourished alongside idealism, religious conviction, and self-sacrifice. While wealthy men purchased 118,000 substitutes and almost 87,000 commutations at $300 each to avoid service in the Union Army, other soldiers risked their lives out of a desire to preserve the Union or extend freedom. It was as if several different wars were under way, each of them serving different motives.

The Strange Advent of Emancipation

At the very highest levels of government, there was a similar lack of clarity about the purpose of the war. Through the first several months of the struggle, both Davis and Lincoln studiously avoided references to slavery, the crux of the matter. Davis told southerners that they were fighting for constitutional liberty. He knew that stressing slavery might alienate nonslaveholders. Lincoln, hoping that a pro-Union majority would assert itself in the South, recognized that the mention of slavery would end any chance of coaxing the seceded states back into the Union. Moreover, not all Republicans were vitally interested in the slavery issue. An early presidential stand making the abolition of slavery, and not the preservation of the Union, the war's objective could split the party.

Lincoln first broached the subject of slavery in a major way in March 1862, when he proposed that the states consider emancipation on their own. He asked Congress to pass a resolution promising aid to any state that decided to emancipate, and he appealed to border-state representatives to consider seriously the idea of emancipation. What Lincoln was talking about was gradual emancipation, with compensation for slaveholders and colonization of the freed slaves outside the United States; until well into 1864, Lincoln steadfastly promoted an impractical scheme to colonize blacks in some region like Central America. The plan was extremely conservative, and since the states would make the decision voluntarily, no responsibility for it would attach to Lincoln.

Lincoln's Plan for Gradual Emancipation

Others wanted to go much further. A group of congressional Republicans known as the Radicals had, from the early days of the war, concerned themselves with slavery. In August 1861, at the Radicals' instigation, Congress passed its first confiscation act. Designed to punish the Confederate rebels, the law confiscated all property used for "insurrectionary purposes"—that is, if the South used slaves in a hostile action, those slaves were declared seized and liberated from their owners' possession. A second confiscation act (July 1862) was much more drastic: it confiscated the property of all those who supported the rebellion, even those who merely resided in the South and paid Confederate taxes. Their slaves were "forever free of their servitude, and not again [to be] held as slaves."

Confiscation Acts

Lincoln chose not to go that far. He stood by his proposal of voluntary gradual emancipation by the states and made no effort to enforce the second confiscation act. His stance brought a public protest from Horace Greeley, editor of the powerful *New York Tribune*. In an open letter to the president, Greeley wrote, "We require of you . . . that you execute the laws. . . . We think you are strangely and disastrously remiss . . . with regard to the emancipating provisions of the new Confiscation Act." Lincoln's reply was an explicit statement of his complex and calculated approach to the question. "I would save the Union," announced Lincoln. "If I could save the Union without freeing *any* slave I would do it, and if I could save it by freeing *all* the slaves I would do it; and if I would save it by freeing some and leaving others alone I would also do that. What I do about slavery, and the colored race, I do because I believe it helps to save the Union."

When he wrote those words, Lincoln had already decided to take a new step: issuance of the Emancipation Proclamation. He waited until an opportune time. On September 22, 1862, shortly after the Battle of Antietam, Lincoln issued the first part of his two-part proclamation. Invoking his powers as commander-in-chief of the armed forces, he announced that on January 1, 1863, he would emancipate the slaves in states whose people "shall then be in rebellion against the United States." The proclamation was less a declaration of the right of slaves to be free than it was a threat to southerners to end the war. Lincoln may not actually have expected southerners to give up their effort, but he was careful to offer them the option, thus putting the onus of emancipation on them.

Emancipation Proclamations

Lincoln's designation of the areas in rebellion on January 1 is worth noting. He excepted from his list every Confederate county or city that had fallen under Union control. Those areas, he declared, "are, for the present, left precisely as if this proclamation were not issued." Lincoln also did not liberate slaves in the border slave states that remained in the Union.

"The President . . . has proclaimed emancipation only where he has notoriously no power to execute it," complained the *New York World*. The exceptions, said the paper, "render the proclamation not merely futile, but ridiculous." Even Secretary of State William H. Seward, a moderate Republican, said sarcastically, "We show our sympathy with slavery by emancipating slaves where we cannot reach

Nearly 180,000 black men fought in the Union army, providing a vital infusion of strength for the northern cause. These soldiers in the 2nd U.S. Colored Light Artillery participated in the Battle of Nashville in December 1864. *Chicago Historical Society.*

them and holding them in bondage where we can set them free."

As a moral document, the Emancipation Proclamation, which in fact freed no slaves, was inadequate. As a political document, it was nearly flawless. Because the proclamation defined the war as a war against slavery, radicals could applaud it. Yet at the same time, it protected Lincoln's position with conservatives, leaving him room to retreat if he chose and forcing no immediate changes on the border slave states. The president had not gone as far as Congress, and he had taken no position that he could not change later if necessary.

In June 1864, however, Lincoln gave his support to the constitutional end of slavery. On the eve of the Republican national convention, he called the party's chairman to the White House and instructed him to have the party "put into the platform as the keystone, the amendment of the Constitution abolishing and prohibiting slavery forever." It was done; the party called for a new amendment, the thirteenth. Lincoln showed his commitment by lobbying Congress for quick approval of the measure.

He succeeded, and the proposed amendment went to the states for ratification or rejection. Lincoln's strong support for the Thirteenth Amendment—an unequivocal prohibition of slavery—constitutes his best claim to the title of Great Emancipator.

Yet Lincoln soon clouded that clear stand, for in 1865 the newly re-elected president considered allowing the defeated southern states to re-enter the Union and delay or defeat the amendment. In February, he and Secretary of State Seward met with three Confederate commissioners at Hampton Roads, Virginia. With the end of the war in sight, Lincoln was apparently contemplating the creation of a new and broader party based on a postwar alliance with southern Whigs and moderates. The cement for the coalition would be concessions to planter interests.

Hampton Roads Conference

Pointing out that the Emancipation Proclamation was only a war measure, Lincoln predicted that the courts would decide whether it had granted all, some, or none of the slaves their freedom. Seward observed that the Thirteenth Amendment was not yet ratified; re-entry into the Union would allow the southern states to vote against it and block it. Lincoln spoke in favor of ratification with a five-year delay. He also promised to seek $400 million in compensation for slaveholders. This financial aid would be an economic incentive for planters to rejoin the Union and would provide capital to ease the transition to freedom for both races. Such proposals were opposed in the North. In the South they were not discussed because of Davis's total commitment to independence.

Before the war was over, the Confederacy, too, addressed the issue of emancipation. Ironically, a strong proposal in favor of liberation came from

Davis's Plan for Emancipation

Jefferson Davis, who was willing to sacrifice slavery to achieve independence. After considering the alternatives for some time, in the fall of 1864 Davis advocated the purchase and arming of slave soldiers and insisted that such soldiers, and later their wives and children, must be freed.

Confederate emancipation began too late to revive southern armies or win diplomatic advantages with antislavery Europeans. But Lincoln's Emancipation Proclamation stimulated a vital infusion of forces into the Union armies. Beginning in 1863, slaves shouldered arms for the North. Before the war was over, 134,000 slaves (and 52,000 free blacks) had fought for freedom and the Union. Their participation was crucial to northern victory, and it discouraged recognition of the Confederacy by foreign governments.

The Disintegration of Confederate Unity

During the final two years of fighting, both northern and southern governments waged the war in the face of increasing opposition at home. The unrest was connected to the military stalemate: neither side was close to victory in 1863. But protest also arose from fundamental stresses in the social structures of the North and the South.

One ominous development was the increasing opposition of planters to their own government, whose actions often had a negative effect on them. Not only did the Richmond government impose high taxes and a tax-in-kind, but Confederate military authorities also impressed slaves to build fortifications. And when Union forces advanced on plantation areas, Confederate commanders sent detachments through the countryside to burn stores of cotton that lay in the enemy's path. Such interference with plantation routines and financial interests was not what planters had expected of their government, and they resisted.

The Confederate constitution, drawn up by the leading political thinkers of the South, had in fact granted substantial powers to the central government, especially in time of war. But for many planters, states' rights had become virtually synonymous with complete state sovereignty. In effect, years of opposition to the federal government within the Union had frozen southerners in a defensive posture. Now they erected the barrier of states' rights as a defense against change. Planters sought a guarantee that their plantations and their lives would remain untouched; they were deeply committed neither to building a southern nation nor to winning independence. If the Confederacy had been allowed to depart from the Union in peace and continue as a semideveloped cotton-growing region, they would have been content. When secession revolutionized their world, they could not or would not adjust to it.

Meanwhile, at the bottom of southern society, there were other difficulties. Food riots occurred in the spring of 1863 in Atlanta, Macon, Columbus, and Augusta, Georgia, and in

Food Riots in Southern Cities

Salisbury and High Point, North Carolina. On April 2, a crowd assembled in the Confederate capital of Richmond to demand relief from Governor John Letcher. A passerby, noticing the excitement, asked a young girl, "Is there some celebration?" "There is," replied the girl. "We celebrate our right to live. We are starving. As soon as enough of us get together we are going to the bakeries and each of us will take a loaf of bread." Soon they did just that, sparking a riot that Davis himself had to quell at gunpoint.

Throughout the rural South, ordinary people resisted more quietly—by refusing to cooperate with impressments of food, conscription, or tax collection. "In all the States impressments are evaded by every means which ingenuity can suggest, and in some openly resisted," wrote a high-ranking commissary officer. Farmers who did provide food refused to accept certificates of credit or government bonds in lieu of cash, as required by law. Conscription officers increasingly found no one to draft—men of draft age were hiding out in the forests.

Such civil discontent was certain to affect the Confederate armies. Spurred by concern for their loved ones and resentment of the rich man's war, large numbers of men did indeed **Desertions** leave the armies, supported by **from the** their friends and neighbors. The **Confederate** problem of desertion became so **Army** acute that by November 1863 Secretary of War James Seddon admitted that one-third of the army could not be accounted for. The situation was to worsen.

The gallantry of those who stayed on in Lee's army and the daring of their commander made the start of the 1863 campaign deceptively positive. On May 2 and 3 at Chancellorsville, **Battle of** Virginia, 130,000 members of the **Chancellors-** Union Army of the Potomac bore **ville** down on fewer than 60,000 Confederates. Acting as if they enjoyed being outnumbered, Lee and Stonewall Jackson boldly divided their forces, ordering 30,000 men under Jackson on a day-long march westward and to the rear for a flank attack. Jackson arrived at his position late in the afternoon to witness unprepared Union troops "laughing, smoking," playing cards, and waiting for dinner. "Push right ahead," Jackson said, and his weary but excited corps swooped down on the federals and drove their right wing back in confusion. The Union forces left Chancellorsville the next day defeated. Although Stonewall Jackson had been fatally wounded, it was a remarkable southern victory.

But two critical battles in July 1863 brought crushing defeat for the Confederacy and a turning point for the war. After finding an advantageous approach to Vicksburg, General Ulysses S. Grant laid siege to that vital western fortification. If Vicksburg fell, United States forces would control the Mississippi, cutting the Confederacy in half and gaining an open path into its interior. Meanwhile, Lee proposed a Confederate invasion of the North. Both movements drew toward conclusion early in July.

In the North, Lee's troops streamed through western Maryland and into Pennsylvania, threatening both Washington and Baltimore. The possibility of a major victory near the Union capital became more and more likely. But along the Mississippi, Confederate prospects darkened. Davis and Secretary of War Seddon repeatedly wired General Joseph E. Johnston to concentrate his forces and attack Grant's army. "Vicksburg must not be lost, at least without a struggle," they insisted. Despite the prodding of his superiors, Johnston did nothing to relieve the garrison. In the meantime, Grant's men were supplying themselves by drawing on the agricultural riches of the Mississippi River valley. With such provisions, they could continue their siege indefinitely. In these circumstances, the fall of Vicksburg was inevitable, and on July 4, 1863, its commander surrendered.

On the same day, a battle that had been raging since July 1 concluded at Gettysburg, Pennsylvania. On July 1 and 2, Union and Confederate forces had both made gains in furi- **Battle of** ous fighting. Then on July 3, Lee **Gettysburg** ordered a direct assault on Union fortifications atop Cemetery Ridge. Full of foreboding, General James Longstreet warned Lee that "no 15,000 men ever arrayed for battle can take that position." But Lee, hoping success might force the Union to accept peace with independence, stuck to his plan. His brave troops rushed the position, and a hundred momentarily breached the enemy's line. But most fell in heavy slaughter. On July 4, Lee had to withdraw, having suffered tremendous casualties in his troops: almost 4,000 killed and approximately 24,000 missing and wounded.

Although southern soldiers displayed a courage and dedication at Gettysburg that would never be forgotten, the results were disastrous. Intelligent southerners knew that defeat lay ahead. The defeats of July 1863 also quickened the pace of the Confederacy's internal disintegration. Southern leaders began to realize that they were losing the support of the common people. Moreover, a few newspapers and politicians began to call for peace negotiations.

By 1864, much of the opposition to the war had moved entirely outside politics. Southerners were simply giving up the struggle, withdrawing their cooperation from the government. Deserters joined with ordinary citizens who were sick of the war to dominate whole towns. Secret societies dedicated to reunion sprang up. Active dissent spread through the South but was particularly common in upland and mountain regions. The government was losing the support of its citizens.

Antiwar Sentiment in the North

In the North, opposition to the war was similar in many ways, but not as severe. There was concern over the growing centralization of government, and war-weariness was a frequent complaint. Discrimination and injustice in the draft sparked protest among poor citizens, just as they did in the South. But the Union was so much richer than the South in human resources that none of these problems ever threatened the stability of the government. Fresh recruits were always available, and food and other necessities were not subject to severe shortages.

Furthermore, Lincoln possessed a talent that Davis lacked: he knew how to stay in touch with the ordinary citizen. Through letters to newspapers and to soldiers' families, he reached the common people and demonstrated that he had not forgotten them. Their grief was also his, for the war was his personal tragedy. His words helped to contain northern discontent but could not remove it.

Much of the wartime protest sprang from politics. The Democratic party was determined to regain power. Party leaders attacked the war, the expansion of federal powers, inflation and the high tariff, and the improved status of blacks. They also denounced conscription and martial law and defended states' rights and the in-

Peace Democrats

terests of agriculture. In the 1862 congressional elections, the Democrats made a strong comeback, and during the war, peace Democrats influenced New York State and won majorities in the legislatures of Illinois and Indiana.

Led by outspoken men like Clement L. Vallandigham of Ohio, the peace Democrats were highly visible. Vallandigham criticized Lincoln as a dictator who had suspended the writ of habeas corpus without congressional authority and arrested thousands of innocent citizens. Vallandigham stayed within legal bounds, but his attacks were so damaging to the war effort that military authorities arrested him. Fearing that Vallandigham might seem a martyr, the president decided against a jail term and exiled him to the Confederacy.

Lincoln believed that antiwar Democrats were linked to secret organizations that harbored traitorous ideas. Likening such groups to a poisonous snake striking at the government, Republicans sometimes branded them—and by extension the peace Democrats—as Copperheads. Though Democrats were connected with these organizations, most engaged in politics rather than treason.

More violent opposition to the government came from ordinary citizens facing the draft, especially the urban poor, who were inducted in disproportionate numbers. Enrolling officers received rough treatment in many parts of the North, and riots occurred in Ohio, Indiana, Pennsylvania, Illinois, and Wisconsin, and in such cities as Troy, Albany, and Newark. By far the most serious outbreak of violence occurred in New York City, in July 1863, where three days of rioting left seventy-four people dead. The riots had racist and class overtones. Many working-class whites feared an influx of black labor from the South, and Irish immigrants resented being forced to serve in the place of others.

New York City Draft Riot

Once inducted, northern soldiers felt many of the same anxieties and grievances as their southern counterparts. Federal troops, too, had to cope with loneliness and concern for their loved ones, disease, and the tedium of camp life. Thousands of men slipped away from authorities. Given the problems plaguing the draft and the discouragement in the North over lack of progress in the war, it is not surprising that the Union Army struggled with a desertion rate as high as that of the Confederates.

Discouragement and war-weariness neared their peak during the summer of 1864. At that point, the Democratic party nominated the popular General George B. McClellan for president and put a qualified peace plank into its platform. Lincoln concluded that it was "exceedingly probable that this Administration will not be re-elected." The fortunes of war, however, soon changed the electoral situation.

Northern Pressure and Southern Will

The year 1864 brought to fruition the North's long-term diplomatic strategy. From the outset, the North's paramount diplomatic goal had been to

Northern Diplomatic Strategy

prevent recognition of the Confederacy by European nations and the military and economic aid it would bring. Confederate leaders, believing that England was dependent on southern cotton, hoped to secure recognition through "King Cotton" diplomacy. Because British cotton mills had a 50-percent cotton surplus when the war began and because England developed new sources for cotton during the war, the South's strategy failed. The British government watched the battlefield and refused to be stampeded into acknowledging the Confederacy. France, though sympathetic to the South, was unwilling to act without the British.

More than once, the Union strategy nearly broke down. A major crisis occurred in 1861, when the overzealous commander of an American frigate stopped the British steamer *Trent* and abducted two Confederate ambassadors. The British reacted strongly, but Lincoln and Seward were able to delay any action until public opinion cooled and they could back down and return the ambassadors. In a series of confrontations, the United States protested against the building and sale of warships to the Confederacy. A few ships built in Britain, notably the *Alabama*, reached open water to serve the Confederacy. In less than two years, the *Alabama* destroyed or captured more than sixty northern ships. But soon the British government began to bar delivery to the Confederacy of warships such as the Laird rams—formidable vessels whose pointed prows were designed to break the Union blockade.

Back on American battlefields, the northern victory was far from won. Most engagements had demonstrated the advantages enjoyed by the defense. As General William Tecumseh Sherman recognized, the North had to "keep the war South until they are not only ruined, exhausted, but humbled in pride and spirit." Yet military authorities agreed that deep invasion was extremely difficult. The farther an army penetrated enemy territory, the more vulnerable its own communications and support became. Moreover, noted the Prussian expert Karl von Clausewitz, if the invader encountered a "truly national" resistance, his troops would be "everywhere exposed to attacks by an insurgent population."

General Grant decided to test these obstacles—and southern will—with an innovation of his own: the strategy of raids. Raids were nothing new, but what Grant had in mind were raids on a massive scale. He proposed to use whole armies, not just cavalry. Federal armies, abandoning their lines of support, would live off the land while they laid waste all resources useful to the Confederacy. After General George H. Thomas's troops won the Battle of Chattanooga in November 1863, the heartland of the South lay open. Moving to Virginia, Grant entrusted General Sherman with a hundred thousand men for a raid deep into the South, toward Atlanta.

Jefferson Davis countered by placing the army of General Johnston in Sherman's path. Davis's political strategy depended on the demonstration of military strength and a successful defense of Atlanta. With the federal elections of 1864 approaching, Davis hoped that a display of strength and resolution by the South would defeat Lincoln and elect a president who would sue for peace.

When Johnston slowly but steadily fell back toward Atlanta, Davis pressed his commander for assurances that Atlanta would be held. From a purely military point of view, Johnston was conducting the defense skillfully, but Davis replaced him with the one-legged General John Hood. Hood attacked but was beaten, and Sherman's army occupied Atlanta on September 2, 1864. The victory buoyed northern spirits, assured Lincoln's re-election, and cleared the way for Sherman's march from Atlanta to the sea.

As he moved across Georgia, Sherman cut a path fifty to sixty miles wide. A Georgia woman described the "Burnt Country" this way: "The fields were trampled down and the road was lined with carcasses of horses, hogs, and cattle that the invaders, unable either to consume or to carry with them, had wantonly shot down to starve our people and prevent them from making their crops. The stench in some places was unbearable." Such devastation diminished the South's material resources. More important, it was bound to damage further the faltering southern will to resist.

In Virginia, the preliminaries to victory proved to be protracted and ghastly. Throughout the spring and summer of 1864, Grant hurled his troops at Lee's army and suffered appalling

Heavy Losses Force Lee's Surrender losses: almost 18,000 casualties in the Battle of the Wilderness, more than 8,000 at Spotsylvania, and 12,000 in the space of a few hours at Cold Harbor (see map). Before the last battle, Union troops pinned scraps of paper bearing their names and addresses to their backs, certain that they would be mowed down as they rushed Lee's trenches. In four weeks in May and June, Grant lost as many men as were enrolled in Lee's entire army. Although costly, Grant's strategy prepared the way for eventual victory. Lee's army shrank until offensive action was no longer possible, while at the same time the Union Army kept replenishing its forces with new recruits.

The end finally came in the spring of 1865. Grant kept battering at Lee, who tried but failed to break through the federal line east of Petersburg on March 25. With the numerical superiority of Grant's army now upward of two to one, Confederate defeat was inevitable. On April 2, Lee abandoned Richmond and Petersburg. On April 9, hemmed in by federal troops, short of rations, and with fewer than thirty thousand men left, Lee surrendered to Grant. At Appomattox Courthouse, the Union general treated his rival with respect and paroled the

The War in Virginia, 1864–1865

defeated troops. Within weeks, Jefferson Davis was captured, and the remaining Confederate forces laid down their arms and surrendered. The war was over at last.

Lincoln did not live to see the last surrenders. On the evening of Good Friday, April 14, he went to Ford's Theatre in Washington, where an assassin named John Wilkes Booth shot him at pointblank range. Lincoln died the next day. The Union lost its wartime leader. For many, relief at the war's end was tempered by uncertainty about the future.

Costs and Effects

The costs of the Civil War were enormous. The total number of casualties exceeded 1 million—a frightful toll for a nation of 31 million. Approximately 364,222 federal soldiers died,

Casualties 140,070 of them from wounds suffered in battle. Another 275,175 Union soldiers were wounded but survived. On the Confederate side, an estimated 258,000 lost their lives, and almost as many suffered wounds. More men died in the Civil War than in all the other American wars combined, before Vietnam.

Although precise figures on enlistments are impossible to obtain, it appears that the Confederate armies claimed the services of 700,000 to 800,000 men. Far more, possibly 2.3 million, served in the Union armies. All these men were taken from home, family, and personal goals and had their lives disrupted in ways that, for those who survived the war, were not easily repaired.

Property damage and financial costs were also enormous, though difficult to tally. Federal loans and taxes during the conflict totaled almost $3 billion, and interest on the war debt was $2.8 billion. The Confederacy borrowed more than $2 billion but lost far more in the destruction of homes, fences, crops, livestock, and other property. Scholars have noted that small farmers lost just as much, proportionally, as planters whose slaves were emancipated.

Financial Cost of the War

Estimates of the total cost of the war exceed $20 billion—five times the total expenditure of the federal government from its creation to 1861. The northern government increased its spending by a factor of seven in the first full year of the war; by the last year, its spending had soared to twenty times the prewar level. By 1865, the federal government accounted for more than 26 percent of the gross national product.

These changes were more or less permanent. In the 1880s, interest on the war debt still accounted for approximately 40 percent of the federal budget and Union soldiers' pensions for as much as 20 percent. Thus, although many southerners had hoped to separate government from the economy, the war made such separation impossible. Although federal expenditures shrank after the war, they stabilized at twice the prewar level, or at 4 percent of the gross national product. Wartime emergency measures had brought the banking and transportation systems under federal control, and the government had put its power behind manufacturing and business interests through tariffs, loans,

and subsidies. Industrialization and large organizations arrived to stay, and in political terms, national power increased permanently. Extreme forms of the states' rights controversy were dead, although Americans continued to favor a state-centered federalism.

Despite all these changes, one crucial question remained unanswered: what was the place of black men and women in American life? The Union victory provided a partial answer: slavery as it had existed before the war could not persist. But what would replace it? African-Americans eagerly awaited an answer, which would have to be found during Reconstruction.

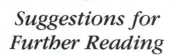

Suggestions for Further Reading

The War and the South

Thomas B. Alexander and Richard E. Beringer, *The Anatomy of the Confederate Congress* (1972); Richard E. Beringer et al., *Why the South Lost the Civil War* (1986); Robert F. Durden, *The Gray and the Black: The Confederate Debate on Emancipation* (1972); Paul D. Escott, *Many Excellent People* (1985); Paul D. Escott, *After Secession: Jefferson Davis and the Failure of Confederate Nationalism* (1978); Paul D. Escott, "'The Cry of the Sufferers': The Problem of Poverty in the Confederacy," *Civil War History*, XXIII (September 1977), 228–240; Eli N. Evans, *Judah P. Benjamin* (1987); J. B. Jones, *A Rebel War Clerk's Diary*, 2 vols., ed. Howard Swiggett (1935); Stanley Lebergott, "Why the South Lost," *Journal of American History*, 70 (June 1983), 58–74; Ella Lonn, *Desertion During the Civil War* (1928); Malcolm C. McMillan, *The Disintegration of a Confederate State* (1986); Larry E. Nelson, *Bullets, Ballots, and Rhetoric: Confederate Policy for the United States Presidential Contest of 1864* (1980); Harry P. Owens and James J. Cooke, eds., *The Old South in the Crucible of War* (1983); Charles W. Ramsdell, *Behind the Lines in the Southern Confederacy*, ed. Wendell H. Stephenson (1944); James L. Roark, *Masters Without Slaves* (1977); Emory M. Thomas, *The Confederate Nation* (1979); Emory M. Thomas, *The Confederacy as a Revolutionary Experience* (1971); Emory M. Thomas, *The Confederate State of Richmond* (1971); William A. Tidwell, *Come Retribution: The Confederate Secret Service and the Assassination of Lincoln* (1989); Bell Irvin Wiley, *The Life of Johnny Reb* (1943); Bell Irvin Wiley, *The Plain People of the Confederacy* (1943); W. Buck Yearns, ed., *The Confederate Governors* (1985).

The War and the North

Ralph Andreano, ed., *The Economic Impact of the American Civil War* (1962); Robert Cruden, *The War That Never Ended* (1973); Wood Gray, *The Hidden Civil War* (1942); Randall C. Jimerson, *The Private Civil War* (1988); Frank L. Klement, *The Copperheads in the Middle West* (1960); Susan Previant Lee and Peter Passell, *A New Economic View of American History* (1979); James M. McPherson, *Battle Cry of Freedom* (1988); Phillip S. Paludan, *"A People's Contest": The Union and the Civil War, 1861–1865* (1989); George Winston Smith and Charles Burnet Judah, *Life in the North During the Civil War* (1966); George Templeton Strong, *Diary,* 4 vols., ed. Allan Nevins and Milton Hasley Thomas (1952); Paul Studenski, *Financial History of the United States* (1952); Bell Irvin Wiley, *The Life of Billy Yank* (1952).

Women

John R. Brumgardt, ed., *Civil War Nurse: The Diary and Letters of Hannah Ropes* (1980); Beth Gilbert Crabtree and James W. Patton, eds., *"Journal of a Secesh Lady": The Diary of Catherine Ann Devereux Edmondston, 1860–1866* (1979); Jacqueline Jones, *Labor of Love, Labor of Sorrow* (1985); George C. Rable, *Civil Wars: Women and the Crisis of Southern Nationalism* (1989); C. Vann Woodward and Elisabeth Muhlenfeld, ed., *Mary Chesnut's Civil War* (1981).

Blacks

Ira Berlin, ed., *Freedom,* Series II, *The Black Military Experience* (1982); David W. Blight, *Frederick Douglass' Civil War* (1989); Dudley Cornish, *The Sable Arm* (1956); Barbara Jeanne Fields, *Slavery and Freedom on the Middle Ground* (1985); James M. McPherson, *The Negro's Civil War* (1965); James M. McPherson, *The Struggle for Equality* (1964); Clarence L. Mohr, *On the Threshold of Freedom* (1986); Benjamin Quarles, *The Negro in the Civil War* (1953).

Military History

Bern Anderson, *By Sea and by River* (1962); Nancy Scott Anderson and Dwight Anderson, *The Generals* (1987); Bruce Catton, *Grant Takes Command* (1969); Thomas L. Connelly and Archer Jones, *The Politics of Command* (1973); Benjamin Franklin Cooling, *Forts Henry and Donelson* (1988); Burke Davis, *Sherman's March* (1980); William C. Davis, ed., *The Image of War,* multivolume (1983–1985); Shelby Foote, *The Civil War, a Narrative,* 3 vols. (1958–1974); William A. Frassanito, *Grant and Lee: The Virginia Campaigns, 1864–1865* (1983); Douglas Southall Freeman, *R. E. Lee,* 4 vols. (1934–1935); Herman Hattaway and Archer Jones, *How the North Won* (1983); Lawrence Lee Hewitt, *Port Hudson, Confederate Bastion on the Mississippi* (1988);

Archer Jones, *Confederate Strategy from Shiloh to Vicksburg* (1961); Gerald F. Linderman, *Embattled Courage* (1989); James Lee McDonough, *Chattanooga* (1984); Grady McWhiney and Perry D. Jamieson, *Attack and Die* (1982); J. B. Mitchell, *Decisive Battles of the Civil War* (1955); Reid Mitchell, *Civil War Soldiers* (1988); Harry W. Pfanze, *Gettysburg: The Second Day* (1988); Robert Garth Scott, *Into the Wilderness with the Army of the Potomac* (1987); Stephen W. Sears, *George B. McClellan* (1988); Stephen Z. Starr, *The Union Cavalry in the Civil War,* 3 vols. (1985); Emory M. Thomas, *Bold Dragoon: The Life of J.E.B. Stuart* (1987).

Diplomatic History

Stuart L. Bernath, *Squall Across the Atlantic* (1970); David P. Crook, *The North, the South, and the Powers, 1861–1865* (1974); Charles P. Cullop, *Confederate Propaganda in Europe* (1969); Frank J. Merli, *Great Britain and the Confederate Navy* (1970); Frank L. Owsley and Harriet Owsley, *King Cotton Diplomacy* (1959); Gordon H. Warren, *Fountain of Discontent* (1981).

Abraham Lincoln and the Union Government

Gabor S. Borit, ed., *The Historian's Lincoln* (1989); LaWanda Cox, *Lincoln and Black Freedom* (1981); Richard N. Current, *The Lincoln Nobody Knows* (1958); David Donald, *Charles Sumner and the Rights of Man* (1970); Ludwell H. Johnson, "Lincoln's Solution to the Problem of Peace Terms, 1864–1865," *Journal of Southern History,* XXXIV (November 1968), 441–447; Peyton McCrary, *Abraham Lincoln and Reconstruction: The Louisiana Experiment* (1978); Stephen B. Oates, *With Malice Toward None* (1977); James G. Randall, *Mr. Lincoln* (1957); Benjamin P. Thomas, *Abraham Lincoln* (1952); Hans L. Trefousse, *The Radical Republicans* (1969); Glyndon G. Van Deusen, *William Henry Seward* (1967); T. Harry Williams, *Lincoln and His Generals* (1952); T. Harry Williams, *Lincoln and the Radicals* (1941).

Saturday, May 16, was a beautiful spring day in 1868. Sunlight and balmy weather bathed the nation's capital. As the morning passed, a crowd gathered in the Senate chamber. Foreign dignitaries filled the diplomatic box, and spectators packed the Senate galleries. Outside the chamber, thousands milled about.

Precisely at noon, the chief justice of the United States entered the Senate. All principals in this solemn drama were present before the High Court of Impeachment except the accused: Andrew Johnson, president of the United States. Johnson, who never appeared to defend himself in person, waited at the White House as Chief Justice Salmon Chase ordered the calling of the roll. To each senator, he put the questions, "How say you? Is the respondent, Andrew Johnson, President of the United States, guilty or not guilty of a high misdemeanor, as charged in this article?" Thirty-five senators answered, "Guilty"; nineteen, "Not guilty." The thirty-five votes for conviction were one short of the required two-thirds majority. The United States had come within one vote of removing the president from office.

How had this extraordinary event come about? What had brought the executive and legislative branches of government into such severe conflict? An unprecedented

15

RECONSTRUCTION BY TRIAL AND ERROR, 1865–1877

problem, the reconstruction of the Union, furnished the occasion; deepening differences over the proper policy to pursue had led to the confrontation.

In 1865, at the end of the war, such an event seemed most unlikely. Although he was a southerner from Tennessee, Johnson had built his career on criticizing the wealthy planters and championing the South's small farmers. When an assassin's bullet thrust him into the presidency, many former slaveowners believed that they had reason to fear Johnson. In the North, the Radicals felt confident that he would deal sternly with the South. When one of them suggested the exile or execution of ten or twelve leading rebels to set an example, Johnson had replied, "How are you going to pick out so small a number? Robbery is a crime; rape is a crime; treason is a crime; and crime must be punished."

Moreover, fundamental change was already under way in the South. During his army's last campaign, General William T. Sherman had issued

Special Field Order No. 15, which set aside for Negro settlement the Sea Islands and all abandoned coastal lands thirty miles to the interior, from Charleston to the Saint John's River in northern Florida. Black refugees quickly poured into these lands; by the middle of 1865, forty thousand freed people were living in their new homes.

Before the year ended, however, these signs of change were reversed. Although Jefferson Davis was imprisoned for two years, no Confederate leaders were executed, and southern aristocrats soon came to view Andrew Johnson as their friend and protector. Johnson pardoned rebel leaders liberally, allowed them to take high offices, and ordered government officials to reclaim the freedmen's land and give it back to the original owners.

The unexpected outcome of Johnson's program led Congress to examine his policies and design new plans for Reconstruction. Out of negotiations in Congress and clashes between the president and the legislators, there emerged first one, and then two, new plans for Reconstruction. Before the process was over, the nation had adopted the Fourteenth and Fifteenth Amendments and impeached its president.

Blacks benefited from having greater control over their personal lives and took the risks of voting and participating in politics. But they knew that the success of Reconstruction also depended on the determination and support of the North. Southern opposition to Reconstruction grew steadily. Most frightful was a secret terrorist organization, the Ku Klux Klan. By the early 1870s, the failure of Reconstruction was apparent. Republican leaders and northern voters had to decide how far they would persist in their efforts to reform the South.

Thus the nation stumbled, by trial and error, toward a policy that attempted to reconstruct the South. Congress insisted on equality before the law for black people and gave black men the right to vote. It took the unprecedented step of impeaching the president. But more far-reaching measures to advance black freedom never had much support in Congress, and when suffrage alone proved insufficient to remake the South, the nation soon lost interest. Reconstruction proclaimed anew the American principle of human equality but failed to secure it in reality.

Equality: The Unresolved Issue

For America's former slaves, Reconstruction had one paramount meaning: a chance to explore freedom. A southern white woman admitted in her diary that the black people "showed a natural and exultant joy at being free." The slaves on one Texas plantation jumped up and down and clapped their hands as one man shouted, "We is free—no more whippings and beatings!" A few blacks gave in to the natural desire to do what had been impossible before. One grandmother who had long resented her treatment "dropped her hoe" and ran to confront the mistress. "I'm free!" she yelled at her. "Yes, I'm free! Ain't got to work for you no more!" Others left the plantation, either to search for family members or just to exercise their new-found freedom of movement.

Most freedmen reacted more cautiously and shrewdly, taking care to test the boundaries of their new condition. One sign of this shrewd caution was the way freedmen evaluated potential employers. If a white person had been relatively considerate to blacks in bondage, blacks reasoned that he might prove a desirable employer in freedom. Other blacks left their plantation all at once, for, as one put it, "that master am sure mean."

In addition to a fair employer, the freedmen wanted land of their own. Land represented their chance to farm for themselves and to have an independent life. It represented compensation for their generations of travail in bondage. A northern observer noted that freedmen made "plain, straight-forward" inquiries as they settled the land set aside for them by Sherman. They wanted to be sure the land "would be theirs after they had improved it."

Blacks' Desire for Land

No one could say how much of a chance the whites, who were in power, would give to blacks. During the war, the federal government had refused at first to arm black volunteers. Necessity forced a change in policy; because the war was going badly, the administration authorized black

1865	Johnson begins Reconstruction; Confederate leaders regain power Black codes; Congress refuses to seat southern representatives	**1870**	Enforcement Act
		1871	Enforcement Act of 1871; Ku Klux Klan Act
1866	Civil Rights Act; Congress approves Fourteenth Amendment Freedmen's Bureau renewed; *Ex parte Milligan* Most southern states reject Fourteenth Amendment	**1872**	Amnesty Act; Liberal Republicans organize Debtors urge government to keep greenbacks in circulation Grant re-elected
		1873	*Slaughter-House* cases; Panic of 1873
1867	Military Reconstruction Act; Tenure of Office Act Constitutional conventions called in southern states	**1875**	Civil Rights Act Congress requires that after 1878 greenbacks be convertible into gold
1868	House impeaches Johnson; Senate acquits him Fourteenth Amendment ratified Ulysses S. Grant elected president	**1876**	*United States* v. *Cruikshank; United States* v. *Reese* Presidential election disputed
1869	Congress approves Fifteenth Amendment (ratified in 1870)	**1877**	Congress elects Hayes; Black Exodusters migrate to Kansas

enlistments. By the spring of 1863, black troops were proving their value. "They fight like fiends," said one observer.

Black leaders hoped that military service would secure equal rights for their people. If black soldiers turned the tide, asked one man, "Would the nation refuse us our rights . . . ? Would it refuse us our vote?" Wartime experience suggested that it would. Despite their valor, black soldiers faced persistent discrimination. For example, the government paid white privates $13 per month, plus a clothing allowance of $3.50. Black troops earned $10 per month, less $3 deducted for clothing. Blacks resented this injustice so deeply that in protest two regiments refused to accept any pay, and eventually Congress remedied the discrimination.

The general attitude of northerners on racial questions was mixed. Abolitionists and many Republicans helped black Americans fight for equal rights, and they won some victories. In 1864, the federal courts accepted black testimony, and New York City desegregated its streetcars. One state, Massachusetts, enacted a comprehensive public accommodations law. Nevertheless, there were many signs of resistance to racial equality. The Democratic party fought hard against equality, charging that Republicans favored race mixing and were undermining the status of the white worker. Voters in three states—Connecticut, Minnesota, and Wisconsin—rejected black suffrage in 1865. For African-Americans, the conflicting signals from the North raised a question: how much opportunity would freedom bring? The answer depended on the evolution of policy in Washington.

Johnson's Reconstruction Plan

Through 1865, the formation of Reconstruction policy rested solely with Andrew Johnson, for shortly before he became president, Congress recessed and did not reconvene until December. In the nearly eight months that intervened, Johnson devised his own plan and put it into operation. He decided to form new state governments in the South by using his power to grant pardons.

Johnson had a few precedents to follow. In December 1863, Lincoln had proposed a "10-percent" plan for captured portions of Louisiana; a state gov-

Lincoln's Reconstruction Plan ernment could be established as soon as 10 percent of those who had voted in 1860 took an oath of future loyalty. Only high-ranking Confederate officials would be denied a chance to take the oath. Radicals bristled, however, at such a mild plan, and a majority of Congress (in the Wade-Davis bill, which Lincoln pocket-vetoed) favored stiffer requirements and stronger proof of loyalty. At the time of his death, Lincoln had given general approval to a plan drafted by Secretary of War Edwin M. Stanton, which would have imposed military authority and provisional governors as steps toward new state governments.

Johnson began with the plan Stanton had drafted. Johnson's advisers split evenly on the question of voting rights for freedmen in the South. Johnson said he favored black suffrage, but only if the southern states adopted it voluntarily. A champion of states' rights, he regarded this decision as too important to be taken out of the hands of the states.

Such conservatism had an enduring effect on Johnson's policies, but at first it appeared that his old enmity toward the planters might produce a plan for radical changes in class relations among whites. As he appointed provisional governors in the South, Johnson also proposed rules that would keep the wealthy planter class out of power. He required every southern voter to swear an oath of loyalty as a condition of gaining amnesty or pardon. Some southern whites, however, faced special difficulties in regaining their rights.

Johnson barred certain classes of southerners from taking the oath and gaining amnesty. Former federal officials who had violated their oaths to sup-

Oaths of Amnesty and New State Governments port the United States and had aided the Confederacy could not take the oath. Nor could graduates of West Point or Annapolis who had resigned their commissions to fight for the South. The same was true for high-ranking Confederate officers and Confederate political leaders. Also barred were all southerners who aided the rebellion and whose taxable property was worth more than twenty thousand dollars. Such individuals had to apply personally to the president for pardon and restoration of political rights; otherwise, they risked legal penalties, including confiscation of their land. Thus, it appeared that the leadership class of the Old South would be removed from power and replaced by a new leadership of deserving yeomen.

Johnson's provisional governors began the Reconstruction process by calling constitutional conventions. The delegates chosen for these conventions had to draft new constitutions eliminating slavery and invalidating secession. After ratification of these constitutions, new governments could be elected, and the states would be restored to the Union with full congressional representation. But no southerners could participate in this process who had not taken the oath of amnesty or who had been ineligible to vote on the day the state seceded. Freedmen, being in the latter category, could not participate in the conventions.

But the plan did not work as Johnson had envisioned. Surprisingly, Johnson played a role in its subversion. He pardoned many aristocrats and chief rebels. By the time the southern states drafted their constitutions and elected public officials, Confederate leaders were in powerful positions. Johnson decided to stand behind his new governments and declare Reconstruction completed. Thus, in December 1865, many Confederate congressmen traveled to Washington to claim seats in the United States Congress, and Alexander Stephens, vice president of the Confederacy, returned to the capital as senator-elect.

Many northerners frowned on the election of such prominent rebels, and other results of Johnson's program also sparked negative comment in

Blacks Codes the North. Some of the state conventions were slow to repudiate secession; others only grudgingly admitted that slavery was dead. Of great concern to northern politicians was the enactment of the black codes. In these laws, southern state legislatures defined the status of freedmen. Some legislatures merely revised sections of the slave codes by substituting the word *freedman* for *slave*. Typical codes compelled African-Americans to carry passes and to observe a curfew. In some cases, restrictions kept blacks out of many desirable occupations and forced them to live in housing provided by a landowner. There were also vagrancy laws, and restrictive labor contracts bound supposedly free laborers to the plantation. Finally, states often denied blacks access to public institutions such as schools and orphanages.

Thus, it was not surprising that northern congressmen decided to take a close look at the results of Johnson's plan. On reconvening, they voted not to admit the newly elected southern representatives, whose credentials were subject, under the Constitution, to congressional scrutiny. The House and Senate established an important joint committee to examine Johnson's policies and advise on new ones. Reconstruction entered a second phase, one in which Congress would play a strong role.

The Congressional Reconstruction Plan

Northern congressmen disagreed on what to do, but they did not doubt their right to play a role in Reconstruction. The Constitution mentioned neither secession nor reunion, but it did assign to Congress the duty to guarantee to each state a republican government. Under this provision, the legislators thought, they could devise policies for Reconstruction.

They soon found that other constitutional questions had a direct bearing on the policies they followed. What, for example, had rebellion done to the relationship between southern states and the Union? Lincoln had always insisted that the Union remained unbroken. In contrast, congressmen who favored vigorous Reconstruction measures tended to argue that war *had* broken the Union. The southern states had committed legal suicide and reverted to the status of territories, they argued, or the South was a conquered nation subject to the victor's will. Moderate congressmen held that the states had forfeited their rights through rebellion and had thus come under congressional supervision.

These diverse theories mirrored the diversity of Congress itself. Northern legislators fell into four major categories: Democrats, conservative Republicans, moderate Republicans, and **The Radicals** other Republicans called Radicals. Although the Republican party had a majority, there was considerable distance between conservative Republicans, who desired a limited federal role in Reconstruction and were fairly happy with Johnson's actions, and the Radicals. The Radicals, led by Thaddeus Stevens, Charles Sumner, and George Julian believed that it was essential to democratize the South, establish public education, and ensure the rights of freedmen. They favored black suffrage, often supported land confiscation and redistribution, and were willing to exclude the South from the Union for several years, if necessary, to achieve their goals. Between the conservative Republicans and the Radicals lay the moderates, who held the balance of power.

Through their actions, Johnson and the Democrats forced these diverse Republican factions to come together. The president and the northern Democrats, insisting that Reconstruction was over and that the southern delegates should be seated in Congress, refused to cooperate with conservative or moderate Republicans. Moreover, Johnson refused to support an apparent compromise on Reconstruction. Under its terms, Johnson would agree to two modifications of his program. The life of the Freedmen's Bureau, which Congress established in March 1865 to feed the hungry, negotiate labor contracts, and start schools, would be extended by one bill; and a civil rights bill would be passed to counteract the black codes. This bill gave federal judges the power to remove from southern courts cases in which blacks were treated unfairly. Its provisions applied to discrimination by private persons, as well as by government officials. As the first major bill to enforce the Thirteenth Amendment's abolition of slavery, it was a significant piece of legislation.

But in the spring of 1866, Johnson destroyed the compromise by vetoing both bills (they were later repassed) and condemning Congress's action. In doing so, he questioned the legitimacy of congressional involvement in policymaking. All hope of working with the president was now gone. Instead of a compromise program, the various Republican factions drew up a new Reconstruction plan. It took the form of a proposed amendment to the Constitution—the fourteenth—and it represented a compromise between radical and conservative elements of the party.

Of the four points in the amendment, the fourth won nearly universal agreement: the Confederate debt was declared null and void and the war debt of the United States guaranteed. The **Fourteenth Amendment** third section, prohibiting prominent Confederates from holding any national or state political office, also gained fairly general support. Only by a two-thirds vote of each house of Congress could these political penalties be removed.

The section of the Fourteenth Amendment that would have by far the greatest legal significance in later years was the first. On its face, this section was an effort to strike down the black codes and guarantee basic rights to freedmen. It conferred citizenship on freedmen and prohibited states from abridging their constitutional "privileges and immunities." Similarly, the amendment barred any state from taking a person's life, liberty, or property "without due process of law" and from denying "equal protection of the laws." These clauses were phrased broadly enough to become in time powerful guarantees of black Americans' civil rights.

The second section of the amendment revealed the political motives that had produced the document. Northerners, in Congress and out, disagreed about whether black citizens should have the right to vote. What was more, Republicans feared that emancipation, which made every former slave five-fifths of a person instead of three-fifths for purposes of congressional representation, might increase the South's power in Congress. If it did, and if blacks were not allowed to vote, the former secessionists would gain seats in Congress.

Most northerners had never planned to reward the South for rebellion, and Republicans in Congress were determined not to hand over power to their political enemies. So they offered the South a choice. According to the second section of the Fourteenth Amendment, states did not have to give black men the right to vote. But if they did not do so, their representation would be reduced proportionally. If they did enfranchise black men, their representation would be increased proportionally—but Republicans would be able to appeal to the new black voters.

Although the Fourteenth Amendment dealt with the voting rights of black men, it ignored female citizens. When legislators defined them as nonvoting citizens, prominent women's leaders such as Elizabeth Cady Stanton and Susan B. Anthony decided that it was time to end their alliance with abolitionists. Thus the independent women's rights movement grew.

In 1866, however, the major question in Reconstruction politics was how the public would respond to the amendment. Would the northern public support Congress's plan or **Southern Rejection of the Fourteenth Amendment** the president's? Johnson did his best to block the Fourteenth Amendment and to convince northerners to reject it. Condemning Congress for its refusal to seat southern representatives, the president urged state legislatures in the South to vote against ratification. Every southern legislature except Tennessee's rejected the amendment by a large margin. In the North, Johnson arranged a National Union convention to publicize his program. Then he boarded a special train for a "swing around the circle" that carried his message far into the Midwest. But increasingly, audiences rejected his views and jeered at him.

The election of 1866 was a resounding victory for Republicans in Congress. Men whom Johnson had denounced won re-election by large margins, and the Republican majority increased. Radical and moderate Republicans gained strength. Thus, Republican congressional leaders received a mandate to continue with their Reconstruction plan.

Recognizing that nothing could be accomplished under the existing southern governments and with blacks excluded from the electorate, Congress, in 1867, passed the Military Reconstruction Act.

Military Reconstruction Act of 1867 The act called for new governments in the South and a return to military authority until they were set up. It barred from political office the Confederate leaders listed in the Fourteenth Amendment. It guaranteed freedmen the right to vote in elections for state constitutional conventions and for subsequent state governments. In addition, each southern state was required to ratify the Fourteenth Amendment; to ratify its new constitution; and to submit its new constitution to Congress for approval. Thus, black people gained an opportunity to fight for a better life through the political process, but their only weapon was the ballot. The law required no redistribution of land and guaranteed no basic changes in southern social structure.

Congress's role as the architect of Reconstruction was not quite over. To restrict Johnson's influence and safeguard its plan, Congress enacted a number of controversial laws. First, it set the date for its own reconvening—an unprecedented act, for the president traditionally summoned the legislature to Washington. Then, it limited Johnson's power over the army by requiring the president to issue military orders through the General of the Army, Ulysses S. Grant, who could not be sent from Washington without the Senate's consent. Finally, Congress passed the Tenure of Office Act, which gave the Senate power to interfere with changes in the president's cabinet. Designed to protect Secretary of War Stanton, who sympathized with the Radicals, this law violated the tradition that a president controlled his own cabinet.

Johnson took several belligerent steps of his own. He issued orders to military commanders in the South limiting their powers and increasing the powers of the civil governments he had created in 1865. He also removed any officers who conscientiously enforced Congress's new law. Finally, in August 1867, he tried to remove Stanton. With that attempt, the confrontation reached its climax.

The House Judiciary Committee, which had twice before considered impeaching the president, again initiated the action. The 1868 indictment concentrated on Johnson's violation of **Impeachment of President Johnson** the Tenure of Office Act. Modern scholars, however, regard his systematic efforts to impede enforcement of the Military Reconstruction Act as a far more serious offense.

Johnson's trial in the Senate lasted more than three months. The prosecution, led by Radical Thaddeus Stevens and others, argued that Johnson was guilty of "high crimes and misdemeanors." But they also advanced the novel idea that impeachment was a political matter, not a judicial trial of guilt or innocence. The Senate ultimately rejected such reasoning, which would have transformed impeachment into a political weapon against any chief executive who disagreed with Congress. Although a majority of senators voted to convict Johnson, the prosecution fell one vote short of the necessary two-thirds majority. Johnson remained in office for the few months left in his term, and his acquittal established the precedent that only serious misdeeds merited removal from office.

In 1869, in an effort to write democratic principles and colorblindness into the Constitution, the Radicals presented the Fifteenth Amendment for ratification. This measure forbade **Fifteenth Amendment** states to deny the right to vote "on account of race, color, or previous condition of servitude." The wording fell short of an outright guarantee of the right to vote because many northern states denied the suffrage to women and to men who were illiterate or too poor to pay taxes. Ironically, the votes of four southern states—compelled by Congress to approve the amendment as an added condition to rejoining the Union—proved necessary to impose even this language on parts of the North. Although several states outside the South refused to ratify, the Fifteenth Amendment became law in 1870.

Reconstruction Politics in the South

From the start, white southerners resisted Reconstruction. Their opposition to change appeared in the black codes and other policies of the Johnson governments, as well as in private **White Resistance** attitudes. Many whites set their faces against emancipation, and the former planter class proved especially unbending. In 1866, a Georgia newspaper frankly declared, "Most of the white citizens believe that the institution of slavery was right, and . . . they will believe that the condition, which comes nearest to slavery, that can now be established will be the best."

Fearing the end of their control over slaves, some planters attempted to postpone freedom by denying or misrepresenting events. Former slaves reported that their owners "didn't tell them it was freedom" or "wouldn't let [them] go." To hold onto their workers, some landowners claimed control over black children and used guardianship and apprentice laws to bind black families to the plantation. Whites also blocked blacks from acquiring land and used force to keep blacks submissive.

After President Johnson encouraged the South to resist congressional Reconstruction, many white conservatives worked hard to capture the new state governments. Elsewhere, large numbers of whites boycotted the polls in an attempt to defeat Congress's plans. Since the new constitutions had to be approved by a majority of registered voters, registered whites could defeat them by sitting out the elections. This tactic was tried in North Carolina and succeeded in Alabama, forcing Congress to base ratification on a majority of those voting.

Very few black men stayed away from the polls. Enthusiastically, they seized the opportunity to participate in politics, voting solidly Republican. Most agreed with one man who felt that he should "stick to the end with the party that freed me."

With a large black turnout, and with prominent Confederates barred from politics under the Fourteenth Amendment, a new southern Republican party came to power in the constitutional conventions. Among Republican delegates were some blacks, northerners who had moved to the South, and native southern whites who favored change. Together, they brought the South's fundamental law into line with progressive reforms that had been adopted in the rest of the nation. The new constitutions were more democratic. They eliminated property qualifications for voting and holding office, and they made elective the state and local offices that had been appointive. They provided for public schools and institutions to care for the men-

tally ill, the blind, the deaf, the destitute, and the orphaned, and they ended imprisonment for debt.

The conventions also broadened women's rights in possession of property and divorce. Usually, the main goal was not to make women equal with men but to provide relief to thousands of suffering debtors. In families left poverty-stricken by the war, the husband had usually contracted the debts. Thus, giving women legal control over their own property provided some protection to their families. Some delegates, however, wanted to expand women's rights further. Blacks in particular called for laws to provide for women's suffrage, but they were ignored by their white colleagues.

Under these new constitutions, the southern states elected new governments. Again, the Republican party triumphed, bringing new men into positions of power. The ranks of state legislators in 1868 included some black southerners for the first time in history. Congress's second plan for Reconstruction was well under way. It remained to be seen what these new governments would do and how much change they would bring to society.

Triumph of Republican Governments

There was one possibility of radical change through these new governments. That possibility depended on the disfranchisement of substantial numbers of Confederate leaders. If the Republican regimes used their new power to exclude many whites from politics as punishment for rebellion, they would have a solid electoral majority based on black voters and their white allies. Land reform and the assurance of racial equality would be possible. But none of the Republican governments even gave this serious consideration.

Why did the new legislators shut the door on the possibility of deep and thoroughgoing reform? First, they appreciated the realities of power and the depth of racial enmity. In most states whites were the majority of the population, and former slaveowners controlled the best land and other sources of economic power. James Lynch, a leading black politician from Mississippi, candidly explained why Negroes shunned "the folly of" disfranchisement. Unlike northerners, who "can leave when it becomes too uncomfortable," former slaves "must be in friendly relations with the great body of the whites in the state." Second, blacks believed in the principle of universal suffrage and the Christian goal of reconciliation. Far from being vindictive toward the race that had enslaved them, they treated leading rebels with generosity and appealed to white southerners to adopt a spirit of fairness and cooperation. For these, as well as other reasons, southern Republicans quickly restored the voting rights of former Confederates. Thus, the South's Republican party committed itself to a strategy of winning white support. To put the matter another way, the Republican party condemned itself to defeat if white voters would not cooperate.

But for a time, both Republicans and their opponents, who called themselves Conservatives or Democrats, moved to the center and appealed for support from a broad range of groups. Some propertied whites accepted congressional Reconstruction as a reality and declared that they would try to compete under the new rules. As these Democrats angled for some black votes, Republicans sought to attract more white voters. Both parties found an area of agreement in economic policies.

The Reconstruction governments devoted themselves to stimulating industry. This policy reflected northern ideals, but it also sprang from a growing **Industrialization** southern interest in industrialization. Accordingly, Reconstruction legislatures designed many tempting inducements to investment. Loans, subsidies, and exemptions from taxation for periods of up to ten years helped to bring new industries into the region. The southern railroad system was rebuilt and expanded. Coal and iron mining laid the basis for Birmingham's steel plants, and the number of manufacturing establishments nearly doubled between 1860 and 1880. However, this emphasis on big business interests produced higher state debts and taxes, took money from schools, and multiplied possibilities for corruption.

Policies appealing to black voters never went beyond equality before the law. In fact, the whites who controlled the southern Republican party were reluctant to allow blacks a share of offices **Other Republican Policies** proportionate to their electoral strength. Aware of their weakness and the level of hostility in the South, black leaders did not push

for revolutionary change. They failed to advocate the confiscation and redistribution of land and, with the exception of some urban mulattos, did not press for civil rights. Instead, they led the fight to establish schools in the region. The schools established, however, were segregated, setting the precedent for segregated theaters, trains, and other public accommodations.

Within a few years, as centrists in both parties met with failure, the other side of white reaction to congressional Reconstruction began to dominate. Some conservatives had always favored fierce opposition to Reconstruction through pressure and racist propaganda. Charging that the South had been turned over to ignorant blacks, conservatives deplored "black domination." The cry of "Negro rule" now became constant.

Such attacks were gross distortions. Blacks were a minority in eight out of ten state conventions (transplanted northerners were a minority in nine out of ten). Of the state legislatures, only in the lower house in South Carolina did blacks ever constitute a majority; generally, their numbers among officials were far below their proportion in the population. Sixteen African-Americans won seats in Congress before Reconstruction was over, but none was ever elected governor, and only eighteen served in a high state office such as lieutenant governor, treasurer, superintendent of education, or secretary of state. Thus, blacks participated in politics but did not dominate or control events.

Conservatives also stepped up their propaganda against the allies of black Republicans. *Carpetbagger* was a derisive name for whites who had come **Carpetbaggers and Scalawags** from the North. It suggested an evil and greedy northern politician, recently arrived with a carpetbag, into which he planned to stuff ill-gotten gains before fleeing. There were a few northerners who deserved this unsavory description. But of the thousands of northerners who settled in the postwar South, only a small portion entered politics. Most of them wanted to democratize the South and introduce northern ways, such as industry, public education, and the spirit of enterprise.

Conservatives invented the term *scalawag* to discredit any native white southerner who cooperated with the Republicans. A substantial number of southerners did so, including some wealthy and prominent men. Most scalawags were men from mountain areas and small farming districts—average white southerners who saw that they could benefit from the opportunities promoted by Republicans. Banding together with freedmen, they pursued common class interests and hoped to make headway against the power of long-dominant planters. Yet this black-white coalition was usually vulnerable to the issue of race, and scalawags shied away from support for racial equality.

Taxation was a major problem for the Reconstruction governments. Financially, the Republicans, despite their achievements, were doomed to be unpopular. Republicans wanted to continue prewar services, repair war's destruction, stimulate industry, and support new ventures such as public schools. But the Civil War had destroyed much of the South's tax base. Thus, an increase in taxes was necessary to maintain traditional services, and new ventures required even higher taxes.

Corruption was another powerful charge levied against the Republicans. Unfortunately, it was true. Many carpetbaggers and black politicians sold their votes. Although white Democrats often shared in the guilt and some Republicans strove to stop corruption, Democrats convinced many voters that scandal was the inevitable result of a foolish Reconstruction program based on blacks and carpetbaggers.

All these problems damaged the Republicans, but in many southern states the deathblow came through violence: the murders, whippings, and intimidation by terrorist groups, **Ku Klux Klan** which most often used the name Ku Klux Klan. Terrorism against blacks occurred throughout Reconstruction, but after 1867, white violence became more organized and purposeful. The Ku Klux Klan rode to frustrate Reconstruction and keep the freedmen in subjection. Nighttime visits, whippings, beatings, and murders became common, and in some areas virtually open warfare developed.

Although the Klan persecuted blacks who stood up for their rights as laborers or people, its main purpose was political. Lawless nightriders made active Republicans the target of their attacks. Promi-

nent white Republicans and black leaders were killed in several states. After blacks who worked for a South Carolina scalawag started voting, terrorists visited the plantation and "whipped every nigger man they could lay their hands on." Klansmen also attacked Union League Clubs (Republican organizations that mobilized the black vote) and teachers who were aiding the freedmen.

Klan violence was not spontaneous; certain social forces gave direction to racism. In North Carolina, for example, Alamance and Caswell counties were the sites of the worst Klan violence. They were in the Piedmont, where slim Republican majorities rested on cooperation between black voters and whites of the yeoman class. In a successful effort to restore Democratic control, wealthy and powerful men organized a campaign of terror in the two counties. These men served as Klan leaders at the county and local levels, recruited members, and planned atrocities.

Elsewhere in the South, Klan violence was all too common. At least 10 percent of the black leaders who had been delegates to the constitutional conventions of 1867 and 1868 were attacked, seven fatally. In Eutaw, Alabama, a Klan raid left four dead and fifty-four wounded. South Carolina Klansmen lynched eight blacks at the Union County jail and committed "at least eleven murders and hundreds of whippings" in York County. According to historian Eric Foner, the Klan "made it virtually impossible for Republicans to campaign or vote in large parts of Georgia." Clearly, "violence had a profound effect on Reconstruction politics."

Thus, a combination of difficult fiscal problems, Republican mistakes, racial hostility, and terror brought down the Republican regimes, and in most southern states so-called Radical **Failure of** Reconstruction was over after only **Reconstruc-** a few years. The most lasting fail-**tion** ure of Reconstruction governments, however, was not political but social. The new governments failed to alter the South's social structure or its distribution of wealth and power. Exploited as slaves, freedmen remained vulnerable to exploitation during Reconstruction. Without land of their own, they had to depend on white landowners, who could use their economic power to compromise blacks' political freedom.

Since they were armed only with the ballot, southern blacks had little chance to effect major changes.

The Social and Economic Meaning of Freedom

Black southerners entered upon life after slavery with hope and determination, but they had too much experience with white people to assume that all would be easy. Expecting to meet with hostility, black people tried to gain as much as they could from their new circumstances. Often the most valued changes were personal ones—alterations in location, employer, or surroundings.

One of the first decisions that many made was whether to leave the old plantation or remain. This meant making a judgment about where the chances of liberty and progress would be greatest. Former slaves drew on their experiences in bondage. "Most all the Negroes that had good owners stayed with them," said one man. Not surprisingly, cruel slaveholders usually saw their former chattels walk off en masse.

On new farms or old, the newly freed men and women reached out for valuable things in life that had been denied them. One of these was educa-

Education for Blacks tion. Whatever their age, blacks hungered for knowledge. When they gained freedom, they started schools and filled classrooms both day and night. Young children brought infants to school with them, and adults attended at night or after "the crops were laid by." The federal government and northern reformers assisted this quest for education. In its brief life, the Freedmen's Bureau founded more than four thousand schools, and idealistic men and women from the North established others and staffed them ably.

Blacks and their white allies also realized that higher education was essential. Between 1866 and 1869, the American Missionary Association founded seven colleges, including Fisk and Atlanta universities. The Freedmen's Bureau helped to establish Howard University in Washington, D.C., and northern religious groups supported dozens of seminaries, colleges, and teachers' colleges. By the late 1870s, black churches had joined in the effort, founding numerous colleges despite their smaller financial resources. Although some of the new institutions did not survive, they brought knowledge to those who would educate others and laid a foundation for progress.

Even during Reconstruction, blacks were choosing many highly educated individuals as leaders. Many blacks who won public office in that period came from the prewar elite of free people of color. This group had benefited from its association with wealthy whites, who were often blood relatives. Some planters had given their mulatto children outstanding educations. The two black senators from Mississippi, Blanche K. Bruce and Hiram Revels, for example, were both privileged in their educations. Bruce was the son of a planter, who had provided tutoring on his plantation; Revels was the son of free North Carolina mulattos, who had sent him to Knox College in Illinois. These men and many self-educated former slaves brought experience as artisans, businessmen, lawyers, teachers, and preachers to political office.

While elected officials wrestled with the political tasks of Reconstruction, millions of former slaves concentrated on improving life at home, on their farms, and in their neighborhoods. They devoted themselves to reuniting their families, moving away from the slave quarters, and founding black churches. Given the eventual failure of Reconstruction, the practical gains that blacks made in their daily lives often proved the most enduring.

The search for long-lost family members was awe inspiring. With only shreds of information to guide them, thousands of black people embarked on

Reunification of Black Families odysseys in search of a husband, wife, child, or parent. By relying on the black community for help and information, many succeeded in their quest. Others walked through several states and never found loved ones.

For husbands and wives who had belonged to different masters, freedom meant the opportunity to establish homes together for the first time. It also meant that wives would not be ordered to work in the fields, and that parents finally would be able to raise their children without interference from whites.

Many black people wanted to minimize all contact with whites. To avoid contact with intrusive whites, who were used to supervising and controlling them, blacks abandoned the slave quarters and fanned out into distant corners of the land they worked. Some moved away to build new homes in the woods. Others established small all-black settlements that still can be found today along the backroads of the South.

The other side of this movement away from whites was closer communion within the black community. Freed from the restrictions and regulations of slavery, blacks could build their own institutions as they saw fit. The secret church of slavery now came out into the open. Within a few years, independent black branches of the Methodist and Baptist churches had attracted the great majority of black Christians in the South.

Founding of Black Churches

The desire to gain as much independence as possible carried over into the freedmen's economic arrangements. Since most former slaves lacked money to buy land, they preferred the next best thing—renting the land they worked. But many whites would not consider renting land to blacks; there was strong social pressure against it. Because few blacks had the means to rent a farm, other alternatives had to be tried.

Northerners and officials of the Freedmen's Bureau favored contracts between owners and laborers. To northerners who believed in "free soil, free labor, free men," contracts and wages seemed the key to progress. For a few years, the Freedmen's Bureau helped to draw up and enforce such contracts, but they proved unpopular with both blacks and whites. Owners often filled the contracts with detailed requirements that reminded blacks of their circumscribed lives under slavery. Disputes frequently arose over efficiency, lost time, and other matters. Besides, times were hard, and the failure of Confederate banks had left the South with a shortage of credit facilities.

Black farmers and white landowners therefore turned to a system of sharecropping: black families worked for part of the crop while living on the landowner's property. The landlord or a merchant "furnished" food and supplies, and the sharecropper, landowner, and furnishing merchant all received payment from the crop. Naturally, landowners tried to set the laborers' share at a low level. Typical arrangements left half the crop to the landowner and half to the sharecropper.

Rise of the Share-cropping System

The sharecropping system originated as a desirable compromise. For landowners, it eased problems with cash and credit. Blacks accepted it because it gave them a reasonable amount of freedom from daily supervision. Sharecropping later proved to be a disaster, both for blacks and for the South. Since blacks were living in a discriminatory society, the system placed them at the mercy of unscrupulous owners and merchants, who had many opportunities to cheat them. As for the South, sharecropping led to an overspecialization in cotton just as the worldwide demand for the crop began to grow more slowly.

The End of Reconstruction

The North had never made a total commitment to racial equality, and by the early 1870s, it was evident that even the North's partial commitment was weakening. New issues were capturing people's attention, and soon voters began to look for reconciliation with southern whites. In the South, Democrats won control of one state after another, and they threatened to defeat Republicans in the North as well. Before long, the situation had returned to "normal" in the eyes of southern whites.

The Supreme Court, after first re-establishing its power, took part in the northern retreat from Reconstruction. During the Civil War, the Court had been cautious and reluctant to assert itself. The *Dred Scott* decision had sparked such a violent reaction and the Union's wartime emergency was so great that the Court had refrained from blocking or interfering with government actions.

But in 1866, a similar case, *Ex parte Milligan*, reached the Court through proper channels. Lambdin P. Milligan of Indiana had participated in a plot

Supreme Court Decisions on Reconstruction

to free Confederate prisoners of war and overthrow state governments; for these acts, a military court had sentenced Milligan, a civilian, to death. Milligan challenged the authority of the military tribunal, claiming that he had a right to a civil trial. In sweeping language, the Supreme Court declared that military trials were illegal when civil courts were open and functioning, thus indicating that it intended to reassert itself as a major force in national affairs.

In the 1870s, interpretations by the Supreme Court drastically narrowed the meaning and effectiveness of the Fourteenth Amendment. In 1873, the Court decided *Bradwell* v. *Illinois*, a case in which Myra Bradwell, a female attorney, had been denied the right to practice law in Illinois because of her gender. Pointing to the Fourteenth Amendment, Bradwell's attorneys contended that the state had unconstitutionally abridged her "privileges and immunities" as a citizen. The Supreme Court rejected her claim, alluding to women's traditional role in the home.

The next day, in the *Slaughter-House* cases, the Court made its restrictive reading of the Fourteenth Amendment even clearer. The *Slaughter-House* cases had begun in 1869, when the Louisiana legislature granted one company a monopoly on the slaughtering of livestock in New Orleans. Rival butchers in the city promptly sued. Their attorney, former Supreme Court Justice John A. Campbell, argued that the Fourteenth Amendment had revolutionized the constitutional system by bringing individual rights under federal protection. Campbell thus expressed an original and central goal of the Republican party: to nationalize civil rights and guard them from state interference.

The Court not only rejected Campbell's argument but dealt a stunning blow to both the scope of the Fourteenth Amendment and the hopes of African-Americans. The justices interpreted the "privileges and immunities" of citizens so narrowly that they reduced them almost to trivialities. Although the Fourteenth Amendment clearly protected citizens' rights, the Court declared that state citizenship and national citizenship were separate.

National citizenship involved only such things as the right to travel freely from state to state and to use the navigable waters of the nation, and only these narrow rights were protected by the Fourteenth Amendment. With this interpretation, the words "No state shall make or enforce any law which shall abridge the privileges or immunities of citizens of the United States" disappeared for decades as a meaningful or effective part of the Constitution. The Supreme Court also concluded that the butchers who sued had not been deprived of their rights or property in violation of the "due process" clause of the amendment. Thus, the justices dismissed Campbell's central contention: that the Fourteenth Amendment guaranteed the great basic rights of the Bill of Rights against state action. In so doing, the Court limited severely the amendment's potential for securing and protecting the rights of black citizens.

In 1876, the Court regressed even further by emasculating the enforcement clause of the Fourteenth Amendment and revealing deficiencies inherent in the Fifteenth Amendment. In *United States* v. *Cruikshank*, the Court dealt with Louisiana whites who were indicted for attacking a meeting of blacks and conspiring to deprive them of their rights. The justices ruled that the Fourteenth Amendment did not empower the federal government to redress the misdeeds of private individuals against other citizens; only flagrant discrimination by the states was covered. In *United States* v. *Reese*, the Court noted that the Fifteenth Amendment did not guarantee a citizen's right to vote but merely listed certain impermissible grounds for denying suffrage. Thus, a path lay open for southern states to disfranchise blacks for supposedly nonracial reasons—lack of education, lack of property, or lack of descent from a grandfather qualified to vote before the Military Reconstruction Act. (So-called grandfather clauses became a way of including illiterate whites in the electorate yet excluding blacks, because the grandfathers of most blacks had been slaves before Reconstruction and unable to vote.)

The retreat from Reconstruction continued steadily in politics as well. In 1868, Ulysses S. Grant, running as a Republican, defeated a Democrat, Horatio Seymour, in a presidential campaign that revived sectional divisions. In office, Grant some-

Election of 1868 times called out federal troops to stop violence or enforce acts of Congress, but only when he had to. He hoped to avoid confrontation with the South, to erase the image of dictatorship that his military background summoned up.

In 1870 and 1871, the violent campaigns of the Ku Klux Klan moved Congress to pass two Enforcement Acts and an anti-Klan law. These laws, for the first time, made acts by individuals against the civil and political rights of others a federal offense. They permitted martial law and suspension of the writ of habeas corpus to combat murders, beatings, and threats by the Klan. Federal troops and prosecutors used them with only partial success, for a conspiracy of silence frustrated some prosecutions.

Some conservative but influential Republicans opposed the anti-Klan laws, basing their opposition on the charge that the laws infringed on states' rights. It was striking that some Republicans were echoing an old and standard line of the Democrats. This opposition foreshadowed a more general revolt within Republican ranks in 1872.

Disenchanted with Reconstruction, in 1872 a group calling itself the Liberal Republicans bolted the party and nominated Horace Greeley, the well-**Liberal Republican Revolt** known editor of the *New York Tribune*, for president. The Liberal Republicans were a varied group, including civil service reformers, foes of corruption, and advocates of a lower tariff. They were united by two popular, widespread attitudes: distaste for federal intervention in the South and a desire to let market forces and the "best men" determine events in the South. The Democrats also gave their nomination to Greeley in 1872. The combination was not enough to defeat Grant, but it reinforced his desire to avoid confrontation with white southerners.

The Liberal Republican challenge reflected dissatisfaction with Grant's administration. Corruption within the administration had become widespread, and Grant foolishly defended some culprits. As a result, Grant's popularity and his party's popularity declined. In the 1874 elections, Democrats recaptured the House of Representatives.

Congress's resolve on southern issues weakened steadily. By joint resolution, it had removed the political disabilities of the Fourteenth Amendment from many former Confederates.

Amnesty Act In 1872, it adopted a sweeping Amnesty Act, which pardoned most of the remaining rebels and left only five hundred excluded from political participation. A Civil Rights Act passed in 1875 purported to guarantee black people equal accommodations in public places, such as inns and theaters, but it was weak and contained no effective provisions for enforcement. Moreover, by 1876, the Democrats had regained control of all but three of the southern states (see dates of reestablishment of conservative rule in map).

Meanwhile, new concerns were catching the public's eye. Industrialization had surged forward, hastening change in national life. Only eight years after the war, industrial production had increased by an impressive 75 percent. For the first time, nonagricultural workers outnumbered farmers, and only Britain had a greater industrial output.

Then the Panic of 1873 occurred, throwing 3 million people out of work and focusing attention on economic and monetary problems. The clash between capital and labor became the major issue of the day. Disturbed by the strikes and industrial violence that accompanied the panic, businessmen became increasingly concerned about the defense of property. Debtors and the unemployed sought easy-money policies to spur economic expansion.

The monetary issue aroused strong controversy. Civil War greenbacks had the potential to expand the money supply and lift prices if they were kept in circulation. In 1872, Democratic **Greenbacks Versus Sound Money** farmers and debtors had urged such a policy, but they were overruled by "sound money" men. Now, hard times swelled the ranks of "greenbackers"—voters who favored greenbacks and easy money. In 1874, Congress voted to increase the number of greenbacks in circulation, but Grant vetoed the bill. The next year, Congress passed a law requiring that after 1878 greenbacks be convertible into gold. The law limited the inflationary impact of the greenbacks and aided creditors, not debtors such as hard-pressed farmers.

By 1876, it was obvious to most political observers that the North was no longer willing to pursue

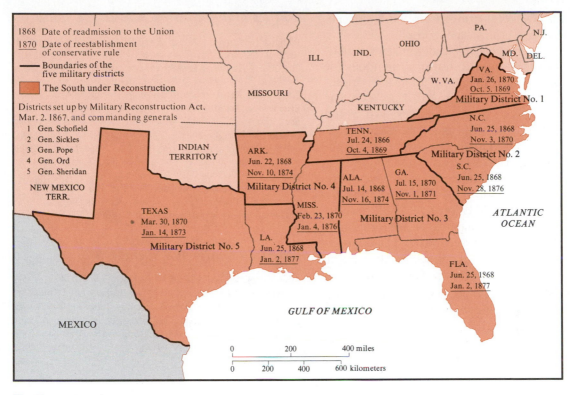

The following map labels appear within the image:

1868 Date of readmission to the Union
1870 Date of reestablishment of conservative rule
— Boundaries of the five military districts
The South under Reconstruction

Districts set up by Military Reconstruction Act, Mar. 2, 1867, and commanding generals
1 Gen. Schofield
2 Gen. Sickles
3 Gen. Pope
4 Gen. Ord
5 Gen. Sheridan

NEW MEXICO TERR.
INDIAN TERRITORY
MEXICO
MISSOURI
ILL.
IND.
OHIO
PA.
N.J.
MD.
DEL.
W. VA.
KENTUCKY

VA.
Jan. 26, 1870
Oct. 5, 1869
Military District No. 1

N.C.
Jun. 25, 1868
Nov. 3, 1870
Military District No. 2

TENN.
Jul. 24, 1866
Oct. 4, 1869

S.C.
Jun. 25, 1868
Nov. 28, 1876

ARK.
Jun. 22, 1868
Nov. 10, 1874
Military District No. 4

ALA.
Jul. 14, 1868
Nov. 16, 1874

GA.
Jul. 15, 1870
Nov. 1, 1871
Military District No. 3

MISS.
Feb. 23, 1870
Jan. 4, 1876

TEXAS
Mar. 30, 1870
Jan. 14, 1873
Military District No. 5

LA.
Jun. 25, 1868
Jan. 2, 1877

FLA.
Jun. 25, 1868
Jan. 2, 1877

ATLANTIC OCEAN
GULF OF MEXICO

0   200   400 miles
0   200   400   600 kilometers

The Reconstruction

the goals of Reconstruction. The results of a dis-

Election of 1876

puted presidential election confirmed this fact. Samuel J. Tilden, Democratic governor of New York, ran strongly in the South and took a commanding lead in both the popular vote and the electoral college over Rutherford B. Hayes, the Republican nominee. Tilden won 184 electoral votes and needed only one more for a majority. Nineteen votes from Louisiana, South Carolina, and Florida were disputed; both Democrats and Republicans claimed to have won in those states, despite fraud on the part of their opponents. One vote from Oregon was undecided due to a technicality.

To resolve this unprecedented situation, on which the Constitution gave no guidance, Congress established a fifteen-member electoral commission. In the interest of impartiality, membership on the commission was to be balanced between Democrats and Republicans. But one independent Republican, Supreme Court Justice David Davis, re-

fused appointment in order to accept his election as a senator. A regular Republican took his place, and the Republican party prevailed 8 to 7 on every decision, a strict party vote. Hayes would become the winner if Congress accepted the commission's findings.

Congressional acceptance was not a certainty, and many citizens feared that the crisis might lead to another civil war. Democrats, however, acquiesced in the election of Hayes. Scholars have found that negotiations went on between some of Hayes's supporters and southerners who were interested in federal aid to railroads, internal improvements, federal patronage, and removal of troops from southern states. But the most recent studies suggest that these negotiations did not have a deciding effect on the outcome. Neither party was well enough organized to implement and enforce a bargain between the sections. Northern and southern Democrats decided that they could not win and failed to contest the election. Thus, Hayes became president, and southerners looked forward to the withdrawal of federal troops from the South. Reconstruction was unmistakably over.

Southern Democrats rejoiced, but black Americans grieved over the betrayal of their hopes for equality. After 1877, the hope for many African-Americans was "to go to a territory by ourselves." In some southern states, thousands gathered up their possessions and migrated to Kansas. They were known as Exodusters, disappointed people still searching for their share in the American dream.

Black Exodusters

Thus, the nation ended more than fifteen years of bloody civil war and controversial reconstruction without establishing full freedom for black Americans. Their status would continue to be a major issue. As the nation turned away from the needs of black citizens, a majority of its people and its government focused attention on the problems related to industrialism.

Suggestions for Further Reading

National Policy, Politics, and Constitutional Law

Richard H. Abbott, *The Republican Party and the South, 1855–1877* (1986); Herman Belz, *Emancipation and Equal Rights* (1978); Michael Les Benedict, *A Compromise of Principle: Congressional Republicans and Reconstruction, 1863–1869* (1974); David W. Bowen, *Andrew Johnson and the Negro* (1989); William S. McFeely, *Grant* (1981); William S. McFeely, *Yankee Stepfather: General O. O. Howard and the Freedmen* (1968); Eric L. McKitrick, *Andrew Johnson and Reconstruction* (1966); James M. McPherson, *The Abolitionist Legacy* (1975); Kenneth M. Stampp, *The Era of Reconstruction* (1965); Mark W. Summers, *Railroads, Reconstruction, and the Gospel of Prosperity* (1984).

The Freed Slaves

Roberta Sue Alexander, *North Carolina Faces the Freedmen* (1985); Edmund L. Drago, *Black Politicians and Reconstruction in Georgia* (1982); Paul D. Escott, *Slavery Remembered* (1979); Leon Litwack, *Been in the Storm So Long* (1979); Willie Lee Rose, *Rehearsal for Reconstruction* (1964); Clarence Walker, *A Rock in a Weary Land* (1982).

Politics and Reconstruction in the South

Richard N. Current, *Those Terrible Carpetbaggers* (1988); W. E. B. Du Bois, *Black Reconstruction* (1935); Paul D. Escott, *Many Excellent People: Power and Privilege in North Carolina, 1850–1900* (1985); W. McKee Evans, *Ballots and Fence Rails: Reconstruction on the Lower Cape Fear* (1966); Eric Foner, *Reconstruction: America's Unfinished Revolution, 1863–1877* (1988); Eric Foner, *Nothing but Freedom* (1983); William C. Harris, *The Day of the Carpetbagger* (1979); Michael Perman, *The Road to Redemption* (1984); Allen Trelease, *White Terror* (1967); Ted Tunnell, *Carpetbagger from Vermont* (1989); Ted Tunnell, *Crucible of Reconstruction* (1984); Michael Wayne, *The Reshaping of Plantation Society* (1983); Sarah Woolfolk Wiggins, *The Scalawag in Alabama Politics, 1865–1881* (1977).

Women, Family, and Social History

Ellen Carol Dubois, *Feminism and Suffrage* (1978); Herbert G. Gutman, *The Black Family in Slavery and Freedom, 1750–1925* (1976); Elizabeth Jacoway, *Yankee Missionaries in the South* (1979); Jacqueline Jones, *Labor of Love, Labor of Sorrow* (1985); Jacqueline Jones, *Soldiers of Light and Love* (1980); Robert C. Kenzer, *Kinship and Neighborhood in a Southern Community* (1987).

The End of Reconstruction

Michael Les Benedict, "Southern Democrats in the Crisis of 1876–1877," *Journal of Southern History*, LXVI, No. 4 (November 1980), 489–524; William Gillette, *Retreat from Reconstruction, 1869–1879* (1980); William Gillette, *The Right to Vote* (1969); Keith Ian Polakoff, *The Politics of Inertia* (1973); C. Vann Woodward, *Reunion and Reaction* (1951).

Reconstruction's Legacy for the South

Robert G. Athearn, *In Search of Canaan* (1978); Jay R. Mandle, *The Roots of Black Poverty* (1978); Nell Irvin Painter, *Exodusters* (1976); Howard Rabinowitz, *Race Relations in the Urban South, 1865–1890* (1978); Roger L. Ransom and Richard Sutch, *One Kind of Freedom* (1977); Laurence Shore, *Southern Capitalists* (1986); Peter Wallenstein, *From Slave South to New South* (1987); C. Vann Woodward, *Origins of the New South* (1951).

Appendix

Historical Reference Books by Subject:
Encyclopedias, Dictionaries, Atlases, Chronologies, and Statistics

American History: General

Dictionary of American History (1976–1978); Robert H. Ferrell and John S. Bowman, eds., *The Twentieth Century: An Almanac* (1984); John D. Buenker and Edward R. Kantowicz, eds., *Historical Dictionary of the Progressive Era, 1890–1920* (1988); George H. Gallup, *The Gallup Poll: Public Opinion, 1935–1971* (1972) and *1972–1977* (1978); Bernard Grun, *The Timetables of History* (1975); Stanley Hochman, *Yesterday and Today* (1979); *International Encyclopedia of the Social Sciences* (1968–   ); R. Alton Lee, ed., *Encyclopedia USA* (1983–   ); Richard B. Morris, *Encyclopedia of American History* (1982); James S. Olson, *Historical Dictionary of the 1920s* (1988); Thomas Parker and Douglas Nelson, *Day by Day: The Sixties* (1983); Harry Ritter, *Dictionary of Concepts in History* (1986); Arthur M. Schlesinger, Jr., ed., *The Almanac of American History* (1983); *Scribner Desk Dictionary of American History* (1984); U.S. Bureau of the Census, *Historical Statistics of the United States* (1975); *Webster's New Geographical Dictionary* (1984); Philip P. Wiener, ed., *Dictionary of the History of Ideas* (1973).

American History: General Atlases

Geoffrey Barraclough, ed., *The Times Atlas of World History* (1979); W. P. Cumming et al., *The Discovery of North America* (1972); Robert H. Ferrell and Richard Natkiel, *Atlas of American History* (1987); Kenneth T. Jackson and James T. Adams, *Atlas of American History* (1978); Adrian Johnson, *America Explored* (1974); National Geographic Society, *Historical Atlas of the United States* (1988); Charles O. Paullin, *Atlas of the Historical Geography of the United States* (1932); U.S. Department of the Interior, *National Atlas of the United States* (1970). Other atlases listed under specific categories.

American History: General Biographies

Concise Dictionary of American Biography (1980); *Dictionary of American Biography* (1928–   ); John A. Garraty, ed., *Encyclopedia of American Biography* (1974); *National Cyclopedia of American Biography* (1898–   ). Other biographical works appear under specific categories.

African-Americans

Rayford W. Logan and Michael R. Winston, eds., *The Dictionary of American Negro Biography* (1983); W. A. Low and Virgil A. Clift, eds., *Encyclopedia of Black America* (1981); Bruce Kellner, *The Harlem Renaissance* (1984); Randall M. Miller and John D. Smith, eds., *Dictionary of Afro-American Slavery* (1988).

American Revolution

Mark M. Boatner III, *Encyclopedia of the American Revolution* (1974); Lester J. Cappon, ed., *Atlas of Early American History: The Revolutionary Era, 1760–1790* (1976); Douglas W. Marshall and Howard H. Peckham, *Campaigns of the American Revolution* (1976); Gregory Palmer, ed., *Biographical Sketches of Loyalists of the American Revolution* (1984); *Rand-McNally Atlas of the American Revolution* (1974).

Architecture

William D. Hunt, Jr., ed., *Encyclopedia of American Architecture* (1980).

Business and the Economy

Christine Ammer and Dean S. Ammer, *Dictionary of Business and Economics* (1983); Douglas Auld and Graham Bannock, *The American Dictionary of Economics* (1983); Douglas Greenwald, *Encyclopedia of Economics* (1982); John N. Ingham, *Biographical Dictionary of American Business Leaders* (1983); John N. Ingham and Lynne B. Feldman, *Contemporary American Business Leaders* (1990); William H. Mulligan, Jr., ed., *A Historical Dictionary of American Industrial Language* (1988); Glenn G. Munn, *Encyclopedia of Banking and Finance* (1973); Glenn Porter, ed., *Encyclopedia of American Economic History* (1980).

Cities and Towns

Charles Abrams, *The Language of Cities: A Glossary of Terms* (1971); John L. Androit, ed., *Township Atlas of the United States* (1979); Melvin G. Holli and Peter d'A. Jones, eds., *Biographical Dictionary of American Mayors, 1820–1980: Big City Mayors* (1981); Ory M. Nergal, ed., *The Encyclopedia of American Cities* (1980). See also "Politics and Government."

The Civil War

Mark M. Boatner III, *The Civil War Dictionary* (1988); Patricia L. Faust, *Historical Times Encyclopedia of the Civil War* (1986); Mark E. Neely, Jr., *The Abraham Lincoln Encyclopedia* (1982); Craig L. Symonds, *A Battlefield Atlas of the Civil War* (1983); U.S. War Department, *The Official Atlas of the Civil War* (1958); Jon L. Wakelyn, ed., *Biographical Dictionary of the Confederacy* (1977); Ezra J. Warner and W. Buck Yearns, *Biographical Register of the Confederate Congress* (1975). See also "Politics and Government" and "The South."

Conservation

Forest History Society, *Encyclopedia of American Forest and Conservation History* (1983).

Constitution and Supreme Court

Congressional Quarterly, *Guide to the Supreme Court* (1979); Leon Friedman and Fred I. Israel, eds., *The Justices of the United States Supreme Court, 1789–1978* (1980); Richard F. Hixson, *Mass Media and the Constitution* (1989); Robert J. Janosik, ed., *Encyclopedia of the American Judicial System* (1987); Leonard W. Levy et al., eds., *Encyclopedia of the American Constitution* (1986). See also "Politics and Government."

Crime and Police

William G. Bailey, *Encyclopedia of Police Science* (1987); Sanford H. Kadish, ed., *Encyclopedia of Crime and Justice* (1983); Michael Newton and Judy Ann Newton, *The FBI Most Wanted* (1989); Carl Sifakis, *The Encyclopedia of American Crime* (1982).

Culture and Folklore

Hennig Cohen and Tristram Potter Coffin, eds., *The Folklore of American Holidays* (1987); Richard M. Dorson, ed., *Handbook of American Folklore* (1983); M. Thomas Inge, ed., *Handbook of American Popular Culture* (1979–1981); J. F. Rooney, Jr. et al., eds., *This Remarkable Continent: An Atlas of United States and Canadian Society and Cultures* (1982); Marjorie Tallman, *Dictionary of American Folklore* (1959); Justin Wintle, ed., *Makers of Nineteenth Century Culture, 1800–1914* (1982). See also "Entertainment," "Mass Media and Journalism," "Music," and "Sports."

Education

Lee C. Deighton, ed., *The Encyclopedia of Education* (1971); Joseph C. Kiger, ed., *Research Institutions and Learned Societies* (1982); John F. Ohles, ed., *Biographical Dictionary of American Educators* (1978).

Entertainment

Tim Brooks and Earle Marsh, *The Complete Directory to Prime Time Network TV Shows, 1946–Present* (1979); Barbara N. Cohen-Stratyner, *Biographical Dictionary of Dance* (1982); John Dunning, *Tune in Yesterday* [radio] (1967); Stanley Green, *Encyclopedia of the Musical Film* (1981); *Notable Names in the American Theater* (1976); *New York Times Encyclopedia of Television* (1977); Andrew Sarris, *The American Cinema: Directors and Directions, 1929–1968* (1968); Anthony Slide, *The American Film Industry* (1986). See also "Culture and Folklore," "Mass Media and Journalism," "Music," and "Sports."

Foreign Policy and International Relations

Gerard Chaliand and Jean-Pierre Rageau, *Strategic Atlas* (1990); Alexander DeConde, ed., *Encyclopedia of American Foreign Policy* (1978); John E. Findling, *Dictionary of American Diplomatic History* (1989); *Foreign Affairs Chronology, 1978–1989* (1990); *International Geographic Encyclopedia and Atlas* (1979); Warren F. Kuehl, ed., *Biographical Dictionary of Internationalists* (1983); George T. Kurian, *Encyclopedia of the Third World* (1981); Jack C. Plano and Roy Olton, eds., *The International Relations Dictionary* (1988); Bruce W. Watson et al., eds., *United States Intelligence* (1990). See also "Peace Movements and Pacifism," "Politics and Government," "Wars and the Military," and specific wars.

Immigration and Ethnic Groups

American Jewish Yearbook (1899–   ); Stephanie Bernardo, *The Ethnic Almanac* (1981); Hyung-Chan Kim, ed., *Dictionary of Asian American History* (1986); Matt S. Meier, *Mexican American Biographies* (1988); Matt S. Meier and Feliciano Rivera, *Dictionary of Mexican American History* (1981); Sally M. Miller, ed., *The Ethnic Press in the United States* (1987); Stephan Thernstrom, ed., *Harvard Encyclopedia of American Ethnic Groups* (1980).

Labor

Gary M. Fink, ed., *Biographical Dictionary of American Labor Leaders* (1984); Gary M. Fink, ed., *Labor Unions* (1977); Philip S. Foner, *First Facts of American Labor* (1984).

Literature

James T. Callow and Robert J. Reilly, *Guide to American Literature* (1976–1977); *Dictionary of Literary Biography* (1978–   ); Eugene Ehrlich and Gorton Carruth, *The Oxford Illustrated Literary Guide to the United States* (1982); Jon Tuska and Vicki Piekarski, *Encyclopedia of Frontier and Western Fiction* (1983). See also "Culture and Folklore," "The South," and "Women."

Mass Media and Journalism

Robert V. Hudson, *Mass Media* (1987); William H. Taft, ed., *Encyclopedia of Twentieth-Century Journalists* (1986).

Medicine and Nursing

Vern L. Bullough et al., eds., *American Nursing* (1988); Martin Kaufman et al., eds., *Dictionary of American Medical Biography* (1984); Martin Kaufman et al., eds., *Dictionary of American Nursing Biography* (1988); George L. Maddox, ed., *The Encyclopedia of Aging* (1987).

Music

John Chilton, *Who's Who of Jazz* (1972); Edward Jablonski, *The Encyclopedia of American Music* (1981); Roger Lax and Frederick Smith, *The Great Song Thesaurus* (1984). See also "Culture and Folklore" and "Entertainment."

Native Americans

Michael Coe et al., *Atlas of Ancient America* (1986); *Handbook of North American Indians* (1978–   ); J. Norman Heard et al., *Handbook of the American Frontier: Four Centuries of Indian-White Relationships* (1987–   ); Barry Klein, ed., *Reference Encyclopedia of the American Indian* (1986); Paul Stuart, *Nation Within a Nation: Historical Statistics of American Indians* (1987); Helen H. Tanner, ed., *Atlas of Great Lakes Indian History* (1987); Carl Waldman, *Atlas of the North American Indian* (1985); Carl Waldman, *Encyclopedia of Native American Tribes* (1988).

The New Deal and FDR

Otis L. Graham, Jr., and Meghan R. Wander, eds., *Franklin D. Roosevelt: His Life and Times* (1985); James S. Olson, ed., *Historical Dictionary of the New Deal* (1985). See also "Politics and Government."

Peace Movements and Pacifism

Harold Josephson et al., eds., *Biographical Dictionary of Modern Peace Leaders* (1985); Ervin Laszlo and Jong Y. Yoo, eds., *World Encyclopedia of Peace* (1986); Robert S. Meyer, *Peace Organizations Past and Present* (1988). See also "Wars and the Military" and specific wars.

Politics and Government: General

Erik W. Austin, *Political Facts of the United States Since 1789* (1986); Mari Jo Buhle et al., eds., *Encyclopedia of the American Left* (1990); Jack P. Greene, ed., *Encyclopedia of American Political History* (1984); Leon Hurwitz, *Historical Dictionary of Censorship in the United States* (1985); Bernard K. Johnpoll and Harvey Klehr, eds., *Biographical Dictionary of the American Left* (1986); Edwin V. Mitchell, *An Encyclopedia of American Politics* (1968); Charles R. Ritter et al., *American Legislative Leaders, 1850–1910* (1989); William Safire, *Safire's Political Dictionary* (1978); Arthur M. Schlesinger, Jr., and Fred I. Israel, eds., *History of American Presidential Elections, 1789–1968* (1971); Robert Scruton, *A Dictionary of Political Thought* (1982); Jay M. Shafritz, *The Dorsey Dictionary of American Government and Politics* (1989). See also "Cities and Towns," "Constitution and Supreme Court," "The States," and the next three sections.

Politics and Government: Congress

Congressional Quarterly, *Congress and the Nation, 1945–1976* (1965–1977); Kenneth C. Martis, *Historical Atlas of Political Parties in the United States Congress, 1789–1989* (1989); Kenneth C. Martis, *Historical Atlas of United States Congressional Districts, 1789–1983* (1982); U.S. Congress, *Biographical Directory of the United States Congress, 1774–1989* (1989).

Politics and Government: Election Statistics

Erik W. Austin and Jerome C. Clubb, *Political Facts of the United States Since 1789* (1986); Svend Peterson, *A Statistical History of the American Presidential Elections* (1963); Richard M. Scammon et al., eds., *America Votes* (1956–   ); G. Scott Thomas, *The Pursuit of the White House* (1987).

Politics and Government: Presidency and Executive Branch

Henry F. Graff, *The Presidents* (1984); Richard S. Kirkendall, ed., *The Harry S Truman Encyclopedia* (1989); Merrill D. Peterson, ed., *Thomas Jefferson: A Reference Biography* (1986); Robert Sobel, ed., *Biographical Directory of the United States Executive Branch, 1774–1977* (1977). See other categories for specific presidents.

Religion and Cults

Henry Bowden, *Dictionary of American Religious Biography* (1977); John T. Ellis and Robert Trisco, *A Guide to American Catholic History* (1982); Edwin S. Gaustad, *Historical Atlas of Religion in America* (1976); Samuel S. Hill, Jr., ed., *Encyclopedia of Religion in the South* (1984); Charles H. Lippy and Peter W. Williams, eds., *Encyclopedia of the American Religious Experience* (1988); J. Gordon Melton, *Biographical Dictionary of American Cult and Sect Leaders* (1986); J. Gordon Melton, *The Encyclopedia of American Religions* (1987); J. Gordon Melton, *The Encyclopedic Handbook of Cults in America* (1986); Mark A. Noll and Nathan O. Hatch, eds., *Eerdmans Handbook to Christianity in America* (1983).

Science and Technology

James W. Cortada, *Historical Dictionary of Data Processing* (1987); Clark A. Elliott, *Biographical Index to American Science: The Seventeenth Century to 1920* (1990); Charles C.

Gillispie, ed., *Dictionary of Scientific Biography* (1970–   ); National Academy of Sciences, *Biographical Memoirs* (1877–   ).

Social Issues, Organizations, and Reform

Louis Filler, *A Dictionary of American Social Reform* (1963); Louis Filler, *Dictionary of American Social Change* (1982); Robert S. Fogarty, *Dictionary of American Communal and Utopian History* (1980); Harold M. Keele and Joseph C. Kiger, eds., *Foundations* (1984); Mark E. Lender, *Dictionary of American Temperance Biography* (1984); Patricia M. Melvin, ed., *American Community Organizations* (1986); Alvin J. Schmidt, *Fraternal Organizations* (1980); Walter I. Trattner, *Biographical Dictionary of Social Welfare in America* (1986). See also "Crime and Police."

The South

Robert Bain et al., eds., *Southern Writers: A Biographical Dictionary* (1979); Kenneth Coleman and Charles S. Gurr, eds., *Dictionary of Georgia Biography* (1983); William Ferris and Charles R. Wilson, eds., *Encyclopedia of Southern Culture* (1986); David C. Roller and Robert W. Twyman, eds., *The Encyclopedia of Southern History* (1979); Walter P. Webb et al., eds., *The Handbook of Texas* (1952, 1976). See also "The Civil War," "Politics and Government," and "The States."

Sports

Ralph Hickok, *New Encyclopedia of Sports* (1977); Zander Hollander, *The NBA's Official Encyclopedia of Pro Basketball* (1981); Frank G. Menke and Suzanne Treat, *The Encyclopedia of Sports* (1977); *The NFL's Official Encyclopedic History of Professional Football* (1977); David L. Porter, *Biographical Dictionary of American Sports: Baseball* (1987), *Football* (1987), and *Outdoor Sports* (1988); David Wallechinsky, *The Complete Book of the Olympics* (1984). See also "Culture and Folklore."

The States

John Clayton, ed., *The Illinois Fact Book and Historical Almanac, 1673–1968* (1970); Roy R. Glashan, ed., *American Governors and Gubernatorial Elections, 1775–1978* (1979); Thomas A. McMullin and David Walker, *Biographical Directory of American Territorial Governors* (1984); Marie Mullaney, *Biographical Directory of the Governors of the United States, 1983–1987* (1988); John W. Raimo, ed., *Biographical Directory of American Colonial and Revolutionary Governors, 1607–1789* (1980); John W. Raimo, ed., *Biographical Directory of the Governors of the United States, 1978–1983* (1985); Robert Sobel and John W. Raimo, eds., *Biographical Directory of the Governors of the United States, 1789–1978* (1978); James W. Scott and Ronald L. De Lorme, *Historical Atlas of Washington* (1988); *The Worldmark Encyclopedia of the States* (1986). See also "Politics and Government," "The South," and "The West and the Frontier."

The Vietnam War

John S. Bowman, ed., *The Vietnam War* (1986); James S. Olson, ed., *Dictionary of the Vietnam War* (1988); Harry G. Summers, Jr., *Vietnam War Almanac* (1985). See also "Peace Movements and Pacifism" and "Wars and the Military."

Wars and the Military

William M. Arkin et al., *Encyclopedia of the U.S. Military* (1990); R. Ernest Dupuy and Trevor N. Dupuy, *The Encyclopedia of Military History* (1977); Holger H. Herwig and Neil M. Heyman, *Biographical Dictionary of World War I* (1982); Michael Kidrow and Dan Smith, *The War Atlas* (1983); Roger J. Spiller and Joseph G. Dawson III, eds., *Dictionary of American Military Biography* (1984); U.S. Military Academy, *The West Point Atlas of American Wars, 1689–1953* (1959); *Webster's American Military Biographies* (1978). See also "American Revolution," "The Civil War," "The Vietnam War," and "World War II."

The West and the Frontier

William A. Beck and Ynez D. Haase, *Historical Atlas of the American West* (1989); Doris O. Dawdy, *Artists of the American West* (1974–1984); Howard R. Lamar, ed., *The Reader's Encyclopedia of the American West* (1977); Doyce B. Nunis, Jr. and Gloria R. Lothrop, eds., *A Guide to the History of California* (1989); Don L. Thrapp, *Encyclopedia of Frontier Biography* (1988).

Women

Maggie Humm, *The Dictionary of Feminist Theory* (1990); Edward T. James et al., *Notable American Women, 1607–1950* (1971); Lina Mainiero, ed., *American Women Writers* (1979–1982); Barbara G. Shortridge, *Atlas of American Women* (1987); Barbara Sicherman and Carol H. Green, eds., *Notable American Women, The Modern Period* (1980); Angela H. Zophy and Frances M. Kavenik, eds., *Dictionary of American Women's History* (1989).

World War II

Marcel Baudot et al., eds., *The Historical Encyclopedia of World War II* (1980); Simon Goodenough, *War Maps: Great Land Battles of World War II* (1988); Robert Goralski, *World War II Almanac, 1931–1945* (1981); John Keegan, ed., *The Times Atlas of the Second World War* (1989); Thomas Parrish, ed., *The Simon and Schuster Encyclopedia of World War II* (1978); Louis L. Snyder, *Louis L. Snyder's Historical Guide to World War II* (1982); U.S. Military Academy, *Campaign Atlas to the Second World War: Europe and the Mediterranean* (1980); Peter Young, ed., *The World Almanac Book of World War II* (1981). See also "Wars and the Military."

Declaration of Independence in Congress, July 4, 1776

The unanimous declaration of the thirteen United States of America

When, in the course of human events, it becomes necessary for one people to dissolve the political bonds which have connected them with another, and to assume, among the powers of the earth, the separate and equal station to which the laws of nature and of nature's God entitle them, a decent respect to the opinions of mankind requires that they should declare the causes which impel them to the separation.

We hold these truths to be self-evident: That all men are created equal; that they are endowed by their Creator with certain unalienable rights; that among these are life, liberty, and the pursuit of happiness; that, to secure these rights, governments are instituted among men, deriving their just powers from the consent of the governed; that whenever any form of government becomes destructive of these ends, it is the right of the people to alter or to abolish it, and to institute new government, laying its foundation on such principles, and organizing its powers in such form, as to them shall seem most likely to effect their safety and happiness. Prudence, indeed, will dictate that governments long established should not be changed for light and transient causes; and accordingly all experience hath shown that mankind are more disposed to suffer, while evils are sufferable, than to right themselves by abolishing the forms to which they are accustomed. But when a long train of abuses and usurpations, pursuing invariably the same object, evinces a design to reduce them under absolute despotism, it is their right, it is their duty, to throw off such government, and to provide new guards for their future security. Such has been the patient sufferance of these colonies; and such is now the necessity which constrains them to alter their former systems of government. The history of the present King of Great Britain is a history of repeated injuries and usurpations, all having in direct object the establishment of an absolute tyranny over these states. To prove this, let facts be submitted to a candid world.

He has refused his assent to laws, the most wholesome and necessary for the public good.

He has forbidden his governors to pass laws of immediate and pressing importance, unless suspended in their operation till his assent should be obtained; and, when so suspended, he has utterly neglected to attend to them.

He has refused to pass other laws for the accommodation of large districts of people, unless those people would relinquish the right of representation in the legislature, a right inestimable to them, and formidable to tyrants only.

He has called together legislative bodies at places unusual, uncomfortable, and distant from the depository of their public records, for the sole purpose of fatiguing them into compliance with his measures.

He has dissolved representative houses repeatedly, for opposing, with manly firmness, his invasions on the rights of the people.

He has refused for a long time, after such dissolutions, to cause others to be elected; whereby the legislative powers, incapable of annihilation, have returned to the people at large for their exercise; the state remaining, in the mean time, exposed to all the dangers of invasions from without and convulsions within.

He has endeavored to prevent the population of these states; for that purpose obstructing the laws for naturalization of foreigners; refusing to pass others to encourage their migration hither, and raising the conditions of new appropriations of lands.

He has obstructed the administration of justice, by refusing his assent to laws for establishing judiciary powers.

He has made judges dependent on his will alone, for the tenure of their offices, and the amount and payment of their salaries.

He has erected a multitude of new offices, and sent hither swarms of officers to harass our people and eat out their substance.

He has kept among us, in times of peace, standing armies, without the consent of our legislatures.

He has affected to render the military independent of, and superior to, the civil power.

He has combined with others to subject us to a jurisdiction foreign to our constitution, and unacknowledged by our laws, giving his assent to their acts of pretended legislation:

For quartering large bodies of armed troops among us;

For protecting them, by a mock trial, from punishment for any murders which they should commit on the inhabitants of these states;

For cutting off our trade with all parts of the world;

For imposing taxes on us without our consent;

For depriving us, in many cases, of the benefits of trial by jury;

For transporting us beyond seas, to be tried for pretended offenses;

For abolishing the free system of English laws in a neighboring province, establishing therein an arbitrary government, and enlarging its boundaries, so as to render it at once an example and fit instrument for introducing the same absolute rule into these colonies;

For taking away our charters, abolishing our most valuable laws, and altering fundamentally the forms of our governments;

For suspending our own legislatures, and declaring themselves invested with power to legislate for us in all cases whatsoever.

He has abdicated government here, by declaring us out of his protection and waging war against us.

He has plundered our seas, ravaged our coasts, burned our towns, and destroyed the lives of our people.

He is at this time transporting large armies of foreign mercenaries to complete the works of death, desolation, and tyranny already begun with circumstances of cruelty and perfidy scarcely paralleled in the most barbarous ages, and totally unworthy the head of a civilized nation.

He has constrained our fellow-citizens, taken captive on the high seas, to bear arms against their country, to become the executioners of their friends and brethren, or to fall themselves by their hands.

He has excited domestic insurrection among us, and has endeavored to bring on the inhabitants of our frontiers the merciless Indian savages, whose known rule of warfare is an undistinguished destruction of all ages, sexes, and conditions.

In every stage of these oppressions we have petitioned for redress in the most humble terms; our repeated petitions have been answered only by repeated injury. A prince, whose character is thus marked by every act which may define a tyrant, is unfit to be the ruler of a free people.

Nor have we been wanting in our attentions to our British brethren. We have warned them, from time to time, of attempts by their legislature to extend an unwarrantable jurisdiction over us. We have reminded them of the circumstances of our emigration and settlement here. We have appealed to their native justice and magnanimity; and we have conjured them, by the ties of our common kindred, to disavow these usurpations, which would inevitably interrupt our connections and correspondence. They, too, have been deaf to the voice of justice and of consanguinity. We must, therefore, acquiesce in the necessity which denounces our separation, and hold them, as we hold the rest of mankind, enemies in war, in peace friends.

We, therefore, the representatives of the United States of America, in General Congress assembled, appealing to the Supreme Judge of the world for the rectitude of our intentions, do, in the name and by the authority of the good people of these colonies, solemnly publish and declare, that these United Colonies are, and of right ought to be, FREE AND INDEPENDENT STATES; that they are absolved from all allegiance to the British crown, and that all political connection between them and the state of Great Britain is, and ought to be, totally dissolved; and that, as free and independent states, they have full power to levy war, conclude peace, contract alliances, establish commerce, and do all other acts and things which independent states may of right do. And for the support of this declaration, with a firm reliance on the protection of Divine Providence, we mutually pledge to each other our lives, our fortunes, and our sacred honor.

JOHN HANCOCK
and fifty-five others

Constitution of the United States of America and Amendments

Preamble

We the people of the United States, in order to form a more perfect union, establish justice, insure domestic tranquillity, provide for the common defense, promote the general welfare, and secure the blessings of liberty to ourselves and our posterity, do ordain and establish this Constitution for the United States of America.

Article I

Section 1 All legislative powers herein granted shall be vested in a Congress of the United States, which shall consist of a Senate and a House of Representatives.

Section 2 The House of Representatives shall be composed of members chosen every second year by the people of the several States, and the electors in each State shall have the qualifications requisite for electors of the most numerous branch of the State Legislature.

No person shall be a Representative who shall not have attained to the age of twenty-five years, and been seven years a citizen of the United States, and who shall not, when elected, be an inhabitant of that State in which he shall be chosen.

Representatives and direct taxes shall be apportioned among the several States which may be included within this Union, according to their respective numbers, *which shall be determined by adding to the whole number of free persons, including those bound to service for a term of years and excluding Indians not taxed, three-fifths of all other persons.* The actual enumeration shall be made within three years after the first meeting of the Congress of the United States, and within every subsequent term of ten years, in such manner as they shall by law direct. The number of Representatives shall not exceed one for every thirty thousand, but each State shall have at least one Representative; *and until such enumeration shall be made, the State of New Hampshire shall be entitled to choose three, Massachusetts eight, Rhode Island and Providence Plantations one, Connecticut five, New York six, New Jersey four, Pennsylvania eight, Delaware one, Maryland six, Virginia ten, North Carolina five, South Carolina five, and Georgia three.*

When vacancies happen in the representation from any State, the Executive authority thereof shall issue writs of election to fill such vacancies.

The House of Representatives shall choose their Speaker and other officers; and shall have the sole power of impeachment.

Section 3 The Senate of the United States shall be composed of two Senators from each State, *chosen by the legislature thereof,* for six years; and each Senator shall have one vote.

Immediately after they shall be assembled in consequence of the first election, they shall be divided as equally as may be into three classes. The seats of the Senators of the first class shall be vacated at the expiration of the second year, of the second class at the expiration of the fourth year, and of the third class at the expiration of the sixth year, so that one-third

---

Passages no longer in effect are printed in italic type.

may be chosen every second year; *and if vacancies happen by resignation or otherwise, during the recess of the legislature of any State, the Executive thereof may make temporary appointments until the next meeting of the legislature, which shall then fill such vacancies.*

No person shall be a Senator who shall not have attained to the age of thirty years, and been nine years a citizen of the United States, and who shall not, when elected, be an inhabitant of that State for which he shall be chosen.

The Vice-President of the United States shall be President of the Senate, but shall have no vote, unless they be equally divided.

The Senate shall choose their other officers, and also a President *pro tempore,* in the absence of the Vice-President, or when he shall exercise the office of President of the United States.

The Senate shall have the sole power to try all impeachments. When sitting for that purpose, they shall be on oath or affirmation. When the President of the United States is tried, the Chief Justice shall preside: and no person shall be convicted without the concurrence of two-thirds of the members present.

Judgment in cases of impeachment shall not extend further than to removal from the office, and disqualification to hold and enjoy any office of honor, trust or profit under the United States: but the party convicted shall nevertheless be liable and subject to indictment, trial, judgment and punishment, according to law.

Section 4 The times, places and manner of holding elections for Senators and Representatives shall be prescribed in each State by the legislature thereof; but the Congress may at any time by law make or alter such regulations, except as to the places of choosing Senators.

The Congress shall assemble at least once in every year, and such meeting *shall be on the first Monday in December, unless they shall by law appoint a different day.*

Section 5 Each house shall be the judge of the elections, returns and qualifications of its own members, and a majority of each shall constitute a quorum to do business; but a smaller number may adjourn from day to day, and may be authorized to compel the attendance of absent members, in such manner, and under such penalties, as each house may provide.

Each house may determine the rules of its proceedings, punish its members for disorderly behavior, and with the concurrence of two-thirds, expel a member.

Each house shall keep a journal of its proceedings, and from time to time publish the same, excepting such parts as may in their judgment require secrecy; and the yeas and nays of the members of either house on any question shall, at the desire of one-fifth of those present, be entered on the journal.

Neither house, during the session of Congress, shall, without the consent of the other, adjourn for more than three days, nor to any other place than that in which the two houses shall be sitting.

Section 6 The Senators and Representatives shall receive a compensation for their services, to be ascertained by law and paid out of the treasury of the United States. They shall in all cases except treason, felony and breach of the peace, be privileged from arrest during their attendance at the session of their respective houses, and in going to and returning from the same; and for any speech or debate in either house, they shall not be questioned in any other place.

No Senator or Representative shall, during the time for which he was elected, be appointed to any civil office under the authority of the United States, which shall have been created, or the emoluments whereof shall have been increased, during such time; and no person holding any office under the United States shall be a member of either house during his continuance in office.

Section 7 All bills for raising revenue shall originate in the House of Representatives; but the Senate may propose or concur with amendments as on other bills.

Every bill which shall have passed the House of Representatives and the Senate, shall, before it become a law, be presented to the President of the United States; if he approve he shall sign it, but if not he shall return it with objections to that house in which it originated, who shall enter the objections at large on their journal, and proceed to reconsider it. If after such reconsideration two-thirds of that house shall agree to pass the bill, it shall be sent, together with the objections, to the other house, by which it shall likewise be reconsidered, and, if approved by two-thirds of that house, it shall become a law. But in all such cases the votes of both houses shall be determined by yeas and nays, and the names of the persons voting for and against the bill shall be entered on the journal of each house respectively. If any bill shall not be returned by the President within ten days (Sundays excepted) after it shall have been presented to him, the same shall be a law, in like manner as if he had signed it, unless the Congress by their adjournment prevent its return, in which case it shall not be a law.

Every order, resolution, or vote to which the concurrence of the Senate and House of Representatives may be necessary (except on a question of adjournment) shall be presented to the President of the United States; and before the same shall take effect, shall be approved by him, or being disapproved by him, shall be repassed by two-thirds of the Senate and House of Representatives, according to the rules and limitations prescribed in the case of a bill.

Section 8 The Congress shall have power

To lay and collect taxes, duties, imposts, and excises, to pay the debts and provide for the common defense and general welfare of the United States; but all duties, imposts and excises shall be uniform throughout the United States;

To borrow money on the credit of the United States;

To regulate commerce with foreign nations, and among the several States, and with the Indian tribes;

To establish an uniform rule of naturalization, and uniform laws on the subject of bankruptcies throughout the United States;

To coin money, regulate the value thereof, and of foreign coin, and fix the standard of weights and measures;

To provide for the punishment of counterfeiting the securities and current coin of the United States;

To establish post offices and post roads;

To promote the progress of science and useful arts by securing for limited times to authors and inventors the exclusive right to their respective writings and discoveries;

To constitute tribunals inferior to the Supreme Court;

To define and punish piracies and felonies committed on the high seas and offenses against the law of nations;

To declare war, grant letters of marque and reprisal, and make rules concerning captures on land and water;

To raise and support armies, but no appropriation of money to that use shall be for a longer term than two years;

To provide and maintain a navy;

To make rules for the government and regulation of the land and naval forces;

To provide for calling forth the militia to execute the laws of the Union, suppress insurrections, and repel invasions;

To provide for organizing, arming, and disciplining the militia, and for governing such part of them as may be employed in the service of the United States, reserving to the States respectively the appointment of the officers, and the authority of training the militia according to the discipline prescribed by Congress;

To exercise exclusive legislation in all cases whatsoever, over such district (not exceeding ten miles square) as may, by cession of particular States, and the acceptance of Congress, become the seat of government of the United States, and to exercise like authority over all places purchased by the consent of the legislature of the State, in which the same shall be, for erection of forts, magazines, arsenals, dockyards, and other needful buildings;—and

To make all laws which shall be necessary and proper for carrying into execution the foregoing powers, and all other powers vested by this Constitution in the government of the United States, or in any department or officer thereof.

Section 9   The migration or importation of such persons as any of the States now existing shall think proper to admit shall not be prohibited by the Congress prior to the year 1808; but a tax or duty may be imposed on such importation, not exceeding $10 for each person.

The privilege of the writ of habeas corpus shall not be suspended, unless when in cases of rebellion or invasion the public safety may require it.

No bill of attainder or ex post facto law shall be passed.

No capitation, or other direct, tax shall be laid, unless in proportion to the census or enumeration herein before directed to be taken.

No tax or duty shall be laid on articles exported from any State.

No preference shall be given by any regulation of commerce or revenue to the ports of one State over those of another; nor shall vessels bound to, or from, one State, be obliged to enter, clear, or pay duties in another.

No money shall be drawn from the treasury, but in consequence of appropriations made by law; and a regular statement and account of the receipts and expenditures of all public money shall be published from time to time.

No title of nobility shall be granted by the United States: and no person holding any office of profit or trust under them, shall, without the consent of the Congress, accept of any present, emolument, office, or title, of any kind whatever, from any king, prince, or foreign state.

Section 10   No State shall enter into any treaty, alliance, or confederation; grant letters of marque and reprisal; coin money; emit bills of credit; make anything but gold and silver coin a tender in payment of debts; pass any bill of attainder, ex post facto law, or law impairing the obligation of contracts, or grant any title of nobility.

No State shall, without the consent of Congress, lay any imposts or duties on imports or exports, except what may be absolutely necessary for executing its inspection laws: and the net produce of all duties and imposts, laid by any State on imports or exports, shall be for the use of the treasury of the United States; and all such laws shall be subject to the revision and control of the Congress.

No State shall, without the consent of Congress, lay any duty of tonnage, keep troops or ships of war in time of peace, enter into any agreement or compact with another State, or with a foreign power, or engage in war, unless actually invaded, or in such imminent danger as will not admit of delay.

Article II

Section 1   The executive power shall be vested in a President of the United States of America. He shall hold his office during the term of four years, and, together with the Vice-President, chosen for the same term, be elected as follows:

Each State shall appoint, in such manner as the legislature thereof may direct, a number of electors, equal to the whole number of Senators and Representatives to which the State may be entitled in the Congress; but no Senator or Representative, or person holding an office of trust or profit under the United States, shall be appointed an elector.

The electors shall meet in their respective States, and vote by ballot for two persons, of whom one at least shall not be an inhabitant of the same State with themselves. And they shall make a list of all the persons voted for, and of the number of votes for each; which list they shall sign and certify, and transmit sealed to the seat of government of the United States, directed to the President of the Senate. The President of the Senate shall, in the presence of the Senate and House of Representatives, open all the certificates, and the votes shall then be counted. The person having the greatest number of votes shall be the President, if such number be a majority of the whole number of electors appointed; and if there be more than one who have such majority, and have an equal number of votes, then the House of Representatives shall immediately choose by ballot one of them for President; and if no person have a majority, then from the five highest on the list said house shall in like manner choose the Presi-

dent. *But in choosing the President the votes shall be taken by States, the representation from each State having one vote; a quorum for this purpose shall consist of a member or members from two-thirds of the States, and a majority of all the States shall be necessary to a choice. In every case, after the choice of the President, the person having the greatest number of votes of the electors shall be the Vice-President. But if there should remain two or more who have equal votes, the Senate shall choose from them by ballot the Vice-President.*

The Congress may determine the time of choosing the electors and the day on which they shall give their votes; which day shall be the same throughout the United States.

No person except a natural-born citizen, *or a citizen of the United States at the time of the adoption of this Constitution,* shall be eligible to the office of President; neither shall any person be eligible to that office who shall not have attained to the age of thirty-five years, and been fourteen years a resident within the United States.

In cases of the removal of the President from office or of his death, resignation, or inability to discharge the powers and duties of the said office, the same shall devolve on the Vice-President, and the Congress may by law provide for the case of removal, death, resignation, or inability, both of the President and Vice-President, declaring what officer shall then act as President, and such officer shall act accordingly, until the disability be removed, or a President shall be elected.

The President shall, at stated times, receive for his services a compensation, which shall neither be increased nor diminished during the period for which he shall have been elected, and he shall not receive within that period any other emolument from the United States, or any of them.

Before he enter on the execution of his office, he shall take the following oath or affirmation:—"I do solemnly swear (or affirm) that I will faithfully execute the office of the President of the United States, and will to the best of my ability preserve, protect and defend the Constitution of the United States."

Section 2   The President shall be commander in chief of the army and navy of the United States, and of the militia of the several States, when called into the actual service of the United States; he may require the opinion, in writing, of the principal officer in each of the executive departments, upon any subject relating to the duties of their respective offices, and he shall have power to grant reprieves and pardons for offenses against the United States, except in cases of impeachment.

He shall have power, by and with the advice and consent of the Senate, to make treaties, provided two-thirds of the Senators present concur; and he shall nominate, and by and with the advice and consent of the Senate, shall appoint ambassadors, other public ministers and consuls, judges of the Supreme Court, and all other officers of the United States, whose appointments are not herein otherwise provided for, and which shall be established by law: but Congress may by law vest the appointment of such inferior officers, as they think proper, in the President alone, in the courts of law, or in the heads of departments.

The President shall have power to fill up all vacancies that may happen during the recess of the Senate, by granting commissions which shall expire at the end of their next session.

Section 3   He shall from time to time give to the Congress information of the state of the Union, and recommend to their consideration such measures as he shall judge necessary and expedient; he may, on extraordinary occasions, convene both houses, or either of them, and in case of disagreement between them, with respect to the time of adjournment, he may adjourn them to such time as he shall think proper; he shall receive ambassadors and other public ministers; he shall take care that the laws be faithfully executed, and shall commission all the officers of the United States.

Section 4   The President, Vice-President and all civil officers of the United States shall be removed from office on impeachment for, and on conviction of, treason, bribery, or other high crimes and misdemeanors.

Article III

Section 1   The judicial power of the United States shall be vested in one Supreme Court, and in such inferior courts as the Congress may from time to time ordain and establish. The judges, both of the Supreme and inferior courts, shall hold their offices during good behavior, and shall, at stated times, receive for their services a compensation which shall not be diminished during their continuance in office.

Section 2   The judicial power shall extend to all cases, in law and equity, arising under this Constitution, the laws of the United States, and treaties made, or which shall be made, under their authority;—to all cases affecting ambassadors, other public ministers and consuls;—to all cases of admiralty and maritime jurisdiction;—to controversies to which the United States shall be a party;—to controversies between two or more States;—*between a State and citizens of another State;*—between citizens of different States;—between citizens of the same State claiming lands under grants of different States, and between a State, or the citizens thereof, and foreign states, citizens or subjects.

In all cases affecting ambassadors, other public ministers and consuls, and those in which a State shall be party, the Supreme Court shall have original jurisdiction. In all the other cases before mentioned, the Supreme Court shall have appellate jurisdiction, both as to law and fact, with such exceptions, and under such regulations, as the Congress shall make.

The trial of all crimes, except in cases of impeachment, shall be by jury; and such trial shall be held in the State where said crimes shall have been committed; but when not committed within any State, the trial shall be at such place or places as the Congress may by law have directed.

Section 3 Treason against the United States shall consist only in levying war against them, or in adhering to their enemies, giving them aid and comfort. No person shall be convicted of treason unless on the testimony of two witnesses to the same overt act, or on confession in open court.

The Congress shall have power to declare the punishment of treason, but no attainder of treason shall work corruption of blood, or forfeiture except during the life of the person attainted.

Article IV

Section 1 Full faith and credit shall be given in each State to the public acts, records, and judicial proceedings of every other State. And the Congress may by general laws prescribe the manner in which such acts, records, and proceedings shall be proved, and the effect thereof.

Section 2 The citizens of each State shall be entitled to all privileges and immunities of citizens in the several States.

A person charged in any State with treason, felony, or other crime, who shall flee from justice, and be found in another State, shall on demand of the executive authority of the State from which he fled, be delivered up, to be removed to the State having jurisdiction of the crime.

No person held to service or labor in one State, under the laws thereof, escaping into another, shall, in consequence of any law or regulation therein, be discharged from such service or labor, but shall be delivered up on claim of the party to whom such service or labor may be due.

Section 3 New States may be admitted by the Congress into this Union; but no new State shall be formed or erected within the jurisdiction of any other State; nor any State be formed by the junction of two or more States, or parts of States, without the consent of the legislatures of the States concerned as well as of the Congress.

The Congress shall have power to dispose of and make all needful rules and regulations respecting the territory or other property belonging to the United States; and nothing in this Constitution shall be so construed as to prejudice any claims of the United States, or of any particular State.

Section 4 The United States shall guarantee to every State in this Union a republican form of government, and shall protect each of them against invasion; and on application of the legislature, or of the executive (when the legislature cannot be convened), against domestic violence.

Article V

The Congress, whenever two-thirds of both houses shall deem it necessary, shall propose amendments to this Constitution, or, on the application of the legislatures of two-thirds of the several States, shall call a convention for proposing amendments, which, in either case, shall be valid to all intents and purposes, as part of this Constitution, when ratified by the legislatures of three-fourths of the several States, or by conventions in three-fourths thereof, as the one or the other mode of ratification may be proposed by the Congress; provided *that no amendments which may be made prior to the year one thousand eight hundred and eight shall in any manner affect the first and fourth clauses in the ninth section of the first article;* and that no State, without its consent, shall be deprived of its equal suffrage in the Senate.

Article VI

All debts contracted and engagements entered into, before the adoption of this Constitution, shall be as valid against the United States under this Constitution, as under the Confederation.

This Constitution, and the laws of the United States which shall be made in pursuance thereof; and all treaties made, or which shall be made, under the authority of the United States, shall be the supreme law of the land; and the judges in every State shall be bound thereby, anything in the Constitution or laws of any State to the contrary notwithstanding.

The Senators and Representatives before mentioned, and the members of the several State legislatures, and all executive and judicial officers, both of the United States and of the several States, shall be bound by oath or affirmation to support this Constitution; but no religious test shall ever be required as a qualification to any office or public trust under the United States.

Article VII

The ratification of the conventions of nine States shall be sufficient for the establishment of this Constitution between the States so ratifying the same.

Done in Convention by the unanimous consent of the States present, the seventeenth day of September in the year of our Lord one thousand seven hundred and eighty-seven and of the Independence of the United States of America the twelfth. In witness whereof we have hereunto subscribed our names.

GEORGE WASHINGTON
and thirty-seven others

Amendments to the Constitution*

Amendment I

Congress shall make no law respecting an establishment of religion, or prohibiting the free exercise thereof; or abridging the freedom of speech, or of the press; or the right of the

---

*The first ten Amendments (the Bill of Rights) were adopted in 1791.

people peaceably to assemble, and to petition the government for a redress of grievances.

Amendment II

A well-regulated militia being necessary to the security of a free State, the right of the people to keep and bear arms shall not be infringed.

Amendment III

No soldier shall, in time of peace, be quartered in any house without the consent of the owner, nor in time of war, but in a manner to be prescribed by law.

Amendment IV

The right of the people to be secure in their persons, houses, papers, and effects, against unreasonable searches and seizures, shall not be violated, and no warrants shall issue but upon probable cause, supported by oath or affirmation, and particularly describing the place to be searched, and the persons or things to be seized.

Amendment V

No person shall be held to answer for a capital, or otherwise infamous crime, unless on a presentment or indictment of a grand jury, except in cases arising in the land or naval forces, or in the militia, when in actual service in time of war or public danger; nor shall any person be subject for the same offense to be twice put in jeopardy of life or limb; nor shall be compelled in any criminal case to be a witness against himself, nor be deprived of life, liberty, or property, without due process of law; nor shall private property be taken for public use without just compensation.

Amendment VI

In all criminal prosecutions, the accused shall enjoy the right to a speedy and public trial, by an impartial jury of the State and district wherein the crime shall have been committed, which district shall have been previously ascertained by law, and to be informed of the nature and cause of the accusation; to be confronted with the witnesses against him; to have compulsory process for obtaining witnesses in his favor, and to have the assistance of counsel for his defense.

Amendment VII

In suits at common law, where the value in controversy shall exceed twenty dollars, the right of trial by jury shall be preserved, and no fact tried by a jury shall be otherwise reexamined in any court of the United States, than according to the rules of the common law.

Amendment VIII

Excessive bail shall not be required, nor excessive fines imposed, nor cruel and unusual punishments inflicted.

Amendment IX

The enumeration in the Constitution, of certain rights, shall not be construed to deny or disparage others retained by the people.

Amendment X

The powers not delegated to the United States by the Constitution, nor prohibited by it to the States, are reserved to the States respectively, or to the people.

Amendment XI

[Adopted 1798]

The judicial power of the United States shall not be construed to extend to any suit in law or equity, commenced or prosecuted against one of the United States by citizens of another State, or by citizens or subjects of any foreign state.

Amendment XII

[Adopted 1804]

The electors shall meet in their respective States, and vote by ballot for President and Vice-President, one of whom, at least, shall not be an inhabitant of the same State with themselves; they shall name in their ballots the person voted for as President, and in distinct ballots the person voted for as Vice-President, and they shall make distinct lists of all persons voted for as President, and of all persons voted for as Vice-President, and of the number of votes for each, which lists they shall sign and certify, and transmit sealed to the seat of government of the United States, directed to the President of the Senate;—the President of the Senate shall, in the presence of the Senate and House of Representatives, open all the certificates and the votes shall then be counted;—the person having the greatest number of votes for President shall be the President, if such number be a majority of the whole number of electors appointed; and if no person have such majority, then from the persons having the highest numbers not exceeding three on the list of those voted for as President, the House of Representatives shall choose immediately, by ballot, the President. But in choosing the President, the votes shall be taken by States, the representation from each State having one vote; a quorum for this purpose shall consist of a member or members from two-thirds of the States, and a majority of all the States shall be necessary to a choice. And if the House of Representatives shall not choose a President whenever the right of choice shall devolve upon them, before *the fourth day of March* next following, then the Vice-President shall act as President, as in the case of the death or other constitutional disability of the President.

The person having the greatest number of votes as Vice-President shall be the Vice-President, if such number be a majority of the whole number of electors appointed; and if no person have a majority, then from the two highest numbers on the list the Senate shall choose the Vice-President; a quorum for the purpose shall consist of two-thirds of the whole number of Senators, and a majority of the whole number shall be necessary to a choice. But no person constitutionally ineligible to the office of President shall be eligible to that of Vice-President of the United States.

Amendment XIII

[Adopted 1865]

Section 1   Neither slavery nor involuntary servitude, except as a punishment for crime whereof the party shall have been duly convicted, shall exist within the United States, or any place subject to their jurisdiction.

Section 2   Congress shall have power to enforce this article by appropriate legislation.

Amendment XIV

[Adopted 1868]

Section 1   All persons born or naturalized in the United States, and subject to the jurisdiction thereof, are citizens of the United States and of the State wherein they reside. No State shall make or enforce any law which shall abridge the privileges or immunities of citizens of the United States; nor shall any State deprive any person of life, liberty, or property, without due process of law; nor deny to any person within its jurisdiction the equal protection of the laws.

Section 2   Representatives shall be apportioned among the several States according to their respective numbers, counting the whole number of persons in each State, excluding Indians not taxed. But when the right to vote at any election for the choice of Electors for President and Vice-President of the United States, Representatives in Congress, the executive and judicial officers of a State, or the members of the legislature thereof, is denied to any of the male inhabitants of such State, being twenty-one years of age and citizens of the United States, or in any way abridged, except for participation in rebellion, or other crime, the basis of representation therein shall be reduced in the proportion which the number of such male citizens shall bear to the whole number of male citizens twenty-one years of age in such State.

Section 3   No person shall be a Senator or Representative in Congress, or Elector of President and Vice-President, or hold any office, civil or military, under the United States, or under any State, who, having previously taken an oath, as a member of Congress, or as an officer of the United States, or as a member of any State legislature, or as an executive or judicial officer of any State, to support the Constitution of the United States, shall have engaged in insurrection or rebellion against the same, or given aid or comfort to the enemies thereof. Congress may, by a vote of two-thirds of each house, remove such disability.

Section 4   The validity of the public debt of the United States, authorized by law, including debts incurred for payment of pensions and bounties for services in suppressing insurrection or rebellion, shall not be questioned. But neither the United States nor any State shall assume or pay any debt or obligation incurred in aid of insurrection or rebellion against the United States, or any claim for the loss or emancipation of any slave; but all such debts, obligations, and claims shall be held illegal and void.

Section 5   The Congress shall have power to enforce, by appropriate legislation, the provisions of this article.

Amendment XV

[Adopted 1870]

Section 1   The right of citizens of the United States to vote shall not be denied or abridged by the United States or by any State on account of race, color, or previous condition of servitude.

Section 2   The Congress shall have power to enforce this article by appropriate legislation.

Amendment XVI

[Adopted 1913]

The Congress shall have power to lay and collect taxes on incomes, from whatever source derived, without apportionment among the several States, and without regard to any census or enumeration.

Amendment XVII

[Adopted 1913]

Section 1   The Senate of the United States shall be composed of two Senators from each State, elected by the people thereof, for six years; and each Senator shall have one vote. The electors in each State shall have the qualifications requisite for electors of [voters for] the most numerous branch of the State legislatures.

Section 2   When vacancies happen in the representation of any State in the Senate, the executive authority of such State shall issue writs of election to fill such vacancies: Provided, that the Legislature of any State may empower the executive thereof to make temporary appointments until the people fill the vacancies by election as the Legislature may direct.

Section 3 This amendment shall not be so construed as to affect the election or term of any Senator chosen before it becomes valid as part of the Constitution.

Amendment XVIII

[Adopted 1919; Repealed 1933]

Section 1 After one year from the ratification of this article the manufacture, sale, or transportation of intoxicating liquors within, the importation thereof into, or the exportation thereof from the United States and all territory subject to the jurisdiction thereof, for beverage purposes, is hereby prohibited.

Section 2 The Congress and the several States shall have concurrent power to enforce this article by appropriate legislation.

Section 3 This article shall be inoperative unless it shall have been ratified as an amendment to the Constitution by the legislatures of the several States, as provided by the Constitution, within seven years from the date of the submission thereof to the States by the Congress.

Amendment XIX

[Adopted 1920]

Section 1 The right of citizens of the United States to vote shall not be denied or abridged by the United States or by any State on account of sex.

Section 2 The Congress shall have power to enforce this article by appropriate legislation.

Amendment XX

[Adopted 1933]

Section 1 The terms of the President and Vice-President shall end at noon on the 20th day of January, and the terms of Senators and Representatives at noon on the 3d day of January, of the years in which such terms would have ended if this article had not been ratified; and the terms of their successors shall then begin.

Section 2 The Congress shall assemble at least once in every year, and such meeting shall begin at noon on the 3d day of January, unless they shall by law appoint a different day.

Section 3 If, at the time fixed for the beginning of the term of the President, the President-elect shall have died, the Vice-President-elect shall become President. If a President shall not have been chosen before the time fixed for the beginning of his term, or if the President-elect shall have failed to qualify, then the Vice-President-elect shall act as President

until a President shall have qualified; and the Congress may by law provide for the case wherein neither a President-elect nor a Vice-President-elect shall have qualified, declaring who shall then act as President, or the manner in which one who is to act shall be selected, and such persons shall act accordingly until a President or Vice-President shall have qualified.

Section 4 The Congress may by law provide for the case of the death of any of the persons from whom the House of Representatives may choose a President whenever the right of choice shall have devolved upon them, and for the case of the death of any of the persons from whom the Senate may choose a Vice-President whenever the right of choice shall have devolved upon them.

Section 5 Sections 1 and 2 shall take effect on the 15th day of October following the ratification of this article.

Section 6 This article shall be inoperative unless it shall have been ratified as an amendment to the Constitution by the Legislatures of three-fourths of the several States within seven years from the date of its submission.

Amendment XXI

[Adopted 1933]

Section 1 The eighteenth article of amendment to the Constitution of the United States is hereby repealed.

Section 2 The transportation or importation into any State, Territory, or Possession of the United States for delivery or use therein of intoxicating liquors, in violation of the laws thereof, is hereby prohibited.

Section 3 This article shall be inoperative unless it shall have been ratified as an amendment to the Constitution by conventions in the several States, as provided in the Constitution, within seven years from the date of submission thereof to the States by the Congress.

Amendment XXII

[Adopted 1951]

Section 1 No person shall be elected to the office of President more than twice, and no person who has held the office of President, or acted as President, for more than two years of a term to which some other person was elected President shall be elected to the office of President more than once. But this article shall not apply to any person holding the office of President when this article was proposed by the Congress, and shall not prevent any person who may be holding the office of President, or acting as President, during the term within which this article becomes operative from holding the office of President or acting as President during the remainder of such term.

Section 2 This article shall be inoperative unless it shall have been ratified as an amendment to the Constitution by the legislatures of three-fourths of the several States within seven years from the date of its submission to the States by the Congress.

Amendment XXIII

[Adopted 1961]

Section 1 The District constituting the seat of Government of the United States shall appoint in such manner as the Congress may direct:

A number of electors of President and Vice-President equal to the whole number of Senators and Representatives in Congress to which the District would be entitled if it were a State, but in no event more than the least populous State; they shall be in addition to those appointed by the States, but they shall be considered for the purposes of the election of President and Vice-President, to be electors appointed by a State; and they shall meet in the District and perform such duties as provided by the twelfth article of amendment.

Section 2 The Congress shall have the power to enforce this article by appropriate legislation.

Amendment XXIV

[Adopted 1964]

Section 1 The right of citizens of the United States to vote in any primary or other election for President or Vice-President, for electors for President or Vice-President, or for Senator or Representative in Congress, shall not be denied or abridged by the United States or any State by reason of failure to pay any poll tax or other tax.

Section 2 The Congress shall have the power to enforce this article by appropriate legislation.

Amendment XXV

[Adopted 1967]

Section 1 In case of the removal of the President from office or of his death or resignation, the Vice-President shall become President.

Section 2 Whenever there is a vacancy in the office of the Vice-President, the President shall nominate a Vice-President who shall take office upon confirmation by a majority vote of both Houses of Congress.

Section 3 Whenever the President transmits to the President pro tempore of the Senate and the Speaker of the House of Representatives his written declaration that he is unable to discharge the powers and duties of his office, and until he transmits to them a written declaration to the contrary, such powers and duties shall be discharged by the Vice-President as Acting President.

Section 4 Whenever the Vice-President and a majority of either the principal officers of the executive departments or of such other body as Congress may by law provide, transmit to the President pro tempore of the Senate and the Speaker of the House of Representatives their written declaration that the President is unable to discharge the powers and duties of his office, the Vice-President shall immediately assume the powers and duties of the office as Acting President.

Thereafter, when the President transmits to the President pro tempore of the Senate and the Speaker of the House of Representatives his written declaration that no inability exists, he shall resume the powers and duties of his office unless the Vice-President and a majority of either the principal officers of the executive department[s] or of such other body as Congress may by law provide, transmit within four days to the President pro tempore of the Senate and the Speaker of the House of Representatives their written declaration that the President is unable to discharge the powers and duties of his office. Thereupon Congress shall decide the issue, assembling within forty-eight hours for that purpose if not in session. If the Congress, within twenty-one days after receipt of the latter written declaration, or, if Congress is not in session, within twenty-one days after Congress is required to assemble, determines by two-thirds vote of both Houses that the President is unable to discharge the powers and duties of his office, the Vice-President shall continue to discharge the same as Acting President; otherwise, the President shall resume the powers and duties of his office.

Amendment XXVI

[Adopted 1971]

Section 1 The right of citizens of the United States, who are eighteen years of age or older, to vote shall not be denied or abridged by the United States or by any State on account of age.

Section 2 The Congress shall have power to enforce this article by appropriate legislation.

POPULATION OF THE UNITED STATES

Year	Number of States	Population	Percent Increase	Population Per Square Mile	Percent Urban/ Rural	Percent Male/ Female	Percent White/ Nonwhite	Persons Per House- hold	Median Age
1790	13	3,929,214		4.5	5.1/94.9	NA/NA	80.7/19.3	5.79	NA
1800	16	5,308,483	35.1	6.1	6.1/93.9	NA/NA	81.1/18.9	NA	NA
1810	17	7,239,881	36.4	4.3	7.3/92.7	NA/NA	81.0/19.0	NA	NA
1820	23	9,638,453	33.1	5.5	7.2/92.8	50.8/49.2	81.6/18.4	NA	16.7
1830	24	12,866,020	33.5	7.4	8.8/91.2	50.8/49.2	81.9/18.1	NA	17.2
1840	26	17,069,453	32.7	9.8	10.8/89.2	50.9/49.1	83.2/16.8	NA	17.8
1850	31	23,191,876	35.9	7.9	15.3/84.7	51.0/49.0	84.3/15.7	5.55	18.9
1860	33	31,443,321	35.6	10.6	19.8/80.2	51.2/48.8	85.6/14.4	5.28	19.4
1870	37	39,818,449	26.6	13.4	25.7/74.3	50.6/49.4	86.2/13.8	5.09	20.2
1880	38	50,155,783	26.0	16.9	28.2/71.8	50.9/49.1	86.5/13.5	5.04	20.9
1890	44	62,947,714	25.5	21.2	35.1/64.9	51.2/48.8	87.5/12.5	4.93	22.0
1900	45	75,994,575	20.7	25.6	39.6/60.4	51.1/48.9	87.9/12.1	4.76	22.9
1910	46	91,972,266	21.0	31.0	45.6/54.4	51.5/48.5	88.9/11.1	4.54	24.1
1920	48	105,710,620	14.9	35.6	51.2/48.8	51.0/49.0	89.7/10.3	4.34	25.3
1930	48	122,775,046	16.1	41.2	56.1/43.9	50.6/49.4	89.8/10.2	4.11	26.4
1940	48	131,669,275	7.2	44.2	56.5/43.5	50.2/49.8	89.8/10.2	3.67	29.0
1950	48	150,697,361	14.5	50.7	64.0/36.0	49.7/50.3	89.5/10.5	3.37	30.2
1960	50	179,323,175	18.5	50.6	69.9/30.1	49.3/50.7	88.6/11.4	3.33	29.5
1970	50	203,302,031	13.4	57.4	73.5/26.5	48.7/51.3	87.6/12.4	3.14	28.0
1980	50	226,545,805	11.4	64.0	73.7/26.3	48.6/51.4	86.0/14.0	2.76	30.0
1990	50	248,656,000[a]	8.9	70.3	NA/NA	48.7/51.3[b]	84.4/15.6[b]	2.64[b]	32.3[b]

NA = Not available.
[a] Projection.
[b] 1988 figure.

Immigration Totals by Decade

Years	Number	Years	Number
1820–1830	151,824	1911–1920	5,735,811
1831–1840	599,125	1921–1930	4,107,209
1841–1850	1,713,251	1931–1940	528,431
1851–1860	2,598,214	1941–1950	1,035,039
1861–1870	2,314,824	1951–1960	2,515,479
1871–1880	2,812,191	1961–1970	3,321,677
1881–1890	5,246,613	1971–1980	4,493,000
1891–1900	3,687,546	1981–1987	4,067,600
1901–1910	8,795,386	Total	53,723,220

Sources: *U.S. Bureau of the Census,* Historical Statistics of the United States, Colonial Times to 1970 (1975); *U.S. Bureau of the Census,* Statistical Abstract of the United States, 1989 (1989).

Major Sources of Immigrants by Country (in thousands)

Period	Germany	Italy	Britain (UK)	Ireland	Austria-Hungary	Canada	Russia (USSR)[a]	Mexico	Denmark, Norway, Sweden[b]	Caribbean (West Indies)
1820–1830	8	—	27	54	—	2	—	5	—	4
1831–1840	152	2	76	207	—	14	—	7	2	12
1841–1850	435	2	267	781	—	42	—	3	14	14
1851–1860	952	9	424	914	—	59	—	3	25	11
1861–1870	787	12	607	436	8	154	3	2	126	9
1871–1880	718	56	548	437	73	384	39	5	243	14
1881–1890	1,453	307	807	655	354	393	213	2[c]	656	29
1891–1900	505	652	272	388	593	3	505	—	372	—[d]
1901–1910	341	2,046	526	339	2,145	179	1,597	50	505	108
1911–1920	144	1,110	341	146	896	742	922	219	203	123
1921–1930	412	455	330	221	64	925	89	459	198	75
1931–1940	114	68	29	13	11	109	7	22	11	16
1941–1950	227	58	132	28	28	172	4	61	27	50
1951–1960	478	185	192	57	104	378	6	300	57	123
1961–1970	200	207	231	42	31	287	22	443	45	520
1971–1980	66	130	124	14	16	115	46	637	15	760
1981–1987	49	24	99	11	9	79	47	474	13	576
Total	6,981	5,323	5,032	4,743	4,332	4,037	3,500	2,692	2,512	2,444

Notes: Numbers are rounded. Dash indicates less than one thousand.
[a] Includes Finland, Latvia, Estonia, and Lithuania.
[b] Includes Iceland.
[c] Figure for 1881–1885 only.
[d] Figure for 1894–1900 only.

Sources: *U.S. Bureau of the Census*, Historical Statistics of the United States: Colonial Times to 1970 (1975); *U.S. Bureau of the Census,* Statistical Abstract of the United States, 1989 (1989).

THE AMERICAN FARM

Year	Farm Population (in thousands)	Percent of Total Population	Number of Farms (in thousands)	Total Acres (in thousands)	Average Acreage Per Farm	Corn Production (millions of bushels)	Wheat Production (millions of bushels)
1850	NA	NA	1,449	293,561	203	592[a]	100[a]
1860	NA	NA	2,044	407,213	199	839[b]	173[b]
1870	NA	NA	2,660	407,735	153	1,125	254
1880	21,973	43.8	4,009	536,082	134	1,707	502
1890	24,771	42.3	4,565	623,219	137	1,650	449
1900	29,875	41.9	5,740	841,202	147	2,662	599
1910	32,077	34.9	6,366	881,431	139	2,853	625
1920	31,974	30.1	6,454	958,677	149	3,071	843
1930	30,529	24.9	6,295	990,112	157	2,080	887
1940	30,547	23.2	6,102	1,065,114	175	2,457	815
1950	23,048	15.3	5,388	1,161,420	216	3,075	1,019
1960	15,635	8.7	3,962	1,176,946	297	4,314	1,355
1970	9,712	4.8	2,949	1,102,769	374	4,200	1,370
1980	6,051	2.7	2,428	1,042,000	427	6,600	2,400
1987	4,986	2.0	2,176	1,003,000	461	7,064	2,105

[a] Figure for 1849.
[b] Figure for 1859.
NA = Not available.

THE AMERICAN WORKER

Year	Total Number of Workers	Males as Percent of Total Workers	Females as Percent of Total Workers	Married Women as Percent of Female Workers	Female Workers as Percent of Female Population	Percent of Labor Force Unemployed	Percent of Workers in Labor Unions
1870	12,506,000	85	15	NA	NA	NA	NA
1880	17,392,000	85	15	NA	NA	NA	NA
1890	23,318,000	83	17	13.9	18.9	4 (1894 = 18)	NA
1900	29,073,000	82	18	15.4	20.6	5	3
1910	38,167,000	79	21	24.7	25.4	6	6
1920	41,614,000	79	21	23.0	23.7	5 (1921 = 12)	12
1930	48,830,000	78	22	28.9	24.8	9 (1933 = 25)	7
1940	53,011,000	76	24	36.4	27.4	15 (1944 = 1)	27
1950	59,643,000	72	28	52.1	31.4	5	25
1960	69,877,000	68	32	59.9	34.8	5.4	26
1970	82,049,000	63	37	63.4	42.6	4.8	25
1980	108,544,000	58	42	59.7	51.1	7.0	23
1987	119,865,000	55	45	59.1	55.4	6.1 (1983 = 9.5)	17

NA = Not available.

Territorial Expansion of the United States

Territory	Date Acquired	Square Miles	How Acquired
Original states and territories	1783	888,685	Treaty with Great Britain
Louisiana Purchase	1803	827,192	Purchase from France
Florida	1819	72,003	Treaty with Spain
Texas	1845	390,143	Annexation of independent nation
Oregon	1846	285,580	Treaty with Great Britain
Mexican Cession	1848	529,017	Conquest from Mexico
Gadsden Purchase	1853	29,640	Purchase from Mexico
Alaska	1867	589,757	Purchase from Russia
Hawaii	1898	6,450	Annexation of independent nation
The Philippines	1899	115,600	Conquest from Spain (granted independence in 1946)
Puerto Rico	1899	3,435	Conquest from Spain
Guam	1899	212	Conquest from Spain
American Samoa	1900	76	Treaty with Germany and Great Britain
Panama Canal Zone	1904	553	Treaty with Panama (returned to Panama by treaty in 1978)
Corn Islands	1914	4	Treaty with Nicaragua (returned to Nicaragua by treaty in 1971)
Virgin Islands	1917	133	Purchase from Denmark
Pacific Islands Trust (Micronesia)	1947	8,489	Trusteeship under United Nations (some granted independence)
All others (Midway, Wake, and other islands)		42	

Admission of States into the Union

State	Date of Admission	State	Date of Admission
1. Delaware	December 7, 1787	26. Michigan	January 26, 1837
2. Pennsylvania	December 12, 1787	27. Florida	March 3, 1845
3. New Jersey	December 18, 1787	28. Texas	December 29, 1845
4. Georgia	January 2, 1788	29. Iowa	December 28, 1846
5. Connecticut	January 9, 1788	30. Wisconsin	May 29, 1848
6. Massachusetts	February 6, 1788	31. California	September 9, 1850
7. Maryland	April 28, 1788	32. Minnesota	May 11, 1858
8. South Carolina	May 23, 1788	33. Oregon	February 14, 1859
9. New Hampshire	June 21, 1788	34. Kansas	January 29, 1861
10. Virginia	June 25, 1788	35. West Virginia	June 20, 1863
11. New York	July 26, 1788	36. Nevada	October 31, 1864
12. North Carolina	November 21, 1789	37. Nebraska	March 1, 1867
13. Rhode Island	May 29, 1790	38. Colorado	August 1, 1876
14. Vermont	March 4, 1791	39. North Dakota	November 2, 1889
15. Kentucky	June 1, 1792	40. South Dakota	November 2, 1889
16. Tennessee	June 1, 1796	41. Montana	November 8, 1889
17. Ohio	March 1, 1803	42. Washington	November 11, 1889
18. Louisiana	April 30, 1812	43. Idaho	July 3, 1890
19. Indiana	December 11, 1816	44. Wyoming	July 10, 1890
20. Mississippi	December 10, 1817	45. Utah	January 4, 1896
21. Illinois	December 3, 1818	46. Oklahoma	November 16, 1907
22. Alabama	December 14, 1819	47. New Mexico	January 6, 1912
23. Maine	March 15, 1820	48. Arizona	February 14, 1912
24. Missouri	August 10, 1821	49. Alaska	January 3, 1959
25. Arkansas	June 15, 1836	50. Hawaii	August 21, 1959

Presidential Elections

Year	Number of States	Candidates	Parties	Popular Vote	% of Popular Vote	Elec-toral Vote	Voter Partici-pation[b]
1789	11	**George Washington**	No party			69	
		John Adams	designations			34	
		Other Candidates				35	
1792	15	**George Washington**	No party			132	
		John Adams	designations			77	
		George Clinton				50	
		Other candidates				5	
1796	16	**John Adams**	Federalist			71	
		Thomas Jefferson	Democratic-Republican			68	
		Thomas Pinckney	Federalist			59	
		Aaron Burr	Democratic-Republican			30	
		Other candidates				48	
1800	16	**Thomas Jefferson**	Democratic-Republican			73	
		Aaron Burr	Democratic-Republican			73	
		John Adams	Federalist			65	
		Charles C. Pinckney	Federalist			64	
		John Jay	Federalist			1	
1804	17	**Thomas Jefferson**	Democratic-Republican			162	
		Charles C. Pinckney	Federalist			14	
1808	17	**James Madison**	Democratic-Republican			122	
		Charles C. Pinckney	Federalist			47	
		George Clinton	Democratic-Republican			6	
1812	18	**James Madison**	Democratic-Republican			128	
		DeWitt Clinton	Federalist			89	
1816	19	**James Monroe**	Democratic-Republican			183	
		Rufus King	Federalist			34	
1820	24	**James Monroe**	Democratic-Republican			231	
		John Quincy Adams	Independent Republican			1	
1824	24	**John Quincy Adams**	Democratic-Republican	108,740	30.5	84	26.9
		Andrew Jackson	Democratic-Republican	153,544	43.1	99	
		Henry Clay	Democratic-Republican	47,136	13.2	37	
		William H. Crawford	Democratic-Republican	46,618	13.1	41	

Year	Number of States	Candidates	Parties	Popular Vote	% of Popular Vote	Elec-toral Vote	Voter Partici-pation[b]
1828	24	**Andrew Jackson**	Democratic	647,286	56.0	178	57.6
		John Quincy Adams	National Republican	508,064	44.0	83	
1832	24	**Andrew Jackson**	Democratic	688,242	54.5	219	55.4
		Henry Clay	National Republican	473,462	37.5	49	
		William Wirt	Anti-Masonic	101,051	8.0	7	
		John Floyd	Democratic			11	
1836	26	**Martin Van Buren**	Democratic	765,483	50.9	170	57.8
		William H. Harrison	Whig			73	
		Hugh L. White	Whig	739,795	49.1	26	
		Daniel Webster	Whig			14	
		W. P. Mangum	Whig			11	
1840	26	**William H. Harrison**	Whig	1,274,624	53.1	234	80.2
		Martin Van Buren	Democratic	1,127,781	46.9	60	
1844	26	**James K. Polk**	Democratic	1,338,464	49.6	170	78.9
		Henry Clay	Whig	1,300,097	48.1	105	
		James G. Birney	Liberty	62,300	2.3		
1848	30	**Zachary Taylor**	Whig	1,360,967	47.4	163	72.7
		Lewis Cass	Democratic	1,222,342	42.5	127	
		Martin Van Buren	Free Soil	291,263	10.1		
1852	31	**Franklin Pierce**	Democratic	1,601,117	50.9	254	69.6
		Winfield Scott	Whig	1,385,453	44.1	42	
		John P. Hale	Free Soil	155,825	5.0		
1856	31	**James Buchanan**	Democratic	1,832,955	45.3	174	78.9
		John C. Frémont	Republican	1,339,932	33.1	114	
		Millard Fillmore	American	871,731	21.6	8	
1860	33	**Abraham Lincoln**	Republican	1,865,593	39.8	180	81.2
		Stephen A. Douglas	Democratic	1,382,713	29.5	12	
		John C. Breckinridge	Democratic	848,356	18.1	72	
		John Bell	Constitutional Union	592,906	12.6	39	
1864	36	**Abraham Lincoln**	Republican	2,206,938	55.0	212	73.8
		George B. McClellan	Democratic	1,803,787	45.0	21	
1868	37	**Ulysses S. Grant**	Republican	3,013,421	52.7	214	78.1
		Horatio Seymour	Democratic	2,706,829	47.3	80	
1872	37	**Ulysses S. Grant**	Republican	3,596,745	55.6	286	71.3
		Horace Greeley	Democratic	2,843,446	43.9	a	
1876	38	**Rutherford B. Hayes**	Republican	4,036,572	48.0	185	81.8
		Samuel J. Tilden	Democratic	4,284,020	51.0	184	
1880	38	**James A. Garfield**	Republican	4,453,295	48.5	214	79.4
		Winfield S. Hancock	Democratic	4,414,082	48.1	155	
		James B. Weaver	Greenback-Labor	308,578	3.4		
1884	38	**Grover Cleveland**	Democratic	4,879,507	48.5	219	77.5
		James G. Blaine	Republican	4,850,293	48.2	182	
		Benjamin F. Butler	Greenback-Labor	175,370	1.8		
		John P. St. John	Prohibition	150,369	1.5		

Year	Number of States	Candidates	Parties	Popular Vote	% of Popular Vote	Elec-toral Vote	Voter Partici-pation[b]
1888	38	**Benjamin Harrison**	Republican	5,447,129	47.9	233	79.3
		Grover Cleveland	Democratic	5,537,857	48.6	168	
		Clinton B. Fisk	Prohibition	249,506	2.2		
		Anson J. Streeter	Union Labor	146,935	1.3		
1892	44	**Grover Cleveland**	Democratic	5,555,426	46.1	277	74.7
		Benjamin Harrison	Republican	5,182,690	43.0	145	
		James B. Weaver	People's	1,029,846	8.5	22	
		John Bidwell	Prohibition	264,133	2.2		
1896	45	**William McKinley**	Republican	7,102,246	51.1	271	79.3
		William J. Bryan	Democratic	6,492,559	47.7	176	
1900	45	**William McKinley**	Republican	7,218,491	51.7	292	73.2
		William J. Bryan	Democratic; Populist	6,356,734	45.5	155	
		John C. Wooley	Prohibition	208,914	1.5		
1904	45	**Theodore Roosevelt**	Republican	7,628,461	57.4	336	65.2
		Alton B. Parker	Democratic	5,084,223	37.6	140	
		Eugene V. Debs	Socialist	402,283	3.0		
		Silas C. Swallow	Prohibition	258,536	1.9		
1908	46	**William H. Taft**	Republican	7,675,320	51.6	321	65.4
		William J. Bryan	Democratic	6,412,294	43.1	162	
		Eugene V. Debs	Socialist	420,793	2.8		
		Eugene W. Chafin	Prohibition	253,840	1.7		
1912	48	**Woodrow Wilson**	Democratic	6,296,547	41.9	435	58.8
		Theodore Roosevelt	Progressive	4,118,571	27.4	88	
		William H. Taft	Republican	3,486,720	23.2	8	
		Eugene V. Debs	Socialist	900,672	6.0		
		Eugene W. Chafin	Prohibition	206,275	1.4		
1916	48	**Woodrow Wilson**	Democratic	9,127,695	49.4	277	61.6
		Charles E. Hughes	Republican	8,533,507	46.2	254	
		A. L. Benson	Socialist	585,113	3.2		
		J. Frank Hanly	Prohibition	220,506	1.2		
1920	48	**Warren G. Harding**	Republican	16,143,407	60.4	404	49.2
		James M. Cox	Democratic	9,130,328	34.2	127	
		Eugene V. Debs	Socialist	919,799	3.4		
		P. P. Christensen	Farmer-Labor	265,411	1.0		
1924	48	**Calvin Coolidge**	Republican	15,718,211	54.0	382	48.9
		John W. Davis	Democratic	8,385,283	28.8	136	
		Robert M. La Follette	Progressive	4,831,289	16.6	13	
1928	48	**Herbert C. Hoover**	Republican	21,391,993	58.2	444	56.9
		Alfred E. Smith	Democratic	15,016,169	40.9	87	
1932	48	**Franklin D. Roosevelt**	Democratic	22,809,638	57.4	472	56.9
		Herbert C. Hoover	Republican	15,758,901	39.7	59	
		Norman Thomas	Socialist	881,951	2.2		
1936	48	**Franklin D. Roosevelt**	Democratic	27,752,869	60.8	523	61.0
		Alfred M. Landon	Republican	16,674,665	36.5	8	
		William Lemke	Union	882,479	1.9		

Year	Number of States	Candidates	Parties	Popular Vote	% of Popular Vote	Electoral Vote	Voter Participation[b]
1940	48	**Franklin D. Roosevelt**	Democratic	27,307,819	54.8	449	62.5
		Wendell L. Willkie	Republican	22,321,018	44.8	82	
1944	48	**Franklin D. Roosevelt**	Democratic	25,606,585	53.5	432	55.9
		Thomas E. Dewey	Republican	22,014,745	46.0	99	
1948	48	**Harry S Truman**	Democratic	24,179,345	49.6	303	53.0
		Thomas E. Dewey	Republican	21,991,291	45.1	189	
		J. Strom Thurmond	States' Rights	1,176,125	2.4	39	
		Henry A. Wallace	Progressive	1,157,326	2.4		
1952	48	**Dwight D. Eisenhower**	Republican	33,936,234	55.1	442	63.3
		Adlai E. Stevenson	Democratic	27,314,992	44.4	89	
1956	48	**Dwight D. Eisenhower**	Republican	35,590,472	57.6	457	60.6
		Adlai E. Stevenson	Democratic	26,022,752	42.1	73	
1960	50	**John F. Kennedy**	Democratic	34,226,731	49.7	303	62.8
		Richard M. Nixon	Republican	34,108,157	49.5	219	
1964	50	**Lyndon B. Johnson**	Democratic	43,129,566	61.1	486	61.7
		Barry M. Goldwater	Republican	27,178,188	38.5	52	
1968	50	**Richard M. Nixon**	Republican	31,785,480	43.4	301	60.6
		Hubert H. Humphrey	Democratic	31,275,166	42.7	191	
		George C. Wallace	American Independent	9,906,473	13.5	46	
1972	50	**Richard M. Nixon**	Republican	47,169,911	60.7	520	55.2
		George S. McGovern	Democratic	29,170,383	37.5	17	
		John G. Schmitz	American	1,099,482	1.4		
1976	50	**Jimmy Carter**	Democratic	40,830,763	50.1	297	53.5
		Gerald R. Ford	Republican	39,147,793	48.0	240	
1980	50	**Ronald Reagan**	Republican	43,899,248	50.8	489	52.6
		Jimmy Carter	Democratic	35,481,432	41.0	49	
		John B. Anderson	Independent	5,719,437	6.6	0	
		Ed Clark	Libertarian	920,859	1.1	0	
1984	50	**Ronald Reagan**	Republican	54,455,075	58.8	525	53.1
		Walter Mondale	Democratic	37,577,185	40.6	13	
1988	50	**George Bush**	Republican	48,901,046	53.4	426	50.2
		Michael Dukakis	Democratic	41,809,030	45.6	111[c]	

Candidates receiving less than 1 percent of the popular vote have been omitted. Thus the percentage of popular vote given for any election year may not total 100 percent.

Before the passage of the Twelfth Amendment in 1804, the Electoral College voted for two presidential candidates; the runner-up became vice president.

Before 1824, most presidential electors were chosen by state legislatures, not by popular vote.

[a]Greeley died shortly after the election; the electors supporting him then divided their votes among minor candidates.

[b]Percent of voting-age population casting ballots.

[c]One elector from West Virginia cast her Electoral College presidential ballot for Lloyd Bentsen, the Democratic party's vice presidential candidate.

Presidents and Vice Presidents

1.	President	**George Washington**	1789–1797	22.	President	**Grover Cleveland**	1885–1889
	Vice President	John Adams	1789–1797		Vice President	Thomas A. Hendricks	1885–1889
2.	President	**John Adams**	1797–1801	23.	President	**Benjamin Harrison**	1889–1893
	Vice President	Thomas Jefferson	1797–1801		Vice President	Levi P. Morton	1889–1893
3.	President	**Thomas Jefferson**	1801–1809	24.	President	**Grover Cleveland**	1893–1897
	Vice President	Aaron Burr	1801–1805		Vice President	Adlai E. Stevenson	1893–1897
	Vice President	George Clinton	1805–1809	25.	President	**William McKinley**	1897–1901
4.	President	**James Madison**	1809–1817		Vice President	Garret A. Hobart	1897–1901
	Vice President	George Clinton	1809–1813			Theodore Roosevelt	1901
	Vice President	Elbridge Gerry	1813–1817	26.	President	**Theodore Roosevelt**	1901–1909
5.	President	**James Monroe**	1817–1825		Vice President	Charles Fairbanks	1905–1909
	Vice President	Daniel Tompkins	1817–1825	27.	President	**William H. Taft**	1909–1913
6.	President	**John Quincy Adams**	1825–1829		Vice President	James S. Sherman	1909–1913
	Vice President	John C. Calhoun	1825–1829	28.	President	**Woodrow Wilson**	1913–1921
7.	President	**Andrew Jackson**	1829–1837		Vice President	Thomas R. Marshall	1913–1921
	Vice President	John C. Calhoun	1829–1833	29.	President	**Warren G. Harding**	1921–1923
	Vice President	Martin Van Buren	1833–1837		Vice President	Calvin Coolidge	1921–1923
8.	President	**Martin Van Buren**	1837–1841	30.	President	**Calvin Coolidge**	1923–1929
	Vice President	Richard M. Johnson	1837–1841		Vice President	Charles G. Dawes	1925–1929
9.	President	**William H. Harrison**	1841	31.	President	**Herbert C. Hoover**	1929–1933
	Vice President	John Tyler	1841		Vice President	Charles Curtis	1929–1933
10.	President	**John Tyler**	1841–1845	32.	President	**Franklin D. Roosevelt**	1933–1945
	Vice President	none			Vice President	John N. Garner	1933–1941
11.	President	**James K. Polk**	1845–1849			Henry A. Wallace	1941–1945
	Vice President	George M. Dallas	1845–1849			Harry S Truman	1945
12.	President	**Zachary Taylor**	1849–1850	33.	President	**Harry S Truman**	1945–1953
	Vice President	Millard Fillmore	1849–1850		Vice President	Alben W. Barkley	1949–1953
13.	President	**Millard Fillmore**	1850–1853	34.	President	**Dwight D. Eisenhower**	1953–1961
	Vice President	none			Vice President	Richard M. Nixon	1953–1961
14.	President	**Franklin Pierce**	1853–1857	35.	President	**John F. Kennedy**	1961–1963
	Vice President	William R. King	1853–1857		Vice President	Lyndon B. Johnson	1961–1963
15.	President	**James Buchanan**	1857–1861	36.	President	**Lyndon B. Johnson**	1963–1969
	Vice President	John C. Breckinridge	1857–1861		Vice President	Hubert H. Humphrey	1965–1969
16.	President	**Abraham Lincoln**	1861–1865	37.	President	**Richard M. Nixon**	1969–1974
	Vice President	Hannibal Hamlin	1861–1865		Vice President	Spiro T. Agnew	1969–1973
	Vice President	Andrew Johnson	1865			Gerald R. Ford	1973–1974
17.	President	**Andrew Johnson**	1865–1869	38.	President	**Gerald R. Ford**	1974–1977
	Vice President	none			Vice President	Nelson A. Rockefeller	1974–1977
18.	President	**Ulysses S. Grant**	1869–1877	39.	President	**Jimmy Carter**	1977–1981
	Vice President	Schuyler Colfax	1869–1873		Vice President	Walter F. Mondale	1977–1981
	Vice President	Henry Wilson	1873–1877	40.	President	**Ronald Reagan**	1981–1989
19.	President	**Rutherford B. Hayes**	1877–1881		Vice President	George Bush	1981–1989
	Vice President	William A. Wheeler	1877–1881	41.	President	**George Bush**	1989–
20.	President	**James A. Garfield**	1881		Vice President	Dan Quayle	1989–
	Vice President	Chester A. Arthur	1881				
21.	President	**Chester A. Arthur**	1881–1885				
	Vice President	none					

Justices of the Supreme Court

	Term of Service	Years of Service	Life Span		Term of Service	Years of Service	Life Span
John Jay	1789–1795	5	1745–1829	Stephen J. Field	1863–1897	34	1816–1899
John Rutledge	1789–1791	1	1739–1800	Salmon P. Chase	1864–1873	8	1808–1873
William Cushing	1789–1810	20	1732–1810	William Strong	1870–1880	10	1808–1895
James Wilson	1789–1798	8	1742–1798	Joseph P. Bradley	1870–1892	22	1813–1892
John Blair	1789–1796	6	1732–1800	Ward Hunt	1873–1882	9	1810–1886
Robert H. Harrison	1789–1790	—	1745–1790	Morrison R. Waite	1874–1888	14	1816–1888
James Iredell	1790–1799	9	1751–1799	John M. Harlan	1877–1911	34	1833–1911
Thomas Johnson	1791–1793	1	1732–1819	William B. Woods	1880–1887	7	1824–1887
William Paterson	1793–1806	13	1745–1806	Stanley Matthews	1881–1889	7	1824–1889
John Rutledge*	1795	—	1739–1800	Horace Gray	1882–1902	20	1828–1902
Samuel Chase	1796–1811	15	1741–1811	Samuel Blatchford	1882–1893	11	1820–1893
Oliver Ellsworth	1796–1800	4	1745–1807	Lucius Q. C. Lamar	1888–1893	5	1825–1893
Bushrod Washington	1798–1829	31	1762–1829	Melville W. Fuller	1888–1910	21	1833–1910
Alfred Moore	1799–1804	4	1755–1810	David J. Brewer	1890–1910	20	1837–1910
John Marshall	1801–1835	34	1755–1835	Henry B. Brown	1890–1906	16	1836–1913
William Johnson	1804–1834	30	1771–1834	George Shiras, Jr.	1892–1903	10	1832–1924
H. Brockholst Livingston	1806–1823	16	1757–1823	Howell E. Jackson	1893–1895	2	1832–1895
Thomas Todd	1807–1826	18	1765–1826	Edward D. White	1894–1910	16	1845–1921
Joseph Story	1811–1845	33	1779–1845	Rufus W. Peckham	1895–1909	14	1838–1909
Gabriel Duval	1811–1835	24	1752–1844	Joseph McKenna	1898–1925	26	1843–1926
Smith Thompson	1823–1843	20	1768–1843	Oliver W. Holmes	1902–1932	30	1841–1935
Robert Trimble	1826–1828	2	1777–1828	William R. Day	1903–1922	19	1849–1923
John McLean	1829–1861	32	1785–1861	William H. Moody	1906–1910	3	1853–1917
Henry Baldwin	1830–1844	14	1780–1844	Horace H. Lurton	1910–1914	4	1844–1914
James M. Wayne	1835–1867	32	1790–1867	Charles E. Hughes	1910–1916	5	1862–1948
Roger B. Taney	1836–1864	28	1777–1864	Edward D. White	1910–1921	11	1845–1921
Philip P. Barbour	1836–1841	4	1783–1841	Willis Van Devanter	1911–1937	26	1859–1941
John Catron	1837–1865	28	1786–1865	Joseph R. Lamar	1911–1916	5	1857–1916
John McKinley	1837–1852	15	1780–1852	Mahlon Pitney	1912–1922	10	1858–1924
Peter V. Daniel	1841–1860	19	1784–1860	James C. McReynolds	1914–1941	26	1862–1946
Samuel Nelson	1845–1872	27	1792–1873	Louis D. Brandeis	1916–1939	22	1856–1941
Levi Woodbury	1845–1851	5	1789–1851	John H. Clarke	1916–1922	6	1857–1945
Robert C. Grier	1846–1870	23	1794–1870	William H. Taft	1921–1930	8	1857–1930
Benjamin R. Curtis	1851–1857	6	1809–1874	George Sutherland	1922–1938	15	1862–1942
John A. Campbell	1853–1861	8	1811–1889	Pierce Butler	1922–1939	16	1866–1939
Nathan Clifford	1858–1881	23	1803–1881	Edward T. Sanford	1923–1930	7	1865–1930
Noah H. Swayne	1862–1881	18	1804–1884	Harlan F. Stone	1925–1941	16	1872–1946
Samuel F. Miller	1862–1890	28	1816–1890	Charles E. Hughes	1930–1941	11	1862–1948
David Davis	1862–1877	14	1815–1886	Owen J. Roberts	1930–1945	15	1875–1955

	Term of Service	Years of Service	Life Span		Term of Service	Years of Service	Life Span
Benjamin N. Cardozo	1932–1938	6	1870–1938	William J. Brennan, Jr.	1956–	—	1906–
Hugo L. Black	1937–1971	34	1886–1971	Charles E. Whittaker	1957–1962	5	1901–1973
Stanley F. Reed	1938–1957	19	1884–1980	Potter Stewart	1958–1981	23	1915–1985
Felix Frankfurter	1939–1962	23	1882–1965	Byron R. White	1962–	—	1917–
William O. Douglas	1939–1975	36	1898–1980	Arthur J. Goldberg	1962–1965	3	1908–
Frank Murphy	1940–1949	9	1890–1949	Abe Fortas	1965–1969	4	1910–1982
Harlan F. Stone	1941–1946	5	1872–1946	Thurgood Marshall	1967–	—	1908–
James F. Byrnes	1941–1942	1	1879–1972	*Warren C. Burger*	1969–1986	17	1907–
Robert H. Jackson	1941–1954	13	1892–1954	Harry A. Blackmun	1970–	—	1908–
Wiley B. Rutledge	1943–1949	6	1894–1949	Lewis F. Powell, Jr.	1971–1987	16	1907–
Harold H. Burton	1945–1958	13	1888–1964	*William H. Rehnquist*	1971–	—	1924–
Fred M. Vinson	1946–1953	7	1890–1953	John P. Stevens III	1975–	—	1920–
Tom C. Clark	1949–1967	18	1899–1977	Sandra Day O'Connor	1981–	—	1930–
Sherman Minton	1949–1956	7	1890–1965	Antonin Scalia	1986–	—	1936–
Earl Warren	1953–1969	16	1891–1974	Anthony M. Kennedy	1988–	—	1936–
John Marshall Harlan	1955–1971	16	1899–1971				

*Appointed and served one term, but not confirmed by the Senate.
Note: Chief justices are in italics.

Index

American Revolution (*cont.*)
resulting from, 117; war debts from, 127
American Society for Promotion of Temperance, 220–221
American System, 155, 225, 228
American system of manufacturing, 166
Amnesty, for Southerners, 276
Amnesty Act (1872), 286
Andros, Edmund, 45, 46
Anglicans: migration of merchants to New England, 43; in Massachusetts, 46; loyalist sentiment among clergy, 90
Anne (Queen of England), 53
Anthony, Susan B., 278
Anti-Catholicism, 208
Antifederalists: opposition to Constitution by, 120–121; ethnic makeup of, 121; representation in First Congress, 124
Anti-Klan laws, 286
Antimasonry movement, 218, 221–222
Antislavery. *See* Abolitionism; Abolitionists
Antiwar sentiment, during Civil War, 266, 268–269
Apaches, 14
Appomattox Courthouse, 271
Apprentice laws, 280
Architecture: African influence on, 58–59; Jefferson's views of, 107; post-Revolution, 107
Argentina, 156
Arizona, acquisition of, 240
Arkansas: political reform in, 191; rejection of secession by, 251
Arkansas River, 144
Armada, 14
Army, U.S.: during War of *1812,* 149, 150; restriction of Johnson's power over, 279
Arnold, Benedict, 102
Arsenals, 165
Art: conflict between virtue and, 106–107; post-Revolution, 107
Articles of Confederation: vs. Constitution, 105; system of government under, 113, 115, 125; ratification of, 113; attempt to amend, 115; weaknesses of, 117; movement toward revision of, 118; on slavery in Northwest Territories, 240
Asante, 34
Assemblies, in 18th-century colonies, 64–65
Assimilation: 18th-century, 53–54; of Native Americans, 210
Associations, in 19th-century urban life, 201–202
Astor, John Jacob, 202, 204
Asylums, 221
Atlanta, Georgia: food riots in, 266; occupation of, 270

Atlanta University, 283
Atlantic trade routes, 43 (ill.)
Attorney general, 125
Augusta, Georgia, food riots in, 266
Awful Disclosures of Maria Monk, 208
Azores, 42
Aztecs, 1, 6

Bacon, Nathaniel, 41
Baltimore, Maryland: free black institutions in, 111; British attack on, 153; impact of transportation advances on, 162; gas service chartered by, 200; free blacks in, 214; Antimason convention in, 222
Baltimore and Ohio Railroad, 162
Banking: political controversy over, 166; 19th-century advances in, 169–170; impact of Civil War on, 260.
Bank of England, 128
Bank of the United States: charter of, 128; Constitution and, 128; expiration of, 154, 169. *See also* Second Bank of the United States
Bankruptcies, 19th-century, 164
Bank stocks, 166
Banneker, Benjamin, 111, 112 (ill.)
Bantus, 8
Baptists, 67, 111
Barbados, 33, 34
Barbary states, 147
Barnraisings, 196
Barton, Clara, 263
Baseball, 201
Battle of Antietam, 258
Battle of Bull Run, 255
Battle of Chancellorsville, 267
Battle of Chattanooga, 269
Battle of Fallen Timbers, 117, 151
Battle of Gettysburg, 267
Battle of Horseshoe Bend, 150, 153
Battle of New Orleans, 153, 154
Battle of Oriskany, 99, 100
Battle of Put-in-Bay, 150
Battle of Queenstown, 150
Battle of Shiloh, 257
Battle of the Thames, 149, 150, 152 (ill.), 153
Battle of the Wilderness, 270–271
Battle of Trafalgar, 147
Battle of Yorktown, 102
Bay Psalm Book, 61
Beach, Moses Yale, 202
Beaver Wars, 39
Beecher, Catharine, 205
Beecher, Mary, 205
Bees, communal, 196, 198 (ill.)
Bell, John, 249
Benevolent activities: of free blacks, 111; during Second Great Awakening, 137, 219–220; involvement of women in, 215
Benevolent societies, 164

Benjamin, John, 87
Benjamin, Sarah, 87
Bennington, New York, 99
Bennitt, James, 182
Bennitt, Nancy, 182
Berbers, 6
Bering Strait, 2
Berkeley, John Lord, 32
Berkeley, William, 41
Bernard, Francis, 81
Bibb, Henry, 214
Biddle, Nicholas, 229
Bill of Rights, 285; Antifederalists and, 120, 121; creation of, 124
Birmingham, Alabama, 281
Birney, James G., 224, 235
Birth control, 196; in 19th century, 205
Birthrate: Southern, 184; decline in, 205
Black churches: as cultural centers, 111; founding of colleges by, 283; founding of, 283, 284
Black codes, 214, 277, 278
Blackfeet, 14
Black nationalism, 214
Black Robes, 13
Blacks. *See* African-Americans
Board of Trade and Plantations, 44
Body of Laws and Liberties (Massachusetts), 25
Boisseau, Alfred, 211 (ill.)
Boom-and-bust cycles, 164, 175
Boston, Massachusetts, 166; settlement of, 22, 23; shipbuilding in, 55; resistance to British taxation, 82, 84–85; free blacks in, 111; riot control in, 202; Irish immigrants in, 207; anti-Catholicism in, 208
Boston Chronicle, 69
Boston Committee of Correspondence, 85
Boston Gazette, 83
Boston Manufacturing Company, 168
Boston Massacre, 82, 83 (ill.)
Boston Tea Party, 84–85
Bouquet, Henry, 75 (ill.)
Bowery boy, 201–202
Bowery Theater, 201
Bowling Green, Kentucky, 161
Braddock, Edward, 73
Bradwell, Myra, 285
Bradwell v. *Illinois,* 285
Bragg, Braxton, 258
Brandywine Creek, Pennsylvania, 99
Brant, Joseph, 99
Brant, Mary, 99
Brazil, 11
Breckinridge, John C., 249
Breevoort, Henry, Jr., 204
Breevoort, Laura Carson, 204
Bremer, Fredrika, 196
British constitution, 112
Brook Farm, Indiana, 198
Brooklyn, New York, population growth in, 199

Inflation: post-Revolution, 115; during Civil War, 259–261
Inoculation, smallpox, 63
Insane asylums, 221
Institutions: for free blacks, 111, 214; development of, 181
Interchangeable parts, 166
Interregnum period, 29
Interstate commerce, Supreme Court decisions regarding, 165
Intervention: proposed U.S.-British declaration against European, 156; Monroe Doctrine's attempt to avoid, 156–157
Intolerable Acts. *See* Coercive Acts
Inventions, 165
Irish immigrants: migration to Pennsylvania, 32; labor in textile mills, 168, 170 (ill.), 171; as landless Southerners, 182; in New York City, 199; in Boston, 207; in 19th century, 207–208; discontent with Civil War, 268
Iron industry, 54, 170, 260, 281
Iroquois, 3, 5, 74; political structure of, 6; drawing of, 40 (ill.); neutrality of, 71, 73; erosion of power of, 93; settlement in Canada, 100; treaty with, 116; religious revival, 137–138
Iroquois Confederacy: Beaver Wars and, 39; neutrality of, 71; split during American Revolution, 99–100; land claims of, 116
Isabella of Castile (Queen of Spain), 10, 11
Islam, in African cultures, 6, 8. *See also* Muslims

Jackson, Andrew, 226 (ill.), 350; role in War of *1812*, 149–150, 153; Indian policy of, 211–212; support by opponents of religious reform, 218; Freemasonry and, 222; in campaign of *1824*, 225; background of, 226; as president, 227–230; opposition to nullification doctrine, 228–229; and Second Bank of the United States, 229; use of veto by, 230
Jackson, Rachel, 226
Jackson, Thomas "Stonewall," 255, 257–258, 267
Jacksonians, 225–228
Jacobites, 53
James (Duke of York), 29, 31–32
James I (King of England), 15, 16, 18
James II (King of England), 45, 46
Jamestown, Virginia, 16, 18
Jay, John: participation at First Continental Congress, 88; as negotiator of Treaty of Paris, 102; campaign for ratification of Constitution by, 121; negotiation of

trade and territorial issues with England, 130
Jay Treaty (1796), 130–131
Jefferson, Thomas, 141 (ill.), 191, 225; views regarding slave system, 60; role in Declaration of Independence, 95; views regarding architecture, 107; views regarding African-Americans, 111; as first secretary of state, 126; view of Bank of the United States, 128; as member of Republican faction, 129; conflict regarding Treaty of Alliance, 129; as vice president, 131; handling of Alien and Sedition Acts, 133; election of *1800*, 134; Republicanism of, 138, 154; inauguration of, 140, 141, 147; appointment of Supreme Court justices by, 142; consolidation of Republican power by, 142; and westward expansion, 144; election of *1804*, 144–145; actions regarding *Chesapeake* Affair, 148; suspension of Non-Importation Act, 148; view of individual freedom, 164–165
Jeremiads, 43
Jeremiah, Thomas, 91
Jervis, John, 160, 162
Jesuit missionaries, 13, 24
Jewish immigrants: in colonies, 54; from Germany, 208
Jews, expulsion from Spain, 10
Jobbers, 169
Johnson, Andrew: and election of *1864*, 269; background of, 273; impeachment and acquittal of, 273, 279; Reconstruction plan of, 274, 276–277; and congressional Reconstruction plan, 277–280; attempt to block Fourteenth Amendment, 278; confrontation with Congress, 279; congressional actions to restrict, 279
Johnson, William, 92, 93, 99
Johnston, Albert Sidney, 255, 257
Johnston, Joseph E., 267, 270
Journeymen, 167
Judaism, 25
Judicial review, 143
Judiciary Act (1789), 125, 126, 143
Judiciary Act (1801), 142, 144, 145
Judiciary branch, revision during Jefferson administration, 142
Judiciary Committee, House, 279
Julian, George, 277
Justice Act, 85

Kansas: resettlement of Indians in, 209–210; organization of territory of, 244, 246, 248; black migration to, 288
Kansas Indians, 209
Kansas-Nebraska Act, 244, 246

Kearny, Stephen, 240
Kemble, Fanny, 177
Kentucky: borders, 92; migration of slaveholders to, 136; War of *1812* enlistees from, 149, 153; alignment with Union by, 251
Kentucky Resolution, 133–134
Key, Francis Scott, 153
King, Rufus, 145, 148, 155
King George's War, 55, 56, 71
King Philip (Metacomet), 41
King's Mountain, 101
Knickerbocker Club, 201
Know-Nothings, 245
Knox, Henry, 126
Knox College, 283
Krimmel, John Lewis, 146 (ill.)
Ku Klux Klan: during Reconstruction, 274, 282; legislation to deter, 286

Labor: slave, 33, 52, 56, 185; specialization on plantations, 59; mill protest over conditions, 171; shortages during Civil War, 259. *See also* Sexual division of labor
Labor force: women in, 111, 204, 259, 285; and boom-and-bust cycles, 164; Irish, 168, 170 (ill.), 171; children in, 171; during Civil War, 259, 261–262; fear of influx of black workers in, 268
Labor movement, 171–172
Labor strikes: by mill workers, 171; by bootmakers, 172; during Civil War, 261, 262
Labor unions: history of, 172; during Civil War, 261–262
Lady of Cofitachique, 6
Laird rams, 269
Lake Champlain, 150, 153
Lake Erie, 150, 161
Lalawethika, 150–151
Land: 18th-century conflict regarding, 65–66; sale of public, 165; value of farm, 172; in west, 175; speculation in public, 229–230; set aside for African-Americans after Civil War, 274. *See also* Property rights
Land grants: railroad construction subsidized through, 165; in California, 175; limited to whites, 213
Lane Seminary, 220
La Salle, Robert Cavelier de, 39
Latin America: racial character of, 12; recognition of governments in, 156; and European noncolonialization in Western Hemisphere, 157. *See also individual countries*
Latrobe, Benjamin H., 59 (ill.), 107
Lawrence, Amos A., 237
Lawrence, Kansas, 246
Leather industry, 170
Lecompton Constitution, 248
Lee, Ann, 197

Lee, Richard Henry, 95; participation at First Continental Congress, 88; opposition to Constitution, 121
Lee, Robert E., 257, 258, 267, 270–271
Legislature, 113. *See also* State legislatures
Leisler, Jacob, 46
Leisure time, African influence on, 59
Leni-Lenapes, 32
Leonard, Daniel, 90
Leopard (ship), 148
Letcher, John, 266
Letters from a Farmer in Pennsylvania (Dickinson), 80
Letters of a Federal Farmer, 121
Letters on the Condition of Women and the Equality of the Sexes (Grimké), 224
Letters to Catharine E. Beecher (Grimké), 224
Lewis, Meriwether, 144
Lewis and Clark expedition, 144, 165
Lewis and Hanford, 168
Lexington Battle, 70
Liability, limited, 170
Liberal Republicans, 286
Liberator, 223
Liberty (ship), 82
Life of Washington (Weems), 107
Limited liability of shareholders, 170
Lincoln, Abraham: on war with Mexico, 239; on Slave Power, 248; debates with Douglas, 249; election of *1860*, 249–251; position on territories, 250; wartime powers of, 252, 262–263; policy during Civil War, 254, 268, 277; avoidance of slavery issue, 263–264; and emancipation, 264–265; and election of *1864*, 269; assassination of, 271; Reconstruction plan of, 276
Lincoln, Benjamin, 100
Literacy: Native American's introduction to, 13; in 18th-century colonies, 62
Literature: post-Revolution, 107; frontier lore in, 173
Little Turtle, 117
Little Women (Alcott), 206
Liverpool, England, 162
Livingston, Robert R., 95, 144, 165
Locke, F. B., 167 (ill.)
Locke, John, 33, 62
Locomotive, 160
London Crystal Palace Exhibition, 166
Long Island, New York, 96
Longstreet, James, 267
López de Santa Anna, Antonio, 233
Lotteries, 221
Louisbourg, 55, 73
Louisiana, 40 (ill.); Napoleon's acquisition of, 144; admission to statehood, 157; prohibition against slavery in, 158; population density in, 181; disruptions to black families

in, 189; secession of, 251; election of *1876* and, 287
Louisiana Purchase, 144, 145 (ill.), 156, 240
Louisville, Kentucky: wheat and hog brokers in, 169; economic development in, 175
Louis XIV (King of France), 46
L'Ouverture, Toussaint, 137
Lovejoy, Elijah P., 223, 224
Lowell, Francis Cabot, 168
Lowell system, 168, 171
Loyalists: in Anglican clergy, 90; extent in colonies, 90–91; actions by Second Continental Congress against, 91; in New Jersey and Pennsylvania, 97; reaction to Burgoyne's surrender, 100; postwar treatment of, 102; post-Revolution confiscated property of, 115
Loyal Nine, 78
Lucas, Eliza, 36
Lumber industry, 170, 181
Lundy, Benjamin, 223
Luther, Martin, 15
Lutherans, 53; German, 208
Lynch, James, 280–281
Lyon, Matthew, 133

MacIntosh, Ebenezer, 78
McClellan, George B., 255, 257, 258, 269
McCormick reaper, 173
McCulloch v. *Maryland*, 155
McGillivray, Alexander, 116
McGuffey's Reader, 201
Machinery, precision-made, 161
Machine-tool industry, 166
Macon, Georgia, 266
Madison, James, 225; as delegate to Constitutional Convention, 118; profile of, 118; campaign for ratification of Constitution by, 121; influence in Congress, 124; on assumption of state debts from American Revolution, 127; on Bank of the United States, 128; as member of Republican faction, 129; handling of Alien and Sedition Acts, 133; and certification of Marbury appointment, 143; as president, 148; and War of *1812*, 149; foreign policy of, 149; election of *1812*, 154; message to Congress, 154; domestic program of, 155
Mail censorship, 224
Mail routes, 175
Maine, 41; admission to statehood, 158; rights of pre–Civil War African-Americans in, 213; border dispute regarding, 231–232; personal liberty law in, 245
Mali, 8
Malnutrition: in colonies, 16

Manassas, Virginia, 255
Manifest destiny, 232–233, 377
Mann, Horace, 201
Manufactured goods, price of, 163
Manufacturing: in 18th-century colonies, 54; slowdown in *1818*, 157; impact of War of *1812* on, 158–159; impact of increased specialization on economy, 161; American system of, 166–167; advances in 19th-century, 168–169; employment of children in, 171; and formation of craft-based associations, 261–262; unscrupulous practices during Civil War, 262
Manumission, 214
Marbury, William, 142, 143
Marbury v. *Madison*, 142–143
Marietta, Ohio, 116–117
Market economy: explanation of, 163–164; boom-and-bust cycles as result of, 164, 175; agriculture and, 172, 173, 175–176; in South, 181; competition in, 215
Marquette, Jacques, 39
Marriage: colonial view of, 109; post-Revolution state of, 109; women's view of, 184; among slaves, 189; 19th-century women rejecting, 206
Married Women's Property Act of 1839, 184
Marshall, James, 174
Marshall, John: as negotiator with France, 132; as Chief Justice of Supreme Court, 142–144, 155, 165, 211
Martin, Betsy, 195
Martin, George, 195
Maryland: founding of, 19; suspension of charter of, 45; alliance with William and Mary, 46; Germans in, 53; Scotch-Irish in, 53; slaves in, 60, 91, 110; slave uprising preparation, 91; acceptance of Articles of Confederation, 113; war debts from American Revolution, 127; protest of whiskey tax in, 128; taxation of national bank, 155; alignment with Union by, 251; Union loyalty during Civil War, 263
Mary (Queen of England), 46
Masons, 202, 218, 221–222
Massachusetts: settlement of, 22, 23; slavery in, 34; as royal colony, 45, 46; witchcraft trials in, 46–47; rifts with British in, 82, 84; organization of revolutionary militias, 94; uprising of farmers in, 104–105; education in, 108, 201; ratification of Constitution by, 121; and American Revolution, 127; industrialization in, 170; county fairs in, 173; population density in, 181; rights of

Property rights: Indian concepts of, 18; and voting rights, 109, 280; of women, 109, 184, 280
Prophet, 150–152, 209
Proslavery theories, 243
Prosser, Gabriel, 137, 189
Prosser, Martin, 137
Prostitution, 219–220
Protestant Association, 46
Protestant reform, religious, 136–137. *See also* Second Great Awakening
Protestant Reformation, 15
Providence, Rhode Island, 25
Public accommodations law, 275
Public schools: development of, 200–201; religion in, 201; Democrats' view of, 227. *See also* Schools
Pueblos: social organization of, 5; political structure of, 6; revolt of, 37
Puritans: origins of, 15; migration to New England, 21, 22, 29; communal ideals of, 22–23; role of family in, 24–25; in English government, 29; Indian attack on, 41; church membership among, 42; Halfway membership among, 42; triangular trade system of, 42–43
Putting-out system, 168, 204

Quakers, 50; settlement in Pennsylvania, 32; religious beliefs of, 32, 61; opposition to slavery, 60, 184, 223; view of slavery, 60; neutral position regarding revolution, 91; agricultural instruction for Iroquois, 137
Quartering Act of 1765, 80, 85
Quasi-War with France, 132, 134
Quebec Act, 85
Queen Anne's War, 48, 71
Quincy, Josiah, Jr., 82, 84, 145–146

Racial discrimination: post-Revolution justifications for, 111–112; Second Great Awakening and, 137; in North, 177, 213–214; federal law and, 213; manifest destiny and, 233; toward black soldiers, 275; grandfather clauses and, 285. *See also* Segregation
Racial equality: conflict between Declaration of Independence and, 105; during Reconstruction, 274–275, 277, 280, 284
Racist theory, 111
Radical Reconstruction, 282. *See* Reconstruction period
Radicals, 264, 273, 276; and congressional balance of power, 277; strength in Congress, 278; and Fifteenth Amendment, 279
Raids, Civil War, 269–270
Railroad industry: impact on commerce, 161; government subsidies for, 166; Confederate regulation of, 259; during Civil War, 260, 262; during Reconstruction, 281
Railroads: redesign of locomotive's wheel assembly, 160; construction of, 160, 162, 165, 166; trade routes created by, 161; transcontinental, 243, 244
Raleigh, Walter, 14, 15
Randolph, Edmund, 118, 128
Randolph, John, 142
Rape, 189
Real Whigs, 76, 83, 121
Reapers, 161, 173
Reconstruction period: opposition during, 274, 279–281; equality and, 274–275; Johnson's plan for, 276–277; involvement of Congress, 277–280, 286–287; and Southern reform, 279–281; impact on African-Americans, 280–284; failure of, 282–283; meaning of freedom for African-Americans during, 283–284; Supreme Court decisions during, 284–285; retreat from, 285–288
Recreation. *See* Leisure time
Reform movements: post–War of *1812*, 217–218; politics and, 218, 220, 225, 235; Jacksonians' views of, 227; impact of, 235; during Reconstruction, 280. *See also* Second Great Awakening
Regionalization, 161–162
Regulator movements, 66
Religion: in early American civilizations, 12–13; tolerance toward, 32; in colonies, 61, 66–67; disestablishment of, 136; evangelical, 136–137; in public schools, 201; 19th-century reform, 218–220. *See also* Christianity; *name of specific denomination*
Religious freedom: New England colonists and, 25; in Pennsylvania, 32; Quebec Act and, 85
Religious persecution, 206; of Quakers, 32; of Mormons, 197; in Holland, 207
Religious revival: First Great Awakening, 51, 66–67; Iroquois, 137–138; of Indians, 152. *See also* Second Great Awakening
Removal Act (1830), 212
Renaissance, 10
Report of Public Credit (Hamilton), 127
Report on Manufactures (Hamilton), 128
Representation: virtual, 76; deliberations of Constitutional Convention regarding, 118–119
Republican faction: beginning of, 123, 124, 129; profile of, 131; conflict with Federalist faction, 132, 141–142; opposition to Quasi-War, 132; opposition to Alien and Sedition Acts, 142; effect of Missouri Compromise on, 158
Republican government: post-Revolution participation in, 105; as embodiment of virtue, 107, 164; reform in education and, 108; role of women in, 108–109; role of African-Americans in, 110–112; state constitutions in, 112–113; Articles of Confederation and, 113–114
Republicanism: definitions of, 105, 106; Jeffersonian interpretation of, 138, 154
Republican party; position on slavery, 238, 248, 253; creation of, 244, 245; and election of *1854*, 245; ideology of, 245–246, 253; political appeal of, 245–246; and election of *1860*, 250; and congressional balance of power, 277; and election of *1866*, 278; black support of, 280; during Reconstruction, 280–282, 285; Ku Klux Klan violence against, 282; opposition to anti-Klan laws, 286; and election of *1876*, 287
Reservoirs, 200
Revels, Hiram, 283
Revere, Paul, 82, 83 (ill.), 93
Revivals: yeoman participation in, 182; evangelical Christian, 218
Revolutionary ideology: impact on education, 108; impact on family, 109; impact on slavery, 110
Revolutionary War. *See* American Revolution
Rhode Island: colonial status of, 45; burning of *Gaspée* by, 82; authority of colonial assembly in, 90; emancipation of slavery in, 110; abstention from constitutional deliberations, 118; ratification of Constitution by, 121; industrialization in, 170; rights of pre–Civil War African-Americans in, 213; personal liberty law in, 245
Rice Coast, 8, 36
Rice cultivation, 36, 52, 56
Richmond, Virginia, 107, 271; population of, 181; as capital of Confederacy, 257; threat by Union forces on, 258; population during Civil War, 259
Richmond Grays, 250 (ill.)
Rifles, 166
Rights of the British Colonies Asserted and Proved, The (Otis), 77, 110
Riots: food, 166, 266; 19th-century urban, 202
Ripley, Sarah, 205–206
Roads, federal funds to build, 155, 165, 228

Roanoke Island, North Carolina, 14–15, 255

Rochester, New York, 169, 219

Rockingham, Lord, 79

Rock Island Railroad, 160

Rolfe, John, 16, 18

Root medicine, 187

Royal African Company, 34

Royal Navy, 147–150, 153

Rural life: development of institutions in, 181; diversity in, 196–199. *See also* Agriculture

Rush, Benjamin, 110

Rush-Bagot Treaty, 156

Russia, and European noncolonialization in Western Hemisphere, 157

St. Augustine, Florida, 13

St. Clair, Arthur, 117

Saint Domingue, 137

St. Leger, Barry, 99

St. Louis, Missouri: wheat and hog brokers in, 169; economic development in, 175; population growth in, 175; immigrants in, 207

Salem, Massachusetts, 23

Salem witchcraft trials, 46–47

Salisbury, North Carolina, 266

Sampson, Deborah, 98 (ill.)

Sanders (Virginia planter), 214

San Francisco, California: growth of, 174; immigrants in, 207

Sanitation: in slave quarters, 185; urban, 200

San Salvador, 11

Santa Fé, New Mexico, 144

Santa Fé Trail, 144, 175

Santa Maria (ship), 11

Saratoga, New York, 99, 100

Savannah, Georgia, immigrants in, 207

Scalawags, 281–282

Scandinavian immigrants, 207

Schools: high school and college enrollment increases, 41; public, 200–201, 227; development of urban public, 200–201; religion in, 201; racial segregation of, 281; establishment for African-Americans in South, 281

Scotch immigrants, 53; in tobacco trade, 56; loyalty to England, 90

Scotch-Irish immigrants, 52–54, 207–208; in Pennsylvania, 32; neutral position regarding revolution, 91

Scott, Dred, 247, 248

Scott, Winfield, 232, 240, 243

Sea Islands, South Carolina, 255, 274

Secession: proposed by New England, 147; proposed by New York, 147; proposed by Federalists, 154; of South, 250–253; as threat to representative government, 262

Second Amendment, U.S. Constitution, 124

Second Bank of the United States, 218; charter of, 155, 169; role in depression of *1818,* 157; closing of, 169; rechartering of, 229

Second Continental Congress. *See* Continental Congress, Second

Second Great Awakening, 124, 217; African-Americans and, 137; women in, 137, 219–220; sources of, 218

Second Party System, 230

Secretary of state, 225

Sectionalism: following War of *1812,* 157; as threat to Union, 158; Missouri Compromise and, 158; economic basis of, 159; political parties and, 245

Seddon, James, 267

Sedition Act (1798), 132–133

Segregation: post-Revolution housing, 111; Northern pre–Civil War, 213–214; in South, 281; school, 281. *See also* African-Americans; Racial discrimination

Seminoles: suppression of, 156; land claims of, 210; resistance to removal, 212–213

Seminole War, 213

Senate, U.S.: on creation of role of president, 125; on assumption of state debts from American Revolution, 127; on Jay treaty, 130; denouncement of British impressment, 148; political balance in commitment to slavery, 157; rejection of annexation of Texas, 233; polarization in, 247; on slavery in territories, 250; and impeachment of Johnson, 273, 277, 279; and power over changes in cabinet, 279

Seneca Falls Declaration (1848), 224–225

Senecas, 39, 99–100

Separate-state secession, 251

Separation between church and state, 25

Separation of powers, 119

Separatists, 21, 199

Seventh Amendment, U.S. Constitution, 125

Seven Years' War, 70, 73, 75–76

Sewage systems, 200

Seward, William H., 264–265

Sex, between slaves and masters, 110, 183, 184

Sex discrimination, 285. *See also* Women

Sexual division of labor: among Native Americans, 5; in West Africa, 8–9; in Europe, 10; among white colonists, 57; among African-Americans, 59, 189; post-Revolution, 108–109; in 19th century, 204–205. *See also* Women

Seymour, Horatio, 285

Shakers, 197

Sharecropping, explanation of, 284

Sharpsburg, Maryland, 258

Shaw, Lemuel, 172

Shawnees: settlement in Pennsylvania, 32; alliance with, 71; confederacy formed by, 116; land claims of, 116; and War of *1812,* 150–152, 209; forced resettlement of, 209–210

Shays, Daniel, 104, 105

Shays's Rebellion, 118

Shelburne, Lord, 102

Shepard, William, 104

Sherman, Roger, 95

Sherman, William Tecumseh, 269–270, 273–274

Shipbuilding: in Boston, 55; 19th-century advances in, 162; during Civil War, 262

Ship fever, 207

Shipping: in colonies, 54; impact of transportation advances on, 161; vs. railroads, 162; Confederate regulation of, 259

Shirt Depot, 167 (ill.)

Shoe industry, 170

Shoemakers' cases, 171–172

Silk industry, 19 (ill.)

Silk Route, 8, 10

Sioux Indians, 13

Sixth Amendment, U.S. Constitution, 125

Slater, Samuel, 168

Slaughter-House cases, 285

Slaveholders: conflict between slaveholding and personal enslavement, 105, 110; westward migration of, 136, 159, 178, 179, 181; lifestyle of, 183; physical and mental abuse inflicted by, 185–186; social and political benefits of, 190–191; conflict between nonslaveholders and, 191–193; Indians as, 211; voluntary freeing of slaves by, 214; in Texas, 233; right to take slaves to territories, 240; in Democratic party, 246; compensation of, 264, 266

Slave Power, 237, 239, 240, 245, 248, 253

Slavery: in Caribbean, 33; economics of, 33, 177–178; establishment of, 33–34; Europeans and, 34; impact on Africa, 34; in Chesapeake, 35–36; in South Carolina, 36; in North, 36–37; in southern colonies, 48; impact on tobacco cultivation, 56; impact on whites, 58–60, 190, 191; Quaker opposition to, 60, 184, 223; white colonists' knowledge of,

Slavery (cont.)
83; Declaration of Independence and conflict of, 105; revision of laws regarding, 110; politics and, 157, 159, 224, 245, 246; as emotional issue, 157; political balance in Senate committed to, 157; emotional attitudes toward, 157–158; in territories, 158, 238–242, 244, 245–249; as foundation of economic and social system in South, 159, 179, 190–191; tactics of advocates of, 224; war with Mexico and, 240; election of *1848* and, 240–241; theories advocating, 243; division of Union over, 247–249; North-South split in Union over, 249–253; avoidance of issue during Civil War, 263–264. *See also* Abolitionism

Slaves: in Muslim Mediterranean, 8; introduction into Europe, 11; in New York State, 31; lifestyle in South Carolina, 36; white male authority over, 58; runaway, 58–60, 237, 242, 263; education of, 62; resistance among, 65, 91–93, 189–190, 237; in Continental Army, 98; in British army during American Revolution, 101; implications of revolutionary ideology for, 110; compensation for slaves who returned to England after American Revolution, 130; westward migration of, 136, 139, 159, 178, 179, 181; sale of excess, 179; as major investment in South, 181; labor conditions of, 184; diet of, 185; physical and mental abuse of, 185–186; attitude toward whites, 187; culture of, 187–188; owned by Cherokees, 211; prohibitions against freeing, 214; plan for emancipation of, 264–265; in Union Army, 266

Slave trade, 20, 33, 35 (ill.); European involvement in, 157; *1807* act closing foreign, 157, 179; interregional, 181

Smallpox: epidemics, 1, 14; inoculation against, 63

Smith, Adam, 164

Smith, John, 16

Smith, Joseph, 197

Smith, Kirby, 258

Smith, Margaret B., 140

Social reform: politics and, 218; 19th-century, 220–222. *See also* Reform movements

Society of the Cincinnati, 107

Soil, exhaustion of, 172, 179

Sons of Liberty, 79, 81, 130

Soto, Hernando de, 12

Sound money, 286

South: basis of economy in, 159,

177–178, 239; regional specialization in, 161; development of transportation in, 181, 182; population density in, 181; rural society in, 181; paternalistic attitudes of slaveholders in, 183; class conflict and, 191–192; growing conflict with North, 238, 240–249; opposition to war with Mexico, 239–240; impact of Civil War on, 254, 258–260, 266–268; anti–Civil War sentiment in, 266, 268; opposition to Reconstruction, 274, 279–280; power in Congress after Civil War, 278; Reconstruction politics in, 280–283

South America. *See* Latin America

Southampton County, Virginia, 189

South Carolina: founding of, 33; slavery in, 36, 52, 60; trade in Indian slaves, 38; as royal colony, 45; antagonism between Africans and Indians in, 54; Stono Rebellion in, 65; Regulator movements in, 66; revolutionary sentiment in, 91, 92; American Revolution in, 100–101; laws regarding slaveholding in, 110; war debts of, 127; political reform in, 191; antiabolitionism in, 223; doctrine of nullification and, 228–229; secession of, 251; naval battles of Civil War off coast of, 255; Ku Klux Klan violence in, 282; election in *1876* and, 287

South Carolina Gazette, 83

Southern Railroad, 160

Spain, 10; colonialism of, 1, 12–14, 37; exploratory voyages of, 11–12; in Florida and Gulf of Mexico, 70, 71; loss of Florida to British, 73; involvement in American Revolution, 100; post–Revolution presence on U.S. borders, 116; Pinckney's treaty negotiated with, 130; Adams-Onís Treaty with, 156; French occupation of, 156; loss of Latin American territories by, 156

Specie Circular, 229, 231

Spirits, 187

Spoils system, 227

Sports, in 19th-century urban life, 201

Spotsylvania, Virginia, 270

Springfield, Massachusetts, 105

Squanto, 22

Squatters, 175

Stamp Act (1765), 77–79, 81

Stamp Act Congress, 79

Standard of living: in colonies, 54–55; during Civil War, 259–261

Stanton, Edwin M., 276, 279

Stanton, Elizabeth Cady, 224, 278

State constitutions: in republican government, 112–113; Reconstruction redrafting of, 276, 280

State court system, 165

State Department: establishment under Articles of Confederation, 125; Jefferson as first secretary of, 126; assistance with agriculture, 165

State government, promotion of economic growth, 166

State legislatures: encouragment of proliferation of corporations, 165; during Reconstruction, 280, 281

Staten Island, New York, 96

States' rights, 286

Steamboats: as agent of economic growth, 160; impact of, 161, 162; and monopoly rights, 165

Stearns, Charles, 206

Stearns, Sarah Ripley, 205–206

Steel plows, 173

Stephens, Alexander, 253, 268, 276

Stevens, Thaddeus, 277, 279

Stobart, John, 178 (ill.)

Stocks, state government investment in, 166

Stono Rebellion, 65

Stowe, Harriet Beecher, 243

Strikebreakers, 262

Strikes. *See* Labor strikes

Stuart, Gilbert, 107

Stuart, James E. B. "Jeb," 258

Stuart, John, 92

Stuarts, 15, 45, 46

Stuyvesant, Peter, 29

Subsistence farms, 161

Suffrage. *See* Voting rights

Sugar Act, 76–77

Sullivan, John, 100

Sumner, Charles, 247, 277

Supreme Court, U.S.: established by Constitution, 124; creation of, 125; first cases of, 125–126; political independence of, 142; under John Marshall, 142–144, 155, 165; efforts to advance national unity, 158; decisions regarding interstate commerce, 165; role in promotion of economic development, 165–166; decisions regarding Indians, 211, 292; on constitutionality of slavery, 247–248; decisions on Reconstruction, 284–285; interpretation of Fourteenth Amendment, 285

Supreme Court justice(s): appointments by Jefferson, 142; reduction of, 142; Chase as, 142, 273; Marshall as, 142–144, 155, 165; Taney as, 166, 247, 248

Susquehannocks, 41

Sutter's Mill, California, 174

Swiss immigrants, 32

Synagogues, 54

Syphilis, 14

Tailors, 167

Tallmadge, James, 157

Taney, Roger, 166

Continuation of copyright page.